RIDICULOUS!

THE THEATRICAL LIFE AND
TIMES OF CHARLES LUDLAM

DAVID KAUFMAN

APPLAUSE
THEATRE & CINEMA BOOKS

Ridiculous! The Theatrical Life and Times of Charles Ludlam
By David Kaufman

Photo research by Ann Schneider. Inside cover photos by Richard Avedon © 1975. BEFORE (INSIDE FRONT COVER, L. TO R.): Bill Vehr, Black-Eyed Susan, Lola Pashalinski, Charles Ludlam, John Brockmeyer, and Jack Mallory. AFTER (INSIDE BACK COVER, L. TO R.): Mallory as Carlton Stone in *Stage Blood*, Brockmeyer as The Magician in *The Grand Tarot*, Ludlam as Marguerite in *Camille*, Pashalinski as Miss Flora Cubbidge in *Bluebeard*, Susan as Tsu Hsi in *Eunuchs of the Forbidden City*, Vehr (in a makeshift costume) as Dude Greaseman in *Corn*.

Book design by Michelle Thompson with assistance from Kate Zimmer.

The Library of Congress has cataloged the hardcover edition as follows:

2002109940

British Library Cataloging-in-Publication Data

A catalog record for this book is available from the British Library

ISBN 1-57783-637-x

APPLAUSE THEATRE & CINEMA BOOKS
151 West 46th Street
New York, NY 10036
Phone: (212) 575-9265
Fax: (646) 562-5852
Email: info@applausepub.com
Internet: www.applausepub.com
Applause books are available through your local bookstore, or you may
order at www.applausepub.com or call Music Dispatch at (800) 637-2852

SALES & DISTRIBUTION

NORTH AMERICA:
HAL LEONARD CORP.
7777 West Bluemound Road
P.O. Box 13819
Milwaukee, WI 53213
Phone: (414) 774-3630
Fax: (414) 774-3259
Email: halinfo@halleonard.com
Internet: www.halleonard.com

EUROPE:
ROUNDHOUSE PUBLISHING, LTD.
Millstone, Limers Lane
Northam, North Devon EX39 2RG
Phone: (0) 1237-474-474
Fax: (0) 1237-474-774
Email: roundhouse.group@ukgateway.net

Praise for *Ridiculous!*

"Whether Charles Ludlam was playing Hamlet, Camille or Maria Callas, he was theatre incarnate—sexy, hilarious and ravishingly demented. This comprehensive biography is absolutely essential, as a portrait of a mad genius, and the world he ruled."
—Paul Rudnick

"Even if you never saw Charles Ludlam and his Ridiculous Theatre, this biography will hold you and make you wish you had. And even if you think theatre per se is ridiculous, it will make you wish you had a Charles Ludlam to shake up your world."
—Arthur Laurents

"A fascinating portrait of an authentic stage genius and the New York avant-garde scene in which he toiled with such demented and dedicated diligence... Superbly researched and impressively presented..."
—*Playbill*

"David Kaufman's *Ridiculous!* is a big book that reads very easily. Generously laced with over a decade's worth of interviews, it is a feast of revelations."
—Andrew Holleran, *The Gay and Lesbian Review*

"The book, like one of Ludlam's epics, moves entertainingly through his life and career, chock-full of funny quotes, strong opinions and outrageous mishaps..."
—Ira Siff, *Opera News*

"With devotion, depth and dishiness, critic Kaufman has turned a 1989 *Interview* article into a decade-long love affair with his subject. The resultant chronology of Ludlam's life reads like backstage gossip... The book portrays not merely the man but his era, explicating Ludlam as more than a product of the 1960s' revolutionary sexuality, politics and art: a shaper of attitudes and ideas sexual, theatrical and artistic..."
—*Publishers Weekly*

"In this amazing and unstoppable biography of Charles Ludlam, David Kaufman captures the times and the man; the wild Manhattan of the 1960s and '70s and the creative crazy genius of Ludlam, who married real learning to raucous laughter in his flamboyant theatre... This is a glorious celebration of the Aristophanes of the 20th century, America's greatest comic spirit."
—Donald Lyons, Drama Critic, *New York Post*

"A rich portrait of Ludlam the conflicted man and artist... Kaufman provides excellent synopses of the plays and revealing examples of Ludlam's comic touch..."
—*Books in Canada*

"This is one helluva piece of work... Kaufman has written a great, big book of love that will keep Ludlam's subversive genius alive, inspire legions of future Ludlamites..."
—Marilyn Stasio, Variety.com

CONTENTS

ACKNOWLEDGEMENTS

This book is dedicated to my life partner Ken Geist, and my friend Bob Olson: their love, generosity, and moral support made it possible. I am also indebted to Jed Mattes, my indefatigable agent and gifted friend, as well as to Steven Samuels, who played so important a part in Charles Ludlam's life and legacy. Steve not only helped clarify my perceptions of Ludlam's work, but also supplied editorial expertise during every phase of the book's development.

Two of my other, dearest friends proved crucial in shaping *Ridiculous!*: Ann Schneider and Robert Gutman. Ann, a Senior Photo Researcher at Vanity Fair, used her professional eye — no less than her warm heart — to help this book become all that it could be visually. An eminent music historian and biographer, Robert contributed a good deal to my understanding of *Der Ring Gott Farblonjet*, Ludlam's parody of Wagner. He also vetted my discussion of *Galas*, Ludlam's tribute to Maria Callas. Robert's authorial wisdom further improved the entire manuscript even after the bound galleys became available, saving me from many an embarrassment. Indeed, Robert's consistently cheerful spirit made his more critical comments that much easier to accomodate.

I would be remiss if I did not rush to include my gratitude for the inestimable help that Black-Eyed Susan, Lola Pashalinski, and Christopher Scott each provided during the past twelve years. Ludlam's life was, first and last, a testament to the collaborative process that is the theater, so perhaps it was inevitable that his biography would prove to be akin to a collaboration as well. Since Susan, Lola and Chris were co-founders of the Ridiculous Theatrical Company, Ludlam's story is also theirs, and they proved unstinting in sharing their memories — even the painful ones. At the same time, they also served to verify or correct everyone else's.

Ludlam's mother Marjorie, his brother Donald, and his lover Everett Quinton all gave me their utmost cooperation. Everett literally handed me Ludlam's Rolodex when I began my extended sequence of interviews. Though it was sometimes difficult for Everett to revisit the past or reflect on certain aspects of his life and relationship with Ludlam, he never shunned my questions or turned me away.

It is a tribute to Ludlam that everyone I interviewed — who either knew or worked with him — not only offered their candid recollections, but also gave me letters, photos, videos, and other precious memorabilia. I am especially grateful, in this regard, to Richard Currie, Tom Harding, Stephen Holt, Leandro Katz, Everett Quinton, Robert Reddy, Christopher Scott, Teriananda, and the late James Morfogen. Thanks also to Frances Scott for providing me with her unpublished memoir of the youthful Ludlam. Nor can I emphasize enough the debt I owe to Walter Gidaly, the executor of Ludlam's literary estate, who encouraged my pursuit of this project, even as he encouraged others to cooperate with me.

To mention that the majority of people I interviewed were bright and articulate speaks volumes about Ludlam, his associates, and thus his accomplishments. The extraordinary cast of characters includes Penny Arcade, Jose Rafael Arango, George Ashley, Paul Bartel, Robert Beers, Eric Bentley, John Brockmeyer, Ericka Brown (aka Eureka), Charles Busch, Frederick Ted Castle, Joyce Castle, John Crosby, David Crownover, Richard Currie, Rick Davis, Ethyl Eichelberger, Charlotte Forbes, Edgar Franceschi, James Gallagher, James Gardiner, Henry Geldzahler, Jeremy Gerard, Walter Gidaly, Peter Golub, Wally Gorell, Martin Gottfried, Richard Hennessy, John Heys, David Hockney, William Hoffman, Stephen Holt, William Hunt, Joseph Hurley, Joe E. Jeffreys, Madeline Kahn, Leandro Katz, Leon Katz, Peter Kazaras, Adam Kilgore, William Kohler, H.M. Koutoukas, Arthur Kraft, Jack Mallory, Paul Martino, Minette, James Morfogen, Georg Osterman, Joseph Papp, Mark Rappaport, Robert Reddy, Jan Reynolds, Jose Rodriguez-Soltero, Thomas Lanigan Schmidt, Stuart Sherman, Michael Smith, Marcia Steiner, Steven Stern (aka Styles Caldwell), Harvey Tavel, Ronald Tavel, Paul Taylor, Teriananda, Steve Turtell, John Vaccaro, Ross Wetzsteon, and Earl Wild.

I want specifically to thank Teriananda for her personal insights into Bill Vehr, and the late, great Minette for opening many a door to me. Both a mascot and a muse to the Ridiculous, Minette graced the company with his other-worldly spirit. He also introduced me to any number of people who were part of the story. While warning me that trying to piece together the early, drug-ridden years of the Ridiculous would be tantamount to "reconstructing the Civil War," Minette proved an infallible guide through that murky period.

However, it was Chris Scott's primary endorsement that opened the floodgates to Ludlam's world for me and catalyzed the biography; I deeply regret that he died within a matter of weeks of being able to enjoy its publication, but I am eternally grateful for his making it happen in the first place.

There is also a mini-saga as to how this book came to be written, entailing another battalion of friends and colleagues who deserve my gratitude. The tale began with Michael Feingold, the longtime drama critic of the *Village Voice*. One of my oldest friends, Michael referred me to Robert Walsh, who in turn invited me to write a piece on Ludlam for *Interview* magazine in 1989 — in conjunction with the publication of *The Complete Plays of Charles Ludlam*. Susan Ralston was the first editor who, subsequently, urged me to write Ludlam's biography. David Groff proceeded to commission the project and, over the years, to supply his talented, hands-on, editorial contributions to a number of chapters. In the end, Mark Glubke of Applause Theatre & Cinema Books acquired the manuscript and deemed it an important volume for the company. During the course of the past year, the Applause team has been both extremely helpful and enthusiastic in making *Ridiculous!* become a reality. I list them here with ongoing admiration for their respective talents and expertise: Jenna Bagnini, John Cerullo, David Hennessy, Kay Radtke, Shannon Reed, Kristen Schilo, and Michelle Thompson. After Mark and Kristen shepherded the manuscript through the early phases of the publishing process — including David's meticulous editing — John and Jenna took up the reins with a care and a precision that most authors would envy. Shannon never tired of tracking down permissions, Michelle frequently worked overtime on her elegant design of the book, and Kay has helped promote *Ridiculous!* with an unflagging energy.

I extend a very special thank you to Richard Avedon, whose inimitable way of seeing things captured the essence of Ludlam and his core players in two remarkable images, which he graciously allowed us to use as endpapers for *Ridiculous!* And for contributing indispensable, last-minute assistance, I thank Deborah Engel and Anne Noonan of the drama department at Hofstra University, J. Hoberman of the *Village Voice*, Pam Jordan of the drama library of Yale University, Jonas Mekas of the Anthology Film Archives, David J. Sleasman of the University of Pittsburgh Libraries, and Robert Reiss, a stranger at my gym, who enriched my anecdotal knowledge of Ludlam's relationship to both Houdini and another great magician named Al Flosso.

For their unwavering support and belief in both me and *Ridiculous!*, I also thank my friends Kenny Nassau and Lee Hebner, David Diamond, John Hochmann, Karl Johnson and Mira Goral, Norman Kleeblatt, Larry Kramer, Martha Labare, Jim Lambert, Larry Lash, Tom McCormack, Nancy Perry, David Samples, Andrew Sichel, and Suzy Troy.

Finally, I want to acknowledge my gratitude to James Rensenbrink, the publisher who let me have my say about the New York theater on a weekly basis for fifteen years in various publications, including the *Aquarian*, the *Soho Arts Weekly*, and *Downtown*. Indeed, it was for Jim that I first wrote about Charles Ludlam and reviewed several Ridiculous productions.

INTRODUCTION: A LIFETIME TO EXPLAIN

The public is wonderfully tolerant; it forgives everything but genius.
— Oscar Wilde

There are things that happen in a day that would take a lifetime to explain.
— Charles Ludlam, *Bluebeard*

When Charles Ludlam died of AIDS in 1987, *The New York Times* proclaimed him "one of the most innovative and prolific artists in the theater avant-garde." As if to confirm that Ludlam's twenty-year run had occurred precisely during a time when the avant-garde merged into the mainstream, his obituary appeared on the front page.

Even as he became noticeably more ill, his star was rising ever higher, with the great downtown playwright-performer extending his influence into many different realms. The first few months of 1987 typified the hectic schedule Ludlam had become accustomed to. While his evenings were occupied with an extended run at his Greenwich Village theater of *The Artificial Jungle*, his twenty-ninth and final play, his days were consumed with his latest obsession — writing a dramatic version of the life of Houdini. During this period, he finished shooting *The Big Easy*, a major studio release in which Ludlam portrayed a quirky New Orleans lawyer. Theatrical juggler that he was, he spent any remaining time researching *Titus Andronicus*, which he was slated to direct that summer for the New York Shakespeare Festival in Central Park, and finally completing the edit on *The Sorrows of Dolores*, an independent film project he had been working on for years. He was also involved in negotiating a new ten-year lease on the Ridiculous Theatrical Company's home. (The tiny bit of property in Sheridan Square where the theater was located would be renamed Charles Ludlam Lane shortly after his death.) Along with the stress of such a grueling schedule, Ludlam was privately grappling with the knowledge that he had AIDS — a fact he shared only with his longtime lover and protégé, Everett Quinton.

At the time of his death in May of 1987, Ludlam's Ridiculous Theatrical Company was twenty years old. A unique and beloved part of New York's thriving cultural life, his repertory theater had amassed an international following. As the tumultuous revolution of the 1960s continued to inform the passing decades, affection for Ludlam proved much larger and more widespread than even his devotees could have imagined. For two decades, Ludlam wrote, directed, and starred in new plays, maintaining his shifting nucleus of bohemian players through extraordinary circumstances and perennial financial hardships.

Early in his career, Ludlam's legendary status was heralded by a coterie of celebrated champions, including Henry Geldzahler, Andy Warhol, Susan Sontag, Stefan Brecht, Bette Midler, Lotte Lenya, Rudolf Nureyev, Donovan, Edmund White, Fran Lebowitz, Christopher Isherwood, Leonard Bernstein, Richard Avedon, Philip Roth, Andrew Holleran, and James Merrill. Although many of his fans never saw beyond his highly charged shenanigans and the homosexuality he flaunted onstage, highbrow theater aficionados and tabloid reviewers alike came to admire his plays and to value the intellect behind them. Parting the curtain of Ludlam's comedy and camp to reveal his more serious intentions, some commentators even compared him to Molière and Shakespeare. Such comparisons referred not only to Ludlam's use of classical forms and grand themes, but also to the fact that all three of these dramatists wrote for, acted in, and directed their own troupes — a far more rare phenomenon than many might suppose.

Ludlam's work endures beyond the era of its creator. At least a dozen of his plays are now being performed in a vast number of unexpected places. (In the years following his death, there have been productions everywhere from Akron, Ohio, Anchorage, Alaska, and Ashland, Oregon to Wheat Ridge, Colorado and White River Junction, Vermont — not to mention the more predictable venues such as Atlanta, Washington, D.C., Tokyo, and Stockholm.) His impact as a major literary force continues to reverberate to this day. He was not only a pioneer of drag performance who paved its rocky runway into the mainstream, but an inventive playwright who combined classical with modernist styles in influential ways. Indeed, Ludlam is a genius on a par with Ionesco, Genet, Orton, and Coward. Though his work has begun to be assimilated in the international culture, he has yet to be properly recognized and comprehended on the larger scale. He prompts us to ask a sadly familiar question with renewed vigor: Why is it that Americans are so quick to embrace foreign geniuses, while neglecting their all too few, homegrown candidates?

From his roots in the revolutionary sixties to the page-one news of his premature death, Ludlam lived a life that encapsulated — and helped to engender — the impulses and upheavals of his time. In the mid-sixties, when the Beatles still wanted to hold our hand, the twenty-two-year-old Ludlam was perfecting his rendition of Norma Desmond, the character originated by Gloria Swanson in *Sunset Boulevard*. Long before androgynous superstars such as David Bowie, Michael Jackson, and Ru Paul would commercialize transvestism, Ludlam was busy creating his own eccentric expression of fractured gender roles. Through the satirist's greatest weapon, exaggeration, he was also anticipating — and fostering — the sweeping changes in sexual mores that would permeate and permanently alter our society, as well as the ways in which we perceive one another.

On the stage, Ludlam was forever toying with a theatrical version of the social chaos he inspired in real life, whipping the cosmic void into his own eccentric vision of coherence. (The title of his second play, *Conquest of the Universe*, declares the mandate he divined for himself.) His personal life reflected similar passions and propensities for danger. Prior to his relatively stable, ten-year relationship with Everett Quinton, Ludlam's numerous liaisons and one-night stands were often highly dramatic affairs. (I fortunately tracked down and interviewed seven of Ludlam's lovers, each of whom was remarkably candid in describing the volatile dynamics of his relationship with him.)

With an emphasis on sex and drugs as a means of liberation, the 1960s spurred on Ludlam's hijinks: His life makes him appear, in retrospect, like a centrifugal force on the culture he came to exemplify. However, there is a danger in ascribing Ludlam to the era he lived in. Though the spirit of the sixties influenced everything he created and performed, he proved the true iconoclast by borrowing more from the past than he absorbed from the present. Thus he transcended the very era he seemed, at first glance, to represent.

By 1970, Ludlam was winning mainstream praise for his sixth opus, *Bluebeard*, a play about a lunatic scientist hell-bent on manufacturing a "third and gentle genital." Based in part on an H.G. Wells novel — as well as on an earlier adaptation of it, *Island of Lost Souls*, a 1932 horror film with a cult following — *Bluebeard* showed how Ludlam synthesized for his own purposes the references he incorporated in his original stage works. Between *Bluebeard* and Ludlam's death seventeen years later, he would write an additional twenty-three plays, with his reputation as a consummate drag performer in *Camille* (1973) and *Galas* (1983) all but eclipsing his other bravura skills. Yet only a handful of the thirty-some characters he created for himself involved cross-dressing.

Ludlam also found energy for numerous projects beyond his Ridiculous Theatrical Company. He taught drama at New York University, Connecticut College, Yale, American University, and Carnegie-Mellon. He also participated in special theatrical events, such as portraying the eponymous *Hedda Gabler* in Pittsburgh in 1984, and staging the American premiere of Henze's *The English Cat* for the Santa Fe Opera the following year — not to mention his involvement in three TV series ("Miami Vice," "Tales From the Dark Side," and "Oh, Madeline!"). He also staged his own adaptation of

Die Fledermaus at Santa Fe, and collaborated with choreographer Paul Taylor on a dance piece. The Ridiculous Theatrical Company enjoyed many tours of the United States and traveled to Europe three times, with performance stops in England, France, Germany, Yugoslavia, Austria, Italy, Switzerland, and Sweden.

"God, if I hadn't discovered theater early on, I would almost certainly have become a juvenile delinquent," Ludlam told Calvin Tomkins for his lengthy profile in the *New Yorker* in 1976, published when he was only thirty-three. As with most autobiographical statements, Ludlam's remark tells half a truth while suggesting the larger one. For what was his idiosyncratic theater if not a self-perpetuating delinquency molded into art? And what was Ludlam, if not an adult who fiercely preserved his childlike imagination and wonder, and used them to confront the world?

Ludlam's theatrical style was born out of defiance, a fierce reaction to his strict Catholic upbringing. After squabbling with his high school drama coach, he formed his own theater troupe near Greenlawn, Long Island, where he had grown up. Relations with mentors at Hofstra University, where he received a scholarship and majored in drama, were equally tempestuous and riddled with rebellion. And if Ludlam's subsequent work was famous for plundering the classics in the course of engendering his own fantastic stories, too little has been written about the rather delinquent way he forged his theater company in the first place. Upon graduating from Hofstra, Ludlam moved to New York City and joined a motley crew of actors under the leadership of John Vaccaro, whose group was an offshoot of that gargantuan vineyard of sixties counterculture, Andy Warhol's Factory. Within a year, in 1967, Ludlam had essentially stolen two-thirds of Vaccaro's troupe to create a rival organization, ultimately preempting the parent company. Nor was that all he appropriated: Vaccaro's company had been called the Play-House of the Ridiculous.

In their recollections, those who knew and worked with Ludlam speak eloquently of the aura of destiny surrounding him from the start. They tend to become less articulate as they relate the mixture of love and hate he stirred within them. Incorporating an extraordinary sexual energy and a Svengali-like magnetism, Ludlam's charisma instantly held sway over practically anyone who entered his orbit. Though he obviously knew how to work such an asset to his advantage — as a con man manipulates his marks — Ludlam's interest in everyone he encountered was quite genuine. But given his egomania and his diabolical impatience — his need to accomplish so very much in the relatively short time he had — the privilege of getting close to him entailed hazards all its own.

༃

My work on this biography started in the summer of 1989, when I interviewed twelve of Ludlam's most intimate associates for a story in *Interview* magazine. As published, the 8,000-word article represented merely a fraction of the 750 pages that were transcribed. I have since conducted innumerable interviews with well over a hundred and fifty additional people — everyone from Ludlam's mother and brother to Jeremy Gerard, who wrote Ludlam's obituary in *The New York Times*.

While Ludlam's legacy endures, his biography is long overdue. *The New York Times* was by no means alone in championing Ludlam throughout his career; nor is it alone in recognizing the influence his works continue to have on the theater in particular and Downtown culture in general. Ludlam's influence is felt today, not only as his plays continue to enter the international repertoire (as confirmed in the *Guinness Book of Records*, one of his plays has become the longest-running theatrical event in the history of Brazil), but by his acknowledged influence on many other creative figures: from Bette Midler and Madeline Kahn to Charles Busch, Buster Poindexter, Paul Rudnick, and Tony Kushner, to name only a few.

When he was asked during an interview how he felt about all those people on whom he had been an influence, Ludlam replied, "The problem isn't that I've influenced them, but that I haven't influenced them enough." Indeed, though Ludlam is famous for being the supreme drag performer, he resisted any such labels. The media continue to perpetuate a number of other misconceptions regarding his work and his significance.

Ludlam resented any attempts to pigeonhole his intentions or to summarize his work in a paragraph that might be suitable for *TV Guide* or a listing in the *Village Voice*. There was an underlying complexity to his designs that defied easy access or the superficial interpretations they often received. As his work repeatedly demonstrated, Ludlam's life was the vital record of someone who — time and again — did everything his own way and succeeded on his own terms.

"One of the problems with accepting a tag like avant-garde or gay theater or neo-post-infra-realism is that you're a bit like an Indian on a reservation selling trinkets to the tourists," Ludlam told an interviewer for his second feature in the "Arts & Leisure" section of the Sunday *Times*. "You have no real interaction with the culture, and whatever impact you may have had on that culture is nullified. That's why I'll always refuse to be typed as this or that. If people take the trouble to come here more than once, they see that I don't have an ax to grind even though I do have a mission. That mission is to have a theater that can offer possibilities that aren't being explored elsewhere. If you ask me why I've lasted so long, maybe that's the answer. I'm here because I keep coming up with possibilities."

How did Ludlam keep on renewing those possibilities? Why, given the obstacles, did he dare to be so original? How, given his eccentricities, did he emerge in the forefront of his generation? What did he do? Why and how did he do it? In this biography, I have endeavored to answer these questions in a chronological account of Ludlam's life, intermingling the man with the work and recreating the context that permitted him to flourish. Beyond scrutinizing Ludlam's achievements in light of his public splendors and private uproars, I hope to have illustrated the unusual degree to which his life and his work were inextricably entwined. And I aim to establish Ludlam's singular place in American culture as one of its enduring, larger-than-life creators. Ludlam may have filled his plays with outlandish characters, but his life shows repeatedly that he was his own most extravagant creation.

SUBURBAN REBEL

Out of the crooked timber of humanity no straight thing was ever made.
— Immanuel Kant

I feel appreciated, although I don't think anyone can ever love me enough.
— Charles Ludlam

"If Jack Kerouac had to live around here, no wonder he went 'on the road'," Charles Ludlam told his younger brother, Donald, about their Long Island home in Greenlawn, New York. Charles's acerbic allusion to Kerouac had far more resonance than he intended. Like that literary pioneer of the previous generation, Ludlam would always remain close to his suburban home and to his mother, no matter where he roamed or how far he believed he and his art had left them behind.

Ludlam and Long Island grew up together, part of the suburban experiment that swept across America in the sprawling boom following World War II. The potato fields of Nassau and Suffolk Counties were converted into plots where small-frame houses sprouted like mushrooms; garages became mandatory to accommodate the cars that were suddenly requirements for domestic life. Long before shopping malls became as familiar an American phenomenon as television, commercial-strip shopping centers began cropping up along the roads that connected these new communities to the larger highways leading to New York City and the rest of the country. People who had grown up cramped in cities suddenly had the opportunity to establish themselves in places that promised them roots and the freedom to move, as well as a newfound security. The fact that the Ludlams, like millions of others in suburban households, customarily left both their house and car unlocked recalls a time when risk seemed to have been removed from domestic life. Sociologists and other commentators would come to renounce the sentimental deceptions of suburban life as perpetrated by 1950s TV fare like "Father Knows Best" and the "Donna Reed Show"; but the ideals represented by those shows reflected real desires for community, safety, and normality in a world everyone knew could be blasted into atoms at any moment.

Within this environment of heightened and self-conscious conformity, Charles Ludlam was viewed as an oddball by his peers. In terms of the cultural rebel Ludlam would become, it seems telling that Robert Mapplethorpe — the bad-boy photographer who also upended cultural values later in life — was born in Floral Park in 1946, only three years after Ludlam was born in the same community. As absolutely distinct as their

I

artistic paths would prove to be, Ludlam and Mapplethorpe both grew up to be gay "outlaws" with a particular penchant for standing sexual mores on end.

No matter how far he would depart from the all-American suburban standards that circumscribed his formative years, Ludlam kept coming home all his life. Always the dutiful son, he frequently made time in his increasingly hectic schedule to return to Long Island for the holidays, as well as for the birthdays, weddings, graduations, and funerals that tend to summon adult children home. His mother claimed that Ludlam never failed to spend Christmas with the family, and he missed only the occasional Thanksgiving dinner when he was touring or otherwise engaged. Though he kept from his parents certain aspects of his life as he became a prominent figure in New York's gay subculture, Ludlam remained close to his mother Marjorie, whose indomitable strength, feisty spirit, and assertive manner he inherited. His relationship with his father, however, would always be problematic, even if Ludlam incorporated Joseph's sense of irony and volatile wit in his own approach to life. Charles Ludlam, master of the mercurial and ephemeral stage, first learned about performance within the dramatic construct of his own family.

℘

Marjorie Ludlam was the youngest of five surviving children. She was born in East Northport, Long Island, in 1913. Her father, Louis Braun, came at the age of fourteen to the United States from Baden-Baden — a popular resort town in the Schwarzwald or Black Forest region of southern Germany — to become a Lutheran minister at a seminary in Georgia. He quickly dropped out of school and became a gardener instead. Marjorie's mother, Bridget Lynch, was an Irish immigrant distantly related to the Bourne family of the Singer sewing dynasty. They sponsored her move to the States in the mid-1890s, when she was about twenty, to become a governess for their children. Bridget shuttled with the Bournes between their posh apartment in the Dakota on the Upper West Side of Manhattan to their mansion in White Plains, as well as to Oakdale, Long Island, where they had yet another estate, which later became La Salle Academy. It was here that Bridget met Louis the resident gardener, and by the turn of the century, they were married.

Louis and Bridget moved to Brooklyn to raise a family of their own. He opened a landscaping business called Braun's Greenhouses in Flatbush, on Canarsie Avenue, across from Holy Cross Cemetery. By the time Marjorie was born, Louis had sold the

Brooklyn operation and opened a larger chain of greenhouses out on Long Island, in Greenlawn. According to Marjorie, when Louis died of throat cancer in 1921, "Mother destroyed everything in a fit of passion. She tore up her marriage certificate and every picture of Father." With a maternal grandmother who acted out her rage in so highly charged a fashion, it would appear as if Charles inherited his knack for the theatrical from his mother's side of the family.

Bridget sold the greenhouse business only to die a year after Louis, of complications from multiple sclerosis, forcing the Braun brood to fend for themselves. The eldest sister, Florence, was already working as a bookkeeper at a lumberyard in Huntington, and May, the next oldest, was employed as a teller at the National City Bank in Manhattan. Charles and Louis, the middle siblings, eventually went to live with Bridget's brother in Brookline, Massachusetts, where they became, respectively, a florist and a factory worker. While her sisters were at work, the nine-year-old Marjorie was frequently left home alone, and thrust into a premature adulthood. By the middle of the Depression, she was attending Drake's Business College in New York and taking odd jobs to supplement her siblings' income.

The girl had grit and strength from an early age. When Bridget's health was deteriorating, an officer from the National City Bank made a house call, ostensibly to pay her respects to her employee's mother, but more likely to confirm the validity of May's extended leave of absence. It was Marjorie who gave the visitor tea. When she was thanked for the beverage, the ten-year-old hostess sassily replied, "You don't know anything! You should be thanking me for my hospitality instead of for the tea."

Charles Ludlam's father, Joseph William Ludlam, was born in 1900 in Long Island's Oyster Bay, with solid Yankee roots he liked to boast about: Joseph's father Charles, also from Oyster Bay, claimed to be a descendent from a passenger on the Mayflower. His mother, Louise McKee, was a Catholic from Syosset. Since a rebellion against the Catholic Church and all that it stood for figured prominently in Charles Ludlam's later life and work, it's intriguing to note that both sets of his grandparents had crossed over the dictates of their respective faiths. His Protestant grandfathers had each married a Catholic a century ago, when it was highly unusual — if not exactly daring — to do so.

Joseph's father ran a livery stable in Oyster Bay until it burned down, after which he became a bartender and worked on highway construction — among other manual labor jobs he could secure over the years. Joseph was the first of four surviving children. His sister Anne grew up to work for the Long Island Lighting Co. His brother — yet another Charles, but nicknamed "Buster" — worked in a pharmacy. His sister Adeline, the youngest, became a legal secretary.

By the time Joseph Ludlam met Marjorie Braun in 1940, he was already a middle-aged man working as a plasterer in the summers and as a truck maintenance man for an oil company in the winters. His first wife, Mary, had died two years before of kidney disease. Joseph was compelled to replace Mary as quickly as possible with someone who could help look after his adolescent son, also named Joseph.

The twenty-six-year-old Marjorie was thirteen years younger than Joseph and still living in Greenlawn with her sisters when she met her husband-to-be. Her brother Louis had married by then, and he eventually opened a greenhouse in East Northport, which would long remain in the family. The prim and proper, lace-curtain Irish sisters Florence and May were slated to be spinsters.

Marjorie had dated a number of men, but never cared for any in particular until she met Joseph. They were introduced by a neighbor of Marjorie's who worked for Joseph's supervisor at the oil company. Their first date consisted of a dinner at a German restaurant in Mineola. Joseph's looks appealed less to Marjorie than his good nature and his youthful manner, which seemed to defy his age. After a year's courtship, they were married in August of 1941, at St. Phillip Neri Church in Northport.

With Joseph's adolescent son providing a ready-made family for the young bride, the Ludlams moved to a two-bedroom apartment above a drugstore in New Hyde Park, on the Jericho Turnpike. Shortly after Joseph left for work on the morning of April 12, 1943 — or sixteen months after they were married — the pregnant Marjorie went into labor. Since the Ludlams had no telephone, Marjorie alerted the owner of the drugstore downstairs, and he in turn notified a neighbor who called Joseph to fetch Marjorie and take her to the hospital. After eight hours of labor, Charles Braun Ludlam was born that night in the Floral Park Sanatorium, which later became a gas station.

According to Marjorie, Joseph Ludlam was jealous of Charles from the moment he was born. Marjorie, for her part, poured most, if not all, of her love and considerable energies into raising Charles. Though Marjorie had already acted as a stepmother, she fell into a familiar pattern that often occurs when a husband and wife redefine themselves as a father and mother, creating a triangular relationship that hinges on their firstborn. In the process, she withdrew her affection from her husband, setting up a resentment of father towards son that became increasingly brutal over the years.

Throughout Ludlam's life and career, his father would be severely disapproving of just about everything his son did, while his mother would support and nurture his efforts. In a three-page autobiographical sketch he wrote later in life, Ludlam described how his mother "used to cry in the dark, which I found very painful. Often I cried too, in sympathy with her." On a more positive note, Ludlam would recall with fondness the stuffed Panda bear ("bigger than myself") that his father gave him. Charles named him Oscar and took particular delight in the bell attached to one of his ears.

Since Joseph Ludlam, Jr. was still living with his father and stepmother when his half brother was born, Charles's crib was stationed in his parents' bedroom. Joseph Jr. joined the armed services shortly thereafter; when he was discharged and returned to the apartment in New Hyde Park, Charles was only three, and Marjorie resented Joseph Jr.'s tendency to stay out late at night and sleep during the day. It became incumbent on her to take Charles out every morning to avoid disturbing the "retired soldier."

Since the Jericho Turnpike was already a well-traveled thoroughfare at the time, Marjorie wouldn't let Charles out of the apartment alone before he went to kindergarten. Without any playmates, Charles invented one of his own, whom he called Willie. Between the ages of three and four, Charles frequently conferred aloud with Willie over how they should play, staging battles with toy soldiers and the like. Charles's attachment to Willie riled Joseph whenever he observed it, and eventually the stern father exploded, insisting that Marjorie forbid such fantasy-like behavior. If Willie was one of the first manifestations of Ludlam's highly charged imagination, it is extremely revealing that Joseph did what he could to suppress his son's creative nature even at this formative stage.

Ludlam would later recount to Steven Samuels — manager of the Ridiculous for the last seven years of Ludlam's life, as well as the future editor of Ludlam's plays and prose — how one day, when he was around six or seven, his father caught him staring at himself in the mirror in what seemed to be an intensely self-admiring fashion. Joseph slapped him and said, "Don't you ever let me catch you looking at yourself in the mirror that way again!" Charles's relationship with his father was difficult from the start, with Joseph ever on guard to suppress any signs of unmanliness. Some years later, Ludlam was deeply hurt when he offered to help uproot a tree in the yard and Joseph replied, "It takes a real man to do this, and you'll never be one."

Countering such harsh and dismissive treatment was the loving attention Charles received from his mother and his two maiden aunts. Florence and May doted on Charles, the child they had never had, who returned their affection in kind. In fact, with little disguised envy, Marjorie claimed that whenever the adult Charles was on tour, "He wrote more to my sister May than he did to me" — mostly picture postcards of the wish-you-were-here variety. May was also Charles's godmother.

The unconditional love he received from his mother and her two sisters induced the future star of Off Broadway to crave and expect adoration from the world at large for the rest of his life. His father's constant rejection, on the other hand, produced a void that Ludlam would spend his life trying to fill — which was, perhaps, the most crucial driving force for his art.

Eventually, Ludlam would bend gender rules in revolutionary ways, and the seeds for those future achievements were sown in New Hyde Park, with the three women for whom he could do no wrong and the one man for whom he could do no right. Re-seeking on a larger scale the approval of these four critical figures from his youth, the adult Ludlam would inevitably astonish the world with his brilliance.

Though Ludlam would later claim he learned how to read from comic books, when Marjorie wasn't taking her young child for walks or on shopping expeditions, she read to him constantly. He obliged her with his curiosity and his omnivorous appetite for information. Before he went to kindergarten, Marjorie even regularly read dictionary entries to Charles.

The two of them also attended the movie house across the street every time the feature changed — which in those days was every week — gorging on Mason Mints from the candy counter as they watched *Miracle on 34th Street*, *Johnny Belinda*, *All About Eve*, *Harvey*, or *A Letter to Three Wives*. As described in his brief autobiographical statement, Ludlam's visual memory of his first home was straight out of the kind of 1940s film noir he would have seen across the street: "The druggist's neon sign in red flashed outside the windows through the organdy curtains and created a fantasy effect. Birds used to nest in the sign and we fed them."

What Ludlam would later tell his *New Yorker* profiler Calvin Tomkins was the most memorable event of his childhood provides more testimony to how inseparable the mother was from the son — and to his early fascination with the peculiar and the perverse. When Charles was six, Marjorie took him to the annual Mineola Fair. Though she refused to visit any of the sideshows because they might frighten her little boy, he managed to slip away and catch some of the freaks on his own. Much later in life, he would specifically remember seeing the fat lady, fire eater, thin man, and armless artists who manipulated chalk with their feet. Equally as crucial to his theatrical calling, Charles also took in a Punch and Judy show offered by Al Flosso, who — as suggested by his longtime moniker, the "Coney Island Fakir" — was much more famous for his magic acts than for his puppetry. (The adult Ludlam would revel in getting to know Flosso and in learning some tricks from the master magician.)

Charles, awestruck, emerged from the sideshow area at the Mineola Fair to be enveloped in the arms of his sobbing mother. The understandably distraught Marjorie had recruited the authorities to help her locate her "lost" son.

However taut the apron strings might have been at this tender age, Charles's fascination with the outside world, and the world of weird make-believe, proved stronger. "Animated cartoons and puppets shaped my life along with movies," he would later declare. Though he never became a TV fanatic like so many of his generation, as a child Charles was an enormous fan of televised puppet shows, including "Howdy Doody," "Foodini and Pinhead," and "Kukla, Fran, and Ollie," whose creator, Burr Tilstrom, became one of Ludlam's most avid fans. Like his invented playmate, Willie, the puppets on these shows were fantasy-based substitutes for the friends he both lacked and yearned for. The little boy's intense sense of solitude — even of being held like a captive in cramped quarters, with nothing but a window to the outside world — was strongly evoked by Ludlam years later: He told Peter Golub, who would serve as composer for the Ridiculous for a decade, how he often sat at the window scribbling down the license plate numbers of the passing cars, as if the information would somehow prove useful. Was he pretending to be a detective, or was he privately hoping to track the drivers down and be whisked away into the real world?

After Charles entered the first grade at New Hyde Park elementary school, Marjorie had him return to the apartment to eat with her every day, instead of packing a lunch for him. He walked home with some schoolmates who lived behind the Ludlams, and then his mother walked him back to school for the afternoon sessions. Marjorie recalled that when Charles came home for lunch on Halloween that year, he complained bitterly because the principal's daughter and her best friend were both wearing costumes, but the other students weren't allowed to. He said he wouldn't go back to school unless he could wear one too. Marjorie telephoned his teacher, who finally consented. "Even when he was five and six, you couldn't tell him anything," said Marjorie. "He knew everything."

He certainly knew he liked to "dress up": Charles actually preferred Halloween to

Christmas because of the costumes. As an adult, he would remember trick-or-treating dressed as a girl, and creating quite a sensation when he attended a Halloween party at school in drag. "When I realized that such dressing up was forbidden I began to practice it regularly in secret using my mother's clothes," he wrote in his recollections of childhood. "People frequently mistook me for a girl anyway." Even after Charles outgrew trick-or-treating, he would make himself up as a ghoul or a monster to greet youngsters at the door. One year, he made it appear as if blood was dripping from his eye as he wielded a burning candle, relishing their giddy fear as he opened the door. And as he grew older, Charles enjoyed creating Halloween costumes for his younger brother Donald, who was both his first audience and his first actor in need of direction.

When Donald was born in 1951, Charles was seven-and-a-half years old. Thanks to Marjorie's acknowledged favoritism toward her first son, and the wide gap in their ages, Charles avoided the jealousy and sibling rivalry that most children experience when their territory is usurped by a newcomer. On the contrary, Charles was uncommonly attentive to and supportive of Donald, often acting more like a parent than a domineering older brother. He created marionettes out of leftover materials from school, and entertained Donald with his own impromptu made-up shows. Much to his brother's delight, Charles also practiced his nascent skills as a ventriloquist. Nearly forty years later, Ludlam would tell a cable television interviewer, "I think all kids of my generation thought they were supposed to become ventriloquists. It was a very popular form of entertainment in the forties, and something to be attained to. But everyone else got over it but me."

By constantly reading to Donald and adopting different voices and dramatic renderings for the various characterizations the stories contained, Charles was already honing his vocal skills as a youth, which would figure so prominently in his theatrical career. Charles also rigorously helped his brother with his homework on a regular basis, which was no minor task, because Donald was dyslexic—long before this reading disability was routinely diagnosed or properly treated.

Charles's half brother, Joseph Jr., had been working in a bowling alley for a spell and generally gallivanting about, much to Marjorie's ongoing distress; after becoming a bricklayer, the twenty-two-year-old married and moved out of the overcrowded New Hyde Park apartment within a year of Donald's birth. The following year, in October of 1953, the then four-member Ludlam family made its first and last move, to the town of Greenlawn, at 20 Lawrence Street, a short walk from Marjorie's sisters' house. The Ludlams settled into a modest stucco home that Charles's father designed and built himself, with help from friends and union chums. He had worked on it for two years, mostly during the summers and on weekends. He completed construction of a living room, dining room, kitchen, and bathroom, as well as two bedrooms on the main floor. He had plans to finish work on two more bedrooms upstairs, but never got around to them. (When Charles was fifteen, he moved out of the downstairs bedroom he shared with Donald and created a living environment for himself amid the rafters upstairs.)

With a hint of yard in front and in back, the house was situated on a quiet, tree-lined street in a relatively rural community, one that was smaller and less commercial than well-trafficked New Hyde Park. Lawrence Street was still being developed when the Ludlams arrived, with only a couple of houses at the lower end of it. It filled out in the next few years and came to resemble most every other suburban road in anywhere U.S.A., circa 1953, but because Greenlawn was both far enough from New York and relatively inland, it still had some potato farms into the 1960s and remained rural enough for Charles to collect tadpoles in the ponds near his house and bring them home in jars. From the very beginning, he was captivated with just about all forms of life.

Charles had long owned a more traditional pet named Pete: a fuzzy, reddish-blond mongrel that clearly had some spaniel blood. Having been cooped up in an apartment on the Jericho Turnpike, Pete succumbed to the newfound risks to roam in Greenlawn — in March of 1954, a month before Charles's eleventh birthday, Pete bounded after his young master as he left the house one day and the dog was killed by a car. Charles was inconsolable for a week, until his parents took him to the pound, saying he could select any dog he wanted as long as it was male. As if it had been prearranged by some canine deity, they discovered a dog that was Pete's twin — in every respect but gender. She was sickly and needed to be nursed back to health. Although the dog was a female, Charles was adamant about calling her Pete. The Ludlams eventually acquired an additional dog, a black and white springer spaniel; because his ears perked up whenever "Topper" was on television, that became his name.

Greenlawn lacked a church of its own when the Ludlams settled there. Since Joseph often worked on Sundays and Marjorie had to contend with Donald, who was too young and restless to behave properly during a service, Charles attended church every Sunday with Florence and May, who took him to St. Anthony's in nearby East Northport. He had already been confirmed at the Church of the Holy Spirit in New Hyde Park, which he had sometimes attended alone in perpetual fascination.

Joseph and Marjorie went to mass only occasionally themselves. They started taking

Donald when he was old enough, but he "never took to it," as Marjorie later claimed, so they stopped. Though Joseph was a practicing Catholic when he married Marjorie, he lapsed over the years and became particularly critical of the changes in the mass enacted by Pope John XXIII in the early sixties. During one newfangled English language mass, he leaned towards his wife in the pew and said, "Never again."

Later in life, Ludlam would also decry the ecumenical changes; but he loved the Church throughout his youth, and not only because it possessed all the pomp and splendor he was denied in his shabby home environment. Charles clearly related to the mystery of the mass, the lavish vestments, and the incense — which, not so incidentally, he would incorporate in the early plays of the Ridiculous. Even at a tender age, Charles found an inextricable connection between the Church and the theater, and he would transfer his youthful adoration of the first into his lifelong commitment to the second.

To be sure, a Catholic service is nothing less than a theatrical event without the reserved seat. Priests are, in a sense, actors reading the Lord's *script*ures and actually reenacting His word in the well-made drama of the mass. As a boy, Charles told his parents he was going to be a priest when he grew up. When he decided to become an actor instead and his mother asked, "What about the priesthood?" he replied, "They're the same thing — they're both here to make people happy."

Also, later in life, Ludlam would draw a far more unusual connection between the Madonna and the transvestite. During an interview for an intended but unwritten biography of the famous female impersonator Candy Darling, Ludlam told Stephen Holt that the Madonna is an "idealized image of woman as a virgin, the inviolable woman," and that "a good argument could be made for the fact that the transvestite is that image, in a way, because it's inviolable, forever virgin, not having female genitalia."

Ludlam's eventual rebellion against the Church and its outmoded ideology would become a recurring motif in many of his plays. Though Catholic guilt was never a part of his conscious vocabulary, it was a motivating force in his life to come. Long before he contended with the Church and its doctrine, he would challenge authority whenever he wanted to win the rights he felt he deserved, or a role he wanted.

He had previously demonstrated that determination with his first-grade teacher in the incident over the Halloween costume, and his unabashed efforts to get what he desired became a manifest theme throughout his school career. Charles's independent streak

won the respect of some mentors but provoked the dismay of others — both when the
boy was on the stage and off.

Charles had his first part in a school play, called *Santa in Blunderland*, when he was in
the second grade. Three years later, he created something of a scene over a role in
another school production. Charles's fifth-grade teacher had already selected another
pupil to play a part that Charles wanted, but with characteristic audacity, Charles
demanded he be considered for the role until the teacher finally relented and left the
decision up to a vote by the students. Charles won the vote and the part — though this
shouldn't suggest that he was particularly popular with his classmates, who treated him
as the loner he was. Perhaps they simply considered him the best candidate for the job.
But, in addition to the part, Charles also secured the lingering disfavor of his teacher.
When Charles's sixth-grade teacher-to-be told his fifth-grade teacher that she couldn't
wait to have him in her class, she was forewarned, "You'll be sorry because he's so fresh
and difficult to deal with."

Even when the prize wasn't a highly coveted stage role, Charles showed the same kind
of righteous willingness to challenge authority. Once in high school, Charles was
disputing a translation question with several of his classmates before a Spanish class
began, when the teacher arrived and entered the fray by correcting Charles, who kept
arguing that he was right. Charles threatened to stage a walkout to prove his point,
and a number of the other students threatened to leave with him — probably as much
to avoid another Spanish class as to side with Charles. The Ludlams were called in to
school and informed of how disrespectful their son had been; but, ultimately, the
teacher had to concede that, in the matter of the translation, Charles had been right.

Charles matched his obdurate independence with his own private version of time and
schedules. As a teenager, he was already developing his lifelong habits as a "night
person," usually reading well into the early morning hours. Naturally, he was slow to
wake up, and his mother indulged him, letting him dash off every day following a little
cereal and juice for breakfast, inevitably late for school. He once wrote a wistful poem
of sorts accounting for his tardiness — "I had to stop and smell the flowers along the
way . . ." — which was pinned up on a bulletin board in the school hallway. Another
time, presumably in high school, Marjorie and Joseph were once again called in, this
time to discuss his chronic tardiness for his first morning class. When he had refused
to follow his teacher's injunction that he tell his parents about the problem himself, the
teacher said, "I'll have to suspend you," and Charles responded, "You won't have to

suspend me: I quit the class." (This same teacher would later become a regular attendee
of the Ridiculous Theatrical Company.)

Charles's manner and attitude may have left a lot to be desired by everyone except his
mother and his aunts, but he was in honors English classes throughout high school. He
was a bright and impressive student who received predominantly A's or B's in everything
but math, which he once flunked and had to make up in summer school.

Beyond his academic accomplishments, Charles began to be notorious for his eccentric,
theatrical behavior and style. New Hyde Park's schools had a dress code but Greenlawn's
did not, which did not stop the teenage Charles from dressing up in his own way. Given
his sartorial care, he appeared terribly overdressed to his classmates, who sported jeans
in junior high. Charles refused to wear them, and they bullied him about it. Donald
remembered more than one instance when Charles came home from school battered
and bruised, trying to cover up the assaults by saying that he had fallen playing ball.

By his junior year at Harborfields High, Charles developed an ostentatiously casual style
less dandy than beatnik, which was more even than this new and highly progressive
school of only 750 students could readily accommodate. He once took a blanket and cut
a hole in the middle, creating a sort of friar's poncho for himself. He crafted a "Chinese
fertility stick" from an intricately carved branch and carried it around school every day
like a cane. He had long, shoulder-length hair a good decade ahead of its time, and he
wore thongs instead of shoes or sneakers to school. Some of his more aggressive tormen-
tors stole his sandals one day, and when Charles was ordered before the principal to
explain why he was attending classes barefoot, the culprits were duly penalized.
However, the episode could not have improved Charles's social standing in a cliquish,
affluent high school hierarchy that would likely have even less tolerance for tattletales
than for outsiders. At that time, Charles's status at home was no better: By then he was
regularly incurring the wrath of his father, who realized he had a "sissy" for a son.

Throughout his youth, Charles turned to the theater to win the attention and approba-
tion he failed to receive through more ordinary channels. Far beyond the puppet shows
he presented on a stage rigged by himself in the basement, he became one of the
leading actors at Harborfields High, which produced two shows a year. Walter Baden,
the school's drama coach, cast Charles as the title character in *Finian's Rainbow*, but
Charles wanted the far showier role of Og, the leprechaun. (It's Og who sings one of
the show's hit songs: "When I'm Not Near the Girl I Love.") He got his wish when
another student agreed to switch roles with him during the rehearsal period.

Our Town and *The Importance of Being Earnest* were among the other school plays Charles was in. But more germane to his own brand of theater-to-be was a slapstick farce, *The Doctor in Spite of Himself*, one of Molière's Sganarelle plays. Like Molière, Ludlam would come to maintain his own troupe of actors for whom he wrote plays, which he starred in and directed himself. And what is arguably Ludlam's most over-looked masterpiece, *Le Bourgeois Avant-Garde*, would be based on Molière's *Le Bourgeois Gentilhomme*.

Charles's involvement with theater as a teenager quickly surpassed the more customary aspiring-actor apprenticeship of performing in high school productions. When he was fifteen, he was introduced to the Township Theater Group in Huntington by Charles Hammond, the son of his aunts' neighbor. Over the next few seasons, not only did Charles perform with this, Long Island's oldest established community theater, but he also directed a number of shows for children, learning about set design and costuming in the process. This was truly extraordinary for one so young.

Working with many older and more experienced amateur actors, as well as ever-volatile children, the budding director undertook versions of *Peter Pan* (in which Charles had a field day playing Captain Hook) and *Jack and the Beanstalk* (a familiar fairy tale he would himself adapt for the stage later in life). He cast his brother Donald as a page in *The Emperor's New Clothes*, a production that was also performed at St. Charles Hospital, a children's infirmary in Port Jefferson. In another fairy-tale play he directed, *The Three Wishing Bags*, one of the young actresses was costumed in a layered net tutu with leotards underneath. She apparently felt that too much of her body was exposed and once showed up with a full skirt under the netting; the decisive Charles just ripped it off.

Also during high school, Charles portrayed the villainous Harry Beaton in a production of *Brigadoon* for the Huntington Choral Society, and he did some onstage narration during dance performances for the Eglevsky Ballet Company in Massapequa. In 1958, Walter Baden even arranged a leave of absence from school for Charles so he could work with William Hunt's Red Barn Theater in Northport, beginning in the late spring.

Like all other summer stock theaters, the Red Barn brought popular Broadway fare to the provinces. Charles was involved with the Red Barn throughout the summer. He had a couple of minor roles in the Broadway hit of three years before, *No Time For Sergeants*. The many notes in his working script for the period comedy indicate how seriously he took even those insignificant parts.

After the Red Barn concluded its season, Charles took William Hunt aside to ask the affable director about his prospects for a future career in the theater. Hunt dodged the question at first, saying that he hadn't seen enough of Charles's work to be able to tell. But when Charles pressed the issue, Hunt told him that one obvious hindrance to any possible success was that he was too effeminate. Curiously, Hunt had the distinct impression that this was the first time anyone had brought the matter to Charles's attention. After a week of pouting and generally feeling sorry for himself, Charles defiantly told Hunt that he would just have to have his own theater then, so that he could be the star he knew he would become.

Charles made the trek to and from the Red Barn on a bicycle. Charles's aunts — who drove an old Dodge sedan, which was kept as spotless as their house — offered to buy a car for their adored nephew. But like his mother, Ludlam would never care enough about driving to even try to get a license. It was highly unusual for someone who came of age in the suburbs in the fifties to choose not to drive when given the opportunity. Unlike other male adolescents of his generation, Charles was far more interested in Shakespeare than in hot rods.

Characteristic of the mama's boy he was, Charles mostly associated with girls instead of boys in high school. One girl he claimed to love romantically was named Kyra, a young woman who struck her classmates as a poetic type, evoking the callow character played by Julie Harris in *The Member of the Wedding*. Another girlfriend, Heidi Hertwig, was in the class below Charles; her parents were German, and she was earthy and sexually liberated in ways redolent of Europe, which made her as much of an outsider to the conformist, suburban culture of central Long Island as Charles. Charles related to Heidi's being different, and he loved her irreverent sense of humor.

Charles also grew close to Claire Weintraub, who lived in the adjacent town of Huntington. Another brainy and precocious teenager, Claire was short and plump and plagued with skin problems. Her awkward appearance left her less interested in fitting in with the crowd than in intellectual pursuits, which naturally made her all the more appealing to Charles. They met when they worked together at the Red Barn, where Claire gave a reading of Anne Frank's *Diary* several years after it was published in English.

Perhaps Charles's most significant relationship with a woman in high school was his profound, platonic bond with Jan Reynolds, who had grown up in Sea Cliff and had attended a parochial school before her family moved to Centerport, when she was in

the sixth grade. The gaunt and uncommonly tall Jan was distinguished by her aristo-
cratic appearance and aloof manner, which reflected her unusually sophisticated
background. Her Catholic father was an executive with Union Carbide, and her
Episcopalian mother traced her roots back "to the Dutch who bought the land from
the Indians," as Reynolds put it.

Jan began attending Harborfields in the eighth grade, and as she recalled, "Charlie
Ludlam was just always there." They were both in the class of 1961, or the second to
graduate from this new and highly progressive school, which had opened its doors
in 1956. Given the vicious attitudes that emerge within close-knit school environments
to taunt outcasts like Charles, it was only natural for him to befriend another loner
like Jan. She was in the Harborfields production of *Our Town* with Charles, but stage
fright got the best of her and she would never act again.

Charles and Jan were brought together by Earl Jacobs, their English teacher, whom they
revered. Jacobs's reading list gives a pretty good indication of just how advanced a
teacher he was for his time: In addition to such challenging books as *Lord of the Flies*,
The Brothers Karamazov, and *The Stranger*, in the coming years Jacobs would assign his
students groundbreaking, provocative works such as Paul Goodman's *Growing Up
Absurd* and Joseph Campbell's *Hero with a Thousand Faces*. "Earl Jacobs was more than
just a 'cool' teacher," claimed Reynolds. "Once, when he found out that Charlie and I
played hooky, his response was, 'You know, I think you can learn more playing hooky
sometimes than coming to school.'"

In addition to recognizing them for the avid students they were, Jacobs realized that
Charles and Jan had a lot in common. It wasn't just that Jan, like Charles, was routinely
tardy for school — sometimes by as much as an hour whenever she happened to miss
the bus. "We were marginal personalities and outsiders who didn't belong," Reynolds
explained, emphasizing how lonely they were before she and Charles met. "I was
extremely rebellious and felt like I was an artist. Then I went to Charlie's house, and I
said to myself, 'Oh, God, here's another one.' But in his case, it was even worse, because
I was somewhat compatible with my mother. Charlie's father was a yahoo. He was a
disgruntled man who never smiled. And Marjorie, who was extremely unattractive,
never talked much when Joe was around. Charlie was also very quiet around his parents
and didn't want to be home. We used to go up in his attic to be by ourselves."

Jan was very impressed with Charles's artistic skills, as displayed by his paintings that
filled the walls of the living quarters he had fashioned for himself in the attic. Earl

Jacobs, who was in his mid-thirties at the time, was also a painter. He had fostered something of an intellectual community within Harborfields High by offering after-school sessions, referred to as "seances," for select students, including Charles and Jan during their junior and senior years. Held on Tuesday afternoons in the Green Room off the school's handsome new theater — or in any available classroom — the discussions dealt with formidable topics such as the virtues or liabilities of utopian communities, Clement Greenberg's art criticism, and controversial theories of education or progressive school environments such as Summerhill. By encouraging his students to think for themselves about so many brash ideas, Jacobs alienated some of his more conservative colleagues, including William Morrisey, a history teacher who also served as the football coach. Morrisey used to declare that Jacobs was a "commie." Predictably, the macho Morrisey also had problems with the fey Charles.

Jacobs clearly had a bohemian sensibility, as did his friends, Dick and Charlotte Koons. Dick Koons was a high school teacher at East Northport who, according to Reynolds, was eventually dismissed for his pro-Communist teachings. The Koons held gatherings for artistic types every weekend at their home in Eaton's Neck, a sparsely settled rural area on Long Island Sound, north of Greenlawn. After Jacobs introduced them, Charles and Jan became regular guests at these affairs, which occasionally included visitors from New York City who were apparently homosexual.

Through Jacobs and the Koons, Charles received the intellectual and emotional suste-nance he craved but failed to get at home. As Henry Geldzahler, the first curator of contemporary art at New York's Metropolitan Museum and a patron of Ludlam's, would explain, "Charles was deeply displeased with his family background. He used to talk about the paucity of understanding when he was growing up, about the inability to show and feel affection at home. When I first knew him in the mid-sixties, he was quite frank about all this. He told me that my support helped to fill up something that had been empty, that my approval was important to him because I was someone who understood him."

Charles and Jan, loners who had banded together, finally came into their own during their senior year, as evidenced by their distinctive yearbook monikers, "Mr. and Miss Individual." That caption appears with a photo of the two of them, posed under a large fishing net bearing a sign: "Fighting Oppression." "During something called 'Brotherhood Week,'" Reynolds recalled, "we had cards saying that we wouldn't care about the race, color, or creed of anybody who lived next to us, as long as they were of good character. I remember being sent to the principal by William Morrisey, the conservative teacher, for distributing those cards in class."

Stressing that Charles was really celebrated at Harborfields for his sensational and antic performance as Og in *Finian's Rainbow*, Reynolds confirms how popular they became. "We finally developed our own group and our own sense of self that final year," she said, "Charlie with theater and me with painting. The whole perception changed: The crowd that was out now became 'in.' We became the place to be." Both Charles and Jan were nothing less than astonished their senior year when Brian Asher, the star of the Harborfields football team, turned to them for advice on how he should pose for his yearbook photo.

Reynolds also felt that Charles conveyed no sense of being superior until that last year, when he suddenly adopted an attitude that he was an artist and, therefore, special. She further believed that Charles's newfound outlook was due mostly to the encouragement of Earl Jacobs, who "came along and said, 'You guys are terrific.' But before that," she continued, "even when Charlie was denigrated by everyone else, he never put down other students. Even when we were suffering a lot, he was quite compassionate."

With the in-school celebrity he found his senior year, Charles felt free to extend the bounds of his theatrical behavior. Far beyond finally feeling accepted for who he was, he found himself being embraced for it.

Probably no one at Harborfields was more impressed with Charles than Christopher Scott. Despite brief periods of estrangement during the next twenty-seven years, Scott would become one of the most significant friends in Ludlam's life.

THE WHOLE WORLD HIS STAGE

To start a theater, you must be a revolutionary. . . . I mean you must be motivated by
dissatisfaction in some way with the status quo.
— Konstantin Stanislavski

I want a blazing career. . . . Acting makes me feel alive. So much of my confusion and
dissatisfaction come from wanting to live every day with the kind of intensity that
is only possible on the stage.
— Charles Ludlam

If Charles Ludlam was an outsider among his peers in high school, he clearly invited such a distinction. He worked hard to be perceived as a renegade and even a weirdo. By the start of his senior year, it was obvious to everyone that Charles was "different," which, on one level, meant gay. Like most other teenagers with this difficult secret, he tried to explore sexual relations with girls. Unlike most other adolescents with homosexual proclivities, he did nothing to disguise them and, in fact, signaled them blatantly. He thrived on his flamboyant mannerisms, since they brought him the attention he craved.

To Charles, the world was primarily a stage to be conquered, and he was already creating a major role for himself as a pansexual Puck. After his flagrant gamble paid off and the misfit was perceived as a maverick, Charles would do whatever was necessary to gain the limelight.

At seventeen, Charles was short and had a compact, muscular body. His best feature was his penetrating, electric blue eyes. As if by flicking a switch, Charles could use his remarkably expressive gaze to appear demonic or angelic. He also had a particular gift for mimicking and duplicating the voices of anyone who entered his orbit — even someone he had only met in passing. But Charles's innate talents and formidable skills could do nothing to disguise the large, bulbous nose that made him at once unattractive and striking. (According to Jan Reynolds, he looked like Cyrano de Bergerac — "a man to his nose attached.") Surprisingly for one so young, he was already beginning to lose his hair as well. Whatever problems he had with youthful self-esteem, however, were more than compensated for by his galloping grandiosity.

By the time Christopher Scott met him, Charles was something of a star at Harborfields High. Anticipating that her sensitive and artistic friend Christopher would like the effusive, proto-bohemian Charles, Jan brought them together. Although he was two years younger than Charles and only a sophomore, Christopher already knew that he wanted to be a painter when he grew up. A quietly intense youth with long black hair, he was another shy, lost adolescent, but he blossomed under Charles's attentions.

In Christopher Scott, Charles found someone who was in awe of him, but he also envied his new friend's more fortunate background. Whereas Charles had one nurturing parent and another who was disapproving, Scott had two who were supportive. Descended from early Quaker and Mennonite settlers in Philadelphia, the Scotts were also affluent in a way Charles had never observed before. Christopher's father, Walter, was an aeronautical engineer at the Grumman Aircraft Corporation, a major defense contractor on Long Island that flourished in the midst of the Cold War. His mother, Frances, was a homemaker whose patrician demeanor her son inherited.

The Scotts, including Christopher's younger brother David, had moved from the nearby town of Huntington to Centerport in 1959. Their large, split-level house, set in an upper-middle-class development called Plaissance, was situated on a waterfront bluff that separated Centerport Harbor from Northport Bay.

Remarkably for a teenager, Christopher had a private entrance to his room, and Charles could visit him without going through the rest of the house. Christopher was also in therapy, which was rare at the time for suburban American parents, let alone their children. But Frances Scott had had several nervous breakdowns, and she passed on her knowledge of Freud's precepts to her two young sons. Christopher himself was in psychotherapy for depression and anomie during his high school years.

Prompted by Jan Reynolds, Christopher phoned Charles in December of 1960 and arranged to meet him during Christmas break. After hitchhiking the two miles from Centerport, Christopher showed up at the Ludlams' modest house and found Marjorie so brusque that she did not even invite him in. But as his friendship with Charles developed, Christopher became a familiar presence at the Ludlam household, whether Marjorie liked it or not. Jan may have found the domestic atmosphere at the Ludlam home subdued several years earlier, but Christopher likened it to a kind of bedlam.

The well-mannered Christopher was always struck by the disarray at Lawrence Street: from the protruding upholstery springs and general clutter everywhere to the way Charles and his family constantly yelled at one another. The pandemonium was only compounded by the pair of large, rambunctious dogs bounding about the small living room and jumping on the decrepit furniture. The house also had a pervasive odor, which Christopher eventually realized emanated from piles of dirty laundry that Marjorie failed to keep up with.

"Charles's mother looked exactly like Shirley Booth," Scott recalled, referring to the beloved actress who was about to become a household name as television's Hazel. "Marjorie had a pronounced New York manner and was always playing a comic role." His additional memories powerfully suggest that Marjorie's dealings with Charles changed as he was about to graduate high school and leave home. "She reacted to Charles's antics with scathing, but obviously affectionate, sarcasm," Scott continued. "She was critical of his every move. When she was really angry, she would rant and rave. But she was hopelessly ineffectual in influencing his behavior. On the other hand, she would defend Charles whenever she felt that he was being unfairly treated by his teachers. When I first met him, Charles mentioned that his mother thought he looked like Greta Garbo — which made no sense to me whatsoever."

"Charles's father," Scott continued, "had the same comic repertoire, but could also be cruel, and was prone to temper tantrums. He was lean and had an eagle-like face as well as a bald dome fringed with gray hair. He wore old-fashioned wire-rimmed glasses, and he generated an aura of virility. He had big, muscular forearms, like Popeye. He usually wore rumpled khaki pants and an old tee-shirt."

Christopher Scott quickly became a part of the suburban, bohemian inner circle at Harborfields High that included Earl Jacobs's "seances" and field trips to the Koons' house on weekends. He believed the Koons were motivated to introduce them to *Giovanni's Room* — James Baldwin's controversial novel about homosexuality — to convey the subtle message that it was all right to be gay. This was something that Charles, Christopher, and Jan Reynolds all needed to hear. Jan was very confused at the time about her own sexuality. Having had an aunt who had a female companion for many years, she knew what lesbians were. She discussed her dilemma with the school psychologist, and she devoured a book on the subject that she discovered in the library. Christopher — who was, after all, younger — was not yet in touch with his homosexual tendencies. Charles, rather than pondering his sexuality, soon began simply to live it.

In the relaxed atmosphere at Harborfields High, these three outlandish musketeers would occasionally cut classes and hang out in the school's music room, or at the nearby and usually deserted Greenlawn Station of the Long Island Railroad's Port Jefferson line. The fact that the depot was heated even when it was unattended made it an ideal assignation spot during the winter.

As they talked, experimenting with various radical notions in the air at the turn of the decade, Charles echoed the liberal views of their teachers, who were highly critical of the cultural establishment and who promoted a rugged individualism to combat the conformity of the Eisenhower era that was then coming to a close. But it was only natural for the young Charles to also subscribe to some of his parents' right-wing views. Among the most shocking was their conviction that the recently disgraced and deceased Red-baiter Joseph McCarthy was a great man and an American hero. Christopher had to work hard to persuade Charles how inconsistent this notion was with his other beliefs.

"One of the reasons I was so drawn to Charles was that he had this absolute confidence in himself," Scott said. "I was very insecure. But Charles had a great verbal gift and he'd talk anyone down. He never let anyone push him around."

That winter — in his bedroom, at the train station and in Christopher's house — Charles talked about his experience at the Red Barn and emphasized how "hokey" and "insincere" such theater seemed to him. He was sure he could do much better with a theater of his own. Frances Scott recalled that Charles always declared he was going to become a part of the New York theater world. And in spite of the obstacles facing him, she had no doubt he would succeed.

Given the opportunity to enjoy the ways a more loving family behaved, Charles seized it. To Marjorie's dismay, he spent more and more time away from home, and much of it at the Scotts' opulent premises. Frances described Charles as the "extra kid who practically lives at your house." During the many evenings he stayed for dinner, she would urge him to phone Marjorie and let her know where he was; sometimes he did, and sometimes he didn't. Christopher's mother also remembered several times when Marjorie called to ask if she knew where Charles was, which Frances usually did. Marjorie had to be doubly offended — not only because Charles did not telephone his mother to tell her what he was doing, but also because Christopher, a more considerate son, always did.

Marjorie was not the only one having problems with the teenage Charles Ludlam. In what emerged as a pattern of irresponsibility that would continue throughout his life, Charles had agreed to provide some more narration for the Eglevesky Ballet Company in Massapequa during his senior year of high school. But then, instead of showing up for the performance, he went on a camping trip with some friends.

The headstrong and competitive Charles had hopes of staging a production himself at Harborfields High. He was much admired by the drama coach; but, due to his unwillingness to take orders and his repeated tardiness, he was expelled from the drama club late that last winter of high school.

Not being allowed to direct a play was all the impetus that Charles needed to form a theater group of his own. Christopher was the first person he approached with the idea. Despite Christopher's misgivings about getting a space and raising the necessary money, Charles was unstoppable. Once he secured his friend's cooperation, Charles phoned Claire Weintraub to recruit her involvement as well. Though they had had some kind of a falling-out since first working together at the Red Barn Theater—"possibly with romantic overtones," according to Scott—she agreed to consider participating in the daring venture if an actual theater materialized.

Shortly after Charles introduced Christopher to Claire, the three of them ventured into Manhattan—the first time Charles had visited the city without adult supervision. Charles had already been to New York on a museum field trip with Donald Kurka, the high school art instructor, but he didn't really know the city at all. He was only too happy to rely on his more experienced friends to show him what it had to offer. With Christopher and Claire as tour guides, they visited Washington Square and took in the Village life around MacDougal and 8th Streets that so captured their budding bohemian imaginations. They had obligatory coffees and pastries at Cafes Figaro and Reggio, which in the spring of 1961 were still redolent of the beatnik era. The sidewalks were teeming with people wearing sandals and sporting beards; and the only thing more unusual than observing a number of interracial couples and obviously gay pedestrians was realizing that they alone seemed to notice them.

Safely back on Long Island, Charles and Christopher went scouting for a theater space for their summer project. They discovered just what they were looking for in Northport, a quaint town on Long Island's North Shore. Above a liquor store on the main street was a large meeting room that had once been used for Odd Fellow functions, but had been vacant for quite some time. Though it had no stage or proscenium, it was equipped with chairs, which the earnest thespians arranged in semicircular rows. In the rear was a small room with a sink and a hotplate. The liquor store owner, a Mr. Blue, was only too happy to add revenue to his monthly income by renting the space, but he was understandably reluctant to deal with minors no matter how confident they seemed. As long as one of their parents signed the lease, the room could be theirs for only $25 a month throughout the summer. Frances Scott came through with both the money and the signature.

During much of the summer, Charles literally lived at the theater, eating and sleeping in the back room. The landlord might have disapproved, but Charles's mother was even more livid. The first time her son stayed overnight in Northport, a distraught Marjorie phoned Frances Scott "several times to ask if Charles was with us. When I next saw him," Frances Scott recalled, "I said, 'Charles, will you please tell your mother that you're living at the theater?' Both Mrs. Ludlam and I worried about what he was eating because he usually had nothing but cans of spaghetti beside his hotplate."

Jan Reynolds recalled that Claire Weintraub seemed to be a moving force behind the makeshift theater troupe that would stage four plays in the summer of 1961, although Christopher Scott denied this. He even remembered that Claire was skeptical, at first, and had to be convinced that the enterprise would work. But surely anyone who observed Charles and Claire interact at the time would quickly realize how fiercely competitive they were. Like Charles, Claire was tremendously energetic and intelligent, with opinions on everything. From which plays they should do to how they should do them, they bickered over every question teenage actor-producers could face. They even argued about what the group should be called. Ultimately, the "Number One Theater" was rejected for the "Students' Repertory Theater."

In the end, the group chose to produce plays that were either obscure, rigorously challenging, or both, and nothing like the Red Barn summer-theater fare being staged just a few towns away: *Madman on the Roof*, a modern Nōh play by Kikuchi Kan; *Theatre of the Soul*, a late-romantic Russian play by Nikolai Yevreinov; O'Neill's *The Great God Brown*; and Strindberg's *A Dream Play*. Given its many characters and the technical demands of its surreal unfolding, *A Dream Play* would have tested the mettle of even the most established of theatrical troupes. If Strindberg's famously expressionistic piece is historically significant for having liberated the theater from the constraints of naturalism, it also prefigured Ludlam's penchant for epic plays that defy time and space. With Charles both directing and starring in the plays, the Students' Repertory Theater further foreshadowed the company Ludlam was destined to form seven years later.

The group charged one dollar for admission. The tickets had been artfully designed with woodcut prints by Christopher Scott. Jan Reynolds was minimally involved — mostly contributing design elements for the O'Neill offering — but a dozen other students made themselves available to Charles throughout the summer.

Charles's expectations for how the plays would be performed were so high, they never could have been realized. When the whole thing was over, he went into a deep depression. Years later, Ludlam told Ridiculous cofounder Black-Eyed Susan that his approach to the Students' Repertory Theater had been far too earnest, and that he had had a "breakdown" after the experience. What's more, he came to feel that he risked going mad again whenever he took things too seriously, as he was inclined to. This, in part, was what motivated him to devote the bulk of his life to writing comedies, as opposed to the terribly dark and somber works he staged in 1961.

Charles walked away from the Students' Repertory Theater with one very important lesson: He had a natural gift for recruiting the support and services of many other talented people. In a brief, unpublished memoir she wrote about Charles, Frances Scott stressed how struck she was by his ability to bring people together to work for him for free, and by his "absolute dogged perseverance." She specifically recalled a time shortly after the Students' Repertory Theater when he needed a sports jacket. He showed up at her doorstep with some fabric and a pattern that he had acquired, asking her for guidance in cutting the material. It was a difficult task she never would have undertaken on her own, but Charles had summoned her to it.

In the face of Ludlam's colossal determination, a remarkable number of people would always do what was necessary to supply him with whatever he needed to create his work. How else could his Ridiculous Theatrical Company have endured for two decades while rarely providing its players with a living wage before its later years?

૭૦

Rather than taking any pride in his son's forming a theater troupe at such a young age, Joseph Ludlam did nothing to disguise his contempt. If anything, his ire was raised a notch or two by the fact that Charles was about to go to college. For years, Joseph had been waiting for Charles finally to graduate high school, get a job, and help support the family. "We never heard how Charles dealt with this problem," Frances Scott claimed. "But nothing would have stopped him. His father — who struck me as a silent, sullen man — was simply overruled."

Under the strained circumstances, the senior Ludlam was certainly not about to help finance his son's college career. But thanks to Walter Baden's endorsement, Charles received a scholarship in drama at Hofstra University in Hempstead, roughly thirty miles from his parents' home on Long Island. From somewhere up her frugal Irish sleeve, Marjorie managed to provide a modicum of financial assistance; in fact, by redeeming an insurance policy she had taken out in her firstborn's name. And as always, his aunts slipped their favorite nephew some spare cash whenever they saw him. Charles would also eke out what living arrangements he could, often with others paying more than their fair share of the expenses. After a couple of months of living with his parents and commuting to school at the start of his freshman year, Charles shared an upstairs bedroom in a private home in Hempstead with Robert Madero, a budding filmmaker.

Charles was accepted as a speech-drama major at Hofstra for the fall of 1961. Although his primary interest was in leading roles, the faculty discouraged the peculiar-looking Ludlam from performing because they didn't think he could secure starring parts in the real world. They steered him instead toward writing and directing, and he would ulti-mately major in dramatic literature.

Nothing, of course, would keep Charles from acting throughout his four-year career at Hofstra. Bernard Beckerman, the chairman of the Drama Department, frequently directed Charles in school productions, but never cast him as the lead. Charles was only a lowly Mariner, for example, in *The Tempest*, which was put on during the spring of his freshman year. He fared much better the following fall, landing the plum part of Banjo (the hyperactive character played by Jimmy Durante in the 1941 film version) in *The Man Who Came to Dinner*. Also during his sophomore year, Charles played the non-singing Finian McLonergan in *Finian's Rainbow* — which happened to be the very same role he had relinquished to portray Og, the leprechaun, in his high school pro-duction. He was typecast as the mischievous Puck in *A Midsummer Night's Dream*, during the spring of 1963. And if he was respectably cast the following year as Decius Brutus, one of the conspirators in *Julius Caesar*, he was really able to strut his stuff during his final semester at Hofstra as Baptista Minola, the put-upon father of Kate and Bianca, in *The Taming of the Shrew*.

By casting him as Baron de Charlus in Tennessee Williams's difficult, poetic, dream play *Camino Real*, and as Squire Acres in Sheridan's classic comedy *The Rivals*, still other fac-ulty members confirmed how Charles was strictly perceived as a character actor. Indeed, one of the primary motivations that led Ludlam to start his own company some years later was to be able to play leading roles — not only gaining himself more stage time but also altering conventional notions of leading roles to suit himself. Time and again, he would also make a philosophical point about received ideas of what constitutes beauty — as well as the way that we perceive ourselves.

Charles achieved something worthy of a footnote in theatrical history in May 1962, when he concluded his first year of college by performing in the world premiere of *Figuro in the Night*, an experimental lyric fantasy by Sean O'Casey, which satirized puritanical aspects of Irish society and furthered the great playwright's long-standing criticism of the clergy. But in an encounter even more important to the development of American theater, Charles — clad in a woman's jacket and hat from the 1940s — approached one of the other cast members backstage during *Figuro*.

"I'd never seen him before," Susan Carlson remembered, "when he just walked up to me and said, 'How do you like my Greta Garbo hat?' He was like a breath of fresh air for me, because backstage were all these terribly unfriendly men who took themselves very seriously. Charles was the opposite: He was open and direct and amiable." His forthright seductiveness with Susan prefigured the way he would introduce himself to others in the future, drawing them into his magnetic field from the moment they met him.

Reared in Shelton, Connecticut, Susan Carlson had just transferred to Hofstra from Emerson College in Boston. She aspired to be a great tragedienne and, given her natural beauty, Susan possessed great dramatic appeal. Charles was captivated by her dark, piercing eyes and her long black hair, which offset her porcelain skin. He would rechristen her "Black-Eyed Susan" in several years, and ultimately she would become the only cofounder of the Ridiculous who remained with the company until Ludlam's death — and beyond, for that matter.

The program credits for *Figuro in the Night* list Susan as a "Dancer" in the production, and she also worked on the costumes. (In addition to playing "1st Old Man," Charles helped construct the set.) Charles encouraged Susan to audition for *A Solid House*, an esoteric one-act by Mexican playwright Elena Garro, a play that he staged in the fall of 1963. After she read for the leading role late on a Friday afternoon, Charles told her that he had several other people scheduled to audition for the part. "But then, as I was leaving the building by the stairwell," Susan recalled, "he came running after me, shouting, 'You have the role! I couldn't let you suffer all weekend!' I realized then how sympathetic he was toward me."

Though *A Solid House* was only twenty minutes long and the cast would be giving only a single performance for other students, Charles spent three months rehearsing it. Only Susan and two other original players stuck it out; other roles continually had to be recast. During the course of the final rehearsals, President Kennedy was assassinated and the campus was abruptly closed down — just as the rest of the country came to a virtual standstill. Susan recalled accompanying Charles to see Beckerman, the department chairman. When Charles insisted, "You have to keep the classroom open so I can rehearse!" a tearful, trembling Beckerman asked the student director if he knew that Kennedy had just been killed. Charles replied, "Yes, I know. It's awful. But I have a play to put on." Contrary to what that exchange might imply, however, Christopher Scott remembered that Charles was deeply affected by the assassination, and wondered what the long-term consequences might be for the country. But clearly, for Charles, theater came before politics or any real-life tragedy.

During the course of *A Solid House*, all of the characters die and enter a tomb. Charles outfitted the actors with skeletal masks on sticks, and then proceeded to paint the masks to resemble their own faces. At the conclusion of the performance, he demanded that the cast members return to their dressing rooms without taking a curtain call, since their characters were supposed to be dead. Yet again, the faculty was troubled by his flouting convention and denying the cast the applause they were entitled to.

Charles believed that he was brighter than his teachers. Not only did he continue to rebel against his Hofstra instructors, as he had argued with his pre-college teachers, but he encouraged others to do so as well. "I was very shy and introverted, and tended to acquiesce," Susan said. "But Charles gave me the power to realize that our teachers had limitations to their vision which had nothing to do with me."

Charles and Susan took several courses together, including Spanish and Playwriting Analysis. When the students were asked in the Analysis class to select a scene from dramatic literature that would feature them playing against type, the fragile and insecure Susan chose the voluptuous, earthy title character in *Anna Christie*. "I was very serious about it," Susan recalled. She wore a black skirt with fringe, high heels, and bright red lipstick for the scene. "After we performed for the class, Charles said, 'Brava. You made the scene.' I responded, 'But I was playing against type. They told me I could never play that role.' And he said, 'You were born to play that role. Don't listen to them.'"

For deliberately shocking and provoking the Hofstra faculty, Charles was penalized in a number of ways. Even though he was obviously one of the more exceptional actors ever to pass through the university's doors, he was excluded from a traveling theater group that performed at various schools throughout Long Island. Charles's file at Hofstra includes an unsigned, undated, end-of-the-year evaluation that was highly critical of his attitude. The "Incomplete" he received for a drama course in the fall of his sophomore year eventually yielded a C grade in the spring. And during his final semester of college, the registrar finally waived the three requisite semesters of ROTC he never got around to taking.

Charlotte Forbes, another Hofstra classmate, declared:

> The one teacher Charles worked a lot with, Bernie Beckerman, could not have respected or loved him more. I remember Charles directed me in *Blood Wedding*, which Bernie was supposed to be directing, but then he got ill and, remarkably, gave Charles carte blanche for staging it. Bernie realized he was out of his depth with Lorca. He also knew that Charles was one of the greatest improvisational people who ever lived.
>
> But the other teachers hated Charles. They were very narrow-minded, and whenever any real talent showed up, they shot it down. There were a lot of very gifted and strange people at Hofstra when I was there. But Charles was the flukiest. I mean, the theater department felt so threatened by Madeline Kahn that they literally threw her out: She transferred into the music department. With Charles, they pushed him into other aspects of the theater [besides acting], as a way of getting rid of him. Other people were more able to play the politics of the situation, but Charles could never bring himself to do that.

Charlotte, who was a class behind Charles, worked with him on a number of shows, including *The Rivals*, in the fall of 1964. Her more vivid memories of being in *The Taming of the Shrew* with Charles the following year, however, demonstrate that Charles would commandeer any stage and make it his own even this early in his career. "I was Kate and Charles was my father. And talk about upstaging! Charles would suddenly walk behind me and say his line. That immediately upstaged me, because I would have to turn my back to the audience to respond to him. We would end up moving all the way to the rear of the stage by the end of that scene. The man was just crazy, you know."

☙

In the summer of 1962, between his freshman and sophomore years, Charles worked with a choreographer who had trained with Edward Villella and the Eglevesky Ballet Company. He also began to explore his homosexuality by visiting local gay haunts. In the company of Christopher Scott and some other acquaintances, Charles had already been to the Hayloft, a large dance bar in Baldwin, Long Island that catered to a gay clientele and was periodically raided. One night when they were there, the police arrived, the lights were turned up, and while some terrified customers ran out a back door, the lesbian and gay dancers who remained abruptly switched to partners of the opposite sex.

The gay couple who had introduced Charles and Christopher to the Hayloft also took them to the Village one weekend, to visit a friend on MacDougal Street, where Charles met Candy Darling, an increasingly famous transvestite who assumed a drag persona both on and offstage. Even though Candy was clad in boy's clothing that day, he looked like a woman who was dressed as a man.

If Charles was by now primed to act on his homosexual orientation, Christopher, who was about to become a senior in high school, was still unwilling to take the plunge. The two friends had their first significant quarrel in June, when Charles proposed that they hitchhike to Cherry Grove, the gay section of Fire Island, and Christopher refused. Although a two-year age difference can be quite irrelevant to adults who have begun to define themselves, it can represent a decade-like chasm to adolescents — especially in this case, when the elder, Charles, was well aware of his homosexual proclivities, and the younger, Christopher, was still suppressing his. The problems between them were considerably aggravated by the fact that Charles found Christopher sexually attractive, but his feelings were not reciprocated. In something of a snit, Charles went alone to Fire Island, and after he returned he reported fabulous sexual adventures, hoping to make his friend envious. He felt even more dejected when he learned that Christopher was planning to accompany his parents on a cruise up the Eastern seaboard to Cape Cod, on his father's sailboat. But then Charles had a brainstorm: He would hitch a ride to Provincetown, another gay resort at the tip of Cape Cod, and if the timing worked out, he would meet up with Christopher there.

Shortly after reaching Provincetown, Charles met a flaming, skinny blond creature named Rene Ricard. Rene was only in his mid-teens at the time, but given his neurasthenic looks and hysterical behavior, it was possible to predict that he would become one of the more notorious gay characters of his era. He would also become a notable poet.

After cruising each other on Commercial Street, the main thoroughfare of Provincetown, Charles and Rene began a wild affair. When Christopher arrived in town and discovered them snuggling on a bench, Charles and Rene were already staying in the East End of town with a man named Prescott Townsend, an "old codger," according to Scott, who had fashioned a driftwood house for himself in a sand dune. Given

Christopher's good looks, Charles predicted he too would be welcome at Prescott's — and he was, until he failed to succumb to their host's advances. After one shouting match too many, Rene went storming out a day or two later, and their ad hoc commune was quickly dissolved.

As his second year at Hofstra began, Charles moved to Long Beach with his former roommate, aspiring avant-garde filmmaker Robert Madero. A onetime summer resort for New Yorkers, Long Beach had become a rather dilapidated community by 1962. The large single room they rented was near the railroad station, in a particularly seedy part of town.

The following spring, Charles spent a weekend at Christopher Scott's and simply insisted that they sleep together. Scott recalled that he was actually relieved to have sex with a man for the first time, since he had secretly wanted to for so long. "But Charles was much too quick and athletic for me — it was almost like a form of wrestling," Scott said. "I discovered that I preferred slow and lingering lovemaking."

During the summer, while Christopher was ensconced at an art school in Aspen, Colorado, Charles spent a good deal of time socializing with Heidi Hertwig, his old high school pal, and with Scott Markman, a new acquaintance with whom he had an affair. When Christopher returned to Long Island for a couple of weeks in August, he too slept with Scott Markman. Charles claimed not to care that they had shared a lover, but Christopher detected an angry undercurrent to his feigned indifference. A pattern of double standards began to emerge, whereby Ludlam would allow himself to pursue any sexual impulse he wanted but fly into a jealous rage whenever he discovered a lover had cheated on him.

Charles's experiences with Scott Markman had somehow turned him against homosexuality, and he was "talking about going straight," Christopher Scott recalled. He went so far as to attempt a liaison with Heidi Hertwig — though nothing came of their making out on the sofa at Christopher's parents' house.

During his Hofstra career, Charles had at least two other significant relationships with heterosexual overtones. While Susan Carlson was under the impression that he had an affair with Naomi Werne, and Charlotte Forbes confirmed that Charles and Naomi were in love with each other, to all evidence he had a far more fraught relationship with yet another classmate named Deborah Rosen. One of the unanswered questions in Ludlam's life is whether or not he impregnated Deborah, as she implied some years later to Stuart Sherman, a New York performance artist who — via Rosen — would befriend Ludlam in San Francisco. According to Sherman, Deborah had the pregnancy aborted. But Charlotte Forbes's perception of the relationship at Hofstra suggests the episode may have been a perverse form of wishful thinking on the part of Deborah, who had her sights set on Charles and persistently pursued him. As the domineering Marjorie Ludlam recalled, "My sister May had to tell Debbie she had no business taking over my kitchen and spending so much time here."

In his junior year, Charles lived in a run-down motel room in Long Beach, on the ground floor fronting the ocean, with a roommate named Irwin Pearl. Deborah Rosen lived with Charlotte Forbes two doors down from them. "Charles and Irwin's apartment was basic Long Island suburban, ghetto-depressed, haphazard, and sloppy," Forbes recalled. "It was such a contrast to our apartment, because Debbie had so home-ified and domesticized it. She had become a pathological housewife: Every day I would come home and the furniture would be rearranged.

"It was Debbie who masterminded getting us all to that motel in Long Beach," Forbes continued.

> It was really all done to entrap Charles. Debbie was ferociously in love with him. She was just mad about Charles, to the point that he was all she talked about. She got us out there thinking Irwin and I would pair up, leaving Charles to her. But her obsessive behavior started driving Charles crazy, and there were many times that he hated Debbie. I can remember one night, Charles came home at two in the morning, and as he walked by our door, he was screaming "You pig!" at Debbie, at the top of his lungs.

As would become increasingly clear throughout his life, Ludlam was an irrepressibly sensual man who enticed many people into his erotic domain. Once he won another person's devotion, however, he could become brutally selfish and inconsiderate of their wants or needs. Not that Deborah was blameless. For one thing, she drove the car the others relied on for getting to and from school, but she proved an unreliable and frequently tardy chauffeur. Deborah may have been stalling to accommodate Charles's customary lateness, but Forbes believed that she punished the three of them because Charles wasn't attentive enough: "She wanted him to come over at night and service her, but Charles didn't want to have anything to do with that." In addition to Charles's ultimate rejection of Deborah, the difficulties with the would-be diva were only exacerbated because she wasn't cast in school plays as frequently as her passengers were, and her resentment became palpable.

"Debbie was like the Glenn Close character in Fatal Attraction," Forbes declared. "The shit she would pull on us was unbelievable. After working our asses off from eight in the morning till midnight, Charles, Irwin, and I would be in a diner at Uniondale at 1:00 AM, plotting her death, because she didn't pick us up as she was supposed to. She had gone somewhere, or done some wild thing and spent all the money we had given her for gas."

All memories of Irwin Pearl, on the other hand, evoke an uncommonly gentle and loving soul. Short, with dark curly hair and beguiling brown eyes, "Irwin was one of those great, fabulous human beings, who never had a mean word to say about anyone," Forbes recalled. "He had this fantastic tenor voice. Even though he never had proper vocal training, he would sing at the top of his lungs in the quadrangle, and classes would come to a halt to hear him." Though Irwin was basically straight, he also dabbled in sexual relations with Charles. According to Christopher Scott, "If one of them was horny in the morning, the other simply furnished a blow job before they went off to their classes."

When Christopher stayed overnight with Charles and Irwin during his Christmas break — between his first college semester at the University of California at Santa Barbara, and his second at the San Francisco Art Institute — Charles instigated a three-way. Christopher found the episode more enjoyable than his first sexual dalliance with Charles the previous summer. But Charles's constant need to dominate proved more of a hindrance to any developing relationship for Christopher. "Because of Charles's egomania and underlying insecurity, he was never willing to think of me, or anyone else, as a partner," Scott claimed. "He desperately wanted me to work with him, but always as a humble subordinate."

No matter how put off Charles was about Deborah Rosen, he was not above seizing the opportunity to spend the summer of 1964 in Manhattan by living with her while he attended acting classes at the well-regarded HB Studio, founded by the imperious actor-director Herbert Berghof and his wife, the celebrated actress Uta Hagen. In what may have been a maneuver calculated to keep Charles within close proximity, Deborah sublet a handsomely furnished apartment at 30 Fifth Avenue and invited him to stay with her. But as Charles explained in a handwritten letter to Christopher — who had a summer job as a short-order cook in Nantucket — their circumstances had changed by July, when the uncooperative lover found his only refuge in acting.

Dear Chris,

My address is changed. I have my own place at last! 250 Broome St. apartment 15 zone 12. Deborah is living with me since we were all evicted from 30 Fifth Avenue. Monday I am going to look for a job here on the Lowereastside [sic]. It is about time since I have been here since the 4th of July. If I don't have some money by the time the rent comes "round" I may be thrown out on my ass! (Although it is not likely.)

Classes at Berghoff [sic] are superior. They have strengthened me as an artist, and completely changed the way in which I attack a role. Strange, my acting seems related to my life[,] which it never was before. And I am searching again, harder than ever — with no cool Olympian detachment, no absurdist point of view. Acting matters more to me than anything else, now more than ever before, because it has become both a refuge and a weapon for coping with the endless chaos.

I ask your forgiveness for not writing. I have, honestly, written and destroyed several letters which seemed to me to be the emissions of a diseased and lonely soul. Too disgusting to look at. I have spared you a good deal of futile pondering. Loneliness is magnified by this city.

You once said something about using the word "obscessed" [sic] instead of love. I feel it now. With you there.

Such a pitifully short letter. But will write at least weekly until I see you again.

Please do not get revenge. Write quickly. The fool hath much pined away.

te amo amigo

Charles

The Broome Street apartment was a dumpy railroad flat in a tenement building between Orchard and Ludlow Streets. Charles did not divulge to Christopher that Deborah was paying the rent. Apparently, he was getting too much out of his acting exercises at HB Studio to look for any work in earnest. He was also writing a play he would ultimately discard, *Edna Brown*, which had a story line that might have been concocted by the young Truman Capote: The title character, a small-town woman, retreats with her nephew into a private universe of their own making.

By late July, Deborah's resentment had peaked. Not only couldn't Charles pay his share of the rent, but he also failed to provide her with the romance she sought. A July 20 letter to Christopher — discussing a recent, disastrous foray to Provincetown — reveals just how confused Charles was about sexual and romantic intimacy when he was twenty-one:

Dear Chris,

I have to explain. I hate explaining because it makes one sound like a character out of an Ibsen play. All they do is explain.

The first note you received from me was a desperate attempt, on my part, to say ever[y]thing in 3 sentences. It was a failure. I meant [what I said in] the letter, but as soon as I mailed it I wanted it back. I knew the effect it would have on you too late. Summers are hard enough without me making them even more unbearable. The post card was another attempt at oversymplification [sic]. Debbie, Irwin, and I drove up for a weekend only. I wanted to undo the damage I had done. Now on reading your letter I see that I have perhaps made things worse. Everything is chaotic. I saw Rene and Prescott. Rene is a horror. He has styled himself as an enfant terrible and I fear he is growing into the image. He is cruel, egomani[a]cal, hysterical, and somehow very charming. I met several people I knew. Scott Markman's X, Charles and a friend of Bennet Yahya's[,] Lucy. Everyone is so lost. A scene that two years ago suited me to a T now seems unbearably meaningless and wasteful. In one year I will graduate. I will feel that I have accomplished something. If I had left school I would still be up there with all of them unchanged, a charicature [sic] of myself, nothing more than a catalogue of mannerisms and eccentricities. Over specialized and unable to communicate outside of my cult, finished. Cults are nice and safe. I reject them.

I don't know what love is. I feel that I need it. But where is it and what are the rules? Fidelity, promiscuity[,] platonic relationships[,] what? Men? Women? I don't know what's going on. The word love like the word beauty deserve[s] to be destroyed — they are meaningless excuses for not exploring in detail the phenomenae [sic] they represent in all their overwhelming complexities. I wish I could cry. But I can't and I won't. There's no answer in that. In a year I will be out of school. I want a blazing career. But it must be honest. An artist must seduce his audience into accepting his ["own" is inserted] fantasies. He must not cater to the fantasies of his audience. Acting makes me feel alive. So much of my confusion and dissatisfaction comes [sic] from wanting to live every day with the kind of intensity that is only possible on the stage. A ["man's" is crossed out] character's whole life on the stage may be played out in 3 hrs., the length of a performance. To live on that level in life is to live only three hours. I don't want to burn out like a meteor in one gawdy [sic] flash, there's no greatness in that. The only greatness is to endure. If you haven't read "The Seagull" by Chekhov read it a few times. (the Russian names are hard to keep straight) (use the Stark Young translation Modern Library) Help! A letter with footnotes! Please stay where you are. At the end of Summer I will be free for almost a month, we'll do something then. Forgive me if these notes upset you. I have always hated writing letters because I have no control over [the] mood of the person at the time he recieves [sic] what I wrote. Another thing is that I tend to write when I am depressed. Also I have lousey [sic] penmanship.

Think of me

Write to me

Charles

Scott saved several more letters that Charles wrote to him during the next few years. They are among the precious few Ludlam left behind. For the most part, they are marked by "the kind of intensity that is only possible on the stage" — as Charles put it. They also tend to predict the life he would lead, to an uncanny degree, even as they set the stage for the art he would create — against all odds and on his own terms.

Though Charles declared in this last letter that he did not know "what love is," he instinctively knew how to elicit, and take advantage of, the dedication of others. He spent his final year at Hofstra commuting from Manhattan, where he continued to live with Deborah Rosen in the Broome Street apartment. While the cultural revolution of the sixties was well under way, New York was the epicenter, luring Charles even before he graduated.

According to Christopher Scott, Deborah was still hopeful that something would develop between her and Charles: She dropped out of school and took a full-time office job to pay the rent. The push-me-pull-you relationship with Deborah continued to be tempestuous, however, and Charles often sought other living arrangements. He camped out for a spell with Robert Madero on the Upper West Side. Susan Carlson, who had an affair with Robert during that period, recalled her lover telling her that she had to meet his roommate Charles — whom she already knew, of course.

Robert Madero used Charles and Susan in a film he was shooting for a grant proposal to fund a longer project. The two of them passed a piece of fruit back and forth via their mouths while the camera was rolling. Charles walked away from the session struck by how cheaply a film could be made — if only the filmmaker were better organized than Robert had been. Thus was planted the seed that would lead to Ludlam's haphazard career as an underground filmmaker.

Though Charles had hoped to direct *Edna Brown* at Hofstra, he kept having problems with the script and finally abandoned it. For his senior thesis, he directed an esoteric play by the seventeenth century Spanish playwright, Calderón. It was also during his senior year that Charles's beloved Aunt Florence died, and that his father had surgery on his bladder, which left Joseph Ludlam somewhat disabled and forced into early retirement.

Charles was still seeing his high school friend, Heidi Hertwig, who was taking courses at the Fashion Institute of Technology in New York. Openly bisexual and more insightful than Deborah Rosen seemed to be, she wrote a telling letter to Christopher Scott. It suggested that she was able to accept the physical limitations in her relationship with Charles that Deborah kept hoping to overcome, and also focused on the overwhelming intensity of Charles's commitment to the stage. "I've grown to love Charles very much," Hertwig wrote:

> His presence is overpowering and confirming. It's a reassurance I need, probably every gay person needs . . . but it[']s more than the gay element, it[']s something else. We joke and say it[']s love. . . . Maybe it is. Romance would destroy (in the classical sense of the word Romance) our friendship, I know.
>
> On New Year's night Charles made some resolutions . . . which I think is a silly custom, but he is silly so the whole bit made sense. Well anyway one of them is not to go out partying anymore. Only to [participate in] "worthwhile" endeavors, such as the theater (number two resolution). He might as well live in a vacuum or sleep and eat on stage . . . build a home on stage and stay there . . . I'm not really putting him down but I think it's a staid thing to do only "worthwhile" things with free time or any time[,] matter of fact. Carrying on is a great tradition, especially for Charles, who is a wonderful camp. It's not that I won[']t have a playmate at parties . . . I'm not that selfish . . . but the notion Charles has about carrying on. Work and relaxation are not one . . . and should not be one . . . I think it[']s a very unhealthful (ha ha) attitude for Charles the person[,] not the performer. I can, I'm happy to say[,] divorce the two.

Do you feel the same way I do about this premise? You paint, but you do not live for painting...you live basically for yourself, of which art has a very large importance...I know Charles does not agree with me...and then again now I'm not so sure you would agree with me[. I] at first thought you might have.

As it turns out, Christopher had decidedly not dedicated his life to painting. After falling in love in the fall of 1964 with a student at UC Santa Barbara named Eric Batt, Christopher dropped out of the San Francisco Art Institute to live near him. Their relationship flourished until June; Christopher remained in Santa Barbara before returning to the East Coast in August. In the meantime, he had sent Charles a letter explaining that he had found out what true love was from his experience with Eric. He also said that he didn't want Charles to have any more illusions that they could be lovers, and that their future together would be as friends and collaborators only. While Christopher was in transit, Charles sent him a fiery response, postmarked August 15, 1965. When Charles then saw Christopher before the letter had arrived, he told his friend to destroy it without reading it. Christopher almost obeyed; he kept but never opened the letter until he rediscovered it in 1993. After reprimanding Christopher, Charles had written at length about his dismay with the commercialization of the art world in New York — a dismay that prompted him to say he would be abandoning the city. The impassioned document reads:

Dear Chris,

My first reaction on recieving [sic] your letter was to write a devastating satire back, complete with pictures of the creature from the black lagoon cut out and pasted in! I didn't mail that letter because I know that form influences content and what I had to say was to[o] important to allow it to be obscured by your probable anger. I want to put this to you straight.

For the past few years you have been going through those very "formative" years known as adolescence. In the earlier days of our friendship I was much more sympathetic to your problems because I too was going through that difficult time. But later on, because I am two years older than you, I came out of it while you had yet to live through the last and perhaps most violent stage. For us the process of maturing was an artistic one as well as a physical and moral one. And so I watched you (and went through my own) go through various kinds of artistic fad[d]ism which (however sophisticated they may have been) I must now call pop art. Our stages of development actually paralleled each other rather neatly[,] come to think of it. This year, (I believe your 20th,) when you have gone through a

severe period of doubt and disillusionment with your work and study[,] is chrono-
logically set at the same time almost to the month as when I went through a
similar period of doubt. If you recall that was the summer that I went to the
Herbert Berghoff [sic] studio on thirty dollars I had to borrow from some friend
of Debby's [sic]. (I was living on Broome St.) Jobless and had one three-hour class
per week [sic]. While you were tucked away safely in Aspen which I believe you
got as a birthday present. That was the year that I confided my doubts in you and
you responded with a letter (which I recently reread and destroyed) telling me that
I was no longer of any use to you because I (lacked/lost) the strength I had always
displayed and which you needed — I have always been strong. I always will be
because I know what I must do. I have always known. But an artist's way is not a
paved road and many side trips are necessary. Believe me Chris, because you are
about to find this out yourself. It is the side trips that require the strength. And so
your mistaken ideas about my development and your inability to forgive me for
not always supplying you with an answer when I myself was busily looking for the
question made our relations difficult. (Not to mention ludicrous attempts to
regard each other as sexual objects.) I have found and you will find that adolescence is even less tollerable [sic] to non-adolescents tha[n] it is to the adolescent.

— this was prologue. [I]f by now your fury over my condescention [sic] has not
led you to destroy the remainder of this letter here is what I truly have to say —

    I am appalled by the state of all the arts in this country. I have taken a good
long look at what is being produced and I don't like it. The avant-garde are
wrong. Everything is moving in the wrong direction. Fad[d]ism and the desire to
make money are destroying the arts. New York City has nothing to offer except
many petty distractions. Super duper pseudo sophistication and hyper refinement
are no longer what can legitimately be regarded as honest advanced work in art. I
want to return to some more primitive kind of communication with my audience.
A popular audience whose tastes have not been so jaded by the shit with which
they have been bombarded that they can no longer respond to an experience honestly with emotion, with imagination. I am abandoning New York. No art can
survive there: No sensitive person can survive. The City has nothing to offer me
or any other honest person. This exile will not be dramatic, because I am not
doing it for effect. This fall and winter I plan to work on Long Island building a
theater[,] laying ground work by next summer. Perhaps we will go further. Success
is not money no matter what we are told. I want to do my work in the world.
That's all. To do my work whose direction is clearer to me every day. [The last

two sentences appear to be squeezed in on a single line, after the fact.] That work is impossible in New York. How can I learn acting when I have so much to teach? How, when my ideas about the actor's art are such that no one can even understand them — yet? It takes great courage to stand against the current of the day. One man must stand even here where the current is a great torrent, an avalanche. If you believe me and if there is anything spon[t]aneous and honest in you (as I know there was once) work in the theater — join me. Or if I drown make your peace with the sea.

Charles

P.S. I have already written a full length play as a first production. Read Artaud's *The Theater and Its Double*. Some of my plans are blueprinted therein.

Instead of reveling in the sudden explosion of artistic possibilities that the counterculture was ushering in — or imagining a place for himself in the limelight anymore — Charles was apparently feeling overwhelmed by it. But perhaps there is a hidden subtext to the ardent diatribe that this letter contains. To extend his closing reference to the "sea," Charles's personality was such that he would rather be a big fish on Long Island than a small one in New York — or so he seemed to believe in the summer of 1965.

Had Christopher read this remarkable letter when it was sent to him that August, Ludlam might have founded his theater company somewhere in Long Island as opposed to Greenwich Village, and his life might have played out quite differently than it did. But in spite of Charles's stated plan to leave New York, by September he was living with Christopher on the Lower East Side, any conflicts implied by the letter having been resolved through the routines of friendship and shared sensibility. They found an apartment at 52 East 1st Street, between First and Second Avenues. The no-frills, $50-a-month tenement dwelling was situated in the rear of the top floor of a building in the midst of a drug-infested neighborhood on the far fringes of artist-friendly Greenwich Village. The Hell's Angels were ensconced a couple of blocks north. Charles and Christopher quickly discovered why their little piece of Manhattan was known as Heroin Alley: It featured basketball courts at the corner, which were extremely conducive to drug-peddling of all kinds both day and night. Charles had by then developed an insatiable appetite for marijuana, so there were decided advantages to the apartment's location, beyond its modest rent.

The neighborhood was made even more vibrant by the presence of the Hare Krishna movement, with a storefront temple nearby on Second Avenue. Ellen Stewart, the bell-ringing Earth Mother of the Off-Off-Broadway theater movement, had started her Cafe La MaMa in a cellar on East 12ᵗʰ Street in 1960, before moving into a second-floor loft above a cleaner's at 122 Second Avenue, near 7ᵗʰ Street. Stewart sponsored a seemingly endless parade of youthful playwrights and theatrical wanna-bes; many of whom would go on to enjoy long and productive careers in the theater. (Indeed, Ludlam and Stewart were fated to have a testy dispute when she became involved with the first production of his landmark play *Bluebeard* in 1970.)

But the real character of this period in Ludlam's life is best revealed by how Charles and Christopher met their neighbor, Jack Mallory, whose apartment shared a fire escape with theirs. According to Mallory's version of the story, his various overnight guests used to turn up with blankets and towels and other furnishings, eventually admitting that they were pilfering the items from the apartment next door, via the fire escape. As soon as he realized what was going on, Jack introduced himself to Charles and Christopher, and returned their belongings.

Scott recalled the circumstances somewhat differently. Jack had invited them over for dinner without bothering to hide any of the items that had been mysteriously disappearing from their apartment. Yet Charles did not have enough of an attachment to private property to bear any residual resentment: Two years later, he would invite Jack to join the Ridiculous. (Mallory always imagined that his frequent and melodramatic fights with his lover, Michael Maloney, were what really impressed Charles, and the reason he asked him to join the company.)

In the summer of 1965, Charles had been to see two short dramatic pieces, *The Life of Juanita Castro* and *Shower*, at an art gallery in the East Village. Ronald Tavel had originally written them as scenarios for underground films by Andy Warhol, but they were presented instead as one-act plays featuring a lot of lewd dialogue as well as ad-libbing and unstructured, illogical plot developments. They would also prove to be the first offerings of the Ridiculous theatrical movement, which Ludlam would essentially co-opt in a couple of years. At the time, however, Charles didn't really see this bizarre and deliberately perverse theater as the sort of thing he wanted to be doing. He had been far more stimulated by plays staged by the Living Theater — Julian Beck and Judith Malina's fervent, revolutionary company, which would come to rely on audience participation, not to mention nudity. Charles was particularly taken with this leftist group's productions of *Tonight We Improvise* and *The Connection*, which made him realize how personal and expressive theater could be.

Charles was also mightily impressed with an underground film he caught that summer at the Film-Makers' Cinémathèque — the early incarnation of Jonas Mekas's Anthology Film Archives, which was devoted to "art" films and located at the time on Lafayette Street, just south of Astor Place. Named for its actor-subject, *Jerovi* was a silent, eleven-and-a-half-minute movie that bordered on the pornographic as it featured "Jerovi" making love, alternately, to a rose and then to his nude self. The film had been made by an ambitious, twenty-two-year-old Puerto Rican named José Rodríguez-Soltero.

Charles was so taken with the movie that he confronted the young filmmaker when he encountered him late one night on the sidewalks of the Lower East Side. "It was 3:00 in the morning," recalled Rodríguez-Soltero. "I was tripping on LSD, and this man was jumping up and down — he seemed like a monkey to me — when he came up and said, 'Aren't you José Rodríguez-Soltero?' I was paranoid, and trying not to freak out. But he said, 'I love your work.' And the funny thing was, even though I was on acid, he made complete sense to me. I thought to myself that this guy can't be putting me on, because he really understood what I was trying to do."

Charles took José home to East 1st Street. "He made me some herbal tea, and he kept instructing me on varieties of teas: Earl Gray, Darjeeling. . . . I thought, 'This guy is more fucked-up than I thought.' I had assumed he picked me up to have sex; but basically, he wanted to teach me about teas. On the other hand, I really liked him."

Indeed, Charles and José did have sex the next time they got together, after which Charles suddenly said, "You Puerto Ricans are all alike: You just want to fuck someone, and then you never want to see them again."

"And he was right," added the droll Rodríguez-Soltero in the midst of recalling the episode. "He was angry at me because I called him a monkey. I mean, to the Japanese and the Chinese, the monkey was like a godhead. And I thought he understood that; but no, he took it as an insult." José felt that Charles was very insecure about his looks; but contrary to what Ludlam's post-coital remark implied, they became fast friends who stimulated each other intellectually. They began going to films together, including rigorous works such as Carl Theodor Dreyer's *Gertrude*, *Day of Wrath*, and *Ordet*, which Charles just loved. "He was the first person I talked to about those films, and he knew just what I was talking about," said Rodríguez-Soltero.

In fact, José accompanied Charles to Tavel's *Juanita Castro* and recalled their speaking with the playwright afterwards. "Charles said, 'I'm going to revolutionize the theater,'" continued Rodríguez-Soltero. "And I thought to myself, 'Another freak — they all talk like that.' But he meant it. And he did it, too."

Charles was intrigued enough with Tavel's plays to take Christopher Scott to them later that summer, when Christopher returned to New York and the plays reopened for an extended run at the St. Mark's Playhouse on Second Avenue. Christopher was more impressed than Charles with what he saw. "It was clear to me," Scott said, "that this was where the future of the theater lay." Christopher was also fascinated with the burgeoning scene at Warhol's "Factory," a magnet for the strays and would-be pop-culture superstars of the era, which is to say just about everyone — and certainly anyone — who craved his or her fifteen minutes of fame. Charles considered it a lot of hype with a vacuous center. He envied all the media attention Warhol was receiving, especially when far more serious work was being neglected. Charles also knew he had more to offer himself; but what would that work be, and when? Back home on East 1st Street — with taped sound effects such as the "Perry Mason" TV theme song supplied by Christopher — Charles was honing his vocal skills by speaking into a tape recorder and applying various voices to outrageous items from Ripley's "Believe It Or Not." This was Charles's equivalent of singing in the shower.

While they lived on East 1st, Charles and Christopher spent a lot of time at an apartment on Abingdon Square in the West Village rented by Debbie Caen, daughter of the San Francisco columnist Herb Caen, which served as a quintessential sixties crash pad. What might have been referred to as a "salon" in an earlier era had acquired a more contemporary edge. The kitchen sink was filled with the same dirty dishes for days, if not weeks. An assortment of visitors would pop in any hour of the day or night to drink, rap, get stoned, make love, or just hang out. Many of the regulars hovered on the fringe of the Warhol phenomenon, which was a large part of the appeal of the place for Christopher. In fact, Debbie Caen herself and Warhol superstud Paul America would eventually become an item. Christopher and Warren Sonberg, who went on to become a filmmaker in San Francisco, also ignited an affair at Caen's. Within a couple of months of moving in with Charles, Christopher vacated East 1st Street to live with Sonberg; but their relationship lasted only a few weeks before Christopher left him for Ed Shostak, a sculptor whom he met through Sonberg.

As soon as Christopher left the apartment at East 1st Street, Joe Franza moved in with Charles. In addition to paying more than his share of the rent, Joe became Charles's lover. According to Scott, Franza was a friend of Deborah Rosen's. He had dark hair, was taller than Charles, and very slender. He was also quiet and laid-back, belying his intelligence. "He had insights on practically every subject," recalled Rodríguez-Soltero, "and Charles was clearly in awe of him." José particularly noted Joe Franza's knowledge of both Oriental philosophy and seemingly all aspects of the art world. He also felt, at the time, that Joe was squandering his talents and doing nothing with his life.

Though memories have blurred as to exactly when Charles left Joe Franza and the East 1st Street apartment behind him, it was at some point in 1966. Lola Pashalinski, who would become a major player in Ludlam's company, recalled, "Charles and Joe were both intelligent, and they could act like Restoration wits together. But they didn't really click chemically. Joe was far more attracted to Charles, who didn't find him sexually exciting."

According to Christopher Scott, the top-floor apartment on East 1st Street was sweltering in the summer. Charles had hung thick, ornate rugs over the broken windows to keep the heat and light out. But then, with the arrival of winter, came cold to match the heat, and since the functioning of the radiators was unpredictable, Charles was compelled to relocate.

Rodríguez-Soltero recalled Charles living with him for a couple of months on Lafayette Street, in a dangerously deserted neighborhood just north of Canal Street. "We argued a lot about gay liberation," said Rodríguez-Soltero. "I wanted to go to these organizational meetings, and Charles would say, 'I'm tired of the Mattachine Society.' In his mind, it was a lot of guys in suits wanting to look straight, so people wouldn't know they were queer." Throughout his life, Ludlam had trouble with anyone making distinctions between gay and straight. As far as he was concerned, everyone should simply act on his or her innate bisexuality.

Between the dubious neighborhood and the escalating arguments, Charles needed to find a place of his own. He discovered an apartment at 524 East 12th Street, between Avenues A and B, on the north side of the block. The rent on Apartment 4D was $45 a month. As was often the case in these old, walk-up tenement buildings, the bathtub was in the kitchen, which visitors entered directly from the hallway. Occasionally when one of his friends arrived punctually to meet for a movie, the dilatory Charles would shout, "The door's open — come on in," even though he was still in the tub. He thought nothing about appearing stark naked in front of any of his guests. (In the years to come, he would appear nude in a number of his plays.)

Nor did he display any shame for the slovenly way that he lived. As Ludlam would later tell a friend, he once cruised a dancer who was on tour in New York, and brought him home to 12th Street. The visitor surveyed Charles's unkempt apartment and said, "Well, I hope you make love like an animal, because you sure live like one."

During the fall, both Charles and Christopher had requisite physicals at the draft board in New York. With the war escalating in Vietnam, a deferral was desirable at any cost. They were automatically relieved of active duty when they presented themselves as homosexuals to the army psychiatrist.

Charles, for one, was taking every opportunity to explore the sexual frontiers the 1960s were opening to urban gay men. His youthful, hormonal years almost make it seem as if he single-handedly brought about the pervasive sexual revolution of the era. Beyond his affair with Joe Franza, he spent regular sessions in New York bathhouses. Although Ludlam would frequent the "baths" for much of his life—and sometimes even work on a play in his rented cubicle, while waiting for a partner to come along—he resented the commercialization of sex they represented. (Years later he would tell Ethyl Eichelberger, the celebrated drag performer who worked with the Ridiculous from time to time, "The baths are filled with masochists who want to suck all your energy out of you.") Charles also often visited the Hudson River piers at the foot of Christopher Street in the West Village, where parked trailer trucks were loaded with untold opportunities for free, raunchy sexual mischief—the kind Charles liked best. A couple months before his twenty-third birthday, he was caught in a raid on the trucks, arrested for indecent behavior, and had to spend the night in jail. He called Christopher as soon as he was released the next day to rant about the capitalistic system that forced you to pay for having sex.

જી

A month or so before his arrest, one of the most significant developments in Ludlam's life occurred—although he wasn't even present when it took place. On Christmas night, Christopher Scott took his parents to a special event for film archivist Jonas Mekas, during which Ed Shostak introduced Christopher to Henry Geldzahler.

Christopher knew that Geldzahler was an important figure in the art world. As the soon-to-be first curator of modern art at New York's Metropolitan Museum, Geldzahler would come to wield huge influence, putting both Warhol and the painter David Hockney on the artistic map. He would become even more powerful when Mayor Edward I. Koch appointed him New York's Commissioner of Cultural Affairs in 1977.

Christopher immediately fell in love with the brilliant, acerbic, and roly-poly Geldzahler. Within a week of their meeting, the two men honeymooned in Palm Beach, beginning a fifteen-year relationship that evolved into a deeply affectionate, though frequently troubled, gay power marriage. Four years after they met, David Hockney would immortalize the couple in a joint-portrait, which would sell for $1.1 million in 1992.

Upon their return from Florida, Christopher Scott immediately moved in with the future CEO of America's visual-arts culture, at his brownstone on West 81st Street. Within a couple of years, Scott would use Geldzahler's money and connections to endow the first few productions of Ludlam's Ridiculous Theatrical Company—and thus Charles would begin to establish his unique place in the American theater.

FLAMING CREATURES

The true artist is known by the use he makes of what he annexes, and he annexes everything.
— Oscar Wilde

This man was willing to do anything for a magical moment onstage.
— Ronald Tavel

Though Charles Ludlam would become most celebrated for inventing a style of theater and playwriting known as the "Ridiculous," few cultural innovators travel uncharted territory alone. The real pioneers of the Ridiculous theater movement were Jack Smith, Ronald Tavel, and John Vaccaro, who had worked primarily as filmmakers — both independently and together — a few years before Ludlam entered their realm.

With the sudden availability of camera equipment and the reduced cost for developing film, the sixties gave birth to a burgeoning art form known as underground film. For anyone who wanted to be a part of the freshly named "in-crowd" or "the scene," the only thing more important than viewing underground movies was being in them — as were many who passed through Warhol's doorway. In addition to Warhol's Factory, Jonas Mekas formed his Film-Makers' Cinémathèque to promote these experimental works.

In stark contrast with these two later-day "studios" was the fiendishly independent filmmaker, Jack Smith. Smith was an Ohio-bred lunatic who created strange and exotic costumes — as well as kitsch and spontaneous performance pieces — out of found items, if not exactly thin air. With a voice and a personality that evoked a hybrid of Truman Capote and Robert Mitchum, he was notorious for his volatile temper. An artist's artist, Smith inspired an entire generation of nascent performers, filmmakers, artists, and writers. His loft at 36 Greene Street in Soho was named the Plaster Foundation. It served as a performance space where he offered free midnight showings of elaborate concoctions with outrageous titles such as *Withdrawal From Orchid Lagoon* (produced by "The Reptilian Theatrical Company"), *Claptailism of Palmola Christmas Spectacle*, and *Gas Stations of the Cross Religious Spectacle*. Like many an artist's artist, anything approaching real fame would elude Smith during his lifetime.

Born and reared in Brooklyn, Ronald Tavel studied Philosophy and Elizabethan Literature at the City University of New York before pursuing a master's degree in Philosophy and French from the University of Wyoming. After returning to New York in 1962 and settling in the East Village, he wrote a peripatetic novel, *Street of Stairs*, based on his travels in North Africa the year before.

Smith and Tavel were introduced to each other by a mutual friend when he realized they were both enthralled by Maria Montez, a Hollywood star of 1940s adventure movies such as *Cobra Woman* and *Arabian Nights*, as well as other outlandish hokum. With Maria Montez serving as the esoteric muse of the Ridiculous movement, Smith discovered a Puerto Rican drag queen and transformed him into Mario Montez — Maria's most palpable, posthumous incarnation.

According to Tavel, Smith was scouting for a "new" Maria Montez, and "for reasons he could not articulate, he decided a transvestite would do the job best. Yvonne De Carlo had tried for years to replace Maria Montez and failed, but Mario would step into her wedgies and keep up the tradition."

Mario Montez made his screen debut in *Flaming Creatures*, Smith's seminal 1963 movie that can best be described as a "filmed orgy." It was immediately banned, but would become a cult classic that had a far-reaching impact in avant-garde circles, both here and abroad. (In more recent years, J. Hoberman in the *Village Voice* declared *Flaming Creatures* "The underground's first *cause célèbre*" and "the only American avant-garde film, whose reception equals that of *L'Âge d'Or* or *Zéro de Conduite*.")

Montez was increasingly agitated when his film career failed to soar following *Flaming Creatures*. "He was a little Puerto Rican boy in his twenties," said Tavel, "who kept complaining [in his thick accent], 'I have five years of beauty left and they don't want to make movies with me. And I tell them I'm going to be finished after that. You understand?'"

Mario Montez was saved from oblivion and essentially rediscovered all over again in December of 1964, when Warhol, who had already made more than a dozen silent films — including one called *Henry Geldzahler* — embarked on his "talkies" phase. On the basis of hearing a tape of Tavel reading from *Street of Stairs*, Warhol approached the author to contribute the scenario to his first sound film, *Harlot* (the title was a pun, referring to Jean Harlow). "It was the old Hollywood system all over again," recalled Tavel. "Mario Montez was introduced to me as a trick for me to sleep with: 'He's a starlet. He sleeps with you and then you will write a screenplay for him.' And Mario thought this was quite wonderful."

The seventy-minute *Harlot* featured Mario in drag, sitting on a sofa next to another wanna-be star, suggestively eating one banana after another, while Tavel, Billy Linich, and Harry Fainlight conducted a banal, off-camera conversation about female movie stars of an earlier era.

Over the next two years, Tavel continued to collaborate sporadically with Warhol every few months, churning out one or two scenarios, acting in some, directing others. His scripts were relatively brief treatments that encouraged the actors to improvise, turning a ten- or eleven-page story into an hour-long film. Of the fourteen-plus movies Tavel made with Warhol, the more significant ones included *Vinyl*—ostensibly based on Anthony Burgess's novel *A Clockwork Orange*—and *Hedy*, about the has-been actress and pathetic shoplifter Hedy Lamarr, portrayed in the film by Montez. Tavel also contributed one of the scripted segments of *The Chelsea Girls* in 1966, which included Montez in its large cast and launched Warhol's breakthrough into commercial cinema.

To pinpoint the birth of the Ridiculous theatrical movement, however, requires backing up to the spring of 1965. Warhol superstar Edie Sedgwick had refused to participate in filming *Shower*, Tavel's send-up of a Hollywood spy movie. In a now legendary remark, Sedgwick claimed that she didn't want "to be a part of Ronnie's perversities anymore." Tavel felt that Sedgwick had been manipulated by Factory compatriots who envied his position as resident screenwriter and wanted to make waves. In any event, rather than contradict his diva, Warhol took his customary path of least resistance. He told Tavel that he liked *Shower*, but decided not to go ahead with it. Suggesting that it might work just as well on the stage, Warhol referred Tavel to the Off-Broadway theater director, Jerry Benjamin.

When Tavel contacted him, Benjamin explained that he was tied up staging *The Toilet*, a controversial play by the provocative playwright Leroi Jones (who would later be known as Amiri Baraka). Benjamin in turn told Tavel about an actor that he knew who wanted to become a director. "I have this feeling he'd be good, too," Benjamin added, "and this is exactly the sort of thing he could do well. He works in a secondhand bookstore on Fourth Avenue. But be careful when you meet him, because he's not quite in his right mind." His name was John Vaccaro.

With thick, black glasses propped on an angular nose, the hyperactive Vaccaro was rummaging through a card catalog when Tavel arrived. "While I was waiting," recalled Tavel, "this woman came into the shop and went up to John and said, 'Sir, do you have any prints of monkeys?' And he replied, 'Did you ever look in a mirror, madam?' She left in a huff, and he sat there laughing his head off. I remember saying to myself, I have to watch myself here."

A native of Steubenville, Ohio, Vaccaro went to Kenyon College in the mid-fifties and transferred to Ohio State in Columbus, where he remained after college and gave beatnik-type readings of pornographic poetry in smoke-filled clubs. After moving to New York, Vaccaro acted with the American Poets' Theater Company and appeared in various Warhol and Jack Smith films.

As Tavel recalled, Vaccaro was quite fed up with the wackiness of actors when he approached him with the script for *Shower*. "He freaked out: 'How dare you come in here! I'm finished with theater. I'll have nothing to do with it anymore. I've never directed a play, and I'm not going to lose my mind by starting now. I have a lover, a good job here. I don't want to be bothered with you crazy people.'" Despite his initial protests, however, Vaccaro eventually read the script and agreed to do it. Together he and Tavel would form the Theater of the Ridiculous.

Since *Shower* only amounted to a one-act play, Vaccaro needed a curtain-raiser and asked Tavel if he had any other scripts. From the half dozen Tavel showed him, Vaccaro selected *The Life of Juanita Castro*, which had just been realized as a seventy-minute film by Warhol in January. Both scripts demonstrated what would become the signature style of the early Ridiculous: a willful incoherence enhanced by non sequiturs and an emphasis on lewd jokes and bawdy behavior.

Vaccaro immediately called on Jack Smith to do the costumes, though they would be ascribed to "Terry Cloth" on the handbill, which Smith also designed. Vaccaro also recruited a group of jazz musicians to play background music. According to Tavel, the "zig-zag effect" of the music perfectly matched his authorial intention to break with conventional playwriting "by abolishing dialectical understanding or linear thinking as a mode of progress within a script."

The rehearsals at Vaccaro's loft on Great Jones Street in the East Village were tempestuous, to say the least. Tavel recalled life-threatening scenes with Vaccaro wielding a kitchen knife, or his phoning at 3 AM and shrieking, "This is not your business!" The temperamental director eventually "dis-invited" the playwright from rehearsals. After Smith said that Vaccaro may have understood the humor and campiness of the plays, but failed to perceive their meaning or "elegance," he too was barred from rehearsals.

And in what would become a pattern for the director, Vaccaro fired one of the actors at the last minute only to step into the role himself. Tavel felt this was an underhanded ploy: Vaccaro still identified himself as an actor first and always intended to take over the plum roles. In the meantime he could devote more of his attention to directing with a rehearsal cast intact. Everybody seemed to remember that Vaccaro was difficult to work with in those early days, with his notorious drug habit contributing to the ordeal.

Since most of the people involved with the Ridiculous were experimenting with one drug *and* another at the time, their subsequent memories proved as slippery as their perceptions were then. Under the elusive circumstances, there emerged a number of versions of how the Ridiculous received its name. Vaccaro ascribed it to Yvette Hawkins, a Method-trained actress and friend who was credited as the "common sense advisor" on the program for *Shower*. While assisting Vaccaro during rehearsals, Yvette once remarked, "But this is just ridiculous!"

Although others claimed that Smith conceived of the nomenclature for the "Theater of the Ridiculous," Tavel remembered it differently. After Smith had a blow-up with Vaccaro, Tavel was commiserating with him one night and mentioned that he wanted a publicity angle for his plays. Smith suggested he might come up with a name for the enterprise to "give the critics a hook" or hand-feed them an approach to the material. "I went home and thought of the Theater of the Ridiculous," Tavel said. He saw it as "the next step after the Theater of the Absurd, a logical progression" — albeit with a premise that emphasized the illogical. According to Tavel, Hawkins's remark at rehearsals was more an affirmation of what he had already come up with, along the lines of "This *is* ridiculous!"

Despite the constant bickering and Vaccaro's hands-off attitude during rehearsals, Tavel ultimately approved of how *Shower* and *The Life of Juanita Castro* were staged. The plays opened in tandem on July 29, 1965 and played for two weekends at the Coda Gallery on East 10th Street. The response was positive enough to reopen them later that summer at the St. Mark's Playhouse. (This is where Christopher Scott saw them, at Ludlam's behest.)

Emboldened by their success, Vaccaro and Tavel decided to continue with their fledgling operation. Partially inspired by Beverly Grant, a Jack Smith "star" who had played the lead in *Shower*, Tavel wrote a new play — his first specifically for the Ridiculous — called *The Life of Lady Godiva*. (Grant, who was tall and slender, ultimately proved unavailable and was replaced by the plump Dorothy Opalach; lines referring to the character's body-type were duly changed.)

Tavel's brother Harvey, who had been living in Europe, returned to New York and joined the company as a producer, beginning with *Lady Godiva*. The single largest sum of money, $800, was contributed for the company's new performance space on West 17th Street by Panna Grady, an alleged Hungarian countess who lived in the Dakota and fancied herself a patroness of the arts. According to Ronald Tavel, Grady was approached by Vaccaro via Warhol. According to Vaccaro, he was introduced to her by Henry Geldzahler. But everyone concurs that it was Geldzahler who, in January or February of 1966, referred Vaccaro to a would-be New York stage actor by the name of Charles Ludlam.

When the twenty-three-year-old Ludlam showed up for an interview, Vaccaro was most impressed with his knowledge of theater history. While Vaccaro had no idea what was in store when he invited Ludlam to join the group, another newcomer claimed that she could instantly tell Ludlam was exceptional. Her name was Regina Hirsch, but she would later become better known as Lola Pashalinski.

Pashalinski grew up in Brooklyn. In childhood, she befriended Harvey Tavel, who later recruited her to become Vaccaro's "script girl," and she was delighted to get a bit part in *Lady Godiva*. During rehearsals, Pashalinski was struck by Ludlam's professionalism. Unlike other members of the motley crew, he would ask Vaccaro questions about blocking and introduce concerns that none of them had taken seriously.

Pashalinski recalled a particularly lascivious moment when she arrived late for a rehearsal following a class at NYU. She took a seat directly behind Ludlam, who grabbed her hand and put it in his crotch as he made some lewd remark. He was "like a little Cupid," said Pashalinski. "He knew he was different — we all did."

Ludlam made his stage debut with the Ridiculous as Peeping Tom in *The Life of Lady Godiva*, which opened in April 1966. He was a last-minute fill-in for Mark Duffy, who had been dismissed after skipping some rehearsals. The week before the opening, Vaccaro had fired another actor and assumed the role of Mother Superviva in the play.

Along with Mario Montez and several others, Pashalinski was in a chorus line of nuns who remained in their choreographed places during the rehearsals. But when this number was presented for the first time to an audience, Montez suddenly lurched forward and created an attention-getting spot for himself.

In his review for the *Village Voice*, Michael Smith declared the play "terrifically entertaining." He further described it as "a combination of *Tom Jones* and *Flaming Creatures*. . . . It is a mocking inquiry in the form of a theater game into the possibility of free will; it is a psychological satire on the subject of women castrating men." Smith also singled out Ludlam's performance as "spectacularly active." But Ludlam would have to wait for the next Ridiculous enterprise before he really made an impression on avant-garde theatergoers of the day.

Given the obscene nature of the plays, the authorities decided to make things difficult for the troupe — and not for the last time. Technical complaints were raised: One concerned the lack of a theater license for their use of the space on West 17ᵗʰ Street, between Fifth and Sixth Avenues. Situated in the parlor floor of what had originally been a townhouse, the large rectangular room featured a makeshift proscenium stage and could accommodate seventy-four theatergoers.

In addition to securing the necessary certificate of occupancy, Tavel resolved the trickier issue of a theater license by renaming the company the Play-House of the Ridiculous, eliminating the word "theater" from the original title. The hyphen apparently made all the difference, allowing the show to go on. Tavel claimed that the "Play-House" designation was also intended as a pun on the notion of "just playing around."

℘

During the winter prior to *Lady Godiva*, Ludlam solidified his new friendship with underground filmmaker José Rodríguez-Soltero. In addition to sharing their impressions of particular movies, the two young men discussed filmmaking methods. Ludlam especially admired Coutard, the raw cameraman for the new, cutting-edge French director, Jean-Luc Godard. He also emphasized his love for *Our Lady of the Flowers*, Genet's highly autobiographical novel, which they talked about making into a film with Ludlam as its star.

"I was just a kid at the time," said Rodríguez-Soltero. "I had studied at the Sorbonne; and I wanted to make films like Buñuel's. But then, after seeing Jack Smith's *Flaming Creatures* and early Warhol films, I thought to myself, 'I want to make films like that.'"

Rodríguez-Soltero was also heavily influenced by von Sternberg's handling of Marlene Dietrich in various films, and by *Scorpio Rising*, Kenneth Anger's groundbreaking, homoerotic movie of 1964. It was actually Anger's sensationalistic book *Hollywood Babylon* — which trafficked in hyperbolic movie star scandals — that gave the Puerto

Rican filmmaker the inspiration for his next movie. Rodríguez-Soltero could not resist the chapter devoted to Lupe Velez, which explained how this Mexican leading lady of the 1930s drowned in her bathroom toilet after trying to take her life with an overdose of drugs.

Given the subject matter, it's hardly surprising that Warhol intended to make a film about Velez as well. "We had a little *contretemps*, and I said, 'Your film would probably be better than mine,'" recalled Rodríguez-Soltero. On the other hand, Rodríguez-Soltero already had a commitment from Mario Montez to star as Velez, and they shot the film off and on throughout 1966. Its working title, *The Life, Death and Assumption of Lupe Velez*, was eventually abandoned and the film was simply called *Lupe*.

Ludlam wasn't going to be in *Lupe* at first, but he was a frequent presence on the shoot and contributed a lot to how the movie evolved. "Charles kept telling me how to film it," recalled Rodríguez-Soltero,

> and he was very helpful sometimes, saying, "Okay, this isn't working. Let's do something else here." He had an incredible knowledge of Greek theater and philosophy. I always thought I was the one who knew such things, but obviously, he did, too. He explained to me that if you're going to develop a character, you should have a chorus, and that's why I added music. He was very influential.

> At one point, Charles was going to play one of Lupe's male lovers. But when we realized that the film wasn't developing as we hoped it would and that we didn't have an ending [that] worked, we came up with the idea of Charles playing her lesbian lover instead, and he finally did. . . . We really weren't very interested in the narrative anyway. It was just a pretext for us to make a film using our friends.

Lola Pashalinski was later added to the film as well, in a bit part portraying a hand-maiden who continually combs out Lupe's hair.

By the time *Lupe* was screened at the Film-Makers' Cinémathèque during the last two nights of January 1967, it boasted of "Fifty Extras" and described itself as "an impro-vised, non-directed, non-scripted film starring Mario Montez." Rodríguez-Soltero recalled taking the fifty-minute movie to festivals in both Cannes and Berlin, where aficionados could decide for themselves whether it mocked or revered the seamy side of Hollywood that it portrayed. Jonas Mekas himself would declare it "an epic of sorts."

If *Lupe* marked Ludlam's first real screen role, his first New York stage appearance occurred on Friday, April 8, 1966, at the Bridge, a hip theater on St. Mark's Place that often showcased controversial events. An ad in the *Village Voice* for the upcoming, midnight, one-night-only event referred to "NIGHT CRAWLERS AT THE BRIDGE/ UNDERGROUND-BENEFIT-BASH." The lineup of ten performance artists began with José Rodríguez-Soltero, whose Vietnam protest piece "LBJ" was promoted as a "live multi-screen scrambled love-hate paradox in USA 1966." Mario Montez was represented by his "DANCE OF THE SEVEN VEILS — superstar of the Underground in person." Ludlam appeared at the bottom of the list with "FOURPAH, AN ORDEAL — Theatre of Blindness and Guilt."

Ludlam's peculiar title was meant to be a pun on "faux pas," and the piece itself was mostly built around his Ripley's Believe-It-Or-Not vocal exercises (incorporating his Mae West voice). Whatever impact he was hoping to achieve that night was completely undermined, however, by Rodríguez-Soltero's "LBJ," which stirred up an enormous uproar when he burned an American flag in the course of his act to the tune of the number-one pop hit of the day, "The Ballad of the Green Berets." Not only did the out-raged response delay the rest of the show — Ludlam ended up performing at 4 AM to a relatively empty house — but the incendiary act also usurped all of the press attention.

In the full-page report of the event in the April 14 issue of the *Village Voice*, Fred W. McDarrah claimed, "Most of the audience, who had never before witnessed such a dramatic anti-American gesture in public, were horrified." Ludlam, for his part, was just livid: He might have agreed that civil disobedience served a purpose in the right con-text, but he resented that such a gimmick monopolized public attention when far more serious work — such as his own — was being overlooked.

Ludlam could at least console himself with his ongoing role in *Lady Godiva*, which opened later that month. He would have to wait until the fall, however, to really make his mark.

⁂

Tavel's next two one-acts, *Indira Gandhi's Daring Device* and *Screen Test*, opened on the same bill at the Play-House of the Ridiculous on September 29, 1966. They played Thursdays through Sundays, with an 8:30 PM curtain. On a single flyer, *Indira Gandhi* was billed as "N.Y.'s first smell-o-drama, with Jeanne Phillips and Charles Ludlam," and

Screen Test as "an intimacy" showcasing Mario Montez, "Off-Broadway's new blaze of excitement!" A press release claimed that with *Indira Gandhi,* the "Play-House of the Ridiculous looks to the land of the Kama Sutra for its latest political satire" and "combines the innovations of theater happenings with ancient liturgy." It also explained that *Screen Test* was written for Mario Montez and constituted "the first important stage role for the most used actor in New York's independent film industry."

Both plays created something of a sensation, although each in different respects. Since *Indira Gandhi* featured an Indian "untouchable" with a three-foot erection as well as a scheme by the titular character to save her starving population, the Indian consul perceived it as an insult. *Screen Test* was rather difficult for its star, Montez, to endure, which led to Ludlam's real breakthrough on a New York stage.

Ludlam had a leading role in *Indira Gandhi* as Kamaraj, the "stud" to the prime minister, played by the husky-voiced Jeanne Phillips; he was not originally cast in *Screen Test,* the curtain-raiser Tavel had compiled from several different scenarios he had already written for Warhol. *Screen Test* depicted the audition of a would-be film star who is abused by a sadistic director. Tavel's nine-page treatment was basically an outline that relied heavily on improvisation — during both rehearsals and performances.

In what everyone had to see as typecasting, Montez played the submissive starlet while Vaccaro, perched on a ladder at the foot of the stage, portrayed the demanding director. When *Screen Test* opened, it could run anywhere from twenty to thirty minutes, depending on how much Montez and Vaccaro ad-libbed during the performance. The script also called for an actress to perform all the directions Vaccaro gave Montez, without verbally interacting with either of them.

Beginning with the rehearsals, Montez told Ludlam how difficult it was to work with Vaccaro. Once the play was up and running, Vaccaro became even more demanding and Montez more distressed. Provoked by Montez's pleas for help, it was some days into the run when Ludlam had a brainstorm. He phoned Tavel and said, "Drop whatever you have planned and be sure to show up for tomorrow night's performance. I have a surprise for you." A few minutes after the show started, Ludlam marched up from behind the audience and interrupted the "screen test." Wearing a black wig donated by Salvador Dalí — via Geldzahler — and a brown silk beaded gown, Ludlam made his drag debut on a New York stage by impersonating Norma Desmond, the Gloria Swanson character from *Sunset Boulevard.*

"Oh, John, what are you doing? Don't let me interrupt you," Ludlam coyly purred, as if he were Swanson and Vaccaro were Cecil B. DeMille in the Billy Wilder film. "Remember the times we used to have down on Second Avenue, John? . . . Oh, please don't let me interrupt you. Continue with your screen test." Referring to Montez and still in character as Norma Desmond, Ludlam said, "Oh, she isn't getting it, let me help her John," as he proceeded to execute Vaccaro's directions. In true Ridiculous fashion, Vaccaro and Montez instantly got into the spirit of the intrusion and played along to winning effect.

At one point, Ludlam left the stage and went to the rear of the audience, where he sat in Tavel's lap. "I could feel him trembling, shaking with tension over what he just did and wondering what the response would be," said Tavel. "But this was when Charles Ludlam first became Charles Ludlam. And it was brilliant. He was Norma Desmond to a T."

Ludlam's outsized personality had emerged considerably earlier, of course. His Norma Desmond merely marked the moment when Tavel became aware of it — and also aware of just what he was up against as a competing artist.

Later in the performance, when Vaccaro instructed Montez to kill her invisible pet panther and then say, "I just strangled my pet panther, Patricia, and I am not upset, I am fatigued," Ludlam returned to the stage and said, "She's doing it all wrong. Let me show her." But after miming the gestures, Ludlam failed to say anything. He just sat back with a satisfied look on his face, until Vaccaro cued him, "And now the line." Ludlam replied, "What line? In my day we didn't need lines — we had faces." In the garish manner of Gloria Swanson performing for the cameras at the end of *Sunset Boulevard*, Ludlam proceeded to twist his arms, grimace, and shake his head until his wig fell off, exposing his balding dome. The audience broke into cheers and extended applause. "That's when I knew that this man was willing to do anything for a magical moment onstage," said Tavel, "even to humiliate himself for the theater."

Following Ludlam's unexpected first appearance in *Screen Test*, his Norma Desmond became a regular part of the show. What had originally required thirty minutes playing time soon consumed an hour or more. Eventually, other members of the company found ways to insert themselves into the piece as well. In keeping with the *Sunset Boulevard* motif, Harvey Tavel once showed up in Eric von Stroheim's role as Desmond's servant, saying, "Norma, your car is ready."

Even later in the run, Ludlam shed his Norma Desmond impersonation for one of Samantha Eggar, the striking actress who had recently become an overnight sensation in William Wyler's film version of *The Collector*. Ludlam used Eggar's pensive style of acting to mock Method training. When Vaccaro gave an instruction, Ludlam would pause until Vaccaro finally said, "I'm waiting." Ludlam would snap back, "I'm getting into character!" Another time, Ludlam pretended to be blind, perhaps in homage to Lee Remick in the stage version of *Wait Until Dark* (which was just then being filmed with Audrey Hepburn); although Ludlam comically bumped into people as he felt his way around the space, he still managed to get to the front of the stage and into the spotlight — which was, of course, the joke.

Initially fueled by a rave review in the *Village Voice*, *Indira Gandhi's Daring Device* and *Screen Test* had a healthy run. There was no charge for admission, but contributions were shared among the players, amounting to little more than subway fare on most evenings.

In the midst of all the shenanigans, the actress on hand to mime Vaccaro's directions became increasingly testy. She was the one genuine female onstage, but she had trouble competing for attention. She once screamed out to the audience, "I'm a real woman! Why do you pay so much attention to these fakes?" At a subsequent performance, Ludlam walked onstage and threw a tampon at her, saying, "Here, dear. You forgot your *real* woman's prop." Eventually, the story circulated that she quit the show on the advice of her therapist.

Any attempt to understand early Ridiculous Theater must take into account the degree to which it incorporated improvisational elements and unexpected developments, both during conception and in performance. Here was a theater that was committed to the ephemeral nature of its being, its premise making for a type of controlled anarchy. Scripts were mere suggestions of what the players were supposed to bring to the dramatic circumstances; they were incomplete products, awaiting the performers' interactions and contributions. They never became finished or set in any way, since every performance was geared to invite mayhem and mishaps, asides and ad-libs, onstage accidents and rescues. For the first couple of years of the Ridiculous, the same show that took one or two hours to present on one night might take three on another.

In ineffable but deliberate ways, each production reflected the particular complexion of its cast. Their different personalities and idiosyncrasies were not only allowed, but encouraged. And since most people were working for free, they felt at liberty to drop out of a production in the middle of a run, requiring last minute fill-ins on a regular basis.

℘

Ludlam's brazen maneuver with *Screen Test* quickly established him as a force to be reckoned with, and there can be no doubt that he intended to run his own company. But it's harder to say when, or even if, he wanted it to be this one. According to Tavel, he already recognized by the time of *Screen Test* that Ludlam would stop at nothing to gain complete control. But the circumstances are far too equivocal to lend themselves to this narrow, and possibly paranoid, view. To be sure, there were a number of other developments before the rift between Ludlam and Vaccaro occurred. The most significant was the split between Tavel and Vaccaro — a split that Tavel believed to have been masterminded by Ludlam.

During the rehearsals for *Indira Gandhi*, Tavel complained to Ludlam about Vaccaro's style as a director. When he said he wanted his plays "done the way they were written" and that "John is ruining my reputation and making me look frivolous," Ludlam defended Vaccaro. "Of course I understand John is not going to be able to get the philosophy or the meaning of your plays," Ludlam told Tavel, "but you should stay with him because this man understands theatricality: how to bring on a chorus; how to take a chorus off the stage; how to build towards a climax..." This meeting took place at Tavel's apartment on the Bowery, which he shared with his brother. Pashalinski, who was present, reinforced what Ludlam was saying by adding that "John could capture the insanity and theatricality of the plays because he lives in a totally insane and theatrical world himself." Afterwards, Ludlam told Pashalinski that he was happy to see he had been of use in bridging the gap between Tavel and Vaccaro and assuaging Tavel's doubts. In fact, Ludlam felt that it was the collision of the two men's personalities that made the resulting stage work so vital.

Tavel accepted Ludlam's advice, at first; but, in addition to his ongoing friction with Vaccaro, he felt a growing antagonism between Ludlam and himself. For one thing, Tavel was in bed with one of Ludlam's lovers when Ludlam walked in on them. "To try and make it look like he didn't care, he just hopped into bed with us, making it a threesome," said Tavel. "But afterwards I could tell he wasn't very pleased with what had happened." Tavel also felt that Ludlam was generally insecure about his looks and envied him on that score. Once, at a rehearsal, he overheard Ludlam saying, "Tavel's very good-looking for a playwright, isn't he?" Another time, when Tavel tried to reas-

59

sure Ludlam that he was attractive, Ludlam snapped back, "I'm ugly, so why don't you just say it!"

But while accounting for his break from the Play-House of the Ridiculous, perhaps Tavel was inclined to invest too much in his personal dynamic with Ludlam, as if Ludlam had more of a hand in engineering the separation than anyone else would confirm. The ultimate dispute centered around Tavel's next play, *Gorilla Queen*, which was loosely based on *King Kong*. At seventy pages, it was easily five times longer than any work Tavel had previously presented to Vaccaro, who was terribly intimidated by its length. "I didn't think the actors we had, or people we knew, could learn all those lines. And also, I didn't like the play at all," said Vaccaro. He proceeded to pull twelve pages out at random, and said, "I'll do these." But since the play's "excess" was part of what Tavel was after, he refused to make any cuts.

"We'd all heard that title, 'Gorilla Queen,'" Ludlam told Calvin Tomkins a decade later for his profile in the *New Yorker*, "which suggested many things — jungle movies, Montez films, the camp idea of a monster gorilla that's gay, that's a queen. Everybody was expecting something lighthearted and campy, and then it turned out to be heavy, very word-heavy. John is not confident with dialogue, and he hated the play."

A meeting was held in Vaccaro's loft for the entire company, then numbering around twenty people. "I refer to that meeting as my 'rude awakening,'" said Tavel, "because I learned that day how innocent I was. It reminded me of *Julius Caesar*, with Brutus making a very rational speech and then Mark Antony making a totally emotional appeal. That's what happened." After Tavel, the self-appointed Brutus in the analogy, attempted to justify and defend his script, Vaccaro said, "This play is filth, it shits on the audience by cursing and insulting them." And then Ludlam joined in the argument.

Ludlam was slated to portray Sister Carrie in the play, a character whose name both mocked the title character in Theodore Dreiser's celebrated novel and toyed with the notion that she "carries" syphilis. According to Tavel, Ludlam said at the meeting, "'I'm not playing a role in which I have syphilis. You're telling the audience that I, Charles Ludlam, have syphilis.' With John shrieking his harangues of filth and garbage, and Charles backing him up, pandemonium ensued when the others agreed with them."

While most people remembered that Tavel chose to leave the company, he felt that he was driven out, and that it was primarily Ludlam who manipulated the circumstances. Ludlam was "envious of my position as resident playwright. He was thinking over this whole situation and working on his own play." Indeed, this was a pivotal moment that led, in due course, to the first production of a play written by Charles Ludlam, *Big Hotel*.

Gorilla Queen would be staged a few months later by Lawrence Kornfeld, the innovative director affiliated with Al Carmines and the Judson Poets' Theater. (It first played at the Judson before transferring to Off Broadway's Martinique Theater on April 24, 1967, and chalking up forty-two performances.) In the interim, Vaccaro resented Tavel's abrupt departure, especially since there were outstanding utility bills at the rented space on West 17th Street, with no show to help pay them. Tavel ultimately met his obligation with *Kitchenette*, a new one-act directed by his brother Harvey, which opened in January 1967.

With a company of players at his beck and call, Vaccaro was anxious for something to do next when Pashalinski mentioned that Ludlam was working on a play. It was really just a collection of favorite lines and vignettes from literature and pop culture, written down in a standard student's composition notebook. The hodgepodge of sources included Ben Jonson, Joyce, O'Casey, Oscar Wilde, Strindberg, Rimbaud, and of course Shakespeare, who was represented by *A Midsummer Night's Dream*, *The Merchant of Venice*, *King Lear*, *The Taming of the Shrew*, and *Macbeth*. There were also lines borrowed from a variety of films, such as *The Red Shoes*, *The Cocoanuts*, *Shanghai Express*, *Dinner at Eight*, *Svengali*, *Cobra Woman*, *Sunset Boulevard*, and *Niagara*. Still more fragments were taken from comic books, cartoons, TV commercials, a French grammar book, and the writings of Marshall McLuhan.

For certain members of the Ridiculous, watching old movies on television had become something of an obsession during the sixties. Montez had become expert at combing through the *TV Guide* to come up with weekly selections for movie parties held at his loft; he had accumulated a vast library of sound tapes by recording the audio tracks from movies on television, and Ludlam plundered them for source material.

The desperate Vaccaro realized he could have a field day staging this potpourri of familiar and less familiar quotations, and he pressed Ludlam into giving his unorganized writings some kind of shape. Ludlam's solution was to model his play on *International House*, a 1933 film concerning an assortment of travelers confined in a Shanghai hotel. The Paramount flick was itself a madcap farce featuring elements of vaudeville, as indicated by its cast: W.C. Fields, George Burns, Gracie Allen, Rudy Vallee, and Cab Calloway. With *International House* providing the framing device for wacky characters to pass through a hotel lobby, Ludlam also incorporated aspects of *Grand Hotel*. This even more beloved thirties film had included Garbo as Grusinskaya, a has-been ballerina, transformed into "Birdshitskaya" in Ludlam's version.

With money supplied by Panna Grady, Vaccaro opened Ludlam's *Big Hotel* at the Play-House of the Ridiculous in February 1967. The play was compelled to close very quickly — ostensibly for another building-code violation, but more likely due to the ongoing scandal that had been stirred up by *Indira Gandhi's Daring Device* the previous year.

Ludlam's first produced play would reopen in the fall. By then, however, Ludlam and Vaccaro had had a series of escalating disputes, culminating in a major confrontation, when eight other members of the company stormed out with Ludlam to form their own troupe. They comprised the nucleus of what was to become, in short order, the Ridiculous Theatrical Company.

GLITTER AND BE GAY

A creator is not in advance of his generation but he is the first of his contemporaries to be conscious of what is happening to his generation.
— Gertrude Stein

Glitter and be gay / That's the part I play
— Richard Wilbur, *Candide*

With the Living Theater, Caffe Cino, and Joseph Papp's Public Theater as precursors, the alternative theater movement was a burgeoning phenomenon by the mid-sixties. The mainstream press was beginning to allocate attention to a number of recently established organizations. Most prominent among these were Ellen Stewart's Cafe La MaMa, Joe Chaikin's Open Theater, André Gregory's Manhattan Project, Richard Schechner's Performance Group, and the Judson Poets' Theater, founded by Al Carmines, who performed his musical confections there after becoming an assistant minister at the Judson Memorial Church in 1961.

Considering the sudden plethora of newcomers, it's even more remarkable that Vaccaro's troupe — with their "heavily made-up performers, their transvestite finery sprinkled with sequins, their rouged faces painted in gold dust" — was looked upon as "the oddest and most outrageously behaved company to be found anywhere in the off off-Broadway scene." This, at least, was the assessment of Stuart W. Little in his textual history of the movement, *Off-Broadway*.

In *The New Bohemia*, published in 1966 and based on his article of the same name that had appeared two years earlier in *New York* magazine, John Gruen claimed, "The present underground theater . . . rides off rapidly in every direction. If there is a difference between it and previous theatrical manifestations, that difference is felt in the total disregard for the formalities of theater. For the most part, all conventions are questioned, if not disregarded."

Any appreciation of Ludlam's theater must begin by distinguishing it from the revolutionary impulses of the 1960s counterculture from which it sprang. In contrast with the Off-Off-Broadway movement that was surging around him in the East Village and always striving to break new ground, Ludlam would embrace abandoned theatrical customs of the past: from *commedia dell'arte* to vaudeville, from Elizabethan theatrics to silent-film acting techniques. In a manner of speaking, Ludlam was uncovering old ground — so old, in fact, that much of his audience would find it new.

In retroactively piecing together the story of the Ridiculous, it is astonishing to realize how quickly it developed a cult following. Strictly on the basis of attending certain shows and admiring what they saw, many creative and influential people would offer their services and affiliate themselves with the company. In addition to Geldzahler's seminal support, Stefan Brecht, son of the great German playwright Bertolt, became an early devotee and patron. He clearly found an underground cause to endorse; and he supported it — both morally and financially — until mainstream attention began to accrue.

Brecht would later account for his initial admiration in *Queer Theatre*, the most thorough eyewitness documentation of the early years of the Ridiculous, albeit an idiosyncratically written one. In one of his more coherent statements, Brecht argued that "To view the theater of the ridiculous as the flaunting tool of pervert coteries — demeaning manliness, humiliating women, expressing self-hatred and alienation by a snide attack on culture, values, reason, 'life itself' — is contemptibly facile. The essential point is that they are exposing and by their mockery opposing a perverse culture."

To be sure, it had become extremely fashionable to upend conventional values and to question all forms of perceived authority. Before becoming ensconced on Broadway, *Hair* opened at the Public Theater in October of 1967 with the cast members celebrating "the dawning of the Age of Aquarius," which was as apt a way of summarizing how the new generation felt about itself as any. But within this heady and topsy-turvy context, the Ridiculous set out to be more revolutionary still.

Ludlam would later describe the formation of a theater reacting against reactionary times:

> We adopted a position of deliberate unfashionableness. . . . We affirmed the currently discarded conventions of the theater; we viewed them as the essence of the theatrical, its language and vocabulary. We used the great traditions of the past as our authority to envision a future diametrically opposed to the one our contemporaries were predicting. We could not accept as avant-garde purely formal experiments which seemed both bloodless and wasteful.
>
> Anyone who defies the narrow limits of fashion and deliberately goes against the current trends runs the risk of appearing ridiculous. And so we decided to strike

the first blow and adopt the name, to create a theatre not about ridiculing others but about the risks of appearing ridiculous to them. This was the birth of America's most original contribution to comedy. Our theater embraced the popular culture, fit it into history and offered it the possibility of a glorious future with a new sense of purpose. We wanted to obviate the American inferiority complex that goes, "Everything European is better." Our work draws its power from a dual vision. The outward appearance is Ridiculous but the intention is serious.

Another person who immediately appreciated the "dual vision" of the Ridiculous was an old-fashioned drag queen and chanteuse, Minette, who happened to catch the initial and quickly aborted run of *Big Hotel* in February 1967 with a free ticket he was given by Mario Montez. Minette was working at the time at Crazy Horse, a club on Bleecker Street. He was also performing that month in a special show at Town Hall called the Miss All-American Camp Beauty Pageant, known more quaintly by those involved with it as "Mind-Blow U.S.A." This one-night affair was put together by the noted drag queen Sabrena, and filmed as part of a documentary called *The Queen*.

"We had all these damn rehearsals for all these production numbers," recalled Minette. "I was doing a single, but I'd be sitting around the rehearsal hall at Eighth Avenue and 50ᵗʰ Street, and in the course of this I met Mario Montez." In the show itself, Minette sang "Am I Blue," and Montez, one of the headliners, made a grand entrance carried down the aisle in a French bathtub, clad in a gold lamé dress, a blonde wig, and a fur wrap, singing "Diamonds Are a Girl's Best Friend."

Though Lady Bird Johnson and Andy Warhol were both supposed to appear as judges, "Mind-Blow U.S.A." was poorly attended, filling only the first six rows or so of the cavernous Town Hall. The event is rather worth mentioning since it introduced Minette to the Ridiculous via Montez. More than becoming the company's first and most loyal fan, Minette became the company mascot. It was his abiding interest in astrology that made the zodiac such a preoccupation for many people in the company.

Though Ludlam would invite him to perform in many a Ridiculous production over the years, as Minette explained, "I could make ten times as much money just staying home and providing some horizontal entertainment in bed. Pansies were popular at the time — this was just before Gay Liberation, which was when people found out they could get 'it' for free."

Gay Liberation was indeed just around the corner, marked as it was by the Stonewall uprising in the summer of 1969, a summer which also marked the first moonwalk as well as Woodstock. It would be another decade before the Ridiculous Theatrical Company founded their permanent home at One Sheridan Square, literally around the corner from where the Stonewall riots took place, in the heart of Greenwich Village.

The production of *Big Hotel* that Minette first saw featured Ludlam repeating his wildly successful Norma Desmond impersonation. Christopher Scott had a brainstorm for evoking a Hanging-Gardens-of-Babylon effect that enveloped the audience during the "Cobra Cunt Ceremony" near the end of the play: With clotheslines and pulley devices, he rigged an overhead system that released strips of cloth over the audience on cue. One was suddenly transported to a jungle and had to peer through hanging vines and Spanish moss to see the stage. In a sense, it was with this show that the look or theatricality of a Ridiculous presentation became equally as important as the material being presented.

It was by now customary for all the players involved in a Ridiculous show to see to their own extravagant costumes and to assist each other in the process. With an emphasis on glitter, sequins, baubles, bangles, and beads, they turned shoestrings into gold laces and created expensive looks out of vintage clothing and found materials. Having learned many techniques from Jack Smith, Montez became a master at this wardrobe alchemy and he willingly shared his makeshift pearls of wisdom with the rest of the cast. Indeed, Montez's loft also served as a workshop for his secondary business: Under the banner Montez Creations, he custom-made unusual apparel for anyone who would pay his fees.

As Montez told Frank Keating for a feature story in the summer 1969 issue of *Queen's Quarterly* — which proudly proclaimed itself on the cover as "The Magazine for Gay Guys Who Have No Hangups" — "It only costs me $50.00 a year for costumes and about $20.00 for makeup." (Ludlam would later claim that everything he knew about applying makeup came from Montez.)

Fifty dollars may sound remarkably inexpensive for the extravagant attire that Montez regularly produced for himself. But his most valuable secret was that the sidewalks of New York proved a treasure trove of discarded items — especially late at night when one could happen upon industrial garbage bins or cartons containing odd pieces of fabric, mylar fragments, and other useful remnants from a busy day at the clothing factories in Soho. (There was a particularly funny incident when the routine plundering backfired. Ludlam was walking in the East Village with Thomas Lanigan Schmidt, an artist and friend, when they discovered a box crammed with rubber gloves. They were trying them on and gloating over their bounty until a foul stench began to permeate the air and they realized the gloves had been used for "medical" purposes.)

ॐ

Though *Big Hotel* was compelled to close early, it played long enough for Ludlam to miss a few performances while he dealt with a bout of pleurisy and went to Long Island to be nursed by his mother. It was also well enough received to encourage Ludlam to write his second play, *Conquest of the Universe*. Given its sprawling, epic proportions, it would be misleading to suggest that *Conquest* was more structured than *Big Hotel*. But it was the first play that Ludlam conceived with the promise of a production in mind, and the difference showed in the semblance of a plot.

Conquest was based primarily on Christopher Marlowe's first play, *Tamburlaine the Great*, concerning Tamerlane, the Mongolian conqueror and descendant of Genghis Khan who had taken over parts of Russia, India, Persia, and Central Asia before his death in 1405, when he was on the verge of invading China. In Ludlam's version, Tamerlane is transformed into Tamberlaine, President of the Earth. His wife Alice (perhaps a reference to "The Honeymooners") calls him a "Mongoloid." He is an interplanetary warrior whose primary motivation stems from his insatiable sexual appetite. As he conquers Mars in the first scene, he asks Bajazeth, the King of Mars, to "kneel and be buggered." Throughout his subsequent victories, as he proceeds to "bugger" just about everybody else onstage, male or female, Tamberlaine retains a certain predilection for Bajazeth, whom he keeps on a leash. After he conquers Mars, Venus, and Mercury, we are told that "Neptune — Uranus — Pluto — Cambodia — Laos — North Vietnam — South Vietnam — West Hempstead" are next. While "West Hempstead" was a throwaway, personal reference to Ludlam's college days at Hofstra, the allusions to Vietnam must have had far more resonance with audiences at the time. But *Conquest* was not as aggressively political as a number of other works that had recently opened Off Broadway and fueled the protests to America's role in Southeast Asia, including Megan Terry's *Viet Rock*, Jean-Claude van Itallie's *America Hurrah*, and Barbara Garson's even more incendiary *MacBird!*

With a juvenile, Flash Gordon-ish quality informing both the text and the staging, *Conquest* is loaded with scatalogical remarks and lewd activities on every page, signaling an ongoing backlash against Ludlam's Catholic upbringing. In terms of its emphasis on flagrant polymorphous perversity and verbal or mimed sex acts, it might well be unprecedented as far as works intended for the stage go: In the second scene, Venus enjoys cunnilingus with Cosroe, a Martian Prince, while being sodomized by Magnavox, King of Mercury, even as she receives Tamberlaine and others in her chambers. In the final scene, Tamberlaine's wife gives birth to nine sons. Proclaiming that he had not "this twelvemonth fucked thee," Tamberlaine has Alice as well as her offspring put to death. At that point, Bajazeth announces that he too has borne Tamberlaine nine "little ones," or turds, "out of my asshole." Even a stage direction parenthetically calls for "A fanfare of farts [to be] heard."

A subplot concerns Cosroe, whose heroic qualities serve as a foil to Tamberlaine's villainy. Cosroe is incestuously in love with his twin sister Zabina. Though this may be an allusion to John Ford's 'Tis Pity She's a Whore, far more obvious are the recurring references that posit Cosroe as Hamlet. As Ludlam told David Scott, Christopher's brother, who ran the sound and lights for *Conquest*, "I would have played Hamlet if I could, but since no one would cast me in the part, I had to write a play with Hamlet in it for myself." In one of the more instantly identifiable scenes, Cosroe encounters a gravedigger who is burying Zabina:

> COSROE: Why, who are you, sir?
>
> GRAVEDIGGER: I am the maker of graves.
>
> COSROE: The opposite of a comedian, you make us grave. Whose grave is it you make, sir?
>
> GRAVEDIGGER: I bury Zabina, one-time queen of conquered Mars. She is a grave woman. A grave womanly offense. Her brother Cosroe, they say, is mad.
>
> COSROE: Is he?
>
> GRAVEDIGGER: They should send him to Earth.
>
> COSROE: Why?
>
> GRAVEDIGGER: They have many psychiatrists there to help him recover his wits. But if he doesn't, 'tis no great matter there.
>
> COSROE: Why?
>
> GRAVEDIGGER: 'Twill not be seen in him there: there the men are as mad as he.
>
> COSROE: (*Picking up a skull*) Alas, poor Urine, he pissed his life away.

Other classical lines worthy of revised notations in Bartlett's *Familiar Quotations* are also inserted with a characteristic Ridiculous twist, such as "My kingdom for a boa."

Since Marlowe is considered the greatest Elizabethan dramatist prior to Shakespeare, Ludlam was sure to pay homage to Elizabethan language while writing predominantly in his own style, which was riddled with contemporary jargon and anachronistic references. Natolia, the Queen of Saturn (who, we're told, speaks "Sauterne") goes back farther still, speaking in Chaucerian Middle English. In one scene, when Natolia is presented with a large package containing Tamberlaine, she responds, "He hadde maad ful many a mariage of yonge woman at his owne cost.... Tamberlaine! As leeve was his hors as is a rake and he was not right fat, I undertake." Another character translates this to mean, "Okay, smarty pants! I'll show all of you I can control my curiosity if I want to! That box means nothing to me."

Conquest is also notable for a "self-conscious" leitmotif, which would become one of Ludlam's signature imprints. For one instance, Cosroe claims, "According to Hoyle, I need the book *I Ching* and the Ting Tripod to make the incantation that would safely allow me to continue in this play." For another, Zabina says, "I need a cigarette. Listen to me, you cocksucker, I've got to have a butt or I'll drop dead! dead! dead! (*Aside*) That was the worst line I've ever had to say in *any* play." And in a more extended dialogue between Tamberlaine and Alice:

> TAMBERLAINE: We'll go to the theater tonight and let everyone see us.
> ALICE: What's playing?
> TAMBERLAINE: *The Conquest of the Universe, or When Queens Collide* by Charles
> Ludlam.
> ALICE: Filth! The insane ravings of a degenerate mind! I won't go! Besides I
> haven't a thing to wear!

The title of Ludlam's second play, *Conquest of the Universe*, could easily be read as a personal mandate for himself. Like Tamberlaine, Ludlam felt "like an explorer on the edge of a new world." Also like Tamberlaine, he set out to "free Mankind from the yoke of reason which weighs upon it." And when Venus defends Tamberlaine's sexual hubris by saying "he's just a kid with a dream," one can detect the author mocking himself.

But relative to the twenty-seven plays that would follow, *Conquest* does not fall high on the list of more successful works by Ludlam. A form of updated burlesque, more raunchy than bawdy, it is amorphous and sprawling by design. It doesn't even abide enough by the categorical rules of farce to be classified as such. Then again, Ludlam was only interested in rules insofar as he could break them.

Though Ludlam would always retain a soft spot and offer a theoretical justification for what he called his "epic" plays — as represented by his first four: *Big Hotel, Conquest of the Universe, Turds in Hell,* and *The Grand Tarot*—the term, as used, is something of a euphemism disguising the fact that they were sloppy, unstructured scenarios. They continued to demonstrate Ronald Tavel's calculated disdain for logic, characterization, and story. They were chaotic, heavily drug-influenced works: performed by people on drugs for people on drugs—and written with that in mind. On the other hand, they are indisputably Ludlam's most original works, stamped by his incipient genius. And they were given uncanny life in performance. But the vitality they expressed and displayed cannot be exactly duplicated. By catering to the moment above all else, they were designed to self-destruct, in a sense. What initial spirit they embodied can no more be recaptured than the original casts can be reassembled.

Clearly it would take some time to "conquer the universe." But Ludlam's more immediate ambitions were delayed and thwarted. Vaccaro rehearsed *Conquest* for a few months in the spring of 1967, while waiting for a theater in which to put it on. The cast included a few newcomers who would later leave with Ludlam to form their own group, though no one would have predicted this except Tavel, who claimed with hindsight to have seen the handwriting on the fourth wall, so to speak.

One of the new members was Hofstra colleague Susan Carlson, whom Ludlam had run into at an all-night grocery store and invited to join Vaccaro's group. Another two, John Brockmeyer and Gary Tucker, had been lovers at Ohio State University before moving to New York together in 1965, where Tucker was studying acting as he had in college. Brockmeyer was then a pharmacist, applying skills he had originally learned in the Navy. He was from Columbus, Ohio and still in high school when he had, coincidentally, seen Vaccaro performing there in the late fifties, in a club called the High Spot Low Spot. It was only after Brockmeyer and Tucker were taken by a mutual friend of Vaccaro's to see *Screen Test* and *Indira Gandhi* that Tucker realized there might be something there worth pursuing.

As Brockmeyer recalled, "John Vaccaro was very attracted to Gary. But we didn't see him for a while, until after the breakup with Ronnie Tavel. We didn't even see that first version of *Big Hotel.* It was when John was putting together the production of *Conquest* that we sort of fell in with the crowd."

Still another Ohio native who came onboard with *Conquest* was Bill Vehr, who, like Brockmeyer, was twenty-six at the time. In fact, Ludlam and Vehr had already slept together and become intimate friends. Of everyone who became affiliated with the Ridiculous early on, Vehr and Ludlam were perhaps the most intellectually compatible.

Like Ludlam, Vehr had an encyclopedic knowledge of old movies. He also had an obsession with James Joyce, which he realized over the years with public readings of *Finnegans Wake*. Vehr was destined to be, in short time, the only person who would ever collaborate on writing a play with Ludlam.

Further reinforcing how small and incestuous their world was, Vehr had already performed with the Ridiculous before returning to appear in *Conquest*. He played the "untouchable" with the huge phallus in *Indira Gandhi's Daring Device*. He had also been in a number of both Jack Smith and Andy Warhol films, sometimes with Vaccaro. He was an underground filmmaker in his own right as well. His most notable movies were *Brothel*— starring Mario Montez as "Maphrodite" and Jack Smith as "Jack the Ripper" — and *Avocada*, which Vehr categorized as a "candle-opera."

Yet another film of Vehr's was called *M.M. for M.M.* Decoded, the title represented Mario Montez for Marilyn Monroe— or vice versa. But apparently this movie was never completed as intended. Only segments of it were shown with other independent movies at various screenings. To try and raise the capital to complete the shooting, Montez signed publicity photos of himself in drag: "We need money to finish film— *M.M. for M.M.* Can you help?" In the lower right-hand corner was stamped: "Send contribution to: Bill Vehr, 517 E. 12th St., Apt. #16."

"Of course, I play Marilyn," Montez told journalist John Gruen during the shooting of the film in January 1967. "I must admit, I don't have her shape, and the bathing-suit sequences will give me some trouble, but I'm sure I'll manage. I'll be singing a lot of her songs, including the 'Heat Wave' number from *There's No Business Like Show Business*. But we're starting out with the bubble-bath scene from *The Seven-Year Itch*."

Ludlam made an appearance in *M.M. for M.M.* as well. Donning an oversized Jerry Colonna-type mustache— which he incessantly twirled in a villainous manner to enhance his mugging— he portrayed a plumber on an emergency call to help Montez extricate his big toe from the bathtub faucet. The sequence was shot in the bathroom of Lohr Wilson, a friend of Vehr's who performed in the first version of *Big Hotel* and who later worked with the Ridiculous principally as a costume designer and occasionally as an actor.

It was a couple of months after *Big Hotel* closed that rehearsals for *Conquest of the Universe* commenced. In addition to having to endure Vaccaro's characteristically abrasive tactics, everyone was getting fidgety since no prospects for a theater space had emerged. Ludlam, who suddenly found himself the company playwright, adopted a grin-and-bear-it attitude when Vaccaro banished his new, black lover Rudy from rehearsals, but he was seething underneath. Though no one can account for the specific incident, Brockmeyer conjectured that "Vaccaro was probably jealous of his big, black dick."

Stunningly beautiful and very sweet, Rudy was indeed extremely well-endowed. Ludlam's affair with him lasted for a couple of months, during which he spent a lot of time at Rudy's apartment on East 10th Street. A fashion designer, Rudy was very domestic and wanted their relationship to become more permanent. But Ludlam was hesitant and it eventually fizzled.

At Geldzahler's instigation, Vaccaro secured the interest of the painter Wyn Chamberlain, whose wealthy connections held the promise of aid in finding a performance space. For a brief period, plans looked firm for a ballroom on the Lower East Side that Chamberlain had located, but they fell through at the last minute. Then, to keep the company together as much as anything else, an outdoor production of *Conquest* was planned for the late spring in Rhinebeck, New York, which was near Woodstock and fast becoming a hippie enclave.

Ludlam, Scott, Pashalinski, and Brockmeyer were driven up to Staatsburg, N.Y., just south of Rhinebeck, by Bill Walters, the company lighting man, and they all spent the night on the floor of Chamberlain's country home. The rest of the company took a bus to Woodstock, where they stayed in unheated cabins, which they complained about the next morning since it proved to have been a chilly spring night. If the whole affair had been arranged to lift the company out of the doldrums, it backfired when the performance was called off the next day. The reasons are as mysterious now as they were then. But there was a resentful rumor circulating at the time that Vaccaro had actually been given some money by Chamberlain for the company — money which he neither acknowledged receiving nor shared.

No one can say with certainty what precipitated the permanent falling out between Ludlam and Vaccaro shortly after they returned to New York. According to Vaccaro, Ludlam just stormed out in the midst of an argument, which was unusual only in terms of his departure, as arguments between them had become standard operating procedure. According to many others, Vaccaro banished Ludlam. Looking back on it, Geldzahler perceived that the breakup was inevitable: "Vaccaro and Charles were both crazy in different ways. Vaccaro became more and more disorganized and demanding at the same time that Charles's creative wings were growing larger and larger. The egomania and lack of discipline on Vaccaro's part, and Charles's fledgling ego, couldn't remain in the same space."

In truth, Ludlam had already discussed with Scott and Vehr the possibility of breaking with Vaccaro and forming their own company, before the pivotal fight occurred during a rehearsal at Vaccaro's loft. Brockmeyer, for one, felt that Ludlam had "instigated the uprising." During this particular flare-up, Ludlam refused to take a direction Vaccaro was giving. In a heated moment, Ludlam called Vaccaro a "dope addict," referring to rumors of his heroin habit. Vaccaro yelled, "You're fired!" While Chamberlain took Vaccaro aside to calm him down, the distraught cast members formed various huddles to try and decide whether to leave with Ludlam or to stay.

For years, Ludlam would tell the story that Vaccaro, in a conciliatory mood, had once phoned him at 5 AM following a fight, asking him to come over and cut his hair. It was only after he refused to be Vaccaro's barber that he was asked to leave the company. Equally fed up with Vaccaro, eight other members of the company left with Ludlam in protest: Christopher Scott, Mario Montez, Lola Pashalinski, Susan Carlson, Bill Vehr, John Brockmeyer, Gary Tucker, and Jeanne Phillips. This group formed the nucleus of what would become the Ridiculous Theatrical Company. They met the next day at Montez's loft, intending to proceed with their own production of *Conquest* without having any idea how it would be done. Though he didn't join them in any official capacity and always retained some distance, Jack Smith was also on hand as a sounding board.

It was Smith who, on the spot, came up with the name of "The Ridiculous Theatrical Company." Rene Ricard, Ludlam's erstwhile Provincetown companion who had been introduced to the Play-House of the Ridiculous via Warhol and Tavel, elected to remain with Vaccaro; but he showed up at Montez's loft, pleading for everyone to forgive Vaccaro and return to the company. He claimed that this was what Vaccaro wanted, though clearly the hot-tempered director had to send an emissary to eat his humble pie. When Ricard realized he wasn't getting anywhere with his peace treaty, he quipped, "When queens collide, the lesser deities get kicked in the ass," referring to the pivotal collision between Ludlam and Vaccaro. *When Queens Collide* was soon to become an alternate name for *Conquest of the Universe*.

Though it would prove more fleeting than he might have expected, Vaccaro had some vengeance before long. Care of Geldzahler, Ludlam was sent a certified lawyer's letter dated October 20, 1967, explaining that "Play-House of the Ridiculous, Inc., producer of *Conquest of the Universe*" had "exclusive stage production rights in the above play." The letter, from the firm of Weissberger & Frosch, further stated: "It has come to our client's attention that preparations are in progress for an additional stage production of the said play. Any such production would be in gross violation of your contract and would cause serious and irreparable damages to our client. In the event you do not terminate such efforts . . . we shall take . . . further action."

If Ludlam had been reluctant to sign a contract for *Conquest* with Chamberlain in the first place, this bitter lesson made him extra leery of contracts ever after. It also confirmed his skepticism towards commercial theater and compelled him to avoid relinquishing rights on his own works to other producers for the rest of his life. Though Broadway would beckon at various points in the future, Ludlam would always back away when he realized he would have to forgo absolute control over the given enterprise. Just as his mother Marjorie had been an overprotective parent, Ludlam would prove to be an overprotective playwright, loath for others to produce any of his works until much later in his life.

Beyond being told that he couldn't stage his own play and being threatened with further action if he did, Ludlam was terribly galled because his name was spelled incorrectly both at the top and the bottom of the lawyer's letter. (From that point on, he would become irate whenever someone spelled his name "Ludlum," usually in confusion with the best-selling novelist Robert Ludlum.) But even as Vaccaro mounted a highly successful production of *Conquest* at the Bouwerie Lane Theater that fall—with a cast that Rene Ricard quickly assembled from Warhol's stable of superstars, including Ultra Violet, Ondine, Taylor Mead, and Mary Woronov—Ludlam circumvented the illegality of producing his own version by renaming it *When Queens Collide*. In addition to picking up on Ricard's remark about the feud between Ludlam and Vaccaro, this alternate title was a variation on *When Worlds Collide*, a popular and corny sci-fi film of 1951.

Vaccaro's version of *Conquest* opened first, in November of 1967. In the *Village Voice*, Michael Smith deemed it "an explosion of talent that leaves the mind in tatters." But it was Martin Gottfried, the theater reviewer for *Women's Wear Daily*, who proved to be the first "Uptown" critic to take the Ridiculous seriously with his review of *Conquest*. Though he dismissed the plot as "a travesty of science-fiction cheapie movie spectaculars and entirely unfollowable," he championed Vaccaro's staging and Ludlam's script for "a freedom bordering on anarchy." He reveled in this "wild, free-for-all theater, so exuberant one could hardly keep from being carried away by it. Post-pop art, post-camp, and so thoroughly obscene that it was nonsexual, it turned out to be the absolutely modern equivalent of burlesque, vulgar in the best, most down-to-earth, basic-theater sense." He described:

> a jester popping up among the vinyl Venetian-Martian-Saturnian trappings with jokes like, "The soldier turned up at his wife's bedside with his discharge in his hand." Or "guest star" Taylor Mead soaring out over the audience on a swing, decked out in green Mary Martin–Peter Pan tights, singing (more or less) "I've Got to Crow" straight-faced (more or less).

> I won't tell you that *Conquest of the Universe* is professional theater, and to be honest its best quality is its antiprofessional attitude. Yet there is a theater intelligence behind it. More important, though, there is a theater excitement — a giddiness of spirit and a joy of invention that make its spontaneity worth almost any price of amateurism.

In her memoir, *Famous For 15 Minutes*, Ultra Violet described her New York stage debut in *Conquest*, in which she played Natolia, the Queen of Saturn, and Ondine played Zabina, the Queen of Mars. "The curtain does not go up until Ondine, in full view of the actors, inserts a needle into his arm, pulls it out and gives the actors' blessing, 'Break a leg.' I respond, 'Break an arm.' Then we go on," wrote Ultra Violet. She also recalled the night she invited Marcel Duchamp to watch a performance. "After the show, Marcel embraces me while puffing on his cigar. He says, 'It's a collage from Brecht, Shakespeare, Adolf Hitler's writing, TV ads. I love you in it.'"

With a regular Tuesday through Sunday schedule and ticket prices ranging from $1.95–$4.95, Vaccaro's version of *Conquest* enjoyed a three-month run. Some of the performances were sold out. There was a special New Year's Eve "Underground Performance" at 9 PM, followed by a "party and dancing."

Legally barred from staging his own version of *Conquest*, Ludlam decided to launch a revival of *Big Hotel* with his new company of players, many of whom had been in Vaccaro's original production. Despite his reservations, he would introduce *When Queens Collide* in repertory fashion shortly after *Big Hotel* opened. Via Geldzahler's bankroll, Christopher Scott donated $400 to the enterprise, which was all that was required for theater rental and start-up costs, considering everyone was willing to work without pay. A performance space had yet to be found, however.

Montez's loft served as the regular rehearsal studio. It was located on the third floor of a building at 180 Centre Street. He had a large rectangular space that stretched the length of the building. A workroom at the end housed his busy sewing machine, and a makeshift wall separated Montez's sleeping area from the living room, which served as the rehearsal space. In his role as director, Ludlam held court from an enormous, elongated couch that reeked of cat urine. (Montez's long-haired white cat, Snowball, was also known as "White Pussy" — and was immortalized in a Warhol film of the same name, as well as in José Rodríquez-Soltero's *Lupe*.)

Since Ludlam needed fresh members to flesh out his new troupe, he got in touch with Jack Mallory, his nutty neighbor back at East 1ˢᵗ Street. Mallory had just returned to New York from an extended stay in San Francisco, his original home, where he had reveled in the bacchanalian delights of the "Summer of Love." Ludlam had actually tried to involve Mallory in the Ridiculous by bringing him to a rehearsal of *Indira Gandhi's Daring Device* the year before, but Mallory was unimpressed with Tavel's play and too intimidated by Vaccaro to pursue any unexplored acting ambitions he might have had at the time. It was different now, however. Ludlam seduced Mallory, like everyone else, into donating his energies to *Big Hotel* and *When Queens Collide*. He would have some incidental roles in the former, and accompany Montez on the piano in the latter.

It would also become a part of Mallory's regular job to prepare and dispense the incense that was so much a part of the early productions. This was the most palpable carryover of Ludlam's childhood fascination with the Catholic Mass. It reflected his conviction that the theater was really a church — without the hypocrisy. Mallory recalled "burning such large quantities of incense that the audience would get up and rush out of the theater sometimes."

Having recently joined the Ridiculous himself, Gary Tucker brought his lover John Brockmeyer to some of the rehearsals. Ludlam asked him if he could do the lighting and stage manage, "And I, being totally inexperienced, said sure," recalled Brockmeyer. "I started acting in a couple of plays later as Mario's leading man, frankly because I was tall," he continued. "I could stand next to the six-foot drag queen in her outrageous shoes and make her look petite." Ergo Brockmeyer's nickname, Big John.

Still another new member was introduced to the Ridiculous by Tucker for the revival of *Big Hotel*. Tucker was working as a salesman at the midtown branch of Sam Goody's, the popular record store, which had several branches in the city. A nineteen-year-old coworker by the name of James Morfogen happened to mention that he had briefly attended some classes at the Academy of Dramatic Arts, of which Tucker was himself an alumnus. Their shared background, coupled with Morfogen's enormous weight, compelled Tucker to invite him to a rehearsal at Montez's loft.

"Charles had piercing eyes and he looked at me very intensely when I met him at the rehearsal," recalled Morfogen. "I was 265 pounds at the time, so there was a lot to look at. My weight was used to advantage in the plays, believe me." It's curious to note that Ludlam was wearing a straight-haired black wig when Morfogen first met him. "I thought it was his real hair," said Morfogen. "I had no idea he was bald."

Exploiting Morfogen's heft, the role of Baby Edgar was invented for him in Ludlam's revival of *Big Hotel*. Clad only in an oversized diaper, Baby Edgar would soon be crawling through the lobby of the hotel set at opportune moments. Morfogen would also replace Jack Smith in some minor parts in the play.

It was probably more than just coincidence that Smith had a falling-out with Ludlam within months of the break with Vaccaro. Though he was always dangerously temperamental, Smith could afford to be cooperative with Ludlam when he viewed him as a colleague. But as soon as Vaccaro was removed from the picture and Ludlam assumed authority, Smith was unwilling to take a subservient role — or so it would seem from his escalating pugnacity.

Though the reasons behind the fight have been lost to the ages — that is, if they were ever very clear in the first place — Ludlam and Smith had already had a memorable confrontation at Montez's loft when Smith screamed, "You bald bastard, you've been wasting my time." Others interceded just as he was about to lunge at Ludlam. Adopting a purely disingenuous attitude, Ludlam responded, "Jack, I love you. Why are you doing this?" But on some level, Ludlam had to appreciate that he was at least as competitive as Smith was.

José Rodríguez-Soltero, who by then also had a loft at 180 Centre Street, recalled a time when Smith "went after Mario with a hammer. He was truly schizophrenic," added Rodríguez-Soltero. "I remember once when Jack was at my place sitting and writing, over and over again, 'Omar the Turk fucked Mario,' with these little drawings and curlicues in the margins. Then he said, 'Mario doesn't love me, because he slept with Omar, the Turk.' And we all knew that there wasn't any Omar, that this was an hallucination of his. But Jack tried to kill a lot of people, and I learned to stay away from him."

It was at a subsequent rehearsal for Ludlam's revival of *Big Hotel* that Smith —

unprovoked and to the astonishment of everyone present—attacked Christopher Scott. "Jack Smith just showed up at Mario's loft one day for a rehearsal and out of the blue, he picked a fight with Chris," recalled Pashalinski. "He singled him out as an enemy." Smith literally punched the bewildered Scott in the face, knocking him to the floor. For Ludlam, it was the last straw. "Charles exploded and, screaming at Jack, he kicked him out," she added.

According to Ronald Tavel, Smith told him some years later that "I suggested to Charles he call it the Ridiculous Theatrical Company to make fun of him, but he never understood that. It was a way of saying the *company* is ridiculous. And by using the word 'theatrical,' it meant they're merely theatrical, not even a theater company. I've been amused all these years that he was too stupid to understand I was putting him down."

Since Ludlam would emphasize in countless interviews that the whole point of the company was to be a mockery of itself, and that both Smith and Tavel had to be aware of this, Smith's claim about mocking Ludlam may have been made to appease Tavel. In any event, Tavel, Smith—and, to a somewhat lesser degree, Vaccaro—each sustained a lingering resentment towards Ludlam, whose career would flourish while their own theatrical legacies languished. Smith, who had always called Ludlam "baldy" behind his back, later referred to him as "the thief." (In an entirely different spirit, Ludlam would acknowledge his debt to the past by calling himself "the thief of bad gags"—which was itself a pun, referring to the classic film, *The Thief of Baghdad*.)

Resentments are usually reciprocal, if not necessarily contagious. It's revealing that Ludlam never saw Vaccaro's version of *Conquest*, considering that it was, after all, his own play. He would, however, see later plays staged by Vaccaro and tell colleagues, "Mine is the theater of beauty. Vaccaro's is the theater of ugliness."

"Vaccaro always ranted about Charles whenever he saw me," claimed Ronald Tavel. "I thought to myself, 'This is probably how he ranted about me to Charles, before *they* split.' It was malicious and slanderous: how dreadful the plays were, how awful the acting was. And the gossip! He carried on this hatred for years and years and years."

Referring to both Ludlam and Vaccaro, Harvey Tavel would complain three decades later: "They stole the theater from my brother and me. I had found the first space, did all the legal work, and raised all the money. I felt terribly betrayed."

As far as the name of the company went, the Ludlam-directed *Big Hotel* would open under the rubric of "The Art Nouveau Ridiculous Theatrical Company." This would be yet another attempt to differentiate themselves from Vaccaro's ongoing Play-House of the Ridiculous.

Before Ludlam could suddenly emerge with a new company, however, there was the obvious need for a space in which to perform. Though performing in art galleries, lofts, and alternative spaces was all the rage in the Off-Off-Broadway movement by 1967, Ludlam specifically wanted a real theater. He was eager to pay homage to the great traditions of theater history, of which he was determined to become a part. He did not specifically say, however, that he also wanted to distinguish himself from the contemporary avant-garde, for which he had less and less tolerance. Ludlam cannily understood that performing in a real theater, as opposed to some fashionably makeshift space, was a very tangible way of making the distinction.

At this juncture, as at every other, being "different" was a key motivation. Ludlam would always resent the tendency to view his work as part of the contemporary avant-garde, or as part of any other movement for that matter. As his own work evolved, he had little respect for the work of other living theater practitioners, to whom he felt superior. And throughout his career, he would struggle with the ongoing need to categorize his work or compare it to anything else that was going on. To call it "gay" or "camp," as most critics and fans would, was perceived as an insult, narrowing the focus of what he had to offer. Inviting comparison with others whose work was exclusively gay or camp demeaned the more serious intent behind Ludlam's exploitation of the same sensibility. Ludlam *knew* he was better than everyone else — that his work addressed loftier goals and contained more meaning — but he wouldn't be satisfied until the rest of the world thought so too.

Even with Scott's largess, an arrangement with any real theater proved price prohibitive. Ludlam reached a compromise by confining his fledgling company to two performances a week, at midnight. The idea for this late hour and limited schedule enabled Ludlam to approach Tambellini's Gate Theater, a run-down movie house on Second Avenue at 10th Street that specialized in avant-garde films. Since the last screening was over well before midnight, Ludlam was allowed to rent the space for a mere $35 for both Friday and Saturday nights.

Though it was then being used to screen movies, the Gate Theater had previously been a Baptist church that was converted into a theater for live performances in 1957. It still featured a cathedral-high proscenium stage, an old light-board, remnants of antique stage machinery, and real theater seats. Jutting out from the rear wall of the stage was a second level or platform, which was used to great effect in Ludlam's stagings. There was even an honest-to-goodness dressing room in the basement, down a long flight of stairs. A separate staircase led from the dressing room to the sound projection booth located in the rear of the balcony. Cast members would often run up there to catch scenes they weren't in.

Midnight performances were an obvious liability in some respects, diminishing opportunities for the mainstream attention Ludlam craved. But they had the unexpected virtue of making a new underground theater company seem that much more underground — and chic. They also targeted the early audience of the Ridiculous for the drug-oriented crowd it was. A number of people who eventually joined the company first became aware of the Ridiculous by showing up for a midnight performance of *Big Hotel* or *When Queens Collide* after popping some speed or dropping acid. They would have no way of knowing that some performances wouldn't begin till 1 AM, or finish before four or five in the morning. But for only $2.50, it was all part of a night's "trip." Stefan Brecht described both plays as "transvestite frolic, horrible fun, street-corner rebellion, all guilty innocence. . . . These plays were endless and had the structure of a firewall collapsing à la Cocteau. They were irresponsible and irresistible."

Big Hotel opened at the Gate Theater on November 24, playing both Friday and Saturday nights for about a month, when it was joined in repertory by *When Queens Collide* on Fridays. A puff piece by Allan Edmands in the January 5, 1968 edition of the *East Village Other* emphasized the mind-altering effects of attending either show. Referring to the Ridiculous as "the neo-Renaissance of Theatre," Edmands wrote, "In his current two intermissionless plays there are enduring stretches of time awareness which are funny in initial impact, hilarious as the prolongation becomes obvious, then perhaps monotonous for awhile, finally hallucinogenic. . . . Barriers around consciousness are relaxed, and the mind is then prepared for the onslaught of forthcoming stimuli," he explained, before quoting Ludlam, "'Our meaning alters with acceleration.'"

While touting "the work of an excellently insane company," Edmands also saw fit to defend Ludlam and friends.

> Once there was only one Ridiculous company, but that was before the wheel-deal power games of an entrepreneur named Chamberlain and a director named Vaccaro forced Ludlam and most of the original company underground. Ludlam didn't read the contract's fine print. Threats of legal injunction prevent[ed] the

Gate's *Conquest* from using that name or from opening before Vaccaro's anathema
Bouwerie Lane production — legally but not morally underwritten by chartered
"Playhouse of the Ridiculous." All this has happened. . . . Worse and worse! The flit-
ting critics of Established Media refuse to come to the Gate after hours:
"Ludlam had his chance at Bouwerie Lane," they screech, yet they ingratiatingly
serve notice to every bit of Neil Simon's Broadway garbage. . . . It is the Gate's
Ridiculous that has all the balls (and even cunt) of spontaneous improvisation.

The level of improvisation was indeed excessive, not to mention eccentric. Even at
rehearsals, Ludlam adopted an anything-goes attitude. Fully aware that he might have
had a rebellion on his hands otherwise, he was determined to be less dictatorial a
director than Vaccaro had been — if only at first. And he brought this nonchalance to
the staging of his first few works.

In accordance with Ludlam's conviction that all the world was a stage, everyone in the
company felt free to invite anyone who claimed to be a performer to come by and do
their "thing" during a performance. As Brockmeyer recalled, "Anybody that showed up
could be in the show. All you had to do was be there that night."

One of the many interlopers was a Puerto Rican, short-lived trick of Ludlam's. He made
what was undoubtedly his New York stage debut by doing lengthy Al Jolson imitations.
With his thick Puerto Rican accent, the results were ludicrous — and just right for the
Ridiculous. But even if his Jolson left a lot to be desired, this would-be crooner was
something of a pro when it came to sexual performance. He was observed one night
"making it backstage" with another member of the company — a mode of behavior that
would prove remarkably common during future productions.

There was also a "nice little Jewish girl" from Brooklyn who played the accordion for a
few weeks in *Big Hotel*. And an elderly woman who used to come by selling bras and
G-strings wound up being in a show after she told Ludlam she had been a hoofer in
vaudeville; she sang Gilbert and Sullivan songs, "quite beautifully," according to
Pashalinski. Even some members of the Hell's Angels ended up onstage because they
were "somebody's trick or other," according to Brockmeyer.

Big Hotel included a natural slot for people to make these guest appearances near the
end of the play, in the so-called "Cobra Cunt Ceremony," which referred to *Cobra
Woman*, the Maria Montez cult classic. The scene was designed in homage to Montez as
a High Priestess — portrayed in *Big Hotel* by Mario Montez, of course — who selected

sacrificial subjects to be thrown down a volcano. *When Queens Collide* also contained a scene which was conducive to guest slots, when the "Fire Women" dance to rescue Mars. Time and again, there was no limit to how many of these subsidiary figures could be accommodated or what inanity they might perpetrate. Candy Darling was among the countless transvestites of the period who showed up for this moment. (After *When Queens Collide*, anyone making a guest appearance in a Ridiculous production would be known as a "Fire Woman": the Ridiculous equivalent of a spear-carrier.)

Thomas Lanigan Schmidt, an artist who specialized in making religious-type icons out of aluminum foil and found objects, never became a member of the company, exactly. But beginning with *When Queens Collide*, he did become a close friend of Ludlam. He had met Scott some months earlier, when they noticed each other and struck up a conversation at the Museum of Modern Art. At Scott's prompting, he finally went to see the play.

"Chris said he was the producer and someone named Charles Ludlam was the director," recalled Schmidt.

> And when I got there they said, "Do you want to be in the play? Don't worry, it's just like making plays in the basement when you're a kid. You just get out there and do it." The next thing I knew, someone slipped this costume on me. It was a half-slip, like a prom dress, with lobster-claw gloves or mitts. And someone else put a bathing cap on my head. I didn't even get the chance to look at myself in the mirror before I went on the stage, but somebody said I looked adorable and that gave me the confidence to go ahead with it. Then I was onstage in some kind of party scene where people were singing church songs. And I remember being swept into the scene the way you would be at an actual party. The actors and the momentum of the scene took care of what was happening.

> I felt that kind of confusion you feel on the first day of school or kindergarten. When I got up onstage there were these different groupings of people and Chris said, "Stay with that group." I remember Mario Montez was wearing an outfit made from clear plastic bags — it was like a wedding gown ensemble. There was this instant sense of communion with people you know you have something in common with that transcends any explanation. You just become a part of something that feels right.

> Backstage, after the play, was very much like being in the play: Everything came

from all these different directions at once. It was my first experience with really good art. Up till then, I had been reading *Art Forum* and thinking more about art-worldish type art. Then seeing that play and becoming a part of it, it was a more primitive kind of art that reminded me of rituals in church when I was a kid. It had the quality of playing as a child and just loving it. It was a matter of feeling at one with a ritual that embodies a belief. It was like suddenly being taken to Lourdes or to the Rome of art, and realizing that this pilgrimage had been transported and was taking place right here in New York. Charles would always say, "The only really great art is in the street."

Another new quasi member of the company was José Rafael Arango. A writer who moved to New York from Colombia in 1963, Arango was tall and gaunt and striking looking. He had a massive nose that almost made it appear as if he were wearing a mask. Ludlam met this new player-to-be when Montez took him to a party at Arango's apartment on Second Avenue in the East Village, "But I first really talked to him when I saw him in *Screen Test*," recalled Arango. "There was a connection right away."

When Arango wanted to become involved with the company, Ludlam put him to work managing the sound for both *Big Hotel* and *When Queens Collide*, which would become a standard way of introducing someone to the family before having them act. The job primarily entailed starting and stopping a tape recorder. "One day I was doing the sound on *Queens* and Charles came to me and said, 'There are no Fire Women — we're short. Please get in drag.' So I did." Arango later assumed the role of Consuela, consort to Venus, portrayed by Pashalinski. According to Arango, when it came time to divide the box office income at the end of any evening, each actor would typically receive two or as much as three dollars.

Though Arango had roles in the next two productions, he remembered feeling that his accent was too thick for him to succeed as an actor. When he said he was considering going back to school to work on his speech, Ludlam replied, "It would be a waste of time: The stage is the best education."

For the actors with the Ridiculous, however, it amounted to an education in learning how to cope with the unexpected. One of the more hilarious incidents occurred at Tamberlaine's banquet during a performance of *Queens*. A piece of fruit accidentally fell off the banquet table into the first row of the audience, and the person whose lap it landed in impulsively threw it back onto the stage. A spontaneous food fight, lasting a couple of minutes, ensued between the cast and audience.

Being high on drugs was not only a part of the festivities for the audience in the auditorium, but very much a part of the onstage activity. Arango remembered Ludlam once exclaiming, "An actor has to prepare" as he was lighting a joint backstage before going on. Though Ludlam and Vehr had a decided preference for marijuana, Mallory favored booze, and still others were into speed and acid. Just about everyone but Montez and Pashalinski was tanked up or stoned on something during a performance. Morfogen remembered one performer in *Big Hotel* named John Foster who was always drunk and "constantly bombed out of his mind. There were even times when he would pass out onstage."

Morfogen was afraid of LSD and never experimented with it, but he remembered that Brockmeyer "always used to tease me that they put acid in my drinks back in the dressing room." More than a tease, Mallory recalled a time when Jeanne Phillips actually did slip some LSD into his beer while he was applying his makeup, and his trip kicked in half an hour into the performance.

Taking drugs in preparation for a performance was part of a much larger ritual. It took everyone quite a while to get made-up — Montez would require over an hour — and gossiping became a favorite pastime during the process. "We'd sit and we'd talk and we'd dish. It was wonderful," said Mallory. "And when you're changing into a woman's clothes, putting on a garter belt and net stockings, you get into the feeling of your character. I remember once Charles told me that if someone was trying to sell *him* on a role, his first question would be, 'Well, what do I wear?' since that would help him understand the character and know if he wanted to play it or not."

Whether or not it was reflected by the antics onstage, the sympatico spirits and shifting allegiances in the dressing room became the glue which brought and kept the motley crew together — in some cases for more than ten years.

"We were a bunch of raggle-taggle queens and dykes who had no acceptance anywhere," said Brockmeyer, "but we found acceptance amongst ourselves. We were never really comfortable with our sexuality. Were we men? Were we women? We were sort of a man-woman phenomenon. Somehow or other that is what sucked me in, because I was a misfit and they were all misfits. We were freaks who found each other. And Charles understood all that, and made it work to his advantage. I mean even the heterosexual Jeanne Phillips had this real deep voice. She was our leading woman, but she sure didn't have a woman's voice. Another thing about the company is that we were all Scorpios working with this Aries."

Ludlam, an Aries, was indeed working with a number of Scorpios, including Brockmeyer, Pashalinski, Black-Eyed Susan, and Phillips. Even Jack Smith and Stefan Brecht were Scorpios. More germane still, the vast majority of the early members of the Ridiculous were all, like Ludlam, lapsed Catholics.

"One of the reasons that we stayed together," continued Brockmeyer, "was that Charles seduced all of us. And I'm not saying that he seduced us in just an intellectual way. I mean he seduced us all sexually. Black-Eyed Susan was Mrs. Charles Ludlam." Referring to the landmark role that would soon catapult Ludlam to the forefront of the Downtown theater scene, Brockmeyer added, "Charles *was* Camille and everyone was in love with him."

Mallory confirmed Brockmeyer's impressions. He described sleeping with Ludlam "on one little occasion. It was like an incidental thing; I was staying at his house on 12th Street. But at one time or another, everyone slept with Charles. You've got to realize this group was mostly a bunch of dead-end kids. We cared primarily about Charles. There was a great deal of sibling rivalry, which I was only partly aware of in myself, my rivalry and my competitive spirit."

For Pashalinski, who also slept with Ludlam once, "Everyone was graced with this incredible sense of humor. That was the most significant thing of all."

Hofstra colleague Charlotte Forbes, who was destined to work with the Ridiculous in the future, recalled the night she slept with Ludlam. "It was in the late sixties," said Forbes.

> We went to Irwin and Anita Pearl's wedding at the Top of the Sixes — it was one of the straightest weddings I had been to. And Charles and I were smashed. Since it was late and I was living up in Washington Heights at the time, I decided to go home with Charles to his place in the East Village. We were fooling around. We debated about whether we should have sex or not. We got undressed and into bed together, and it was very touchy-feely. We were just giggling and having a great time, but it just didn't work.
>
> Finally I said, "You know Charles, I have to go to work tomorrow." And he said, "Well don't worry about it. I've got plenty of clothes here for you to wear." Needless to say, I get up in the morning, I open up his closet looking for something and figure everyone has a basic black dress. But no, with Charles everything was sequins. So I go to the American Can Company — which in those days was as

conservative as IBM — wearing this sequined frock. Everybody just took one look at me and nobody even asked where I had been the night before.

☙

A.D. Coleman's review of the revival of *Big Hotel* in the *Village Voice* (January 18, 1968) was far from favorable. Coleman called the play a "spectacular failure" and proceeded to attack the very approach Ludlam was aiming for.

> The author heaps ingredients onto the stage in the vain hope that some rich and heady brew will concoct itself. A vast and numberless cast of characters flops around uselessly for several hours, striking few sparks and starting no fires. Compounding his errors by serving as his own director, playwright Ludlam permits his cast to stretch every scene well past its breaking point, each collapsing like a deflated balloon. The result is suspension in a state of endless and total boredom.

In keeping with Ludlam's ambition to create a theater that would strike the first blow by appearing ridiculous itself, Coleman's negative review was transcribed verbatim on company stationery and used for promotional purposes. Flaunting such a response, rather than suppressing it, can be seen as another manifestation of Ludlam's lifelong reaction to authority figures. Throughout his school career, disapproval had always been perceived as a challenge, goading him on to greater and greater offenses. In this instance, he literally tried to transform the flagrant disapproval into a palpable advantage.

To offset any disguised or lingering injury over Coleman's pan, Ludlam could more than console himself with a rave review of *Big Hotel* by Dan Isaac in *Show Business*. Isaac called the play, "A triumph of the theater of the ridiculous" and "A wild improbable farce that means nothing and everything. . . . Blondine Blondell and Norma Desmond, played by Mario Montez and Charles Ludlam, provide the best comedy to be seen anywhere in the city," he gushed. "Charles Ludlam is the theater's newest triple threat man, for he also directed the play that bears his authorship."

Even though Ludlam was already perfecting his skills as an expert seducer and manipulator of people — skills that would enable him to hold a company together for two decades against perpetual adversity — he wasn't able to come to terms with the critics until late in his life. He would long harbor an ambivalent attitude towards those who could have an impact on his success. (After Michael Feingold became the lead theater critic for the *Village Voice*, Ludlam often referred to him as "Michael Findfault.")

There was one member of the critical fraternity, however, who first caught Ludlam at a midnight showing of *When Queens Collide* and quickly became an unwavering advocate as well as, eventually, a friend: Eric Bentley, the distinguished playwright, translator, and critic. "Despite the outward appearance of being crude and raunchy, the Ridiculous had a kind of delicacy to it," said Bentley, "as did Charles, when I got to know him later. Instead of being a loud or raucous personality, he was rather quiet, rather subtle and ironic, and very benign. You know, he was closer to a saint than to a devil."

&

Already at work on a new play and confident that he would have some sort of a theatrical troupe to return to in the fall, Ludlam took time off during the summer of 1968. He visited Christopher Scott and Henry Geldzahler at the house they rented in Provincetown, where they all gallivanted with John Waters. (Waters would make his debut as a high-camp filmmaker in only two years, with *Mondo Trasho*.) But Ludlam allocated far more time that summer for a visit with Deborah Rosen in San Francisco.

Given his fear of flying, he made the cross-country trek by train, and enjoyed several hard-boiled detective novels along the way. As soon as Ludlam arrived, Rosen put him to work making beaded flowers with herself and her friend, Stuart Sherman, who went on to become a performance artist as well as Ludlam's confidant.

Rosen and Sherman had recently met in a community theater production of *The Importance of Being Earnest* in San Francisco. According to Sherman, the domineering Rosen was so dissatisfied with the way the director had handled things, she practically took over the production. Rosen also hoped to start her own theater on the West Coast, and intended to stage a play by Jackie Curtis, who was on the verge of becoming a Warhol superstar. But apparently nothing came of this.

As he planned on extending his Western trip with an excursion to Mexico, Ludlam invited Rosen and Sherman to accompany him, but both declined. If Susan Carlson's memory is correct, it was during the bus ride south of the border that Ludlam really discovered Proust and had a related epiphany in the desert.

Ludlam apparently injured his ankle, either during the bus trip to Mexico or shortly after he arrived. In a letter addressed to Geldzahler and Scott at 853 Seventh Avenue, from Hotel Marin, Ciudad de Mexico DF, Ludlam wrote:

Dear Henry and Chris,

The doctor says my muscle is torn and I must see him again on Monday. I now have a plaster splint on my ankle and I can hardly walk. I may need a plaster cast. Mexico is lovely but not for a cripple. Thanks for the money. The doctors haven't mentioned money yet but I think I will need more to pay them. I wish I were home. I want to start work on the play. I will wire you Monday about any further developments. But it will go to your apartment in New York since I only have your telephone number in E. Hampton.

Chris, I think you will play Charon the oarsman on the river Styx. I have a beautiful song for you too — lifted from the *Inferno* of Dante.

Lovers are plentiful here. Due to some cultural differences I am considered quite handsome here and the queens flip over me. (Only that one was an evil hustler) the others are all terribly Romantic. Although I must admit the hustler had quite a line (He wasn't Mexican he was from Guatemala) Of course everyone here is my type. My confidence is soaring.

Since I have to stay over the weekend (God I hope no longer) I think I'll go and see another bullfight tomorrow. They are fantastic. Sado-masochism elevated to an art form.

There seems to be a revolution brewing here. The soldiers killed a number of students and professors during the demonstration. It[']s quite frightening. Americans caught demonstrating were deported. I'm glad I wasn't ["involved" is inserted above] caught. I went to the Burlesque before the demonstration reached its climax. There are soldiers and tanks everywhere. The students are agitating to get rid of the President whom they refer to as "the son of Johnson[,]" "hijo de Johnson." Very serious business. I love you both very much and hope to see you soon. If the doctor permits me I will leave Monday. In any case I'll send a telegram. Try to be in New York to recieve [sic] it if possible.

Your grateful pal

Charles

As the letter implies, Ludlam was by now accustomed to relying on Scott for financial support. While most of Scott's expenses were already taken care of by Geldzahler, he received a $75 weekly allowance for managing his lover's accounts, and he shared his bounty with Ludlam. Except for recurring periods when he was on the outs with Scott, these regular handouts supplemented what income Ludlam managed to eke out in the late sixties by hustling, among other things. As Stuart Sherman would recall in a brief memoir written after Ludlam's death, both he and Ludlam placed ads as "escorts" in the fall of 1968.

Though few people were ever aware of this facet of his life, Ludlam would later tell the inner sanctum that his experiences as a prostitute helped him create his landmark role of Camille. Initially, Ludlam approached hustling as a lark and an adventure. But he also complained that he usually couldn't achieve orgasm during intercourse with the men who hired him. And no matter how dire his circumstances, Ludlam could not tolerate sex when it was a form of work — in any sense of the word.

WITH THE FORCE FROM MY EMERALD EYE

Acid, booze, and ass
Needles, guns, and grass
Lots of laughs, lots of laughs
— Joni Mitchell, from "Blue"

"Our goal in those days was that the audience would become part of the theater, that the theater would expand to encompass the world," Ludlam told Calvin Tomkins for his profile in the *New Yorker*, while reflecting on the first few plays of the Ridiculous. "I didn't really care what happened in those plays so long as I could put over my own scenes. Also, I was very influenced then by the ideas of John Cage. I wanted to find ways of getting beyond my own personal taste and avoiding aesthetic decisions. I wanted to get rid of that no, and to say yes to everything."

It's revealing that during the earliest days of the Ridiculous, Ludlam was primarily interested in being able to "put over my own scenes." His major concern, in other words, was with his own acting. But he wanted it to be on his own terms: in roles that he coveted — not to mention, created — and without some dictatorial director interfering with his technique.

Though his mentors at Hofstra had felt he was too eccentric ever to succeed as an actor and encouraged him to explore playwriting and directing instead, acting was still his first choice in the late sixties. In a similar vein, Ludlam would come to appreciate over the years that writing roles specifically for others was a way of keeping them in the company despite impoverished circumstances. Earning a living wage from acting is one thing (even if no one in the Ridiculous would for some years), but having a character designed with you in mind was an even sweeter reward and tribute. And as everyone from Molière to Terrence McNally would explain, it can be much easier to work on a play with a particular actor's voice in mind.

Despite Ludlam telling Tomkins that acting had been what he most cared about and that he wanted "to get rid of that no, and to say yes to everything," there was one "yes" he said in 1968, which is still surprising in retrospect. Apparently without any hesitation or misgivings, he agreed to put on *Whores of Babylon*, a new play by Bill Vehr, as the company's third offering. This was the only play written entirely by someone other than Ludlam that the Ridiculous Theatrical Company would ever stage prior to Ludlam's death. There is no doubt that Ludlam admired the play, since he went on to stage it three times; but the timing may have had something to do with his decision.

When the eight core members left Vaccaro to form a company of their own in the summer of 1967, no rules or guidelines of any sort had been stipulated. Though Ludlam immediately became the ringleader, this emerged as an unspoken development. Despite Ludlam's claim later in life that he had been voted in as director, nobody really questioned his appointment at the time, nor did anybody really affirm it, for that matter. It was just accepted as a given. In the same casual and comradely spirit, it was only natural for Vehr to write a play if he wanted to; and it would have been awkward for Ludlam to protest its presentation.

On the other hand, it's hard to imagine that Ludlam would have been so cooperative had the upstart been anyone other than Vehr. Though Ludlam was extremely competitive by nature, Vehr had a way of circumventing the attendant tension whenever rivalry was prone to surface. There was something about Vehr that eliminated the threat. Both Vehr and Ludlam had an abiding respect for all people. But Ludlam could also be harshly critical and easily enraged by others, in ways that Vehr could not. Though they were both invested in helping everyone bring out the best in themselves, Ludlam's need to prevail, or to capture the limelight, often superceded this aspect of his personality. Ludlam thrived on Vehr's emotional and intellectual support, while Vehr was ultimately willing to confine his own creativity to the company's backseat.

While looking back on the early years of the company, many recall Vehr as an ameliorating influence and the keeper of the peace within this highly-charged mixture of theatrical and competitive personalities. He was a great diplomat: private and discreet. But he could also be brutally honest. With time, people learned to turn to him to hash out any problems they might be having with Ludlam. By the same token, whenever someone begged to differ with a direction Ludlam was giving, Vehr usually rushed to Ludlam's defense. Vehr became the one person who could publicly question Ludlam and be taken seriously by him. Vehr neither deferred nor flattered so much as he nourished and boosted. Along with his intellect, this was part of what earned Ludlam's trust and respect, and part of why Ludlam would be so amenable to staging one of his plays.

In spite of their mutual admiration, Vehr had to be aware of the rivalry his play might induce in Ludlam, since he even mocks the matter in *Whores of Babylon*, in the first scene between Mano and the Emerald Empress (played respectively by Vehr and Ludlam). In the script, the scene is introduced with the stage direction: "THE EMERALD

EMPRESS *is discovered reclining. A gigantic hand forces its way into her chamber. The hand is* MANO'S."

> EMPRESS: Didn't you ever learn to knock?
> MANO: I have no need for knocking! I enter when I please!
> EMPRESS: State your business and leave! I'm busy!
> MANO: I have a proposition for you, Empress! You and I could work together....
>   Take over this [space]ship and escape to another galaxy! Together we
>   could rule the Universe!
> EMPRESS: You're a fool, Mano! It would never work...We're too much alike!
>   We'd always be at each other's throats!
> MANO: So...maybe I'll *convince* you!
> EMPRESS: I'll do the convincing — with the force from my Emerald eye!

On the stage — as in life — Vehr could appear to be a Slave to Ludlam, the Master. Though he proposed, as Mano, that "together we could rule the Universe," he ultimately gave in to Ludlam, the "Empress" with the final word on all matters. And Ludlam's Svengaliesque sway over everyone, including Vehr, was by now so transparent that it becomes a throwaway joke of Vehr's, ironically to be uttered by Ludlam: "I'll do the convincing — with the force from my Emerald Eye!" The most revealing line in this passage, once again given to Ludlam, is: "We're too much alike." It's further evidence that Vehr realized Ludlam viewed him as a peer. When it came to writing a play, treating Vehr as an equal was a privilege Ludlam would never again extend, to Vehr or to anyone else.

With "a war of space weapons" ensuing between Mano and the Emerald Empress, it's easy to see the influence of *Conquest of the Universe* on *Whores of Babylon*. (The hint of an s&m relationship between Ludlam and Vehr was also suggested by Ludlam in *Conquest,* in which Vehr played Bajazeth, the dethroned King of Mars who is willingly led around on a leash by Tamberlaine.)

Yet another exchange between Mano and the Empress can be read as an explanation of the drag element in the Ridiculous, ending with a quote from Eleanora Duse:

> EMPRESS: It is a woman who is speaking to you, Mano. Do you understand?
> [LONG PAUSE]
> MANO: How well I understand that struggle in you between the warrior-artist and
>   the woman.

93

EMPRESS: The woman, the woman! Don't you know that there are a thousand
women in me, and that I am tormented by each one in turn?

But even if the banter between Mano and the Empress divulges a good deal about the
personal relationship between Ludlam and Vehr, these characters seem to have little to
do with the rest of the play. *Whores of Babylon* is another stubbornly incoherent work
that is hard to apprehend from the script alone. While the play uses a circus motif, with
a Ringmaster as narrator (portrayed by Lola Pashalinski), the main characters are taken
from the Bible, mythology, and comic books. Samson is represented, as is a chorus of
three Delilahs. (Vehr's working title for the play had been *Circus Delilahs*.) Adam and
Eve make an appearance, as do Frankenstein and Superboy. The drug-popping audience
members would have been especially gratified when Superboy was seen sleeping in front
of Mano and the Empress, and Mano exclaimed: "Some dreams are too intense. They
awake the sleeper. We must take care. For we are the dream of one who sleeps so pro-
foundly that he is not even aware that he is dreaming us."

Prior to Ludlam's summer trip to the West Coast, *Whores of Babylon* replaced *Big Hotel*
in the spring of 1968 and ran on weekends in repertory with *When Queens Collide* at the
Gate Theater. For a brief period, the company renamed itself "The Trockadero-Gloxinia
Magic Midnight Mind Theater of Thrills and Spills," and it was under this name that
Whores and *Queens* were presented. "Trockadero" was a reference from Proust, and
"Gloxinia," a type of flower, referred to Ludlam's abiding love of plants. (With Ludlam's
blessing, "Trockadero Gloxinia" would be borrowed by Larry Rée — a dancer who per-
formed frequently in early Ridiculous productions — when he subsequently formed his
own drag dance troupe called the Trockadero Ballet.)

On the subject of names, Ludlam appeared in the cast list of *Whores of Babylon* as
Constance Bedlam. This pseudonym had already appeared on the program for the
Ludlam-directed *Big Hotel*, as had Clairene Bedlam and Charlotte Bedlam. Such names
were shuffled in the various programs since Ludlam usually doubled up in different
roles. But they were also intended to distinguish him from the author of the play. The
pun itself alluded indirectly to his father, Joseph, who had years before been nicknamed
"Mr. Bedlam" by his neighbors, referring to the unkempt environment and general disarray typical of the Ludlam household.

Other members of the company were also playing the name-game for one reason or
another; the most practical being that an alternate moniker was useful in terms of
underreporting income, such as it was, to the IRS. When Jack Smith created a flyer for

Big Hotel, Ludlam, Scott, and Smith came up with the name of Inez "Bunny" Eisenhower for Regina Hirsch, without her approval. Even more to her dismay, they included her real name on the flyer as well. But by the time of *Whores of Babylon*, she had assumed the more permanent alias of Lola Pashalinski. Also by then, Susan Carlson, who played Eve, was calling herself Black-Eyed Susan. Ludlam had invented the name for her, obviously referring to the flower as well as to her stunning, dark brown eyes. (He may have also been thinking of an 1829 play by Douglas Jerrold called *Black-Ey'd Susan*, which was included in an anthology of nineteenth century plays that Ludlam had studied.) Somewhere along the line, Ultra Violet started calling Gary Tucker "Eleven," and that became his stage name. In *Whores of Babylon*, James Morfogen played Second Delilah under the name Mae Moon. Though the alias was actually lifted from a dress shop in New Jersey, this rather hefty male was also impersonating Mae West in the play.

The handbill for *Whores of Babylon* includes a subtitle that doesn't appear elsewhere: "Nights in a Cuban Garden." This may have referred to Vehr's sexual preference for young Latinos, not to mention males of any ethnic background who were noticeably deformed in one way or another. (Whenever the company toured in the future, the attractive Vehr became the unofficial procurer of "sweet young things" for other male members of the company.)

In their world of rampant promiscuity, there was one night following a performance of *Whores of Babylon* when Ludlam, Scott, and Vehr were at Mario Montez's loft commiserating about how difficult it was to connect sex with love and have an honest-to-goodness, long-term "boyfriend." Vehr said, "Wouldn't it make life easier if the four of us could just have sex together?" And spontaneously, they did. But predictably, there weren't any real fireworks.

☙

Though *Whores of Babylon* proved to be the only play written by someone else that Ludlam would ever stage under the auspices of his own company, it paved the way for an anomaly of a different sort. The company's next and fourth offering, *Turds in Hell*, was cowritten by Ludlam and Vehr. It turned out to be the only play that Ludlam ever collaborated on with another writer. In a sense, most of Ludlam's plays were collaborations, however, since they frequently relied on input from the cast members, many of whom interpolated lines or stage business of their own during both rehearsals and performances.

The difficulty in differentiating between Ludlam and Vehr's contributions to *Turds in Hell* is powerful testimony to how similar their ideas were at this point. Though partially based on *Satyricon* (Fellini's film version of the classic text was on the verge of being released with a lot of advance hoopla), the play was structured very much like the preceding Ridiculous works. In other words, it wasn't really very structured at all. Its real inspiration, which Ludlam would later take credit for, came from meeting Arthur Kraft, who was introduced to the Ridiculous by Minette.

Minette and Kraft had first encountered each other in 1957, in a flea-bitten antiques shop in the Village called Ye Olde Thrifty Shoppe. A decade later, Minette knew that he had to bring Kraft and Ludlam together. He kept telling Kraft about the Ridiculous shows at midnight until they finally went to see *When Queens Collide* and visited Ludlam backstage. Ludlam invited Kraft to be a "Fire Woman" on the spot.

No stranger to show business, Kraft, who was born in 1918, started performing in vaudeville when he was six: first as a child singer, then as a comedian. "I played Loew's Lincoln Square with Jack Benny on the same bill," he said in a voice part Mel Brooks, part Spanky from "Our Gang," and all nasal Brooklyn growl. "Truth is stranger than fiction. Fiction is stranger than truth. And I'm stranger than both," he added, to ensure that he wouldn't be mistaken for a "normal" person.

Not that anyone would have ever made such a mistake. Of all the crazy characters who gravitated to the Ridiculous, Kraft seemed to be the looniest. There were reasons everyone referred to him as "Crazy Arthur." Even into his seventies, Kraft exhibited a childish nature: petulant on the one hand, shy on the other, but nonetheless oversexed and rather aggressive in his lascivious come-ons.

Since Kraft was at once a part of theater history as well as a ready-made Ridiculous personality just waiting to be exploited on a stage, Ludlam adored him. In *Turds in Hell*, the part of Orgone, "the Hunchback, Pinhead, Sex Maniac," was written for Kraft. His childlike manner is embedded in the character: an abandoned orphan who leaves his baby carriage to be raised by a gypsy until he embarks on a quest for his real mother. (Kraft's real mother had died when he was only five.) But Orgone emerged from his perambulator — actually, a metal-wire supermarket cart — with a thick, two-foot long, erect penis strapped to his groin. Kraft was also costumed with a cone-shaped pinhead cap that sometimes lit up on cue, as well as the fur-covered legs of a satyr and flippered feet, none of which disguised his bare flabby chest and protruding stomach. (This cone-domed Pinhead preceded the Coneheads of "Saturday Night Live" by seven years.)

The play's title was a phonetic reworking of Turzahnelle, a name belonging to one of Vehr's aunts. In the play, Turzahnelle is Orgone's mother, who abandons him on a mountaintop in the opening scene. A brief prologue is delivered to the audience by the Devil: "The play you are about to see is a mortal sin. Any person witnessing this play takes part in that sin and thereby risks his immortal soul."

With various scenes set in a convent, a monastery, a brothel, and a yacht on the River Styx, *Turds in Hell* became another frontal attack on the Church and all that it stood for. While Tucker played the Devil and Vehr the Angel, Ludlam portrayed Saint Obnoxious, "the great prophet of Nazareth in Galilee," who first appears in the play overturning the tables in the dishonored Temple. The scene ends with Saint Obnoxious extending an invitation to his disciples: "Let us go into the sanctuary and take the Last Supper. I'll pick up the tab." Not only is Hail Mary recited in Pig Latin, but Saint Obnoxious also tempts the Devil to have carnal relations with him. Another canonized figure, appropriately named Saint Frigid, has the dubious task of protecting wayward nuns from each other. When Orgone, disguised as Santa Claus, sneaks into a convent to seduce some nuns, he confronts a roller-skating novice and asks her, "Are you a nun or are you straight?"

As suggested by the play's title, the scatalogical references in Ridiculous productions reach a new height throughout this script, and the by-now obligatory orgies as well as simulated sex scenes are strewn throughout the play. For example, the Devil advises, "Suck a dick a day or die," and there's an extended recitation of "a recipe for cookin' human balls." Later on in the play — courtesy of Minette, who came up with the rhyme — a chorus of whores sing, "Spermatozoa / I love you so-a / I want to know-a / When you will come. You are so tasty / I want to taste ye / I will not waste ye / Please give me some. Yum yum yum yum."

Though ad-libbing was part of the protocol for the Ridiculous, Kraft became the most notorious of all actors for inventing lines during a performance and then repeating them on subsequent evenings. "In *Turds*, when some other character asked me what I was, I said, 'I'm a try-sexual: I'll try anything.' Then I'd sing, 'I'm trisexual, in metaphysical drag for Jesus,'" recalled Kraft. Some other remarks he added to the script included "Cookies for Jesus" and "Mother's got a box in heaven for you." This last line became an identifying refrain for Kraft and earned him his second nickname within the company, "Mother." He was, in fact, known affectionately by the early members of the Ridiculous as "the mother of us all."

"In *Turds*, Mario played my gypsy mother who found me, and in a scene she said,

'Beyond the forest is the whole world,' and I added, 'Yeah — Forty-Second Street' [relayed with a Jimmy Durante spin]. I decided to imagine that I was in Bryant Park and that was the forest. That made it more real for me," said Kraft.

The need to make the scene "more real" was pretty pronounced for Kraft. Half an hour after the curtain was supposed to go up for the opening night performance on November 8 at the Gate, there was no sign of Kraft in his dressing room. Ludlam began to put on Kraft's outlandish costume while Minette and Stefan Brecht rushed down to Kraft's apartment on Monroe Street, on the Lower East Side.

According to Kraft, he was working as a messenger for RCA at the time and, accustomed to napping in the evenings, he simply overslept. But legend has it that Minette and Brecht discovered a naked Kraft, tripping on acid. They threw a coat on him and whisked him back to the theater in Brecht's Volkswagon. A fuming Ludlam relinquished the costume, which was quickly transferred to Kraft, who was wheeled out onstage in his perambulator. When the show finally went on at one AM, an hour later than scheduled, Kraft peered over the edge of the shopping-cart that contained him and audibly groaned, "What a fucking lousy trip this is going to be."

Penny Arcade, a protégé of Jack Smith and a future Downtown performance artist, recalled being at the opening night of *Turds*. Moments before it finally began, Jack Smith ran down the aisle with her in his arms and then pretended to copulate with her onstage. "I was horrified," claimed Arcade, "and frightened that Charles would think we were trying to upstage him." But Ludlam was far too upset with Kraft's irresponsibility to let Smith's relatively benign tomfoolery upset him as well.

Printed on regular sheets of paper, the program for *Turds in Hell* was the most extensive yet. Its lengthy bios reveal more than just a characteristic sense of humor. For example, the Inez "Bunny" Eisenhower who appeared in *Turds in Hell* as "Turtle Woman" was not Lola Pashalinski, but a man by the name of Ed Dame. He was a drifter who first performed with the company as a "Fire Woman" in *When Queens Collide*. (According to his program bio, Dame "worked in an amateur theater group after the Air Force" with roles in *Father of the Bride*, *Mr. Roberts*, and *Suddenly Last Summer*. "Left group to complete a novel, do day labor in Chicago, hotel work in Los Angeles, pick lemons in Santa Barbara, then on return to New York started at his seventh college." Eventually Ed Dame would become a transsexual, surgically transforming himself into a woman, only to live with another woman as a lesbian.)

RIGHT: One of the earliest photos of Charles, taken in 1945 or 1946 — when he was still the obedient child. Photograph courtesy Marjorie and Donald Ludlam.

BOTTOM LEFT AND BOTTOM CENTER: No, they are not the original Bonnie and Clyde, but Marjorie and Joseph Ludlam, ca. 1928. (Poised as a hood ornament, Marjorie looks remarkably like Charles in drag.) Photograph courtesy Marjorie and Donald Ludlam.

BOTTOM RIGHT: Marjorie and Joseph Ludlam in the beginning, when it seemed like nothing but smooth sailing ahead. Photograph courtesy Marjorie and Donald Ludlam.

Top: With his mother's two maiden sisters showering their love on him, Charles was virtually reared by three mothers. Aunt May (top left) and Aunt Florence (top right). Photographs on this page courtesy Marjorie and Donald Ludlam.

Left: Charles on his graduation day, playacting with his younger brother, Donald, who was his very first audience in all matters theatrical.

Opposite top: The modest house at 20 Lawrence Street, in Greenlawn, Long Island, which Joseph Ludlam built with union buddies, and in which Charles grew up. Photograph courtesy Marjorie and Donald Ludlam.

Opposite bottom: Charles is hugging a stuffed bear as Christopher Scott, his best friend, poses for the photographer. This snapshot was taken in the summer of 1961, when they hitchhiked to Northeast Harbor, Maine, to visit Earl Jacobs, who was teaching at an art school there. Photograph courtesy Christopher Scott.

TOP RIGHT: A publicity photo of Jack Smith looking his most virile (ca. 1970). His aptly named *Flaming Creatures* — an underground film that was banned in the 1960s — could have been describing himself. Photograph © The Plaster Foundation, Inc.

CENTER RIGHT: With cigarette in hand, John Vaccaro — the intense maestro of the Ridiculous — peers at Charles. Photo taken by Christopher Scott, probably in the spring of 1966. Photograph © Christopher Scott.

BOTTOM LEFT: In another snapshot, Christopher Scott captured a plaintive Mario Montez in the foreground, with a blurred Charles Ludlam in the back (ca. 1966). Photograph © Christopher Scott.

BOTTOM RIGHT: Minette, mascot and muse to the Ridiculous, published a photocopied version of his memoirs in 1979. Though "the words are Minette's," *Recollections of a Part-Time Lady* was "edited and condensed" by Steven Watson. Its many photographs were "re-worked" by Ray Dobbins.

Minette

Recollections of a part-time La

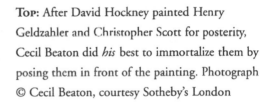

Top: After David Hockney painted Henry Geldzahler and Christopher Scott for posterity, Cecil Beaton did *his* best to immortalize them by posing them in front of the painting. Photograph © Cecil Beaton, courtesy Sotheby's London

Far left: Bill Vehr's photo-card of Mario Montez presents him in an archetypal pose. This was sent out to raise money for Vehr's independent film, *Mario Montez for Marilyn Monroe* (or vice versa). (Mid-1960s.)

Center left: Jack Smith: self-portrait, collage (ca. 1980). "His loft at 36 Greene Street in Soho was named the Plaster Foundation. It served as a performance space where he offered free midnight showings of elaborate concoctions with outrageous titles such as *Withdrawal From Orchid Lagoon. . . .*" Photograph © The Plaster Foundation, Inc.

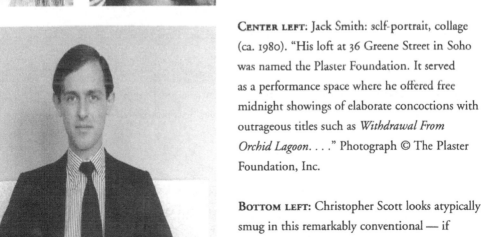

Bottom left: Christopher Scott looks atypically smug in this remarkably conventional — if elegant — portrait by the bad-boy photographer Robert Mapplethorpe. Christopher, 1976 © copyright the estate of Robert Mapplethorpe. Used with permission.

Top LEFT: Jack Smith designed this flyer for Ludlam's *Big Hotel* and *When Queens Collide*, incorporating a still from the 1954 film *Elephant Walk*, starring Elizabeth Taylor.

Top RIGHT: As designed by Christopher Scott, this mock-up, or study, for an ad for the first two productions of Ludlam's Ridiculous Theatrical Company featured Lola Pashalinski, Mario Montez, and Charles Ludlam.

OPPOSITE TOP: Christopher Scott took this head shot of Black-Eyed Susan as Birdshitskaya in *Big Hotel*. "She aspired to be a great tragedienne and, given her natural beauty, Susan possessed great dramatic appeal. She would become the only cofounder of the Ridiculous who remained with the company until Ludlam's death — and beyond, for that matter." Photograph © Christopher Scott.

OPPOSITE BOTTOM: Lola Pashalinski (as Venus, LEFT) and Ted Castle (wrapped in garden hose, as Ortygius, RIGHT) in a loft performance of *When Queens Collide*. Castle's apartment, where the performance took place, was referred to as "the 13th Street Loft." Photographs © Leandro Katz.

LEFT: With a subtitle that says it all, this issue of *Queen's Quarterly* featured an article on Mario Montez, encompassing a two-page spread of a dozen photos demonstrating his transformation into drag. The summer of 1969 — or date of the issue — also marked Woodstock as well as the first moonwalk and the Stonewall riots, which launched Gay Liberation.

BOTTOM: The hefty James Morfogen backstage, getting into makeup — and into character — as "Baron Bubbles in the Bathtub" for *Turds in Hell*. Photograph © Norman Glavas.

LEFT: This flyer for *Turds in Hell* features co-author Bill Vehr (as the Angel) and Ludlam (as Saint Obnoxious). Notice the stigmata on Ludlam's hand.

TOP: "Crazy" Arthur Kraft as Orgone, "the Hunchback, Pinhead Sex Maniac," in *Turds in Hell*. "Since Kraft was at once a part of theater history as well as a ready-made Ridiculous personality just waiting to be exploited on a stage, Ludlam adored him." Photograph © Leandro Katz.

THIS PAGE: Two production shots of the famous sex scene from *Bluebeard*, which was performed in the nude. After lunging at the buxom Miss Cubbidge (Lola Pashalinski), Bluebeard (Ludlam) has his way with her. Photographs © Leandro Katz.

OPPOSITE: A melancholy portrait of Ludlam, taken by Christopher Scott during the period of *Bluebeard*. "Charles was quite in control of how he manipulated people. But I don't think he was in control of that desperate quality of needing to be at the center of things." (Wally Gorell.) Photograph © Christopher Scott.

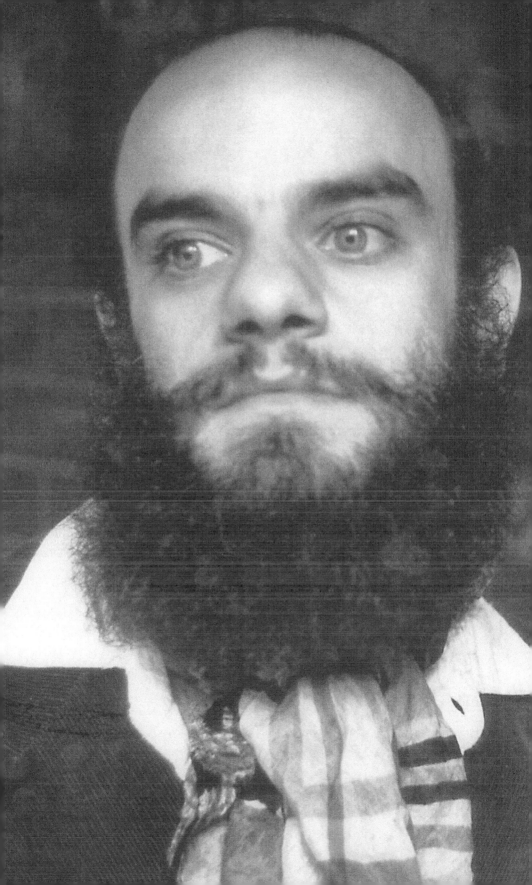

TOP: Edgardo Franceschi's costume designs for the second edition of *The Grand Tarot* (1971) evoked the Follies of a previous era. Drawings © Edgardo Franceschi.

ABOVE LEFT: John Brockmeyer leads the parade during a rehearsal for *Eunuchs of the Forbidden City*. He is followed by Lola Pashalinski, Ludlam, Lohr Wilson, and Black-Eyed Susan. That's Stefan Brecht in the rear, under the umbrella. Photograph © Tom Harding.

ABOVE RIGHT: A scene from *Eunuchs of the Forbidden City*: Ludlam as An Te Hai, the Chief Eunuch, is "servicing" Black-Eyed Susan as Tsu Hsi, the last empress of China. Photograph © Leandro Katz.

LEFT: This handbill for *Eunuchs of the Forbidden City* was designed by Edgardo Franceschi, with appropriately ornate lines.

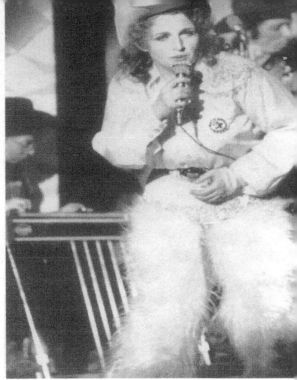

TOP LEFT: That's Charles Ludlam — not E.T. — behind those Foster Grants, as captured by Edgardo Franceschi in front of the Museum of the City of New York (ca. 1972). Photograph © Edgardo Franceschi.

ABOVE: Lola Pashalinski as Lola Lola, the country-western star of *Corn*. "Along with Virgil Young and his musical combo, Pashalinski performed a midnight spin-off of *Corn*, and James Morfogen joined them for the hootenanny." Photograph © Tom Harding.

MIDDLE LEFT: Former theater student, early follower of macrobiotic guru Michio Kushi, and six-month lover of Ludlam, Wally Gorell. This photo was taken during a vacation in Mexico, in the summer of 1973. Photograph courtesy Wally Gorell.

BOTTOM LEFT: John Brockmeyer as Maw McCoy in *Corn*: "Ow, my sacroiliac! I'm havin' an attack. God is punishin' me with ungrateful children and a bad back." Photograph © Les Carr.

Top left: Richard Currie as Duval Sr. imploring Marguerite Gautier — aka Camille — (Ludlam) to relinquish her hold over his son, Armand Duval. "Come, come, let's not exaggerate. You're not going to die. What you feel is the melancholy of happiness, knowing that even love can't last forever." Photograph © Richard Currie.

Left: This publicity shot for *Camille* features a withering Ludlam as Marguerite, renouncing her love for the dashing Armand (Bill Vehr). Photograph © John Stern.

Top right: Ludlam and Vehr, again, figure prominently on the program cover for *Camille*. (Note how the Barnum & Bailey–like typeface is instantly contradicted by the play's subtitle: *A Tearjerker*.) Program courtesy Teriananda.

Top: With typically fetching results, Black-Eyed Susan posed for Peter Hujar's camera backstage during the run of *Camille*. Photograph © Peter Hujar, courtesy Matthew Marks Gallery, New York.

Right: Peter Hujar's companion photo of a pensive Lola Pashalinski, also taken backstage during *Camille*. Photograph © Peter Hujar, courtesy Matthew Marks Gallery, New York.

ABOVE: Peter Hujar's often-reproduced photo of a wistful Ludlam, 1975. "By writing, directing and starring in his own plays, he created the context in which he could be loved, respected, adored, and marveled at, in precisely the ways he wanted and needed." Photograph © Peter Hujar, courtesy Matthew Marks Gallery, New York.

Ludlam's bio doesn't even refer to his professional training:

> CHARLES LUDLAM — CONSTANCE BEDLAM — BUTCH BEDLAM (Saint Obnoxious)
> was discovered by José Rodríguez-Soltero who featured him, as The Lesbian, in
> his Puerto Rican epic *The Life, Death and Assumption of Lupe Velez*, starring Mario
> Montez. In his New York stage debut, he created the role of the Peeping Tom in
> *The Life of Lady Godiva*; and then Kamaraj in *Indira Gandhi's Daring Device*; and
> Norma Desmond in *Screen Test*, all confections by Ronald Tavel, and later
> recreated the title role in the author's skit *The Life of Juanita Castro* at Rutgers
> University. After these triumphs he became the protégé of the lecherous John
> Vaccaro. Ludlam was then forced to write plays when Tavel's jealous feud
> with Vaccaro left the Ridiculous Company scriptless. His first play *Big Hotel*
> produced by the Ridiculous is considered by many to be an underground master-
> piece. Mr. Ludlam wrote *Conquest of the Universe*. Later, Vaccaro, in cahoots with
> the slippery Wyn Chamberlain, tried to swindle Ludlam and Co. out of the play.
> Forced further underground by a threat from Elizabeth Taylor's lawyer, they
> changed the title of the play from *Conquest of the Universe* to *When Queens
> Collide*, revived *Big Hotel* and wrought a true repertory out of the petty indignities
> of a past at which they do not look back.
>
> Mr. Ludlam staged Bill Vehr's *Whores of Babylon* and played the Emerald Empress.
> Tonight he plays the role of Saint Obnoxious in the play he co-authored with Bill
> Vehr, *Turds in Hell*. He plays the role of the plumber in Vehr's "Federal Rap
> Celluloid" *Wait for Sugar* [*M.M. for M.M.*], the life story of Marilyn Monroe,
> judged obscene under US Code 1305, Title 19.

Ludlam would later explain that he and Vehr had set out with *Turds in Hell* "to evoke
actual demons and to stage a black mass — and it couldn't be done. The resulting
mess and debris was the work of art. I was always good at creating extremely original
material by failing."

But in his review of the play for the December 5 issue of the *Village Voice*, Martin
Washburn claimed that he "personally found it approached a kind of ideal" and
that he wanted to "see it again." (He had already seen it twice.) "It is very ingeniously
staged," wrote Washburn, "with unrelated scenes — simultaneously presented, focus
shifting from one to the next, somewhat in the manner of a complex baroque
painting."

Turds in Hell played for three weekends at the Gate Theater, until the owners raised their rental fees to prohibitive levels. Brecht told a self-described "disciple" of his, Ted Castle: "Charles needs a theater. We have to find him something."

Brecht had already taken Castle to see *Big Hotel* and *When Queens Collide* at the Gate, as he had many others. And Castle proved an instant convert: "I knew the theater quite well," said Castle, who grew up in Upstate New York but came to the city regularly to attend shows with his mother, who was herself an actress. "But when I saw Charles, I felt that I had never been to the theater before, that this was *really* the theater. In fact, everyone who became involved with the Ridiculous just referred to it as 'The Theater,' and you knew what they were talking about. Right from the beginning, I thought to myself: 'I know the Shakespeare of my time.'"

An art critic, journalist, novelist, and poet, Frederick Ted Castle had met Brecht through an editor at *The New York Times*. Castle was working on his second novel at the time, though it wouldn't be published until 1986. *Gilbert Green: The Real Right Way to Dress for Spring* proclaimed itself on the jacket cover "A Novel of 1968." It was a *roman à clef* that captured the New York underground scene of the period by focusing on a songwriting "poet-superstar" who, typical of the times, becomes a filmmaker.

In the novel, two characters attend the Ridiculous: "They were half an hour late for the midnight performance by Charles Ludlam at the Gate," explains the omniscient narrator.

> It didn't bother them at all. They went right in and sat right down just in time to see Charles Ludlam make his entrance playing Norma Desmond and himself. They laughed and clapped and loved the scene. The incense was almost suffocating. During the fight between the actors they were hit with a banana peel and half an orange which they threw back on the stage. They had seen the play five times before but once again it was completely new and utterly exhausting. By the time it was over, nobody had the energy to clap or bravo very much. As they left, they repeated a few choice lines to each other as they walked along. . . . They felt weak with laughter and drained by fantastic visions of the past and of the future.

When he learned from Brecht that the Ridiculous was in need of a space, Castle phoned Yvonne Rainer, the avant-garde dancer and filmmaker. She, in turn, referred Castle to a man who owned a network of theaters. "I called him up and he was this very rough guy," recalled Castle. "He said, 'Yeah. We can give you a theater. What do you want? What about one of the porno theaters on West 42nd, where they watch "beaver" films? Why don't you come over and we'll show you one?'

"So I called Charles and we went to see it," continued Castle. "It was the Masque Theater. There were all these guys jerking off to rear-projection screenings of porno films. We got in on Friday and Saturday nights, at midnight, when they were finished with their regular showings. We loved the fact that it was called the Masque."

Located on the South side of 42nd Street between Ninth and Tenth Avenues, the Masque was a small house, but it offered dressing rooms and a sloped auditorium with built-in seats. (It was destined to be torn down a decade later as part of a major urban renewal project designed to revitalize the tawdry area with a series of thriving, Off-Broadway houses, known as Theater Row.)

By finding a space, Castle felt as if he had ingratiated himself with Ludlam. He also offered to do "whatever else needed to be done," and began by cleaning the auditorium before performances ("picking up cum-filled newspapers and things") and assuming the duties of ticket-taker. In short order, he became the sound manager on *Turds in Hell* by contributing his 3-M Wollensak tape recorder, which was used primarily for Mario Montez's dance routines. Recalling how drug-ridden those days were, Castle said, "I remember one time I raced down the stairs to the dressing room and I said, 'Charles, you're on!' And he looked at me with this knowing, sheepish expression on his face and said, 'I'm not *on* yet.'"

It was just before he was introduced to Ludlam that Castle met Leandro Katz, with whom he proceeded to have a relationship for the next decade. Originally from Argentina, Katz moved to New York in 1965. He was a poet and writer who became involved with the performing arts through his connections with Castle and Ludlam.

At Castle's instigation, Katz went to see *Turds in Hell* when it opened at the Masque in December of 1968. He took another friend, David Johansen, with him. They were both tripping on acid. David Johansen eventually became a member of the group called the New York Dolls and later came to be known as "Buster Poindexter." "David was just a child then, a street kid," said Katz. "In fact we had met in the street. He was just hanging out, playing the ukulele and saying he was going to be a performer. Back then, you met everyone in the street, literally. There was more of a sense of community. You saw someone who looked like a character and got to know them.

"That time in New York City was like a moment of epiphany," continued Katz.

> Everything that happened was just so grandiose and had an intensity about it. But
> you can't recall that intensity, that sense that you were changing the world, the
> insanity of some of the things you would do. The intensity of *Turds in Hell* was
> not only because we were tripping on LSD. Even without the drugs, the second
> time I saw *Turds in Hell*, everything that happened seemed to have a greater
> meaning. I knew I was witnessing a tremendously revolutionary event that was
> challenging my sense of sanity. It was extraordinary. And it wasn't very easy to
> impress me at that point, because I had seen many things by then: the Living
> Theater . . . the be-ins . . . Judson Church. But with Charles, the tremendous sense
> of chaos and beauty, the breaking-of-the-rules transported you. You were trans-
> ported into a very visual spectacle. It was the overall effect of anarchy and excess.

Part of the lunacy and beauty of *Turds in Hell* had to do with the staging. Soap flakes
were used to invoke falling snow in the opening scene, when Turzahnelle deposits her
baby on the mountaintop. In a subsequent sequence, Montez performed an "under-
water ballet" during a storm-at-sea scene; while he danced behind a sheet of plastic,
stagehands hurled buckets of water at him. Montez was followed by Larry Rée and a
corps of ballerinas, who would slip and slide across the stage on the soapy floor.

"It was totally insane," recalled Katz.

> Sometimes you couldn't really tell what was happening. While half of the dancers
> were running after Mario trying to pull his bikini off, you couldn't see all of what
> was going on because there were extra layers of gauze curtains, and the incense
> and smoke, and lights flashing. . . . It was truly an hallucination, with or without
> any drugs.

The audiences at the Masque consisted of a rapidly accruing cult following as well as
newcomers to the Ridiculous. But there were also porno clients of the theater itself:
men who strayed in expecting to see pornography, or leftover patrons from the
evening's previous showings. The actors once became alarmed when they realized an
audience member was participating by urinating into a whiskey bottle. He came up to
the stage during a scene between Black-Eyed Susan and Vehr, and said, "Drink the fluid
from my body." In character, Vehr said to Susan who was playing Vera, "Don't drink,
Vera. Don't drink." The apparently inebriated stranger proceeded to pour the contents
of the bottle on the stage.

The onstage sexual hijinks of *Turds in Hell* sometimes spilled out into the auditorium as well. Both Minette and Katz recalled Larry Rée stopping the performance with a slide-whistle, going into the audience, and caressing various men. There were even stories of his accompanying some of the more obliging customers down to the men's room for some full-blown hanky-panky.

"There were also many sex scenes backstage," said Katz, "and many love affairs. I had a fling with Charles myself. The company gave a context to my relationship with Ted Castle. But in another way, it also gave our relationship an uneasiness because of all the criss-crossing of sexual energy. My idea of a relationship was more sedentary and less filled with promiscuity." In fact, Castle and Katz were both already married and had children when they first got together.

A flyer for *Turds* in its "7th Smash Week" advertised "10 Gorgeous Drag Queens 10" and "3 Real Women 3." It also promoted "Top Comic Arthur Kraft" and quoted from Stefan Brecht's critique in *The Drama Review*: "Polymorphous sexuality and the contemporary religion of this country: *pervert* heterosexuality." Another flyer quoted the *East Village Other*: "Spontaneous combustion affair . . . beyond camp, beyond boredom, beyond everything."

Initially, *The New York Times* refused to run any advertisement for *Turds* because of its obscene title. For the sake of securing an ad in the paper, the play was retitled *The Garden of Earthly Delights*. By its "20th Smash Week," another ad for *Turds in Hell* in the April 10, 1969 issue of the *Village Voice* announced, "guest star Candice Darling as Saint Frigid." At Ludlam's invitation, Candy Darling replaced José Rafael Arango, who had obtained a new job with an airline and was shipped off to Spain for preliminary training. Though Candy was in the show only briefly, she made quite an impression one night when, in her scene with Ludlam, she pulled off his loincloth, exposing his privates.

Even earlier in the run, Jackie Curtis — another famous drag queen who portrayed both a gypsy dancer and Bijou in *Turds* — was asked to leave the company. As Castle remembered the episode, "Jackie was a fabulous person and a great performer. But Charles needed more control. Like all born leaders, Charles couldn't have ambitious people around him for very long. My function during this episode was to pat Jackie and tell him he was great, which I did."

Jackie Curtis became a playwright and director in his own right. Shortly after he left the cast of *Turds in Hell*, one of his first plays, *Heaven Grand in Amber Orbit*, was staged by

John Vaccaro. And while Ludlam and Candy Darling talked about getting married and throwing a big wedding as a publicity stunt, Jackie Curtis beat them to the fictional altar when he "married" Warhol star Eric Emerson.

Ludlam later claimed that "The main thing about Candy and Jackie Curtis was that they took female impersonation into the street — off the stage and into their lives. They tried to *live* it, twenty-four hours a day." Ludlam, on the other hand, was an advocate of "the Dionysian principle":

> [Y]ou're drawing on your own personality [as an actor]; you are committing an act of self-destruction, because you are obliterating your own identity to create another one. And so we have these periods in which we must revive ourselves. You give a performance and come offstage, and you've got to get into yourself and rest, reconstruct your own true personality, indulge it. Only then can you go back and play the role again.

> But once you start playing the fantasy twenty-four hours a day, you may have obliterated your personality on a more or less permanent basis. A mask can be a protection to preserve what's inside, but in the case of Jackie and Candy . . . they were always . . . giving so much they didn't leave anything for themselves.

Ludlam himself took female impersonation "into the street" at least once, but with a telling difference. It developed as something of a dare, when Stuart Sherman offered to buy himself and Ludlam a pair of front-row center seats to *Conduct Unbecoming* — a British play that had been imported to Broadway — if Ludlam would go in a dress. They often attended Wednesday matinees on Broadway together, only this time Ludlam indeed showed up in drag regalia, with a string of pearls. To compete with suburban dowagers and elderly women who had their Bergdorf and Bonwit Teller shopping bags in hand, he acquired a bag from Tiffany's, which he filled with tissue paper. But this was also during the period when Ludlam wore a long, scraggly beard. Along with his exposed bald head, the image he created was patently ludicrous. "As all eyes focused on Charles going down the aisle," recalled Sherman, "he took my arm and acted totally oblivious, talking to me as if no one were noticing us." Unlike Jackie Curtis, Candy Darling or other female impersonators who lived the roles they were playing, even when Ludlam took drag into the real world, he had to demonstrate that it was an act.

Ludlam believed that "drag embodies the paradox of acting" and "is always super-charged with theatricality." He quickly became determined never to do a play "in which

I did not cast someone in the role of the opposite sex." But contrary to the general, posthumous impression, in terms of his own acting career, "my male roles outnumbered the female ones. My flaw as a female impersonator lay in this: I always played women who wished they were men. I always feel like a lesbian in drag. I am never content."

A Lower East Side artist and political activist by the name of Teriananda was an early fan of the Ridiculous who particularly admired the sexual politics behind the plays. She first met Ludlam and several other cast members backstage, after a performance of *When Queens Collide*. She became particularly close to Bill Vehr, who later lived with her for several months on East 6th Street.

"I had been a teenage beatnik," recalled Teriananda, "and I had nothing but disdain for the whole flower-child, Hippie phenomenon, which I felt had been created by the media and was not getting at the heart of the real changes that needed to be made. And that's what attracted me to the Ridiculous: the fact that they were dealing with the guts of it. They were changing theater not just by playing to the reviewers or to get a big audience. They were doing what they did with integrity."

"Being young, and virile, and full of himself, Ludlam was unstoppable," she continued.

> It was almost impossible to make contact with him, except through his work. He was just like this madman who was the ringmaster of this circus. I mean, Crazy Arthur and Mario Montez were among my favorite people. And I loved Charles for allowing them to be themselves. The fact that he was putting these insane people on the stage was beyond words. It was very groundbreaking, and seemed very genuine in comparison to the superficial sixties thing that was going on at the time.

∽

In the midst of the extended run of *Turds in Hell*, Ludlam conceived of a new version of *Whores of Babylon* incorporating elements of Indonesian shadow puppetry illuminated by rear-projection. Katz designed and supervised the exotic effects by manipulating nine projectors with different colored gels and spotlights. A huge screen masked the stage entirely, and behind the screen were two additional scrims. Microphones were added to project the actors' voices to the front of the stage.

Roughly a dozen performances of this version of *Whores of Babylon* were inserted in repertory fashion that spring at the Masque. At a certain point, Montez rebelled, saying,

"I'm not going to spend all that time getting dressed and made-up only to perform behind a screen and not be seen." He gradually spent more and more time in front, which prompted others to do the same. Ludlam, in drag, performed a tantalizing striptease in silhouette from behind the screen, while Black-Eyed Susan was dancing nude on the other side of the stage. As Susan recalled, "Charles began to feel that the audience couldn't relate to the characters behind the screen, so he encouraged everyone to make some appearances in front."

A nude David Johansen portrayed a lion, with his hair teased into a mane. As the lion, he had a wrestling match with Samson, played by Brockmeyer. There was one night when Brockmeyer had a severe backache and he couldn't easily win the match as he was supposed to. The fight went on and on, much to the titillation of the audience who had longer to gawk at the naked Johansen.

Though Vehr's *Whores of Babylon* was, if anything, more fragmented than Ludlam's first two plays, it was also more stunning to behold in this rarified, short-lived format. Brecht described the shadow-puppet version as "someone else's dream that, imagine! you have been privileged to see: and when a few of the performers from time to time broke through the self-contained surface, stepped out front and did a scene, it was a gathering of small boys out on the street at night after supper, unsupervised, enchantedly playing something...."

ε⌃

There was one glorious Friday afternoon in mid-April when various members of the company attended a performance event on West 14th Street involving conceptual "body" art. It was sponsored by Street Works and organized by the art critic John Perrault, the artist Scott Burton, and the poet Hannah Weiner. Perrault had invited Katz to participate, and he in turn brought Ludlam and the gang along. Clad in his loincloth "Saint Obnoxious" costume, Ludlam played a flute. Vehr, wearing his white chiffon "Angel" regalia, strummed a zither that belonged to Johansen. And Katz, walking in shoes decorated with play-money, played a portable xylophone. Pashalinski wore a pig mask that Katz had made for her. With Minette also in attendance and everyone stoned or tripping, the group passed out flyers advertising both *Turds in Hell* and *Whores of Babylon* at the Masque Theater. They also distributed Ridiculous "dollar bills" that had been designed as a promotional gimmick. Resembling a Medieval band of merry revelers, the troupe was led by Ludlam down Sixth Avenue to 8th Street, where they paraded into different shops to hand out their materials. They were joined en route by passers-by in a Pied-Piper-of-Hamlin fashion and gathered quite an entourage.

By the summer of 1969, which was also the summer of Woodstock and of the Stonewall Riots, the company lost the Masque. Though none of the actors had earned any money from the run of the two plays, there had been just enough box office revenue to pay for the theater rent and various ads. Vehr, who was working during the day as a bank clerk, would rush the weekend box office receipts in on Monday mornings to cover the weekend overdrafts. Such pressure continued for six months, until May, when the paying customers began to dwindle.

For the night of the Summer Solstice in 1969, Katz and Castle organized a special event through the Poetry Project at St. Mark's in the Bowery Church, across from the Gate Theater on Second Avenue. They called the fesitivity "Midsummer Madness." It began with a street procession leading into the church, where they offered poetry readings and selected scenes from Ridiculous plays. The cast members had donned their costumes across the street in a crafts shop named Elephants Are Contagious, which Katz owned.

With church organ accompaniment, Katz read some "absurdist" poetry he had written for the occasion. Ludlam and David Scott performed the scene from *Whores of Babylon* in which the Emerald Empress cuts a lock of Superboy's hair and then smokes it in a pipe, only to complain about not getting high. Minette interpolated a couple of classic songs: "If You're a Viper" and "Am I Blue." (Susan turned to Minette at one point before he went on, and exclaimed, "My God, you're wearing less makeup than I am!") Ludlam and Montez recreated their Svengali-and-Trilby scene from *Big Hotel*. In a purely melodramatic manner, Inez "Bunny" Eisenhower performed a wild *divertissement* of his own invention, ripping off his clothes while imagining he was being raped by an invisible manhandler.

Of course, the craziest bit of all belonged to Crazy Arthur, who, in priestly robes, delivered a homophobic sermon from the pulpit. Minette heckled Kraft from the audience during the homily, as he warned him he might. "That's what put over the act," said Minette. But midway through the program, Minette noticed that the audience was leaving in droves, and he abruptly advised Ludlam to "collect the money now, before they all get away."

Kraft's anti-gay sermon went over well enough for Ludlam to incorporate it into his next play. In the meantime, the company offered a few makeshift performances of *When Queens Collide* in Ted Castle's loft at Broadway and 13th Street, where the rent was free and it didn't really matter how many customers showed up. The audience was seated around the playing area in the middle of the room. For this version of the play, Ludlam added a twenty-minute musical interlude to the final banquet scene, in which Tamberlaine has his wife and her progeny slaughtered. Ludlam wanted all the performers to play musical instruments for this interpolation. Katz plucked a guitar, and Montez jangled a tambourine. Susan, who possibly took Ludlam more seriously than anyone else — including himself — learned how to play the Italian mandolin from a music book.

After abandoning Castle's loft, performances of *When Queens Collide* continued through June in a screening room at the Millennium, again in a theater-in-the-round setting. It was Katz who knew the director of this venue that specialized in experimental films and was located on Great Jones Street in the East Village. *The Grand Tarot*, Ludlam's fourth play and the fifth produced by the Ridiculous Theatrical Company, had its premiere at the Millennium in the fall.

Though anyone who had been following the Ridiculous would have considered *Turds in Hell* the apogee of whipping chaos into some sort of shape and calling it a play, *The Grand Tarot* was designed to be more arbitrary still. It was the most sprawling yet of Ludlam's epic plays; but in another sense, it was also the most schematic. All of the characters were based on the archetypal figures derived from Tarot cards used by fortune-tellers. At the beginning of each performance, the cards themselves were dealt out to determine the sequence of the play's twenty-two scenes. In this way, it was quite literally subject to chance, which was by now governing Ludlam's life in more ways than he would endure for much longer.

In addition to his fascination with the aleatory experiments of composer John Cage, Ludlam was a proponent of the theories of Antonin Artaud. A French theater practitioner and writer whose vision matured in the 1930s, Artaud was an anarchist who sought to break down barriers between theater and life — as well as between one human being and another — through performance. He invested a lot in exploring the possibilities of chance, but is perhaps best known for inventing the Theater of Cruelty. Artaud's legacy posthumously wielded an enormous influence on many avant-garde performance artists of the fifties and sixties, including both Cage and Ludlam.

It is perhaps equally appropriate to see *The Grand Tarot* as a natural outgrowth of the chaos in Ludlam's life — as "a culmination of the diffusiveness that was happening," in Brockmeyer's words. To have every performance depend upon an arbitrary shuffling of the cards was a sherwd attempt to control the uncontrollable, to acknowledge life as a source of random events; to bring into being a threater with chaos as its organizing principle.

In a written preface to the play, Ludlam explained the rationale behind his conception:

> Before each performance, we lay out the twenty-two cards. The order in which they fall determines the order in which the scenes will be played. Taken as a narrative (the play is in the epic tradition), we could say that the story is never the same twice. Asked a question, the play becomes an oracle. The sequence of scenes is everything. Compare two different performances or compare a performance with a reading of Tarot cards given on the same night. But I must remind you that science has little empire over the subject of fortune telling, for it is imagination and intuition that reign over this charming kingdom.
>
> Ask a question of the oracle before we shout the sacred name of God, Yod He Vau He, and watch the future of your fates.

The preface was signed, "CHARLES LUDLAM: Inventor."

Giving chance free rein in a performance, however, led to any number of problems. One of the recurring ones had to do with costume changes. Tarot card figures, wonderfully illustrated over the ages, offered marvelous opportuniries for the most gorgeous and fabulous costumes yet concocted by the Ridiculous (in this case, credited to "Montez Creations"). Yet they could also present obstacles depending on the sequence of the cards or scenes. Black-Eyed Susan, for instance, played both the Moon and the Sun: She wore all silver makeup and glitter for the first, all gold for the second. This led to dead time onstage whenever her cards turned up back-to-back. Brockmeyer remembered instances when "we would just sit onstage and chant 'na-na-na-nam' while people were trying to get into their costumes." Susan recalled one performance when Mallory noticed the stage was vacant and filled in the time by playing a trumpet — virtually in the nude. "I played Richard Strauss," said Mallory, "but when I finished the piece, still no one had come out onstage, so I declared a ten-minute intermission. Charles was furious at me for that. He said, 'Don't you ever, ever do that again.'"

There were preliminary performances of *The Grand Tarot* at Castle's loft before the play opened at the Millennium in September 1969. It played at 9 PM on Saturday nights only, through October 4. Ludlam would later revise the script, adding nine scenes to the scenario and eliminating the drawing of the Tarot cards, so the play would always be performed in the same sequence. It was this codified version of the play that received a modicum of success when it finally opened. But that wasn't until February of 1971. In the interim, Ludlam gave birth to *Bluebeard*, his fifth play, and the one that proved to be exactly the milestone he intended. It was *Bluebeard* that put the Ridiculous on the mainstream map of New York culture.

"The nadir came when we lost all the other outlets and finally performed *Grand Tarot* up in Mario's loft," claimed Mallory. "After we did a half-performance one night with only four or five people in the audience, Mario made us stop."

The first version of *The Grand Tarot* was not only a culmination of the chaos that held sway over the company up to that point, but also something of a last straw for Ludlam. It represented the anxieties that such uncertain circumstances had wrought over an extended period of time. More than two years of labor had stirred up underground sup-port and produced a cult following; but the company wasn't even earning enough yet to sustain the rental of a proper theater space, let alone provide its members with consis-tent subway fare. Anarchy, like freedom, had its price.

It was while the company was performing at the Millennium that Pashalinski lost her job. She had been working for nearly a year as a credit correspondent for the International Institute of Engineering, which was near her apartment on East 49th Street. As she devoted more of her life to the Ridiculous, Pashalinski had become lax at work: increasingly late or absent, and chronically tired from lack of sleep the night before.

After borrowing some money from her parents to pick up the slack, Pashalinski dis-cussed the matter with her therapist, who felt it would be healthier for her to collect welfare. The ease with which she achieved this, via a letter from her shrink, inspired Ludlam to do the same. He had been working briefly at a secondhand clothing store in the East Village, and he had had it by then with his forays as a hustler.

Ludlam started seeing a female therapist who, like Pashalinski's, supplied him with a letter to qualify for welfare. Mallory was also on welfare, and within a couple of years, Brockmeyer would follow suit. Though Vehr still had his job at Amalgamated Bank and Black-Eyed Susan was working for Nonesuch Records, the legend was quickly cir-culating that just about everyone in the company was on relief. But even as some members turned to welfare in order to support their theater habit, the Ridiculous seemed to be losing ground.

According to Brockmeyer, "It was during the first production of *The Grand Tarot* that we realized we weren't going anywhere fast." Ludlam would later confide, "I began to feel I was pouring everything into an abyss. I felt drained, and yet we went on and did *The Grand Tarot*, which was even more complex. . . . It was performed in pieces in many places. It was like an opera, like a Wagnerian *Ring*. The twenty-two cards of the Tarot deck were like twenty-two plays. The idea that it could be a finished play would be folly. . . . That was the period when I began to see everything falling apart. That's when I decided to abandon the epic form and write a well-made play."

A WELL-MADE PLAY

In retracing our history we will see that as much innovation happened inside tradition as in the revolution against it.
— Guy Davenport

On the face of it, everything seemed to be coming to a halt by the end of 1969. With no new play or revival on the boards, everybody was questioning where the company was headed and wondering if it had a future at all. The wild, free-for-all antics of the past year could disguise underlying problems and tensions for only so long.

During this vacant period, Ludlam expressed uncertainties about what he wanted to be doing and doubts about even continuing with the company. According to Lola Pashalinski, there was a misanthropic side to Ludlam, "that wanted to keep the 'stink' of humanity away from him and close himself off from the rest of the world." And it was this side that surfaced after the failure of *The Grand Tarot*. "On some level, it seemed like he just wanted to go off and be a lonely genius," remarked Pashalinski.

The elitist side to Ludlam inevitably provoked some animosity in the lower ranks. Pashalinski, Black-Eyed Susan, and John Brockmeyer all felt somewhat excluded from Ludlam's relationship with Christopher Scott and Henry Geldzahler, and they made catty remarks about it amongst themselves. Brockmeyer used to refer to Scott as "Her Royal Highness" behind his back. In a year or so, Scott would receive an anonymous letter. Whether or not he was right in deducing that the letter was from Stefan Brecht, it demonstrates just how venomous other Ludlamites were feeling towards him at the time.

Chrissie Boy—

You must be the worst mistake Ludlam *ever* made. . . . A boil on the nose of an otherwise accomplished and brilliant company. You are *drowning*, out of your league, pitiable. Go back to your uptown hustling—that's where your lamentable talents lie. Get wise Baby—Ludlam is just trying to keep you off the 42nd St. circuit—At least that's what he told a certain ex-uptown soubrette [Scott assumed this referred to Black-Eyed Susan]. The word is leech honeybun. That's the word around[,] anyway.

My name is

Sonny

With hindsight, Pashalinski believed that they all envied Ludlam's abiding love for Scott. In the same reflective breath, she recalled a time when Susan said, "It's all very well for them to sit up there, *fanning* themselves and discussing art." "Up there" referred to Scott and Geldzahler's opulent quarters at the Wyoming, an apartment building on West 55th Street and Seventh Avenue. They resided there from 1967-1972, and Ludlam periodically stayed overnight on a daybed in the dining room. But it was the kitchen at the Wyoming that kept the core members of the Ridiculous together throughout these vague winter months, when nothing was happening for them theatrically.

More specifically, it was Scott's intense interest in a vegetarian diet — and the way of life it represented — that united them. He mobilized the group by hosting a series of macrobiotic cooking lessons at the Wyoming. With Scott as the galvanizing force, Ludlam, Black-Eyed Susan, Brockmeyer, Jack Mallory, Gary Tucker, and Minette all participated. Pashalinski and Bill Vehr attended these sessions less frequently. Convinced they were all out of their minds, Mario Montez simply refused — though he dropped by once or twice just to visit. "We already felt like we were on a spiritual journey together," said Pashalinski, "and this became part of that. It was a way of staying close, but also a cleansing thing, to cure ourselves and try to get a grip on things."

Their altered diet represented a crucial turning point for the Ridiculous in other respects as well. Having cavorted for several years like avant-garde infants in a cultural playpen had served its creative purpose. Now, in the 1969 winter of his discontent, Ludlam made a very deliberate and disciplined effort to become more mature. Following the fiasco that *The Grand Tarot* proved to be in its first installment, Ludlam finally seized control of himself and the company, as if the moment for doing so had been preordained. (He would shortly refer to himself as a "benign despot.") It's no mere coincidence that his next play, *Bluebeard*, was about a controlling madman, nor that it marked his most carefully composed writing up to that point.

Both Brockmeyer and Mallory felt the Ridiculous did not really become a company until *Bluebeard*. According to Brockmeyer, "Everything had gotten too big, too epic, too sloppy. But then with *Bluebeard*, Charles said, 'We're going to do a well-made play that is going to be a big success,' and it was. And that's when we wound up becoming a company." As Mallory viewed it, "We all knew Charles could write dialogue, but we didn't think he could put together a play — until *Bluebeard*. At that point, he said, 'I'm going to write a play that will work.' And it did."

Without a theater to perform in, Ludlam "took a winter off [to write] a play that was very traditional and formal, much more focused and carefully worked out than our pre-vious ones." By aiming with his fifth opus to write a well-made play, Ludlam was really making a well-calculated play for mainstream attention. But even Ludlam, great manip-ulator that he was, must have been surprised by how well the ploy worked. Not only did he prove to have an innate grasp of how to appeal to a wider audience, but he achieved it with remarkable success as soon as he put his mind to it. By appealing to the crowd, the *cognoscenti*, and the mainstream critics all at once, the Ridiculous Theatrical Company came of age with *Bluebeard*.

Bluebeard is Ludlam's first relatively conventional play. It boasts a beginning, a middle, and an end — not to mention a coherent plot. Ludlam had recently developed an appetite for story line by reading the novels of Anthony Trollope, which Geldzahler introduced him to. And even though Ludlam once identified Chekhov's *The Seagull* as a specific influence on *Bluebeard*, it more obviously incorporated elements of "mad doctor" horror movies.

Bluebeard was based on H.G. Wells's *The Island of Dr. Moreau* as well as *Island of Lost Souls*, the classic 1932 film adaptation of the novel. Depicting a crazed scientist who transforms animals into humans through vivisection — creating half-breed monsters in the process — the film starred Charles Laughton and Bela Lugosi. In Ludlam's brilliant variation, Moreau becomes the eponymous Bluebeard. The island is no longer situated in the South Seas but off the coast of Maine, and we're told that sailors call it "the Island of Lost Love." Though Bluebeard is another mad scientist, unlike Moreau he is not interested in giving animals human characteristics. He is rather hell-bent on devel-oping a "new and gentle genital" by experimenting on human subjects.

While referring to this fantastic notion in his opening monologue for Khanazar von Bluebeard, Ludlam was back in an Elizabethan mode and borrowing heavily from Marlowe's opening monologue for Doctor Faustus. But in the course of mimicking Marlowe's cadences, Ludlam modified the speech to his own ends. In contrast with Marlowe ("Settle thy studies, Faustus, and begin / To sound the depth of that thou wilt profess. . . . Is, to dispute well, logic's chiefest end?"), consider:

> Give up your passions, Bluebeard, and become the thing you claim to be. Is to
> end desire desire's chiefest end? Does sex afford no greater miracles? Have all my
> perversions and monstrosities, my fuckings and suckings, led me to this? This
> little death at the climax followed by slumber? Yet chastity ravishes me. And yet
> the cunt gapes like the jaws of hell, an unfathomable abyss; or the boy-ass used to

buggery spread wide to swallow me up its bung; or the mouth sucking out my life! Aaagh! If only there were some new and gentle genital that would combine with me and, mutually interpenetrated, steer me through this storm in paradise! (*The sound of a foghorn*) They said I was mad at medical school. They said no third genital was possible. Yang and yin, male and female, and that's that. (*Laughs maniacally*) Science suits a mercenary drudge who aims at nothing but external trash. Give me a dark art that stretches as far as does the mind of man; a sound magician is a demigod.

The very idea of a third genital can easily be interpreted not only as Bluebeard's goal, but also as Ludlam's mission in life. He wanted to see himself as neither male nor female so much as both. At least metaphorically, he wanted to discover "some new and gentle genital" that would better manifest his pansexuality, even while guiding him through the "storm in paradise" that was his life. In his own commentary on his aims, Ludlam claimed that "Bluebeard is an intellectual who really doesn't like either of the existing sexes, so he's trying to make a new one. To me, the third genital means the synthesis of the sexes."

Ridiculousness prevails in the play, however, and Bluebeard's quest for a "third genital" is clearly presented in preposterous terms. A couple of other principal characters are Bluebeard's servant Sheemish and his housekeeper Mrs. Maggot. Both are failed experiments of their cruel master. Whenever Bluebeard wants to exercise the upper hand, he need only mention "the House of Pain," referring to his laboratory. This prompts his underlings to wince and clutch their groins in memory of the anguish Bluebeard inflicted upon them there. With a towering humpback and a lumbering gait, Brockmeyer portrayed Sheemish à la Boris Karloff. Tucker played Mrs. Maggot, an old deformed crone, in drag.

The plot commences when Bluebeard's ingenue niece, Sybil (Black-Eyed Susan), arrives on the island. She's accompanied by her foppish fiancé, Rodney (Vehr), and her ludicrous governess, Miss Cubbidge (Pashalinski). Since he was expecting Sybil to arrive alone and intending to use her for his next genital transplant, Bluebeard views Rodney as an interference. He recognizes Miss Cubbidge, who constantly utters hilarious malapropisms, for the silly woman she is. But for the sake of getting to Sybil, Bluebeard relaxes his prohibition against the uninvited, and plays host to all three of his guests by having dinner prepared for them.

The dinner scene is typical of Ludlam's self-mockery, making fun of both his own dramaturgy and the company's newly acquired, offstage vegetarian diet. (We're told by Sheemish that meat has not been "seen in the palace in nineteen years.") As the guests are assembling for dinner:

> RODNEY: Strange, all the places are set to one side of the table.
>
> BLUEBEARD: That is because of a little surprise I have for you. There will be an entertainment tonight while we are taking our evening meal, a little play I wrote myself.
>
> SYBIL: What, a play?
>
> RODNEY: Jolly!
>
> MISS CUBBIDGE: Wrote it yourself? You've a touch of erosion, I see, Baron. And yet you studied medicine?
>
> BLUEBEARD: I write for amusement only.
>
> MISS CUBBIDGE: Were you indoctrinated? I mean, did you receive the doctorate? On what theme did you write your dissipation? Which degree did you receive?
>
> BLUEBEARD: I received the third degree.
>
>   (MRS. MAGGOT *places a platter of meat on the table.*)
>
> RODNEY: This meat looks delicious.
>
> BLUEBEARD: (*Having a seizure*) Meat? Meat? (*Turning on* MRS. MAGGOT) You dare to serve them meat?
>
> MRS. MAGGOT: Eh?
>
> BLUEBEARD: (*In a blind rage*) Take it away at once, blockhead! Do you want to ruin my experiment? (*He throws the meat at* MRS. MAGGOT *and then leaps up on the dinner table like a wild man, roaring*) What is the Law?
>
> MRS. MAGGOT and SHEEMISH: (*Bowing before him as though he were an idol on an altar, they link their arms together and chant, swaying back and forth rhythmically*) We are not men. We are not women. We are not men. We are not women. His is the hand that makes. We are not men. We are not women. His is the House of Pain. We are not men. We are not women. That is the Law!
>
> BLUEBEARD: (*Rolling his eyes savagely*) Now get out! (*Turning on the guests*) All of you!
>
> MISS CUBBIDGE: (*Horrified*) What about dinner?
>
> BLUEBEARD: I've lost my appetite!
>
> RODNEY: What about the play?
>
> BLUEBEARD: I detest avant-garde theater.

Ludlam intended to include a scene from this play-within-the-play, but he didn't like the way it unfolded onstage and dropped it after a few performances. Bluebeard's temper tantrum proved more effective, even as it revealed his savage madness to the other characters.

In one of the play's longest scenes, performed as a seduction that culminates in the nude, Bluebeard rapes Miss Cubbidge. He subsequently ravishes Sybil as well, and with hair-trigger timing proceeds to play each woman against the other in another hilarious scene. With each of them he privately feigns marriage intentions. To both he gives a key to his laboratory, but forbids their using it, knowing this will entice them into his lair and facilitate his surgical procedures. When Sybil arrives in the anteroom to his laboratory near the end of Act II, Bluebeard says in an aside, "Curiosity killed the cat. But it may have a salutary effect on the pussy." He then hypnotizes her into submission.

Earlier in the play, Rodney was warned of Bluebeard's fiendish ways by Lamia "the Leopard Woman" (Montez), another one of the doctor's failed experiments. She explains how she was seduced by Bluebeard:

> No woman can resist him, I tell you. . . . I didn't know if I was coming or going. . . . His idealism . . . his intensity . . . the Clairol Blue of his beard! His words carried me away. He had a strange look in his eyes. I felt strange inside. . . . If you love [Sybil], get her off this island before it is too late."

It's the old "Emerald Eye" all over again — Ludlam as Svengali — on the stage as in life.

But even forewarned, Rodney cannot prevent the foul deed from being perpetrated on Sybil's genitalia. Sybil emerges from the surgery wrapped in bandages like a mummy. "When she is completely nude except for her fuck-me pumps, the [new] genital [a chicken claw with a bit of sponge] begins to move," reads the stage direction. She "moves like the bride of Frankenstein, with stiff, jerking movements of the head and neck."

In a Dickensian plot twist that becomes the play's denouement and refers specifically to *The Importance of Being Earnest*, Mrs. Maggot realizes that she is Sybil's mother. Along with Miss Cubbidge, Rodney, and the mangled Sybil, she returns to "normalcy." Bluebeard is left alone with Sheemish and Lamia on the Island of Lost Love.

There is a bit of Ludlam mocking himself in Sheemish's speech about his master, who, as he says, turns "to ridicule everything we believe in." Two other lines, uttered by Bluebeard and Sybil respectively, are bald statements of Ludlam's evolving manifesto:

"Heart! Talent! These are nothing, my boy. Mediocrity is the true gift of the gods," and "The human heart...who knows to what perversions it may not turn, when its taste is guided by aesthetics?" This last remark is taken from Proust, as is another of Bluebeard's lines that Black-Eyed Susan brought to Ludlam's attention: "Do you think that the envenomed spittle of five hundred little gentlemen of your mark, piled one on top of the other, could succeed in so much as slobbering the tips of my august toes?"

Confirming Brockmeyer and Mallory's mutual impression that everyone knew Ludlam had finally written a real play and the company had become a real company, Pashalinski recalled that Ludlam changed even in his capacity as a director with *Bluebeard*. He was suddenly "more practical," she claimed. "He cut to the chase more quickly. And in the same way that he felt more sure of himself, we felt more sure of ourselves. There was suddenly this feeling that we knew what we were doing."

Held in Mario Montez's loft as usual, the rehearsals reflected the difference. They were both "more unified and more sheer fun," according to Pashalinski. They also required roughly half the rehearsal time of the earlier works: one month as opposed to two. "This went along with the sureness of what we were doing," continued Pashalinski.

> In a sense, everyone was playing a comic version of who we were ourselves. Everybody had ideas and gravitated towards their roles instantly. We finally had real characters to work on that had beginnings, middles, and ends to their development, and carried through to the finish of the play. Finally, we had acting we could sink our teeth into. It was the first time that I felt like I had become an actress. The reassurance I had been looking for finally came through. Though the "sacred weed" was still being sucked up, drugs were now taking a subsidiary role [and were even less prevalent during performances].

One member of the company who was less in tune with the *Bluebeard* breakthrough was Gary Tucker. Tucker was more career-oriented than most of the other players, and he had started to cultivate his interest in music by forming a rock group called Eleven's Black Sabbath — a name which incorporated his alias for the Ridiculous. The group included Warhol superstar Ultra Violet, as well as James Morfogen. It was highly theatrical, with exploding powder effects and light shows.

In fact, Tucker originally declined to be in *Bluebeard*. Ed Dame (Inez "Bunny" Eisenhower) attended the first few rehearsals, taking the role of Mrs. Maggot, until Tucker relented and deigned to assume the role. Ludlam proved unforgiving, however.

How could anyone choose another career over what he had to offer? Though he tried his best to disguise it, Ludlam had a tendency to perceive anyone's leaving the company as a personal betrayal. Tucker and Ludlam frequently squabbled during both the rehearsals and performances of *Bluebeard*.

As Pashalinski recalled,

> Charles was hard on Gary. They had an argument over who was going to bring on the chairs in the dinner scene. Charles felt Gary should and Gary said, "Charles! Chairs are not an actor's props." Gary was ambitious and wanted to be more professional. He had Warhol connections that were pulling him away. And in response to this, Charles nagged and picked on him all the time.

The friction Tucker felt with the company was also infiltrating his relationship with Brockmeyer. Though it was Tucker's acting connections that introduced the couple to the Ridiculous and Brockmeyer had initially played a subsidiary role in the company, their positions were now changing. Brockmeyer, a delicious gossip and more congenial fellow, simply fit in better with the group.

Morfogen recalled that Ludlam was also having a "little feud" with Bill Vehr during the *Bluebeard* rehearsals.

> I had lost ninety-five pounds over the past year, and Charles came to me and said, "You know, you look very good James. If Bill doesn't behave, you'll have his part in the play." I didn't like the idea of being used as a pawn in some game he was playing with Bill. Bill should have the part, but leave poor James alone — don't hold the carrot out or taunt him that way.

Even before Ludlam finished writing the play, scenes from *Bluebeard* were included in a larger program that also contained the Trilby and Svengali segments from *Big Hotel* and the "Venus Fucking scene" from *Conquest of the Universe*. The event — called *Tabu Tableaux* — took place a couple of weekends in February of 1970. It came about when Ludlam was invited to contribute to a revue to be staged at Christopher's End, a sleazy gay bar that derived its name from its location at the foot of Christopher Street in Greenwich Village — very near where he had been arrested for indecent behavior several years earlier. A dressing room had been rigged in a narrow alcove with a curtain in front. Without a backstage bathroom at their disposal, the male members of the company urinated in jars.

Within a month or so, Ludlam was invited back to Christopher's End to perform the completed version of *Bluebeard*. A wooden platform was set up on the bar to extend the playing area. Incredible as it sounds, this is where the Uptown critics attended the play to deliver their rave reviews.

But *Bluebeard* had originally premiered in March of 1970 at Cafe La MaMa, under the sponsorship of Ellen Stewart. Stewart had initially promised the Ridiculous a four-week run of the play, but Ludlam balked when she presented him with her standard contract. It was by now customary for theater companies to request a percentage of royalties on subsequent productions of plays they initiated. But Ludlam wasn't aware of such terms until it was too late to make any other arrangements. Furious about the contract and still smarting at the memory of Wyn Chamberlain's ownership of *Conquest*, Ludlam refused to sign. Stewart reduced the run from four weeks to one and didn't invite any press. Pashalinski recalled being in the dressing room with Ludlam on opening night and peering over Stefan Brecht's shoulder as he studied the contract and deemed it preposterous.

In one of his rare diary entries, Ludlam wrote:

> Ellen Stewart wants me to sign a contract giving her an option on the complete rights to *Bluebeard* or 5% of the royalties for the next fifteen years. Just because she let us perform there at La MaMa for five nights. She promised me $400 for the actors [to share among the group], but only came through with $350. The bureaucratic bitch.

Though Ludlam and Stewart remained cordial with each other throughout the years and he always supplied her with the obligatory kiss on the cheek whenever they met, he did nothing to prevent the rest of the world from knowing his true feelings: that she was an uneducated amateur who didn't deserve the prominent position she held within the theatrical community. Stewart claimed to be aware of his opinion of her, but she wasn't privy to the satirical impersonation he would perform whenever her name was mentioned.

The first review of a Ridiculous production in *The New York Times* was for *Bluebeard*, when it reopened in April at the newly christened "Christopher's End Theater." (It played a Tuesday through Sunday schedule.) In his piece, Mel Gussow gushed that the play "serves successfully as both a loving paean and a lunatic parody" of "every mad-doctor movie ever made." While recognizing that it was based on *Island of Lost Souls*, he cited the "infinite revisions and elaborations by the devious Ludlam. There are intimations, for example, of *Faust* and Bartók's *Bluebeard's Castle* is playing as the entertainment begins."

Appreciating "Ludlam's consistently amusing linguistic conceits," Gussow added, "The plot is complicated and digressionary, and great fun to follow." He particularly praised Ludlam's bravura performance as Bluebeard, which he described as

> deliciously rococo, and obviously he has infected everyone in his Ridiculous
> Theatrical Company. For one thing, the masklike make-up, which is credited
> to the entire company, is near-miraculous (a knobby-faced slavey, a gilt-
> skinned angel.) . . . In a beard that looks like blue Brillo, his eyes blazing with
> mad menace, [Ludlam] is a monstrous, but oddly ingratiating fiend. "When
> I am good," he boasts, "I am very good. When I am bad . . ." He pauses,
> considers his catalogue of turpitude, and concludes, "I'm not bad." As a vil-
> lain, he is not only not bad, he is terrific.

Gussow also had particular praise for Black-Eyed Susan (who "merits some sort of cita-
tion for the self-confidence with which in the last scene she wears that third genital") and Brockmeyer (for his "Karloffian servant"). Montez, however, couldn't have been too thrilled by Gussow's observation that "Led by Ludlam, a truly terrible actor like Mario Montez . . . seems exactly right."

The *Village Voice* provided not one but two reviews of the play in consecutive issues, both of them raves and both in response to the production at Christopher's End. In the first, Martin Washburn focused on the acting to explain how he was won over by an otherwise absurd play. "For some reason," he wrote,

> the details of the story, which are absurd nonsense are not dismissable
> as absurd nonsense. . . . The nonsense of the story supports the actuality
> of the actors, and vice versa. . . . Their secret is utter faith in the words
> and gestures they have arrived at. . . . Their reverence for their vehicle,
> this silly story about a sex-obsessed Bluebeard, is absolute. It makes their
> acting unique. . . . To see the serious way in which Charles Ludlam is
> ridiculous is to see the testimony which is at the heart of the theatre. . . .
> Bluebeard is not a role for Ludlam, the actor — he *becomes* Bluebeard,
> because he knows all the passwords, the right way to do this and that
> movement. Frequently his movements have the uncanny grace and preci-
> sion of a dancer.

Black-Eyed Susan has a kindred sense of distance from her role, which gives her great power as an actress. Her face is a stage within the stage, and fortunately the theatre is small enough to see it clearly. With the tiniest of movements, she writes whole tracts on the tenor of events. I became impressed by her powers as a humorist when I realized that, though she had taken all her clothes off, I was still looking at her face.

The second *Village Voice* review, by Richard Schechner, the theater director and theorist, was a more earnest investigation that compared Ludlam to Molière and declared *Bluebeard* an "exemplary performance." Exemplary performances, Schechner explained, are landmarks that both refer to the past and point to the future. "They do not mark out new ground," he wrote, "but show clearly how well what was recently undoable is now done superbly. From their vantage we can see more clearly where to go next." Salvaging the best from past traditions while creating something unique and of the moment was exactly what Ludlam was aiming for.

Schechner also felt that "Marked against the utter irrelevancy of most theatre, [*Bluebeard*] is nothing short of an achievement." The play itself he saw as a "brilliant" and

> extraordinary collage that cannibalizes sources from the Bible to Shakespeare to Wells to contemporary TV programs. But [Ludlam's] text is not a hodge-podge, or an exercise in second-quoting. It is an authentic theatre text, made in the theatre the way Molière made his plays and, I think, as fine a *whole experience* as Molière.

Recognizing the title figure as "a titanic and masterful hybrid of Dr. Moro [sic], Bluebeard, Faustus, Don Juan, and Ludlam," Schechner spared no kudos in describing the performance. "Ludlam," he wrote,

> is a genius of redemption, whose total commitment to his face, his body, the *shape* of his words makes us understand again what a *star* is. . . . A master of doing, showing, and *enjoying* showing. . . . Ludlam is able to gather and mobilize his face and throw it across a room; or to bend his body as a bow is bent and then suddenly — preposterously and absolutely — aim and release all that energy. His company is also gifted, but they are infected too. And, I think, Charles Ludlam is their plague.

It is important to emphasize here that Ludlam's genius as an actor was being celebrated both Uptown and Down not for a drag performance, but for a male character.

Putting his finger on Ludlam's intentions more precisely than anyone else had up to this point, Schechner continued,

> It is not parody, though there is much parody in it; nor is it farce, though its greatest moments are farcical. *Bluebeard* is contemporary high comedy. That is, Ludlam's company is showing the only way that traditional theatre — the theatre of texts, costumes, stages, impersonations, stage lights — can flourish in our society. [It] is exemplary of the continuation of the Grand Tradition in the theatre.

(Schechner's momentous response to *Bluebeard* may have played a part in the decision to include the script for Ludlam and Vehr's *Turds in Hell* in a subsequent volume of *The Drama Review*, dated September 1970.)

There were additional raves from John O'Conner in the *Wall Street Journal* ("A drawing room grotesque right out of Bela Lugosi with Noël Coward thrown in for good measure... bizarre, more than a little mad and hilarious"), Martin Gottfried in *Women's Wear Daily* ("Ludlam's concept is staggering for its sheer creativity...nothing short of a comic masterpiece"), and Emory Lewis in New Jersey's *Bergen County Record* ("A fascinating play... Ludlam is magnificent... a splendidly controlled artist, and his voice can range from an unearthly squeak to a booming growl").

Given all the attention in the *Village Voice* and the response to *Bluebeard* in general, it is hardly surprising that Ludlam won a *Village Voice* Obie Award, the company's first of many. He received one of six Special Citations at the fifteenth annual Obie Awards presentation on May 26, 1970, presided over by Dustin Hoffman. The panel of judges that year consisted of Jack Kroll of *Newsweek*, John Lahr of the *Village Voice*, and John Simon of *New York* magazine.

Thomas Lanigan Schmidt, whose youth was as steeped in Catholicism as Ludlam's, compared seeing *Bluebeard* to "attending Easter Mass at the Church of the Holy Sepulcher." In mid-April, Stefan Brecht had taken Lotte Lenya and Douglas Fairbanks, Jr. to see *Bluebeard* and they became admirers of the company, as had Leonard Bernstein when he saw *When Queens Collide*. But given that Schechner ran the Performing Garage, here was a supporter in a position to help the company, following his critical praise in the *Village Voice*. He invited Ludlam to take a look at his larger space and, by early May, *Bluebeard* had moved from the relatively cramped quarters at Christopher's End to a more genuine theater in Soho.

The audience members at the Performing Garage were seated in bleachers, and as Lamia the Leopard Woman, Mario Montez would slink through the rows and wind up in their laps during the performance. In keeping with the company's new macrobiotic diet and the way it was humorously worked into the play, a note at the bottom of the program advised that "Macrobiotic food and drink will be sold in the lobby during intermissions."

Bluebeard played at the Performing Garage for four months, in blisteringly hot conditions without air-conditioning throughout the summer. Fortified by the Obie Award, rave reviews in the *Times* and elsewhere, and glowing word-of-mouth, the audiences never diminished. But the space had to be relinquished in the fall, when Schechner retrieved it for his own purposes.

Along with the company's runaway success came pressures of a different sort. As Mallory perceived it, the personal dynamics within the company changed during the *Bluebeard* period. "In the same way that Khanazar Bluebeard is in charge of everything," said Mallory,

> I'm afraid that everyone in the company suddenly made Charles the boss and something of a father figure. He never really wanted to be responsible for all of us in the way we made him be, because there were times when it interfered with his creativity. Charles was put in this position of being our father onstage and off, but you could tell that he really wanted freedom from all the garbage it sometimes entailed.

Concurring in a way with Mallory, Schmidt claimed:

> Probably more people were possessive of Charles than he was of them. He was so good at giving uniquely to each person something they needed. He made you feel like he was the long-lost mother/father figure who understood things about you no one else did. I felt that way, and it took me years before I realized he made many people feel that way.

> On a more primitive level, Charles was like a shaman who was maybe biologically male, but then female in temperament. And he combined those elements to become a mother-father-priest figure. But that's a big burden for a person to carry, because beyond that, he's a human being too, with the same needs as everyone else.

Black-Eyed Susan recalled times when Ludlam would say, 'I'm not a father figure, and people have to stop treating me that way."

While acknowledging that even Brecht told her Ludlam reminded him of *his* father, Pashalinski felt that Ludlam rather assumed the paternal position as opposed to their demanding it of him.

"I was beginning to see Charles in a more detached way," Pashalinski explained.

> I was starting to take more for myself when I was out onstage. It was part of making the giant leap for me to become an actress. You have to be selfish. And that was part of the continuing challenge with Charles, because the stakes kept getting higher and higher. These things didn't matter so much in the earlier plays, but they started to with *Bluebeard*. It reached a culmination with *Camille* [a few years later], when we all had to fight him for every fucking moment on that stage.

Bluebeard's seduction of Miss Cubbidge became the most celebrated scene in the play. Its success hinged on the precision timing of Ludlam and Pashalinski's cat-and-mouse maneuvers and the classical comic routines they entailed. With winning results, the scene set out to mock heterosexual relations. But what no one was aware of was the degree to which this scene reflected the complexities of their offstage relationship.

If Scott and Vehr supplied Ludlam with the intellectual support he required, Pashalinski came to see herself as the emotional fulcrum in his life. They had even had sex once, a couple of years earlier. Their evening began with a party at Vaccaro's loft, and ended at Ludlam's apartment. It marked the first time Ludlam dropped acid, which was something he had been afraid to do. It was a good thing Pashalinski was on hand in a more sober state to look after him, since he went off the deep end when he hallucinated and believed himself to be Jesus Christ.

The emotional dynamic between Ludlam and Pashalinski was embedded in the seduction sequence in *Bluebeard*: Their off-stage relationship informed both Ludlam's conception of the scene as well as the way they developed it together. They had, of course, worked out the basic structure of the physical business in rehearsals, but the scene continued to evolve in front of audiences.

Pashalinski recalled Lohr Wilson telling her during the run of *Bluebeard* at the Performing Garage, "Charles is getting laughs at your expense and taking the scene away from you." This prompted her to fight back during a subsequent performance. "I began to work on my role in a more analytical fashion," said Pashalinski, "and I stole the scene. And as soon as we left the stage, Charles exploded. He said, 'Why do you think I trust you out there, if I didn't think you were great? But don't you ever do that again!'"

A part of what allowed Pashalinski to begin to detach herself from Ludlam was the fact that she was now "involved" with somebody else. It was during the run of *Turds in Hell* that Bill Vehr took Pashalinski to the Judson to see *Camille Has a Right to Complain*, a play by Fran Winant. Through Winant, Pashalinski met Flavia Rando in the spring of 1969 and proceeded to have a six-year relationship with her. This was the first time since the Ridiculous was formed that a member of the core group fell in love with someone outside the company, and it clearly had repercussions.

With sadness, Pashalinski recalled the precise moment she first said "no" to Ludlam. He had phoned her late at night, as he often did, to share a scene he had just written. But she was preoccupied with Rando and told him that she couldn't talk.

There were evidently ways in which the intimacy that brought everyone together now started to drive them apart. Though it was subtle and unspoken, Ludlam showed signs of feeling secretly threatened whenever members of the company turned their attention elsewhere. Affairs with others brought pressures to bear on the special relationship that everyone had with Ludlam. Vehr was infatuated with David Johansen, and the two of them took off for the West Coast in the summer of 1969. Even before that, Black-Eyed Susan and Stefan Brecht started having an affair, which was complicated by the fact that Brecht's wife Mary designed costumes for the company.

As for the others, Scott and Geldzahler were still going strong, even though they both liked to stray sexually and maintained an open relationship. And as Brockmeyer and Tucker became more assimilated into the company, the competitive strain began to erode their long-term relationship, which would be abruptly terminated altogether within a year of *Bluebeard*.

In the midst of all this was Ludlam, a catalyst for the others who was himself stuck between the rock of promiscuity and the harder place of wanting a romantic attachment. "He was a very romantic and vulnerable person who often got hurt," said Pashalinski. "He was looking for Mr. Right — there was no question about that."

It was on his twenty-seventh birthday, in April of 1970, while *Bluebeard* was up and running at Christopher's End, that Ludlam met a potential Mr. Right. His name was John Heys. Following that evening's performance and a typical post-theater dinner with the gang, Ludlam went solo to the Hippodrome, a popular dance club where one was apt to encounter gays, straights, and everything in between. Ludlam was dressed in white pants and a white tee-shirt, with his long, dyed, blue-black beard offsetting the ensemble.

After cruising and flirting outrageously, and then dancing for a spell, Ludlam invited Heys to his apartment on East 12th Street. They became sometime lovers for the next six months. "Charles courted me," claimed Heys,

> and we had a lot of fun together. But he had his sadistic tendencies too. As the public knows [since he appeared naked so many times onstage], Charles was enormously well endowed. But he had a penchant for certain things. He liked to fuck almost exclusively, and it was pretty one-dimensional in that respect. For Charles, that's what constituted sex. But it wasn't as passionate as I had hoped for. He was very aggressive, but he would turn passive in the middle of it.

With his gaunt figure, angular features, extremely prominent nose and long hair, Heys would have stood out in any crowd. "I think Charles found me attractive because of my hair," said Heys. "He was always very generous with compliments about the way I looked. Many years later, he painted a portrait of me. I think he was captivated by my face."

Although he had never met Ludlam before the Hippodrome, Heys had been taken by another boyfriend to see *Turds in Hell* when it was playing at the Gate Theater. He found it lacking, or as he put it, "too too . . . I just couldn't digest it."

When he met Ludlam, Heys was the editor of *Gay Power*, a pioneering, visually oriented, biweekly tabloid that claimed to be the first gay newspaper in New York. (The centerfold in one issue featured a photo of Nureyev nude.) With offices above the Fillmore East on Second Avenue, it was brought out by the publisher of the *East Village Other*, from August of 1969 to August of 1970.

Even though Heys remained outside the company, Ludlam still found ways to benefit his own career through their connection. More than most artists and perhaps less than none, there was ultimately no separation between life and work for Ludlam. With Heys as the conduit, Ludlam wrote an essay for *Gay Power* on "Why I Use Drag Queens in

My Plays," which took a classical and historical approach to the subject before evolving into a more personal manifesto. "The greatest and most restrictive bond on one's identity is sex," he wrote.

> It is fixed biologically or bio*ill*ogically at birth. Anatomy is destiny. When we impersonate the opposite sex we are freed from one prison only to enter another. . . . The female impersonator is not one who is freed from the rituals of sexual identity. He understands the rituals better and knows the passwords. He can pass back and forth. While others are content with one sexual identity he has two. He is a great actor because he has prepared himself for both roles all his life.

In a mischievous coup worthy of Shaw or Wilde, Ludlam also wrote a review of *Bluebeard* — obviously, it was a rave. It appeared in *Gay Power* under the pseudonym "Althea Gordon," which probably referred to the female black tennis player, Althea Gibson, who was once rumored to be a transsexual. (Ludlam would also use the name of Althea Gordon for an incidental character in a future play called *Caprice*.) In terms of his own review of *Bluebeard*, Susan recalled Ludlam "laughing and talking about Althea Gordon and saying, 'It's such a perfect name. How could anybody doubt that it's real?'"

"The play is a gothic thriller featuring the slick art-nouveau acting that has made the Ridiculous Theatrical Co. the toy of intellectuals and the hub of a little known religious cult," wrote Ludlam under the guise of an impartial reviewer. Ms. Gordon claimed the play to be "flawlessly structured" and referred to the seduction scene as "one of the funniest and most daring love scenes ever performed before a live audience." S/he ends the review: "The shock ending alone is worth the price of admission. The rest is superb farce and great entertainment."

Had Ludlam met Heys a year earlier, he probably would have put him onstage, as he had the various tricks and potential lovers he happened upon during the first few years of the Ridiculous — whether they had any performing talents or not. But *Bluebeard* proved too important to be tampered with or violated in this fashion. It would be more than a decade after their affair dissolved before Ludlam included Heys in three Ridiculous plays, beginning with *Galas* in 1983. But it was through his affiliation with Ludlam that Heys became a performance artist in his own right.

Though the relationship lacked romance or passion even for the half year it lasted, it was with Heys that Ludlam demonstrated the first signs of craving some sort of domestic arrangement. This was yet another symptom of the settling down process that

Bluebeard entailed. He stayed at Heys's apartment on East 6th Street much of the time, and they cooked meals together. Heys recalled that whenever Ludlam spent the night, there was always a residue of black flakes in the bathroom sink from the seaweed tooth powder he used. Heys also said, "A lot of the time was spent sitting there and listening to Charles talk. It was always that way. But there could also be awkward silences when we were together."

Their affair ended shortly after it peaked, when they went on their "honeymoon" in Montreal for a week. They took a midnight bus from Port Authority, immediately following the closing performance of *Bluebeard* at the Performing Garage, at the end of the summer. They stayed in this "charming little guest house," recalled Heys. "And the minute we got there, early in the morning, Charles ordered a beer."

By now, Ludlam was a quasi macrobiotic who frequently held court at the Paradox and the Cauldron, two popular macrobiotic restaurants in the East Village. (Indeed, it was over a lunch at the Paradox that Ludlam and Scott had originally hatched the idea for *Bluebeard*.) But his version of the diet permitted beer and cigarettes, and Ludlam could be fiendish in his consumption of both.

Ludlam's relationship with Heys didn't suddenly flare up and then quickly burn itself out, the way many others would, so much as it slowly fizzled. In fact, Heys would go on to have a more meaningful and enduring friendship with Bill Vehr. (A rock music aficionado at the time, Vehr wrote a feature article on the Velvet Underground that was also published by Heys in *Gay Power*.)

Vehr often stayed at Heys's apartment through the first half of the 1970s, and particularly when his host made annual pilgrimages to Morocco or Spain. "Bill was a prince of the earth," according to Heys. "He had a gift for not making waves. More than anybody else in the group except maybe John Brockmeyer, Bill held Charles in such profound respect and he took every one of the roles that Charles created for him as a gift.

"But when the curtain came down, Bill had this amazing ability to go off into his own world and truly do what he liked," continued Heys.

> We often met at Max's Kansas City. He liked to do glamorous things. But he could also be quite content with nothing more than a comfortable chair, his coffee and cigarettes, and his Joyce or his Proust. He spent a lot of time reading.

We also had a lot of fun going to the baths together. Bill developed some mysterious and perverse relationships with various men, some of whom were noticeably handicapped either physically or mentally. His relationship with [a lover nicknamed] Shorty was very significant and very long — and Shorty was handicapped.

Susan recalled that when Vehr was going with Shorty, he told her: "When I first met him, I saw this black cloud, a person with nothing but bleakness in his life, and I wanted to offer him some light." Shorty had reportedly been abused by his father as a child, and he was so obviously mentally deficient that there were rumors he had been lobotomized. Shorty's afflictions made him even more appealing to the openhearted Vehr.

Heys also recalled many instances when someone was organizing a dinner or throwing a party and Vehr refused to go. "Instead of just accepting Bill's privacy, his being at the baths or whatever, Charles would always press him to attend these events." Sometimes Vehr would relent, sometimes not. "But what Bill cherished most was quality time between two people. He could be devious, but it was always with a facade of incredible charm."

When Vehr returned from the West Coast with David Johansen in the fall of 1969, he announced that he had decided to become a great actor and that he knew Ludlam was the person who could help him become one. But having written *Whores of Babylon* and cowritten *Turds in Hell*, which were produced earlier in the year, it was almost as if Vehr then stepped aside in order for Ludlam to seize the playwriting limelight sans competition.

ↄ

After *Bluebeard* had closed and Ludlam returned from Montreal with Heys, he met a man cruising in Stuyvesant Park. "I was sitting on a bench when Charles came up to me and said, 'Do you have a dog in this park?'" recalled Edgardo Franceschi. "I looked around and said, 'Of course not — there are no dogs in this park,' at which point, we both broke out laughing."

The blond and delicate Franceschi was a couple of years younger than Ludlam. After growing up in Puerto Rico, he attended an art school in Maine. He became a painter and had moved to New York earlier that year, in the beginning of 1970. On the night they met, Franceschi accompanied Ludlam to his apartment on East 12th Street. He was particularly impressed by a large willow tree Ludlam had painted in homage to the French fashion designer, Paul Poiret. It was painted directly on the walls and the ceiling, hovering over Ludlam's mattress in the corner.

Shortly after they slipped into bed, there were some repeated knocks on the apartment door, which Ludlam chose to ignore. Within twenty minutes, the police showed up and cast their flashlights on the startled young couple nestled beneath the sheets. Having dropped by just before and discovered no one at home, Ludlam's brother Donald was alarmed to find the door unlocked and worried that the place had been broken into. He returned with the police to investigate the matter.

Franceschi lived with Ludlam for a couple of months on 12th Street, until he was mugged in the foyer of the building and decided he had had enough of the dicey neighborhood. Since the recession of 1970 had already hit and Alphabet City was becoming increasingly dangerous, Ludlam took extra precautions whenever leaving or returning home. He advised, "If you spot any kids wearing sneakers, start running no matter what." There was one afternoon when Ludlam was writing and he took a break to make a sandwich in the kitchen. When he returned to his desk, he discovered that his Olivetti typewriter had been stolen.

According to Franceschi, Ludlam was a passive lover and sex was not a predominant part of their relationship. They rather became great admirers of each other's work as well as theatergoing companions. Franceschi recalled that when they saw Richard Schechner's *Commune* at the Performing Garage during the winter, Ludlam was so moved that he broke down and cried. Given Schechner's published praise for *Bluebeard*, Ludlam was primed to appreciate what he saw — even though many others found this collection of improvised scenes on current events rather incoherent. Far more characteristic of the competitive Ludlam was the contempt he showed for the New York Shakespeare Festival production of *Hamlet*, starring Stacy Keach, which he saw with Franceschi in the summer of 1972.

With Ludlam prodding him, Franceschi would apply his considerable artistic skills to designing for the theater. He worked on a handful of Ridiculous shows over the years (including, more than a decade later, the company's most extravagant offering, *Salammbô*).

At the time he met Franceschi, Ludlam was still earning a modest wage as a part-time salesman at a used-clothing store in the East Village, where friends would come by and schmooze in the afternoon. He didn't have to think twice, however, about taking a couple of weeks off to visit Stefan Brecht's country house in Great Barrington, a rural area in the southwest corner of Massachusetts. Ludlam was working on a new play, and Brecht invited him to develop it away from the distractions of the city. Ludlam referred to the upcoming excursion in a July 15, 1970 letter to Christopher Scott, who was touring the Côte d'Azur with Geldzahler that summer:

Dear Chris,

Thank you for your congratulations and your long awaited letter. That childish morass of petty details and materialism which you are fond of calling "the adult world" has bade me enter and I have accepted the invitation without misgivings. It is Karmic, I believe. In August I and the company will retreat to Stefan's country house and woods to prepare the new production; a detective story set in Chinatown involving the Tong wars entitled: *The Curse of Sanpaku* [Sanpaku is a macrobiotic term for drooping eyelids, a sign of poor health.] It will not espouse a macrobiotic philosophy. Rather it will show the Oriental's eagerness to adopt American customs. Focusing on the age of dietary anarchy, I will show how people are made foolish and then subjugated.

In consulting the *I Ching* I have drawn the first hexagram. I will try to prove worthy of it. Summer is a difficult time to write a play. My diet is fraught with errors as you can imagine. The wide diet is so hard to balance but narrower eating does not provide me with the proper bridge between the ability to imagine and the ability to execute. Changes are gradual but continuous. I am learning patience. My new interest in concentric dramatic construction has led me into a study of mystery stories. Aristotle said that plot is the soul of drama. It must be so. The more I discover about my own inner nature the more carefully I plot my plays.

Your drawings of us have been widely admired and your set [for *Bluebeard*] has proved equally effective in three different theaters. I am looking forward to further collaborations and of course the pleasure of your company. My best to Henry.

Your devoted,

Charles

With a magnanimity that transcended mere patronage, Brecht had encouraged Ludlam to bring the entire company with him to Great Barrington. Susan, Brockmeyer, Vehr, Pashalinski, Morfogen, Mallory, and Lohr Wilson were among the regular guests. Mary

Brecht was present only part of the time. Scott came up for a spell, as did Flavia Rando, Pashalinski's lover, and the gentle Franceschi, who was quickly perceived as Ludlam's new boyfriend.

Tucker and Mario Montez, however, failed to visit Great Barrington. Tucker was simply falling out of the company, as well as Brockmeyer's life. And Montez, for his part, was still anxious to become more established as a movie star. He was also reluctant to travel, and tended to shun communal situations.

With an enormous front porch overlooking the grounds, the Brecht homestead was thoroughly isolated on a large estate, commanding a view of a mountain in the distance. It was furnished primarily with top-quality Shaker furniture. But since the house could barely accommodate so many people at once, visitors came and went in a rotating fashion. The house tended to swell with guests on the weekends. Ludlam and Franceschi had a room to themselves. Pashalinski had private quarters to accommodate Rando's visits, while Susan shared a room with Lohr Wilson. Several people would spend the night on the floor of the unfinished attic.

Though Brecht had phoned everyone individually to extend personal invitations, some of them felt this respite from the city was a gift from Ludlam. "Charles wanted to pay people back for all the hard work we had done by then," said Pashalinski. "He was being generous with somebody else's hospitality by giving so many of us a kind of holiday in this beautiful spot, and by including us in the process of working on a new play.

"It was very much like summer camp," continued Pashalinski,

> or like "the fresh air fund," taking the impoverished kids to the country during the summer. It was especially wonderful to observe the transformation in Jack [Mallory]. He was like this inner-city rat, and you watched the barnacles drop off him and saw the innocence that was lurking underneath. It was Jack who won the corn-eating contest.

Brecht posted a large list of household chores on the kitchen wall, for everyone to participate in maintaining some order. Everyone was involved in preparing the meals or cleaning up afterwards, but it was primarily Brockmeyer and Susan who oversaw the macrobiotic cuisine.

A vegetable garden near the house yielded a lot of produce. Susan remembered that they discovered burdock growing naturally on the grounds. People walked or hitchhiked the three or four miles into town for other provisions, and Brecht's Volkswagon convertible was sometimes available as a backup. Morfogen remembered once going into Great Barrington with Brockmeyer, who stole some packaged pastries. The macrobiotic diet had obviously been too much for him — or rather, not enough.

Given the abundance of guests, the septic tank was overtaxed and the plumbing eventually failed. The cellar was flooded with the overflow, emitting an awful stench. Morfogen and Mallory went down in hip boots, with shovels and buckets, to clean it up.

While others were enjoying the countryside, Ludlam would disappear for long stretches of time to work on his new play. At one point, he told Morfogen, "Stefan wants me to write in a very regimented fashion, but I can't work that way." Ludlam had arrived in Great Barrington with some scenes already written for *The Curse of Sanpaku*, which bore the alternate title *Terror of the Tongs*. It was conceived as a Charlie Chan-type murder mystery about gang warfare in Chinatown. One scene was set in a Chinese restaurant called "The Szechwan Fire" (pronounced to sound like "set you on fire"), and it was riddled with esoteric macrobiotic jokes.

But as Ludlam worked on the script, the Charlie Chan element was abandoned altogether in favor of his newfound interest in prerevolutionary China. That interest had been sparked by his discovery of *Imperial Woman*, Pearl Buck's fictionalized biography of the last empress of China, which Lohr Wilson had given to him. Originally, Ludlam had thought of playing the empress, Tsu Hsi, himself. But as they were reading some of the preliminary scenes in Great Barrington — more than a year before the play would premiere as *Eunuchs of the Forbidden City* in Berlin — he realized that Black-Eyed Susan was more suited for the part. Ludlam became An Te Hai, the chief eunuch, instead.

Susan was known for her black moods and temperamental nature. According to Morfogen, she became particularly irritable when she ran out of amphetamines in the country. Morfogen made some silent home movies of the Great Barrington expedition, and a two-minute segment of the group on an outing at Umpechene Falls captured Susan's volatility. Everyone was wearing a bathing suit but Ludlam, who donned a red shirt, bright red sneakers, and blue jeans rolled up to his knees. Morfogen recalled that Susan, "in her Greta Garbo phase," asked not to be photographed at first. But then, in more of a Bea Lillie mode, "she took her breast out as the cameras were rolling."

After returning to the city, Ludlam, who was still dilatory in most things, sent his brother Donald a belated birthday greeting on October 10.

> Dear Donald,
>
> I'm sorry I didn't send you a card on your birthday. It's not that I forgot, exactly. I thought about it quite a bit. Nothing seemed suitable. And anyway, what can a card say, really? I'll try to make it up to you when I come out for a visit. What do you think of Joplin and Hendrix? I couldn't believe it. It looks like they both wanted to split from the scene. But I think there's something fishy about the story I read in the papers about Janis's OD'ing. When a person OD's he doesn't have time to run out and dump the needle, etc., in the garbage can. They go into a coma immediately with the works still stuck in their arms. Somebody was with Janis in my opinion, and stashed the evidence, and let her die rather than get involved with Alice in Blue Gown and Billy Law or Fugs. Well I'm no Dick Tracy but what do you think? Call me up some time. So long for now. Love and [a peace sign was drawn here] and flowers and jewels, Charles.

ⰔⱭ

The company reopened *Bluebeard* in November at the Gotham Art, a tiny theater space at 455 West 43rd Street that had once been a funeral parlor. Ludlam found the Gotham through Michael Abrams, son of the art book publisher and yet another influential admirer of the company. Abrams considered producing a film version of *Bluebeard*, and Ludlam entertained hopes of its coming to pass. But as Pashalinski recalled, Ludlam's attitude towards Abrams quickly turned suspicious and any plans for the film eventually collapsed. "Charles tended to shy away from people he thought might exploit him," said Pashalinski, and evidently this was how he came to view Abrams. The camp filmmaker Paul Bartel also intended to render *Bluebeard* on film, but his plans never materialized either.

In the midst of the *Bluebeard* revival at the Gotham, Bill Vehr sent a serial letter to ex-roommate Teriananda, which he began composing on December 30, 1970. "I have been meaning to write to you for sometime [sic] and am now finally getting around to it," he wrote.

> I'm at a rehearsal for *The Grand Tarot* and it['s] getting better and better all the time. We plan to open it on February 2 (James Joyce's birthday) — it['s] been

a tradition with us to try and open a new production every year on Joyce's birthday.... Have you seen "Gimme Shelter" yet? Did I tell you what Trish and I did when the Kinks were in town? Trish had her car and after the Fillmore concert on Saturday nite we waited at the stage door in the car — and when the Kinks got in their car we followed them all over New York City. They couldn't believe it. I had written a beautiful letter to Ray Davies (lead Kink) and filled the envelope with dried rose petals and [a] small postcard of a beautiful painting by Ingres. Anyway we followed them to a bar on Eighth Avenue [at] 48th St. where they were having a private party. We knocked on the door and a tall man in a tuxedo and a British accent answered and wouldn't let us in — so I said: "In that case, will you give this letter to Ray Davies?" He said he would and we left, dancing up Eighth Ave to our car....

Happy, happy New Year!!! I am writing this on New Year's Day, 1971.... Last night (New Year's Eve) we (everyone, that is) went to John Vaccaro's New Year's party — it ended quite effectively with Everyone (with a capital "E") being thrown out by John who went into a mad rage (one of his many mad rages). Some got the hint (not very subtle at that) and left[;] others were thrown out bodily. IT WAS A CAMP. His rage was provoked by a girl... who stole $50... and stuck it in her underpanties. Anyway, nearly everyone progressed to Max's [Kansas City] which was opened [sic] till 8 AM, with the discotèque upstairs playing Rolling Stones till 7 AM, and snow falling profusely on all the living and the dead (if I may misquote Joyce).

Jan 2 1971. Well, it looks like we're into 1971 now, whether we like it or not, and by the looks of it, it's gonna be a bitch. But as they say, "A bad dress rehearsal, a great performance," or, "It's always darkest before the dawn." At any rate, last night we had a terrible fight backstage between Charles and Jerry Fabian (Mrs. Maggot) [during a performance of *Bluebeard*]. [A replacement for Tucker, Fabian had been introduced to the Ridiculous by a friend of Mary Brecht's.] It seemed to begin onstage and became more intense as the evening progressed. Tonight Jack Mallory will play Mrs. Maggot....

Anyway, it's January 6 now, and yes, we all did get drunk and/or stoned, and it was a magnificent performance with lots of heavy luminaries of the New York "scene" in the audience. Rodney Parker [Vehr's own role] was especially fabulous. (I say that in all modesty, believe me.) Did I tell you Rudolph Nureyev was in the audience two weekends ago?

Ludlam's newly restructured and more stabilized version of *The Grand Tarot* joined *Bluebeard* in repertory at the Gotham that winter. A year after the phenomenal success of *Bluebeard* had commenced, it was only natural for the critics to take notice of the earlier play, which — fortunately — they had bypassed in its first incarnation. Though he eliminated the use of the Tarot cards to determine the sequence of the scenes, Ludlam retained an element of chance by having the cast members step out of character and relate their dreams, intentions, ambitions — or whatever else might occur to them.

Even in this altered format, however, *The Grand Tarot* could not draw audiences the way *Bluebeard* did — even if Cecil Beaton, the great British designer and photographer, reportedly attended a performance. But the fabulous costumes for *Tarot* — including some new ones designed by Edgardo Franceschi — prompted a pictorial spread in *Vogue*, with fawning commentary by Martin Gottfried. The lavishly reproduced photographs depicted Ludlam as the Holy Fool, Black-Eyed Susan as the High Priestess, and Pashalinski as the Empress. In spite of the accompanying photos, Gottfried devoted the bulk of his editorial space to *Bluebeard*.

Even more significant than Gottfried's approval in *Vogue* was Mel Gussow's in the *Times*. With his second review of a Ridiculous play, Gussow was already establishing himself as a champion in the most important outlet of all. While acknowledging that *The Grand Tarot* "is not as precise or as funny as Mr. Ludlam's *Bluebeard* . . . it too is charged with cosmic comedy and theatrical energy." He recounted an announcement at the end of the play that this is "a work-in progress — the plot is still trying to emerge from the mire of the playwright's mind." "I admire the mire," he quipped.

> Mr. Ludlam is an exploded pack of Tarot cards, a one-man harlequinade — with his feet firmly rooted in silly red sneakers. His bedlam-eyes dance merrily. The "heavenly fodder" accent gives a hilarious buffoon dimension to his clown. I would love to see him as a Shakespearean fool, or a movie villain, but in traditional trappings would Ludlam still be Ludlam?

Referring to her personal confession within the show, Gussow described how,

> The voluminous Lola Pashalinski states that she intended to play The Empress as Helen Hayes would (a mind-boggling juxtaposition of actresses), then thought of her as a cross between Helen Hayes and Mae West, and finally acted her as Sophia Loren would. Actually she plays The Empress as Lola Pashalinski — with spectacular gusto.

In his own aside to the audience, Ludlam explained how the play is an "attempt for me to elevate self-destruction to the level of religious experience."

A name new to the cast list of *The Grand Tarot* was that of Sebastian Swann. This was actually a stage name for Stefan Brecht, whose son was named Sebastian. According to Minette, "He took his son's name and besmirched it with his awful acting." While all concur that Brecht wasn't much of an actor, he reportedly loved playing the Marriage card, in a striking costume designed by his wife. Half of Brecht's body was clad as a tuxedoed bridegroom, the other as a blushing bride, with appropriately schizophrenic wigs and makeup completing the effect.

A highly unusual cast member who received no credit in the program was Larry, Brockmeyer's pet boa constrictor. Larry was "worn" by Brockmeyer both as a belt and as a coil around his cone-shaped Magician's hat. Minette recalled one particular performance when Larry nuzzled Brockmeyer's crotch during a kissing scene with Black-Eyed Susan. "They tried to train Larry to do it again, but he never did after that."

Ludlam assembled the cast one night before going on with *Tarot* to tell them that there would be no performance on a particular evening the following week. "We're all going to Carnegie Hall to see Judith Anderson as Hamlet," he explained. Without a trace of irony, he added, "She's come out of retirement to show me how to play the role."

There was another night when Larry Rée arrived before the performance and announced that Stravinsky had just died. During the intermission, he donned a tutu and put on a tape of the "Rite of Spring," improvising his movements under his *nom de ballet*, Ekatrina Sobechanskya.

By the time of the *Tarot* revival, Brockmeyer, Tucker and Black-Eyed Susan were living together on two floors of a house they had rented on Staten Island. Their household income had to be stretched to feed other mouths as well: In addition to Larry the snake, they cared for a myna bird. They also had a frequent houseguest named James Eichelberger who always brought his large afghan, Amy Lou, with him. (According to Minette, Amy Lou resembled Carole Lombard.)

Tucker and Eichelberger had been acting students together at the American Academy of the Dramatic Arts in New York in the mid-1960s. Long after Eichelberger adopted the performance name of "Ethyl," he would tell Ronn Smith (for an article in *Theatre Crafts* magazine) about the first time he ever saw Ludlam. Tucker had taken

Eichelberger to a rehearsal of Ludlam's *Big Hotel.* "I'll never forget it," said Eichelberger twenty-two years later:

> No one ever forgets their first meeting with Charles. . . . This very short, balding man with long hair would jump up whenever it was his turn, do his rehearsing, and then, when he finished, just sit down. One time, however, he jumped up and said, "Wait a minute." He ran to this stuff piled at the back of the loft, picked out a piece of chintzy green satin, and wrapped it around himself. When he turned around, he was that great actress Norma Desmond. No makeup, nothing, just this piece of cheap material. It was incredible, a total transformation. . . . It was one of the most amazing things I had ever seen. And it changed my life.

After he graduated from the Academy in 1967, Eichelberger became an actor with the Trinity Repertory Company in Providence, Rhode Island. But while staying with the gang on Staten Island whenever he visited New York, Eichelberger gradually became enmeshed with the Ridiculous and eventually joined the company.

&

Though Ludlam's affair with Franceschi proved relatively tame and short-lived, he quickly became involved in a stormy relationship that entailed physical violence and public spectacles before it ended a year later. The source of this turmoil was Robert Liebowitz, who had pursued Ludlam after seeing him in the buff in *Bluebeard* and being impressed by his sizable endowment. While Franceschi, his previous lover, designed the sets for *The Grand Tarot* at the Gotham, Ludlam invented the incidental role of the Sphinx for Liebowitz in the modified version of the play. (He was listed in the program as "Robert Player.")

According to Pashalinski, "Whenever Charles brought new lovers into the company, it must have felt like the Addams Family was waiting for them. There was this sense of being put through a crucible of fire — the poor things."

Apart from the public fights that later came to define his relationship with Ludlam, Liebowitz was naturally shy. He tried to ingratiate himself with the company without any success, despite his joining them on their first European tour in the fall of 1971.

Without the wider appeal of *Bluebeard* as a box office draw, the audience for *The Grand Tarot* quickly faded and both shows closed in the spring. Ludlam preserved his bushy "Bluebeard" whiskers on film by appearing in *Pink Narcissus*, the fantastically gay erotic movie by James Bidgood, released in 1971. Ludlam portrayed a vendor in a sleazy Times Square sequence, selling oversized dildos and "artificial anuses" to a clergyman.

The summer was used to design and rehearse *Eunuchs of the Forbidden City*, which was scheduled to have its world premiere in Vienna as part of a much larger European visit. But what could best be summarized as a "starvation tour" got off to a bad start. Vienna, where the company had planned on having their longest stay, proved to be the most inhospitable city of all.

The tour had been organized by Catherine Farinon-Smith, the company's first official business manager. Farinon-Smith became affiliated with the Ridiculous during the run of *Bluebeard* at the Performing Garage, where she held an administrative position. She also ran a company called New Arts Management, a promotions firm for the performing arts that specialized in international bookings.

The roster of travelers included Ludlam, Liebowitz, Vehr, Brockmeyer, Pashalinski, Black-Eyed Susan, Brecht (sans Mary), Mallory, Lohr Wilson, and Mark Giles, a dynamic and attractive lesbian who had become a stage manager for the Ridiculous at the Gotham. At his mother's bidding, Ludlam also took his brother Donald along. And Pashalinski's lover, Rando, paid her own way as a traveling companion, only to end up handling the company's business affairs as the trip continued.

As for those who stayed behind, Tucker was simply out of the picture by then, following his flare-ups with Ludlam the previous season. Chances are Morfogen would have been included to fill out the cast list if Liebowitz had not arrived on the scene. The biggest absentee, however, was Mario Montez.

Like Ludlam, Montez was superstitious about flying. He was also working with other directors and hoping that his film career would blossom into something more substantial. Indeed, Montez had become increasingly irritable and Ludlam was beginning to fear he might lose him at any point. During a weekend visit at Geldzahler's house in the Hamptons, Ludlam turned the threat around by inviting Thomas Lanigan Schmidt to replace Montez. But Schmidt saw through the manipulative gesture, just as Morfogen had earlier, when Ludlam suggested that *he* might replace Vehr.

The troupe members embarking on the European tour had to see to their own travel arrangements. But given the lineup of performances they were scheduled to give in

Belgrade, Zagreb, Vienna, Berlin, Copenhagen, and finally London, Ludlam assured them they would be earning enough to pay room and board during their travels. Unfortunately, it didn't quite work out that way.

The plan was for everyone to meet in September in Belgrade where they would perform *Bluebeard* at a summer theater festival. Pashalinski left a month early with her lover to visit Rome and then scout out Rando's paternal relatives in Sicily. Pashalinski had gotten a clerical job earlier in the summer to combine with her welfare payments and pay for this preliminary trip. Apparently the bureaucracy was doing nothing at this point to cross-reference sources of income, and all sorts of scams prevailed, with some people collecting both unemployment and welfare simultaneously.

Since he was deathly afraid of flying and, like his mother, never had flown, Ludlam went by ship to Europe. With Liebowitz and "six hundred kilos of scenery and costumes" for *Bluebeard*, *The Grand Tarot*, and *Eunuchs of the Forbidden City* in tow, he left on August 13, 1971 for what would be his first and last trans-Atlantic crossing by ship. The first few days of the cruise engendered some of the most extensive journal entries of Ludlam's life.

"There were rumors at 11:00 PM that the captain was delaying the departure until after midnight because he didn't want to leave on Friday the thirteenth," begins the first of three entries.

> But at eleven fifteen the tugboats came and towed us out into open waters. The waning moon in a crescent appeared a molten slab of copper watermelon. Moabe, the Japanese boy — who is circling the globe by motorcycle — pointed it out. I agreed with him that it was "some" moon. I picked the bits of potato out of my succotash at lunch although I suspect a few bits of ham slipped by my evening screening of an omelette. My spirits were high when they brought in what appeared, in its lemon garnish, to be filet of sole, and sank when they revealed it was veal.

Other anecdotes in the journal recreate conversations with fellow passengers and the ship's waiters. Liebowitz is referred to variously as "my roommate" or, more naturally, Robert. There is a lengthy description of the third day, when "almost everyone is seasick," including Ludlam:

> Only about eight people showed up for lunch....I left the table with my

head reeling. The ocean became more and more turbulent. We are passing through a hurricane it turns out. Outside my portal I see nothing but sea and sky alternately. I am staying in bed. Surprisingly Robert offers me hashish which I decline for fear that it might intensify the seasickness. But finally I yield and discover that the "hash" has made the rocking sensation into an amusement and I no longer feel seasick. Perhaps they should sell hashish in a drugstore or should I say pharmacy to be purchased by prescription only for the relief of seasickness?

My reading and writing obsess my mind. The old compulsion to finish my articles on costume and makeup fetishism and the sexual act, and my "Seven Levels of Theater." From Ohsawa's seven levels of judgement. 1) Mechanical. 2) Sentimental (sensational). 3) Intellectual. 4) Moral. 5) Economic. 6) Social. 7) Supreme. To tie up the loose ending of *The Grand Tarot*. But as always I long to begin a new play.

The ship landed in Italy. Ludlam and Liebowitz visited Sardinia, Casablanca, and Tunis before making their way to Belgrade via train. (Ludlam found a long, striped, and hooded caftan in Casablanca, and for many years he could be observed walking around Greenwich Village clad in this cherished robe.)

In the meantime, seven other woebegone travelers encountered problems from the outset that should have warned them about the trip ahead: Vehr, Brockmeyer, Black-Eyed Susan, Mallory, Giles, Wilson, and Donald Ludlam congregated at the airport only to discover that the booking agent had failed to confirm their charter flight reservations. They spent a couple of nights cramped in an airport hotel, and then, in true vagabond fashion, they spent another at the gate, before finally boarding a plane early the next morning.

Since they were low on funds from the beginning, the seven of them shared two rooms and two double beds during their stopover night in London. Though the train to Dover and the ferry to the Continent were without incident, problems resumed once they boarded a train in Belgium to wend their way to Belgrade. The group was confined to a single compartment, traveling second class without sleeping cars and without any food service. This required pit stops whenever the train pulled into various stations; and in Cologne, they failed to reboard in time.

Like a sequence out of a Preston Sturges movie, one misstep led to another. On the next train, different cars had different destinations, with transfers made at various depots late at night. The next morning, the beleaguered company learned they were headed for Stalingrad as opposed to Belgrade, so they needed to change trains yet again.

The most frightening — and ultimately humorous — leg of their journey occurred when they arrived at the Yugoslavian border. There appeared to be some problem with Vehr's visa and, at first, they all assumed this was why they were detained. "When we pulled into the first stop in Yugoslavia, we were all pulled off the train," recalled Donald Ludlam.

> No one spoke English and we thought we were being arrested. The police came on and took Bill off first, then everyone who was traveling with him, and no one could explain to us what was happening.

> Then suddenly we were divided up into two groups and put in the back of a couple of limousines. It was the first time since we left New York that we had any elbow room. We were being rushed to an airport. We didn't know where we were going, we just knew we were being rushed. Finally, at the airport a translator explained that we were being flown to Belgrade because we had to be onstage in less than four hours. Since there wouldn't be a minute to spare after flying there and getting from the airport to the theater, everyone started putting on their makeup and getting into costume on the plane.

"When the company got to London they didn't have enough money to fly to Yugoslavia," Ludlam later explained.

> I was in Belgrade, and the head of the festival said, "Is your company coming or aren't they?"

> John Brockmeyer called from London and said, "Don't worry, we're getting on a train, we'll be there for the opening." The head of the festival said, "Train is completely wrong! They must fly!"

> Three trains were stopped at the Yugoslavian border. The actors were taken off the train and driven to the airport. They didn't know what was happening. . . . I was at the theatre setting up all by myself. I worked with the lighting man in sign language. He said, "Do you want simple lighting or complicated?" I said complicated. We had thirty or forty minutes to go and no company, but I kept working.

All of a sudden I looked down and saw John Brockmeyer on the stage in complete costume and makeup, and I hadn't even started. He always was ready before I was —and I'd been there a week.

It was a unique performance. The cast hadn't slept for days. We hadn't seen each other since two months before in New York.

The company performed *Bluebeard* over a four-day period in a large, modern, luxurious, state-run theater in Belgrade. "Everything [else] at the festival was Grotowski-oriented," Ludlam complained.

It was disgusting. There was a Rumanian *King Lear* in plastic laundry bags. The front curtain hadn't been used at the festival in six years [until the Ridiculous employed it]. . . . The second night, after word got around [about the hilarity of *Bluebeard*], they were standing in the aisles, and we got standing ovations. They were so relieved to laugh. Everything else was coming on like gangbusters, trying to reform the audience's terrible vices. . . . *Bluebeard* won second prize in the BITEF festival of avant-garde theater in Belgrade. The first was a Serbo-Croatian *Hamlet*.

Susan remembered that during their stay in Belgrade, Ludlam was summoned to a meeting with the administration of the festival. "Charles later told us that in bickering over what we were to be paid, he was being argued down. And in order to be heard, he removed his shoe and beat it on the table in pure Khrushchev fashion."

Belgrade was followed by a four-day stint in Zagreb, where once again only *Bluebeard* was offered. "We played at the state-run comedy theater there, with old wooden seats," said Pashalinski. "And they went insane for *Bluebeard*. During and after the rape scene, there was this incredible rattling sound as the audience was shaking their seats and stomping on the floor with their feet, creating thunderous sounds."

Ludlam was particularly gratified by the "fantastic gothic set" which the Zagreb crew designed for *Bluebeard*, with a cuckoo clock and large burning candles. Adding some local color, the prop woman placed a statue of the Virgin Mary on the piano. In a fit of inspiration, Ludlam as Bluebeard caressed and fondled the icon to commence the seduction scene, before beginning his onslaught of Pashalinski.

After Zagreb came Vienna, where it seemed like everything that might go wrong did.

Perhaps in the effort to preserve their city's old-world charm, the Viennese were fiercely conservative. While "flower power," peace signs and other elements of the Love Generation had already infiltrated the rest of the Western world by 1971, anyone resembling a Hippie was scorned by the Austrians. Genuine American-bred Hippies were considered worse still. There was one incident when Vehr and Black-Eyed Susan entered a Viennese restaurant only to be impolitely escorted out by the proprietor. Susan recalled Vehr telling her that the owner of another restaurant indicated a sign in the window saying, "No Dogs Allowed," while pointing to Vehr's long hair.

A large part of the ungracious attitude the Ridiculous encountered in Vienna was indirectly related to John Vaccaro. Vaccaro's Play-House of the Ridiculous had participated in the festival in Belgrade simultaneously with the Ridiculous Theatrical Company. But while Ludlam's group went to Zagreb immediately following the festival, Vaccaro's went to Vienna. As Donald Ludlam recalled:

> Vaccaro and the Play-House of the Ridiculous had been run out of Vienna for being vile and obscene just before we got there. And once we arrived, there was some confusion between us because of the similarities in our names. The Viennese were set up to give us a hard time no matter what happened. We had to move around from place to place every other day.

In Vienna, the group stayed in youth hostels and student dormitories. This led to all sorts of problems, however, because many of these places had strict 10 PM curfews and imposed fines if you transgressed. "Each of us was making less than two dollars a day performing in Vienna," recalled Donald Ludlam, "and the fine for getting back into the dormitories was maybe five dollars a night. Sometimes we couldn't get in again."

But the real problem in Vienna was that the work was not well received. Given the conservative attitudes, the company was prohibited from exhibiting any nudity onstage, without which the actors were thrown off pace, and *Bluebeard* did not go over very well. Then too, the space they had to perform in was hardly conducive to success. "They put us in a PTA meeting hall," Ludlam explained. "There were fluorescent lights on the stage, linoleum on the floor of the theatre, folding chairs — it was just horrible.... We couldn't have any sex in the play. There was no advertising, just a poster on the door, and it was in a back alley."

With poor attendance and ultimately an aborted run, the actors weren't even earning enough to eat proper meals every day, and many of them actually went hungry. Ludlam had recently received a Guggenheim grant, which helped carry him through these rough days and provided for Liebowitz as well during their tour. Brecht "tried to show a little kindness by taking us out one by one for an occasional meal," said Pashalinski.

> But it was a very desperate situation. Also, people had to go off their macrobiotic diets, which was hard. There wasn't a vegetable to be eaten in all of Vienna. There were potatoes and pork, and wonderful pastries, of course. And you know, Jack [Mallory] had actually brought a suitcase of pots and pans with him so he could be macrobiotic throughout the tour.

The enterprising Brockmeyer stole some Viennese cookies and Grand Marnier from a grocery store, and later told Calvin Tomkins this is what he lived on "for several days."

There was also growing resentment as others realized that Ludlam and Liebowitz were dining in relative splendor while they were starving. "We complained to Charles all the time, and he was unhappy about it," continued Pashalinski.

> But the agreement was we were supposed to be living off the box office, and simply not enough people were coming. Lohr Wilson became especially irate about the sense of deprivation we were enduring, and he blew off steam at Charles on a bridge over the Danube. He threatened to throw Charles into the river. This made it easier for the rest of us, after he vented our hostility. He got it off all of our chests and then we felt better. But poor Lohr felt considerably worse.

Adding a bit of unwanted irony to the company's travails, the Vienna portion of the tour was supposed to be the most extended leg of the itinerary. Though there were a couple of unsuccessful performances of an expurgated version of *The Grand Tarot*, the planned premiere of *Eunuchs of the Forbidden City* was canceled, and the stay in Vienna was cut down from three weeks to two. The company pushed ahead to Berlin, the next stop on the agenda. Though Berlin became the most extensive and delightful part of the tour, a premature arrival proved tricky.

After some cries of desperation and haggling on Ludlam's part, the director of the Forum Theater in Berlin—where the troupe was scheduled to perform *Bluebeard*—managed to unearth cash advances. There remained the question of where they would stay. The majority spent a couple of nights on the outskirts of the city with a communal group of vegetarians. The living conditions were rather squalid, however. The basement apartment, if it could be called that, was unheated, and the nights were frigid. The company ate nothing but beans the first night and slept on a cement floor with a sort of campfire in the middle of the room.

Only later did the theater director explain that he had gone out of his way to find accommodations with other macrobiotic people, when it would have been just as easy to put them up in a regular hotel. More comfortable arrangements were quickly made with various friends and patrons of the theater for housing in vacant apartments or spare rooms. The director also provided each with a daily food allowance, which proved a mere pittance compared to what was to be earned once *Bluebeard* became a runaway hit in Berlin.

Donald Ludlam stayed with a Hare Krishna member for a couple of weeks. Pashalinski and Rando were guests of a member of the theater's board; they lived in a room off the pantry, which was a common kitchen for the entire apartment house. Black-Eyed Susan stayed in the rear of a macrobiotic food store with the couple who owned it; but she also made the mistake of having an affair with an artist, which became very torturous for her when she learned he was married.

Whereas Ludlam and Liebowitz were, to all evidence, monogamous during the tour, Vehr had numerous romantic encounters. Brockmeyer fell hopelessly in love with a Berliner and proceeded to have a torrid affair with him, no matter how he was feeling about Gary Tucker back home. Indeed, Brockmeyer was visited by his new German lover in Copenhagen, after the company wended its way there as the next stop on the performance tour.

As reported by Pashalinski, the most peculiar romantic circumstance was when Brecht "put the make on" Rando. Though he was thoroughly aware of her entanglement with Pashalinski, Brecht went so far as to invite Rando to accompany him on a side trip to Switzerland. She declined.

Brecht organized a more local excursion one night to East Berlin, on the other side of the Iron Curtain. He took Ludlam, Liebowitz, Brockmeyer, and Black-Eyed Susan to the Berliner Ensemble, his late father's company, where they saw *In the Jungle of Cities*. After the performance, they went with Brecht's sister Barbara to the actors' canteen. But there was a problem in returning to West Berlin. Regulations required travelers to return via the same route by which they had entered. Brecht had arrived earlier via "Check Point Charlie," which was open all night, but the rest had come via another portal that was now closed until morning.

"We tried returning with Stefan," recalled Susan,

> but they wouldn't let us over the border. When I protested, one of the guards
> cocked and clicked his gun, and Charles said, "Susan, he's not kidding!" We ended
> up spending that night at Barbara's home. The next morning, the cleaning lady
> arrived as we were preparing to leave. And when she saw Charles and John with
> their long hair, she ran into the streets screaming, "Polizei! Polizei!"

It's impossible to say just how much Stefan Brecht's formidable reputation and influence helped make the Ridiculous such a success in Berlin; but *Bluebeard* was embraced by both the critics and the public alike. Its run was extended at the Forum, where there were also well-received performances of *The Grand Tarot*. According to Ludlam, the Forum was "the only avant-garde theatre in Berlin. All the young, beautiful, gifted people go to that theatre. It's all focused, just the opposite of here."

Bluebeard's popularity prompted a nightclub called the Reichskabaret to invite the company to perform. This is where *Eunuchs of the Forbidden City* had its world premiere, after it had been canceled in Vienna the month before. The cramped quarters were difficult to play in, given Wilson's extravagant set and costume designs, with enormous wigs and headdresses and long, flowing Oriental robes. The audience sat in old wooden classroom chairs with inkwell stands now accommodating their beer steins. With Rando functioning as a business manager and scrutinizing the nightly income, the cast received a percentage on the sale of the beverages at the Reichskabaret. According to Pashalinski, "We were each earning ninety dollars a week in Berlin" and living in relative splendor.

Susan remembered that, "In keeping with his inclination to involve amateurs in the productions, Charles invited some local Germans to appear as extras in *Eunuchs*, in non-speaking roles. Of course, they were young and quite attractive, and scantily clad."

"The German press received [*Eunuchs*] with gratitude and enthusiasm," Ludlam observed. "Critics saw our style as a welcome alternative to the 'Living Theatre approach,' which dominated the European theatre scene then. Europeans appreciated our extensions of tradition — the habit of mining out, redefining and exploiting traditions rather than merely destroying them." The play was referred to as a *Kostume Klamotte*, German slang for a ragbag of fancy costumes or thrift-shop chic.

Apart from Black-Eyed Susan, who was tormented by her deceptive lover and their affair gone wrong, everyone was having a grand time in Berlin, where they ended up spending a month. They were especially pleased that hashish was so readily available. Vehr had discovered one street full of young boys sitting on stoops, shaving off the hash from huge logs and selling it for a pittance.

A minor crisis occurred during the run of *Eunuchs*, however. Ludlam was out walking one day when he suddenly doubled over in excruciating pain. At first, Brecht accused him of exaggerating his ailment; but after Ludlam was rushed to the hospital, it was discovered that he had kidney stones. He was anesthetized and had to remain still for hours so the stones could pass without doing any internal damage. Ludlam never really forgave Brecht for initially pooh-poohing his distress. This may have contributed to the permanent rift lurking in the near future for the two of them. But Ludlam was having still other problems with Brecht, who was frequently late and may have even missed a rehearsal or two in Berlin. Subsequently, Ludlam would tell Eric Bentley, "The greatest pleasure in my life to date was firing Stefan Brecht."

The company performed briefly in Frankfurt, before moving on to their next stop in Copenhagen. Having endured so many trials and challenges on the tour, Ludlam mustered the courage to fly for the first time. He went by plane with the company to Denmark. They played there for less than a week, in a space so small that the audience was seated in the rafters. But with the nude scenes intact, *Bluebeard* went over as well with the Danes as it had with the Germans. Among the funnier-if-you-had-been-there anecdotes of the trip, Vehr invented a phrase, "Bravelschnitz Feenerschnab," which he kept inserting in conversation whenever the whim dictated. The theater in Copenhagen had a backstage sign-in sheet for the actors, and Vehr got a lot of mileage out of making these words his signature. It perplexed the theater personnel who kept asking questions about who this strange Feenerschnab was.

After finishing the run in Copenhagen, there were a few days to kill before the company was scheduled to perform in London, the final leg of the tour. While almost everyone including Ludlam pressed on to England, Pashalinski and Rando visited Amsterdam, and Brockmeyer returned to his lover in Berlin.

At first, everyone apart from Ludlam and Liebowitz stayed in an inexpensive, out-of-the-way hotel in London. But they quickly transferred to bed-and-breakfasts when they realized they were equally accommodating and even more economical.

Bluebeard opened on November 16 at the Open Space, a Fringe theater, which is the London equivalent of Off Broadway. The Open Space was run by Charles Marowitz, with whom Ludlam and Liebowitz stayed. It was a small house, with the performances given on the floor while the audience sat on risers. Though there were at least a dozen reviews, the English critics just didn't get it. To this day, the London press has not been favorably disposed toward Ludlam's plays. For one thing, British theater has an older and more respected tradition of drag performance than the American, and the response to the Ridiculous may have entailed a proprietary interest — as if to say that British actors could do better what Ludlam had appropriated from them in the first place. It was also symptomatic of the larger war for theatrical superiority being waged on both sides of the Atlantic.

As Ludlam later griped,

> The critics in London seemed annoyed with me. All the plays on words were lost on [them]. Then there'd be these incredibly lame lines from Trollope and they'd get a big resounding laugh every night. You felt like you were playing for a non-English-speaking audience.... In the reviews they praised the play but insulted our appearance. The phrase "these Americans" kept recurring. The reviews were admiring but grudging: "Americans Attempt Play."

Pashalinski recalled one of the critics writing: "The sex scene was enough to discourage any further displays of sex in public or in private." The only positive review was by Frank Marcus, the British playwright, who had recently had quite a hit in New York with *The Killing of Sister George* and risen above any British chauvinism.

Despite the notices, *Bluebeard* eventually enjoyed positive word-of-mouth in London. Having already seen the play in New York, Nureyev came one night and brought an army of friends. Though it finally caught on once the Mod crowd discovered it, *Bluebeard* ended its run shortly thereafter, as scheduled.

The day before returning to New York — in ample time to spend Christmas with his family, as always — Ludlam phoned his mother. "He said, 'We decided to stay over and won't be home until January,'" recalled Marjorie. "The next night, I was at my sisters' house and there was a knock on the door. It was Charles. He just wanted to surprise us this way. He had hidden his luggage in some bushes behind the train station, since he couldn't carry it all by himself."

IN THE FORBIDDEN CITY

Banners and furbelows, teeny umbrellas teetering on long poles, wigs like puff pastry, gilded
sneakers and combat boots — plus an occasional coach, sampan and palanquin — colorfully
evoke this fantastical Oriental empire.
— Mel Gussow, on *Eunuchs of the Forbidden City*

That desperate quality of needing to be at the center of things. . . .
— Wallace Gorell

Despite any hardships endured during the trip, the company's first European tour
proved, in retrospect, to have been an exhilarating experience. "It was a peak for
everyone, with nothing but highs and lows every day," said Lola Pashalinski. "It was
very romantic, being gypsies that way and the freedom it entailed.

"The trip had also been a maturing experience," continued Pashalinski. "On the one
hand, it was reassuring to see that the plays worked in so many different countries.
On the other, it made us realize we had to become more business oriented, that there
was more to maintaining a theater than catch-as-catch-can. The tour made us stronger
and a lot less naive."

Nevertheless, after the company returned, John Heys remembered having heard how
"Charles had fabulous accommodations while everyone else had horror stories to
report." There were horror stories of another sort to be reckoned with once they got
home, however.

With no advance notice, Gary Tucker had vacated the group house on Staten Island
and moved to Chicago, taking all the furniture with him. He also took along a
new lover, a fun-loving Italian guy whom everyone, including John Brockmeyer, had
met before the tour but believed to be just a friend. According to James Morfogen,
"Gary and I were hanging out a lot while they were all in Europe, and Gary didn't like
John's being there. John's increased position within the company, coupled with Gary's
difficulties with Charles, ultimately led to their breaking up."

In fairness to Tucker, he might have been forced to leave the Staten Island address. The
landlord, a Greek Orthodox priest who also lived in the building, was homophobic
and anti-Hippie. According to Susan, while she and Brockmeyer were on their extended
European tour, the landlord placed their personal possessions in the street to be

ransacked by neighbors. But even as they were fuming about having to relocate without their belongings (Susan found a three-room flat in a tenement building on Mulberry Street and Brockmeyer eventually moved in with her), Ludlam became furious with Tucker for an entirely different reason: This Ridiculous renegade reportedly staged his own version of *Turds in Hell* after settling in Chicago.

Ludlam was also contending with some unresolved conflicts that promised to disrupt his relationship with Robert Liebowitz. Though Liebowitz appeared to be quiet and overly submissive, he could actually be even more obstinate than Ludlam.

The two of them spent a relatively tame New Year's Eve with Pashalinski and Flavia Rando shortly after their return from Europe. More characteristic of Ludlam and Liebowitz's deteriorating relations was the night they had a public fight at a Gay Liberation dance. What began as a typical spat escalated into violence, with the couple hitting each other and needing to be pulled apart. (Minette, who happened to be present, was terribly embarrassed and pretended not to know them.) Brockmeyer often told the story of yet another evening when Ludlam phoned and begged him to come over, saying it was urgent. Just as Brockmeyer arrived, Liebowitz was taking off in a cab with Ludlam chasing after him screaming, "I'll kill you! I'll kill you!"

Their final fight, in the kitchen of their new apartment at First Street and First Avenue, where they lived only briefly, was equally violent. They threw Ludlam's beloved Fiesta Ware at each other, destroying the prized collection. In a fit of temper, Liebowitz stormed out of the building and jumped into a cab again. At first, Ludlam ran after him. But as he later told Pashalinski, he stopped running and asked himself, "What am I doing? This person is leaving me. Let him go." Ludlam finally grasped how destructive the relationship had become for both of them, and that was the end of it.

After the breakup, Ludlam wrote his occidental version of a haiku: "I hate all ex-lovers/ Want to risk it?" He later claimed that Liebowitz's addiction to speed had been the primary problem, without allowing for his own contributions to the emotional turbulence. The fact is, all of Ludlam's long-term romantic entanglements were volatile. He could never give what he could never get, which was the total devotion he craved. But the intensity with which he craved it was obvious to all of his intimates.

Despite Ludlam's continuing enmity, Liebowitz wanted to renew their relationship. Once he sensed Ludlam was unshakable in his resolve to shun him, he phoned Christopher Scott out of desperation. By then Ludlam had made it clear to Scott that "there wasn't a chance in the world they would get back together again." Scott invited Liebowitz over to the Wyoming and spoke to him on Ludlam's behalf, explaining how "it would never be." (Some years later, Ludlam was walking down Christopher Street with a friend and noticed Liebowitz approaching. Ludlam quickly crossed the street to avoid him.)

In the spring of 1972, Ludlam relinquished the apartment on First Avenue he had found with Liebowitz and briefly moved into the St. Mark's Hotel. This is where Viola, a cat his mother had given him some years earlier, was impregnated by a big white tomcat that slipped in through an open window. Viola was part calico and part Persian, with a big bushy tail. According to Minette, she had Ludlam's personality: dynamic and very talkative.

In keeping with her master's suddenly peripatetic existence, Viola had her litter that summer at Ludlam's next residence, a borrowed apartment on East 6th Street between First and Second Avenues. He was staying in a large parlor room in the rear of a townhouse, overlooking a garden. But within a month or so, he had to relocate again. He lived briefly in an apartment on 11th Street and had an affair with a married man who lived in the building, while the man's wife and child were in California.

Ludlam also spent a couple of months with Richard and Anne Roberts in a townhouse on Tompkins Square North. To supplement his welfare income, Ludlam worked part-time at the Roberts' health food store, down the block from the Paradox restaurant. Ludlam next stayed temporarily with Scott and Geldzahler in their new home on West 9th Street. Geldzahler had recently purchased this traditional Village townhouse with Arthur Lambert, a roommate at the Wyoming, and moved there in February with Scott. At first, Ludlam stayed in Lambert's quarters on the top floor; but after Lambert returned from a trip, he moved downstairs into the maid's room.

Ludlam's further foray into the western — and more notoriously gay — section of Greenwich Village prompted him to forsake his longtime roots in the East Village. At Scott's suggestion, he went to a well-established real estate agent, Mrs. Courtney Campbell, and found a rent-controlled apartment on Morton Street — a few blocks south of Sheridan Square and just west of Seventh Avenue — where he would live for the rest of his life. It was a prewar, Deco building, relatively large for the neighborhood, and situated on a quiet, tree-lined block. The rent, $135 a month, seemed steep at the time; but with a sunny southern exposure commanding a view of the lower Manhattan skyline, the top-floor apartment had a lot of charm. With a narrow corridor connecting the tiny rooms, Ludlam made the larger area in front his living and sleeping quarters. There was a smaller room in the rear, which became his overcrowded office and library; the hallway connecting them led to a miniscule bathroom and a cramped kitchen.

After many months of shuffling from apartment to apartment — often as a guest or as a boarder — Ludlam's living arrangements finally acquired some stability in the fall of 1972. This was part and parcel of Pashalinski's impression that the company's first European tour had proved to be a maturing experience. Just as the obstacles encountered during the trip compelled Ludlam to become more business oriented in managing the company, he was trying to bring some order into his personal life as well.

It was roughly half a year before Ludlam moved to Morton Street that *Eunuchs of the Forbidden City* had its New York premiere. The play opened in March, three months after the company returned from Europe, at the Theatre for the New City. This new theater space was located at the foot of Bank Street in Westbeth, a phone company building near the Hudson River that had been converted into subsidized apartments for artists. (The Theatre for the New City would become more established after moving into what had been the Gate Theater on Second Avenue, where it remained until the early eighties, after which it relocated to First Avenue.)

Eunuchs was stylistically a hybrid play for Ludlam. It incorporated both the sprawling properties of his earlier "epic" pieces and the more coherent tendencies of *Bluebeard*. It meandered in terms of scope and structure, yet it had a cohesive plot.

With five acts consuming more than three hours of playing time, the long, byzantine saga follows the corrupt history of Tsu Hsi (1834-1908), the last Empress of China. When the play begins, Tsu Hsi (Black-Eyed Susan) bears the name of Orchid Yehonala. She is one of a number of concubines paraded before the Emperor, Chien Feng (John Brockmeyer), who is obliged to sire an heir. (Additional concubines are named Pervading Fragrance and Welcome Spring.) The conniving Yehonala increases her chances of being selected by bribing An Te Hai (Ludlam), the Emperor's villainous Chief Eunuch.

Against his mother's wishes, Chien Feng chooses the "immodest" Yehonala for her beauty, at which point, An Te Hai (pronounced "Auntie High" — an obvious pun about marijuana, and also possibly on the schmaltzy song from *South Pacific*) offers an aside to the audience, with all but a twirl of his Fu Manchu mustache: "What we eunuchs find most deplorable is the cocky attempts men and women make to distinguish between love of beauty and licentiousness, forgetting that one always leads to the other."

The next scene jumps a year ahead. Chien Feng is on his deathbed and Yehonala (now Tsu Hsi — "Toots" for short) coerces him to sign an "Edict of Succession," naming their infant son heir to the throne and thereby seizing control of the empire for herself. The Emperor's two brothers try to intervene and plot to kill their nephew, but the sly Tsu Hsi outfoxes them. The Boxer Rebellion, a revolution commenced by the peasants, ensues.

Despite the idiocy of her son, T'ung Chih (also played by Brockmeyer), Tsu Hsi will stop at nothing to maintain her power. Addressed, like all the emperors, as the "Son of Heaven," T'ung Chih develops into a spoiled brat, fond of Western toys such as electric trains and chemistry sets. When T'ung Chih is of age and on the verge of assuming the throne, his mother sees to it that he dies. "Yes, of course I destroyed him," says Tsu Hsi in her calculating, cutthroat manner. "I destroyed the infant to create the boy. I destroyed the boy to create the man. And now I destroy the man to create an empire. His end will be excruciating, protracted, agonizing, perfect." After many other murders and intrigues set in the Forbidden City, Tsu Hsi — who has become known as "Our Dragon Lady of the Eunuchs" — also kills a cousin.

As deviously evil as Tsu Hsi is, An Te Hai, the Chief Eunuch, proves equally duplicitous. It is Ludlam's marvelous conceit to suggest that all of the emperors of the Manchu dynasty were "born sterile" and secretly sired by the Chief Eunuch. Though eunuchs are castrated by definition, An Te Hai's gonads are intact. Near the end of the play, he is about to be beheaded for having "eaten out the twats of our virgins and sucked the cocks of our young boys until they have shot off their hot loads of come into your mouth and rammed their stiff little rods up your backside. For these sacrileges we must decapitate the eunuch who usurped the pomp of the Son of Heaven." Just as the ax is about to fall, An Te Hai exclaims, "It was heaven. For six hundred years, the Sons of Heaven have been born sterile. I am no eunuch. I am Hung (*He whips out his schlong*), Father of Emperors. The secret weapon of the concubines!"

The gory and serious-minded story is relieved, of course, by jokes throughout. The script is peppered with Confucian-style puns ("One rat dropping spoils a pot of rice," "Two barrels of tears are no substitute for plastic surgery," and "It is a careless rat that chews on a cat's tail") as well as with plays on words ("Ah, why so blue, my wanton little Won Ton?"). The stage is overladen with concubines and eunuchs, permitting no end to Ludlam's trademark lascivious humor.

When the imbecilic T'ung Chih comes of age, a concubine named A Lu Te (Bill Vehr) is sent to him:

> A Lu Te: It is time, Lord of Ten Thousand Years.
>
> T'ung Chih: Time for what?
>
> A Lu Te: It is time for you to pluck my cherry blossom.
>
> T'ung Chih: Pluck your cherry blossom? What do you mean by that?
>
> A Lu Te: It is time for you to drink the wine in my cup.
>
> T'ung Chih: What wine? What cup? What are you talking about?
>
> A Lu Te: It is time for your horse to enter my valley.
>
> T'ung Chih: (*Aside to* li lien ying) Is she crazy or is she drunk?
>
> Li Lien Ying: (*Aside to* a lu te) Remove your robe. That should turn him on.
>
> A Lu Te: (*Slipping her robe down over her shoulders*) It is time for you to find yourself in me and I in you.
>
> T'ung Chih: What do you want? Speak plain Chinese.
>
> A Lu Te: I have come to make love. Roll in hay. Get laid. Do the business. Fuckee fuckee. Get it?
>
> T'ung Chih: I've never done anything of this kind before. Are you a eunuch?
>
> A Lu Te: No, something better. Something special. (*She climbs on top of him*) Feel anything?
>
> T'ung Chih: No.
>
> A Lu Te: (*Kissing him*) Feel anything now?
>
> T'ung Chih: Nothing.
>
> A Lu Te: (*Rubbing her body against him*) Anything?
>
> T'ung Chih: Nothing.
>
> Li Lien Ying: (*Aside to* a lu te) Try this on him.
>
> A Lu Te: What is it?
>
> Li Lien Ying: It's a special preparation the eunuchs know to assist in the art of love, where all else fails. It's called a popper.

Since only eunuchs and women are allowed in the Forbidden City at night, Tsu Hsi is sexually frustrated. The following is one of the funnier sex scenes:

> Tsu Hsi: We have been so bored. Everything is so boring.
>
> An Te Hai: Boredom is the absence of yum-yum.
>
> Tsu Hsi: Yum-yum?
>
> An Te Hai: Yum-yum.
>
> Tsu Hsi: Oh, pooh! What can a eunuch do?

AN TE HAI: Let me satisfy you the unique way. (*Aside*) Hope I don't muff it. (*He eats her out*) Slurp! Slurp!

TSU HSI: Enough! You eunuchs are strictly for vegetarians. A queen needs a piece of meat once in a while. Why do they castrate you guys, anyway?

AN TE HAI: I don't think of myself as castrated. I think of myself as extremely well circumcised.

TSU HSI: That's funny, you don't look Jewish....

The script also contains the obligatory praise for an androgynous state of being: "There is none like you under heaven," Li Lien Ying tells Tsu Hsi. "You are not male or female, Majesty, but more than either, greater than both."

By now, the notion of being neither male nor female, "but more than either" and "greater than both," had become a credo for Ludlam. While he explored this theme in *Bluebeard* through the mad scientist's search for a "third genital," he was investigating it here through the concept of a eunuch. As a castrated creature, however, a eunuch is neither "more than either" a male or female, nor greater than both. But by presenting An Te Hai as a eunuch impostor, Ludlam got to have his androgyny and his "schlong" too.

The play ends on a signature, self-mocking note, as Tsu Hsi positions herself on a "tiny stage" upon the stage and A Lu Te inquires, "What kind of play is this?" Li Lien Ying responds, "Pages full of unlikely words / Handfuls of hot bitter tears / They call the author a silly fool / Because they know not what he means." By ridiculing himself directly in this fashion — as he tended to do in a number of his plays — Ludlam was undermining any criticism others might hurl at him by beating them to it. Self-ridicule was part of his manifesto and his theater.

The production of *Eunuchs of the Forbidden City* was fortified by a $10,000 grant from the National Endowment for the Arts and a smaller one from the New York State Council on the Arts. These represented the company's first public grants and were yet another reassuring sign of progress and maturation. It cannot be overemphasized just how seriously Ludlam viewed the responsibility conferred by such grants over the years. Time and again, referring to public funds he and the company had received, he would say, "My country has called on me."

In the case of *Eunuchs*, most of the money was poured into the show's fabulously extravagant costumes and sets. At least one critic felt the money was misspent. In his review for *Women's Wear Daily*, Martin Gottfried, who had been the company's first mainstream champion, attacked Ludlam for making such decisions. "Money is endangering the Ridiculous Theatrical Company," began Gottfried's review:

> but true to its tradition of reversed logic, the danger is not a lack of money but an
> excess of it. Charles Ludlam's divine institution is hardly lolling in dollar bills (an
> appropriate image) but it has used badly needed funds for handsome costumes
> and scenery rather than for technical equipment, a financial cushion and perhaps
> some small pay for the actors. Ironically enough, the new-found good looks of
> production have weakened one of this company's greatest assets — its look of
> tacky opulence.
>
> This irony tells something about Ludlam's thinking. Though he has always
> insisted that his productions do not mock (old movies, old styles, old extrava-
> gance) but emulate, it has always been tempting to disbelieve him because who,
> after all, would really admire obsolete vulgarity?
>
> Quite clearly, Ludlam would, as he is the first to say. The sequins were shabby
> simply because classy ones were too expensive. Now that they can be afforded,
> they are there.... Were Ludlam's true love for cultural relics less true, the grand-
> ness of his work could never be possible, for it depends on sheer honesty. Yet, in
> appreciating everything that he has done — his work has been classically theatrical
> and elating — have we been laughing at or with him? (If you laugh at him, he will
> laugh at you.)

Most of the other reviews were quite favorable. Mel Gussow wrote a glowing notice
in *The New York Times*. He found *Eunuchs* "an exuberant and robust work, one of
Ludlam's most polished and comic inventions." He had special praise for the performances by Black-Eyed Susan and Ludlam, and went on to explain: "The words are a
heady blend of movie taglines, puns, cartoon balloons, pop-tune lyrics, perverse
anachronisms, fabricated Confucianisms... and pure Ludlamisms."

Unlike Gottfried, Gussow reveled in Lohr Wilson's sets and costumes, which he labeled
"spectacular," as his description went on to suggest: "Banners and furbelows, teeny
umbrellas teetering on long poles, wigs like puff pastry, gilded sneakers and combat
boots — plus an occasional coach, sampan and palanquin — colorfully evoke this fantastical Oriental empire." Gussow also included a wonderfully evocative description of
Ludlam: "Glowingly robed, ribboned and garlanded, his hair pointed like spires of

shish kebabs, his fingers knuckled with blue baubles, Ludlam is a resplendent and madcap clown."

In his review for the *Village Voice*, Michael Smith took a rhapsodic approach. "I'm at a loss how to convey the idiosyncrasy, charm, and distinction of Ludlam's style," he wrote. "The play is conventional in form, harking back to such classical models as Racine and W.S. Gilbert. In a way it is restrained, dignified, almost stately. At the same time it is, by its own claim, ridiculous."

In addition to his review, Smith interviewed Ludlam for the *Village Voice*. "I feel that I'll define what ridiculous is as a genre," said Ludlam, who continued:

> The actor is a person who can believe anything. Theatre of the Absurd refused to take anything seriously, sabotaging seriousness. Ridiculous takes everything seriously, searching for its meaning. It's ecological theatre — we take the abandoned refuse, the used images, the shoes from abandoned shoe factories, the clichés, and we search for their true meaning. We are recycling culture. My problem has been to go beyond the circular cyclical structure of the absurdists which represented a morbid philosophical position they had come to. We represent the positive side of nihilism. Instead of negating anything we try to find its inherent value. If you learn to use the waste of society you can not only make yourself very prosperous but bring an era of prosperity for everyone.

Given who the reviewer was — or more to the point, who she was to become — perhaps the most intriguing response to *Eunuchs* was written by Fran Lebowitz, in an East Village publication called *Changes*. While recognizing the play as an "ambitious" and "epical" work, Lebowitz had serious reservations. "The sex scenes are too broadly played for my comic tastes, and the play is somewhat burdened by the now almost obligatory gender switches. The attempts at humor do not always come off and, when they do, it is often due to the acting rather than the writing."

Though *Eunuchs* never achieved the popularity of *Bluebeard* or a number of subsequent works, it played at Westbeth through April 16 before offering a sequence of midnight shows on weekends at the St. Mark's Cinema. It then transferred to the Performing Garage, where it played from mid-May to the end of June 1972. Apart from the mixed responses of Gottfried and Lebowitz, the majority of the critics were enthralled with *Eunuchs of the Forbidden City*, and apparently more so than the larger public. It is, to be sure, one of Ludlam's more difficult works. There is an unresolved tension in the script — between the serious and the inane moods, as well as between the epic and well-made play formats — which relied too much on the performance to tip the scales one way or the other.

If the lurid references and scenes in Ludlam's plays seem excessive several decades after they were written, they also reflected the country's libido during those years. As Eric Bentley recalled, when he went to see *Eunuchs*: "I had arrived late, and the ticket man was actually screwing a man in the box office. I thought, only with the Ridiculous Theater can one be a voyeur for a real fuck before getting into the theater."

It was also around the time of *Eunuchs* that Bentley encountered Ludlam at Man's Country, a bathhouse on West 15th Street. Bentley felt very awkward about it, but he joined Ludlam in his cubicle, and they proceeded to have a lengthy discussion about the theater. What struck Bentley most about their session was how casual it all seemed for Ludlam: They might as well have been chatting at home or in a restaurant, even though they were both naked underneath the towels wrapped around their waists. Whether or not this was the first time they actually had a full-fledged conversation, "It was certainly the time we opened up to each other," said Bentley. "And Ludlam had removed my sexual embarrassment by making it clear that that was not what we were about to do at all."

⁊⁊

At first, Mario Montez did not rejoin the company for *Eunuchs*. But he made a couple of guest appearances as a concubine in the "selection" scene during the play's run. Ludlam added the character, called Broken Blossom, specifically for him. Though Montez's film career seemed to be waning rather than waxing as he had hoped it would, he was otherwise engaged on the stage at the time. When *Eunuchs* opened at Westbeth, Montez was costarring in an all-male version of *The Trojan Women* with Jackie Curtis. Christopher Scott, on the other hand, returned to the acting fold with *Eunuchs* to play Su Shun, the Grand Councilor. (Though Scott had served in various design, business, and advisory capacities on intervening shows, this was his first performing role since *When Queens Collide*.) Two new people — Georg Osterman and Richard Currie — joined the Ridiculous with *Eunuchs* and remained with the company even after Ludlam's death.

Osterman had moved to New York in August of 1971, shortly after graduating high school in Great Falls, Montana, where he had grown up. One of a dozen children, Osterman had had a strict Catholic upbringing, as did so many who gravitated towards the Ridiculous. He attended parochial school and loved performing in school pageants and plays. He had moved to New York to become an actor, but first got a job as a "gofer" at an advertising studio, and was living at the YMCA on West 63rd Street.

The sexual revolution that had started the previous decade was now in full swing, as Osterman's memories of his early days in New York attested:

> The "Y" was a totally frightening experience for me. Here I was, this eighteen-year old "chicken" [youthful gay sex object], surrounded by all these old men forcing themselves on me. I had never experienced anything like that before, except when I was thirteen and Father Kendricken took me to the movies. But that's another whole can of worms. Anyhow, the "Y" was driving me crazy. I couldn't sleep at night for all the advances. One guy chased me back to my room and put his foot in the door. I slammed the door several times on his foot.

Though Osterman quickly began a three-year affair with a young, would-be musician named Michael Angarola, it was via a detour that would have confounded even Cupid's aim. "While I was staying at the 'Y'," said Osterman,

> Al Carmines' production of *Everyman* — starring Geraldine Fitzgerald — was playing next door at the Ethical Cultural Center. I snuck in on a rehearsal one afternoon and sat up in the balcony, fascinated with the whole thing. There was this really cute boy there named Billy whom I kept noticing around the neighborhood. This girl I knew from Montana was in the production and she finally introduced me to Billy. He was Puerto Rican and so cute. I just fell head-over-heels.

> Billy had a lover at the time named Bobby. I left the "Y" and moved in with Billy and Bobby, and we had a little *menage à trois* for a brief time. I found out later that Bobby wanted to kill me after he discovered Billy and me in bed. I think Bobby purposely introduced me to Michael [Angarola] in hopes that he would lure me away from Billy.

Osterman moved in with Angarola that November, in an apartment on West 16th Street. "Our apartment was so outrageous," Osterman said.

> We were paying $245 a month, which was more than anyone we knew was paying

to live in New York. We found out that we could get a bigger place for half the price in the East Village, so we moved. Everybody moved around like crazy back then. We never stayed in an apartment more than a year.

Anyway, at first I was totally monogamous with Michael, except for some instances. Michael had recently met Bill Vehr and they had had this little fling. The company had just returned from their European tour and Bill told Michael all about it. He also said they planned on expanding *Eunuchs of the Forbidden City* and would be adding some extra roles. So Michael told Bill about me and my interest in the theater.

Vehr phoned Osterman and invited him to John Heys's apartment on East 6th Street, where he was living at the time. They talked for a while until Vehr noticed the time and suddenly announced, "We better get going." They immediately went to the first rehearsal of *Eunuchs* at Westbeth, and Osterman was struck by the energy and pandemonium. "Charles was saying, 'We need some concubines here,'" recalled Osterman, "and I hadn't a clue what a concubine was. Bill told me, 'It's a little tart,' and I understood that perfectly."

Osterman had been terrified about meeting the Ridiculous clan: He had been a great admirer of the troupe from afar, having read the published script of *Turds in Hell* in *The Drama Review* before coming to New York. It was like the proverbial dream-come-true for an eighteen-year-old hick from the sticks. But as anxious as Osterman was, Ludlam instantly made him comfortable during the rehearsals, and he also felt somewhat protected by his alliance with Vehr.

"I had a kind of crush on Bill," continued Osterman.

He was one of the funniest people I ever met. I remember once when Bill and Charles together convinced me that female clowns were known as "cloons." At first, I didn't believe them. But they were dead serious and it was such wonderful acting on their part. I was always learning so much great theater history from both of them, and I thought this was part of that. I remember thinking to myself, "I'm not this little ignorant country bumpkin anymore: I know what a 'cloon' is."

Of the many practical jokes Ludlam and Vehr collaborated on, the most novel — in a decidedly pre-AIDS era — involved a heterosexual couple who were patrons of the Ridiculous. The woman had announced that she had no trouble accepting homosexuals as friends, but kept insisting that she could not understand "how one man can swallow another man's sperm." Ludlam and Vehr invited the couple over for a Chinese dinner they had prepared. It was Vehr's idea for both of them to ejaculate into the first course — *Egg Drop* soup! The unsuspecting patrons raved about the unusual taste and texture of the soup, but they were never told the secret ingredient.

Ingesting sperm related to another of Osterman's memories. During the run of *Eunuchs* at Westbeth, both Ludlam and Osterman were living within a couple blocks of one another in the East Village, and they often walked home together. "Charles and I 'got it on' once during *Eunuchs*," recalled Osterman.

> Charles started the ball rolling by kissing me after inviting me up to his place. . . . It was the first time anyone ever came in my mouth, and I didn't know how to handle the situation. With this garbled voice, I asked Charles, "What do I do now?" He looked at me like I was from Mars, and he told me to spit it in a plant over in the corner.

Osterman had no way of knowing that "making it" with Ludlam was tantamount to an initiation rite for company newcomers. Though Ludlam was still smarting from his recent breakup with Robert Liebowitz, and floundering as he frequented the baths in his desperate search for another attachment, his onetime interlude with Osterman was part of a different program. Sex was his way of greeting anyone who came onboard, a way for both securing adoration and establishing a bond. (As Ethyl Eichelberger would succinctly summarize the situation, "You had to sleep with Charles, or he didn't trust you.")

Osterman also verified what many others have reported: "Though we were all involved with Charles to some degree or another, he and Susan would push and pull at each other during rehearsals in a different way, very much like a married couple."

It became apparent that Ludlam would apply different directing methods with each of the core members of the company. He tended to be analytical with Brockmeyer, demonstrative with Pashalinski, and impatient with Mallory. With Vehr, he would often step aside and have a private conversation to make a point or iron out a problem. With Black-Eyed Susan, he could become outright vicious. "I think he innately understood how tough I was," recalled Susan, "even though I didn't know it. We both had tempestuous, fiery temperaments." The variations in Ludlam's approach as a director obviously reflected the different relationships he established with each of these people, and revealed just how mercurial he could be.

Osterman particularly appreciated the way Ludlam encouraged everyone to make the character they were playing his or her own by introducing personal props or costume enhancements. "During this opium-smoking scene, when all the others were passing around a pipe, I brought in my own bubble pipe and blew bubbles," recalled Osterman. Though he considered Lohr Wilson's costume designs "amazing" and "gorgeous," he also recalled, "They were the most painful costumes I ever wore. Wearing those enormous wigs was like putting your head in a vice. They were made with wires and extremely tight as they pressed into your temples. It was because they weighed so much, probably more than five pounds. Mine had little chopsticks with tassels hanging off the ends."

Osterman also remembered drugs, and especially marijuana, being ubiquitous during the run of *Eunuchs* — although Ludlam now frowned upon them in the theater. When the show was transferring to the Performing Garage, Ludlam attempted to adjust one of the scenes. He wanted Su Shun, the Grand Councilor, to appear more lecherous — so he added some concubines for him to chase after, portrayed by Osterman, Edgardo Franceschi, and Arturo Esguerra (a printmaker and friend of various members of the company). But the three actors were so high on dope that they missed their cue the first night this business was to be inserted. "Charles was not happy about it at all," said Osterman. "In fact, he was furious, and decided then and there to cancel the addition. So it never really happened."

According to Richard Currie, who did the lighting design for *Eunuchs*, "As far as I was concerned, the show was totally undirected. I would sit in the lighting booth every night and block it in my head as it was taking place, because it was never really blocked at all. And it was very, very slow. It was very self-indulgent. It had lots and lots of magic in it, but it just took forever to perform."

Though Currie didn't join the Ridiculous until *Eunuchs*, he had crossed paths with the company a number of times before then. Indeed, his background indicates just how incestuous the theatrical community can be.

Currie was born in Rochester in 1938, making him five years older than Ludlam. Like Ludlam, he had staged puppet shows and other children's entertainments during his grammar school years. After studying theater at Ohio State University, he became a lighting designer. John Vaccaro was an acquaintance of Currie's in Ohio. "John wasn't in school," said Currie, "but he lived right there. We hung out at the same coffee shop and I saw him in a couple of school productions. He was also the only beatnik any of us knew. He smoked marijuana, which was unheard of in 1959. He gave messy poetry readings in a basement coffeehouse. One time I took him to a gay bar in downtown Columbus to read some of his poems. It was called Rosemary's, after the woman who ran it, and there was a stage in the bar for entertainers and shows. John was hooted off the stage."

After graduating from Ohio State in 1962, Currie affiliated himself with Brown Ledge, a summer theater in Colchester, Vermont, where he has spent most every summer since. The mid-sixties entailed a lot of theater work for Currie, including various Off-Broadway theaters, bus-and-truck gigs in the Tristate area, and finally a number of shows at the Public Theater in 1968, including *Hair* and the Martin Sheen version of *Hamlet*. In the fall of 1968, while Ludlam and the Ridiculous were performing *Turds in Hell*, Currie got together with a few friends and opened a drug-oriented club called Cerebrum.

A cross between an old-fashioned speakeasy and a newfangled "happening," Cerebrum was the outgrowth of a more makeshift project Currie had previously formed with the same trio of friends — Ruffin Cooper, Bobjack Callejo, and John Brown — who were all involved with theater. After countless sessions of smoking dope and playing around with music and lighting effects at home, Cooper proposed that they cater "loft parties." As Currie explained, "People were smoking socially, and we would come in with tambourines and projection equipment and weather balloons. We'd project images, take care of the music, and give them participatory instruments to play."

Cerebrum was a far more elaborate concept. "The Electric Circus was in full swing at the time, and one could go there and be stoned and have a nice time," continued Currie.

> So we started talking about putting together a club, and created Cerebrum. You arrived at the southeast corner of Broome and Crosby Streets [in Soho] and there was no sign or anything, just a lighted doorbell. You pushed the bell, a door opened and shut behind you, and you were suddenly in a totally black box. This voice said, "Welcome to Cerebrum. Do you have a reservation?" After you identified yourself, a wall slid aside and you stepped into what we called the Orientation Room, where you removed your shoes. Then you paid the entrance fee. Originally it was two dollars on Tuesdays, three dollars on Wednesdays, four dollars on Thursdays — something crazy like that.
>
> After you paid, you turned this corner where you were greeted by a guide in a

white robe, who was obviously naked underneath. You got into a robe yourself, and you were taken up a ramp and turned another corner at the top, where you suddenly came upon this elongated room that was entirely white. There were seven floating platforms down either side of the room, with a runway in the center, all done in white carpeting. Each platform could hold four to six people, and for the next couple of hours, you'd spend twenty minutes at each of the environments. Each platform had a control panel in the center. The first would be upbeat music: You could listen to headsets and play tambourines. There were slide projections and we filled the room with fog.

Several people said that it always looked like it was going to become an orgy at any moment. And sometimes after the fog would clear, we'd have to stop couples from fucking. They were sitting together with their robes over each other. One night, Eugenia Shepard [a fashion columnist] fell off of a platform and broke her leg, which gave her and us lots of publicity.

Cerebrum opened in the fall of 1968 and closed the following spring. But it's telling that the club's pioneers were approached by some businessmen who wanted to franchise the operation in college towns across the country. "At that point everyone thought that marijuana would be legalized within the year," recalled Currie.

Having seen them in *When Queens Collide*, Currie recognized Ludlam and Pashalinski when they patronized Cerebrum. According to Currie, Ludlam was a frequent visitor. Considering his subsequent, longtime tenure with the Ridiculous, it's curious to note that Currie was not a fan of the early plays. "A group of us had been to see *Queens*," claimed Currie. "We were all traditionally trained theater people, and we thought it was crude and scattered. It was fun, but it was too chaotic. I really fell in love with the Ridiculous with *Bluebeard*."

Currie knew Robert Liebowitz prior to joining the company with *Eunuchs*. "We used to hang out and smoke dope together," said Currie. When the company returned from Europe and Ludlam was scouting for a lighting designer for the American premiere of *Eunuchs*, Liebowitz mentioned Currie's name. Then Ludlam ran into Bobjack Callejo at a party. Vaguely connecting Callejo with Currie because of his visits to Cerebrum, Ludlam asked him if he thought Currie might be interested in doing the lighting. Callejo replied, "Yes, *we* would."

Though Callejo was primarily a set designer, Lohr Wilson was already fulfilling that role for *Eunuchs*. Callejo seized an assistant lighting credit with Currie as a means of lining up future design work with Ludlam. Together, they brought in the third Cerebrum entrepreneur, John Brown, to supervise the sound on *Eunuchs*.

According to Currie, Ludlam never interfered with someone else's lighting design, "because it had never been his field." But this was apparently only the case in terms of his collaborations with Currie. In fact, he often intervened in other aspects of a production. After Callejo started designing for Ludlam, he complained to Currie, "Charles takes all the fun out of theater because he wants to do it all himself, and it's no longer a group effort."

ço

During the run of *Eunuchs* at the Performing Garage, Ludlam met yet another lover. Two years younger than Ludlam, Robert Beers was an extremely bright and striking youth. "I was born in Pennsylvania, went to school in Connecticut and Ohio, and then I came to New York because I found myself in the middle of this revolution called the sixties," said Beers.

Beers quickly fell in with the Warhol crowd by frequenting Max's Kansas City. In the spring of 1971, Beers befriended Jackie Curtis, who persuaded him to participate in his play *Vain Victory: or The Vicissitudes of the Damned*. An apotheosis for Curtis, this was the underground megahit of the season, which ultimately had four different incarnations. Featuring a rotating cast of countless performers, six-page monologues, and impromptu developments, it was the Off-Off-Broadway equivalent of a DeMille epic. Beers also performed with the Living Theater during the extensive run of their signature piece, *Paradise Now*. He had been attending Ludlam's plays "as they came out," and considered them "sensational."

One night before Beers saw *Eunuchs*, he and Bill Vehr were both stoned and picked each other up cruising on the street. "We didn't get along sexually at all," claimed Beers. "But he saw that I had James Joyce in my house. We both liked opera and baseball. He was the only other gay person I knew who liked baseball."

When Vehr eventually introduced them, Beers told Ludlam how much he admired *Eunuchs* and mentioned that he would like to work with the Ridiculous. It was a couple of months later, or sometime in the summer of 1972, when Ludlam and Beers ran into each other at a bookstore and had their first substantial conversation. Beers had a rental on Fire Island, and Ludlam accompanied him there several times for what evolved into a summer fling.

"Charles was a genius, and geniuses are all of a piece," said Beers,

> the way they eat, the way they fuck, the way they speak, think, dress, read. They have the crystalline simplicity of the cosmos at their disposal. Charles was a very, very, very strong personality. He could also be extremely benign. He was a force for good, for light, for laughter, for love, for beauty. One of the reasons his work was so fabulous was because his personality imbued every centimeter, every costume, every line, every bit of set and staging. Everything bore his unified imprint.

Beers emphasized that Ludlam and he were not lovers, per se. It was more a matter of "having an affair and becoming friends with an erotic history together," explained Beers.

> Now that I'm older, it seems to me that sex is so simplistic, but society tries to make it more complicated. In order for it to happen there has to be a positive and a negative polarity, and I think everybody gravitates towards that polarity which is most comfortable for him or her. Charles and I in a sense shared a polarity — we were both very dominant personalities. But I was in love with him, so I adjusted myself sexually to him. I had to be submissive. But I certainly couldn't have made a steady diet of it.
>
> In all modesty, I could keep up with Charles intellectually and he liked that. But I couldn't keep up with him sexually because he was an Aries: It was slam-bam-thank-you-ma'am sex. And I'm a Scorpio. For me sex was an entire universe. I set aside whole weekends to do nothing but have sex with a particular person. For Charles, sex was an act like eating, defecating, sleeping. After a certain point, we didn't have sex anymore. We became very good friends and it was just talking, talking, and talking. When one is in the presence of that sort of visionary, you would have had to have been very stupid not to shut your mouth and just listen.

In addition to becoming a lifelong friend of Ludlam, Beers inevitably joined the company and performed in the next few plays. He did not, however, consider himself an actor. Ludlam gave Beers a role in *Corn*, his next opus. But even before then, Beers played Hecate, the Devil's advocate, during a benefit performance of *Bluebeard* in October. The event was held at Sammy's Bowery Follies, a long-abandoned dive of a nightclub where the rich went slumming during the Depression. Since it had been neglected for many years, it was filthy and creepy—which made it an ideal venue for *Bluebeard*. But with no curtain, no backstage, and no wings, it was hardly appropriate for a performance. The players had to keep going "across and under and back-and-forth and up-and-down to this pit" of an unkempt basement to reach their makeshift dressing room. Worse yet, there was only one narrow, railing-less staircase for making the trip. (Between the traffic jams and her anxiety over reports of rats in the basement, Black-Eyed Susan missed a cue one evening.)

To play Hecate, Beers wore a dress for the first time in his life. Originally owned by Helene Weigel, Bertolt Brecht's wife and Stefan's mother, it was an antique, "bat-like" creation with protruding spikes on the shoulders. In the scene where Bluebeard gives Hecate a snake (Larry, John Brockmeyer's pet), Beers was flustered and his dress came undone, revealing his privates. Luckily, a smoke bomb went off as part of the staging, glossing over the mishap. But bewildered, and finding the live snake particularly difficult to deal with, Beers flung poor Larry back at Ludlam.

Since Mario Montez proved unavailable for the *Bluebeard* benefit, Ludlam offered the part of Lamia "the Leopard Woman" to Georg Osterman. Osterman recalled that during the performance, "a lot of people were on acid, and Charles was totally unaware of how many of us were doing drugs. This was when Charles was into his macrobiotics, and when Charles was really into something, he wanted everybody else to be, too."

As Beers saw it, "Charles was consistently inconsistent. Over the years, he either smoked a lot of cigarettes or none at all. He smoked marijuana or he didn't. He drank or he didn't drink. He had hamburgers or he was totally macrobiotic."

એ

Christopher Scott brought a visiting friend, Wallace Gorell, to the special benefit performance of *Bluebeard*. After meeting him later that night, at a post-performance party, Ludlam proceeded to have one of the more significant and revealing love relationships of his life with Gorell.

"Before going to the play, Chris told me that Charles was a genius and that it was going to be the funniest thing I had ever seen," said Gorell. "We sat in the back row because we arrived late, and Chris just sat there hooting and howling and having a ball. But I sat there appalled. I had studied acting at Carnegie Tech, and I had a very clear idea of what was good theater. And this definitely was not it. It was a travesty!"

As soon as the performance was over, Scott told Gorell he wanted him to meet the company. "I was just terrified," recalled Gorell. "I let Chris know what my reaction to the play had been, but I didn't know what I was going to say to anyone else. But then Chris dragged me down into this pit, and there was the company, with their grubby little makeup boxes. It just seemed so sad to me, their thinking it was real theater."

In fact, Scott could enjoy the production more than Gorell because he brought with him his experience of the play's previous incarnations. Gorell had arrived with high expectations, only to encounter a thrown-together version of the play, within an extremely squalid environment. But despite Gorell's abominating *Bluebeard* and his terror of meeting Ludlam, "I immediately liked him," said Gorell.

> It was astonishing to me, because I was in a state of real dread. But Charles was so friendly and attentive and interested in me. I don't think it had to do with me as much as with the moment. The whole question of what I thought about the play seemed beside the point. And although I didn't find Charles the least bit attractive during the play, I found him very attractive as soon as I met him.

A large group of the players went for a post-performance supper, and then to a private party on West 11th Street. Ludlam, Scott, and Gorell sat together on the floor of the large studio apartment, rapt in conversation.

Before long, Gorell discovered himself with Ludlam on a mattress in a corner of the room. "We were on the bed where all the coats were piled," reported Gorell.

> We ended up having sex while the party went on around us. We had chatted each other up, then we started kissing, and then we had sex. It was oral sex, mutual sixty-nining, and everyone around us took it in their stride. It was beyond thinking. It was complete intoxication. It was also very much of that period. Everyone was stoned but me. But Charles and everyone else had been smoking lots of grass. . . . And then we had this six-month relationship.

Gorell, who was twenty-seven when he met Ludlam, had only had sex with a man twice before, and considered himself "more heterosexual, or possibly bisexual. I just wasn't capable of identifying myself as a gay man." But following their public spectacle at the party, "We spent all of our time together for the remainder of my stay in New York, or the next few days," recalled Gorell. "We spent a lot of time at his place. Charles had just gotten the Morton Street apartment, and we went looking for furnishings. We also spent a lot of time in bed. And we went for walks. He took me to delis on the Lower East Side and to a funny reptile shop on Bleecker Street."

Gorell's father owned an aluminum storm window factory in Pennsylvania, which conducted a lot of business in and around New York City. "I made sure I was on the company plane every time it came to New York," said Gorell. This is what enabled Ludlam and Gorell, despite the distance, to pursue their affair over the next six months. They saw each other weekly for a few months, and every other week after that. Their visits consisted of three- or four-day weekends. Though Ludlam and Gorell never corresponded, they spoke frequently on the phone when apart.

Whenever they were together, they led a highly active sex life: "as many as three, four, or five times a day," said Gorell. "Charles was very physical. We were all over the place, but it was all just oral and manual kinds of sex. There was never any fucking in either direction."

Given his rampant promiscuity, it's curious that Ludlam frequently introduced the topic of monogamy in his discussions with Gorell. "He insisted many times that he was monogamous by nature," continued Gorell,

> That he had extensive periods of having sex with lots of different people, but that when he was in a relationship, he didn't want to have sex with anyone outside. This was a recurring theme in our conversations while we were having the affair. He wanted to be assured that I wasn't seeing anyone else, and he wanted to assure me that he wasn't.

Gorell was apparently the first person to whom Ludlam expressed such views. According to Gorell, the subject came up at a dinner party they attended at Scott and Geldzahler's. Unbeknownst to Ludlam, Geldzahler had previously seduced Gorell himself; and now he asked Ludlam, "What would you do if you found out Wally was seeing someone else?" A livid Ludlam replied, "I'd throw my miso soup in his face."

"Henry loved playing the 'bad boy'," added Gorell, "and he loved that the communication had taken place without Charles realizing that it had."

The fact that Gorell considered himself a heterosexual — albeit a flexible one — intrigued Ludlam even as it presented him with a challenge. But his yearning for a monogamous relationship was further indication that, following both the European

173

tour and his tempestuous relationship with Liebowitz, Ludlam longed for some sort of stability. It may have also been prompted by his recent recovery from a bout of hepatitis, a common sexually transmitted disease within the gay fast lane.

Gorell knew better than to share his negative response to *Bluebeard* with Ludlam. When he finally and foolishly did, "Charles was horrified," recalled Gorell. "He wasn't defensive, but offensive. He became very arch, and said that he hoped I would get beyond such a narrow-minded perspective."

In view of Gorell's having studied acting at Carnegie Tech, Ludlam pontificated further:

> Yuck! The stuff they teach you in drama school nowadays is so stupid — all that naturalistic blather. It's dis-empowering and unhealthy, and not what one wants from a theatrical experience. Unless you live the reality of the play and remain outside the reality of the play at the same time, you're being denied the theatrical experience. Trying to win over the audience into imagining that they're a fly on the wall, or that they should lose themselves in the experience, robs them of just how glorious it can be.

Ludlam and Gorell strongly disagreed on a number of issues. Gorell remembered being particularly startled when Ludlam revealed he was against abortion. Rather than acknowledge any residual Catholic influence, Ludlam justified his position by saying he was sure that many of his friends had been "unwanted" children. (His vehemence on the matter may have had much to do with his unresolved relationship with his father, and his feeling unloved by him.)

The biggest source of strife between Ludlam and Gorell concerned their relationship. Ludlam was anxious for them to live together on a permanent basis, and Gorell kept resisting until he finally flat-out refused. "Very early in the relationship," said Gorell, "Charles acted with absolute certainty that he wanted me to move to New York and live with him. He thought it was perfectly appropriate that I would share his life in the theater, since I had studied acting." But Gorell was more inclined at the time to a bucolic existence. He intended to move to the country and run a farm.

The conflict was exacerbated during their fourth month together. While Gorell's parents were away on a vacation, Ludlam visited him in Indiana, Pennsylvania. One morning, Ludlam pressed the issue of Gorell's moving to New York and Gorell responded, "It's just too urban for me." Later that afternoon, when they were alone in

Gorell's father's office, the persistent Ludlam resumed the argument. "He said, quite perceptively, that he thought the reason I didn't want to live with him was because I was a gay homophobe," recalled Gorell. "He said it in a very needling way, as I was walking past him to get to a filing cabinet. I kicked him in the shin, and for days after that, whenever there was a lapse in conversation, he said 'I just can't believe you kicked me.'" In fact, Ludlam referred to the episode for months afterwards. He would always prove hard-pressed to put any hostilities behind him.

Gorell eventually admitted to Ludlam that he couldn't view himself as a gay man. There was, however, another reason he chose not to live with Ludlam, which he didn't dare bring up. "I never told him that he was a very difficult man," said Gorell, "overpowering, and very trying for me whenever we were in the company of others. The shift in the way he treated me when others were present, from when we were alone, became intolerable."

When it was just the two of them, Gorell felt like "a full and equal partner, someone whose concerns and interests were on a par with his own." But as soon as anyone else entered their realm, he felt like "this person Charles just met on the street for whom he had no concern whatsoever, and whose ideas were certainly of no interest."

When Gorell confronted Ludlam with this behavioral pattern,

> Charles became huffy. He essentially said that it didn't make any difference how he treated me around others because I knew how deeply he felt about me. He also said that he needed to maintain a certain persona in public. But I couldn't help concluding that he was driven to behave that way in public for more deeply seated reasons. When others were around, it was like he was afraid that he wasn't going to get his share of attention.

Gorell observed this same dynamic between Ludlam and other members of the company. Once he won someone's adoration, Ludlam no longer needed to perform for them in the same way.

"It was this desperate quality he had," explained Gorell,

> his really needing attention. But when we were alone, he was completely relaxed and there was none of that desperation. In a group of people, Charles did not draw anyone out as to their opinions, except to deflate them, or to use them as a springboard for his own ideas. Charles commanded an absolute deference from

everyone. He accepted input from others, but he was always the arbiter as to whether something was or wasn't a good idea. At rehearsals, he always had the prerogative to go off on lengthy digressions. But if someone else wanted to, he would say in this imperial way, "Can we get on with this?"

In one of the best-articulated perceptions of Ludlam's personal motivations, Gorell continued:

> Charles was quite in control of how he manipulated people. But I don't think he
> was in control of that desperate quality of needing to be at the center of things.
> There was clearly the need to be approved of and loved, even if it came across as
> insecurity at times. But Charles had designed for himself the opportunity to get
> that love in exactly the ways he wanted it. By writing, directing and starring in his
> own plays, he created the context in which he could be loved, respected, adored,
> and marveled at, in precisely the ways he wanted and needed.

The inevitable breakup between Ludlam and Gorell was at first protracted, then finally abrupt. It was catalyzed at a New Year's Eve party where Gorell met a woman — ironically, through Christopher Scott again — whom he eventually married. Her name was Diane Wolff, the only woman with whom Scott had ever had an affair. Gorell latched onto this budding liaison as a defense against his relationship with Ludlam. Initially, it was Wolff who pursued Gorell, calling him up while he was staying with Ludlam and inviting him out. Detecting a threat, Ludlam put his foot down and said he didn't want her phoning Gorell at Morton Street anymore.

Gorell stayed in Pennsylvania for a while, and phoned Ludlam before his next visit to announce that he would be staying with Scott and Geldzahler instead. "He was very hurt," said Gorell, "But he was still being considerate, and acted as if I were going through a rough patch I would soon get over. He was miffed and distant, but agreed to it."

Whenever Gorell saw Ludlam during his subsequent New York visits, Wolff was always with him. There was one especially catty encounter when Ludlam — with "heavily-laced irony," according to Gorell — told Wolff that he would "claw her eyes out." Although he offered the remark as a joke, there was a bitter edge to it.

While reflecting on his relationship with Gorell, Black-Eyed Susan recalled Ludlam telling her, "A person who claims to be thoroughly pan- or bisexual uses the male and female figures as parental figures, becoming the child who plays the mother against the father." But none of Ludlam's rationalizations could compensate for the degree to which he was hurt by Gorell's rejection, or his overwhelming need to be in a relationship again, following his previous breakup with Liebowitz.

❧

Corn, Ludlam's seventh play, opened in November of 1972, when his affair with Gorell was at its peak. During rehearsals at Sammy's Bowery Follies, Ludlam had to contend with a number of last-minute cast changes. Though Ludlam intended for Equity actor Tony Azito to play the part of Ruben, he left during the reading phase for a union job. Since Ludlam maintained his company on a shoestring budget by avoiding Actors' Equity and its minimum salary requirements, such defections always threatened and infuriated him the most. In this instance, he quickly gave the part to Robert Beers.

Another cast change occurred a couple of weeks into rehearsals. After leaving the company before their first European tour in the fall of 1971, James Morfogen attempted to make a comeback with *Corn*. Ludlam had, in fact, written the part of Moe Hatfield with him in mind, and Morfogen actually began to rehearse the role. But according to Morfogen,

> I sensed that I was being punished by Charles for having left the company in the first place. There was this how-dare-you-leave-me attitude, and I was having to pay for it now, when I returned. One day, Charles came up to me and asked me point blank why I had left. I could tell he was hurt. I liked him too much to be able to explain that I had felt like I was being persecuted at the time. I could tell that the company was evolving back then, and that Charles's tone towards me was changing.

Morfogen's defection actually stemmed from his buried dismay at being excluded from the European trip the year before. Ludlam replaced Morfogen in *Corn* with Richard Currie, who was already scheduled to do the lighting. Ludlam knew that Currie had some acting experience, and proceeded to use him regularly as a replacement player over the years.

Though Georg Osterman had played a concubine in *Eunuchs*, the role of Melanie in *Corn* became his first speaking part for the Ridiculous. "He still didn't give me much direction," said Osterman. "He probably figured that my 'hick' background worked well for the role. And it did."

If *Eunuchs of the Forbidden City* had been an unwieldy synthesis of the two predominant writing styles Ludlam was employing up to that time, *Corn* was a departure from both. Mel Gussow began his review by calling it "a change of pace and of face" for Ludlam. "A Finger Lickin' Good Country Western Musical," read the legend beneath the title on the handbill.

Not knowing where to go after *Eunuchs* or what to write next, Ludlam turned to Christopher Scott for advice. It was Scott, after all, who had helped Ludlam conceive of *Bluebeard*, his previous breakthrough. This time Scott, who was more and more heavily invested in Eastern mysticism and occult phenomena, consulted the *I Ching*, an ancient Chinese system used for predicting the future. Scott told Ludlam that "a play with a happy ending involving the union of lovers" was in the stars. Recognizing that comedies categorically have happy endings but that none of his plays had thus far, Ludlam instantly favored the idea.

Beyond being Ludlam's first — and ultimately, his only — musical, *Corn* abandoned the more serious undercurrents of his earlier works. It also dispensed with the androgynous themes he seemed to be exploring with increasing clarity up until then. *Corn* was more juvenile in tone, and designed primarily to entertain. It was also noticeably less lurid than any of his previous plays — it was good, *clean* fun, as opposed to the more naughty kind that had previously prevailed.

When *Corn* was in its conceptual phase, Ludlam described it as "a cross between *The Blue Angel* and the Lulu plays of German playwright Frank Wedekind, in country-western" style. His original name for *Corn* was "The Bluegrass Angel." But apart from the character named Lola, there is no other residual evidence in *Corn* of either Wedekind's plays or the classic film starring Marlene Dietrich. *Corn* is rather based on the hillbilly legend about the feud between the Hatfields and the McCoys.

In *Corn*, Wedekind's Lulu becomes Lola Lola (played by Lola Pashalinski), a fabulously successful country singer who has it all but wants to return to her roots. She's fearful of becoming "just another pop-art product, like old Kentucky recipe frozen TV dinners." With an element of mystery, her roots are in Hicksville, a small Appalachian town where "the Hatfields and the McCoys are still a-feudin'." Though her agent Dude (Vehr) is opposed to the idea, Lola Lola wants to offer the people of Hicksville "a free country-western jamboree" with her backup group, "The Lucky Stars." Since they're anticipating a crowd on the scale of Woodstock ("We're expectin' Rednecks, Rubes, Crackers, and Yokels from miles around"), their problem is locating a space large enough to present the show. The only solution would be if the Hatfields and McCoys were to agree to donate their adjoining cornfields.

In a shack on one side of the stage reside Maw McCoy (Brockmeyer) and her two daughters, Rachel (Black-Eyed Susan) and Melanie (Osterman). In a shanty on the other side live Paw Hatfield (Ludlam) and his two sons, Ruben (Beers) and Moe (Currie). Their properties are divided by a barbed-wire fence located center stage.

Ludlam conceived of Rachel as a mute character who winningly spoke her own symbolic language, "the language of the flowers." This actually came about after Susan told Ludlam that she had had too much dialogue in *Eunuchs of the Forbidden City* and would prefer less in the next play. "In *Eunuchs* I was wearing twelve-inch, hand-carved shoes which inhibited my movement," said Susan. "And since I had so many lines, I related to my character on a verbal level. This time, I wanted to be more in touch with my role physically."

In *Corn*, Dude approaches Maw McCoy while Lola Lola calls on Paw Hatfield, in hopes of gaining their mutual assent to combine their lands for the concert. But given the notorious feud that has passed down from generation to generation, the appeals only rile Maw and Paw.

> LOLA LOLA: Looks like this is gonna be a tough nut to crack, Dude. Seems like
> the Hatfields went and killed off all of the McCoy menfolk and the
> McCoys killed off all the Hatfield womenfolk. These are the only six
> left! We got the battle of the sexes on our hands.
> (*Shots are fired by the* HATFIELDS.)
> LOLA LOLA: Those male chauvinist pigs!
> (*The* McCOYS *fire a volley in return.*)
> DUDE: There's women's liberation for you.

Just when they're about to give up and return to New York, Lola Lola and Dude "notice Ruben and Rachel exchanging a kiss over the back fence," and realize they may be able to reach the parents through their children.

An overt parallel to lovers from feuding clans is drawn with the Capulets and the Montagues. As Dude says in the middle of the first act, "Why, this is a regular backwoods *Romeo and Juliet*!" — which is as succinct a way of summarizing *Corn* as any. Comparison with the Shakespearean tragedy is reinforced after Lola Lola learns in the denouement that she is actually the "illegitimate daughter of the thwarted love of Jebediah McCoy fer Mavis Hatfield;" since their families' feud had forbid them from marrying, "they took th' Lover's Leap," or committed joint suicide.

In the spirit of the Ridiculous, however, *Corn* is more of a comedy than a tragedy. Since it entails mistaken identities, and three feuding couples are "hitched up" in the end (Rachel and Ruben, Melanie and Moe, and even Maw McCoy and Paw Hatfield), its climax is straight out of *As You Like It* or *A Midsummer Night's Dream*, both pastoral romances. Indeed, *Corn* is a pastoral romance, though it could be better described as "rural" or "corny."

The equivalent of the *Dream's* Puck in *Corn* is Aunt Priscilla (Mallory), the town elder and local faith healer whose various spells and healing powers bring the three couples together. In her warning against sugar — an inserted bit of Ludlam's macrobiotic "propaganda" — Aunt Priscilla says, "Well, yer sweet tooth may say, 'Yes-yes,' but yer wisdom tooth better say, 'No-no.'"

Ludlam's most straightforward, lightweight comedy yet, *Corn* opened in mid-November at the 13th Street Theater. It pleased both critics and audiences alike and ran for ten weeks. Some performances were so oversold that additional seats were set up on the perimeter of the playing area to accommodate the overflow.

Though Mel Gussow conceded that "The fun is not primarily in the script, but in the performance," his review in the *Times* still qualified as a rave. Declaring the show "a thoroughly enjoyable entertainment," he praised Brockmeyer as "hilarious," Susan as "delightful," Ludlam as "antic," and Pashalinski as "a show-stopper." While acknowledging that "this is really more of a comedy with music added than a musical comedy," Gussow noted the "good traditional hillbilly" songs by Virgil Young, an aspiring composer who had already supplied technical support on a revival of *Bluebeard*. Young's Memphis background made him ideal for writing the show's songs. (His mother ran a beauty salon back home called Helen of Memphis, which inevitably became his nickname with company members.)

Michael Smith's review in the *Village Voice* was equally enthusiastic: "Ludlam has constructed the play with even more than his customary wit, decorative richness, and expertise, lightly turning every dramaturgic trick to the end of sheer delight. The good humor and transparent ease of *Corn* are irresistible and, it seems to me, an admirable direction for this talented company to have taken." Both Ludlam and Pashalinski would win Obie Awards for their performances.

Corn averaged a weekly box office income of $700. Confirming that Ludlam was developing a keener interest in business matters, he experimented with a new payment schedule for the actors. Each performer was guaranteed $25 a week, and the box office receipts were further split after expenses.

A backhanded sign of *Corn*'s success arrived later on in the mail, when the Ridiculous received a letter from an attorney for Kentucky Fried Chicken claiming the "Finger-Lickin' Good" phrase was copyrighted and could not be used in the show's publicity. This was near the end of the run, however, so nothing came of the matter.

Even more indicative of *Corn*'s success, Ludlam was approached by producer Jeff Britton, who had recently had a big hit with *The Me Nobody Knows*, an upbeat musical revue. Britton wanted to move *Corn* to Broadway, and at first Ludlam seemed amenable to the idea. Virgil Young worked on additional songs, and auditions were arranged with the Shubert organization. Much to Pashalinski's chagrin, Bette Midler, a fan of the company, was being considered for the lead. (Though it sounds rather apocryphal, Osterman claimed he was told that the Shuberts wanted him to transfer with the show — until they found out he was actually a man!)

In the end the Shuberts retreated. But, according to Pashalinski, it was Ludlam who ultimately backed out of any further negotiations after learning that Britton was talking to Lucille Lortel — the celebrated Off-Broadway producer — about moving the show to her own Theatre De Lys on Christopher Street. Jo Anne Worley, fresh from her overnight success in TV's "Laugh-In," had been approached to play Lola Lola. (After he had dinner with Worley at a "fancy" restaurant at Britton's expense, Ludlam assured Pashalinski that Worley's "only interest was in a free meal.") Though Ludlam claimed he was still willing to sell *Corn* as a property, he now refused to be in it himself. He was focusing instead on his next play, *Camille*, which commenced rehearsals at the 13th Street Theater two weeks after *Corn* closed at the end of January 1973.

Despite the reasons given, however, Ludlam's ambivalence over Britton's ambitions to move the show was part of a larger, defensive pattern. As much as he craved success, his fear of relinquishing control proved stronger. His past experiences with John Vaccaro (over *Conquest of the Universe*) and with Ellen Stewart (over *Bluebeard*) only reaffirmed his lifelong problem with authority figures, beginning with his father.

There was also the question of how to define success. Ludlam was much too critical of — and blatantly hostile towards — the Broadway establishment to receive an invitation to perform there with anything less than ambivalence. Correctly or not, he believed that he could not have the success of a Neil Simon without the mediocrity of a Neil Simon — nor could he know which came first, the successful chicken or the mediocre egg. Unlike the rest of his generation, he would take the counter-cultural message and clarion call of the sixties well into the seventies and eighties — and to his grave, for that matter.

In another respect, Ludlam also sensed — or was it feared? — that his appeal might be limited after all. If he moved to Broadway, how long would he be able to fill a large house? How quickly would he determine the extent of his audience and exhaust it? Was it a risk he could afford to take? Though he already considered himself the Shakespeare and Molière of his day, as more and more would gradually come to see him, was there really room for a Shakespeare or a Molière in a commercially-driven, common-denominator environment? Why test those hazardous and murky waters? Especially when he was doing so well on his own smaller scale — in his own way and on his own terms. Worse still, any company members who moved with the show would have to finally join Actors' Equity, thereby jeopardizing one of the key elements in maintaining the Ridiculous.

Though Ludlam eventually imagined that his Ridiculous Theatrical Company would become the classic American comedy repertory of its era, permanently installed at Lincoln Center, it would always be easier for him to sustain the dream by avoiding the address. The important thing was to continue to achieve, but without the setbacks that any failure on a large scale might inflict.

Lola Pashalinski, who had become something of a sensation as Lola Lola in *Corn*, implored Ludlam to reach an agreement with Britton and take the show to Broadway. Ludlam told her, "I know that if I followed your advice, I would become commercially successful. But it's not my way." For Ludlam — who, Minette emphasized, was a dominating Aries — success could only be accomplished in his own "way," on his own in-control-of-everything terms.

Looking back on those days, Pashalinski sees the conflict over moving *Corn* as a turning point for herself — one that came full circle seven years later, in 1980, when she finally left the company she had helped to create. With *Corn*, she began to realize that she was more eager for popular success than Ludlam or any other member of the core group. Though part of Ludlam wanted it too, he couldn't bring himself to make the compromises or risk his artistic integrity, an unavoidable pitfall he believed such success entailed.

In the meantime, Pashalinski, along with Virgil Young and his musical combo, performed a midnight spin-off of *Corn* at the 13th Street Theater in early March of 1973. (James Morfogen joined them for the hootenanny.) It was a country and western jamboree called "Lola Lola and the Lucky Stars," as if the characters from the play had taken on a life of their own. They repeated this musical entertainment the last two weekends of the month at the Theatre for the New City, also with midnight performances. Though it was very much the ensemble acting that made *Corn* work as well as it did, Pashalinski remained the star of the show, and this was the first time she experienced the sense of "having a separate career apart from the company."

Although he wasn't exactly relinquishing control, Ludlam did, in fact, suddenly demonstrate a willingness to take a backseat in terms of his company and his colleagues. Though he originally intended to play the part himself, Ludlam had given Black-Eyed Susan the plum role of Tsu Hsi in *Eunuchs of the Forbidden City*, virtually making it *her* play instead of his own. (Ludlam boasted that after Blanche DuBois, Tsu Hsi was the second greatest female role in American drama.) And in *Corn*, he made Pashalinski the star, once again as opposed to himself. Ludlam's primary motivation was gradually changing. The actor who wrote and directed plays in order to be able to perform was becoming the playwright and director who also acted. This was partially a conscious effort on Ludlam's part to remove himself from the plays so that he could view them more objectively and better mark his progress as a playwright. In a few years he would actually write and direct a play (*Der Ring Gott Farblonjet*) without even being in it — at first, anyway.

Though a pattern was emerging whereby Ludlam would dedicate successive works to different core members, *Camille*, his next play after *Corn*, was a gift to himself. It would become, arguably, the greatest role of his life.

THE ULTIMATE MASOCHISM

It is fatal to be a man or a woman pure and simple;
one must be woman-manly, or man-womanly.
— Virginia Woolf, *A Room of One's Own*

I think that I am the Camille of our era.
— Charles Ludlam

When looking back at a life, certain developments acquire the illusion or mystique of
having been inevitable. In the case of Charles Ludlam, perhaps none seems more preordained than his portrayal of Marguerite Gautier, better known as "The Lady of the
Camellias" or Camille. She was not only a courtesan, but also a tragic heroine whose
fictional history made her the subject of many different works.

Marie Duplessis, a celebrated Parisian courtesan who died of tuberculosis in 1847 when
she was only twenty-three, first appeared in fiction in 1848 as the central character of
the French novel *The Lady of the Camellias* by Alexandre Dumas, *fils*. But it was four
years later, in a drama by the same author, that she really captured the hearts of the
Parisian public and became an immortal figure. Next came Verdi's opera, *La Traviata*,
based on the Dumas play. The American silent film version of 1927, featuring Norma
Talmadge and Gilbert Roland, was followed by George Cukor's 1938 film, starring Greta
Garbo and Robert Taylor. There were even a couple of subsequent ballet versions by
John Taras and Sir Frederick Ashton. Though Ludlam incorporated elements from both
Dumas and Verdi, his adaptation was most faithful to the Cukor film.

Ludlam, who considered the original *Camille* "the most successful play ever written,"
had seen the Garbo film version when he was in college and had been "destroyed by it.
It moved me to tears," he later told Calvin Tomkins for his profile in the *New Yorker*.
"I developed such an identity with the role I began to think I *looked* like Garbo." As
Christopher Scott remembered, Marjorie Ludlam had — curiously — told her son
that she noticed a resemblance when he was just a boy, and Ludlam had clung to this
peculiar delusion.

Ludlam's attraction to the character "had a lot to do with my feelings about love and the
nature of love in one of its highest expressions. Is love, in fact, self-sacrifice, or is there
another way of expressing love?" Though he "always wanted to play Camille" and long
talked about it, he may have been a tad too intimidated to tackle his revered subject

during the first six years of the Ridiculous. He needed to feel more secure, and in time did, emboldened by the success of both *Bluebeard* and *Corn*. But when he finally went about the task of writing *Camille*, he nearly finished it in less than a month, completing the third and final act — the death scene — the week before the show opened.

"When I finished writing my adaptation, the comic and the tragic converged perfectly," he exclaimed with characteristic immodesty. "It went through a lot of changes, but it never lost that balance."

Camille is the story of a woman who lives by her beauty and charm, and who ultimately sacrifices everything for love, including love itself. Given all its tragic and campy excesses, the subject was a natural choice for Ludlam, who was becoming an expert at recycling what had long been considered culturally effete and turning it into something fresh and viable — or at least outrageous. But if *Camille* was destined to become one of Ludlam's greatest hits and to expand his audience even beyond the widening cult he had gained a few years earlier with *Bluebeard*, it may have been due more to his performance than to his script.

Ludlam portrayed Marguerite in a manner that both was and wasn't "drag." Metaphorically speaking, his performance as Marguerite can be viewed as the realization of Bluebeard's quest for a "third genital." Though, as others perceived, Ludlam evoked just about every grand dame of the Silver Screen from Garbo to Bankhead in his vocal effects, his voice would also descend occasionally into a more masculine register during the performance. And although he wore fabulous gowns and wigs in the part, he did nothing to disguise his chest hair, which announced itself prominently beneath the *décolletage* or open neckline of his costume in the opening act.

This daring maneuver was the single most commented-upon feature of the show. In spite of this slap-in-the-face to conventional drag, this toying with suspended disbelief by displaying masculine characteristics in a woman's dress, many critics described how they were convinced Ludlam *was* Marguerite, and how he brought them to tears in the tragic death scene. (*Camille* was, indeed, the most heavily reviewed show of the Ridiculous to date, with subsequent feature stories in *The New York Times* and elsewhere helping to extend its run.)

"I didn't want to engage in the kind of trickery that would make people think I was a real woman and then suddenly unmask at the end," Ludlam told Tomkins. "I wanted to lure them gradually into forgetting, to make it more amazing later on."

"I wanted the audience to keep in mind that I was a man playing the role," he also observed. "That's why I deliberately showed the hair on my chest through the open neck of Marguerite's gown in Act I. I was not trying, like the transvestite, to see how completely I could conceal my male identity. Wanting to look like a woman was not the point. Wanting to create the illusion of Dumas' heroine was.

"I pioneered the idea that female impersonation could be serious acting, an approach to character," he further boasted. "I became known as the actor who does real acting in drag."

In his portrayal of Marguerite, Ludlam was deliberately impersonating an aging actress who was in turn undertaking a youthful role. He was fascinated by the phenomenon of opera divas and older actresses tackling younger parts, as Bernhardt and Duse had each been famous for doing. He played the twenty-three-year-old character as if he were a fifty-year-old actress. Though it went unrecognized or at least unremarked upon by the critics, this subtext to the performance added yet another dimension to Ludlam's remarkable rendition of Marguerite, and made it even more poignant.

As Ludlam told many people, here was a character he felt born to play. Like Marguerite, he depended on the force of his personality to sustain himself, and he discovered love only after years of being buffeted by failed affairs and experimentation with rampant sex. There were other respects as well in which he clearly identified with her. Following his turbulent and ultimately unrewarding relationship with Robert Liebowitz, Ludlam's "marriage" proposal to Wally Gorell had only recently been rejected when he started work on the play.

Certain lines of Marguerite's seem to express how Ludlam himself was feeling at the time. When asked if she "believes" in love, Marguerite replies, "I don't know what it is. It's hard to believe in it if you've never had it." And when she finally begins to succumb to the advances of a new suitor near the end of Act I, Marguerite says, "Is it possible that he does love me? Or can I even be sure that I love him, I who have never loved?" But earlier in the scenario, she says, "I have nothing against love. It just makes such dull conversation." Ludlam, who felt he had been "through the mill" relationship-wise, was indeed feeling cynical at the time. If the pathos was to be found in an older actress speaking the lines of an ingenue, Ludlam could relate to both.

Other lines of Marguerite's can be read as a kind of confessional for Ludlam: "If I were to begin to take care of myself, I would die. Don't you see that it is only the feverish life

I live that keeps me alive? The moment that I am no longer amusing to people, they leave me . . ." and "I came up from grinding poverty and it stinks. I never want to go back to work in a shop and live in two little rooms with cucarachas and ratóns. No, no, I'll never go back! There are only two ways a woman may rise from the gutter and become a queen: prostitution or the stage. And believe me . . . I'd rather peddle my coosie in the streets than become an actress!"

Like Marguerite, Ludlam also led a "feverish" life and seemed to operate at a quicker tempo than most mortals. He exploited his daunting ability to be charming and "amusing," albeit often in aggressive ways. Rather than setting out just to secure adoration, he was also motivated by his obsession to avoid boredom. According to Christopher Scott, Ludlam was constantly preoccupied with his own hedonistic, urban gay lifestyle at the time, and turning to macrobiotics was a conscious effort to compensate for its punishing toll.

Marguerite's line about becoming "a queen" induced shrieks of laughter from gay audience members. But few in the house would have known that Ludlam had indeed peddled his "coosie" a number of times before writing *Camille*. Then too, his greatest ambition had always been to be an actor — or "actress," as the case may be.

Finally, Marguerite's protracted death scene seemed to relate directly to Ludlam's obsession with mortality. As he frequently told others, "No one is promised tomorrow." (Steven Samuels would later refer to this as Ludlam's "mantra.")

Not only was Camille a custom-fit role for Ludlam, but the story was an ideal choice for his paradoxical designs as a playwright. "Drama at its greatest is paradox," he stated. "To ask unanswerable questions is the secret to capturing the imaginations of humanity eternally." The play's sentimental nature coupled with its tragic overtones made it the perfect vehicle for his special brand of ridicule mixed with earnestness. Finding the comic in the tragic, and vice versa: This was Ludlam's mission in the theater as in life. On the hundreds of occasions Ludlam played the part, members of the audience could be found weeping at the end, even though they had been howling with laughter only moments before.

The first act, set in Marguerite's Paris drawing room on her birthday in 1848, establishes her appetite for an extravagant life as well as her aversion to love. She believes that one precludes the other. She is still contending with coughing fits and other symptoms of the consumption that had begun to assail her a year before. (When a friend arrives and says, "You're looking well," Marguerite responds, "I always look well when I'm near death.")

Christopher Scott recalled that Flaubert's novel, *The Sentimental Education*, was another influence on Ludlam's *Camille*. "Charles was astonished by the similarities between the life he was leading in New York during this period and Flaubert's luminous depiction of the Parisian demimonde of the 1840s, with its intermingling of the bohemian, the bourgeois, and the nouveau-riche worlds. Charles highlighted the connection in an esoteric line that drew a big laugh from the more knowledgeable theatergoers. As Nanine, Marguerite's servant, is setting the table, Marguerite exclaims: 'Not the Melmac, Nanine, the Limoges.'"

The Sentimental Education figured particularly in the hilarious party scene in Ludlam's version of *Camille*, where Marguerite's guests encompass the gamut of French society. For her birthday celebration, Marguerite is surrounded by her faithful servant Nanine; her chief paramour and benefactor the Baron de Varville ("I like older men. They're so ... grateful," says Marguerite regarding her duplicitous relationship with Varville, in a line that's actually adapted from Garbo's character in *Two-Faced Woman*); her naive childhood friend Nichette Fondue (the line "No, No, Nichette!" was Ludlam's throwaway reference to the 1925 musical *No, No, Nanette*, which was concurrently enjoying a successful revival on Broadway); her gossipy neighbor Prudence Duvernoy; another friend, Olympe de Taverné; and Olympe's lover, Saint Gaudens. Prudence arrives with the playboy Gaston Roué and a young romantic figure named Armand Duval, who is introduced to Marguerite as "the man who is more in love with you than any man in Paris." (As Prudence puts it — with buried references to both a Duke Ellington song and the cult classic film version of Clare Boothe Luce's play *The Women* — "He's got it bad and that ain't good. Ah, l'amour, l'amour!")

By the second act, set three months later, Marguerite is captivated by the sincerity of Armand's love, which she had dismissed in Act I but now reciprocates. She renounces the Baron and his wealth to summer with Armand in a country house she has rented. To finance their idyll, Marguerite has secretly been selling her expensive jewels and gowns.

One afternoon, while Armand is away in Paris, his father pays Marguerite an unexpected visit. He has come to implore her to "leave Armand altogether." He explains that, given her checkered past, she is destroying Armand's future chances for a worthwhile life. Seeing the wisdom of Duval Sr.'s logic, Marguerite abruptly terminates her affair with Armand and returns to Paris. By the time in Act III that Armand discovers his father's intervention, it is too late. He returns to Marguerite, but she is now on her deathbed. As she tells Armand, "If your coming hasn't saved me, nothing will. I have lived for love. Now I'm dying of it."

During the rehearsals for *Camille*, Ludlam told his cast that the audience would be in tears by the end of the play. He even subtitled the play "A Tearjerker," without meaning to be ironic. The cast was dubious because the play was strewn with Ludlam's typical puns and farcical wisecracks. Even the death scene had more than its share of zingers, as when Marguerite, confined to her bed, exclaims: "I'm cold. Nanine, throw another faggot on the fire!"

> **NANINE:** There are no more faggots in the house.
> **MARGUERITE:** (*Plaintively looking out at the audience*) No faggots in the house?
> Open the window, Nanine. See if there are any in the street.

Ludlam's phenomenal success in the role stemmed primarily from the conviction of his identification both with the character and with the aging actress portraying her. While playing for laughs, he also emphasized the underlying tragedy. It was similar to the unconventional way he approached the drag element of the performance by exposing his hairy chest framed by Marguerite's gown.

But it wasn't only the audience that was "lured into" suspending their disbelief and experiencing Marguerite's grief. Robert Reddy, a recent addition to the Ridiculous, recalled one night when he was standing next to Black-Eyed Susan backstage, during Marguerite's death scene. Reddy, who portrayed Susan's lover in the play, Saint Gaudens, was also responsible for working the snow machine. "The snow began to fall as the lights faded out of Marguerite's window," explained Reddy.

> And this one particular night as I was getting ready to do the scene, Susan was standing beside me and I could see her profile in the stage light. There were tears running down her cheek. And as I noticed that, I realized there were also tears running down my own. That had been happening every night, but we hadn't noticed it. We were absolutely reacting to the reality of that moment, in a play we were performing in ourselves.

Reddy had first joined the company when Richard Currie, a classmate at Ohio State University, invited him to help operate the sound for *Corn*. It was during the run of

Corn that Ludlam shrieked one night that he desperately needed some pipe cleaners before going on. "When I came back with them, Charles said, 'I'll put you in my next play for that,'" recalled Reddy.

Reddy was flattered to have the part of Saint Gaudens written with him in mind. It proved the first of a number of roles for him with the company. Reddy was amazed by Ludlam's schizophrenic methods as a director. "If you were reading from the script and left out a comma [in your interpretation], you heard about it from Charles — often at length. But there were also times when he'd just give you the idea for some lines and leave it up to you to create them. 'This is what I want to have,' he'd say, 'You fill it in.' It always seemed odd to me that he could go both ways."

Georg Osterman, who played Nichette, said, "Charles gave me readings of lines only a couple of times. For our tea scene in *Camille*, the funny thing was, we had played out that scene many times in real life. During the period Charles was writing *Camille*, we'd often talk about love and relationships and being with someone. He wanted to know what I thought about marriage. The relationship I had with Michael [Angarola] at the time, which was pretty monogamous, was something Charles wanted too, and this became the basis of Nichette's relationship with [the offstage character] Gustave."

Camille was rehearsed primarily at Robert Beers's apartment in Soho. The lengthy rehearsal period focused on the first two acts, however, since Ludlam refused to write the death scene till the eleventh hour. "He just couldn't bring himself to kill off Marguerite," recalled Richard Currie. "And he kept saying, 'This is going to be *Camille: A Tearjerker*,' and we all kept saying to ourselves, 'Oh, yeah, sure.' Because up until then, it was all pretty much fun and games during Acts I and II."

With the final act relatively unrehearsed, the last dress rehearsal went on till four or five in the morning. "Charles had unlimited energy, and he assumed everybody else did too," said Reddy.

> On all the shows, the last rehearsals would be extra long for all of the technical additions. With *Camille*, we had been rehearsing from four in the afternoon, and then at three in the morning, he'd say, "Now we'll work on the curtain call." As soon as someone rebelled and suggested we work on the curtain call tomorrow, it meant we would have an even more elaborate, meticulously rehearsed one, then and there. Whenever Charles was challenged, he became more obstinate and persistent.

A challenge of another sort was presented on opening night when Alexis Delago, a famous New York drag queen, arrived in a Camille-type getup of his own. Accompanied by a tuxedo-clad escort, Delago wore a magnificent gown embroidered with countless pearls and beads, offset, of course, by a period wig and makeup. While Delago sat in the front row and proceeded to laugh louder than anyone else in the auditorium, he further drew attention to himself by going to the bathroom several times. Ludlam took it all in stride by choosing to simply ignore the upstart, who, in fact, attended the opening night party.

During the extended run of the play, Ludlam had to prime himself to create Camille nightly. As he later explained:

> I had to convince myself that I was beautiful before I went on. If I believed it [the audience would believe it too]. Belief is the secret to reality. The Catholic Church understood that and made specific beliefs a virtue and thereby seized control of reality. . . . My belief in what I was doing made me gullible, the ultimate dupe, as well as a hypnotist. Self-hypnosis [leads to] mass hypnosis.

Perhaps part of what allowed Ludlam to believe he was "beautiful" had something to do with his nightly state of inebriation. Not only was alcohol a dressing room staple, but Ludlam was consuming it during his performances *onstage*. Robert Beers played Gaston, Marguerite's friend who visits her on her deathbed and hands her some medicine in "a little demitasse cup and saucer." According to Beers, "Her *medicine* was pure, unadulterated bourbon — it was Wild Turkey every night."

Beers recalled a particular performance when he advised the stage manager to fill the cup only three quarters to the brim, since he was wearing white gloves for the part and always feared spilling some of the drink on Camille's oyster-colored silk nightgown. "Charles was furious," reported Beers. "When I said, 'But it's much less dangerous that way,' Charles replied, 'Don't you realize the audience senses the danger? That's what keeps them watching. Without the element of danger, they'd fall asleep.'"

This was clearly not a macrobiotic period for Ludlam. The Cedar Tavern, a bar and restaurant that had been fashionable with Village artists in years past, had become his favorite, post-performance dining spot. Though he never really showed it, he would sometimes arrive in a semi-looped state, order a hamburger with fries, and drink countless beers while smoking his favorite, Nat Sherman cigarettes.

Regarding his nightly battle with the role of Camille, Ludlam claimed:

> When the audience laughed at my pain, the play seemed more tragic to me than
> when they took it seriously. A solemn audience trivialized the event. This [irony]
> of *Camille* was the ultimate masochism. I went out there to try to have a happy
> ending every night and got knocked down by every peripeteia of the plot. How
> could I continue such a pessimistic enterprise? Even in a boxing match both
> sides have a chance to win, but not me. I had to pretend that I had a chance.
> No wonder I was mad and sought all kinds of sensation and ran away from the
> boredom of mediocrity.

Though Ludlam embraced what was mediocre in the culture for the sake of transforming it into art, there was nothing he feared more than appearing mediocre to
himself or to others. Though he was a pioneer of camp and one of its greatest
exponents and practitioners (the term had been legitimized — although according
to Ludlam, bastardized — by Susan Sontag in her landmark 1964 essay, "Notes on
Camp"), he resented being labeled a "camp-meister." By its mainstream acceptance, the
camp movement had been misappropriated and had become too misunderstood for
Ludlam to be categorized this way, dismissing his other aims in the process. "Camp is a
way of looking at things, never what's looked at," Tomkins quoted him as saying.

Once the iconoclast, always the iconoclast: Since much of the breakthrough terrain
Ludlam already traversed had become acceptable and even chic to mainstream audiences — and drag had become so ubiquitous on New York stages by 1973 — he had
to give cross dressing some new twist. As a rule, whatever was acceptable to others
became objectionable to Ludlam. He was an obstinate contrarian first and last, always
ready to contradict himself at a moment's notice.

But Ludlam did not resent the mainstream attention that began to accrue with
Bluebeard, picked up momentum with *Corn*, and now brought him his greatest fame to
date with *Camille*. In response to the play's premiere at the 13ᵗʰ Street Theater in April
1973, the reviews were ecstatic. "This is no facile female impersonation, but a real performance," wrote Gussow in the *Times*, while also pointing out that "Ludlam never
forgets his gender, and neither do we."

Writing for the *Bergen County Record*, Emory Lewis exclaimed, "I have seen many stage
Camilles. Susan Strasberg was surely the most inept and miscast. Colleen Dewhurst was

the healthiest. In many ways, Ludlum [sic] is the most touching. . . . He manages to catch a quality of essential goodness and purity in the character. He plays on two levels at once — parody and true sentiment. It is an astonishing tour de force."

While noting how "the company is perfectly in key with Ludlam's own performance, which skillfully combines the best of Mary Pickford, Tallulah Bankhead, and the Wicked Queen from *Snow White*," Michael Feingold in the *Village Voice* wrote: "The sentimental story of a loose woman dying of TB is burlesqued by having a new sentimental story impasted over it: the one about an old drag queen's misery as he watches his young lover turn to real women."

In a briefer notice the following week in the *Voice*, Michael Smith took Feingold to task for reading into the play "a second layer of sentiment" that wasn't there. "Charles isn't playing an old drag queen . . . he is playing Camille," rebutted Smith. "Ludlam and his company may not do *Camille* straight, but they certainly do it fully. . . . Ludlam is one of my favorite actors, and he plays the role with the love it deserves."

Despite any internecine battles at the *Voice*, Ludlam was given his third Obie Award by the paper for his performance as Camille. This helped extend the run throughout the summer at the 13th Street Theater. It had a 10:30 PM curtain, Thursdays through Sundays. A puff piece in the *Daily News* (in Ernest Leogrande's "Night Owl Reporter" column) reported that, "When the dying Camille shivers in the third act and complains of being cold, it takes on an extra dimension to see the tricklets of perspiration from Camille's forehead and armpits." While the entire cast had suffered in the underheated 13th Street Theater the preceding winter, when they were clad in *Corn*'s skimpy Appalachian costumes, they now sweltered — under the heavy brocades and velvets of *Camille* — without air-conditioning.

♋

Camille's already extensive run would have probably continued had it not been for the company's previous commitment to a second European tour. They performed both *Bluebeard* and *Camille* in Geneva, Zurich, and Brussels, spending a week in each locale between October 1 and 21, 1973. Whereas the first European tour had been poorly organized and underfinanced, the second was relatively problem-free and profitable. In addition to comfortable accommodations and meals for everyone, there was even a petty cash fund maintained by Pashalinski, who recalled returning to New York with $2,000.

Part of the success of the second European tour had to do with its economies of scale. Not only was it more modest in scope — three weeks as opposed to three months, three cities as opposed to six — but Ludlam also limited the number of people involved. He eliminated the Saint Gaudens and Gaston characters from *Camille*, redistributing their lines to others. It was this pared-down version of the play that entered the company's repertoire for all future tours.

Beers, who played Gaston, was deeply upset at having been excluded. "I desperately wanted to go, and I was hurt," said Beers. "I understood the financial bind, and that he had to provide work for those members of the company who had been with him longer. But that was the benign aspect of it. It was also a kind of rejection.

"The thing about it was, the only time one really got to see Charles was when you were working with him," continued Beers. "The socializing was totally within the company. And I realized that, after I wasn't part of it anymore, I wouldn't be seeing him very much."

The nine-member troupe that embarked on a Swiss Air flight for Geneva included the core group — Ludlam, Black-Eyed Susan, Lola Pashalinski, Bill Vehr, John Brockmeyer, and Jack Mallory — in addition to relative newcomers: Georg Osterman, Richard Currie, and Richard Gibbs, who was then the company stage manager.

There was an incident in Geneva that became one of the company's beloved legends. Vehr and Brockmeyer were staying in a pensione run by an embittered, anti-American Swiss woman who enforced a peculiar curfew. In keeping with the regimentation for which the Swiss are famous, the bathroom was off-limits late at night. Out of necessity, Vehr was forced to defecate into the sink in the room. Brockmeyer observed him laboriously trying to wash his excrement down the drain and couldn't wait to share the story with the rest of the clan. (This circumstance would eventually become a recycled anecdote in *Stage Blood.*)

There was also a small brouhaha of sorts during the final leg of the trip, when *Bluebeard* was being performed at Theatre 140 in Brussels. The nude seduction scene created such a scandal on opening night that the police mobilized for the second of four performances. Jo Dekmine, the artistic director of the theater, feared that they would be closed down. At the last minute, Ludlam complied with Dekmine's request to eliminate the scene altogether. Since the rest of the trip had gone so smoothly and the company had been so well received, he didn't want to rock any moral boats in this, the final stretch.

In place of the seduction scene, Bluebeard and Miss Cubbidge merely shook hands. Ludlam said, "*Voulez-vous couchez avec moi, Madame?*" to which Lola replied, "*Oui! Oui! Monsieur!*" And since the "third genital" was deemed too phallic, the loofah sponge rigged with a chicken's foot was replaced by a head of cabbage with sparklers protruding from it. After Black-Eyed Susan was unwrapped like a mummy, Ludlam ignited the sparklers and said, "*Ah, mon petit chou.*"

Not that Susan required any extra illumination: She was having an impassioned affair with the theater's lighting director. After Ludlam learned about their liaison, he told her, "How very clever of you. No wonder he favors you in directing the spots."

There was some offstage drama when the company was departing Brussels and Bill Vehr was detained at the airport. The authorities had discovered some rolled joints in his cigarette pack and held him back. While everyone else boarded the plane, Ludlam remained behind to look after his colleague. Rushing to Vehr's defense, he went to the police station to try and straighten out what could have become a crisis. But it was only after the theater manager intervened that Vehr paid a nominal fine and was released later in the day. Ludlam and Vehr returned home the next morning, a day after the others.

Following their second European tour, the company performed *Camille* at Connecticut College in New London as part of the 27th American Dance Festival. Others participating in the annual event included Meredith Monk, whose company (The House) staged a new piece called *Paris Chacon*, and André Gregory's Manhattan Project, which presented its avant-garde version of Chekhov's *The Seagull*. But, as a follow-up report in the *Daily News* claimed, "few [of the offerings] ranged as far as Ludlam's *Camille*." To the eyes of a middlebrow *Daily News* critic, cross-dressing still seemed more outrageous in the mid-seventies than even the brazenly avant-garde work of Monk or Gregory.

As if to confirm that his theater was grounded in classic, comic traditions, Ludlam began offering Monday night workshops in *commedia dell'arte*, along with several company members. (Dating back to the sixteenth century, *commedia dell'arte* is based on improvisations within generic situations.) They acquired their students — anywhere from ten to twenty-five per session — by placing ads in the *Village Voice*. Though they worked out different *commedia* scenes for each class, they exploited their individual quirks by always playing the same stock figures. With her kewpie-doll demeanor and air of naiveté, Black-Eyed Susan was predictably the ingenue, Isabella. The privately vain Vehr was the handsome but impoverished Octavio. Pashalinski, who was perhaps the most independent-minded member of the company and certainly the eldest, did double-duty as both Captain Spavento, the braggart soldier, and an old crone. The lanky and fun-loving Brockmeyer was Pantalone, the foolish merchant; and bad boy Mallory was the pedantic Doctor, sometimes called Graziano. Ludlam, naturally, was Arlecchino or Harlequin, the clown. Their fabulous costumes were derived from traditional, *commedia* designs.

The short-lived classes in *commedia dell'arte* commenced soon after the company took up residence at the Evergreen Theater with *Hot Ice*. By the time this, Ludlam's ninth opus, began performances in January 1974, he could feel that his lifelong dream of running a repertory company was finally coming true. For the first time, the Ridiculous had what appeared to be a permanent home. Ludlam signed a three-year lease on the Evergreen Theater for $1,300 a month. It was located on East 11th Street, near Broadway. Though it had no fly or wing space, it had been recently refurbished with new seats and could accommodate 140 people.

Ludlam first got the idea for *Hot Ice* two years earlier, while he was living with Richard and Anne Roberts and working in their East Village health food store. While Ludlam admired the couple's holistic approach to life, he was never entirely comfortable with their espousal of euthanasia. His opposition to mercy killing stemmed from his Catholic upbringing: Such a background may have prompted a hyperactive and highly theatrical rebellion, but its fundamental precepts remained firmly entrenched in his psyche. But in addition to any Catholic doctrine, Ludlam also had an abiding love of and respect for life in any form.

When it came to heated political issues, Ludlam would often adopt an unfashionable point of view just to be contrary and to stimulate debate, even if it meant taking a position that contradicted his own. Everyone in the troupe remembered instances of this contrariness. Black-Eyed Susan recalled a particularly startling moment when a woman came backstage following a performance. After she made some reference to an upcoming antinuclear march, Ludlam launched into a diatribe supporting nuclear power and all the good it did. He rolled his eyes in a mischievous way afterwards, to let Susan know he was being facetious.

It was his Shavian proclivity for arguing any two sides against an equivocal middle which very much prompted *Hot Ice*. In contrast to euthanasia, Ludlam was aware that

Salvador Dalí was investigating cryogenics and planned to have himself frozen before he expired, in hopes of being revived in a medically advanced future. These opposing impulses presented themselves to Ludlam as "a conflict that was not really a conflict," or in other words, "a paradox — the perfect ridiculous idea." Indeed, the play's title is a perfectly self-contained paradox — an oxymoron.

The plot of *Hot Ice* was inspired by Raoul Walsh's *White Heat*, a classic, 1949 gangster film starring James Cagney. (Though Ludlam had no respect for Woody Allen, an unacknowledged but more contemporary inspiration may have been the filmmaker's *Sleeper* (1973), about a health food store owner — no less — who is restored to life two hundred years after being frozen.) Ludlam drafted an outline that concerns a euthanasia police force versus a mother and son who run a cryogenics operation. The play that emerged from this scenario went over very well with both critics and theatergoers — for a while, at least. It proved a difficult birth, however, for many of those who participated in its creation.

Ludlam now felt compelled to write plays not only to satisfy personal goals, but also to fulfill grant commitments. Whether he was aware of it or not, he treated *Hot Ice* like a chore he resisted finishing. If the final script feels somewhat thrown together, the confusion began when the company commenced rehearsals with only the barest of outlines and a few pages of dialogue. There was a distinct lack of clarity from Ludlam on how the play should evolve. Everyone was encouraged to contribute not only lines, but also any ideas they might have for the story and its structure. And practically *everything* was tried — not only during rehearsals, but during performances as well.

There was one day when Ludlam and Georg Osterman were already late for a rehearsal, but they were famished and Ludlam said, "Well, why don't we just stop in at John's and get a pizza?" With a slight modification to the line — "Well, why don't we just send out for a pizza?" — an onstage "pizza break" was built into the performance every night. Since Jack Mallory consumed beer the way most others drink water, a bit was added for him to urinate on cue every night. (Ludlam was particularly proud of the magical effect created by focusing a light on the steam that rose from the warm liquid pool.)

Since Bill Vehr had always wanted to be a narrator, a narrator was added to the scenario. Theoretically, the commentator was supposed to move the action along — but on the written page, he tends to slow it down. The performance was literally interrupted every night by four planted actors who impersonated audience members. They halted the proceedings to argue about the virtues and drawbacks of euthanasia with the actors onstage, prompting Ludlam to step out of character and complain, "Great, audience participation! My favorite theatrical device." The play features alternative endings, each of which is also interrupted. While this may have been the inevitable outcome of Ludlam's delight in advocating opposing viewpoints, the artifice also contributes to the impression that Ludlam never really knew where he wanted the play to go.

The story commences when Ramona Malone (Black-Eyed Susan) shows up at the Euthanasia Police station seeking help. After her husband died, she was obliged by the terms of their wedding contract "to keep him in a state of cryogenic suspension indefinitely and at my own expense." As run by the evil Irmtraut "Moms" Mortimer (Lola Pashalinski) and her imbecilic son Max (John Brockmeyer), the Cryogenics Foundation has been milking poor Ramona ever since, bringing her to the verge of bankruptcy.

In a setup that both exploits and parodies the hard-boiled fiction devices of Dashiell Hammett and James M. Cain, Ramona is first interviewed by Tank Irish (Richard Currie), the Chief of Euthanasia Police, and then by Buck Armstrong (Ludlam), a detective on the force who agrees to take on the case. (Armstrong was a deeply macho character, quite the opposite of Ludlam's previous portrayal of Camille.) To discover the whereabouts of the Cryogenics Foundation, Ramona poses "as a corpse with the aid of a sleeping draught" and Armstrong impersonates "the widower seeking to place his wife in the deep freeze of cryonic suspension."

> NARRATOR: At his very first opportunity, Buck will plant a transmitter, which can
> be made from any radio, in her vagina.
> RAMONA: Cunt.
> NARRATOR: And Buck will insert.
> BUCK: Ram.
> NARRATOR: Mona's.
> BUCK: Shove it.
> MISS ENRIGHT: Up her cunt.
> RAMONA: Twat.
> BUCK: Vagina.
> NARRATOR: Discovering the secret storage vaults. Fly in the map of New York City.
> (*Map flies in*) Squad cars equipped with the proper antennae will pick
> up a signal when they are within a twenty-mile radius of the transmitter.

This passage is typical of the crude level of humor in *Hot Ice*. A more serious note is interjected near the end of the first act by a female heckler planted in the audience. "I suggest you just close the play down," she shouts, before explaining that her mother "was a vegetable" being fed intravenously for thirteen years "in an iron lung." But, one day, long after "the doctors gave up hope," her mother miraculously recovered.

A "kid in the audience" pipes in, arguing the euthanasia point of view. "I think it's disgusting to resort to heroic measures such as heart transplants and iron lungs to extend life beyond its natural limits, with no thought to the quality of the life you are extending," he says.

Georg Osterman, whose boyfriend, Michael, was running the box office, recalled,

> There were a couple of nights when the fights in the audience were so real that people would run out to Michael and say, "You better call the police, because there are these people in there who are really flipping out." The first time, Michael went into the house to see what was wrong before realizing it was part of the show. But some people would get so upset, they'd leave. That's where we would stop and have our pizza break.

Robert Reddy, who played one of the plants in the audience, considered *Hot Ice* "goofy, and certainly not one of Charles's best plays." But he also found the prearranged disruption thrilling. "To be in an audience when they don't know what the hell is going on is wonderful. One night, this woman next to me just grabbed my arm and said, 'Is this part of the play?' I'd been shouting at someone across the theater at that point. I turned to her and said, 'Lady, I haven't a clue. I'm just sitting here like you are.'"

Reddy remembered another night when,

> a big Puerto Rican fellow got up out of the audience and just walked very quietly up onstage and put his arm around the actress who had been disturbed about her mother. He started talking softly to her and walked her up the aisle while everyone onstage just stared in amazement, not knowing what to do. I thought to myself, well, where are we going to go from here? During the intermission she told us, "He was very sweet. He was just trying to calm me down, and he said that he's going to take me out after the show and see if he can find some professional help for me."

Richard Currie claimed that "I used the word 'genius' to describe Charles a lot until *Hot Ice*, but that's when he began to call himself one. And I remember telling myself,

I'm never going to call him a genius again. That was a particularly bad period for everybody, the most painful of all. One day during rehearsals, Charles would say, 'These are
my words and don't anybody dare change them.' The next day he'd say, 'Does anybody
have anything they want to put into the play?'"

According to Currie, part of the problem was that Ludlam wasn't "in love" with anyone
at the time. Black-Eyed Susan concurred: "I always felt much better when Charles had a
lover." As Currie further explained, "Things always went more smoothly when Charles
was in love, because then he fought with his boyfriends instead of with us. How Susan
ever survived *Hot Ice*, I'll never know. Charles ran her into the ground, ragging her
daily. He'd say, 'You piece of shit' and blah-blah-blah.... Then he'd defend such
behavior, saying she loves it."

Currie's problems with *Hot Ice* were to some degree shaped by his resenting the fact
that, through Geldzahler, Ludlam brought in the fashionable artist Edward Avedisian to
design the sets and costumes. "Charles was enamored of 'art' people. I think he was a
bit of an art and a literary snob. So he made this big deal out of having Avedisian, while
my friend Bobjack [Callejo] was put on hold again."

The rehearsals were also hard on Robert Reddy, who was "fired" in the midst of them.
"Originally there were only a few pages of script, and we went over them again and
again," said Reddy, who continued:

> Charles was improvising the play and writing it as we went along. I was ad-libbing
> a scene as "Dr. Quick," the joke being that somebody became ill and someone
> else would say, "Get a doctor, quick!" I'd come out of the audience and say, "I'm
> Dr. Quick."
>
> Well, nothing much was happening at these rehearsals for me, and after about two
> weeks, I went to visit my family for the Christmas holidays. When I returned sev-
> eral days later, Charles was very cool to me. We barely sat down when he said, "By
> the way, Bob, I won't be needing you anymore. I'm going to cut that part in the
> play." He was efficient and brusque about it. So I just gathered my things and left
> the rehearsal. But it was clear to me that it was because I had stayed away for a
> week while he was working that I didn't deserve to be in the play.
>
> Lola phoned me right after that and said, "Bob, that was the cruelest thing I've
> ever seen anyone do, and you took it so well. I can't believe it. I wouldn't have

taken it so well." Then Charles called me, mortified, saying that he had been mad about this and that, and having a temper tantrum. "But do come back and we'll find something for you to do."

Robert Beers experienced the thorough commitment that Ludlam required from everybody in a similar fashion. "He couldn't share people in any way," said Beers.

> It was a totally dominant thing. He wanted to rehearse in the afternoon, do a performance at night, and have a repertory theater company. You couldn't really have any other real job. You couldn't have a relationship with someone else because there wouldn't be time for it, and Charles didn't like lovers loitering around. He shook the company down to the people who said "Yes" or "Fine" to that deal.

> Charles and I had a falling-out later. He got into this mode of saying, "I'm not going to write all these plays for all these people anymore. It's just going to be *Les Six*" — the six people who were there from the beginning. But I've always traced the basis for this conversation back to *Hot Ice*, which was when I fell in love with Ted Spagna, a photographer and filmmaker. Though I had stopped sleeping with Charles by then, I was still an acolyte and a devotee. But when I started my relationship with Ted, I sensed that Charles resented it. He just couldn't share anybody. That's why very few of the people who were with him for a long time ever had long-standing commitments of any kind with anyone else.

Although Ludlam wasn't "in love" during the period of *Hot Ice*, there was a new person on the scene by the name of Randy Hunt. He played "the kid in the audience" who is worked into the play. "I think everybody was dabbling with 'pretty' Randy," recalled Currie. Indeed, Osterman reported, "Randy was like this really cute hustler kid who hit on me. He was bright in some ways, but didn't realize what he was doing. He and I continued to have this little fling a few times. Next he started making it with John [Brockmeyer]. Randy really hurt John when he went directly from him to Charles. And then when he did the same thing to Charles, Charles really didn't like it at all."

Living up to his first name, Hunt even had a brief affair with Black-Eyed Susan, who with hindsight felt that he was a lot more manipulative and aware of what he was doing than anyone thought at the time. But even though Hunt managed to fit Susan into his busy carnal schedule, it was Henry Geldzahler who came between him and Ludlam.

"When I went to see *Hot Ice*," said Geldzahler,

> there was this blond boy handing out the programs who was such a staggering
> beauty, my heart stopped. When I went backstage after the show, Charles was sit-
> ting there and this lovely creature was sitting next to him. *Sotto voce*, I told Randy
> I'd definitely love for him to come visit me someday, and by the time I got home
> later that night, there he was sitting on my steps.

Randy Hunt had been staying with Ludlam for a few weeks when they had an enormous fight and Ludlam kicked him out. Then, when he moved in with Geldzahler,
Ludlam recanted and wanted Hunt back, but it was too late.

"Charles was chilly with me for a while after that," recalled Geldzahler. But as
Christopher Scott claimed, he himself had to deal with Ludlam's wrath over the matter.
Although Ludlam usually presented an "on-top-of-the-world" attitude, "There was
another side to him," said Geldzahler, "a self-critical mode, a mode in which he wasn't
'cock of the walk' and entirely proud of himself. There were depressive moods or states
of mind that could go on for quite a while sometimes."

Unable to equal his success with *Camille*, Ludlam's self-critical mode prevailed during
the period of *Hot Ice*. He was floundering with the play, and his bad mood was clearly
beginning to take its toll on some members of the company. Others, however, remembered having a good time with the play. More than a decade later, Brockmeyer would
look back on it as "one of my favorite plays and roles." Black-Eyed Susan also liked her
character, and was in favor of reviving the play, when Ludlam proposed the idea several
years later.

Pashalinski recalled some background tensions during the period of *Hot Ice*, but she,
too, appreciated her part. "This was our first contemporary piece," she pointed out,
"and it was refreshing and freewheeling after all the costume epics. It was kind of a conspiracy, knowing that we all had to put it together, and it showed us our own strengths.
The improvisations produced some brilliant results, and the audience participation
meant we all had to be quick on our feet every night. It just felt like new depths were
being plumbed by working on it."

In fact, the level of improvisation that Ludlam required from the cast during rehearsals
for *Hot Ice* was a throwback to the early Ridiculous shows. As with *Big Hotel, Conquest*

of the Universe, Whores of Babylon, and *Turds in Hell,* the surviving script is at best a reconstructed roadmap of what actually occurred during any given performance. But it was apparently easier for the older members of the company to contend with this level of improvisation than it was for the newcomers.

Considering all the backstage ill will that *Hot Ice* engendered, in retrospect it was miraculous how well it went over — at first. With ticket prices ranging from $4 to $6.50, this was the first Ridiculous production to feature an official "On Stage" playbill. The play's opening for the critics was delayed until February 10, while Ludlam kept tinkering with the production. Once it opened, however, the reviews were more than generous. While conceding that, "This is not one of Mr. Ludlam's tightest scripts" and "at times it even seems inchoate," Mel Gussow claimed, "there is a madness in his method," and he found "enough sense beneath the nonsense to make the evening frozen food for thought."

From his perch at the *Village Voice,* Michael Smith was elated, referring in his opening sentence to this "brilliant, hilarious, outrageous new play [that] puns and plays on too many levels for a simple accounting." Though he arrived ten minutes late because of a snowstorm, it didn't prevent him from pronouncing the play "indefatigably artful, tastily offensive, as profound as it is preposterous, as serious as silly . . . the actors go right on touching all bases with the precision, bizarre individuality, and good nature that make the Ridiculous Theatrical Company a treasure and delight."

In addition to such praise, the play became a popular hit that enjoyed a total of eighty-four performances. (The script was also eventually published in *The Drama Review.*) As he demonstrated time and again, however, Ludlam had a tendency to keep even his successful shows running too long, and far beyond the time they exhausted their audiences. Late in the run of *Hot Ice,* "We were doing two performances on Fridays and two on Saturdays, where we were outnumbering the people in the audience," recalled Currie. "But Charles would not cut back on the performances. 'If they can do it on Broadway, we can do it,' he'd say. Unfortunately, Walter Kerr came on one of those dreadful Friday nights, when there were maybe ten people in the house, and he let us have it in the *Times* the next week."

Among the most influential critics of his day, Kerr was known for his conservative views. He had nothing but contempt for *Hot Ice,* which he dismissed by referring to "the spectacle of bald, full-breasted hermaphrodites camping as before." The play closed shortly after Kerr's notice appeared. As Ludlam would later tell Calvin Tomkins, he firmly believed that "Walter Kerr really killed *Hot Ice*." But Currie's memory of dwindling audiences, even before Kerr saw the show, suggests otherwise.

With a hefty monthly rent to pay for the Evergreen, *Camille* was instantly revived after *Hot Ice* closed. The glowing reviews that greeted *Camille*'s premiere production the previous year were nothing in comparison to the flood of raves that welcomed the play's return engagement the following spring. Confirming that the Ridiculous had truly entered the mainstream with *Camille*, *The New York Times* assigned Clive Barnes, its chief drama critic at the time, to cover the play's reopening on May 13, 1974. Prior to this, the *Times* had relegated coverage of the Ridiculous to Mel Gussow, their second-string critic whose domain had been, and would continue to be, Off and Off-Off-Broadway.

Barnes's review, which was read over the phone to Ludlam and the gang at an opening night party and later blown up outside the theater, was rapturous. "That fine hairline between comedy and tragedy is lovingly and most skillfully etched in Charles Ludlam's *Camille*," it began:

> In a strange way, it is oddly touching. It is also one of the most hilarious and unbuttoned camp evenings in New York. You can, and possibly will, laugh until the tears run down your cheeks — but remember to question yourself whether all the tears are those of laughter.... This is no ordinary drag act played for laughs. The remarkable thing is that while Mr. Ludlam takes very little pains to convince us that he is a woman — this must be the first Camille in history with a hairy chest — it soon becomes unnoticeable. He is a completely convincing Camille.
>
> His dramatic and histrionic methods are unvarying. He plays every scene with total sincerity — but that sincerity is occasionally punctuated with what might be called subtitles of humor. It is the art of the melodramatic comic aside seen in terms of the movie camera. The wit is throughout the piece intensely cinematic.... We are never far away from Garbo's Camille, but Mr. Ludlam is too smart merely to copy Garbo. His portrayal indeed seems to be a composite of Garbo, Bette Davis, Nancy Walker, with even a touch of Joan Sutherland and Margot Fonteyn thrown in to keep the message pure.

The ebullient endorsement of their chief critic prompted the *Times* to run their first extensive feature on Ludlam, two months later. It was written by Elenore Lester, a theater professor at New York University who was filling in for the vacationing Walter

Kerr, and it was prominently positioned, beginning on the front page of the Sunday "Arts & Leisure" section.

Lester declared Ludlam "a master of theatrical parody [who] has the ability to breathe new life into threadbare fantasies." Based on interviews with Ludlam and other members of the company, Lester's insights into the Ridiculous are a perfect representation of how Ludlam wanted himself and his work to be perceived; they confirm that Ludlam had become expert at manipulating the media to his own purposes. After a preliminary discussion of *Camille*, Lester downplayed the drag element while recounting the company's history and explaining what Ludlam was about.

"His works constitute a comic anthology of theatrical references," wrote Lester. Ludlam borrowed material for his plays from so many "diverse sources," she explained, "just as playwrights have traditionally gone to history and folk tales for characters and plots." Since it had become so "diluted" and "promiscuously used," the notion of "camp" (which is coyly offset by quotation marks) "is useless in describing Ludlam's energetic and complex farces," she wrote.

Better still, Lester placed the Ridiculous in a class by itself, above the other, trendy Off-Off-Broadway companies of the day. She described it as being "as far from" them as it was "from the naturalism of the Broadway stage," neither of which Ludlam could tolerate. Lester continued:

> The Living Theater, Open Theater, Performance Group and the Manhattan Project have all struggled grimly for "honesty" and "self-revelation" in their performances and have broken down the audience-performer barrier in strenuous efforts to involve their audiences in experiences that are liberating both sensually and intellectually. The results, in many cases, have been academic and sterile, despite nudity and regimented orgies of audience-performer "communication."

> Ludlam and company, on the other hand, rejoice in the artifice and buffoonery at the heart of theater — exuberantly offering their audiences childish fantasies of murder, mayhem and sexual anarchy. They employ virtually every trick in show biz from elaborate costuming and Marx Brothers bedlam to sophisticated Pirandellian and Brechtian breaks in illusion.

Lester's discussion ends on a similar note, suggesting that there was a vitality to the Ridiculous lacking in other contemporary theater: "In the early days, Ludlam's nihilism was out of style, shared by only a tiny minority. Today, however, at a time of widespread disillusionment, it is mainstream theater which is irrelevant and in financial trouble, and it is Ludlam who is able to say, 'I think theater is in a regenerative state.'"

Only seven years after he first performed on a New York stage with John Vaccaro's Play-House of the Ridiculous, and only six after he formed his own company, Ludlam was established enough to have a major write-up in *The New York Times*—referring to his "early days," no less. And given the hit he had with *Camille*, he could afford to say that "theater is in a regenerative state," taking particular glee in the notion that his success was, indirectly, at the expense of more mainstream theater. No wonder Ludlam could tell the *New York Post*, in yet another feature story, "Tradition isn't a stale thing that holds you back—it's a profound thing that feeds you. My feeling is that I'm coming at precisely the right moment."

As the raves kept pouring in from the provinces and as articles began to appear in national magazines, the barriers began breaking down between what had been considered avant-garde and what was mainstream. A write-up in *Vogue* compared Ludlam to Marcel Duchamp, for their shared ambition "to lampoon life, to fracture the square." In his review for the *Long Island Press*, William A. Raidy called Ludlam "an artist in a field of paper daisies." In a combined review and feature story for the *Washington Star-News*, David Richards wrote, "Tallulah Bankhead, Lillian Gish, Bette Davis, Maria Callas, Cleopatra and Joan Crawford could all probably successfully file for copyright infringement, except that Ludlam's Camille goes beyond them all to land in some riotous dreamworld where the late-show movies of the 1930s and the sexual ambivalence of the 1970s coalesce in a grand guignol of drag." As Ludlam told Richards, "I am the Camille for the 1970s."

John Simon delivered a dissenting view of *Camille* in his bloodthirsty column for *New York* magazine. He began by disputing Barnes for claiming that *Camille* was not "a drag show." Simon found it "the very essence of a drag show; the difference is merely that the previous efforts of the Ridiculous were not even good enough for a good drag show." Demonstrating his penchant for dismissing any artistic achievement for the sake of promoting his own wit, Simon continued, "Now, however, the company has progressed from the slime to the ridiculous." Venting his spleen still further, and revealing his homophobia in the process, Simon exclaimed, "What Charles Ludlam has done to [Marguerite] shouldn't happen to a dog.... One hates oneself for laughing at Marguerite being travestied by a short, stocky, homely man in drag, who is outrageous even when by his or certain reviewers' standards he is playing it—you must excuse me—straight. . . . For his ruining her for people—or trying to—I shall not readily forgive Charles Ludlam."

Simon's was not the lone pan. Richard Watts was a bit of an old fogy by then, still maintaining his column at the *New York Post*. He found *Camille* "hopelessly un-funny," defensively adding, "If this is 'camp,' you are welcome to it." But there would eventually be yet another negative reaction to *Camille* that Ludlam had to take more personally. Stefan Brecht, who had been such a crucial patron of the Ridiculous, claimed in *Queer Theatre* that, "Ludlam's artistic career seems to have ended with Camille."

In fact, Brecht was already disenchanted with the preceding play, *Corn*, which he felt marked "Ludlam's descent into professionalism and ostentatious harmlessness; his [earlier plays] were minor demonstrations of mastery in the genre of burlesque comedy; funny, intelligent, in good taste, excellently acted, with a faint glitter of philosophy." Though he acknowledged that "*Corn* was *great* fun," he lamented that "there was no evil in it, none of those sloppy crevices through which Ludlam once seduced you into the fissures in your soul in which incipient truths lurk, unguarded by definition."

Nor was Brecht the only insider who would turn against Ludlam. Some years following his involvement with Ludlam and the first few productions of the Ridiculous, Jack Smith would tell Penny Arcade, "Charles started out doing powerful political theater but decided to appease the powers that be, stopped being serious, and wound up doing farce."

As Brecht indirectly revealed in his discussion of *Corn* he had more personal reasons for turning against the Ridiculous. He resented that his imprimatur was no longer necessary to Ludlam. "The success of *Bluebeard*," he wrote, "generated . . . the support of the uptown critics . . . an uptown middle class audience . . . and steady financial support from the foundations and government." With moral and financial assistance suddenly being bestowed by the "uptown" enemies, Brecht had less of an interest in maintaining his own support. He could no longer turn his friends on to an underground cult phenomenon they wouldn't have known about otherwise.

But there was also some validity to Brecht's noticing that the work was changing. Both *Corn* and *Camille* were indeed without the "sloppy crevices" that seemed to define the earlier "epic" works. They each had a consistency and a coherence—a "through-line" —that made them more palatable for a mass audience.

There was, however, something else even more obvious that Brecht failed to put his finger on: Both *Corn* and *Camille* lacked the more sordid dialogue and prurient sex scenes of the earlier plays — and of *Hot Ice*, for that matter. If *Hot Ice* seemed like a throwback to the "sloppy crevices" Brecht yearned for, it also marked a syndrome for Ludlam that would become even more obvious later in his playwriting career: Any mainstream success he bargained for and won drove him back to his bawdier — and frequently "epic" — roots.

In all likelihood, *Camille* would not have received the boost it did from *The New York Times* had it adhered to the raunchiness of Ludlam's earliest works. With *Corn* and *Camille*, Ludlam was beginning to make himself more acceptable to a mainstream audience in ways that his rebellious nature did not earlier permit. But whatever compromises this transition entailed for Brecht (or Smith) had little to do with Ludlam. From Ludlam's perspective, it was all still being done his own way; and the wider admiration he was suddenly receiving was what he felt he had always deserved.

Camille was fated to become not only Ludlam's signature performance, but also the company's trademark production. For the next decade, it became the most frequently revived show, both in New York and on various tours. Along with *Bluebeard*, it was brought in at the last minute to bail the company out of a tight financial hole whenever a newly introduced work was failing. This was, after all, a primary benefit of running a repertory theater company.

The first revival of *Camille* at the Evergreen introduced yet another person to the company: Steve Turtell, who ran the show's lights for several months. "I saw Charles do Camille sixty times, before I ever saw Garbo in the film," said Turtell. "Then, when I finally saw Garbo, I thought to myself, 'My god, she's so butch!' She just seemed so mannish to me in comparison to Charles. I mean, Charles had it all over Garbo."

Turtell had been introduced to Ludlam by Sydney Chandler Faulkner, a Greenwich Village eccentric who reportedly had an impassioned affair with Ludlam. "They were pretty hot for a while," claimed Turtell, who added that Faulkner's terraced apartment on West 11th Street was the equivalent of an open house. "You never knew who you were going to run into there. People would just show up, and Sydney would play impromptu host all the time."

In addition to standing in as the butler in *Camille* for a spell, Faulkner had been one of the players planted among the audience in *Hot Ice* earlier in the season. As Turtell recalled, it was during this period that, "Sydney had the most amazingly wonderful getup. When you arrived at his place, Sydney would greet you at the door wearing a snood, his red-lacquered nails, and his red tights with his crotch cut out and his dick just dangling there. He never knew who was going to be at the door, and it was kind of like this test he would give them, to see how they would handle it."

೧೦

While it was *Camille* that first brought the "bridge and tunnel" crowd to the Ridiculous, celebrities kept attending as well. "*Camille* was when I first became aware of who our audience was," claimed Osterman. "Nureyev, Warhol, Jasper Johns, Richard Avedon. . . . I wasn't really nervous onstage at that point, except when I knew those people were in the house. It was during *Camille* that Bette Midler came backstage while I was taking off my makeup in front of the mirror. I could only see these boobs in the mirror, not her face, as she said, 'I'd like to see what you look like with it off.' And I didn't know if she meant my pants or my makeup."

Bette Midler was by then a well-established fan of the Ridiculous. She would graciously acknowledge that she had patterned part of her act after Black-Eyed Susan. Geraldine Fitzgerald also became a longtime aficionado. Among other celebrities who came to see *Camille* were Lotte Lenya — accompanied by Douglas Fairbanks, Jr. — and Baryshnikov.

There was a regular — though less famous — fan of the company whom everyone knew as "Bruce." He always brought along a large party of gay friends, making the evening a special event. For *Camille*, everyone wore wrist corsages and displayed badges with the legend, "I SAW *CAMILLE* WITH BRUCE." They also brought a multitude of bouquets to toss to the diva at the end of the performance. It was precisely this "fan club" type of adoration that Ludlam loved the most. As much as anything, it was such support that persuaded him to maintain his company on its relatively modest terms: A fear of losing such followers contributed to his ambivalence over being a more commercial or mainstream success.

Even more special for Ludlam was the night his mother attended with his Aunt May. While they were waiting for him to remove his makeup and emerge from the dressing room, Pashalinski asked them how they felt about Ludlam's performance. With a remark that simultaneously underscored and relieved the tension in the air, Marjorie responded, "He does a good woman!" But it was Pashalinski who had the last word: "He doesn't do a bad man either."

Richard Currie had to leave the revival of *Camille* at the Evergreen for his regular summer stint at Brown Ledge. He was replaced in the role of Duval Sr. at the last minute by Adam Kilgore. A member of Actors' Equity, Kilgore adopted the pseudonym of "Adam McAdam" to avoid any union problems when he began working with the non-Equity Ridiculous.

Born in Detroit, Kilgore came to New York "to work in the theater" in 1956, when he was twenty-one. "At an early age, I realized it was bullshit about *not* sleeping your way into the theater," he said. "I decided that if I could get anyone to sleep with me, I'll come and move in with them, and that's how I can get to New York. And that's what I did. He was a designer."

After studying children's theater in college, Kilgore cofounded Nicolo Marionettes with Nicholas Coppala, a subsequent lover, in New York. Kilgore had been a fan of the Ridiculous beginning with *Bluebeard*, and Ludlam was, in turn, a fan of Kilgore's, having seen his puppet version of *Cinderella* at the Cottage Marionette Theater in Central Park. It was some days after Ludlam went backstage to greet the puppeteer that Kilgore coincidentally ran into the cast of the Ridiculous at a party. He learned that Currie was leaving for the summer and thought he would be "perfect for the part. But I didn't have the courage to ask Charles directly at the party," recalled Kilgore.

> Then I was encouraged by a friend to just call him up. I got really drunk, phoned him, and said, "I understand that Richard's going away and I'd be perfect in his role." Charles said, "Can you go into the show tomorrow night?" He told me Bill Vehr had a script and sent me over there that night to get it.
>
> Apparently they had already been rehearsing someone else, but there had been money problems and he backed out at the last minute. So Bill was going to play the role himself, in addition to playing Armand. But he was relieved when I took over. I stayed up all night studying the script, and then showed up a wreck the next day. When I went on that night, I didn't remember line one. I was in this daze. I just had to do it. So I improvised my lines with Charles, playing this real tough, moralistic character. And I got an enormous exit applause. Charles was

furious because I didn't say one line in the script. He didn't tell me this at first. He just said, "You have to work harder on the lines." And it was another week or two before I got them all right.

As he was getting into costume one night, Kilgore realized he had forgotten to bring his freshly laundered black socks with him: He salvaged the situation by painting his ankles black with shoe polish. He also remembered "the high level of wit with Bill and John in the dressing room at the Evergreen as being better than the show."

At the Evergreen, there was a tiny dressing room upstairs shared by Ludlam and Mallory, and a larger communal dressing room downstairs for the rest of the cast. Ludlam would often run down fifteen minutes before curtain time to wish everybody luck, and sometimes to provide one or two of the actors with notes he had made the night before. Since Ludlam was onstage for practically the entire performance, most of the cast took up some form of knitting to occupy themselves between their cues in *Camille*. This included just about everyone except for Black-Eyed Susan and Pashalinski, the only two female cast members. Robert Beers and Robert Reddy both became needlepoint experts, as Brockmeyer and Ludlam already were.

Ludlam also used his more private upstairs dressing room whenever he had special business to transact between scenes. With great sadness, Robert Beers recalled Ludlam saying, "I want to talk to you," as he called him into his dressing room one evening. "He was sitting there in his curls and his ball gown, telling me, 'I'm writing a new play, and there's no part for you in it.' He said that he liked my work as an artist, that he loved me as a friend, and that he could even see us collaborating. But my role was not as an actor for him. And the night we closed *Camille*, I went up on the stage before the play began and cried like a baby, even more than when my mother had died."

While it was sometimes difficult for Ludlam to tell others they weren't going to be in the next show, a number of the secondary players also found it hard to confront him when they wanted to leave, knowing he would take it personally. It almost felt like breaking up with a lover: Would Ludlam be explosive or act dejected?

"People always came to me, to have *me* tell Charles that they were quitting," claimed Brockmeyer. "That was one of my roles in the company in the seventies. They couldn't tell Charles, but they'd tell me and I would tell him, 'So and so is not going to be in the company,' or 'So and so is not going to be in the show.'

"And when we did *Stage Blood*, Charles very consciously said, 'I've had it! We're doing a six-character play next,'" continued Brockmeyer. "And that's when it really came back down to the core group: It was just Charles, Lola, Susan, Bill, myself and Jack Mallory."

Robert Beers, in other words, was not the only one for whom there would not be a part in Ludlam's next play. But beyond the core group — who had taken to calling themselves "Les Six" in reference to the group of celebrated French composers of the 1920s — there was a relative newcomer to the company who claimed to be instrumental in providing Ludlam with the inspiration for *Stage Blood*. Though Ludlam had always wanted to play Hamlet, it wasn't until Bobjack Callejo showed him his latest school project that he figured out how to tackle this cherished challenge.

"Everything that I designed for Charles was a reflection of what I was studying at Lester Polakov Studios," said Callejo.

> At the time of *Camille*, I was studying forced perspective — instead of something being just straight on, squared off, all the scenery was forced in to make it look deeper, to give it more dimension. But the $400 budget [for *Camille*] was used mostly for glitter and paint.
>
> Then, just before Charles wrote *Stage Blood*, we were in my tiny apartment on Thompson Street, smoking marijuana, and he was just rattling off all these titles of plays he hadn't written yet. He always kept this list of titles — "I Beg Your Pardon" and "The Butler Did It" were a couple of them. Then Charles said that he always wanted to play Hamlet, and I told him that I was studying working with a revolving stage at the time. And I remember us sitting there at my kitchen table and cutting a circle out of a piece of cardboard. And we played with it, smoking one joint after another, and that's literally how *Stage Blood* came about. That was the one show where the scenery came first.

Given his long-standing ambition to play Hamlet, a revolving set was all the inspiration Ludlam needed to write what is one of his most underrated works. The elaborate scenario of *Stage Blood* was such that Ludlam first envisioned it as a film, but a revolving stage could serve the same purpose. The story concerns a family of actors who perform *Hamlet* in the sticks. During the course of the play, their backstage intrigues come to mirror the plot of *Hamlet*, like an infinite number of Chinese boxes folded one within the other. The revolving stage concept permitted Ludlam to swing back and forth —

frequently with overlapping sequences — between the performance of *Hamlet* and the backstage story that mimics it. After a certain point, the characters in *Stage Blood* truly become interchangeable with the characters they portray in Shakespeare's play.

The head of the troupe, Carlton Stone (Mallory), is an archetypal actor-manager in the nineteenth century tradition, traveling from town to town with a repertoire of classic plays. Now elderly and alcoholic, Stone complains bitterly in the opening scene, "I used to be Hamlet.... Now I'm just the ghost. Poetic justice. I'm a ghost of my former self."

Other members of Stone's troupe, called "The Caucasian Theatrical Company," include his wife Helga Vain (Pashalinski), his son Carl (Ludlam), Jenkins (Brockmeyer), and Edmund Dundreary (Vehr). Jenkins is the stage manager, Edmund a would-be play-wright, and they both act in the company. "Our company may be small, but it's pretentious," claims Stone.

Intimidated by the prospect of following in his father's footsteps, Carl is reluctant to play Hamlet. But even more problematic is the loss of the actress who was to play Ophelia. She left in a snit just as the company was coming to Mudville, Stone's home-town. Stone had been critical of her acting "because she was Stanislavski-trained." When Jenkins points out that she worked "honestly and truthfully," Stone launches into a diatribe: "What do you know of honesty and truth? I call it lies and deception. Deceiving the audience into believing in surface reality, illusion. The great actor gives you a glimpse beneath the surface. Something that lies beyond your honesty and truth."

The company is stranded without an Ophelia, but salvation arrives when a local, "stagestruck, small-town girl" named Elfie Fey (Susan) appears at the theater and is instantly cast. "Do I have what it takes to be an actress?" she asks Carl. "Can you starve, Elfie?" he replies.

The first act of *Stage Blood* ends just after the opening "ghost" scene of *Hamlet* is per-formed. There is a "bloodcurdling scream" as the stage rotates to reveal the dressing room: "Helga stands with blood on her hand," reads the stage direction. "Stone lies dead, his head in the toilet, blood issuing from his ear." The second act begins as Helga, who plays Gertrude, confides to Edmund, who, of course, plays Claudius, that she murdered her husband "to get the company for you, my baby." They conspire to pre-vent her son Carl from assuming management of the company.

Though Carl suspects that his father was murdered, it isn't until Stone's ghost appears before him in the dressing room that he implicates his mother. "You are the dispossessed son: I am the murdered father: Your mother is the guilty queen," says "Stone's voice." Thus the plot of *Hamlet* is replicated in *Stage Blood* both backstage and on.

Ludlam further complicates the scenario with the introduction of a seemingly superfluous character, Gilbert Fey, Elfie's father, who implores Carl to "prevent my daughter from going on the stage." Wielding a bottle of "stage blood," Carl claims it won't be easy for him to interfere with Elfie's theatrical ambitions. "It's not real blood," he explains, "it's the blood we use onstage. That's what your daughter has in her veins."

In the meantime, Carl helps stage manager Jenkins, an aspiring writer, work on an "avant-garde" play he's written called *Fossil Fuel*, in hopes that Helga will agree to stage it, thereby expanding the company's repertoire beyond the classics. While functioning as the play that Hamlet arranges to trap his stepfather, this play-within-the-play is an even more direct parody of Treplov's juvenile drama in Chekhov's *The Seagull*, as well as avant-garde offerings of the 1970s.

Jenkins's defense of *Fossil Fuel* could be a description of Ludlam's own attitude towards *Stage Blood*: "This is the tightest plot that has been constructed in the last four hundred years. . . . No! . . . In the whole history of drama. Someday some poor sucker will be writing his doctoral thesis on the relationship between my writings and my bowel movements."

Gilbert Fey divulges in the closing scene that he is actually Stone in disguise. He only pretended to be murdered by using some "stage blood." Elfie is not his daughter, but his "mistress." Upon this revelation, Elfie says, "I'm sorry, Carl. You're just too immature for me," and Stone adds, "Sorry to cut you out of the action, son." "That's all right, you two," replies Carl. "I'm having a rather interesting 'experimental' relationship: With Jenkins!" And Helga adds, "It's a mother's dream come true. To have a son who's gay!"

Since *Stage Blood* is entirely about the theater, it gave Ludlam the opportunity to show off his considerable knowledge on the subject. The title is an obvious *double entendre*, referring both to fake blood used by actors and to the cliché about having the stage in one's blood, as Ludlam clearly did. In addition to sending up Stanislavski and Method training, *Stage Blood* contends that "the plays of Shakespeare were, in fact, never written by Shakespeare," but rather "by another playwright of the same name." References to everything from *Oedipus Rex* and Grotowski to Marlowe and *The Mousetrap* (the longest running play in London history) abound. Even a luncheon order concerns the theater: "I'll take turkey," says Helga. "I don't think turkey's good luck on opening night, Mother," responds Carl. "Better give me ham," she decides.

There are a number of esoteric, personal references embedded in the script as well. Stone's line, "What you do to Shakespeare shouldn't happen to John Simon," was Ludlam's retaliatory quip for Simon's mean-spirited review of *Camille*. When Carl, on the topic of Mudville, says, "It could be worse, Mother. We could be in Vienna," Ludlam was clearly alluding to the company's first European tour and the disasters they encountered there.

> HELGA: Ah, Vienna, the city of my nightmares. The only town we played where
> we had to go back to our hotel rooms to take a piss.
> CARL: What about the night that Edmund Dundreary [actually, Bill Vehr in
> Geneva during the company's second European tour] was discovered in
> his hotel room forcing a load of shit down the sink with his thumb?

Though it ran for three months and was, for the most part, perceived by the critics to be the intelligent work it is, *Stage Blood* was not popular with Ludlam's audience. As he later told Calvin Tomkins, "I got a feeling of disappointment from the audience. They'd come expecting something else — expecting a product, something they were used to from me. Nobody was in drag in *Stage Blood*, although the Hamlet character, you feel, turns out in the end to be homosexual."

If *Stage Blood* is among Ludlam's better plays, it is also one of his more serious, and it simply wasn't "ridiculous" enough for his regular following. It is heavily academic in spots, as Ludlam reveled in inserting long disquisitions on the art of acting and stage-craft, only sometimes modified by his penchant for punning. (*Stage Blood* would also receive the honor of being included in *Theatre of the Ridiculous*, an anthology of three plays that was the first to recognize the Ridiculous as a genuine genre of playwriting. In her Introduction to the 1979 volume, Bonnie Marranca distinguished Ludlam's *Stage Blood* from the other two works — Kenneth Bernard's *The Magic Show of Dr. Ma-Gico* and Ronald Tavel's *The Life of Lady Godiva* — by citing it as "an example of the literary side of the Ridiculous.")

What emerged as Ludlam's most studied and rigorous play to date was simply an anomaly for his regular audience. He would encounter their resistance, their disappointment, again and again — whenever he strayed from the more lighthearted path of raucousness. The majority of Ludlam's fans did not admire his intelligence or cleverness, per se, so much as his irrepressible need to stick out his tongue at anything held sacred. But for Ludlam, *Hamlet was* sacred.

Perhaps in tandem with Ludlam's more earnest concerns, *Stage Blood* is also highly autobiographical in its psychological revelations. As he told Tomkins,

> Such amazing things happened when I was writing [*Stage Blood*]! There's a speech that I do in my dressing room [within the play], that I took from Joyce's *Ulysses* and changed around — about the relation between a father and son. "The son unborn mars his mother's beauty: born, he brings pain, divides affection, increases care. He is a male: his growth his father's decline, his youth his father's envy, his friend his father's enemy." And at that moment the ghost of my father appears to me. I'm nude — I'm changing from my street clothes, which are all black leather, into the black Hamlet costume — and my father appears and touches my hand in that gesture of Michelangelo's God in the Sistine Chapel, and he delivers a speech from Kyd's *Spanish Tragedy*. It's the same speech that Joyce was parodying in *Ulysses*. He says, "My son! and what's a son? / A thing begot within a pair of minutes, there about / . . . Methinks a young bacon, / Or a fine little smooth horse colt, / Should move a man as much as doth a son; / For one of these, in very little time, / Will grow to some good use; where a son . . ." And suddenly, when I was writing this, I remembered my own father saying, "Children! I should have raised pigs, I'd be better off!" The real murderer of the father was me — killing my father in fantasy, working through and finally forgiving him. It was a milestone for me.

In spite of what Ludlam told Tomkins, it would be a number of years before he would truly "forgive" his father. The paternal disapproval he had endured as a child he now had to endure as an adult. Though Ludlam's mother and brother had been to see a number of his plays by the time of *Stage Blood*, not once had his father deigned to attend a Ridiculous production. Of course Ludlam was hurt by this, and he did nothing to disguise his feelings from everyone in the company.

But if, contrary to his father's expectations, Ludlam had achieved a personal dream by proving himself to be a consummate actor in *Camille*, he achieved an ancillary ambition by showing that he could be a consummate writer as well with *Stage Blood*. He was right to consider it "a milestone" for himself. And at first, the critics concurred.

Mel Gussow, in the *Times*, recognized this as a more earnest work for Ludlam. "Laughs are freefalling, but the play is less wild and untidy than usual Ludlam," he wrote.

"There is a slight loss in madness and nonsense but a gain in structure and discipline. This is a crisply wrapped comic package, with a clear plot and smart staging."

In his review for the *Village Voice*, Dick Brukenfeld wrote: "If our commercial theatre lifted its embargo on new American plays, Charles Ludlam's *Stage Blood* might share the success now monopolized by British imports. It's cut from much the same cloth." After comparing it favorably to *Equus, Sleuth, Rosencrantz and Guildenstern Are Dead*, and *The Real Inspector Hound*, Brukenfeld explained, "*Stage Blood* has a quality that sets it apart from those British successes — a satiric nonchalance in the performing which keeps a fine balance between playing out the story and sending it up."

Now writing for the *New York Post*, Martin Gottfried exclaimed, "Having hit upon an idea that captures the very essence of his sublimely Ridiculous Theatrical Company, Charles Ludlam threw all his (considerable) craft as well as (considerable) spirit into the making of *Stage Blood*. The new show that opened last night at the Evergreen Theater is one of the company's best ever — tight, consistent, madcap, literary and terribly funny." He also conjectured that "Shakespeare would have loved it." And in a notice in the *Post* a few months later, Gottfried declared it "as purely theatrical and gloriously funny a show as I have ever seen."

Famed photographer Richard Avedon also loved *Stage Blood*. It was shortly after he attended a performance accompanied by Verushka, the celebrity model, that he took a series of photographs of the troupe.

There were, however, two dissenting reviews in response to the show's opening night performance at the Evergreen on December 8, 1974. After referring to the play's "promising premise," Allan Wallach (in *Newsday*) felt that "it's undermined by the performing of the Ridiculous Theatrical Company, which is reaching the level of self-parody." And while Emory Lewis, in the *Bergen County Record*, acknowledged that Ludlam "is one of the funniest men in the New York Theater," he felt this production was "one of [his] lesser efforts."

The "killer" notice came a month later, on January 12, when Julius Novick panned the play in a "Guest View" piece for the all-important Sunday *Times*. While recognizing that Ludlam "appears to have become more disciplined, more fastidious, less outrageous and less obsessive" than he had been, Novick wrote: "To do what Ludlam is trying to do in *Stage Blood* takes more wit, more intelligence, more talent, than he has been able to muster." The dialogue, he opined, "is not wild enough in its badness to function successfully as parody, nor is it good enough to be worth much taken straight."

Having already suffered the blows inflicted by Walter Kerr's devastating reaction to *Hot Ice*, Ludlam was furious over Novick's remarks in the same paper. But Ludlam realized how important this play was, both personally and professionally, and he continued to work on it in hopes that it would be better perceived in revival. It was *Stage Blood* that enabled Calvin Tomkins to say: "What began as ridicule and rebellion has become, in both cases, an infatuation with much older theatrical values."

Having sustained a repertory theater company for seven years, Ludlam felt sufficiently encouraged by *Stage Blood* to tell Tomkins, "I do think of myself as part of a viable tradition in theatre. . . . The romance of the theatre gives me energy and inspiration: Molière acting in his own plays, with his wife and his two brothers-in-law; Shakespeare playing a lead in Ben Jonson's *Every Man in His Humour*; Marlowe and Kyd sharing a room in London. I feel a part of all that."

Of the twenty-nine plays Ludlam would write, *Stage Blood* was his most direct tribute to the theater and to the theatrical tradition of which he felt a part. As Lola Pashalinski recalled,

> Charles was very happy working on that play, and we were all thrilled because it was just the six of us working on these classic roles in this undiluted fashion. We truly were the Caucasian Theatrical Company, with our raggedy ass. But it was a second flowering for all of us, demonstrating that we had the ability to do it "straight" as well as fool around, proving that we were these great actors. Here was the play [*Hamlet*] where any actor proved himself worthy of the label.
>
> At the very first rehearsals, we started out by reading *Hamlet*, and discussing or interpreting it. Charles's identification with the role of Hamlet was very profound. He was a very boyish Hamlet from the beginning.

Though rehearsals for *Stage Blood* were atypically restricted to only a few weeks, the script — as usual — wasn't finished when the actors began. They were already rehearsing the play on a completed set before Ludlam had composed the bulk of the second act.

"I wanted to write a ghost story/murder mystery," he later explained. "I borrowed a book from a friend called *How to Write a Murder Mystery* and there was a list in it of things you should *never* do in writing a murder mystery. I did them all. It was the only list in the book, so that was the easiest way."

Black-Eyed Susan recalled that it was also during this period that Ludlam "was steeped in reading about Henry Irving, the famous actor-manager of the nineteenth century. He said that he intended to emulate him, and in fact he did." This, too, was clearly a direct influence on *Stage Blood*.

As already observed, no matter how personally rewarding the play proved to be for Ludlam and Les Six, it wasn't the crowd-pleaser the company's following had come to expect. Ludlam had been driven to mock what he loved and to love what he mocked, a delicate balance that began to give way with *Stage Blood*: Here the adoration proved stronger than the mockery. It wasn't really Novick's pan as much as the lukewarm audience reaction to the show that closed it earlier than expected.

The last paragraph of Novick's review referred to another event that Ludlam was staging solo at the Evergreen on Saturday afternoons during the run of *Stage Blood*. A puppet show called *Professor Bedlam's Educational Punch and Judy Show*. Novick recommended it whole-heartedly. "Here," Novick wrote, "[Ludlam's] affection for artifice is put to good use: He understands the Punch and Judy tradition, with its extravagant farcical violence, and works freely and entertainingly within it. . . . Less than an hour of knock-about puppeteering, [it] is a much better taste of Ludlam's quality than *Stage Blood* with all its complications."

With a relatively sophisticated puppet stage designed and constructed by Bobjack Callejo, Ludlam was now performing professionally what he used to stage as a child in his basement. In the meantime, since the centuries-old Punch and Judy puppet show had its roots in *commedia dell'arte*, the exercise enabled him to make use of his recent studies of the genre tradition by improvising performances primarily for children.

According to Ludlam, "With hand puppets, it's your hand that's acting. Your hand becomes a metaphor for the whole human body. . . . It is almost the most pure expression of the performer in the sense that the *mise en scène*, or scenic element, and the performer are one. The puppet has unlimited expressive possibilities."

Punch and Judy was only the beginning of what would develop over the years into a regular subsidiary children's theater for Ludlam and the Ridiculous, encompassing another matinee puppet serial, *Anti-Galaxie Nebulae*, as well as Ludlam's adaptations of *Jack and the Beanstalk*, *A Christmas Carol*, and a more original work, *The Enchanted Pig*.

Ludlam claimed to be "astounded" by the success of *Punch and Judy*. "I started doing children's theater because I thought it would be fun," he said. "Not having any children of my own — and I won't — it's a very high experience performing for them."

Though Ludlam never did have children, he eventually entered into a gay marriage with someone he met late one night, cruising on Christopher Street, a week or so after *Stage Blood* closed on February 9, 1975. His name was Everett Quinton. After their initial one-night stand, Ludlam met up with Quinton again six months later, and they proceeded to live together for the rest of Ludlam's life. Here, finally, was the lover and mate he had always wanted.

CAPRICE ITSELF

Ugliness, no matter where it is, always has a beautiful side; it's fascinating to uncover beauty where no one else can see it.
— Yvette Guilbert on Toulouse-Lautrec

I would like to lead people out of materialism ... to bring frivolity to Mankind, know many people, take chances, risk everything, live as though I were Caprice itself!
— Charles Ludlam, *Caprice*

"I met Charles on a cold night in February," recalled Everett Quinton. "It was two o'clock in the morning. He was walking down Christopher Street while I was standing in a doorway on the other side. And then I was looking up the block, and when I turned around he was standing next to me. We chatted and he invited me home. He told me he was writing a play about a gay hero, and that was something I needed to hear at the time. I was twenty-two and just coming out. We spent the night together and had breakfast the next morning. But I didn't see him again after that. I lost his phone number. I ran into him the following August, and the first thing he said to me was, 'So you're not a dream! You do exist!' And that's when we became lovers."

Given Quinton's tendency to cruise Christopher Street while standing on the stoop of his apartment building, H.M. Koutoukas — a playwright and sometime actor with the Ridiculous — had christened him "the doorway Madonna." When Ludlam and Quinton met, Ludlam was wearing a black knit cap and a battered leather jacket. With shoulder-length hair and an impish Hippie look, Quinton was clad in a long, blue regulation Air Force overcoat.

After countless one-night stands, the thirty-two-year-old Ludlam had no way of knowing that his first encounter with Quinton would lead, six months later, to the relationship he had yearned for. Ludlam had very much wanted to form a relationship with Wally Gorell two years earlier, so he was clearly poised to enter into a mature partnership with a lover. And following the lessons he had learned from his failed efforts with Robert Liebowitz, he was better equipped to make the sacrifices a lasting relationship entailed — to a point.

The timing of Ludlam's union with Quinton was also part of a larger pattern. Though Ludlam had not really forgiven his father in the course of writing *Stage Blood* — as he would soon tell Calvin Tomkins he had — his "Hamlet" play rather marks a time when he was coming to terms with the father in himself. This was manifested by his concomitant exploration of children's theater, by his recently having become a teacher, and also by the Pygmalion-like relationship he would develop with Quinton, ten years Ludlam's junior.

In the process of their coming together, however, Quinton established a deep dependency on Ludlam. As fostered by Ludlam, the dependency would only escalate at first, and then take years to work itself out. In addition to Ludlam's intensity, this volatile couple had to contend with Quinton's notorious drinking problems. The first five years of their relationship would be marked by violent episodes causing physical injuries to one or the other, as well as a suicide attempt.

Like Pygmalion, Ludlam found in Quinton an unstructured lump of clay waiting to be molded. When he met Ludlam, Quinton's only stage experience had been in a high school production of *Rip Van Winkle*. He had also taken some theater courses at Hunter College as part of a Liberal Arts program he never completed.

Although Quinton didn't exactly know where he was headed, he knew what he was running from. "I came from an incredibly abusive family," said Quinton, "alcoholic and violent. Mother was terribly abusive, and each of us got it — there was no target child. It was drunken violence that would make a movie-of-the-week look tame."

The second eldest of twelve children, Quinton had a lower-class Brooklyn upbringing, with Irish Catholic roots. Like everyone else, Ludlam was impressed by the care and concern Quinton demonstrated towards his many siblings. Quinton's parents had separated when he was a teenager, and he did what he could to help raise his brothers and sisters — some of whom would eventually work for the Ridiculous.

When he was twenty years old, Quinton found himself living in Portsmouth, New Hampshire: "Just running away," as he put it. In retrospect, he realized that his abusive childhood had led to ongoing problems with authority figures. "I brought those problems to my relationship with Charles," he said. "I always felt threatened. If Charles said, 'Move left,' I'd have this insane, irrational reaction and feel, 'Well, what's wrong with moving to the right?' But I became dependent on Charles and I think he came to resent my dependence. He'd always throw it up to me that he was supporting me."

Shortly after Ludlam met Quinton and *Stage Blood* closed, a revival of *Bluebeard* was rapidly thrown together to pay the rent at the Evergreen. Mario Montez returned to the

Ridiculous to play Lamia "the Leopard Woman," a role he had originated. The revival was rereviewed with glowing notices and played for nearly three months. It was this production that filmmaker John Waters and friends, including Divine, attended one night. According to Pashalinski, they "were knocked out by what they saw." Divine, of course, had already been a huge presence at the company's parties and social gatherings, and there had often been talk of his/her appearing in one of the shows, but s/he never did.

In the summer of 1975, Connecticut College offered an intensive training program for would-be actors, dancers, and performers. The roster of visiting artists displayed a decided emphasis on the avant-garde: Richard Foreman, André Gregory's Manhattan Project, Mabou Mines, Richard Schechner's Performance Group, Pilobolus, and Twyla Tharp all participated. In addition to performing *Bluebeard*, Ludlam and company — including Black-Eyed Susan, Pashalinski, Vehr, Brockmeyer, Osterman, and Mallory — offered their classes in *commedia dell'arte*.

In the fall, while the company was rehearsing Ludlam's newest play, *Caprice*, the Evergreen Theater was sold to the Baha'i Foundation, and the Ridiculous lost its lease on the space. With the recycled title of *Tabu Tableaux*, a benefit was quickly launched to raise funds. Henry Geldzahler was recruited to sponsor the one-night event. He sent out a letter dated November 6. "Dear Friends," it began:

> During the past eight years Charles Ludlam's Ridiculous Theatrical Company has produced the most innovative and amusing plays in New York. Few of us have seen them all. On November 20th at 9:00 PM at the Evergreen Theater the Company will present a benefit evening *Tabu Tableaux*, a two-hour retrospective highlighting the outrageous fantasy and trenchant wit that have been a revitalizing force in the theater. This anthology will be composed of one scene from each of the eleven plays produced to date:

Big Hotel (1967)
Conquest of the Universe/When Queens Collide (1968)
Whores of Babylon by Bill Vehr (1968)
Turds in Hell by Ludlam/Vehr (1969)
The Grand Tarot (1969)
Bluebeard (1970)
Eunuchs of the Forbidden City (1971)
Corn (1972)
Camille (1973)

Hot Ice (1974)
Stage Blood (1975)

The evening will be capped with a scene from Ludlam's newest comedy *Caprice*, which will open later this season.

Since 1971 The Ridiculous Theatrical Company has received grants from the National Endowment to [sic] the Arts and The New York State Council on the Arts. These institutions have made it a condition of future funding that the Company show its ability to raise money from private sources as well. Last year government grants remained at the same level while production costs continued to increase. We need your help to keep this joyous company at the top of its form.

In order to ensure the continuation of government support and meet current expenses, we are asking you to contribute $25 per ticket (tax deductible) for each of the 140 seats at this gala evening of good humor and reckless virtuosity by our only serious comic theater.

The letter was signed "Sincerely, Henry Geldzahler."

Just about everybody played their original roles in *Tabu Tableaux*, which was held on November 20. Robert Beers returned for this one-night event to play Ruben Hatfield in the scene from *Corn*. But even though Arthur Kraft was on hand to play the "Potted Guest" in *Big Hotel*, his more notorious Orgone from *Turds in Hell* was undertaken by Adam Kilgore. Ethyl Eichelberger, who was then calling himself Eric, made his Ridiculous debut as an actor in the segments from *Bluebeard*, *Corn*, and *Camille*. (Unbeknownst to most members of the company, Ludlam and Eichelberger were already engaged in a surreptitious, backstage affair by then.)

Richard Currie recalled that "lots of people left at intermission, because they didn't know *what* they were seeing. It was just snatches from the earlier works that didn't make any sense strung together." The otherwise successful fund-raiser was upset by a tiny incident that prompted gales of laughter in the audience but greatly disturbed Ludlam during the *Camille* part of the program. In the midst of a scene between Marguerite and her maid Nanine, Jack Mallory's necklace came undone, and its pearls went scurrying across the stage like so many wayward marbles. "Charles and I were fiercely competitive in *Camille*," said Mallory, "and he suspected I had rigged the necklace to break on purpose. He didn't invite me back to the theater after that."

In fact, Ludlam and Mallory had already had a falling-out some weeks before the *Tabu*

Tableaux benefit. Though Mallory was initially cast in *Caprice*, he had missed some of the first rehearsals, which had been held at the Evergreen. "We were having early morning rehearsals, and it was just an outrageous hour for me," said Mallory. "Anyway, Charles called me to find out why I had missed a rehearsal or two, and he started screaming at me over the phone. After a certain point, I just hung up on him. When I showed up for rehearsals the next day, he struck me and screamed at me to 'Get out!'"

Missing rehearsals is justification for being fired from any production, and Mallory was neither the first nor the last to be dismissed by Ludlam for such behavior. But Mallory was one of the oldest members of the company, and it *is* surprising that Ludlam would choose to curtail their longtime association over a single episode. There were, however, other reasons.

As Mallory saw it, it had to do with Ludlam,

> being put in this position of being the father figure for all of us, and suddenly he didn't want that any more. It really began with *Bluebeard*, when he was suddenly thrust into the position of being a real director. This whole cast of people had turned him into a father figure and we no longer functioned like the collective group we had been before then. But now Charles wanted freedom from dealing with other people's lives and all the garbage it entailed. He was only interested in his art.

John Brockmeyer also felt a change coming over Ludlam, starting the year before, when he pared down the company and deliberately wrote *Stage Blood* for Les Six. It was a matter of focus, of becoming more protective of his overextended energies. It's hardly coincidence that he was now writing plays at a far more rapid clip, and would maintain this rigorous pace for the rest of his life — producing nearly twice as many in roughly the same amount of time. (Ludlam wrote ten plays between 1967 and 1975, and a remarkable nineteen plays between 1976 and 1986.) In the years ahead, he would even begin to experiment with allocating responsibilites to others, inviting Pashalinski, for instance, to direct the company's next production after *Caprice* — *Jack and the Beanstalk*.

Ludlam's newfound focus was also a part of what enabled him to embark on his committed relationship with Everett Quinton. Though it would take a few years for the relationship to stabilize and prove beneficial in terms of Ludlam's productivity, the impulse to focus evidently preceded it.

By the time rehearsals for *Caprice* commenced in the fall, Quinton was living with

Ludlam at his tiny Morton Street apartment. The one-night *Tabu Tableaux* benefit had been the only Ridiculous work Quinton had seen before joining the company with *Caprice*. But even when the need arose to replace Mallory in a large role, Ludlam did not consider Quinton, who lacked previous stage experience. He rather invented a bit part for him as a "Slave of Fashion" — what in earlier years had been known as a "Fire Woman" role. Ludlam also put Quinton in charge of wigs and wardrobe, which became regular jobs for him with the Ridiculous.

As with previous lovers whom Ludlam brought into the theater, Quinton felt like an outsider; awkward and intimidated by this close-knit troupe of players. "I was very shy and afraid to even go to the theater, frightened by all these grand actors," recalled Quinton. "I remember going to a Christmas party and being afraid of everyone. I was especially frightened of Lola. Here was this fabulous actress at the table with me. She was very open and warm and gracious. But I was like this little bird and felt out of my element. It took me a while before I could open up and trust that I'd be all right in these situations."

Adam Kilgore recalled that when Ludlam proposed a "Fire Woman"-type role for Quinton in *Caprice*, "At first, Everett said, 'No way! You'll never get me onstage.' Everett seemed totally untheatrical. He was in awe of Charles and he seemed very shocked by all these people."

It's interesting to note how thoroughly Ludlam had conceived of *Caprice* before writing it or introducing it into the repertoire. But this was by no means uncharacteristic of Ludlam: By the mid-seventies, he had more ideas for plays than anyone could keep track of — including himself. Some of them would come to fruition much later than intended. Still others would remain nothing more than a title or a reference in one document or another.

In an artistic statement prepared for the National Endowment for the Arts at the end of 1975, Ludlam boasted about his plans for a busy year ahead:

> We are going into rehearsal for a new production, *Caprice*, which will open in mid-March. . . . In August and September we are planning a San Francisco run of *Camille*. We are planning three productions next season! The first, *Utopia, Incorporated*, will be an Aristophanic satire on a concept of Utopia as a static economic state; an attempt at a politico-economic philosophy. The second, *The*

Enchanted Pig, will be our children's production and the third, *Black and Blue*, will be Blue's chronicle of the Civil War in honor of the Bi-centennial.

The fact is, the company did not perform *Camille* in San Francisco until 1978, or three years after Ludlam had intended. *Utopia, Incorporated* also appeared three years later than announced in the fund-raising statement, and *The Enchanted Pig* a year later still. And despite any patriotic spirit Ludlam meant to exploit by approaching a government agency for funding in the Bicentennial year of 1976, *Black and Blue* was never to be.

In terms of *Caprice*, Ludlam shared his ideas for the play with the company a good two years before they began working on it. Richard Currie recorded an eloborate description of *Caprice* in his journal entry of October 13, 1973, when the company was finishing their week in Zurich during their second European tour. This was just before *Hot Ice* opened in New York, and offers further proof that *Stage Blood*—yet another intervening work—was written in a fit of inspiration.

As Currie wrote in his journal:

> Charles is currently planning to open the season with *Caprice Or Fashion Bound*, not *Jack and the Beanstalk*. It's episodic and stunning. Charles will play Claude Caprice, homosexual designer, inventor of the bra and live models.
>
> In the opening scene he is discovered asleep with his lover Adrian in a swan-boat bed in a swamp bedroom. Adrian is a Randy [Hunt] type (Charles is secretly in love with Randy . . . and he will definitely be a Euthanasia Policeman [in *Hot Ice*]). John Brockmeyer will play Babushka—the first live model (the [character's] name is mine). Susan has turned up her nose at playing Baroness Von Rothschild who receives the curse of Caprice—"Out of fashion for 6 months!" Perhaps she'll be TaTa, Claude's androgynous secretary. Steven Sterne [aka Styles Caldwell] will be perfect as Lady Gloriana Kaufman. The role of Bertha her cheeky maid is still open. Bill Vehr will apparently be a rival designer. Lola will play Leah the international lesbian. A name on the urinals here is Tywfford Adamant [a European manufacturer of toilet bowls] — Charles likes that, and Lola thinks a character should be called "Stella Artois" after the ubiquitous beer signs.
>
> Charles says this play will prove we're not a homosexual company. We ridicule even *that*! There are other roles but that's all I know. Claude will not appear in

every scene, it's not meant to be a vehicle for him [Charles]. Some of the scenes
are very poetic. It should be a lush [Ronald] Firbankian project. I hope we do it.

Though there were a number of cast changes, the play finally opened at the Performing
Garage in February 1976 — or two and a half years after Currie's journal entry — is
quite similar to this preliminary concept. Claude Caprice (Ludlam) is an internationally
renowned fashion designer whose creations are instantly knocked off by competitors.
He is the inventor of everything from the brassiere and the live model to "the gownless
evening strap."

The secret to his success is that "Caprice designs the ugliest clothes in the world." As
Baroness Zuni Feinschmecker (Black-Eyed Susan), his principal customer and
patroness, explains: "The uglier my clothes, the more beautiful I appear by contrast. So
many designers want all the attention to go to their clothes. But not Caprice, he makes
clothes ugly and women beautiful."

(Hofstra colleague Charlotte Forbes took credit for this last line: "I remember telling
Charles in college that I always wore ugly clothes, because they make me look more
beautiful. Charles and I would have long conversations about what true beauty is. We
both maintained that to be truly beautiful, you needed to have some aspect of you that
was ugly.")

The farce in *Caprice* escalates when Zuni rejects one of Caprice's designs and he rele-
gates her to "rack and ready to wear." Despite her entreaties to be reinstated in "the
House of Caprice," he tells Zuni, "You can wear sackcloth and ashes for all I care." In
her desperation, Zuni expatriates to the salon of Caprice's chief rival, Twyfford
Adamant (Bill Vehr).

A fashion show was added to many of the performances, involving a long, burlap sackcloth with a half-dozen holes for heads to pop through. This became the "Fire Woman"
segment of *Caprice*, and a good number of the old gang made guest appearances in the
scene, including Crazy Arthur, Minette, and Marsha P. Johnson, celebrated for being
one of the drag queens who initiated the Stonewall riots in 1969.

The "sackcloth and ashes" reference in *Caprice* was not only a barb at Catholicism, but
also, perhaps, a direct reference to a famous episode from the TV series "I Love Lucy."
In their search for original designer gowns, Lucy and her friend Ethel are tricked by

their husbands into wearing potato-sacks. The scheme has ironic repercussions when various fashion houses in Paris steal the look.

In a slightly veiled way, Ludlam claimed that the character of Twyfford Adamant was a takeoff on Warhol. "Twyfford was more of an s&m type," he said, "an asexual who is a voyeur, loves to have other people have sex while he watches. A lot of these characteristics were from people we knew, many celebrities in the art world." Warhol was notorious for being an asexual voyeur. Caprice himself was based on Paul Poiret, the early twentieth century French fashion designer who popularized Oriental styles in the Occidental world and had inspired Ludlam's willow tree wall mural in 1970.

Basically a parody of the fashion industry and — less directly — of the art world, *Caprice* is also a mockery of homosexuality. As confirmed by Richard Currie's journal entry, it was conceived to be a send-up of the most stereotypical notions of being gay. Though many might find it surprising, this was the first time that Ludlam played a specifically gay character, and a ludicrous one at that. But by capriciously gnawing on the hand that fed him, Ludlam alienated a portion of his large gay audience with this play. *Caprice* epitomizes Ludlam's tendency towards self-mockery, or what some might see as his perverse aesthetic.

On the other hand, as Ludlam had told Quinton in regards to *Caprice*, he was writing a play about a "gay hero." While making fun of homosexual stereotypes, the play also set out to defend and celebrate them — to say, in essence, that there's nothing wrong with being a flaming queen.

Several of those involved with the production, however, had problems with the inherent contradictions. Mario Montez returned to the Ridiculous to play the incidental character of Babushka, the "live fashion model." But, as Pashalinski phrased it, this proved to be "Mario's Armageddon." Montez had finally found the macho Latin lover he had always dreamed of — a paramour who told him, "Why are you doing this? You look foolish and silly up there on the stage." Ludlam tried to reason with Montez, pointing out that he should not sacrifice his celebrated reputation as a drag queen just to suit his lover. But Montez, who had been one of the primary inspirations behind the Ridiculous, renounced drag and never performed again with the company after *Caprice*.

Though Adrian, Caprice's "divine love," was played by Brockmeyer, the character was clearly based on Quinton. When the play begins, Adrian and Caprice have just been reunited after a terrific fight. "I found him in the same doorway he was standing in the night we met," says Caprice, directly describing Ludlam and Quinton's first encounter. "I felt like a heel after all the terrible things I said about him and the poor bunny's been suffering for weeks. He can't live without me."

Upon hearing that "Adrian has come back," Zuni exclaims, "You can't be serious. After that last scene I thought they'd never speak to each other again." "On the contrary, they're closer than ever," explains Tata, Caprice's servant. "Scenes are as necessary to the progress of love as wars are to the progress of civilization."

It's important to recognize that the relationship between Caprice and Adrian is presented in a healthy, positive light. Although the play mocked homosexuals, it was even more scornful of heterosexuals, as embodied by the problematic relationship between Zuni and her husband, Harry Feinschmecker.

As played in drag by Pashalinski, Feinschmecker is an oversexed character. "Like Scheherazade I have dished up a thousand and one nights of perversion to hold him under my spell," explains Zuni.

> Once when he began to get bored I had him frigged while he kissed the asshole of one girl while a second frigged his ass and a third his prick. Then I had him lick the cunt of another while a fourth licked his asshole. Then I had them all switch positions so that when all was said and done he sucked a beshitted ass, had a tongue frig his beshitted asshole, encunted the friggeresses, swallowed their balm, and all three of them had their asses kissed.

Feinschmecker's perversity progressed to the point where "he had a young boy dressed in mare's skin, his asshole smeared with mare's fuck, and surrendered this small boy to an excited horse. He observed their struggles and the boy's death." This grotesque act had been inspired by Feinschmecker's having seen "*Equus* the night before. He was always an intellectual, a theatergoer."

According to Susan, "Charles specifically wanted me to have this speech, which was adapted from the Marquis de Sade, because he thought I looked the most innocent of anyone in the company and those words would have a greater impact coming out of my mouth." Susan also recalled one particular night when Martin Gottfried brought some producers from the Shubert organization who fled after this speech.

To avoid the unexpected arrival of Zuni, Harry Feinschmecker hides in Caprice's steam room, where he's "initiated into the rites of homoerotica." He turns "queer" and changes his name to "Marcel," specifically in homage to Proust. Though he's had an antagonistic relationship with Caprice up until this scene, he now wants to become his "cosmetician" and "a man who lives for one thing only . . . (*Runs out screaming*) Makeup!"

"I'm a little worried about the Baron," says Caprice. "He'll be all right. Some people overreact at first," replies Adrian.

After emerging from the steam room, Pashalinski "settled for a lisp" to convey the Baron's homosexual transformation. But from the very beginning, Pashalinski found *Caprice* the most difficult show she ever worked on. "*Caprice* was hard for me," she admitted. "It started out with the casting. First I was going to be a lesbian journalist named Stella Artois. And for some reason, I couldn't find myself in this role as a lesbian. I was even uncomfortable about doing it, but I didn't tell Charles that." Pashalinski continued:

> Charles wanted me to give the character more pizazz, but there wasn't really much of a role there, and it just kept coming out flat. We kept switching roles too. I even read Zuni, once, because Susan was having problems as well. He didn't have anyone to play Harry Feinschmecker at first, and a number of people read it at different times, beginning with Jack Mallory. But then when I read it, it took off. It was dynamite chemically between Susan and me. But also very hard.

Part of the problem was that this was Pashalinski's first — and last — drag role in a Ridiculous play. "It was hard doing drag," she recalled,

> exposing my inner fantasies and making me feel very vulnerable. I had difficulty finding the right makeup. I felt I never looked right and tried to disguise myself completely. I also felt as if I were sacrificing myself for Charles by doing this drag role, which wasn't a romanticized portrait but rather grotesque. I felt as if it was exposing me as a lesbian more than playing a lesbian would have. It exposed my masculine side, involving the stereotypes that accrue to gay women, and it brought up a lot of garbage from my psyche.

If Pashalinski found it difficult being an out-of-the-closet lesbian playing a male character who turns homosexual, the gay issues and tomfoolery of *Caprice* had to be equally hard on Black-Eyed Susan, the lone straight member of the company at the time. It was during *Caprice* that Pashalinski and Susan had their first real fight.

According to Susan, part of the problem was that *Caprice* was somewhat unfinished when they began staging it.

> And Charles was always hard to get along with when the plays were unresolved. We often had cold wars, but he was being especially hostile and aggressive toward me during this period. I thought the best way to deal with him would be just to back off. In fact, by the time of *Caprice*, I hadn't spoken to Charles outside of the theater for several months.

Pashalinski claimed that, "My scenes with Susan became this real power struggle both onstage and off. It felt like I wasn't Lola any more to Susan. She behaved differently with me all of a sudden. We were sharing a dressing room when we moved to the Provincetown Playhouse [with *Caprice*], and even had a 'fistfight' backstage one night. I was so incensed, I slapped her in the face, and she went crying into the boys' dressing room."

Susan's bad mood spilled over and affected the rest of the cast. When Brockmeyer heard that Pashalinski had slapped Susan, he responded, "Somebody had to."

Pashalinski recalled appealing to Ludlam to try and help resolve the difficulties with Susan, "But I didn't get much sympathy from him." The slapping episode occurred well into the run of the play, long after Pashalinski and Susan had been feeling upstaged by each other. Pashalinski was especially furious over the opening scene in Act II. As the transformed and "homoeroticized" Feinschmecker, s/he comes home to Zuni, imploring her to "let me do your hair.... How's about a wash and set? Or something really camp, like a frosting?" "If there's one thing I cannot tolerate it's effeminacy in women," replies Zuni.

During the scene, Pashalinski was supposed to take Susan by the hand and lead her to a chair across the stage where she would redo her hair. "And Susan always resisted, standing there like a ton of bricks every night. It was almost impossible to move her," recalled Pashalinski. "After this had gone on for a number of performances, I finally exploded one night. That's when I slapped her."

According to Susan,

> The next day, Lola phoned me to discuss the incident. She said we should talk

about our relationship with Charles, which she felt was the core of the problem. She thought we were both competing for Charles's attention. But I told her I hadn't spoken to Charles outside of the theater for a long time. This just made her more furious. I really think she was irate with me because she just hated playing a man, and I was the only other woman in the show.

Though the original production was fraught with backstage headaches, *Caprice* emerged as one of Ludlam's wittiest works. He continued his ongoing attack against Catholicism in some of Adamant's lines: "I might mention to the good sisters how you urinated in the holy water they sent to be scented and told them it was bitter rhodium sacred to Saint Jerome.... Or how you have been known to distill your own rankest farts into frankincense for the Holy Father himself in Rome."

But all hidden agendas aside, *Caprice* was far less frivolous or "capricious" than it seemed on the surface. A prologue hints at the more serious intentions behind the play: Ludlam plays a "Hermit" who is visited by a "Wayfarer" (Bill Vehr). The Hermit has "no worldly connections, no luxuries," but he shares what little he does have with his visitor in need of food and shelter. The Wayfarer or pilgrim proves to be a Bodhisattva — someone who has attained Enlightenment and become a Buddha for future ages. Out of gratitude, the Bodhisattva offers the Hermit the chance to "enter into nirvana." But with one of the most autobiographical speeches that Ludlam ever inserted into a play, the Hermit chooses instead to,

> live yet another life to help others to become enlightened.... I have lived a life of seclusion, balance, order, and reason. For my last life, I should like its opposite. I would like to lead people out of materialism. But in a different way. A way wholly unlike hermitage. I would like to bring frivolity to Mankind, know many people, take chances, risk everything, live as though I were Caprice itself!

The Hermit, in other words, becomes Caprice, whose self-chosen mission — like Ludlam's — is to enlighten others, to denigrate materialism and to "bring frivolity to Mankind." While spiced with puns and jokes, the script also sustains this ulterior theme. Caprice is "more than a king of kings — he is a king of queens!" When he invents "the world's first brassiere," Zuni asks him, "How much do you want, Caprice? Name any sum."

> CAPRICE: (*Embarrassed*) No, no, I did it for Womankind. I could not accept payment.
> ZUNI: (*With warmth and understanding as though she were comforting a child*) We

cannot *pay* for Art. You know that, Caprice. I give you this money. You
give me your brassiere. Shall we call it foundation support? . . .
CAPRICE: (*Overcome*) I shall study deserving.

Caprice also says: "Art is like a blindfold that stands between Man and Nature. If we
could truly see Nature we would not need Art. But alas, it is easier to see Nature in Art
than it is to see Art in Nature." Ludlam identified particularly with the Caprice who
tells Adrian, "The fact is . . . that when the period in which a man of talent is condemned to live is dull and stupid, the artist is haunted, perhaps unknown to himself, by
a nostalgic yearning for another age."

After the play was up and running, Ludlam got it into his head that he wanted
everyone to appear naked onstage. He borrowed a gag from French farce: One character
had his clothes stolen, then he or she in turn stole someone else's, until practically
everyone had been exposed. When he first proposed this, Mario Montez responded, "I
don't mind if I'm naked for three or four minutes, but after that it's exhibitionism." The
business was tried for a few nights without getting the desired laughs, after which it was
abruptly dropped.

Adam Kilgore remembered that during the previews for *Caprice*, Ludlam asked him, "Is
there anything really *wild* you'd like to do onstage, like being whipped? I'll write it in
for you." "He just kept asking everybody for all these sensational things," said Kilgore,
"hoping they'd fit together."

Ethyl Eichelberger solidified his new involvement with the company by undertaking
three bit parts in *Caprice*: La Fleur, a parfumeur; Bertha, Adamant's maid; and Althea
Gordon, an interviewer. Though content at the time to be doing anything with the
Ridiculous, he would come to feel that his own considerable talents were squandered in
such small roles.

∽

With its blend of humor and seriousness, *Caprice* did quite well when it opened at the
Performing Garage. But the space lacked Ludlam's beloved proscenium stage. Edward
Avedisian's set designs did their best to compensate with a large canvas backdrop that
had pieces of fabric collaged on it. The production then moved to the Provincetown
Playhouse — which did have a proscenium — and it was here that it opened to the
critics in April 1976.

Caprice received only fair notices. In the *Times*, Gussow pronounced it "lesser Ludlam ...far below the author's *Bluebeard*, *Camille* and *Stage Blood*." Gerald Rabkin, writing for the *Soho Weekly News*, felt that one reason *Caprice* didn't "measure up... is because the play does not afford Ludlam the comic actor an opportunity to do what he does best. Claude Caprice is too obvious a comic target; the world of fashion is itself a form of self-parody. Ludlam as performer is at his best when he plays *against* the character he is embodying, when he amplifies its absurdity through manic invention."

Ludlam rightfully resented the response to *Caprice*, a better play than the critical record allows. But it was especially the reaction to the gay issues that upset him. As Richard Currie viewed it, "*Caprice* was to prove once and for all that we were not a gay company, because Charles wanted to show the world that we could make fun of gay people, too. It was a little vendetta behind the play."

Beneath it all was Ludlam's lifelong resistance to being categorized or pinned down. His stubbornly paradoxical nature would take exception to anyone's defining his theater one way or the other. He particularly needed to combat the "drag," "camp," and "gay" labels that had accrued to the company from the very beginning. By mocking gay stereotypes in *Caprice*, he hoped to avoid this trap once and for all. But he unwittingly set himself up for another in the process.

Ludlam complained,

> People have preconceptions about what you should be doing. As a parodist it's diffi-
> cult, because you're making fun of things. In *Caprice* I showed the gay world, and
> gay people were the ones who were most offended. Some thought it was great and
> understood it; others thought that we should only be presenting a so-called positive
> image of gays. I would never stoop to presenting a positive image — of anything.

It was directly after *Caprice* closed that Georg Osterman had a falling-out with the company. "In the play, I played a mechanical doll called Copelias who is sent by Twyfford Adamant to destroy Caprice by winning his heart and giving him nothing in return." (As Adamant reveals his scheme: "This doll, shrouded in deathless beauty, will tell him anything he wants to hear. But try though he may, it will never give him one drop of human feeling.") At the end of the run, Osterman sent Ludlam a letter. "I said that it didn't feel like a family anymore and I felt like an outsider," recalled Osterman. "Although it was coming from a position of feeling hurt, it could have been interpreted as anger, and I know I hurt Charles's feelings. After the letter we didn't speak for a while."

Only in retrospect did Osterman come to see that "I was going through a psychological problem then. I had been cast only in female roles and I was beginning to feel like I was stuck and if I ever wanted to do anything else, I wouldn't be able to. But I didn't say any of that in the letter." It is nonetheless telling that in Ludlam's next play, *Der Ring Gott Farblonjet*, Osterman was cast in a male role.

Though it was hard for Ludlam to accept the response to *Caprice*, he evidently took to heart the end of Rabkin's review in the *Soho Weekly News*. "I'd like, for once, to see Ludlam as playwright work without having to service Ludlam the star performer," wrote Rabkin. "Perhaps Ludlam could put down one of his hats from time to time and invite guest collaborators."

Not only would Ludlam soon have Pashalinski direct *Jack and the Beanstalk*, but far more remarkable, he wouldn't even write a part for himself in his subsequent play, *Der Ring Gott Farblonjet*. It was also during the period of *Caprice* that Ludlam began to embark on outside projects.

With Broadway as the intended destination, he accepted a commission from producer Adela Holzer to rewrite the book for a musical about Catherine de Medici and the St. Bartholomew Day Massacre. (The controversial Holzer would later be indicted for her role in an immigration scam.) With music by Will Holt and lyrics by Gary William Friedman, the original book by Tom Topor had been deemed a failure. When Ludlam told Holzer his working title, *Isle of the Hermaphrodites, or The Murdered Minion*, she said, "Wonderful! Murder and hermaphrodites — two of my favorite subjects," but no production emerged. Ludlam wrote the book with an eye on possibly performing the play at the Ridiculous one day. Although readings were eventually held, the play was never produced in Ludlam's lifetime.

Reaching out to children's theater was another gambit to secure additional funding. Following the success of *Professor Bedlam's Educational Punch and Judy Show* at the Evergreen, Ludlam was approached by the New York State Council on the Arts to write something for their "Younger Audience" program. The result was his short and subversive adaptation of *Jack and the Beanstalk*, performed for children at the Brooklyn Academy of Music. The ten-page script amounts to perhaps his least substantial work. An author's note dictates that "the duration of the performance should not exceed forty-five minutes."

Predictably, Ludlam made some adjustments to the nursery tale. When Jack is forced by his mother to sell his beloved cow ("Bossie," played together by Ludlam and Quinton in a cow suit), he happens upon an Ex-Butcher. "I used to be a butcher who cut up animals to make meat," says the Ex-Butcher. "But now I'm so sorry that I just want to take a cow home as a pet and lavish all the good things in life on her." And in a typical Ludlam mode, the beans the Ex-Butcher exchanges for the cow are soybeans. "They have just as much protein as meat," he explains. "They don't take up as much room. And you don't have to eat your pets!"

The otherwise straightforward adaptation included some politically provocative material. The first scene is set in "The tenement apartment of Jack and his mother, Mrs. Beanstalk." A stage direction reads, "The style should be socialist realism." Far more subversive was Ludlam's interpolation of an anti-establishment "Man-in-the-Moon," whom Jack encounters on his climb up the beanstalk. "I don't understand why the government spends billions of dollars to put men on the moon," says this fanciful figure.

Apart from the startling leftist perspective, there was an uproar by the management of BAM following the first performance because the play proved so short. They had been expecting a ninety-minute show and were outraged by its brevity. They were also disturbed by Ethyl Eichelberger appearing in drag as the Giant's Wife, and threatened to withhold royalty payments. As Osterman, who played Jack, remembered, "They didn't want to pay us, because they said we were spreading communist propaganda to little children."

Nor did the production really look right. Callejo's painted backdrops for *Jack and the Beanstalk* filled only a fraction of the cavernous space at BAM. For the second performance, Ludlam had the cast improvise and interact with the audience to extend the running time. But the play's scheduled run at BAM was abruptly terminated after only two performances.

Though Ludlam never told Pashalinski directly, he complained to others that he should have directed the play himself. For her part, Pashalinski was somewhat defensive about being the "chosen one" — the first other person to direct one of Ludlam's plays since the rift with Vaccaro. And she felt "responsible when it got the response it did."

Ludlam later observed that it "was an ill-fated production. I have since learned that when you do plays for children, you are really not being judged by the children but by the parents."

There was a single, subsequent performance of *Jack and the Beanstalk* at the Egg in Albany. The company flew up and took the train back after the matinee. "It was this huge, coliseum-like space," said Osterman, "and it was packed with screaming children. Since we weren't miked, I don't think they could hear us at all. But Ethyl made his entrance by roller-skating down this ramp to the stage and that went over very well."

The Ridiculous had already taken *Camille* on a brief tour of Upstate New York earlier in the year, shortly before *Caprice* reopened at the Provincetown Playhouse in April. They gave two performances at the Carrier Theater in Syracuse, where Ludlam also offered his *Punch and Judy* puppet show at II AM on Saturday.

A rather memorable example of Ludlam's willingness to offer directions while onstage occurred during a performance of *Camille* at the Carrier. Given its size, the theater employed microphones, with which the Ridiculous players were thoroughly unfamiliar. When Ludlam was unhappy with the way Mallory delivered a line, he muttered *sotto voce*, "Have you given up acting, darling?" The laughter wafting through the house made it only too clear that he had been far more audible than he had meant to be.

The company proved an even bigger hit at the Studio Arena Theater in Buffalo — the end of a local review (by Hal Crowther) demonstrates just how well *Camille* went over in this provincial town: "[Ludlam] does things with his shoulders and his hands that would have extended the careers of Cleopatra and Mata Hari. In fact, as this style of womanhood vanishes . . . Ludlam may become the sole repository for everything another era revered as feminine. If Greta Garbo had half as much talent as Charles Ludlam, she could have played Abraham Lincoln."

Richard Currie recalled an explosive incident involving Quinton during their upstate visit. "At first, Everett was just this person on the fringes," said Currie.

> He was quiet and seemingly shy. But he was hanging around all the time, and we all understood what was happening — that he was someone Charles was seeing. Then in Syracuse, I was hanging the sets and getting the lights cued for *Camille*. I had maybe half an hour before curtain and I was about to get made-up to play the butler in the first act when Charles asked me if I could teach Everett to play the part. I blew up at him and said, "Are you kidding? Not only have I got to finish cuing and get this show ready, but everything the butler does is much too busy. There are too many cues, too many entrances of the guests, to show him all

of it in a half hour." I was furious that Charles would think that Everett could replace me at the last minute like that.

In a quieter moment, Currie pointed out to Ludlam that he disliked playing the butler in the second party scene as well, since this suggested that the character had "turned on Marguerite and was now working for Olympe. If you want Everett to go on, let him be the butler at Olympe's, because there's nothing to know. He only needs the cues to introduce the various guests, and then Olympe comes over and kicks him and says, 'Say dinner is served.' And we finished that tour with Everett playing the butler for the Olympe party scene."

The Ridiculous took both *Camille* and *Stage Blood* to Chicago as well, right after the second installment of *Caprice* closed at the Provincetown Playhouse on May 9, 1976. In retrospect, the most notable development during their week in the Windy City entailed the introduction of Charles Busch, the drag-diva-to-be, to the company.

Busch first became aware of the Ridiculous by way of the article in *Vogue* on *The Grand Tarot*, when he was living in Manhattan with the aunt who raised him. The young acolyte's enthusiasm for Ludlam picked up momentum when he saw *Eunuchs of the Forbidden City*. It further blossomed during the company's stint in Chicago, where Busch was in his senior year at Northwestern University. Busch attended a symposium the Ridiculous held at the University of Chicago, in conjunction with their performing there.

"Charles was answering these very academic questions," recalled Busch. "I added my two cents on some subject or other, and he seemed to appreciate what I had to say. Then, I was waiting in the lobby as Charles and the other members of the company started coming out the door." Though Ludlam was aloof, Busch instantly bonded with both Georg Osterman and John Brockmeyer. "When I mentioned that I was going to be seeing *Stage Blood* that night, they told me there would be a party afterwards and invited me to go along with them," continued Busch.

After the performance, but before the party, Busch went backstage and helped strike the set. "I had this one, very weird, 'All About Eve' moment," he claimed. "When we were packing up the costumes, somebody tossed Camille's ball gown to me; and as I was holding it up, I noticed Charles watching me with this odd look: I put it down *very* quickly."

The posh soiree was given by a local patron of the arts. Since it ended quite late, and

Northwestern was on the other side of town, Busch accompanied his newfound friends to their hotel instead of returning home. Brockmeyer shared his bed with Busch, who was somewhat surprised — and perhaps a tad dismayed — that his host proved to be the perfect gentleman.

Adding still more to their academic credentials, the company was invited to instruct theater students at American University in Washington, D.C. during the summer. With Quinton participating more as a pupil than a teacher, Ludlam and Eichelberger offered classes in *commedia*. Black-Eyed Susan and Adam Kilgore directed an all-student pro-duction of *Bluebeard*, and Pashalinski and Vehr supervised one of *Corn*, in which Quinton undertook the role of Moe.

According to Pashalinski, Ludlam "loved both productions when he saw them, but he was particularly pleased with the seriousness with which Susan had approached the project." Susan claimed that Ludlam liked the way *Bluebeard* came across, "because it was different than when he directed it."

Following their Bicentennial summer in the District of Columbia, the company embarked in early August on their third European tour. (This was in lieu of going to San Francisco, as Ludlam had planned the preceding fall.) In addition to Ludlam, the relatively small troupe consisted of Brockmeyer, Vehr, Pashalinski, Black-Eyed Susan, Osterman, Eichelberger, stage manager Richard Gibbs, and of course Quinton. It was scheduled to be a two-week visit to Florence, where they performed *Camille* and *Stage Blood* as part of an international theater festival. (La MaMa also participated in the fes-tival with Andre Serban's highly praised, avant-garde interpretation of three classic Greek plays.)

Osterman claimed, "We were very well received in Florence. Ethyl would always tell the story that the press said I was the most beautiful woman on the Italian stage. I think they thought I really was a woman. Italian men sure liked me. And I liked them. I was a big slut in Florence. I was really bad, but I had a ball."

One of the company's biggest fans in Florence was Kathryn Keene, sister of the onetime governor of New Jersey. Known as K.K., she was an artist who had worked with Red Grooms and Robert Wilson. Keene had a large villa outside of Florence where she spent half the year, and she invited the company out for a couple of days. Surrounded by olive groves, they feasted on home-cooked meals and drank gallons of the local Chianti.

The Ridiculous went over so well in Florence that a French scout invited them
to extend their European visit and perform *Camille* at an upcoming theater festival
in Nancy. Founded more than a dozen years earlier by Jack Lang and a group of
students and artists, the Festival Mondial du Théâtre ("The World Theater Festival")
had evolved into a major annual event with companies attending from all over
the world. The previous year's festival, in 1975, had reportedly drawn more than
200,000 visitors, and the architecturally splendid town of Nancy did all it could to
welcome them.

Though it was an honor to be invited, there would be a couple of weeks before the
engagement began, and the festival could not afford to pay any salaries to cover this
lead time. The management offered minimal accommodations in a dormitory and meal
tickets for a student cafeteria prior to the official opening on September 3, when the
company was moved to a more proper hotel and provided with a regular stipend.

Given the circumstances, Brockmeyer, Black Eyed Susan, Vehr, and Eichelberger
declined to accompany the others to France. According to Pashalinski, "It was another
exercise in self-sacrifice and they just didn't want to make it this time. They weren't
going to be fooled by Charles anymore." As Susan recalled, for her it was more a matter
of returning to her job and fulfilling previous commitments in New York.

With eleven different theaters or sites engaged simultaneously, the focus of the 1976
Nancy festival was on popular comic theater. (A brochure referred to that year's edition
as "Carousel Round the Comic Muse" and explained that the emphasis would be
on "descendants of the *commedia dell'arte*" tradition.) Ludlam was pleased to perform
in the Grand Théâtre, the city's major opera house, which had been damaged during
the Second World War and recently renovated. Mabou Mines and Italy's beloved Dario
Fo were among the thirty-three groups and performers that played in other venues.
A hallmark of the ten-day festival's opening weekend was an outdoor event, "Ubu à
Nancy," with jugglers and acrobats winding their way through the center of town and
evoking an almost medieval atmosphere.

According to Pashalinski, Ludlam was "grumpy" in Nancy. Though he made the best of
it, he was indeed bothered by the departure of Susan and the others. He could not
understand how anyone could turn down the opportunity to work with him, even if it
was to return to a job. Regardless of the practical considerations, it was simply in his
nature to interpret such behavior as a personal betrayal.

There were also problems between Ludlam and Quinton while they were in Europe. Though they were celebrating their first anniversary abroad, dark moods prevailed and it was all the others could do to get them to speak to one another. At other times the rest of the troupe wished they were *not* communicating—in view of what they had to say to each other.

Ludlam had even more serious problems to contend with when his pared-down group arrived in Nancy. Though they had been invited to perform *Camille*, it was hardly feasible with only half the cast. Ludlam took advantage of the two free weeks before the festival began by starting on a new piece called *The Fearsome Adventures of the Fearless Fucker Carigos*.

Only working notebook pages and fragments of the script survive. It was partially cobbled together with dialogue from earlier shows, including *Turds in Hell* and *Bluebeard*. But the characters as well as the situations were freshly invented. Ludlam played Kharagoz ("Carigos"), derived from Karaghiozi, a Turkish folk character and prankster who customarily appears as a shadow puppet. Ludlam had already begun to work with the idea of Kharagoz in his *commedia* classes.

In *The Fearsome Adventures*, Ludlam turned Kharagoz into the sex maniac implied by the title. In the opening scene, Kharagoz instructs his bedraggled sidekick Gluteous Maximus (Quinton) in how to pursue sexual escapades, the chief preoccupation of their so-called "adventures." They visit a bathhouse run by Madame Geets, played by Pashalinski. (Madame Geets was the actual name of a memorable, domineering concierge the company had to contend with in Brussels, during their previous European tour.)

Kharagoz arrives at the bathhouse with a foam-covered bat representing a huge erect penis. Clad only in towels, a dozen or so students from local schools were recruited to play other patrons. With Kharagoz and his Beardsleyesque phallus following them surreptitiously, they roam from one enormous column to another, emit a scream from behind as he catches up with them, and emerge rubbing their rear ends as if they had just been penetrated.

The rambling scenario included a vignette concerning King Stanislaus, a local hero who had ruled over Nancy in the eighteenth century and built many of the city's rococo buildings. Ludlam invented an allegorical figure, the Virgin of Lorraine (Osterman), who is rescued by Stanislaus after having been attacked by a forest of "tree lesbians" that wanted to "impregnate" her. Ludlam got the idea for the tree lesbians from a comic book he happened upon in Florence. They were played by the students who wore brown paper bags representing tree trunks and who held branches over their heads.

The evening also featured an eating contest between Kharagoz and Madame Geets. *Divertissements* were performed during their feast, including a mock ballet from *Swan Lake*, done in drag by one of the students. This was followed by the rape scene from *Bluebeard*, and then by Quinton and Osterman performing Moe's seduction of Melanie from *Corn*.

In addition to *The Fearsome Adventures*, Ludlam also performed the death scene from *Camille* by simultaneously playing Armand and Marguerite. Borrowing Mary Brecht's half-bride, half-groom design from *The Grand Tarot*, Osterman constructed a bi-gendered costume for Ludlam. With a snow machine contributing to the effect, the scene commenced with Marguerite painfully dragging herself from her sickbed to the window, where she watches a passing parade consisting of gigantic Mardi Gras-type heads. Via a mirror, Ludlam appeared to be holding a glass in each hand, so the lovers could toast one another.

Osterman also designed the costume for Kharagoz: oversized, zebra-striped balloon pants. As Madame Geets's niece Convulvula, Osterman wore a flower-patterned sarong and a blonde bouffant wig spiked with flowers. Quinton, who helped make the costumes, designed for himself a woolly coat that was slit open in the back, exposing his naked derriere, or his "Gluteous Maximus."

There was only a moderate turnout the first night. But once the critics had expressed their outrage, the Ridiculous had a full house every night for the rest of the festival. As Osterman recalled, "They basically wrote that we were mad and should be locked up, and never allowed onstage again. After those reviews, every night was packed to the rafters. And the audience loved it."

Though they all had a ball doing the show in Nancy, the excursion marked another turning point for Pashalinski, who felt the need for some distance from the company and from Ludlam's domineering personality. "Before, the only thing that seemed to matter was what Charles wanted and when it was good for him," said Pashalinski. "When he took his vacations was when we had ours. But I was now turning forty-one and just saw that the company was not going to fulfill my every need. After ten years with the company, I needed to be much more in control of my life.

"The emotional complexities were working against me as a person," continued Pashalinski.

> On the one hand, Charles was my pal; on the other, he was my boss. I needed his approval, but in other respects, he needed mine. I realized that I was the eldest member of the company, and felt like I was the most practical, the most level-headed one. [Pashalinski was eight years older than Ludlam and seven years older than Vehr.] But it was time for me to start pulling away from the feeling that the company should be or could be something it wasn't. Why couldn't we have a steady salary? There was also my need for more personal recognition. I was also beginning to realize that the company could be a burden for Charles, and that he had resentments as well.

In terms of Pashalinski's craving "more personal recognition," she had to be impressed with the profile of Ludlam and the Ridiculous which appeared in the *New Yorker* on November 15, 1976, shortly after they returned from France. Here was a long, in-depth analysis of the company and its history, appearing in one of the country's most prestigious publications on all matters cultural. Though it gave the Ridiculous the recognition that followers felt it had deserved for years, Ludlam obviously dominated the piece — as he did the company.

Having one's profile in the *New Yorker* was a tribute of the highest order under any circumstances; but since Ludlam was only thirty-three, the honor was even more exceptional. This was especially true then, when the venerable William Shawn was still overseeing every aspect of the publication, and before he was replaced by a series of editors who endeavored to appeal to a younger audience.

Actually, Henry Geldzahler had given the idea for the profile to Calvin Tomkins, the art commentator and journalist, a few years before it was written. At this stage in his career, Ludlam could not have asked for a more incisive or sympathetic spokesman than he found in Tomkins. Based on extensive interviews with Ludlam and other members of the company, Tomkins's piece promoted Ludlam as an important artist who should be taken more seriously by the critical establishment than he had been.

The Ludlam whom Tomkins met was "a small, wiry, nervously energetic man of thirty-three, with thinning hair, melodramatic blue eyes, and a large nose and mouth, [who] has a compelling stage presence." From Tomkins's perspective, the work of Richard

Foreman, Robert Wilson, Richard Schechner, and André Gregory "has occasioned daunting critical essays here and abroad. So far, however, hardly anyone has given a serious thought to Charles Ludlam . . . and though the critics have treated him by no means unkindly, he sometimes feels that they have consistently overlooked the dramatic values and the serious ideas at the heart of his comic oeuvre."

The profile featured a caricature of Ludlam in his Hamlet costume from *Stage Blood*, rendered by Koren — the regular *New Yorker* cartoonist — with his distinctively jagged lines. Beyond analyzing the background of the Ridiculous and discussing Ludlam's development as an artist of the first rank, Tomkins summarized the company's first eleven shows with telling anecdotes and insightful commentaries. The dense article concluded with lengthy quotes from Ludlam talking about his acting methods, his current problems as a writer, and finally, a reference to his work-in-progress, *Der Ring Gott Farblonjet*.

"In school," Ludlam told Tomkins,

> there was all that emphasis on the Method, and feeling your way into the part, and it was always sort of schizophrenic for me; there were too many different things to juggle. But now I think I'm really a Stanislavski actor par excellence. I go into a sort of trance onstage and believe in my role completely. Of course, I also know I'm onstage and people are watching — I'm admitting I'm acting — but on another plane my belief is total. People talk about great performances, most of which are luck — the right role coming along at the right time for an actor. But I'm seeing to it that I get the role. I've created it, written it, directed it. My immersion is total!

> My main problem as a writer now is with language. I love the language. I'm hung up on words. In the early plays there was always a motif, and the language would be a parody of that motif — science fiction or *Grand Hotel*, or gothic horror story. In *Eunuchs*, I tried aiming for an Oscar Wilde sort of headiness, a very elevated diction. In *Corn*, I was able to get by on clichés and country dialogue. The problem is, when you're not parodying a genre anymore, how do people talk? The minimal vocabulary was Beckett's solution — also Racine's. I can see that as a possibility. But I want something richer than that. Passion sings in opera; in the theatre, it has to do something else. It is richness that I want — that panoramic quality, the allusiveness of language.

"Ludlam, at any rate, is convinced that Ludlam improves each year as a writer, director, and actor, and new projects abound in his head," added Tomkins.

> And although he complains of feeling oppressed by the notion that his work must be funny at all times, he is halfway through the writing of a ridiculous opera, a four-hour spectacle entitled *Der Ring Gott Farblonjet*, for which he has merrily plundered Wagner's entire *Ring* cycle and an early Ibsen play called *The Vikings at Helgeland*, among other sources. Wagner's score is to be performed in a "collaged" version by (he hopes) a brass band, and Ludlam is looking for people who can sing it "in the manner of Florence Foster Jenkins.... My Valkyries are lesbian motorcyclists, and Valhalla is Lincoln Center, which we'll burn down in the last act. The staging is so complex that I'd planned not to act in it at all, but I may not be able to resist."

Only a lunatic would have the audacity to compress and stage Wagner's mammoth *Ring* cycle of four operas, which was first performed in its entirety in 1876. Only a genius could bring it off in a manner that would be even halfway acceptable to experts and aficionados of this towering work. Lunatic *and* genius that he was, Ludlam succeeded on both counts — even if the first production was to fare badly with the majority of the critics.

Given the *Ring*'s reputation as a monumental creation — its grandeur and its excesses — it was simply an irresistible choice for Ludlam to plunder and make his own. Along with *Camille* and *Hamlet*, it was among the handful of "great works" Ludlam kept saying he wanted to do long before he finally got around to them.

It was John Brockmeyer who ultimately prompted Ludlam to undertake his adaptation of *Der Ring* in 1976. "I was never billed as a leading man and I was always comfortable with seeing myself as just a character actor," said Brockmeyer. "It was fine with me to be a comic character actor. But I had this one desire to play Siegfried, who was a juvenile lead. So I was always after Charles, saying, 'Come on, when are we going to do the *Ring*?'

"Although I've always been a very youthful looking person," continued Brockmeyer,

> at that time I was going to be thirty-seven. I mean I still looked sensational, but I started pressuring Charles that in a couple of years I would be too old to play Siegfried. And then I got to play it. Talk about fulfilled dreams! To me, he's the

ultimate juvenile in all literature: the kid, the kid with the dream. And I was able
to do it and I had a sense of real accomplishment when I did it.

Though Brockmeyer was among the very few whom Ludlam had in mind for a specific
role, *Der Ring* was one of the rare plays that was completely finished before rehearsals
began. To create such a gargantuan work presented a formidable challenge in itself, and
Ludlam planned to serve only as author and director out of the desire to excel in both
capacities. In view of the universal kudos he had already received for his performances
— especially in *Bluebeard* and *Camille* — Ludlam by now felt like a consummate actor
and didn't need to prove his acting abilities anymore. But he still wanted to hone his
skills as a director, which he could better achieve by remaining offstage, both to increase
his objectivity and consolidate his focus.

Running three-and-a-half hours and including an abundance of design demands, *Der
Ring* was the most epic of Ludlam's "epic" works. Based on Germanic, Scandinavian,
and Icelandic myths and sagas, Wagner's work defies not only summary but also comprehension. It involves dragons and beasts, gods and goddesses, giants and dwarfs, most
of whom are seeking to either gain or protect a ring forged from gold and stolen from
the Rhine River, a ring that endows its owner with control over the entire world.

While accounting for both his attraction to Wagner's *Ring* and his methods of adapting
it, Ludlam explained, "I love the incredibly inflated theatricality, the preposterousness
of opera. I followed the plot from different libretti of the *Ring*, including Wagner's own
libretto, as a scenic structure, used it as an outline. Then I improvised; in a sense,
invented the dialogue. I employ a selective attitude, like arranging gems in a setting,
using words as objects.

"It was influenced by Joyce," he continued,

> but I didn't really invent new words, which he did in *Finnegans Wake*. I felt that
> each word would be understood, although you might need an expanded vocabu-
> lary. *Der Ring Gott Farblonjet* abandoned literal speech and went into a completely
> abstract poetical language. Because it was about the evolution of man and thought,
> it was also the evolution of language. People had debates, rational discourse, and
> the medium of speech suffered through vaudeville and German Yiddish. It strug-
> gled out through all these different permutations. . . . I wanted to play with the
> idea of showing an evolution of speech. The characters speak different ways, using

words that ring of certain periods of history. I gave the characters linguistic leit-motifs: the Nihilumpens speak in potato-German; the Gibichungen speak an elevated revenge-tragedy Elizabethan speech; the Valkyries — chaste, heroic, virgin lesbians — have Gertrude Steinian speech. . . . I presented a kind of history of English and German compacted: the Forest Bird speaks in plain English, then Siegfried tastes the dragon's blood and suddenly understands birdsong, so he starts to understand English — at least, that was my justification.

Of course, the biggest challenge was simply reducing a nineteen-hour extravaganza, spread out over four separate evenings, into a single evening's entertainment. Given the compressed circumstances, what most impressed eminent Wagnerian scholar Robert W. Gutman about Ludlam's version is how faithful he managed to be to the complete story. Anyone familiar with the original would also notice an imbalance in the treatment, however. Ludlam's adaptation of *Das Rheingold* ("The Rhinegold"), the first opera in the cycle, is noticeably more complete and accurate a rendering of its source than the subsequent three. It may be that as Ludlam proceeded to write *Die Walküre* ("The Valkyrie"), *Siegfried*, and *Götterdämmerung* ("The Twilight of the Gods"), he recognized the need to be more concise. But it's harder to say why he didn't then rewrite *Das Rheingold* to adjust the ratio and maintain Wagner's original proportions.

With so many demented tangents and confusing developments to be travestied, Ludlam recognized that the *Ring* was already an absurd parody of itself. He more or less confined his *ridiculous* spin on it by punning in terms of both language and incidents. His loving attack begins with his new title for Wagner's magnum opus: *Der Ring Gott Farblonjet*, which combines the German and Yiddish term for God with the Yiddish for "fucked up." The title can roughly be translated as "God, Is This Ring Fucked Up!" or "The Ring God Fucked Up!" The inclusion of Yiddish throughout his adaptation is itself a joke, given Wagner's notorious anti-Semitism.

Though Ludlam retained most of the characters' names, there are puns in the few he altered. Wotan becomes Twoton, further described in the program as "Nobodaddy of the Gods"; Alberich becomes Alverrück, incorporating the German word for craziness (*verrückt*); Mime becomes Ninny; Fasolt becomes Fasdolt; Donner, the God of Thunder, becomes Dunderhead; Erda becomes Eartha; The Nibelungs become Nihilumpen; *Die Walküre* becomes "The Dyke Bikers at Helgeland," from Helgeland, New Jersey, "before the discovery of America."

Equally outrageous is the dialogue, which is a contrast of high and low diction, referring in some instances to comic vaudeville German à la The Katzenjammer Kids. To take but one of countless examples, Alverrück says to Ninny: "Kam hier you craftische zwergende Dwarf! Tapfer gezwickt sollst du mir sein. Where is the golden ring I ordered you to make? Is it finished?" Craftische suggests "crafty," but it's actually close to the German word for "strong" (*kräftig*). Zwergende is a construction derived from the German word for dwarfish (*zwergenhaft*), so he's essentially saying "dwarfish dwarf."

There are also touches of New York slang as well as predictable anachronisms. Consider this exchange: LOGE: "Don't cry over spilt milk! Help is on the way." NINNY: "Ich bin all smacked up! My brother has made me his slave." Far more preposterous is the dialogue between Fricka and Twoton after Fasdolt and Fafner have taken Freia away and the gods begin to age:

> FRICKA: (*Panicky*) Twoton, do something! It's your fault. You got us into this with
> your wheeling and dealing!
>
> TWOTON: For God's sake don't nag me, woman. I did it for you. Schlack! Schlack!
> Schlack!
>
> FRICKA: Schlemiel!
>
> TWOTON: Schlemasel!
>
> FRICKA: Schlepp!
>
> TWOTON: Schloomp!
>
> FRICKA: Schlub!
>
> TWOTON: Schmo!
>
> FRICKA: Schnook!
>
> TWOTON: Schnorrer!
>
> FRICKA: Schnozzle!
>
> TWOTON: So now it's schnozzle! How could you insult my nose? That's hitting
> below the belt. I'll descend through the thicker lower atmosphere to
> Nibbelhome where Alverrück's race the lowly Nihilumpen dwell.
>
> FRICKA: You, ride a subway? This must be a depression we're in.
>
> TWOTON: To get the Gold I must degrade myself.

One of Ludlam's more subtle conceits was to supply Siegfried with only pidgin German and Yiddish until he unites with Brunnhilda, who, according to Wagner, brings him love and wisdom. When he encounters the Wood-Bird, Siegfried says, "Zingk yidlach zingk! [Sing, little Jew, sing!] I lischten to yer zong! I burn. I'm on fire." When he confronts Twoton disguised as a "Wanderer," Siegfried says, "You talk funnische! Ha ha ha!" and "Dodderink schtill? Aus mein way alte cocke!" When he arrives to rescue

Brunnhilda and arouse her from her long sleep, he says, "The olde man shake-'is-speare for the last time. Ich hab his spear gebroken!" After Brunnhilda has transformed Siegfried, all traces of his "funnische" dialect disappear, as when he tells her, "Religion, myth, and poetry cannot be eradicated by conquest or education."

Ludlam's focus on language knows no bounds in *Der Ring*. There's a self-contained parody of Gertrude Stein's playful prose in a dream that Sieglinda relates: "Is there to stay? To stay is there? Is there to stay (we stay) in there. Is there to stay? Is there to stay? Is there? Is there?" His "too Jung to be Freudian" is more delightful still.

Ludlam also pays particular homage to Wagner's love of alliteration in the original libretto for the *Ring*. Loge says: "Here's Nibblehome. Home sweet Nibblehome deep in the bowels of the earth! In tunnels and caves the lowly laboring lazy louts the lascivious Nihilumpen dwell. Far from the light of day." Ninny says: "Ohe! Ohe! Ow! Ow! Let go of my ear! Cease and desist from this pitiless pinching! Please, I moiled and toiled from morn to midnight."

Without explanation, Ludlam contrived one minor adjustment that contradicts Wagner's text: After Siegfried drinks Hagen's potion, he retains his memory of Brunnhilda. This makes his subsequent renunciation of her and his concomitant agreement to marry Gutruna somewhat baffling. Equally baffling is Ludlam's reason for making the change, since he clearly took great pains to be so faithful to other subtleties in the byzantine plot.

ↄ

With nineteen cast members required to fill out more than forty roles in *Der Ring*, new people had to be recruited. One of them was Ericka Brown, who would later refer to herself as "Eureka." Born in England and raised partly in Upstate New York, where her father taught theater, Eureka had attended Antioch College "in the mad sixties." She majored in theater and graduated in 1969, when she moved to New York City and quickly became affiliated with Nicolo Marionettes in Central Park. She had been working with Adam Kilgore (alias McAdam) for seven years, when he told her that Ludlam wanted her "to come and read for something," meaning *Der Ring*.

Ludlam had seen a number of the puppet shows that Kilgore and Eureka had staged together, beginning with Kilgore's own version of *Punch and Judy* called *Punk and Tudy*. It was performed in Central Park and at various other outdoor locations in and around the city in 1974. Ludlam happened to catch the show in Greenwich Village on an extremely hot summer afternoon.

"I just will never forget the first time I saw Charles," recalled Eureka. "I had already heard a lot about him from Adam. Then, we were standing on this platform which was extended from the back of our truck. And as we were performing, I looked down and there was this little guy wearing a tee-shirt, with his hands in his jeans pockets. His eyes looking up at us were just amazing, those huge blue eyes with all of this brilliance shining out of them."

In the intervening years, Eureka had seen Ludlam's own puppet shows, as well as *Camille* and *Caprice*. "To be honest, I don't think the first time I saw *Camille* was one of Charles's good days," said Eureka. "There were times when Charles got tired of *Camille* and he'd camp-up the third act more than he should have. But I saw it again when he was 'on,' and he was wonderful. Still, it was when I saw *Caprice* that I knew I was encountering the only authentic genius I was ever likely to find in my life."

It was during the period of *Caprice*, the year before *Der Ring*, that Kilgore wrote another puppet show called *The Reluctant Dragon*. By then Kilgore and Eureka were recording their voices for the performances, and Ludlam was invited to portray the dragon on tape. "Charles's voice as the dragon was very laid-back, very stoned," recalled Eureka. "I was on the tape in several other parts, and after the recording session, Charles told me that he liked my work: my acting and my voice."

As for her being asked to participate in *Der Ring*, Eureka emphasized: "I weighed 250 pounds and was extremely large at that point, and Charles was very drawn to physical extremes. I was never very comfortable with the idea that some of us were brought into the company because we were extreme or freakish. But I remained that size until after Charles died."

Kilgore remembered Ludlam telling him that "he felt it was such a treat for an audience to be able to see a truly fat body: Most of us don't get to see that our whole lives."

Though *Der Ring* was slated to open at the Truck and Warehouse Theater on East 4th Street, directly across the street from La MaMa, the initial rehearsals occurred at the Performing Garage. The first consisted of a reading of the play. Ludlam was noticeably proud of providing everyone with a completed script. "He made a big deal out of the fact that it was finished," recalled Eureka, "and we had to get it exactly right, exactly the way it was written on the page." This wasn't very easy, however, in view of the heavily accented, sometimes invented, language peppering the script.

All of the bit parts were up for grabs and cast in a rather haphazard fashion at that first reading. "It wasn't really a matter of casting," recalled Eureka, "so much as Charles saying, 'Who wants to do this? Who wants to do that?' He asked me to read one of the Rheinmaidens, but I ended up being a Norn, too. And when he asked 'Who wants to be Valtrauta,' I put my hand up right away."

Der Ring was rehearsed "all over the place." Following the initial sessions at the Performing Garage, the cast congregated for a couple of weeks at Ethyl Eichelberger's large loft in the Flower District. Eichelberger, who would get to display his range as an actor by portraying both Fricka and Gunthur in *Der Ring*, was not a particularly neat housekeeper. Everyone had to move around the room carefully to avoid the piles of petrified turds left by his dogs: a black scottie named MacDuff, the enormous afghan Amy Lou, and a saluki named Zeke. There was an abundance of marijuana, and it wasn't unusual to observe Ludlam just reclining on the sofa, staring at the others and "not saying a hell of a lot." There were days when everyone would show up at the designated time only to wait around for what seemed like hours, while Ludlam continued to address some minute detail. There were other times when the scheduled rehearsal didn't happen at all.

Throughout the extensive rehearsals for *Der Ring*, Eureka recalled:

> If you asked Charles a question about something, you got this feeling that you were supposed to know the answer just from the text. He was a stickler for every syllable being pronounced as it appeared on the page. But some of it was in pidgin German, or pidgin Yiddish, or just plain nonsense. I remember rehearsing "Hiya! Hiya! Hiya!" for hours, and he'd get quite impatient if you didn't just see it there and read it the way he had heard it in his head.
>
> His directing techniques varied enormously. Most of the time he was pretty laid-back with *Der Ring*. But he also had moments of incredible brilliance as a director — he could be very insightful and supportive. I think the marijuana had a lot to do with some of those long, long rehearsals when nothing much got done.

After the first run-through at the Truck and Warehouse, Ludlam gave his actors extensive notes and then made them go through the entire play once again. Considering that the play ran more than three-and-a-half hours, the evening proved an exhausting exercise for all those involved. This was, however, the first time that Ludlam adopted the technique of taking notes, rather than interrupting the rehearsal to make his points.

The notes were rapidly scrawled on scraps of paper with the actor's initials on top. On any given one, Ludlam shrewdly tended to temper his criticism with compliments. One of a couple dozen notes to Pashalinski said, "'Unburden your heart' . . . good reading . . . implement physically" (meaning that he wanted her to gesture more when Brunnhilda says, "Unburden your heart"). Another read: "'Guilty me' . . . better [if] ambiguous . . . does she [Brunnhilda] mean it?" Yet another: "Don't break up. You sabotage other actors." More than one note to Pashalinski indicates just how quick Ludlam was to let people know what worked for him. "Some of the going-to-sleep business yesterday were [sic] good," said one. "Laugh [is] brilliant," said another.

In the midst of the second run-through at the Truck and Warehouse, Ludlam threw up his arms in exasperation: "If I give you a piece of direction and we go back and do it over, please do *something* different," he implored the cast. "I don't care if you follow my specific direction or not, just do something different so I don't feel totally useless. You have to protect me from this feeling of uselessness."

Since he wasn't performing in *Der Ring*, it was inevitable that Ludlam, an actor first and foremost, would feel particularly superfluous once the show opened. He had a devilish time adjusting to being merely the author and director. Though he wasn't in the play for the first two-thirds of its run, he attended practically every performance to wait for Quinton, who played Ninny as well as a Rheinmaiden and a Norn.

Ludlam sometimes made a nuisance of himself backstage while others were preparing to go on. As part of his ever-burgeoning love of puppetry, he had recently purchased an expensive, hand-carved ventriloquist's dummy. Ludlam later explained his motivation for working with a dummy: "I hold these conversations with myself—two parts of myself, divided and always set in opposition." He also believed that he resembled the particular dummy he unearthed at Tannen Magic, an esoteric shop in Manhattan that specialized in such items. Playing on his overidentification with his new pal, Ludlam named him Walter Ego (as in "alter ego").

Everyone recalled Ludlam badgering them with Walter Ego backstage during *Der Ring*, and he was sometimes humorous, but more often annoying. There was something pathetic about his having to get into the act indirectly, as it were, via his sidekick. The communal dressing room was already something of a madhouse, having to accommodate so many actors and so many costume changes in an awkward, U-shaped backstage area. Eventually, the players gave up on any semblance of modesty as they frantically ran around, sometimes stark naked, looking for their next outfit.

In the midst of the ensuing mayhem, Ludlam would casually approach individuals with Walter Ego, saying, "Hi, how are you tonight?", chattering on and on and distracting them while he practiced his ventriloquism. There was one incident when Ludlam cornered Eureka. Along with Quinton and an actress named Beverly Brown, she was one of the three Norns who shared a long piece of connected fabric as their single costume, though they would enter onstage one after the other. "One time when Charles was talking to me with Walter Ego, I looked down and noticed the Norn dress was trailing off without me," recalled Eureka. "I quickly stepped on the end of it, stopping the other two short onstage. I climbed in at the very last minute while they were standing there waiting for me."

If Ludlam punished himself as well as his cast because he was not in *Der Ring*, he was in turn punished by the critics when the play finally opened on April 27, 1977, following two weeks of previews. As Gerald Rabkin succinctly put it, "Ludlam the playwright-director-designer has denied himself the Ridiculous Theatrical Company's greatest asset: Ludlam the actor. Obviously, this absence is keenly felt, as no single performer in *Der Ring* possesses his comic inventiveness."

Ironically, it was Rabkin who had said — in his earlier response to *Caprice* — that he was eager to see Ludlam write a play that was not a vehicle for himself. Even more ironic, in view of what he was now saying, Rabkin's review of *Der Ring* for the *Soho Weekly News* was one of only two positive notices the production received. Though time and reputation would come to convey that *Der Ring* was among the company's better-received shows, the reviews were, in fact, either lukewarm or damning. Nor was the problem only with the critics: The audience tended to thin out during one of the two intermissions on any given night. Even Michael Feingold conceded, in his relative rave in the *Village Voice*, that the length was "excessive," and that "certain individual scenes drag on too long." But Feingold rather admired the combination of Ludlam and Wagner, which he, like others, saw as having been inevitable. "Ludlam has found his ideal subject matter: a myth which is serious because it is silly," he wrote. "Like all the great burlesquers of the *Ring* — Tolstoy and Anna Russell come to mind — he puts down the work for the purpose of putting it up higher."

The stodgy Douglas Watt began his pan in the *Daily News* with a surprising admission: "Having successfully avoided the Ridiculous Theatrical Co. for eight years, on what turned out to be the sound advice of friends, I was finally drawn to this troupe of amateur, or at least non-Equity, performers when the other night they . . . present[ed] no less than a three-hour version of Wagner's four-evening *Ring* operas. I stayed through the first three works, unable to witness the mutilation of *Götterdämmerung*, the final opera and my personal favorite." Watt concluded by dismissing Ludlam's *Ring* as "a pointless and boring effort" as well as "a ghastly mistake."

In his brief but venomous notice on *Der Ring* for *New York* magazine, John Simon also revealed his predisposed prejudice against the Ridiculous. "I was warned when I took this job that, sooner or later, I'd have to come up against the work of Charles Ludlam," began the first of two paragraphs devoted to the production. "The piece is diffuse," ends the second, "it betrays its gags by repetition, and the inadequate work of Mr. Ludlam's company . . . prevents even the better ideas from making their point."

The always generous Mel Gussow offered a mixed review in the *Times*. "Give Mr. Ludlam points not only for nerve, but for ambition," he wrote. "This is unquestionably his most massive undertaking, a comic grand opera — with a score by Jim McElwaine that ranges from Wagnerian arias to the Rheingold beer commercial (played by a tiny, versatile orchestra). The plot is as thick as a briar patch, the characters are comprehensive . . . and the canvas sweeping. . . ."

Along with the other critics, Gussow's chief problems with *Der Ring* concerned the length, as well as the inherent difficulties of parodying a parody. "Seeing *Farblonjet* is almost like downing all of Wagner in a single swallow. One tends to gag." The evening's major "delectations" for Gussow were to be found in the "zesty Mae West presence" of Pashalinski, "the adorable, doll-like" Black-Eyed Susan, and the "stalwart" Brockmeyer. "Absent onstage and definitely missed is Mr. Ludlam himself," added Gussow. "This time he makes his primary contribution as a designer, a capacity in which he echoes his writing by cleverly recycling old material."

Gussow was by no means alone in praising the ingenious designs. As described by Feingold:

> The set and costume designs — the most consistently successful part of *Der Ring*
> — are the work of an artist with a vision such as one rarely sees onstage; they

made me think of David Hockney's Grimm illustrations, which use contemporary modes and junk objects the same way, for epic effects. A Valhalla made from slide projections of Lincoln Center and St. John the Divine, Gibichung cloaks that look like black plastic garbage bags, Mime's forge built of glued-together egg crates, all end up being noble and beautiful, as do the dwarves' striped knee socks and the Rhine maidens' blue-lamé cocktail gowns.

Ludlam, in fact, won a special Obie Award — his fourth — for his design of *Der Ring*. Pashalinski won her second Obie for her portrayal of Brunnhilda.

Bobjack Callejo, who had designed the last few shows for Ludlam, recalled being "disappointed and a little bit upset" when he wasn't invited to do *Der Ring*. "I would probably have been angry if someone other than Charles did it," explained Callejo. "After I saw the show, I remember going backstage and telling Charles I had expected to hate it, but I loved it. He broke all the rules, but it was great."

One person who was not very happy with the technical aspects of the production was Richard Currie. In addition to portraying Fafner, Hagen, and Hunding onstage, Currie functioned in his more regular capacity as the lighting designer. But he also felt like he contributed far more to the appearance of the show than he received credit for, and he had a blowup with Ludlam when he first saw the program.

"Charles's set for *Der Ring* was not representational, so the lighting had to take you all those places," said Currie,

> the mountaintop, the forest, etc. But achieving this was a particularly arduous task since the Truck and Warehouse was such a vast space. Charles and I had gotten together a lot on how we were going to do various things, and I really helped him a lot. Then the program came out and it said, *"Der Ring Gott Farblonjet*: Written and Designed by Charles Ludlam, Music by Jim McElwaine."* I was pissed because I wasn't getting the recognition I deserved for doing at least a third of what was being seen on that stage. And when I complained to Charles, he shrugged it off as being something Cathy Farinon-Smith [the company business manager] had done.

Richard Currie was far from alone in registering dissatisfaction with the way that *Der Ring* was working out. Given the negative reviews and the mixed audience reactions, it was a strain on everyone to perform this gigantic work six nights a week. It became even more stressful when Currie left for his regular summer job at Brown Ledge, and Ludlam put himself in the play as his replacement. Ludlam later reflected on how his entering the production disrupted the proceedings:

> I watched it forty times and I couldn't even think of an improvement. Then an actor left and I went into the play to take his role. Immediately *I* was what was wrong. I hadn't been rehearsed, and no one had the objective eye. The whole thing changed. Everyone changed. I would start doing things and they'd say, "Oh! You can do that?" and I'd say, "Well, why not?" They'd say, "Oh! Well! If *you* can do *that*.... You wouldn't have let us get away with that!" I said, "You never tried anything," and they said, "We didn't know we were allowed."

> It was the difference between having an authority figure outside of the play and being in the play. Suddenly everyone started to take the liberties that I was taking. It didn't change the vision one bit. They didn't compromise the things that were perfect about the play. But a new spirit came over it.

More specifically, Ludlam suddenly began to sing his spoken lines. And with far from lilting results, others began to imitate him by singing theirs as well. As Kilgore recalled, "When Charles came into the show, he did all the things that he had directed us not to do. He'd play it tremendously slow. And then his singing turned the words into these long, boring arias. When any of us did that during rehearsals, he made us stop."

But even before Ludlam joined the cast onstage, the backstage spirit that reigned over *Der Ring* was by many accounts far from pleasant. Although Jack Mallory wasn't in *Der Ring*, he had real problems with Ludlam during its run. Having been asked to leave during the rehearsals for *Caprice* the previous year, Mallory tried to elbow his way back into the company by offering to run the concession stand at the Truck and Warehouse. Ludlam agreed, but in the midst of the run, "He threw me out of the theater," recalled Mallory. "The excuse was that I was selling some chocolate candies during the first intermission; and people would eat them and then get sleepy during the second act."

While simply denying that the play was unwieldy and too long, Ludlam looked for whatever excuses he could find to explain its failure to win over an audience. Near the end of the extensive run of *Der Ring*, he took to blaming the poor box office returns on just about everything but the play itself. He cited the location of the theater as a problem, pointing out that Tennessee Williams's *Small Craft Warnings* had failed in the same space several years earlier, never acknowledging that it, too, was a problematic play.

Nearly a year later, Ludlam would tell journalist Glenn Loney (for a feature story in the *Los Angeles Times*) that doing *Der Ring* "was like climbing Everest. It was a turning point in my life. I wanted to come to terms with the paradoxes of that work. Look, there are no mistakes in art. Malpractice, maybe. . . . What's great about a work of art is often what's wrong with it."

With characteristic obstinacy, Ludlam kept *Der Ring* running long after it had exhausted its audience. By the beginning of July, he reduced the performance schedule to Sunday nights only, reviving *Stage Blood* on Fridays and Saturdays. To meet the rent at the Truck and Warehouse, Ludlam offered Saturday matinees of his one-man, twenty-two-character *Punch and Judy Show*. And Bill Vehr did what he could to boost the box office by presenting readings of his beloved *Finnegans Wake* on Thursday nights.

But everything closed with *Der Ring*. This was in spite of fresh reviews of *Stage Blood* (a positive one in the *Soho Weekly News* somewhat offsetting Richard Eder's negative review in *The New York Times*), and even more significantly, a gift from Mel Gussow in a Friday edition of the *Times*. With a headline that read "LUDLAM'S A SUCCESS IN A RIDICULOUS WAY," Gussow wrote a glowing feature article on Ludlam and the company's various offerings. It appeared on July 22, only two and a half weeks before everything folded. Gussow's intended boost was evidently not effective enough to surmount the mixed word-of-mouth that *Der Ring* had been receiving from theater-goers, many of whom left before the final act.

There was one person, however, who came to Ludlam's rescue on the basis of Gussow's article. Having already seen and adored both *Caprice* and *Der Ring*, William Kohler, a wealthy arts patron from Philadelphia, was particularly struck by news that the company was in financial straits. "Despite 10 years of almost continuous performance, the company is still non-profitable," wrote Gussow. "The actors live from grant to grant, with an occasional European tour to boost the income. 'In one way, it's easier if you have no money,' Mr. Ludlam says, philosophically. 'Then everyone is exploited, including yourself.'"

After reading that paragraph, Kohler phoned the company and spoke to Farinon-Smith, the business manager. "I said, 'I want to give you five thousand bucks,'" recalled Kohler. His one stipulation was that he wanted to meet Ludlam. "And she said, 'I'll take care of it.'" It was arranged for Kohler to arrive at Ludlam's Morton Street apartment on a Sunday morning. Ludlam strategically saw to it that Quinton was not home. Extending his hand, the first thing Ludlam said to the seventy-five-year old Kohler was: "You know, I don't grant sexual favors."

According to Kohler, who became a lifelong sponsor and friend:

> I told Charles that I liked his Jewish sense of humor [referring to *Der Ring*]. And he said, "But I'm Irish." We instantly liked each other. When you meet important people, they either look down their nose at you or they take you seriously. Charles listened to me, he took me seriously.

> I never wanted to sleep with Charles or with anyone else in the company. Our relationship was strictly a friendship. He was a very pleasant companion, an interesting man. He was very much alive, and you find very few people who are. Charles was not appreciated to the degree that he wanted to be. But he did what he wanted to do, and this is what we all strive for. He lived the life he wanted to live. He was independent, and he was recognized.

Born in Germany in 1902 to a Jewish mother, Kohler came to New York in 1934 where he studied law at Columbia and then Cornell. He settled in Philadelphia where he became a highly successful lawyer for a large chemical firm. In his later years, he served as a board member for various musical and theatrical foundations, culminating with his leadership of the Walnut Street Theater Foundation in 1975.

As a gay man, Kohler came to New York "frequently on weekends, to go to the theater and to fuck. I couldn't do it here [in Philadelphia] for fear of blackmail." Kohler made Ludlam a regular part of his New York visits. He would attend evening performances at the Ridiculous or elsewhere, and then have dinner with Ludlam and Quinton afterwards. These were usually at McBell's, a local Greenwich Village tavern and restaurant Ludlam frequented — or, at Kohler's preference, the Cornelia Street Cafe. There were also Sunday breakfasts at Tiffany's, a coffee shop at Sheridan Square. Occasionally Kohler accompanied Ludlam on Saturday afternoon shopping expeditions, and he would slip him a hundred dollars or so. "Charles never asked for money," said Kohler. "But whenever he brought out a new play, I always gave him some."

Over the years, Kohler took Ludlam and Quinton to the opera several times. He went alone with Ludlam to various gay bars and sex clubs. "Charles used to go to the porno bookstores with stalls in the back," said Kohler.

Once I went with him to the Mine Shaft. They didn't want to let me in because I was overdressed. But Charles argued with them, explaining that I was from out of town. I remember that after we were inside and he disappeared for a while, Charles returned all covered with excrement, because he had had sex in a corner where someone had defecated. We also went to a dangerous s&m club, and Charles came out, saying it was too much, even for him.

Though Ludlam and Quinton suggested to interviewers that they were monogamous, neither of them relinquished a penchant for "extracurricular" activities. After Quinton arrived on the scene, Ludlam refrained from introducing tricks to the company, as he often had in the past. But the ongoing promiscuity put a strain on their relationship. Callejo recalled "running into Charles at the baths when he was doing *Der Ring*. We'd always smoke dope together at the tubs." Christopher Scott also remembered encountering Ludlam in the backroom of the gay bookstore at the corner of Christopher and Hudson Streets. "Frequently during the early eighties," said Scott, "whenever I went, he was there."

Georg Osterman said,

It was during *Der Ring* that Everett began having his fits in the theater. He could go from being very sweet to being this monster when he was drinking. Everett suddenly became very cold and I felt like he hated me. Charles would sometimes get very upset and we'd all feel it. But there were other times when he'd just carry on and try not to show how bothered he was.

Osterman abruptly left the show a week before it closed. "It was the first time that so many people who hadn't worked with the company before were being introduced, and I started feeling disoriented," recalled Osterman. "Also, Charles didn't give me much direction. He did tell me to get into the sword fight more; but I had a broken hand and I was really having problems with it."

One of the newcomers that Osterman found "disorienting" was Stephen Holt, a playwright and actor who had interviewed Ludlam the previous January for a biography he was pursuing on Candy Darling — a project he never completed. In the meantime, Ludlam had been impressed enough with Holt to cast him as a Valkyrie and in other incidental roles in *Der Ring*.

In a letter he sent to Richard Currie on August 10, or three days after the show folded, Holt wrote:

> The *Ring* closed suddenly. I did not even know till *Götterdämmerung*, really, that it was all over. I did a Norn for the first and last time Sunday night. Beverly [Brown, who played a Norn as well as the Forest Bird] and Georg [Osterman] both left the show *last* week, and *this* week everyone was rehearsing the replacements like crazy. Charles and Lola had a big knock-down-drag-out fight on Wednesday à la Jack Mallory and Charles told *me* to learn Brunnhilda and Helga Vain in *Stage Blood*. Too much, too much. Of course, I was flattered, but I knew Charles and Lola would never part company, at least in this way. Kathy [sic] Smith told me it was a big financial dip that caused the closing this week, but I think it was just because Charles was tired and bored with the whole thing. I don't know. Who can say? The *Ring* certainly had its run . . .
>
> Georg seems to have had it with Charles at the moment. Everyone was shocked at *his* leaving. Beverly they all expected and wanted to leave. Klaus [Nomi, who replaced Beverly Brown] as the Rheinmaiden and the Wood Bird was not to be believed! He was really brilliant. I couldn't get over it. He really knew just what to do with both those roles whereas Beverly never did. I did the Norn and Larry Rée did Helmvige [another Valkyrie] for one night. It was a night to remember, to be sure. Klaus was so good that you never would have known it was his first performance. And that voice! . . .
>
> The problem was replacing Georg. Charles got a weight-lifter whom he had met at a party to do Siegmund. And he did Loge himself. Just between you, me and the history books, the weight-lifter stank and Charles wasn't so hot as Loge. The stage manager [Richard Gibbs] did Fafner and the Dragon and Bob Reddy came back and did Dunderhead. It was pure madness, let me tell you. Charles's Hagen, though, that last night, was quite something.
>
> I think it was after the first act [that] he realized he really didn't have it together as Loge and decided to shutter the whole thing. And Susan was spitting with the weight-lifter, he was so bad. She was giggling and laughing as I carried her across the stage as Sieglinda in the Valkyrie scene, and mumbling, "This is Ted Mack's Amateur Hour," and she was right.

As Holt's letter documents, the final weeks of *Der Ring* were chaotic — a trial for everyone involved with the show. With so many last-minute dropouts, Ludlam was acting more like an activities coordinator than a director. But Holt's letter also demonstrates that Ludlam had what it took to persuade old-time regulars like Robert Reddy and Larry Rée to drop everything and quickly memorize some lines — if only for a night.

As for Ludlam asking Holt to learn Pashalinski's roles in *Der Ring* and *Stage Blood*, this wasn't just the same old petty power ploy it had been in years past, when he had asked Thomas Lanigan Schmidt to consider taking over for Mario Montez, or James Morfogen to possibly replace Bill Vehr. Regardless of her "big knock-down-drag-out fight" with Ludlam — which she did not remember having — Pashalinski recalled that her life was coming together during *Der Ring*. But she also confirmed that Ludlam suddenly had reasons to question her long-term commitment to the Ridiculous.

When the company was performing *Caprice*, Ludlam encouraged Pashalinski to go on a diet. "He told me he was concerned, because I had gotten to be very heavy and I was sweating so much onstage," she recalled.

> He said he was worried I was going to have a heart attack, and there were so many more roles he could write for me. Then I went on a diet in January, in preparation for *Der Ring*. At first I felt very ill. But by the time of *Der Ring*, I had lost a tremendous amount of weight. I looked fabulous, and I had this wonderful role as Brunnhilda.
>
> I was also adopting a sort of Zen attitude about giving up my desires for the company and becoming more detached about it. I pulled back emotionally and objectified the company a bit more. I was really achieving that and it made me much more comfortable with myself.

At the time he asked Holt to learn Pashalinski's roles, Ludlam apparently detected that she was becoming somewhat distant, and he felt threatened by it. According to Pashalinski, "I also fell madly in love with someone new during *Der Ring*, and the relationship I had formed with Debra proved instrumental for my pulling back from the company."

Having amicably terminated her long-term relationship with Flavia Rando in the summer of 1975, Pashalinski was more than ready for a fresh attachment. She found one with Debra Crane. Yet another newcomer to the company, Crane was a New York University student whom Ludlam had recruited from his *commedia* acting classes to be an intern with *Der Ring*. Crane played Siegruna, and embarked on what was to become a five-year relationship with Pashalinski, who was twenty-three years her senior.

Though Pashalinski claimed that "Charles liked Debra very much," she also recalled a time when "I accused him of being jealous, and he denied it." According to Pashalinski, Crane could be very "cheeky" with Ludlam. Whenever Pashalinski complained about him, Crane would tell her, "Well, why do you take that from him?"

In another letter, Stephen Holt elaborated further on Pashalinski's behavior towards the end of *Der Ring*. "The *Ring* closed suddenly and unexpectedly last night," he wrote to his friend Billy Edgar on August 8.

> Charles is *so* capricious. Although I think the company wanted to shutter it since they (and everybody else) were not getting paid. Charles had a *huge* fight with Lola last week and I think that sort of sealed things. She's really fed up with him and now wants to do "the story of a flaming butch dyke lesbian who is triumphant" — *with me!* . . . And when an Obie-winning goddess such as Lola Pashalinski drops the handkerchief before one, well, a gentleman *must* pick it up, if, indeed he is a gentleman at all. "The Company should be broken up!" Lola was screaming, "It's gone on too long, and everybody should go out on their own." And the fact that *I* am the one she is turning to in her hour of need is, well, I can only describe it as "an honor."

Pashalinski's "hour of need" wasn't quite as urgent as Holt anticipated, however. Although she would go on to perform in some of his plays, their collaboration would have to wait a couple of years, while intervening outside projects permitted her to test the murky waters away from the Ridiculous, and from the security it represented.

More immediate plans had called for the Ridiculous to take *Camille* and *Stage Blood* on an Australian tour that winter. But when they fell through, the company went to Toronto instead. Quinton, who suddenly had more acting responsibility as Nichette, recalled that Maria Callas died while they were in Canada — on September 16, 1977, to be precise. Ludlam was an enormous fan of the great opera singer, and devastated by the news. Although he determined then and there that he would write a play in tribute to her, *Galas*, his second most celebrated drag role after *Camille*, would not be produced until 1983.

It was not unlike the day in 1968 when Tallulah Bankhead had died. Grief-stricken and weeping, Ludlam had sought consolation from a new friend named Regina Hirsch. But when Callas died a decade later — long after Regina Hirsch had become Lola Pashalinski — allegiances were shifting, and Ludlam was turning elsewhere for emotional support.

A TALENT LIKE THIS

All the leaves are brown, and the sky is gray
I've been for a walk on a winter's day
I'd be safe and warm if I was in L.A.
California dreamin' on such a winter's day.
— The Mamas & the Papas

I thought, this is the greatest actor in America, and I'm gonna use him. . . .
A talent like this had to be used.
— Mark Rappaport

Ludlam walked away from all the emotional turmoil that surfaced with *Der Ring* by going to the opposite extreme with his next project. With so much backstage strife occurring as one cast member after another abandoned the production, Ludlam would have the last word by writing a play for only two actors. Whereas his tribute to Wagner had been his most ambitious work to date, *The Ventriloquist's Wife*, Ludlam's fifteenth play, would be his most modest. Its relatively small scale made it that much easier for Ludlam to fulfill his commitment to teach playwriting at the Yale School of Drama — on a CBS fellowship grant — during the 1977-78 academic year. In terms of its content, however, *The Ventriloquist's Wife* is far from modest, and arguably Ludlam's most ego-maniacal work. Initially conceived of as a solo piece to be performed by Ludlam with his beloved new sidekick, Walter Ego, it evolved into a three-character play for two actors plus the dummy.

Before developing *The Ventriloquist's Wife*, Ludlam had been working with Walter Ego in various venues — not only backstage at the Truck and Warehouse, where he annoyed various cast members of *Der Ring* with his ventriloquial shenanigans. He did an act with Walter at Little Peter's, a run-down Bowery bar frequented by transvestites and rough trade. As arranged by Larry Rée, this mini-review also included Klaus Nomi, who sang, and Pashalinski who, clad in a tuxedo, acted as the emcee. There were a number of performances over a couple of weeks in August — before the company took *Camille* to Toronto — but Pashalinski was only present for the first. "I was not sufficiently pre-pared," she claimed.

While he was perfecting his techniques as a ventriloquist, Ludlam and Walter Ego showed up in even more unlikely places that autumn. These included passing-the-hat performances in Washington Square Park and on the steps of the New York Public

Library, as well as stints at a Ukrainian restaurant, and even aboard the Staten Island Ferry. Performance artist Stuart Sherman had received a grant to offer street shows of his own, highly idiosyncratic work, and Ludlam tagged along for some of those as well.

The various venues were well documented in yet another *New York Times* feature story that appeared on November 18, 1977, written by the ever-faithful Mel Gussow. "Wherever he goes, Walter is a traffic stopper," wrote Gussow, for whom Ludlam proceeded to perform with Walter during the course of the interview:

> "The minute he is out of the box," said his master, "a crowd forms. It's instant theater."
> "They love me," said Walter.
> Walter was sitting on Mr. Ludlam's knee. Swiveling his head, Walter asked him, "What's a ventrickolist?"
> "Ventriloquist," corrected Mr. Ludlam. "It's an act where a comedian and a dummy..."
> "Which one is you?" asked Walter.

Gussow was merely one of many who were treated to personal sessions with Ludlam's alias. There is no question that Ludlam overidentified with his (W)alter ego during this period. On the one hand, Walter was the "child" a part of Ludlam always wanted but would never have; on the other, he tended to represent the more mischievous aspects of Ludlam's own personality. Bill Vehr claimed it was "the last straw" when Walter, not Ludlam, phoned him, and Ludlam later insisted that he never made the call. The spirit behind this little prank, so innocuous on the surface, took on a far more sinister dimension when worked into the script of *The Ventriloquist's Wife*.

If Ludlam's involvement with Walter Ego suggested he was entering an introspective phase and consolidating his energies, yet another project that came to fruition during this period manifested his newfound independence from the company. *Aphrodisiamania*, conceived of as a dance piece for Paul Taylor's company, was the first of a growing sequence of outside projects Ludlam would work on during the coming decade.

Though Taylor was accustomed to collaborating with composers and designers, it was rare for him to work with anyone else in terms of a scenario. "I had been following Charles's work from the very beginning, and I approached him," explained Taylor.

> I was affected very much at that time by what I'd seen of his. I just loved in

particular his actors — they were such lovable, offbeat freaks. I was charmed by
the vulgarity of it all. It was so vulgar that it was childlike. It didn't offend me in
the least. But that element of a kind of wide-open view of sex, and the childlike-
ness of it, and the humor, of course, appealed to me. I wanted to do something
like that: I didn't know exactly what, but it would have a story. And my dancers
had never spoken onstage, or sung, and I loved that idea. So I called him, and we
had a meeting, and I asked him if he could think up a kind of plot.

But once Ludlam agreed to the collaboration, Taylor had to repeatedly goad him into
fulfilling his commitment. "It was like pulling hens' teeth to get anything out of
Charles," he said.

> I had a four-week deadline from the time we started rehearsals. And nothing had
> happened from the time I approached him until we began rehearsals. I only
> had the names of the characters and some vague idea about *commedia dell'arte*. I
> phoned him and said, "Well, tell me at least how this piece begins." And he
> told me something and it was enough to put together the first rehearsal. And then
> I'd call him, and say, "Well, what happens next?" He'd tell me a tiny bit more,
> and I'd do that. And that's the way it went. I don't think either of us had a real
> plan. But somehow he'd just toss out developments of the plot. As I remember,
> he never came to rehearsals.

In fact, Ludlam attended several rehearsals. He once invited Pashalinski to join him,
and Susan recalled being "hurt" that he never invited her, especially since she loved
dance. But Taylor's difficulties with his collaborator proved typical of Ludlam the
procrastinator.

"From the very beginning, I told him, 'I'd love to get these dancers to look like your
people,'" continued Taylor.

> Although he was polite about it, I could tell he didn't really go for that. He loved
> dancing, and like most people who love dancing, he loved the beauty of the
> dancers' bodies. He thought of them as gods and goddesses. And I was trying to
> think of them as freaks. So we never had a meeting of the minds. He won, really,
> because my dancers were so beautiful. But he was very, very nice. I would have
> thought that someone like him would want to get his hands on things that he was
> involved with. But I don't remember him ever stepping in or intruding in any
> way. He was quiet and very polite about it all.

Taylor further remembered being disappointed with the result. "I didn't think it was very good and I never thought it was worth bringing back," he said. "It didn't stay in the repertory." Curiously, he has no recollection of the rave review *Aphrodisiamania* received from Anna Kisselgoff in *The New York Times*.

Describing itself as "a Macaronic Imbroglio After the Commedia Dell'Arte," *Aphrodisiamania* opened at BAM on November 29, 1977, where, according to Kisselgoff, this "decadent delight" had "settled in for a very welcome week-long run." In the opening paragraph of her review, Kisselgoff pronounced *Aphrodisiamania* "an outrageous new theater-cum-dance piece conceived by Paul Taylor in conspiracy with Charles Ludlam." Her description of the piece emphasized the "phallic imagery" that abounded. "All the jokes about snakes and swords locate this particular commedia somewhere between Naples and Milan, possibly Peoria," she quipped. "The humor never does get out of hand, although Mr. Ludlam's provocations are very much in evidence both in specific images and as author of the scenario. Yet Mr. Taylor is a moralist and the resolution is of course, clean cut."

Exactly where Ludlam was headed with Walter Ego and his new play proved far less "clean cut." But once he decided to add the ventriloquist's "wife" to the scenario, it was only natural for him to give the part to Black-Eyed Susan. According to Susan, "Charles specifically wanted to see if he could adapt a play for a cabaret. This meant it would have to be short, amusing, and highly entertaining." The early report in circulation was that Ludlam was working on "a two-character play about Jack the Ripper." Certainly, he was accustomed to taking his inspiration from other sources. And when it came to pursuing his longtime obsession with ventriloquism, he could not have turned to a more successful vehicle than "The Ventriloquist's Dummy."

Based on a story by John V. Baines, "The Ventriloquist's Dummy" was one of five separate segments of a 1945 British horror film called *Dead of Night*. Due primarily to Michael Redgrave's bravura performance as the ventriloquist, it remains the most celebrated of the film's several episodes. With a homosexual subplot, it tells the story of Maxwell Frere, a paranoid ventriloquist whose demonic dummy, Hugo, gradually assumes control over his master. Fearing that Hugo is going to leave him and work with another ventriloquist, Frere ultimately murders his rival. He claims that Hugo is "more to blame than me." In the end, Frere becomes Hugo, in the same way that Norman Bates's split personality is utterly inhabited by his mother's persona at the close of Hitchcock's *Psycho*. As a doctor explains Frere's case, with a pun worthy of Ludlam: "The dummy got the upper hand entirely."

To flesh out *The Ventriloquist's Wife*, Ludlam shrewdly grafted elements from the plot of "The Haunted Mirror," another story in *Dead of Night*, onto his scenario. Also based on a story by Baines, "The Haunted Mirror" describes a wealthy couple driven mad by the husband's hallucinations in an antique mirror. When he looks in the mirror, he sees himself reflected in a mysterious room from an earlier era, and he progressively goes insane. His desperate wife visits the antiques shop where she had originally purchased the mirror, only to learn that the previous owner of the mirror had murdered his wife and then himself, and that the mirror had borne witness to the crime. In Ludlam's variation, the wife (named Black-Eyed Susan) calls the pawnshop from which her husband (named Charles Ludlam) purchased the dummy (Walter), and discovers that the original owner had murdered his wife.

Perhaps another resource for *The Ventriloquist's Wife* was *Magic*, a best-selling novel by William Goldman, which was on the verge of being released as a major — if mediocre — film, directed by Richard Attenborough and starring Anthony Hopkins. It also concerned a diabolical dummy — named *Chucky*, no less — who compels his master to commit murder.

In terms of the performance, Susan recalled perhaps the most important influence of all. "During the rehearsals for *The Ventriloquist's Wife*," she said, "we listened to endless tapes of old radio shows. Edgar Bergen and Charlie McCarthy and Mortimer Snerd."

Ludlam developed his script over the course of several months. To embellish the give-and take between himself and Walter Ego in the routines they performed together within the play, he referred to several joke books filled with standard one-liners and vaudville turns. This was the first time that Ludlam actually wrote the bulk of a script by dictating the lines to Susan, who typed the dialogue in his apartment while he paced the room in fits of inspiration.

The result was as diabolical as "The Ventriloquist's Dummy," but far more lewd and hysterical, making *The Ventriloquist's Wife* among Ludlam's funniest scripts — if also one of his briefest. In the play, Ludlam portrayed Charles Ludlam, a stand-up comic and cabaret performer who returns home one day with a freshly purchased dummy. "No more schlepping!" he tells his wife Susan. "No more weddings! No more birthday parties. No more Elks lodge! No more girdle manufacturers conventions! No more being hailed by millions just because I'm driving a cab. . . . I got a gimmick!" The gimmick is Walter.

At first, Walter is shy when Charles introduces him to Susan. But he quickly becomes lascivious:

> WIFE: You're fresh. If you were my kid, I'd kill you.
> WALTER: You wouldn't have to. If I were your kid I'd commit suicide.
> WIFE: I'd like to take you over my knee and give you a spanking!
> WALTER: If you do, you'll get a handful of splinters. Did you ever see a
> woodpecker? I've got twelve inches, but I don't use it as a rule.

In the second of six scenes, Charles performs his act with Walter on the "stage of a beatnik nightclub in Greenwich Village," during which Walter begins to gain control.

> VENTRILOQUIST: We go together like, well, like spaghetti and meatballs.
> WALTER: Yes, and we know which one is the meatball, don't we?
> VENTRILOQUIST: Walter, please, show a little more respect. You are talking to an
> expert ventriloquist.
> WALTER: And you're talking to yourself.
> VENTRILOQUIST: I throw my voice.
> WALTER: Well you can throw it in the garbage. I'm gonna expose this whole racket.
> VENTRILOQUIST: Ventriloquism isn't a racket, Walter. Ventriloquism is a profession.
> WALTER: So's ragpicking, but it's still trash.

Back home in scene three, Susan receives an obscene phone call from Walter.

> VOICE OF WALTER: Hello there, Susan. This is Walter.
> WIFE: (*Laughing*) Oh, hello, Charles. I was just thinking of you.
> VOICE OF WALTER: This isn't Charles. This is Walter. (*Does heavy breathing*)
> WIFE: You're a riot. You should go on the stage.
> VOICE OF WALTER: Susan, I had a dream about you last night.
> WIFE: Did you?
> VOICE OF WALTER: No, you wouldn't let me. Do you know what's big and hairy
> and sticks out of my pajamas at night?
> WIFE: Walter!
> VOICE OF WALTER: My head. What's hard that you hold to your mouth?
> WIFE: (*Indignantly*) I wouldn't know.
> VOICE OF WALTER: The telephone! heh, heh, heh. (*In a hoarse whisper*) Susan, I
> want to tell you something. I want you to sit on my face.
> WIFE: Charles.

VOICE OF WALTER: I told you this isn't Charles. What do you want to hang
    around a loser like him for?
WIFE: This isn't funny.
VOICE OF WALTER: (*Heavy breathing*)
WIFE: (*Outraged*) Charles, stop it. It isn't funny anymore.

Ludlam gave Susan additional "acting turns" by having *her* do Walter's voice on occasion. Though the audience thought it was Ludlam from behind the curtain, it was actually Susan who delivered Walter's lines when he made the obscene call. "Charles taught me how to throw my voice," she recalled. "And in a sense, I had to be even better than Charles, because I didn't have the dummy to distract people, so my lips couldn't move visibly at all."

After Charles returns home with Walter in tow, both master and dummy insist they didn't make the call. When Charles asks, "You know the difference between right and wrong, don't you Walter?" Walter replies, "Sure I do. Wrong is usually more fun." There's no stopping Walter, who bites Ludlam's hand as he's returned to his case, and curses his master with a line from *The Exorcist* while his head spins around: "Your mother sucks cocks in hell! Your mother sucks cocks in hell!"

For their second cabaret performance within the play, Charles and Walter have graduated to "a high-class nightclub." They begin with the standard blindfolded "Swami" act, in which the Swami (Walter) guesses what objects members of the audience are holding up in their hands, as his assistant (Charles) works the room. The joke, of course, is that Charles is also Walter the Swami, so both know what's being exhibited. It becomes particularly humorous when Walter fails to guess the third item. "It isn't easy to read minds with a hand up your ass," Walter snaps defensively.

Since Walter has become more and more uncontrollable, Charles abandons ventriloquism for his next nightclub act. He employs Susan instead for a standard magic trick. ("Don't worry, Susan. The last woman I sawed in half is alive and well and living in Paris and London. And now, ladies and gentlemen, I shall indulge for your delectation a deceptively benign form of sadomasochism.")

Even when he stops working with Walter, Charles continues to have a mental breakdown. In the final scene, he accuses Susan of "cheating" with Walter. "It's just as I suspected. You like Walter better than me," he rants. "He told me how you go in his room at night and fondle his controls!" He tries to strangle Susan with a telephone cord, but she breaks away and smashes the dummy's head with a hammer. At this point, Charles the ventriloquist "turns into" Walter — "laughing maniacally," reads a stage direction. But he is also transformed into a psychiatrist, consoling Susan as if they were suddenly in the midst of a traumatic therapy session.

"By the way, Susan," says the ventriloquist as the doctor, "last week your check came back." "So did my neurosis," she adds in the play's closing line. As the lights fade, a dummy's hand rises from her dress and begins to strangle her.

Ludlam had long proven his innate talent for manipulating his voice and creating vivid characterizations with it. But the phenomenal success of *The Ventriloquist's Wife* was due, in large part, to his previously untapped skill for throwing his voice. As described by Mel Gussow in his review for the *Times*,

> Mr. Ludlam's manipulation of the dummy — physically and vocally — is masterful. Goggling his eyes and bobbing his neck, Walter is not only a versatile piece of wood, he is also a marvelously animated actor.
>
> When Mr. Ludlam, furious at Walter's repeated mischief, crams the dummy back into his cardboard suitcase, Walter's whimpers of protest, muffled by his enclosure, are breathtakingly expressive. Later, when Walter responds to the abuse by refusing to speak, the figure suddenly loses its spryness and vitality. He is as limp as a beanbag; it is as if he had died. Then, just as suddenly, as if shot through with adrenaline, he springs back to life.

The Ventriloquist's Wife began its preview performances at the Wonderhorse Theatre. The single-sheet, handwritten program featured a Rorschach inkblot illustration and described the play as "a psychodrama for cabaret, conceived and executed by Charles Ludlam." With "special thanks" to the New York State Council on the Arts and the National Endowment for the Arts, the program further credited Everett Quinton as Stage Manager. Susan's "frock" was designed by Steven Burdick, John Brockmeyer's new lover. And without a credit, Susan's mother knitted a sweater worn by Walter.

The play transferred to Reno Sweeney the last week in December. It was scheduled to have a limited two-week run (excluding weekends) at this heavily booked, popular nightclub in Greenwich Village, where Ludlam and Susan gave two performances a night. It opened there to such rave reviews, however, that it was instantly guaranteed a longer life at other venues. Gussow declared it "a diabolically comic *coup de théâtre*...."

The script is one of Mr. Ludlam's most inspired creations, and the actors — all three of them — are mesmerizing. [It] raises ventriloquism to a high comic art."

Clive Barnes, who had recently lost his position at the *Times* and moved over to the *New York Post*, found Ludlam "a superb ventriloquist — recalling in some of his sketches the great Señor Wences in his vaudeville prime." Like other critics, Barnes also had special praise for Susan's "perfectly reproducing the dummy's voice" during the obscene phone call scene. "It is a curious, succinct and fascinating experience to watch Ludlam at work on the audience and on himself," continued Barnes. "His sin is that of the occasional self-indulgence. His virtue is that of comprehending the actual magic of theater."

Even the *Village Voice's* Erika Munk, whom Ludlam would later view as one of his harshest critics, sent her readers to the show. "All feats of skill I don't understand or can't approach doing delight me, and Ludlam's ventriloquist act is grand," she wrote. "It's pure pleasure [and it has] redeeming anti-social value, allowing us to be mean, wide-eyed, and sophisticated all at once."

In the middle of the two-week run at Reno Sweeney, Ludlam, Susan, Quinton, and the show's lighting designer, Robert Fuhrman, took *The Ventriloquist's Wife* to Philadelphia at William Kohler's instigation. They gave two or three performances of the play during the last weekend in 1977, encompassing New Year's Eve. Susan recalled that Ludlam was so impressed by the outrageous and decorative costumes in the Philadelphia Mummers' Parade they attended on New Year's Day, that they inspired his own fantastic costume designs for his next play, *Utopia Incorporated*.

The Philadelphia excursion was the first of many engagements for the play at various venues and nightclubs throughout the country. After closing at Reno Sweeney on January 8, 1978, Ludlam, Susan, and Quinton took *The Ventriloquist's Wife* to the 99-Cent Floating Theater in Pittsburgh in the middle of January. They were guaranteed $900 for six performances over three nights, including traveling expenses. Ludlam also received an additional $150 for three "after school" performances of his *Punch and Judy* puppet show while in Pittsburgh.

Following Pittsburgh, there were several performances of *The Ventriloquist's Wife* at the Bottom Line, another Greenwich Village nightclub, before the play settled in for a two-month run at the Village Gate in the heart of the Village. There would be more performances at nightclubs and theaters in California, Nevada, and Wisconsin during the coming year. (Since there were only two actors and *The Ventriloquist's Wife* was such an inexpensive show to tour, it proved to be one of Ludlam's more lucrative properties, and would help him to secure a lease on the theater at One Sheridan Square.)

By this point, Ludlam had become more cavalier about publicity and more capable of manipulating it to his own ends. In the brief note he sent along with the signed contracts for the Pittsburgh booking, he wrote: "I love interviews but it is more efficient to do it all at once than it is one at a time. Could you arrange a press conference early on? We'd be happy to answer questions and explain."

This was a one-shot, provincial deal, and Ludlam had no way of knowing that it would lead to an important new contact. Along with Susan and Quinton, he stayed at the home of Leon Katz, a theater professor at the University of Pittsburgh and director of the University's 99-Cent Floating Theater, which was committed to "experimental" theater. It was Katz who had invited them in the first place.

An author, playwright, and theater scholar, Katz instantly hit it off with Ludlam, and they became lifelong friends and colleagues. Over the coming years, Ludlam would occasionally call on Katz, using him as a long-distance dramaturge to iron out any problems he encountered with the development of a play. "We had a kind of immediate recognition of one another," said Katz about his first meeting Ludlam. "I knew him, and he knew me, and that was it. It was really quite remarkable.

"Despite his reputation and public image for being camp and drag and all that, the first thing that struck me about him was the intent seriousness with which he spoke," continued Katz.

> He would say things that were in conventional terms outrageous. His style of thinking was habitually to invert the commonplace. His mind literally worked that way. He wasn't just being paradoxical. He inverted the cliché. But it was never with the Oscar Wildean tone of "Aren't I bright?" or "Isn't this an interesting way of putting words together?" He simply said what he meant.

Katz found Ludlam and his work to be one and the same, inseparable. But he also felt that Ludlam had never been properly understood or assimilated by the culture at large. "Even during that first weekend, I noticed the kinds of things that fascinated him when we went shopping for some little five-and-dime items," said Katz.

> He collected what on the face of it would be considered junk. He loved the

iniquitous, the tacky, just as he loved the detritus of American culture, the underside of it. But it was a genuine affection. I subsequently discovered that he loved the same thing about the theater and drama. He loved what was totally ludicrous, what was trashy in itself, what was conventional to the point of being unbearable. But it wasn't that he was laughing at these things. He was paying homage with affection to things that were the reverse of what accepted opinion suggested they should be. His response was literally the reverse. He was a true original. So much so, that he was mistaken for the opposite. He was mistaken for being deliberately camp, kitsch, and so on, which was absolutely not the case.

Even people who loved his work: What they told him when they praised him would really discourage him. He would feel horrible even about the rave reviews he got, because the characteristics the critics were attributing to him were the opposite of what he intended. I saw this over and over again: his absolute hatred of even the articles that praised him to the skies. He would always be in despair because they just didn't get it. It wasn't gotten because it was too similar to what was normally understood to be camp or drag. His work was similar, but wasn't the same at all, and its implications were really the opposite. Charles thought of himself as a very serious revolutionary in the theater, and one of the things he was rebelling against was the avant-garde. He hated the idea and rationale of the avant-garde because he looked backward. He loved tradition. He loved particularly the tackiness, the badness of tradition. He loved what was understood to be beyond the pale and culturally unacceptable.

It's much like a bag lady who loves all the crippled animals she finds in the street. Charles loved what was crippled in the culture and really raised it to an extraordinary level. But he did it with affection, by blowing it up, exaggerating it, going to the limit of its absurdity and thereby redeeming it. And I adored it in him, because the integrity of it was absolute. He wasn't kidding anybody. He wasn't being Barnum. He wasn't being a showman in that sense at all.

Katz recalled having some underlying anxieties when he first met Ludlam. He had only recently inherited the stewardship of the 99-Cent Floating Theater: *The Ventriloquist's Wife* was the first of ten events he had programmed and he was "concerned about whether anyone would show up." He remembered arriving at the theater the first night, "and I heard nothing but silence as I walked the length of the corridor that led to the box office. But there were two hundred some-odd people lined up." The show proved so successful that they added an additional performance beyond the scheduled January 12—14 run, which was also a sellout.

Ludlam apparently was less apprehensive. He had mounted a large banner that simply read "LUDLAM, LUDLAM, LUDLAM, LUDLAM" as it ran along the facade of the theater. After the reactions in New York and Philadelphia, he knew he had a hit on his hands; enough so to keep it running at the Village Gate—once they returned to New York —until the company had embarked on a prearranged tour of the West Coast in April of 1978.

Camille and *Stage Blood* had been booked for a rigorous tour of various colleges of the University of California, beginning with a one-night performance at UCLA on April 10, followed by two nights each at Santa Cruz, Santa Barbara, Berkeley, and San Diego. This was all a prelude to a return to Los Angeles for two-weeks at the Improvisation (April 22 to May 8), where the company proved so popular that another week was added to the run. Ludlam and Susan also performed *The Ventriloquist's Wife* at Studio One, an L.A. nightclub, on May 1.

It was a wild and heady time for the group, which consisted of Ludlam and Quinton, Black-Eyed Susan, Pashalinski, Vehr, Brockmeyer, Currie, Kilgore, and Robert Fuhrman, who looked after the sets and costumes. There was ample time to explore the natural wonders of the environment, such as the rugged coastline of Big Sur. Debra Crane, Pashalinski's new lover, joined them upon their return to Los Angeles late in April.

When they arrived in Santa Barbara on April 13, there was an impromptu champagne gathering by the hotel's pool belatedly to celebrate Ludlam's thirty-fifth birthday. While walking to the campus later that afternoon, they stopped on a footbridge to admire a rainbow. Expressing what they all felt, Brockmeyer remarked, "We're in California. We've found our pot of gold." The first night in Santa Barbara, Ludlam happened to catch Alexander Korda's classic 1942 film *To Be or Not To Be* on TV, and he worked some of Jack Benny's shtick from the film into his performance of *Stage Blood* the next night.

Ludlam also enjoyed visiting his ex-lover Wally Gorell, who was completing his master's degree in the Rhetoric Department at UC Berkeley and caught a performance of *Stage Blood* there. Gorell recalled taking Ludlam and Quinton to the Berkeley Botanical Gardens one afternoon.

"Charles was really wowed by their collections of cacti and succulents," said Gorell.

> He mentioned that he was always so envious of people who lived in California
> because their geraniums grew like shrubbery and you could have jade trees
> growing in your front yard. He had this glimmer in his eye, and you just knew
> that he was amazed to suddenly feel like there could actually be another place in
> the world worth living besides New York City. Although I knew he'd never leave
> New York, I remember thinking then that he'd at least come back for a vacation.
> But he never did.

Since the formation of the company in the late sixties, Ludlam had never really taken a
"vacation" in any normal sense of the word. This was yet another respect in which his
life and work could not be separated. On the other hand, he felt like he took mini-vaca-
tions every day, that is, whenever he found himself distracted from a current play or
project, or whenever he drew or painted — as he frequently did.

Though the company appreciated the parties the various UC theater departments
hosted for them, and were grateful for the predominantly glowing reviews in the local
papers, nothing could match the thrill of the attention they received after they returned
to Los Angeles. They stayed at the Tropicana, which was the L.A. equivalent of the
Chelsea Hotel in New York, and popular with rock stars.

Ludlam was scheduled to give yet another interview on a day when everyone else had
planned an excursion to Disneyland. With Quinton encouraging the rebellion, Ludlam
skipped the interview and went on the outing instead. They arrived early enough to avoid
the crowds, and as Pashalinski recalled, most of them were inevitably stoned for the rides.

Dan Sullivan's mixed reviews of *Camille* and *Stage Blood* in the *Los Angeles Times* were
offset by an advance feature in the April 9 Sunday edition that inaugurated the
California tour. The troupe was even more compensated by the positive notices both
plays received in the *Los Angeles Herald Examiner* and the *Hollywood Reporter*. But who
needed the critics anyway, when there was a whole new contingent of West Coast
celebrities joining the Ridiculous bandwagon?

Richard Currie recalled,

> One night after *Camille*, I was in the public restroom in the basement washing

the gray out of my hair. And as I was coming up from the sink with my eyes full of soap, this curly-haired man handed me some paper towels. As I looked at him more clearly, I realized it was Donovan. When I returned upstairs and as I was about to burst into the story, Charles introduced me to Bob Dylan and then Donovan.

The company's biggest West Coast fans included the famous English novelist Christopher Isherwood and his lover Don Bachardy. They saw *Camille* several times and encouraged their friends to attend as well, including George Cukor, the director of the Garbo film version that had been a primary resource for Ludlam's adaptation. According to Cukor's biographer Patrick McGilligan, "Here was the director of Hollywood's classic *Camille* watching an avant-garde cross-dressing road company from New York. Yet Cukor was disoriented by the show. He was, if anything, horrified. He just didn't get it." McGilligan, who claimed that the event took place in "the early 1970s," failed to mention that Cukor left during the second intermission, missing the third and final act.

Isherwood and Bachardy also attended the first of two performances of *The Ventriloquist's Wife* at Studio One on the lone Monday night it played there. They loved it so much that they called a number of friends to catch the second show, which they stayed for as well.

In the middle of the run at the Improv, Isherwood and Bachardy gave a dinner party for the company at their home in Santa Monica. The wine flowed freely, and Robert Fuhrman became particularly inebriated. Bachardy, a much-admired artist, drew portraits of Ludlam, Quinton, Susan, Pashalinski, Brockmeyer, and Currie. His more special gift was the surreptitious sexual tryst he had with Ludlam, which Ludlam apparently divulged only to Christopher Scott. Ludlam did, however, make a point of telling Pashalinski that at this point in their long-term union, Isherwood and Bachardy had an "open" relationship.

There was another party for the cast, cohosted by the actress Sally Kirkland. It was attended by "hundreds of Hollywood people," according to Pashalinski, and it made them feel like they were the toast of the town. The high note that this first California tour seemed to sound for everyone was reinforced by the knowledge that they would be returning to a new home theater in New York, finally permitting the Ridiculous players to function as the repertory company they knew themselves to be.

৵

After the Evergreen Theater was sold to the Baha'i Foundation in the fall of 1975, the Ridiculous played wherever it could while looking for a new space to call its own. As the search for a theater dragged on, Pashalinski recalled accompanying Ludlam to Tambellini's Gate, which proved only too available. Since they had performed their first two productions (*Big Hotel* and *When Queens Collide*) at the Gate a decade before, it held a certain nostalgic appeal. But the awful disarray they found it in was shameful, and Ludlam felt returning there would be going backward. He had had his heart set on the Cherry Lane, a quaint theater in the West Village that was a landmark in Off-Broadway theater history. The Cherry Lane was far more like the jewel box theater Ludlam always dreamed of having. But it was doing quite well on the basis of show-by-show rentals, and proved too expensive for any long-term leasing prospects. He instead found what was to become the company's new home while he was performing *The Ventriloquist's Wife* at Reno Sweeney, in the autumn of 1977.

This basement theater at One Sheridan Square had been used in a variety of ways. It was most celebrated over the years as Café Society, a nightclub that opened in 1938 and featured such performers as Billie Holiday, Lena Horne, and Imogene Coca. An ad for Billie Holiday proudly claimed that the club was "The Wrong Place for the Right People." "Café Society was New York's only truly integrated nightclub, a place catering to progressive types with open minds," wrote David Margolick in *Strange Fruit*, a book whose title refers to the harrowing ballad that Holiday sang at the site.

Prior to Café Society, the space had been a speakeasy during Prohibition, as well as a magic theater called the Shrine of the Orient. Decades later it became a jazz club called Salvation, where Jimi Hendrix, among others, performed. It had also been a gay bar, and, most recently, the Greek Revival Theater. Ludlam's first lease on the space covered a six-year period, beginning March 1, 1978, with an optional extension effective through February of 1988.

In fact, Ludlam had first stumbled upon One Sheridan Square six years earlier. He described the space in a letter to Lola Pashalinski on August 16, 1972, before choosing the Evergreen Theater instead. "Things are chuggin' along," it began.

> I found a theater that is available at #1 Sheridan Square. It used to be the Haven, a gay bar. They want fifteen hundred per month and a long-term lease. We won't have any new grant money until the middle of September, but perhaps a deposit would hold it. Everybody I've talked to says it's a great — even a posh — place.

They say it has low ceilings. It might be the perfect home theater for us. I'm going to see the place today. The location is the "end."

After inspecting the premises, Ludlam resumed:

> Just got back from seeing the theater. It is the *perfect* thing for us. They've had trouble with it in the past because of Mafia connections and the gay after-hours joints that were in there. Our competition for the place want to open a nightclub. The super and the agent seemed to lean more toward a respectable legit theater (that's us all over). If they will let me put a deposit on it I'll do that with my money to hold it until mid September or October, when the grants come in. You can't imagine how excited I am about it. Incidentally the ceilings aren't bad since they've put in a sunken dance floor. It's run down. We'd have to clean, paint, put in seats etc. But it would be all ours. And we could really expand our repertory and playing schedule. Not to mention building up a subscription audience. Lots of room. Bar kitchen. Men's and Ladies' rooms and lots of dressing room space. Keep your fingers crossed.

Ludlam's initial glowing impressions glossed over some definite drawbacks, which were discovered once he took over the space. Though it could accommodate 155 theatergoers, a couple of large, structural support columns obstructed a number of views. From the performance perspective, the elongated but narrow thrust stage was made smaller still by what were, indeed, low ceilings — which also made the challenge to set designers that much greater. And there was less space for the ample dressing rooms than Ludlam had anticipated.

But with a backlog of plays just waiting to be performed in repertory, such problems did not seem insurmountable. Following the West Coast tour in the spring of 1978, everyone pitched in to do the necessary renovations in preparation for opening the theater the last week in May. This entailed a pretty extensive cleanup job, but numerous friends also volunteered their help. The uncomfortable seating left behind by the Greek Revival Theater, the last tenant at One Sheridan Square, remained something of a nuisance. The seats were, in fact, pews made of concrete and arranged in the manner of an amphitheater. (In the process of choreographing a revival of *Corn* in the fall, Richard Goldberger — who, as a dancer in Larry Rée's ballet company, called himself Olga Plushinskaya — had the bright idea of making pillows to soften the effect of the concrete on patrons' derrieres. He organized sewing parties to create cushions in surreal, Daliesque shapes. Several years later, a Trans-Lux movie chain, in the course of renovating one of its houses, donated some theater seats, after which visitors to the Ridiculous could sit in conventional comfort.)

Along with the company's new permanent home came new responsibilities. According to Christopher Scott,

> The NEA [National Endowment for the Arts] and NYSCA [New York State Council on the Arts] wanted the Ridiculous to transform itself from a New York experimental theater into a miniature national cultural institution. Charles asked me to help, and since I was having a rocky time in my relationship with Henry [Geldzahler] and felt vulnerable, I seized the opportunity.

Both renewing and formalizing the role he had played in the first few years of the Ridiculous, Scott became its Executive Director in 1978. At first, he worked side-by-side with Catherine Farinon-Smith, who continued as the business manager until 1980, when he officially replaced her.

"Although Cathy had worked very hard and fast for Charles throughout the seventies, she was terribly imprecise in business matters," said Scott. "It was always haphazardly done. She was notorious for the sloppiness of her budgets with the NEA. Of course, she was the one who got Charles to apply for the grants in the first place. But there came a point when Charles almost lost his status as a charitable organization because she failed to file the necessary papers on time."

"There were lots of financial problems," continued Scott. "Cathy had just dropped the ball, and eventually she disappeared. I discovered stacks and piles of unopened mail from the IRS and others left behind in garbage bags. The IRS was freezing our bank account for employee withholding taxes. There was even a secret bank account."

But in other respects, the Ridiculous could finally begin to function like a repertory company. They started life at One Sheridan Square with performances of *Camille*, *Stage Blood*, and *The Ventriloquist's Wife* in rotating rep. Plans for later that summer called for revivals of *Bluebeard* and *Corn*, as well as the introduction of *Utopia, Incorporated*. (*Utopia*, Ludlam's newest play, would have to wait until November to make its bow.)

By July, Ludlam was also offering *Anti-Galaxie Nebulae* on Saturday afternoons. As improvised and performed with Quinton and Vehr, this was a weekly sci-fi puppet serial inspired primarily by the phenomenally successful film *Star Wars*. But since each episode was unique, it evolved over the months into its own wacky concoction for "warpable young minds of all ages" — according to a review in the *Soho Weekly News*.

During its first year at One Sheridan Square, the Ridiculous would give a whopping 279 performances of nine different plays selected from its repertory. To maximize the income while running his own theater, Ludlam would also occasionally lease the space out on dark nights, or for late-night performances. The first to ever take advantage of such an arrangement with the Ridiculous was Charles Busch — in fact, only two months after the company moved into One Sheridan Square. But as Busch recalled, he was really the moving force behind the development himself, and Ludlam was rather ambivalent about it.

Busch had just moved back to New York from Chicago in the spring of 1978, bringing his one-man show, "Hollywood Confidential," with him. "Because Ludlam was my idol, I really wanted him to think I was talented," said Busch. "So I went on this campaign to get his attention. First, I wrote him a letter inviting him to come see my show. No response. Then, I put up posters near the theater at One Sheridan Square. Next, I saw [Black-Eyed] Susan on the street, and I asked her if she would put some flyers inside the theater, and she did."

Though Busch became terribly excited the night he learned that Ludlam and Quinton were — at last — in the audience, he was crestfallen when they failed to come backstage after the performance. But with the determination of a stagestruck starlet, Busch persisted. He had noticed that Ludlam was soon slated to receive a special comedy award, and made sure he was present at the event. Following the presentation, Busch visited Ludlam's table, where he finally received fulsome praise from his Ridiculous hero. According to Busch, it was then and there that Ludlam invited the budding comedienne to offer his current act as a late-night performance at the company's brand new home, and even said that the Ridiculous would advertise the show for him.

Busch was thrilled, of course, but then disappointed all over again when nothing seemed to come of the offer. "I hadn't heard from Charles, and he wouldn't return my calls," said Busch.

> Then I went backstage after one of his shows at Sheridan Square to say hello, and I said, "I guess I should talk to someone about when I can start having tech rehearsals." He looked at me with this blank expression and said, "Oh. Oh. I think you should talk to Cathy Smith, our business manager." So I went to see

her. She was very busy and *fartootst* [Yiddish for bewildered or disoriented]. She said, "I'm sorry. We couldn't possibly have you at our theater now. We're at the end of our season and we don't have our new funding money yet. There's just no way that we could ever produce you. Charles never should have suggested that." I said, "Please, if you just let me use the space it won't cost you anything."

Busch performed his one-man show at One Sheridan Square on Fridays and Saturdays at midnight for several months, beginning in July. He split the box office revenues "fifty-fifty" with the Ridiculous. "Being in Ludlam's theater gave me a certain legitimacy in that milieu," Busch acknowledged years later.

In spite of any ambivalence he felt about this highly ambitious rival, Ludlam called Busch one afternoon during the revival of *Bluebeard*, which also opened in July, and invited him to go on that very night as Hecate. Busch gave half a dozen or so performances in the part, and found it a very trying experience. "If I had ever entertained a fantasy of working with the Ridiculous Theatrical Company, doing Hecate got it out of my system," claimed Busch. "I remained a great admirer of Ludlam's. I mean, Charles was fascinating, but he was such a dominating personality to all of them, and I didn't feel like being part of that."

Indeed, the old-timers were also having their customary problems with Ludlam. As a number of different plays were being offered — and still others rehearsed — each week, Pashalinski found this a "killing" period. Susan remembered one night following a performance of *The Ventriloquist's Wife* when: "Charles lashed out at me, claiming I did this and that wrong. But I knew that I had given a good performance. He was projecting because he hadn't done so well himself."

In addition to the problems he was having with his cast at the theater, Ludlam had to cope with ongoing stress at home. For one thing, Quinton became terribly insecure once he got wind of Ludlam's affair with Ethyl Eichelberger. Though he was under the impression that they were no longer sleeping together, Quinton had a highly intense confrontation with Eichelberger at Boots and Saddles, a tacky gay bar on Christopher Street. As Eichelberger later told his close friend Steve Turtell, a drunken Quinton had screamed, "He's mine, and you can't have him!"

"Whenever I mentioned Everett's name, there would be this tension with Ethyl," said Turtell, "until he finally told me about that incident with Everett." According to Turtell, Eichelberger found it hard to understand what Ludlam saw in Quinton. "Ethyl would only fall in love with someone who was an artist he could respect; and he thought it should be the same for Charles. He would get really irritated with people who didn't have the same training or knowledge that he did."

Nor is it likely mere coincidence that, while he relinquished any hold he still had on Ludlam during this period, Eichelberger also withdrew as a regular member of the Ridiculous. In his unpublished biography of Eichelberger, Ridiculous scholar Joe E. Jeffreys quotes from a Ph.D. dissertation by Uzi Parnes, conveying that Eichelberger "realized it wasn't [Ludlam's] company I was emulating. It was him that I wanted to be. I felt all along that I wanted to be in his company, and I was, [but] I kept wanting more." Regarding the actor's departure from the company in the late 1970s, Jeffreys explains that Eichelberger finally realized he would rather be doing his own shows. (Indeed, Eichelberger went on to have a significant career directing and performing in his own pieces, predominantly in the East Village. He would also return to the Ridiculous from time to time, in various capacities — including a star-turn in *The Artificial Jungle*, Ludlam's final play.)

Looking back on the first few years of his relationship with Ludlam, Quinton recalled, "I was a frightened and troubled person, unkind and unprofessional. I wasn't fun to be with. It was like pulling teeth for Charles to get me to do what he wanted. But Charles could be very unyielding and demanding, too."

Ludlam showed up one day for a rehearsal of the *Corn* revival with his right hand in a cast. Though he tried to cover it up at first, the truth eventually leaked out: He had had another violent fight with Quinton and broken his hand. And even as Ludlam was becoming more entangled with Quinton, his own behavioral patterns were changing noticeably within the company. The two of them went off on their own more and more after the performances, and the core members felt Ludlam pulling away from them.

Ludlam was suddenly less the child seeking attention from others and, at the same time, less the parent who was there for them. In the process of devoting himself more exclusively to Quinton, he gained more control over his own life.

Given his injured hand, however, Ludlam couldn't go on as Paw Hatfield in *Corn*. According to Adam Kilgore, who had been cast as Aunt Priscilla, "It happened just a few days before the opening and Charles was fretting about how he could play his role. I suggested we switch parts. I mean, I was playing this old lady and I told him he could put a shawl over his hand and nobody would know the difference. But there was no way he could play Paw and do all those athletic things with a cast on his hand."

Nor, evidently, could Ludlam write at the time. But this was due as much to his customary writer's block as it was to any physical injury. Although Ludlam had started working on *Utopia, Incorporated* some years before and planned to open it along with the revival of *Corn,* at the end of the summer, he still didn't have a script.

A confused reference to the play had appeared a year earlier, in a letter Stephen Holt sent to Billy Edgar in August 1977, shortly after *Der Ring* closed: "Charles working feverishly on new play called *Utopia, Inc.* which is said to be written around him, or written around Susan, or written around Lola, or written around John, depending on whom you speak to."

But even if Ludlam was feeling somewhat "feverish" about the play, he was never "working feverishly" on it. According to Kilgore,

> He only had three pages of *Utopia* written, and we kept rehearsing those three pages over and over and over again for months. He just had this awful time getting the plot together and getting the scenes done. Even when we got close to opening, it was still relatively formless. It was hard to believe it was ever going to happen. And when it finally seemed to sort of gel, you could tell that even Charles didn't believe it would. Somehow, the production made it happen more than the writing.

The protracted genesis of *Utopia, Incorporated* was like a throwback to the troubled creation of *Hot Ice.* In each case, Ludlam had a rough idea of what he wanted the play to be about, but he had great difficulty realizing it. The bulk of the dialogue in *Utopia* was comprised of material from the joke books he had acquired to help shape his routines with Walter Ego.

Without any real idea for a story to guide him, Ludlam borrowed plot elements from *The Tempest, Lost Horizon, Journey to the Center of the Earth,* and *Gulliver's Travels,* as well as the "Road To . . ." movies of Bob Hope and Bing Crosby. (As Gerald Rabkin summarized the matter in the *Soho Weekly News*: "God knows what else . . . has lodged in Ludlam's fervid imagination.") The throwaway scenario concerns Captain John Gullible (Bill Vehr) and his shipmate Botchup (Ludlam), a pair of drug-smugglers who are whisked into the Bermuda Triangle, which transports them to a subterranean land.

They encounter Anarch (John Brockmeyer), the ruler of this "uninhibited island," and his daughter Phyllis (Black-Eyed Susan), obvious stand-ins for Shakespeare's Prospero and Miranda.

Not everything is perfect in Anarch's ostensibly utopian kingdom, however. Rosalba (Lola Pashalinski), the "High Priestess of the Happy Isle," is plotting an insurrection against Anarch with the aid of her two minions, Hyacinth (Everett Quinton) and Martok (Adam Kilgore). They seize the good-for-nothing Botchup as their savior, God Erunam (that is, "dog manure" spelled backwards), whose arrival had been prophesied thousands of years before; he, they believe, will help them gain control of the island.

In another subplot, Gullible plans to marry Phyllis. But Gullible is imprisoned after he is revealed to be the son of Anarch's former partner on Earth, who ruined him. Phyllis helps him to escape and agrees to return to Earth with him. As they confront a mugger, a waitress, and a derelict, their visit becomes an excuse for one lame joke after another, which in essence is all the play is comprised of — albeit, intentionally.

In the end, Botchup has "industrialized" Utopia and become President of the Corporation. Rosalba, now Botchup's secretary, answers a series of phone calls in rapid succession: "Utopia, Incorporated. He hasn't come in yet. Utopia, Incorporated. I expect him any minute. Utopia, Incorporated. He sent word he'd be in a little late. Utopia, Incorporated. He's been in but he went out again. Utopia, Incorporated. He's gone to lunch."

The satire of the business world in the final scenes of the play are its funniest. But much of the audience usually vacated their seats long before reaching that point. The following exchange between Anarch and Botchup is typical of the script:

> ANARCH: Tell me, where was the Declaration of Independence signed?
> BOTCHUP: At the bottom? . . .
> ANARCH: How do you find the weather in Utopia?
> BOTCHUP: You don't have to find the weather in Utopia. You just walk out the
> door and there it is!

Ludlam would claim that he set out to write a play consisting almost exclusively of old comic routines with *Utopia, Incorporated*. The result struck many as uninspired. A character's advice in the middle of the play, "Just take it at farce value," seems as good a description of the vacancy at the core of the work as any.

Kilgore recalled,

> As Martok, I never got any direction, I never got any comments. I'd go up to
> Charles and say, "How am I doing?" And he'd say, "Wonderful — if you had any
> problems, I'd tell you." But I just felt lost in this play. What was I doing here in
> this green wig with rubber nipples glued to my breasts? There was this one scene
> where I had to bend over with my bare ass while he passed out a pin-the-tail-on-
> the-donkey game to everyone. They'd all be blindfolded to pin the tails on me.
> But it took forever and the audience was bored to tears. That whole scene was
> dropped after a few nights.

Predictably, the critics were uniformly displeased when the play opened to the press
the first week in December. Gussow found it "an evening of lackadaisical Ludlam."
Feingold cited "a confused plot, laborious action, and a lot of banal dialogue." In
the *Post*, Marilyn Stasio grumbled that it was "an anemic letdown from past triumphs"
and quipped, "This time around, the Ridiculous isn't." In a fit of typically perverse
inspiration, Ludlam placed an ad that highlighted the devastating quotes and cited the
critics, including: "Awful — and hoary with age" (Gussow) and "The puns come so
thick and fast that one's reactive groaning becomes rhythmic. I recognize the method
in this badness" (Gerald Rabkin, the *Soho Weekly News*).

Far more impressive than the play were the freshly painted murals in the lobby of the
theater. As conceived and painted by artist Richard Hennessy, they were coordinated
to be finished in time for the opening of *Utopia*. A fan of the Ridiculous almost from
the beginning, Hennessy first met Ludlam at a party at Scott and Geldzahler's in 1971.
Though it was Scott who invited Hennessy to do the decorations, what Hennessy
most appreciated was the freedom Ludlam allowed him to do what he wanted with
the lobby.

While reflecting on the project, Hennessy described a Ludlam who was far less competitive than his theatrical colleagues found him. "Charles was absolutely amazing," said
Hennessy.

> There was never a question of, "Oh, well, you know, I like green, or why have you
> done this or that." Every day he would come in and think it was absolutely won-
> derful, encouraging me to do more and more. I realized that Charles was a very
> great artist who didn't compete with other artists. He wanted others to do their
> absolute best, and wouldn't get in their way.

Hennessy's colorful squiggles and large, amoeba-like shapes filled the walls, floors, and ceilings of the staircase leading down to the lobby as well as the lobby itself. As reported by John Russell in his *New York Times* art column, "A sense of parody and a sense of fun are everywhere evident, but there is also something more fundamental: a chromatic energy that communicates itself to the visitor and persuades him that something extraordinary will happen to him before he makes it back up the stairs."

Unfortunately, *Utopia* hardly made for an "extraordinary" event. Though it was a dismal failure with audiences and critics alike, with customary obstinacy Ludlam kept it running for an incredible two months. It was precisely because it didn't go over so well that Ludlam latched onto it as one of his better, if "misunderstood" plays. As Hennessy experienced this behavior over the years,

> Of course, there were always the hits, the *Bluebeard*s and the *Camille*s. And there were always the misses. But it was always the play that *wasn't* accepted, that they just didn't get, which Charles would talk about the most. He was constantly fighting that sense that everybody was trying to bury him after a hit like *Bluebeard*, that sense of "let's make somebody a phenomenon of just the moment."

Steven Samuels, who would soon join the Ridiculous, recalled, "Charles often pointed out that both *Der Ring* and *Utopia* were outgrowths of his search for a modern stage language, and belong to his highly modernist period. Each, in a way, is impossible, and seemingly impossible to take, perhaps precisely *because* they fulfilled his theoretical intentions."

In a brief note inviting Leon Katz to *Utopia*, Ludlam referred to it as "our excursion into philosophical fantasy" and proclaimed it "a major breakthrough for me. I think you will agree." But no matter how much Ludlam could disregard the critical reaction to the play, he could not ignore the poor box office revenues and the grave financial circumstances they led to. Though *Anti-Galaxie Nebulae* was still selling tickets on Saturday afternoons, its income wasn't sufficient to meet the new monthly rent. Nor could it maintain the cast, whose weekly earnings were dwindling to practically nothing.

Though the core members had endured financial hardships for ten years, it had to be particularly disheartening to be working so hard now, in their own home, without being able to sustain themselves. Outside influences and interferences were also beginning to take their toll. Susan recalled that Steven Burdick, who was "very devoted to John," waited for Brockmeyer "every night at the theater" during the run of *Utopia*.

"Steven would often get on my case," she said, "telling me 'You should all be earning more money. Where is all this grant money going to?' When it was clear to me that it was going into the productions." To some degree, however, Burdick's unfair and misguided accusations clearly influenced others, including Pashalinski.

Through William Kohler's connections, the company went to Philadelphia the last weekend in January — right after *Utopia* closed — to put on *Camille* at the University of Pennsylvania. While they were there, Pashalinski told Ludlam that she had been approached by Harvey Perr to do a reading of his play, *Gethsemane Springs*, at Playwrights Horizons. Well aware that Perr had already had an affair with Ethyl Eichelberger, Ludlam responded, "Harvey Perr — I don't want to ever hear that name again." Out of sheer perversity, Pashalinski smugly replied, "Harvey Perr, Harvey Perr, Harvey Perr." Though they both had a good laugh over it at the time, this was a far more significant development than it appeared. The reading marked the first theatrical venture outside of the Ridiculous for Pashalinski, and the beginning of her discovery that she could make a career for herself without Charles Ludlam.

Ludlam, in the meantime, had a far more dramatic incident to contend with during the *Camille* weekend in Philadelphia — worthy of the character he was playing onstage. Kohler, who hosted a large party for the company at the Art Alliance, recalled that after the first evening's performance, "Everett tried to hang himself in the bathroom. They just cut him down at the last minute. It was at a Holiday Inn near the university where they were all staying."

According to Adam Kilgore, "Charles and Everett's worst times publicly were during the touring productions of *Camille*. They'd have these terrible episodes when Everett was playing Nichette during the tea scene. Everett was shaking all the time because he was so nervous, and his teacup would bang against the saucer. Charles would whisper directions to him behind his hands, saying nasty things to him and kicking him under the table. Everett would come off the stage furious, saying, 'I quit!'"

In terms of their first night in Philadelphia, Kilgore remembered,

> After having a fight with Everett, Charles came to sleep in my room. Richard
> [Currie] came knocking on my door later that night to explain that Everett had
> tried to hang himself. [It was Currie who discovered Quinton in the nick of time.]
> He was taken to the hospital and Charles stayed with me. It seemed to me that
> almost all of their fights had to do with Everett feeling humiliated by being

directed by Charles, either onstage or off. He was so resistant to Charles's trying to direct him in a role. And when he got drunk, he would lash out about it.

The urgent need to replace Quinton as Nichette led to Georg Osterman's return to the Ridiculous after a yearlong hiatus. "Richard Currie called me from Philadelphia," recalled Osterman.

> He said that Everett had had an "accident," and could I catch the next train and come down. It was John [Brockmeyer] who spilled the beans about the suicide attempt once I got there. Although I couldn't find my copy of the script and it had been a couple of years since I played Nichette, I went through the role in my head and it all came back to me on the train.

After Ludlam's turbulent affair with Robert Liebowitz some years previously, such problems were all too familiar to members of the Ridiculous — if not exactly on such a scale. But from the beginning, the stakes with Quinton seemed to be higher. "There were dramatic incidents at restaurants, with either Charles or Everett getting up and storming out — stuff like that, that went on for a good long time," recalled Hennessy. "But Charles had to be impossible to live with. I mean that kind of intensity, and his always being so obsessed. We can't imagine what it must have been like for Everett. But Everett obviously wanted to learn how to act. And this made it perfect. He was able to live that closely with Charles, which was extraordinary."

Looking back on their early years together, Quinton acknowledged,

> It was a tempestuous relationship, with ups and downs. It was happy. It was sad. It was also hard because Charles was my lover as well as my boss. He was my acting teacher. And there was an awful lot coming at me from different directions at once. It was a lot to digest. So it got pretty heavy at times, and I didn't learn how to deal with the working together and living together till later, when I could make the switches more comfortably.

Some years would pass before the beneficial aspects of their relationship really began to manifest themselves in both Ludlam and Quinton. In the meantime, the return to New York from Philadelphia in February of 1979 was filled with a number of hardships, the most pressing being financial.

According to Steven Samuels, the poor box office of *Utopia* "catapulted the company into hyperactive repertory" in the spring of 1979. Along with the warhorses such as *Camille*, *Corn*, and *Bluebeard*, there were as many as six different shows in a single week. This was in lieu of staging Oscar Wilde's *Salomé* with Ludlam in the title role — a tantalizing proposition which had been announced to the press the preceding fall, but which never came to pass. Apart from Bill Vehr's *Whores of Babylon*, it would have been the only work by another playwright produced by the Ridiculous in Ludlam's lifetime.

Ludlam was, nevertheless, busy with other projects. Quinton's bio in the playbill for *Utopia* announced that he was "currently creating the title role in *The Sorrows of Dolores*, a motion picture by Charles Ludlam which will be presented by the Ridiculous Theatrical Company at One Sheridan Square in the spring."

Though Ludlam had already started making this silent black-and-white film — which costarred Minette and featured other Ridiculous players — he would still be working on it at the time of his death eight years later. Filming was done over the years with 16 millimeter camera equipment that had been given to him by William Kohler, when he learned that Ludlam was interested in making a movie. Kohler had originally purchased the equipment for a trip to Libya. "What I saw of the film didn't impress me," said Kohler. "Charles didn't have the eye for making movies. But he did things his own way and it was always fine with me."

But it wasn't always fine with Pashalinski, who began to seek roots outside the company. At least as far back as the original production of *Corn*, Pashalinski had been considering how she could function apart from the Ridiculous.

After her reading at Playwrights Horizons, Pashalinski's first real acting job without Ludlam entailed a good number of Ridiculous connections. The play was *Mirandolina*, an eighteenth century comedy by Goldoni, the Italian equivalent of Molière who was very much in the Ridiculous vein. Even more noteworthy were the other colleagues from the Ridiculous involved with the production: It was directed by Robert Reddy, designed by Lohr Wilson, and featured Adam Kilgore.

According to Pashalinski, Ludlam "cautiously encouraged" her to take on this external project. "It didn't overwhelm him with joy, but he made the best of it." Ludlam even went so far as to rearrange the playing schedule at One Sheridan Square to accommodate her. Since *Mirandolina* played Thursdays through Sundays at the Theater for the New City, Ludlam inserted *The Ventriloquist's Wife* in those time slots. It was the only play in the Ridiculous repertory that didn't require Pashalinski's presence. In fact,

Camille could still be performed twice on the weekends, since *Mirandolina* didn't go on until midnight on Saturdays and gave a matinee on Sundays. Ludlam attended the last matinee and was effusive in his praise for Pashalinski's performance.

Though Ludlam evidently refrained from sharing any misgivings with Pashalinski regarding her branching out, he was more than willing to share his concern over the matter with Black-Eyed Susan. She recalled that it was during this period that Ludlam began to "confide" in her more. Up until then, she had always felt that Pashalinski had been more his confidante.

According to Susan, "In trying to cope with his sense of rejection, Charles would turn it around and find fault with the person who was leaving. He felt that Lola didn't want to work as hard as she had been working. But he'd also implicate her whole nature. It was a defense mechanism."

Though neither of them is particularly willing to admit it even today, there was a tremendous, long-standing competition between Pashalinski and Susan. Their rivalry transcended the practically universal ambition to capture Ludlam's love and attention, in answer to his demand for the absolute devotion of everyone around him. Rather, Pashalinski and Susan had been in contention with each other as the only female members of the company. And in a less palpable but more deep-seated way, they were also grappling with the woman "in" Ludlam.

Susan recalled Ludlam once asking her, "Are you jealous that you're not playing the leading actress [in *Camille*]?"

> I replied, "The problem isn't that I'm jealous, but that you abuse me when you're in drag." And he said, "Just a minute. For that accusation we need a third opinion." He called in Debra Crane, and said, "Susan says that I mistreat her when I'm in drag. Do you think it's true?" And she replied, "Yes, it is." I believe he was really shocked, because he honestly never saw his behavior, nor my reactions, objectively. But I do think he became extra competitive whenever he was in drag, because he felt that's the way a woman behaves.

༂

It may have been relatively easy for Ludlam to rearrange the sequence of plays performed in rep during the three weeks Pashalinski was in *Mirandolina* in the spring. But it proved far more problematic when she left *The Enchanted Pig* in the middle of its extended run to portray the Queen in the annual Renaissance Festival in Upstate New York.

Ludlam's seventeenth play, *The Enchanted Pig*, was one of those works that was quickly thrown together to try and raise some much-needed capital. As Adam Kilgore recalled, "There were tremendous discussions and fights over money when Charles submitted a grant proposal for us to do *The Enchanted Pig* together as a puppet production. He used my name in the proposal. But at that point, the play was barely an idea. Once the grant came through, he rapidly wrote it and had a complete script before we went into rehearsals."

In an effort to make the proposal even more foolproof, Ludlam used another name he hoped would impress the grant-bestowing committee: Bobjack Callejo. Callejo, who hadn't worked with the Ridiculous since *Jack and the Beanstalk* back in 1975, was reunited with Ludlam in the summer of 1978. "I bumped into Charles and Everett one weekend in Cherry Grove, and they came back to my Fire Island house with me that afternoon," recalled Callejo. "When Charles next needed to do a children's play in order to get funded, he used me on the application, because I looked very good: I had another major career going. Later, when I read the script, I had this image of Rousseau. And so I designed all the sets as if they had been painted by Rousseau — faux-primitive and naïve."

With a subtitle, "A Fairy Tale for the Disenchanted," that referred to Ronald Firbank's label for *Odette* ("A Fairy Tale for Weary People"), the play indeed appeared to be naïve in its conception. After his ineffectual attempt to incorporate *The Tempest* into *Utopia, Incorporated*, Ludlam turned to an equally challenging Shakespearean tragedy for his next venture. *The Enchanted Pig* is a highly improbable but charming blend of *King Lear* with any number of fairy tales, including elements of *Beauty and the Beast*, *The Frog Prince*, *Cinderella*, and *Rumplestiltskin*.

Ludlam's interest in *Lear* had recently been aroused when he was approached to play the Fool to Richard Burton's King at Lincoln Center, with John Dexter directing. But Burton's ambition to play Lear was aborted when the great Welsh actor refused to offer more than six performances a week.

Though *King Lear* is the foundation of the story, *The Enchanted Pig* rather marks the apotheosis of Ludlam's love of children's theater. Given that it was written primarily to secure endowment dollars, Ludlam never dreamed it would become the success it did. Nor, for that matter, was he in the play, which made its long run all the more remarkable.

Like *Corn*, *The Enchanted Pig* was polished off in a couple of weeks, and as a result it has a similar coherence and purity of spirit. The story concerns King Gorgeous and his three daughters: Princess Gonda and Princess Wanda, who are wicked, and Enfanta Eulalie Irene, who is good. Just as Lear mistakes the motives of Cordelia, his one sincere daughter, King Gorgeous banishes Eulalie Irene to her fate. While Gonda and Wanda marry princes respectively from the East and the West, it is Eulalie's misfortune to marry "a pig from the North."

When he arrives to claim his wife, the Pig insists that "garbage and swill" be served at the wedding feast. "And after the banquet we'll have dancing and we'll all roll in the mud." At first reluctant, Eulalie submits to the Pig, just as Beauty does to the Beast. But as the title suggests, this Pig is "enchanted," and she discovers on their wedding night that he turns into a man while asleep.

In Eulalie's efforts to cure her husband of his strange malady, she comes upon Mother Wormwood, a witch "who knows all the magic arts." "Why is [my husband] a pig by day and a human being by night?" asks Eulalie. "It could be worse. It could be the other way around," responds the witch. As it turns out, it was Mother Wormwood who had placed the curse on the Pig.

After being separated from the Pig, Eulalie Irene must endure many trials before she can undo the curse. With the help of the Mother of the Moon, the Mother of the Sun, and the Mother of the Wind, she is finally reunited with the Pig, only to discover that he is really Prince Charming.

The sillier jokes — which were a hallmark of Ludlam's scripts and overwhelmed *Utopia, Incorporated* — were kept to a minimum in *The Enchanted Pig*. When the Prince from the East asks King Gorgeous for "the hand of your eldest daughter," the King replies, "Her hand? What's wrong with the rest of her?" As Eulalie Irene gets into bed with her new husband, she says, "Don't hog the covers."

Given the play's simplicity, it's surprising that it should have proved so popular for so long. Without either the campy excesses or the more serious messages that usually inform his other works, it remains something of an anomaly for Ludlam. Certainly it is not "in a class with such vintage Ludlam extravaganzas as *Bluebeard* and *Camille*," as Mel Gussow found it to be.

But Gussow was far from alone in declaring it a "delirious new merriment." In the *Daily News*, Don Nelsen went so far as to exclaim: "Ludlam here has all the makings of a success equal to that of another fairy tale, *The Fantasticks*." William A. Raidy (*Newark Star Ledger*) called it "sublime" and "a masterpiece of childish nonsense." James Leverett (*Soho Weekly News*) wrote that it "will cure the most ennui-struck sophisticate — not to mention captivating you, your kids, and your great-aunt from Sioux City." Jan Hoffman (*Village Voice*) considered it "perhaps Ludlam's most compact, elegant production." Even Terry Helbing wrote in the *Advocate* that "it ranks as one of the best plays in the RTC repertory."

The night that Clive Barnes covered the play for the *Post*, Ludlam noticed from backstage that he was dozing in his seat. Before they went out for the scene in which they're supposed to run offstage screaming, he told the two actresses playing the bad sisters (recent Ridiculous additions Deborah Petti and Ghislaine Chantelle) "to scream extra loud in the direction of Clive Barnes, to wake him up."

After opening in April to across-the-board raves, *The Enchanted Pig* ran for six months. Though it's a slight work, it embraced a positive, life-affirming attitude. And like the critics, the audience responded more to the production than to the play. For one thing, it was stunning to behold. Callejo won an award for his designs and both Adam Kilgore and John Cunningham were roundly complimented by the press for their magical masks and puppetry effects. There was also special praise for Gabriel Berry's imaginative and elegant costumes.

Without Ludlam to compete against onstage, the cast performed at their peak. Susan held center stage as Eulalie Irene. In his most important role to date, Quinton played the Pig, wearing an enormous snouted mask. (Peter Hujar, the highly respected photographer who often took candid shots of Ridiculous cast members backstage, felt that *The Enchanted Pig* was Ludlam's way of trying to show everyone else in the company why he loved Everett so much.) Brockmeyer was in his element as King Gorgeous and Pashalinski was in hers as Mother Wormwood. Vehr and Currie played the princes from the East and West, and Adam Kilgore was the Mother of the Moon. During the run, Kilgore also had to replace Brockmeyer as the King.

Brockmeyer had already missed one Sunday matinee when he ostensibly forgot about the performance and went to a movie instead. But while *The Enchanted Pig* was a run-away hit that extended its run, Brockmeyer proved unwilling to make the kind of sacrifices he had in the past — especially with Burdick, his new lover, encouraging him not to. They would follow through with their vacation plans for a New England camping trip late in the summer.

But personal, lover-oriented plans were one thing. It proved even more threatening and intolerable for Ludlam when Pashalinski left the show to participate in the Upstate Renaissance Festival. Even though Ludlam wasn't in *The Enchanted Pig* himself, he was angry that Pashalinski and Brockmeyer felt free to just remove themselves this way.

Pashalinski suggested that she could easily be replaced for those performances she would be missing, and, although he displayed some underlying annoyance, Ludlam went along with her proposal. With only a few days for rehearsals, Eureka played Mother Wormwood. She had not performed with the company since *Der Ring*, but she had already seen *The Enchanted Pig*. "Charles said something wonderful to me," recalled Eureka. "He said, 'I don't want you to be like Lola. I want you to do your own thing with this. And in your way, I think you can be even better.'" Ludlam was not only diabolically competitive himself, but clearly he knew how to use such means to motivate others.

Though Ludlam wasn't in the play, he attended many of the performances. This was despite an unbelievably busy schedule caused by his suddenly having to negotiate various other projects, including a course of his own design called "Eccentric Comedy," which he was teaching in the Experimental Theater Wing at New York University.

Early in the run of *The Enchanted Pig*, Ludlam had reintroduced the idea of staging Wilde's *Salomé*. This time a reading was actually held — with Ludlam in the title role, Pashalinski as Herodias, Brockmeyer as John the Baptist, and H.M. Koutoukas as Herod.

Though nothing came of *Salomé*, to further boost box office income Ludlam put together yet another piece, which was offered at midnight on Saturdays, beginning in June 1979. It was called *Elephant Woman*, playing off the title of *Elephant Man*, which served as a very loose inspiration. Promoting itself as "a midnight frolic," *Elephant Woman* was a sort of Victorian-style vaudeville of carnival sideshow acts and circus freaks. Ludlam, who was never in the show himself, simply gave a frame to the evening, and then invited everyone who participated to invent their own shtick. Quinton played what amounted to a master of ceremonies, introducing the various acts. The show would radically change from week to week, depending on the cast's availability. John

Brockmeyer was the only one of the five remaining core members to appear in it. (He played a nurse in drag, and evoked Eve Arden.) Adam Kilgore portrayed "the Faceless Woman," and Robert Reddy returned to the Ridiculous to play "Madame Beluga," the bearded lady. But *Elephant Woman* had been conceived primarily as a vehicle for several new people who were students of Ludlam's at NYU, and had already been helping out both on and backstage: Vicki Raab, Ed McGowan, Deborah Petti, Ghislaine Chantelle, and Kevin Kelleher.

Georg Osterman, who played "Nurse Friendly" in *Elephant Woman*, claimed that it was "a very funny, very twisted piece. Everybody added their own little thing to it. I missed some of the shows because I was having a relationship with a wealthy man I met during *Der Ring* and traveling a lot with him. But I remember Charles Busch was in it some times, and so was Robert Whitehead, another actor." As Busch recalled, it was Osterman who phoned him to ask if he would go on "as the nurse in this burlesque skit. It was just chaos," added Busch.

Elephant Woman was archetypal Ludlam, not least because it was ephemeral and subject to the vagaries of constant mutation, even as it referred in its way to a form of entertainment that seemed lost to the ages. It also referred to the wide-eyed wonder of the little boy who disobeyed his mother and went off on his own at the Mineola Fair to observe the sideshow freaks she had hoped to protect him from. Here he was, thirty years later, recreating that significant moment of his childhood by assembling and directing "freaks" of his own invention.

෨

Though it's curious that Ludlam chose not to appear on his own stage during most of 1979, he was still fulfilling his primary love of acting by costarring in a film called *Impostors*. It was being made by Mark Rappaport, an independent filmmaker who had already established his reputation in art circles with at least two of his four previous feature-length films, *The Scenic Route* and *Local Color*.

Rappaport had admired Ludlam from a distance ever since he had seen *Bluebeard* six years earlier. He appreciated that Ludlam "was not camp. He was classical. He transcended everything he did with his mercurial acting style, his ability to stop on a dime, and making it a million different things at the same time."

After attending *Camille* in Los Angeles — the very same performance from which

George Cukor had fled — Rappaport conceived of *Impostors* with Ludlam in mind. "I was knocked senseless by his *Camille*. I thought, this is the greatest actor in America, and I'm gonna use him; I'm gonna work with this guy. I was astonished that no one had used him in films. A talent like this had to be used."

From the beginning, Rappaport pictured Ludlam in the "top hat and tails" Michael Burg had already donned for the filmmaker in *Local Color*. Rappaport envisioned Ludlam and Burg playing twins, "or something like that," when he began working on the screenplay of *Impostors* in the fall of 1978.

A note in the script conveys how suited Ludlam was to the role of Chuckie. As it's described, Chuckie's relationship with Mikey (Burg),

> must be played like an amalgam of the Marx Brothers and Peter Lorre, the Three Stooges mixed with Dostoevsky. There is also a broad streak of amiable Mel Brooks vulgarity running through it. In short, they are always playacting. . . . But underlying it all is a menacing dead seriousness that is unsettling — two psychopaths, refugees from trashy horror films, on the loose.

The willfully cryptic story concerns a pair of pathological killers who may or may not be twin brothers. They are more likely impersonating a pair of twin magicians, whose act they stole after murdering them. Their real motive is the search for an ancient Egyptian treasure. While Chuckie is gay, his symbiotic relationship with his partner is fueled by Mikey's girlfriends, many of whom have become Chuckie's victims. This may or may not come to include Tina, the assistant in their magic act with whom Mikey is currently involved. Tina, meanwhile, is being courted by Peter, a wealthy romantic, but she is also in love with Gina, a gymnast, with whom she has a shadowy history.

As with most of Rappaport's films, the plot is the least interesting aspect of *Impostors*. Ludlam was more responsive to the underlying themes of obsession and love, as best expressed by a character who declares, "everything we know about love we've learned from the movies." Like all of Ludlam's plays, Rappaport's script for *Impostors* is loaded with literary and film references. Of course, Ludlam also responded to a role that was custom-made to showcase his own bravura abilities.

"I called Charles up and he was as sweet as he could be," said Rappaport.

> I sent him as much of the script as I had written, and he said he'd love to do it. I

had thought to myself, "Oh, God! He's going to be such a pain in the ass, because he's a writer and director himself. He's going to want to rewrite. He's going to want to direct." But on the contrary: For him it was like a vacation, because he didn't have to write or direct. He could just act, which he loved doing. And he was a dream to work with.

After reading the script, Ludlam asked Rappaport if he could play both Chuckie and Mikey. "It would be just like those Bette Davis movies," he suggested, referring to both *A Stolen Life* and *Dead Ringer*. "I'd be the bad sister and the good sister." But he made no further entreaties when Rappaport decided to adhere to his original concept.

According to Rappaport, a couple of friends had recommended Peter Evans for the role of Peter in *Impostors*. Rappaport was totally unfamiliar with this much-admired stage actor, and therefore surprised when he proved hard to get. "The only thing that attracted Peter to the project was that Charles was in it," said Rappaport. "He needed to be convinced, and Charles became the major selling point. He idolized Charles's work."

Following two weeks of rehearsals in Rappaport's Soho loft in June of 1979, they spent twenty-eight days shooting the film over the bulk of July. "When we were rehearsing," recalled Rappaport, "Charles would do everything different every single time. He loved rehearsing. It meant more time for him to be the center of attention. And then during the shooting, Charles kept getting hotter and hotter. Thirty takes wouldn't be enough for him. He'd be heating up and getting more and more extravagant."

During rehearsals, Rappaport sensed that Michael Burg was nervous and intimidated by the prospect of working with Ludlam. "It was a nightmare at first," said Rappaport. "I had to convince Mike that he had to do it. I said to him, 'Mike, you're going to be playing the straight man to Charles, but that doesn't mean you're going to disappear from the screen.' Charles is the whirlwind whenever they're on together, but Mike is the solid rock that makes the whirlwind possible. Otherwise the whole thing would seem out of control.

"But Mike was afraid that Charles was going to walk away with the movie," continued Rappaport,

> and he does. It was amazing. No matter what you did, somehow or other Charles was always center stage. Even when he would be in three-quarters profile while another person was facing the screen, the other person was like somewhere in the

shadows. He had this instinct for where the lights were and where the camera lens was, and he just knew how to upstage everyone else. Not in a malicious way, however.

Though Rappaport invited him to write or rewrite his own part, Ludlam ultimately contributed only a single line. Since the role had been written for him, it was already designed to exploit his quick-change artistry, his mugging, his remarkable vocal and facial expressions, his ability to "go from being manic to being sullen in a moment."

Ludlam himself recognized that Rappaport "saw something about my acting, was sensitive to an aspect of it that I had not seen too many people be that clear about, which is the ability to slip in and out of characters and make an amalgamation of a character out of pieces of other characters and impressions."

For what may have been the first time in his life, Ludlam was always punctual for the shoot. There were several days of nighttime filming at both a mansion in Westchester and an old movie theater on Staten Island. The setups sometimes required so much time that the camera wouldn't start rolling until two or three in the morning. But even after the other actors had fallen asleep, Ludlam was always alert and ready for action. He consistently had this "where's-the-camera?" attitude. "And he was never, ever ornery, as actors often are under such conditions," reported Rappaport. "Everybody on the crew adored him. He kept saying, 'Oh, all the guys working on this film are so gorgeous.'"

Each of the actors received fifty dollars a day for working on the picture. Ludlam's lawyer, Walter Gidaly, was hard-nosed with Rappaport and insisted that his client receive an additional 5 percent of any profits the film might enjoy. However, this never amounted to anything.

Though it would come to be admired in subsequent years, *Impostors* initially received poor notices. (*The New York Times* claimed it was "almost funny.") But it remains the most telling, extant record of Ludlam's unique talents as an actor. It was conceived to cater to his special gifts, and it does so extravagantly. Though there are primitive video versions of some of Ludlam's later plays (shot during performances at One Sheridan Square), as well as a handful of other films and TV specials that he participated in during the eighties, none of these gives as clear or as extensive a picture of his multi-dimensional acting abilities. If working on *Impostors* was part of what prevented Ludlam from appearing onstage in *The Enchanted Pig*, posterity should be grateful for the obstruction.

~

Near the end of the run of *The Enchanted Pig*, Pashalinski and Brockmeyer's rebellious attitude was becoming both more overt and more unavoidable. Among the plays that Ludlam considered reviving next was *Hot Ice*. When he proposed it, an uppity Pashalinski responded, "I'd like to reread it first." Ludlam was terribly offended, and he substituted *Conquest of the Universe*. When he announced that he wasn't going to be in it himself, Pashalinski presented a list of her "dream cast," with herself as Alice, as opposed to Venus, the lesser role she had originated. But Ludlam had Quinton in mind for Alice, and he refused to make even this compromise to appease Pashalinski.

Both dreading and prompting the inevitable breach with two of his cofounders, Ludlam became more remote and unapproachable. Pashalinski tried to reason with him by discussing things in "professional" and "unemotional" terms. When she confronted him directly and said that it felt like he was creating a fresh company out of newcomers, he simply dismissed the notion. He also resisted the idea that the nature of the company was changing, that old-timers could and would seek outside work. Though he himself was suddenly taking on more and more such work, he was both too possessive and too insecure to settle for anything less than a total commitment from the rest of the troupe.

In retrospect, Pashalinski claimed that on a certain level they had simply become "bored" with one another, a notion that Ludlam refused to acknowledge. He also refused to face the fact that both Pashalinski and Brockmeyer had outgrown the arbitrary ways of the Ridiculous and were eager to have new experiences, to assume new lives. As Pashalinski succinctly put it, "He was my father and I had grown up. I had to leave home. It had to happen." But for Ludlam, the impending crisis was just too threatening. It was not unlike the double standards and no-win situation he brought to his love relationships, where he insisted on promiscuity for himself but monogamy for his partners.

The power struggle between Ludlam and Pashalinski became even more blatant over the revival of *Conquest*. Though she declined to be in it when he refused her the role of Alice, at least Brockmeyer was going to play Tamberlaine — at first. But Ludlam was still smarting over Brockmeyer's having left *The Enchanted Pig*, and when he showed up for a rehearsal without knowing any of Tamberlaine's lines, Ludlam asked him to leave the show. (Though he was never known to turn down a Jack Daniels, Brockmeyer was drinking more heavily than usual during this period. It was his escape from feeling torn between Ludlam, who was behaving like an old rejected spouse, and his lover Burdick, who had instigated much of the friction.)

With Susan and Vehr still in his court, Ludlam glossed over the problems with Brockmeyer and Pashalinski and put together a cast of subsidiary Ridiculous players. Though the two insurrectionists attended a Halloween party at One Sheridan Square, they had to be upset because Ludlam was proving he didn't need them to continue the company they had helped create a dozen years before. Indeed, Susan recalled that it was "the rumblings about Lola and John leaving" that prompted Ludlam to revive *Conquest*. "He wanted to gather a whole new group around him," and the script called for a relatively large cast — certainly larger than *Hot Ice*.

Ludlam had to appreciate the greater irony regarding the emergence of any rift with the core members over a revival of *Conquest of the Universe*. With its alternate title *When Queens Collide* to commemorate the event, the original production of *Conquest* had marked the pivotal moment in 1967 when Ludlam and the rest of the troupe split from John Vaccaro and the Play-House of the Ridiculous. History was now on the verge of repeating itself, even if the battle lines were being differently drawn.

With completely abstract sets designed by Richard Hennessy, Ludlam directed the revival of *Conquest* in a professional and somewhat aloof manner. His work as a teacher had given him something he never really had had before — patience. At one point in a rehearsal, when Ludlam told Vicki Raab, "I don't think you're getting it," he detected that she was crushed, and instantly altered his approach. "I had no idea you were such a sensitive actress," he told her. "I feel like I've been playing a Stradivarius with a chain saw."

There were two other newcomers involved with the revival of *Conquest* who would become key figures in the company: Steven Samuels and Peter Golub. Golub, a young composer who had already written concert works and some theatrical music for the Public Theater, first became aware of the Ridiculous when he saw *Caprice*. "It was a revelation to me that just turned my head around about what the theater could be," said Golub. After seeing other Ridiculous productions, Golub finally met Ludlam at "one of Mary Brecht's soirees. I asked him if he would ever need a composer and he seemed kind of intrigued with the idea."

Though nothing came of his request at first, Golub went backstage to speak to Ludlam after seeing *Camille* a "second or third time." He followed up his visit with a letter, once again offering to write music for the company. Ludlam replied with a postcard: "It's probably too late to write music for our new show, but why don't you come by and we'll see what you can do."

The "new show" was *The Enchanted Pig*, which became Golub's first score for the Ridiculous. As composer-in-residence, he would write incidental music and the occasional song for all the plays Ludlam subsequently produced. Like Richard Hennessy, Golub was struck by the amount of freedom Ludlam gave him in their collaborations. "Charles respected the other artist as well as his craft," said Golub.

> He let you come up with your own ideas, but he also knew what he wanted and what he didn't want. He did not have an antipathy towards modern music, unlike many people in the theater, and particularly in the avant-garde theater. In fact, he liked modern music and wanted really classy music in his theater.
>
> Charles would come up with incredible ways of conveying what he wanted. He would always find helpful adjectives to describe the sense of a scene. He would say, "This should be even more *Tristan* than *Tristan*," for instance. After a while, I learned that Charles didn't ever want to have music under him when he was speaking. He quoted Bette Davis as saying that "[film composer] Max Steiner always got to the top of the stairs before she did," and he didn't want to be upstaged that way by the music.

Golub composed music for the revival of *Conquest*, which is when he intoduced Steven Samuels, a Bennington classmate, to the company. Samuels had seen the original production of *Bluebeard* at the Performing Garage in 1970, when he was only sixteen, and it left an indelible mark on him. His first job with the Ridiculous was running sound for *The Enchanted Pig*, followed by his managing the lights on *A Christmas Carol*, the next production. He eventually became the company business manager, seeing the Ridiculous through its most successful years. (Following Ludlam's death, Samuels would edit both *The Complete Plays of Charles Ludlam* and *Ridiculous Theatre: Scourge of Human Folly*, a compendium of Ludlam's prose and interviews.)

"My first impression of Charles, personally," he explained, "was of this absolutely dapper and distinguished maniac, poking his head into the sound booth and screaming at me, 'Who is this? Who is running the sound? Who is that person? I've never seen him before. Peter! Peter! What's going on? The press is coming and I don't even know who this is!'"

Though the newcomers apparently enjoyed themselves during the revival of *Conquest*, Ludlam's heart wasn't really in the production. Susan felt, "It wasn't much fun to do, because none of the original inspiration was there." Eureka, who played Venus, remembered that Ludlam "wasn't around very much" during its limited run, which began in late October and lasted for less than a month. He was busy at the time working on an adaptation of *A Christmas Carol.*

What is most remarkable about Ludlam's version of this classic is its utter faithfulness to the original. Much of the dialogue was taken directly from Dickens, and much of the prose was incorporated as stage directions. For the most part, the production was played very straight as well. It remains the only play by Ludlam that didn't have some other edge to it in either the script or the staging. But in portraying Scrooge — a larger-than-life figure Ludlam "was born to play," as many of the reviewers were quick to point out — there was no need to do it otherwise. As conceived by Dickens, the role relied on histrionics: Scrooge's scowl and bombast were archetypal Ludlam, as was the terror Scrooge experiences in the presence of the Ghost of Christmas Future — which played on Ludlam's personal obsession with mortality.

Bill Vehr was typecast as the self-effacing Bob Cratchit opposite Ludlam's Scrooge; Quinton portrayed Marley's Ghost; Pashalinski played Christmas Past, and Brockmeyer, Christmas Present. To fill out the unusually large cast of eighteen, Ludlam recruited two of Quinton's younger siblings, John and Mary Ann. Two more children's roles were given to Katina and Renée Pearl, daughters of Ludlam's Hofstra colleague, Irwin. Irwin's wife Anita was on hand to supervise her daughters by playing both Mrs. Fezziwig and Mrs. Dilber. In the only cross-dressed role in the production, Renée Pearl portrayed Tiny Tim, earning high marks from the reviewers. Behaving offstage like a cross between W.C. Fields and Scrooge himself, Brockmeyer became quite vocal about his resentment over having to share his dressing room with all "the brats," which he perceived as punishment for having acted up in previous months.

In addition to Ludlam's impeccable performance, the highly beloved production owed much of its success to Gabriel Berry's period costumes and to Callejo's storybook set designs. While working on this, his last collaboration with the Ridiculous, Callejo recalled that Ludlam was in "a very nasty mood."

"I applied everything I knew as an artist, and it all came out on that stage," said Callejo.

> It was like an illustration, an etching from a children's book. One side of the stage was Scrooge's bedroom, which was major forced perspective: the floor raked up, the walls raked in, the ceiling came down. There was this tiny bed, which Charles complained about, but it looked wonderful. On the other side was Cratchit's

office. I had this idea of putting Scrooge six feet off the ground on a stool at his writing desk, with Cratchit far below. When I first installed it, Charles said, "What's this? It's not gonna work. How are we going to focus on each other?" And we had this horrible argument over it until I said, "Why don't you just give it a try?" Finally he relented. But then he spent an eternity climbing up the ladder to the stool, to show me how impossible it was for him to get up there. Then, only five minutes into the scene, he stopped and said, "Bobjack, how high off the stage am I? And how high is Bill? You know what we oughta do, I think we should cut a foot off of Bill's chair," exaggerating the difference still further.

The effect of Ludlam's miserly Scrooge looking down at Vehr's Cratchit from on high was specifically applauded by many of the critics. All of the reviewers were charmed by the adaptation, except for the *Village Voice's* Erika Munk, who chose to rise above the sentimentality inherent in the story. (Munk's criticism was particularly unfair since it was based on an early preview performance she insisted on attending, before the company was ready for the press.) Ludlam led the audience in a rendition of "Joy to the World" at the end of each performance, and everyone left the theater suffused with good will.

One person in particular who couldn't resist Ludlam was Steven Samuels, who worked the lighting for *A Christmas Carol*. "Before each performance, Charles would sit back-stage getting ready, babbling into the mirror at himself about 'how difficult it is to turn this gorgeous, thirty-six-year-old man into this old fellow [Scrooge],'" recalled Samuels.

> It was very crowded backstage with all these people running around. And I guess nobody wanted to listen to Charles anymore, even though he never stopped talking. But I had just arrived and I found him endlessly fascinating. So, after running my little light-check, I would dash backstage and sit at his feet, listening to him babble.

> I worked very closely with him for a couple of years before he heard me utter a complete English sentence, which those who know me would find very odd. But Charles could *really* talk, and he didn't really seem to care to whom he was talking. If I hadn't been there, he would simply have talked to the mirror.

Scheduled to run through New Year's Eve, *A Christmas Carol* was extended into January. There was no performance on Christmas night, permitting Ludlam to attend the annual family dinner in Greenlawn with Quinton in tow. Though Pashalinski and Brockmeyer had returned to the fold in *A Christmas Carol*, this second, self-created family continued to trouble Ludlam, and prompted him to turn to newcomers, such as Samuels and Golub, for attention.

According to Callejo, "John complained a lot about Charles during *A Christmas Carol*. He was jealous of Everett. They were all competing for Charles's attention." In a "what next?" sort of manner, Pashalinski was particularly dismayed when they learned that Ludlam had once again resurrected the notion of launching Oscar Wilde's *Salomé*— this time with Quinton, as opposed to himself, in the title role. Quinton was not yet the actor he would become under Ludlam's loving tutelage, and Ludlam alone recognized his potential: No one else took Quinton seriously yet, including himself.

જ

Though there had been no question that Pashalinski and Brockmeyer would participate in *A Christmas Carol*, they had no idea it would be their last new play with Ludlam and their farewell performance at One Sheridan Square. Brockmeyer did, however, have hesitations about going on the company's second West Coast tour, which immediately followed the close of the show in early January 1980.

According to Pashalinski, "John didn't want to leave his day job. He didn't want to leave Steve [Burdick]. Although I ultimately think he would have come anyway, I remember telling him, 'I can't imagine anyone else in your roles or traveling without you on the road. It would make me very unhappy.'"

In the end, Brockmeyer was persuaded by the high expectations surrounding the tour. After their unbridled success in California two years earlier, practically everyone anticipated an even finer reception this time — the notable exception being Ludlam himself, though he was eventually caught up in everyone else's enthusiasm.

There was even talk of establishing an alternate home for the company: a West Coast branch, to be inaugurated in the course of an extended stay in San Francisco. Ludlam envisioned giving the premiere of *Isle of the Hermaphrodites* in the Bay City, then taking it to New York in triumph, and leaving behind a clone company. It was to be formed by means of a contest to find actors resembling those of the New York troupe. Ludlam and Quinton even came close to renting an apartment in San Francisco, shortly after arriving there the first week in February.

Though it wasn't articulated as such, California was being seized as a kind of renewal for the company, to resolve the interpersonal tensions and internecine battles that had recently climaxed. Given such heady ambitions, who could have predicted that this, the company's last tour in Ludlam's lifetime, would prove to be as disastrous as their first a decade before — only with even more dire consequences?

The tour began with weeklong engagements in both Vancouver and Seattle, where everyone had fun behaving like tourists, and where they performed *Camille* and *Stage Blood.* (*Bluebeard* would join them in repertory once the company arrived in San Francisco.) As arranged by Richard Currie, who had always wanted to sample moose steak, there was one night in Seattle when they had all planned to go to a suburban restaurant that specialized in this rather uncommon fare. Everyone assembled at the appointed time in the hotel lobby, but there was no sign of Ludlam or Quinton. Currie phoned their room and realized they were going to be late: The "Ludlams" were having another one of their tiffs, putting their colleagues on hold. When they finally came down an hour later, everyone — ravenous and enraged — piled into the car in icy silence, and not a word was spoken during the entire ride to the restaurant.

But it was one thing to wait for Ludlam while he was off in the wings having another domestic squabble. It was quite another to wait for all the promises he had made to come true. The last straw came in San Francisco, when the critics began pummeling the company. Given the horrible notices and several weeks of equally disappointing houses, everyone's mood quickly soured. With typical obstinacy, however, Ludlam adhered to his dream of success in California. Despite the practically empty houses, he wanted to keep on running long enough for word-of-mouth to take hold — even without any indications it ever would. And with typical audacity, he fully expected the others would be willing to indulge his unwarranted optimism, by agreeing to take a reduction in pay. According to Kilgore, "Most of the problems and arguments in San Francisco had to do with money. When Charles wanted us to build up momentum in spite of the bad reviews, it was primarily Lola and John who were against accepting any salary cuts." They had been through it all before with Ludlam, which explains both why he would expect them to go through it again, and why they refused.

Culminating with the permanent departure of Pashalinski and Brockmeyer, the disappointing California tour of 1980 would become a line of demarcation, separating what the company had been from what it would become. But no one ever seemed to understand why the Ridiculous failed so dismally in San Francisco: While everyone seemed to come up with a different explanation, none seemed to suffice.

As Richard Currie looked back on the company's final tour, he recalled how,

> We all had this fantasy of a split season: six months in New York and six in San
> Francisco. It just seemed that since we were doing so well in New York, it would
> only be natural for us to take San Francisco by storm. This was the home of
> Charles Pierce and the Cockettes, so the Ridiculous should fit right in. What we
> didn't count on was the "*Beach Blanket Babylon* syndrome." That's what repre-
> sented camp to San Francisco, and we must have looked very amateurish by
> comparison. Their version of drag was already fairly established, with amazingly
> polished, classy tap dancing and singing. And we just didn't fit into that.

According to Pashalinski, "Charles and Everett and I were on the bus one day, talking
about why we weren't going over so well there. I said that I thought it was because we
were too energetic, performing at such a boiling point that Californians just couldn't
get it. And a gay man sitting in front of us, who had seen us, turned around and said,
'You know, you're right.'"

Kilgore recalled that,

> The opening night of *Camille* was one of our worst performances. Out of the
> blue, Charles had decided the night before to cut all the pauses. He wanted the
> lines to clip right along. He wanted the play to be shorter and lighter, with a
> more rapid pace. But doing it that way cut so much of the texture of the play, and
> all the beautifully choreographed laughs were gone. Charles was also very stoned
> on pot on opening night.

Many, including Ludlam, put the blame for their awful San Francisco reception on the
location of the theater. The venerable and elegant On Broadway Theater was in the
North Beach area, a distance from the Castro or any gay center. According to this theory,
they were simply in "the wrong part of town," and their audience never found them.

A more objective inquiry suggested far more complicated reasons. At the heart of the
problem was the ongoing competition between the West and East Coasts in all matters
cultural, a competitive spirit that was only exacerbated by the gay issues. Perhaps even
more significant was Ludlam's characteristic refusal to be categorized or catalogued in any
way as an artist, and more specifically his resistance to his company's being labeled gay.

Though it was originally intended to promote the Ridiculous, a feature story in the

February 8 edition of the *Sentinel*, a weekly gay paper, probably did more harm than good. As written by Steve Warren, it began:

> "If you say you're not a gay theatre they say you're saying you're not gay." So says Charles Ludlam, whose Ridiculous Theatrical Company has settled in for what he hopes will be a long stay at the On Broadway Theatre in North Beach. Although Ludlam and most of his company are gay and attract a largely gay audience, and Ludlam's writing and direction are heavily influenced by a "gay sensibility," he distinguishes his work from other "gay theatre" in that it's less overtly political.

Whatever the company's reputation had been within the large gay contingent of San Francisco, it couldn't have been helped by Ludlam's distinguishing his work from "other gay theater." Especially not in 1980, when gay politics had reached an outspoken peak. Ever since the Stonewall riots a decade before, gay politics had picked up momentum, making it increasingly fashionable to be "out" and proud of being gay. Ironically, this would begin to taper off only a few years later, when the onset of AIDS complicated the relevant issues and created opposing factions within the gay community.

A celebrated gay interloper from New York who was alienating his hardcore audience, Ludlam might have sounded wishy-washy to straight San Francisco theatergoers as well. In any case, the ambiguity made it much easier for local critics to exercise their chauvinistic, anti-New-York-theater attitude, and to dismiss the Ridiculous out of hand, without inviting any backlash.

But Ludlam had an amazing capacity to absolve himself of responsibility and to place the blame for failure on outside factors. In the final analysis, he decided that San Francisco was theatrically provincial, and left it at that. He may have understood that without the critics on his side, he simply wasn't going to reach the more sophisticated segment of the population, which he correctly identified as one of his target audiences. But it's as if he never grasped that by failing to endorse the politics of being gay in the brave new post-Stonewall world of gay pride, he ran the risk of losing his gay constituency as well.

Perhaps a major reason the Ridiculous players went over so poorly in San Francisco was their fatigue with putting on the same plays again and again and yet again — Ludlam most of all. The vitality that *Bluebeard, Camille,* and *Stage Blood* had exuded in the past no longer came across the footlights. Whatever impact the gay political issues may have had on attendance in San Francisco, it is just as likely that an important factor in the company's failure lay in the quality of its work.

At the same time that Ludlam refused to identify his theater as gay, the company's sexual identity was changing back home in New York. As evidenced by the recent involvement of Peter Golub, Steven Samuels, and several of the actors Ludlam brought on board from his classes at NYU — all of whom were heterosexual — the company was, in a sense, becoming "straighter." There's a curious reference to this notion near the end of the feature in the *Sentinel*. Ludlam told Warren that the company "became a family for us in a way. . . . Being gay — except for Susan — we needed that tribal thing, a sense of belonging. The gayness is a bond. But in New York we have a larger company with a lot of heterosexuals and that's an even more marvelous blend."

ↄ

The "bond" that had held the company together for a dozen years abruptly collapsed with this second California tour. Though it had been a long time coming, the fracture was nevertheless painful and traumatic for everyone. Both Brockmeyer and Pashalinski emphasized a lack of financial security as their justification for leaving the company. But Ludlam understood that there were other reasons.

Pashalinski recalled asking Brockmeyer how he broached the subject with Ludlam, and he replied, "I told Charles that he would have to guarantee me $500 a week in order for me to stay, because that's what I need to meet the expenses of my life. And I added, 'I know you can't do that.'"

A decade after the fact, Brockmeyer latched onto this easy "out" before exploring other, emotional explanations. "The reason I left was purely for financial reasons," he said.

> We had had very bad management, those many years. And I felt a certain responsibility to my lover and my home. We left for California with this big brouhaha, that we were going to become a big success in San Francisco. But it didn't happen.
>
> While we were away, I asked Cathy [Farinon-Smith] to see to it that Steven [Burdick] received checks for the mortgage — which was a brand new word in my vocabulary. She assured me she'd take care of it. But when the show was over I called Cathy from San Francisco and asked her if she'd sent Steven the check. She said, "Oh, I forgot." I said, "When I get back to New York, I'm going to come to your place on Washington Street, and I'm going to punch out your face."

According to Susan, "Charles was very hurt and felt like John and Lola hadn't given him the real reasons for their leaving."

> He told me that one of the reasons they left was because they didn't like all the work we were doing in the new theater [at One Sheridan Square]. But he didn't resent their leaving, so much as he was worried that he had disappointed them or let them down in some way. Lola felt that Charles's name was first and foremost in the theater, and she wanted to step out and make a name for herself.

Quinton, in turn, recalled:

> There was a very unhappy atmosphere in the company at the time. Lola and John were unhappy. They wanted to move on. And it took a lot of courage for them to assert their unhappiness and leave, because it's very easy to stay in a company and be provided for. Charles was definitely angry for a while. He felt abandoned by them at first. But eventually it turned around. He came to understand they had to leave and he felt free, free to make other choices. He had been writing for them all those years, and now he said he was not going to have to write with their specific voices in his head.

In hindsight, Pashalinski described an element of "answered prayers" to her break with the Ridiculous. "The dream I had had," she said,

> had come true. We had relatively steady salaries, and we finally had a home. But somehow, some way, it wasn't enough. Rather than feeling satisfied by having reached these certain goals, I felt chained and conflicted, ambivalent and without the motivation I used to have. It had come too late, and there had been internal changes that had taken place which I couldn't undo or ignore. But it filled me with a great deal of sadness.

"I didn't leave because I *hated* Charles Ludlam, which everyone wanted me to say," added Brockmeyer.

> One of the things that definitely influenced me at the time was my lover Steven Burdick. But it was true of all of our lovers: they were all jealous. Each of them knew we were in love with Charles, and they found it hard competing with him. Steven did it by harping on how he was always being paid. Steven was making $800 a week as Carol Channing's dresser, and he was constantly on my case,

"Charles doesn't pay you so and so." He'd always say to me, "Well, where is all this box office money?"

Ludlam let everyone know that he was tired of pulling out *Bluebeard*, *Camille*, and *Stage Blood* to solve financial problems. He had come to feel trapped by those plays, and particularly annoyed that his new works tended to be unfavorably compared to them. He would later claim, "I'm not out to write the Great American Play because if they won't forgive me for my success with *Bluebeard* or *Camille*, what will they do to me for that?" But Ludlam would never admit that he encouraged a dissolution of the core group in order to bring about the internal changes he needed as an artist. Though he expressed feeling abandoned and blamed Pashalinski and Brockmeyer for leaving, he was more responsible for the breach than he would ever acknowledge — even to himself. He was, after all, a master of passive-aggressive manipulation.

Quinton, who had greater access to Ludlam's inner motives than anyone, explained, "Charles was letting go of his history. He wanted to break with his past accomplishments. He was growing to another level of artistic consciousness."

Brockmeyer hinted at this as he remembered,

> Charles had said something very significant the year before the break had come. He said that we "tyrannize" his life. I sort of knew all along that that's what the relationship was about. But I didn't want to be that person anymore. Charles took on whatever role he had to take on. But this was the first time I became aware of how much we as individuals drew off of him, because we weren't normal people. That skinny little runt of a man wrote roles for us for twelve years. And when he said that, I thought to myself, "I can't do this to him forever."

Adam Kilgore recalled that even before the fatal San Francisco tour, Ludlam had "stopped consulting with" the core members of the company.

> It was no longer a group. He became the tyrant who made all the decisions, more so than ever before. And when we came back from California, I remember him talking about it, saying, "You know, I can't have these people hanging on to me all of their lives. They should have their own lives." He developed this attitude that they had become too dependent on him, and he reached a point where he said, "I want them all off my back."

Peter Golub, who was relatively new to the company and could bring some objectivity to the situation, detected "the kind of tensions that exist when you're establishing your independence and the parent both wants you to be independent but also doesn't, in a way. The difficulties between Charles and Lola and John had that kind of parent and child aura to them."

After the Ridiculous, Pashalinski would continue to evolve and develop as an actress, working steadily with any number of writers, directors, and other companies. For Brockmeyer, work would prove more sporadic in subsequent years. But he never had the acting ambitions that Pashalinski did. In a way, his twelve-year involvement with the Ridiculous had owed as much to the family he found there, as to the work.

Susan recalled how much Brockmeyer specifically loved being recognized in public, "in the streets and in bars. He would brag about it. He also attracted more tricks that way." But he wasn't driven to get beyond a coterie of local admirers, the way Pashalinski and Ludlam were.

"Except for Charles, who knew so much theater history, we weren't really aware of what we had," said Brockmeyer.

> From day one, Charles always said we were going to take over Lincoln Center and become the national comic theater. And I swallowed it hook, line, and sinker. Basically he said to us, come on this ride. I never really had dreams of being a rich man or a movie star from all this. I had no aspirations to be nationally known and interviewed. I simply wanted to be a New York theater star. And I was. So in a sense, my dreams had been fulfilled.

As for the impact of the core group's rupture on the two who remained, Susan claimed that "Bill retreated somewhat after Lola and John left. But it was more a matter of his simply becoming more involved in his other interests." The path-of-least-resistance Vehr would carry on good-naturedly no matter what the circumstances.

For Susan, the long-term effect was more troubling. Without Pashalinski and Brockmeyer to act as buffers, her difficult relationship with Ludlam became even more unhealthy. Kilgore, who became much closer to her after the San Francisco debacle, recalled many late night phone calls from Susan during subsequent years.

"I've had it with Charles!" she'd say. "Do you know what he did to me today? Do you know what he said to me? I'm never, ever going to work with the man again." And I'd say, "Well, Susan, maybe it's time. You've got to do what you've got to do." This went on and on for years, her calling me regularly with what amounted to the same story. But of course she never left him.

Though it would take a while for Ludlam to recover from his wounded pride, he eventually found the breakup of the core group in the spring of 1980 to be a liberating experience. For at least the better part of a year, however, as Christopher Scott experienced it, "I had to listen to Charles ranting and raving about Lola and John's ingratitude. You'd have to let that go in one ear and out the other. Because if you dared contradict him, Charles would just turn things around and start screaming at you."

Susan had a similar reaction. "Charles talked about Lola and John for several years," she said. "But I'd reached the point where I tried to steer the conversation in other ways. He wasn't saying anything new, and I was just getting bored with it."

Through it all, Ludlam continued to harbor dreams of his troupe becoming "the national comic theater company" — dreams now nursed by the renewed, hands-on involvement of Christopher Scott. Without the past holding him back, Ludlam worked that much more effectively to achieve his ambitions. Without the constraints of having to write so many roles for specific actors, his creative juices flowed more easily, and he would go on to produce his most accomplished works.

SECRET LIVES

He is unclassifiable, which in a world of –isms and –ologies is also unforgivable.
— Bruce Chatwin, on Malraux

Husbands are chiefly good lovers when they are betraying their wives.
— Marilyn Monroe

In "The Seven Levels of the Theatre," a Ludlam manifesto based on his readings of George Osawa and the tenets of Zen Buddhism, Ludlam identified seven overlapping levels of "judgment" theater: Mechanical, Sentimental, Intellectual, Social, Economic, Moral, and Supreme. In an afterword, he cautioned that these are "purely imaginary" categories, and that all "real" theater is based on a combination of at least two of them. But it is the last category, the "Supreme," that best describes Ludlam's own modus operandi.

"The supreme theatre is intuitive," Ludlam claimed in 1971, when he was only twenty-eight years old and wrote his manifesto. "The artists of this theatre have mastered and internalized the first six levels of judgment," he continued.

> They are spontaneous and lucky. At the supreme level there are no ulterior motives, no striving for one thing to the exclusion of others. If there is anything these artists enjoy as much as complete success it is a real fiasco. They get better as they get older, giving all they have. Because they have suffered, they accept their applause with gratitude. Their secret is that of the ancient Chinese marksman whose every arrow was found in the dead center of a chalk circle. They shoot their arrows first and draw the circle afterward.

Though it's hard to say who really initiated the shot, the breakdown of the core group became something of a Zen arrow around which Ludlam was now beginning to draw his circle, giving himself the bull's-eye. Having already decided to "wash his hands" of *Bluebeard, Camille,* and *Stage Blood,* Ludlam vowed after the company's last California tour that he would produce no more revivals whatsoever. He was especially aggravated since theater reviewers — unlike dance critics — refused to cover revivals even when there were significant cast changes. From now on, he would provide only new plays to buoy any dwindling box office receipts.

But as Paul Taylor discovered when he collaborated with him on *Aphrodisiamania,* Ludlam procrastinated when it came to putting words on paper. This was true of everything from grant proposals to plays and letters. His terror at writing just about anything only intensified whenever he was working against a deadline. How could it be otherwise for a man who loved the ephemeral and shunned whatever was permanent or irrevocable? Of his twenty-nine plays, it was the rare ones that were anywhere near completion before rehearsals began. Most of them were still being cobbled together well into the rehearsal process, and sometimes even after performances had been given before an audience. *Reverse Psychology*, Ludlam's next and nineteenth opus, fell into the latter category.

When the California trip was unexpectedly aborted, however, Ludlam could justify delaying work on his next play. Since the company had planned on being in San Francisco through the spring, the theater at One Sheridan Square had been sublet to Jane White for performances of her one-woman autobiographical musical, "Jane White, Who? . . . ." It played for two months and closed at the end of March.

Ludlam busied himself during this period by working on his silent film, *The Sorrows of Dolores*. One of the scenes had been shot at Les Amants, a quiet, neighborhood bar at the corner of Hudson and Morton Streets. Its friendly proprietress, Marie, was featured in the scene.

Peter Golub frequently met Ludlam at Les Amants as they further established their working relationship. The night the company returned from California, in fact, Ludlam phoned him. Along with Quinton and Golub's girlfriend, Anna, the four congregated at Les Amants where Ludlam ranted about Pashalinski and Brockmeyer, as well as the lack of sophistication in San Francisco.

Golub recalled another night when he received a desperate call from Ludlam at five in the morning: "Peter! You've got to come over here! Everett is trying to kill me!" Though he attempted to "talk some sense" into Ludlam over the phone, Golub refused to intervene. He did not want to become any more embroiled in their personal problems than he already was.

In addition to the routine turbulence that circumscribed their relationship, Ludlam and Quinton were also contending with impoverished circumstances in the spring of 1980. There was simply no money coming in. Christopher Scott slipped his old friend some cash when he could, but Golub's assistance proved even more creative. Having just received a commission to write an orchestra piece for the Sage City Symphony in Bennington, Vermont, Golub went to Steven Samuels and asked if their fledgling theater company, Empty Hands, could also give a $250 fee to Ludlam to contribute a libretto. As Samuels recalled, Golub told him, "Charles is *starving*. He needs money to buy rice."

Written for a mezzo-soprano and an actor, their collaboration, *The Production of Mysteries*, concerns a widower named Harry who seeks the aid of Ms. Wisteria, a medium, to try to contact his deceased wife. In a simulated trance, Wisteria instructs Harry to establish a "nonprofit, tax-exempt, charitable organization." In the end, Harry exposes Wisteria for the fraud she is.

Though the text never specified Houdini as Harry's last name, *The Production of Mysteries* stemmed from Ludlam's lifelong fascination with the famed magician. (In fact, Houdini spent considerable energies during his lifetime trying to communicate with the dead — just as he told his loved ones that he would attempt to reach them after his demise.) It also served as a preliminary sketch for the last play Ludlam would attempt to write, a play in which he intended to portray Houdini himself.

The twenty-minute piece was performed by a community orchestra in Bennington later that year. To attend to costumes and other staging matters, Quinton accompanied Golub to the show. He returned with a program that included Ludlam's libretto, but omitted any copyright insignia. Ludlam "went ballistic," claimed Golub, who tried to reassure him that such a provincial production would not lead to any copyright infringement. (There were subsequent performances some years later at The Brooklyn Academy of Music and Cooper Union, with Lukas Foss conducting, as part of a larger program. Kimball Wheeler sang, and Robert Sherman, of WQXR Radio, portrayed Harry, a spoken role.)

Amounting to only a couple pages, Ludlam's script for *The Production of Mysteries* was hardly taxing for his quick-study methods. But Golub recalled that he was late delivering it. "I remember we both smoked dope one afternoon, and then I literally forced him into the chair in front of the typewriter to finish the thing."

Beyond making some headway with *The Sorrows of Dolores*, Ludlam was beginning to formulate his ideas for *Reverse Psychology*. At Christopher Scott's urging, he set out to write a play with a small cast in order to keep expenses down. While focusing on a piece for only four actors, he produced one of his wittiest scenarios. It concerns two psychotherapists who are married to each other, but having affairs with one another's patients, who are also husband and wife. None of them is aware of the incestuous entanglements until they're all brought together in the second act. Patterned in part on

Noël Coward's *Private Lives*, the script was loaded with contemporary references as well as examples of Ludlam's wisecracking sensibility.

But Ludlam was talking about *Reverse Psychology* more than he was writing it. It was one of the many plays he worked out verbally more than on paper. When it was still in the idea phase, Ludlam described the play to former Hofstra colleague Charlotte Forbes during a chance encounter at a birthday party for their college chum, Irwin Pearl. The two of them spent a lot of time together on the balcony of the Pearls' high-rise apartment behind Lincoln Center, when Ludlam offered Forbes the part of the female therapist.

Though she had attended several Ridiculous shows in the intervening years, Forbes had not really seen Ludlam since Irwin and Anita Pearl's wedding in the late sixties. Nor had she performed with him since Hofstra, and she suddenly found the thought of working with him very appealing. "Acting with Charles was one of the greatest things a person could do in a lifetime. He was a true professional — he had everything mastered, and yet it was mastered to the point where he could be tremendously spontaneous. So you never knew. You were always on the edge with Charles onstage. He would be very playful in scenes. Charles and I had many run-ins with upstaging."

But Forbes had not been involved with theater for ten years, and the opportunity to act again was only a part of why she agreed to be in *Reverse Psychology*. "I had just started my own advertising business, and I had no money," recalled Forbes.

> So I said, "Charles, what do you pay?" He offered me $150 a week, and at that point I wasn't earning anything. So I said, "Well, that sounds pretty good." I also figured in the back of my head, "Well, this will be great because I'll be able to work with Charles, make this extra money, and still get my new company off the ground because it won't last that long," since most of Charles's plays didn't run very long.

Although Ludlam hoped for a commercial hit with *Reverse Psychology*, even he could not have anticipated that it would continue to draw audiences for seven months, encompassing an intervening revival of *A Christmas Carol* that following December.

Casting himself and Forbes as the married therapists, Ludlam gave the roles of their patients/lovers to Black-Eyed Susan and Bill Vehr. Though there was no role for Quinton in the play, Forbes remembered him as a constant presence at rehearsals. Ludlam wanted it that way — to keep an eye on him as much as anything else. (Susan recalled Ludlam once telling her, "Don't ever have a lover who's *not* in the theater, because he'll always know where you are every night at eight o'clock, but you won't know where he is.")

To accommodate Forbes and Susan's day jobs, the rehearsals were held at night. Ludlam didn't really start writing the play until rehearsals began in the summer. He'd bring in the scenes written on index cards and panel boards and then further work out the script with his cast. This went on for two months until he produced a play.

Black-Eyed Susan felt that Ludlam became much more objective in his approach as a director than he had been prior to this point. "Bill had a harder time during the rehearsals," she said, "because he was such a creature of habit. Having to change his style to work with newcomers presented a real challenge, and he became somewhat disengaged." Vehr's detachment had a great deal to do with the absence of Pashalinski and Brockmeyer, and the inescapable sense that the "family" was no more.

"Sometimes we'd talk for maybe two hours before we even started rehearsing," said Forbes, discovering what others had long become accustomed to. "But then we were just finessing the play all the time. We kept trying different scenes in different order. He hadn't even finished the play when we opened, because he still wasn't sure about the ending, and we kept trying different ones."

After attending more than one of those extended, preliminary rehearsals, Christopher Scott quickly became fed up. "Charles was smoking enormous amounts of grass during that period," he said. "And fifty percent of the rehearsal time was spent on feeding his own ego. They were just terribly inefficient, and I found them boring."

Scott had enough confidence in the play itself, however, to see to it that along with all the major critics, Barnabus McHenry (a representative of the Lila Acheson Wallace *Reader's Digest* foundation) and Gerald Schoenfeld (of the Shubert organization) attended the opening night on September 15. "Schoenfeld hated it," reported Scott. "There was simply no mention of the play when I had dinner with them and their wives afterwards."

But such a negative reaction to *Reverse Psychology* was unusual. The frequently full houses over the next seven months testified to the show's popularity. Even those reviewers who cited an overload of comic styles or genres tended to find the play one of Ludlam's "most entertaining" pieces. Many recognized it for what it was — Ludlam's most mature and conventional play to date — and they reveled in its hilarity.

Basically a contemporary sex farce à la Feydeau, the play opens in "a cheap hotel room." Dr. Leonard Silver and Eleanor have just met in a bar and checked in at the hotel for some extramarital hanky-panky. Neither is aware that Leonard's wife, Dr. Karen Gold, is Eleanor's therapist; nor that Eleanor's husband, Freddie, is Leonard's patient.

Set in the Metropolitan Museum of Art, the second scene is similar to the celebrated opening sequence of *Dressed To Kill*, Brian de Palma's popular film that had just been released in July, while Ludlam was working on *Reverse Psychology*. Karen and Freddie first meet in a museum gallery, before embarking on *their* clandestine affair. By conceiving of Freddie as an impoverished painter, Ludlam could slip in his customary digs at the art world, which he felt was becoming more fashionable and less legitimate all the time.

But beyond the fun it has with contemporary art and sexual mores, *Reverse Psychology* is primarily a wicked send-up of the therapeutic profession. Ludlam particularly ridicules the therapists during two discrete scenes depicting therapeutic sessions. Early in Eleanor's session, Karen takes some notes, which her patient is anxious to see.

> ELEANOR: Doctor, did you write down something about me?
>
> KAREN: Yes, I sometimes take notes. It helps me to review the patient's case. It's hard to remember everything that's said.
>
> ELEANOR: What did you write about me?
>
> KAREN: I'd rather not tell you just now.
>
> ELEANOR: Why?
>
> KAREN: Why does it matter?
>
> ELEANOR: What if someone reads it?
>
> KAREN: No one is going to see this but me.
>
> ELEANOR: What does it say, damn it!
>
> KAREN: You're getting hostile.
>
> ELEANOR: (*Angry*) I am not getting hostile. I just want to know what that damn note says.
>
> KAREN: These are my own confidential notes for my own confidential files.
>
> ELEANOR: (*Screaming*) Give me that goddamn note!
>
> KAREN: Why are you upsetting yourself?
>
> ELEANOR: (*Raging through her tears*) Give me that note! Give it to me! Give it to me! (KAREN *calmly hands her the note*) "Pick up chopped liver." I don't get it.
>
> KAREN: It was a note to myself, Eleanor.
>
> ELEANOR: Chopped liver.

KAREN: You don't trust me completely yet, Eleanor.

ELEANOR: Chopped liver. What a relief! (*Laughs*)

Later in the scene, just as Eleanor is on the verge of a penetrating childhood memory, Karen rudely interrupts the session by accepting a phone call. Though none of the characters have made the connections yet, the audience by now realizes that it's Eleanor's husband Freddie who is calling. At the end of the session, while Eleanor is having a revealing "breakthrough," Karen interrupts her again, announcing that "time is up." Before leaving, Eleanor explains she's "a little short of cash" and asks if she can postpone payment for a week. "Learning to spend money on things that are worthwhile and good for you is part of your therapy, Eleanor," says Karen. "Did you bring a check?" As soon as Eleanor leaves, Karen calls Lutèce, among the most expensive restaurants in New York, to make a dinner reservation, presumably for herself and Freddie.

Leonard's session with Freddie begins with vaudevillian banter, before Freddie announces that he's "gotten a new psychiatrist" and "I'm leaving you." Though it's presented as farce, Leonard's response reflected some of Ludlam's feelings about the recent departures of Pashalinski and Brockmeyer, which he was deeply wounded by, but managed to objectify and mock in the play.

LEONARD: How can you do this to me? Not after all we've been through together.

FREDDIE: I'm sorry, but I feel we've gone as far as we can go. I'm grateful to you
    for the years we've had together. But people change. Their needs
    change. Sometimes they grow apart. There are some things we have to
    leave behind.

LEONARD: Oh, so that's what I am, huh? Some *thing* you're going to leave behind!
    That's all I've meant to you.

FREDDIE: Now, Leonard, don't be upset.

LEONARD: Don't be upset! Don't be upset! You waste the best years of my life and
    you say don't be upset. Who is he? Some little Freudian you've been
    seeing on the sly?

FREDDIE: She's into Gestalt.

LEONARD: (*Exploding*) Ha! So it's a woman! You're leaving me for a woman. You'd
    better be careful there, Freddie. If you go to a woman psychiatrist,
    people are going to think you're gay. I always suspected you were latent.

At the prospect of being abandoned by his patient, Leonard becomes increasingly petulant and vindictive. He eventually tells Freddie, "You're sick. You know that, don't you?

You're sick. Two weeks out of my care and you'll be completely out of control." And, "I hate you and I hope you die!"

Presenting therapists as more irrational than their patients is only one of the ways in which roles are reversed and psychotherapy is upended in *Reverse Psychology*. The real engine driving the plot concerns the overlapping affairs the characters have with each other's spouse. They do not become aware of what is going on until Act II, set in the "Calypso Beach Resort Boatel," to which both couples have retreated for their surreptitious lovemaking.

After they recognize their mutual deceptions, Karen suggests they experiment with a new clinical drug called "R.P." It stands for "reverse psychology," which Eleanor explains is telling "a person to do the opposite of what you want them to do knowing that they'll do the opposite just to be stubborn or independent." A variation on the magic devices in *A Midsummer Night's Dream*, R.P. is designed to make "you strongly attracted to the person you would normally be least attracted to."

A sequence of farcical reversals is played out, ultimately reversing the skewed attractions and returning both couples to their proper married status. But then, in an "Epilogue" to the play, there are still more reversals: Eleanor and Freddie have ostensibly come to visit a straightjacketed Leonard in "Funny Hill Farm Sanitarium," where Karen is a presiding doctor. Once they leave the room, however, the entire situation is revealed to be a therapeutic ruse to cure them. As Karen explains their "regression" therapy: "The first step is their willingness to accept that they are the patients and that this is a hospital. Once they take that step the rest will follow easily."

Though it contains its share of routine gags and jokes ("Instead of a marriage license you should have gotten a learner's permit"), the level of humor in *Reverse Psychology* is more subtle and sophisticated than Ludlam had achieved in the past. In a pivotal scene between Leonard and Karen at the breakfast table, their domestic quarrels are, of course, punctuated by psychobabble and a tendency to attack each other with overanalysis, based on what they know of their respective backgrounds. (It's worth noting that Ludlam deliberately set out to evoke Strindberg in his composition of this scene.) But while trafficking in psychological clichés, Ludlam squeezes in his typical social commentary:

> LEONARD: Please don't look at me like that. It reminds me of your mother. And
> you know how I *love* your mother.
> KAREN: Leave my mother out of this. And don't be sarcastic.

LEONARD: In fact I think you're turning into just as big a bitch as your mother.

KAREN: You seem to forget everything she's done for you.

LEONARD: Don't throw that up again!

KAREN: Well she did set you up in private practice. You'd still be strapping drug
 burnouts to their bedpans at Bellevue if it weren't for her. You'd still be
 a straightjacket man.

LEONARD: They're not using straightjackets anymore. They're using chemical
 restraint. And you'd know that if you'd read the professional journals
 instead of *Redbook*!

KAREN: You're just jealous because they published my short story and rejected yours.

LEONARD: It's easier for a woman to get published today. They all want woman
 authors. It used to be blacks. Next it will be gays. It's hopeless for a
 white Anglo-Saxon Protestant male. We're just effete and genetically
 debilitated. An oppressed majority. The pallid afterglow to the sunset of
 Western civilization. All there is left for us now is jogging.

Recalling how competitive Ludlam was onstage, Charlotte Forbes claimed,

> Every time we did the breakfast scene over the newspaper, it was a dare. We would
> just look at each other. It was an unspoken dare . . . who, who was going to get the
> biggest laughs? Even before we would go on, we'd talk about it. How big do you
> think the count is gonna be on this line tonight? We would just look at each other
> and go, one-two-three-four . . .

According to Susan, "Charles was really in an 'up' mood during *Reverse Psychology*.
Charlotte's being there had a very positive effect on him, because she had a great sense
of humor and she could put him down in a joking manner and really get away with it.
It was clear that he enjoyed the repartee they had going." And as Everett Quinton summarized it, Forbes was quite literally "like a breath of fresh air," since she was a
newcomer to the company. But since she was also from his more distant past, Forbes
helped smooth the transition for Ludlam who was operating for the first time without
two of his cofounders and longtime compatriots.

After some months of economic insecurity, Ludlam was also in an "up" mood because
Reverse Psychology put the company back on its feet financially, just as he hoped it
would. Though the reviews in the *Daily News*, the *Post* and the *Village Voice* were favorable if "mixed," the *Times* offered what's known in the trade as a "money review" (that
is, highly quotable).

It's significant that the review in the *Times* was not written by Ludlam's longtime champion, Mel Gussow. Even as *Reverse Psychology* marked the beginning of a new era for Ludlam, the recent appointment of Frank Rich as Chief Drama Critic marked a new era of New York theater coverage for the *Times*. Beginning with his response to *Reverse Psychology*, Rich would become every bit the champion of the Ridiculous that Gussow had been, only far more influential. According to Quinton, the arrival of Rich "was just what Charles wanted, because suddenly those comparisons with *Bluebeard* and *Camille* were gone," comparisons that had become like the proverbial albatross whenever Ludlam introduced a new work.

"If you ask me, it may be time for Charles Ludlam's Ridiculous Theatrical Company to change its name," began Rich's review of *Reverse Psychology*. "Mr. Ludlam's latest farcical brainstorm . . . is a lot of things, but ridiculous is the least of them. Silly? Perhaps. Clever? Certainly. Funny? Absolutely. But ridiculous? When a play is as well-crafted and sharply written as Mr. Ludlam's, honest-to-God respect must be paid."

While the review raved about the play itself and put Ludlam-the-author on a par with Feydeau, Alan Ayckbourn, and Preston Sturges, Rich's reservations had to do with the ensemble's performance. "Were it not for a production that sells the writing short by a substantial measure, this would be one of the funniest evenings in town," he wrote.

> While the actors are game and energetic, their exaggerated performing style is better suited to campier Ludlam projects than this one. . . . Mr. Ludlam's own performance, though, is as precisely considered as his play. He whines to his wife in the puffy, tight-lipped manner of Tony Randall; he traumatizes his patients with frenzied, manic-depressive mood swings worthy of Gene Wilder. In *Reverse Psychology* Mr. Ludlam amply demonstrates that even in the ridiculous there is ample room for art.

The problems Rich cited with the performance when the play opened became more pronounced as the run was extended. Even members of the company noticed that Forbes became increasingly shrill: She had never been in a play for more than a few weeks and had no idea how to keep her performance fresh as the weeks stretched into months.

Christopher Scott recalled trying to approach Ludlam on this and other matters with *Reverse Psychology*. "Charles felt that I was usurping his role as director," said Scott.

He couldn't really direct the play after it was up and running, because he was onstage himself. I was out in the audience seeing it more objectively. But he just couldn't take any criticism. It was terribly frustrating, because I could spot immediately when and why something wasn't working. Yet telling him about it would only make him furious. There was an art to trying to tell him anything. I would have to use every manipulative skill I had, to try and catch him at just the right moment and make suggestions without his going into a screaming rage.

A problem of another sort arose only a month into the run, when Ludlam was invited to guest-direct William Wycherley's *The Country Wife* with student actors at the Carnegie-Mellon drama school in Pittsburgh. It was scheduled to play November 19 through December 13, in rotating rep with *The Suicide*, a Russian satire that was being directed by Mel Shapiro.

Ludlam loved Wycherly's bawdy Restoration comedy, which was considered obscene and even banned during the Victorian era. "It's all about sex, love and possessiveness," he told Donald Miller for a feature in the *Pittsburgh Post-Gazette* in conjunction with the play's opening. "In many ways, the 17th century was a more open period than now. We're still in the wake of Victorianism. I graduated from Hofstra University on Long Island in 1965. There has been an incredible conservative backlash since then.

"I'm not sure that this is a totally bad thing," Ludlam continued. "Back in the '60s, students were throwing too many things out. They weren't interested in Shakespeare's history plays because they were about dead kings and stuff. The '70s were a reconstruction period and the '80s are *fin de siècle*, a time for masterpieces."

Though he very much looked forward to working on *The Country Wife*, there was the question of scheduling trips to Pittsburgh while maintaining the run of *Reverse Psychology* at One Sheridan Square. At first, Ludlam considered replacing himself as Leonard with Ian McKay, a performer with Hot Peaches, the openly gay, politically in-your-face theater group. While Ludlam went to Pittsburgh every Monday through Wednesday, Susan, Vehr, and Forbes rehearsed with McKay. But there was a great deal of stress for all those involved when Ludlam was absent. Though they all felt there were problems with McKay, no one would tell Ludlam that he just wasn't working out in the role. But when he finally saw McKay in action, Ludlam realized it himself. He chose instead to alter the playing schedule of *Reverse Psychology*, so that another actor would not be needed after all.

Even more unusual was Ludlam's decision to interrupt the sellout run of *Reverse Psychology* in order to bring back *A Christmas Carol* for the month of December. It was practically unheard of to close a show that was doing so well, but Ludlam remembered his obligation for children's theater to his funding organizations; and he intended to make his version of the Dickens classic an annual holiday offering.

According to Forbes, when Ludlam announced that he was going to close *Reverse Psychology* to bring back *A Christmas Carol*,

> For me it was a relief. But we were doing so well that it seemed like a crazy thing to do. How many people have a hit play and close it midstream? I can't tell you how many people on the subway or in the streets would stop me and say, "Oh, you're Karen Gold!" And I didn't really know if we were going to come back and do it again. I had just figured we had ended it and that was that. Then when I learned we were bringing it back in January, I couldn't believe it. I remember saying to myself, "We're gonna do it *again*?" After we came back, it was beginning to feel more like a job.

Susan and Vehr directed the early rehearsals of *A Christmas Carol* while Ludlam was in Pittsburgh with *A Country Wife*. "Neither Bill nor Susan appeared to have had much experience directing," said Steven Samuels. "Working out a modus operandi was rather difficult for them, and the whole thing floundered. Charles had very little time to attend to it, and I don't think he was particularly interested in it. His performance wasn't anywhere near as good in the second go-round either."

At Marjorie Ludlam's insistence, it was with this second production of *A Christmas Carol*, in December of 1980, that Joseph Ludlam finally consented to attend one of his son's plays — the only work by his son he would ever see. Perhaps not so coincidentally, it was also among the most innocuous and straightforward plays in the Ludlam canon.

The expedition from Long Island to Greenwich Village became even more of a Ludlam family affair when Joseph's brother, Buster, agreed to accompany them. "I don't think either one of them was impressed," recalled Marjorie. "My brother-in-law said, 'That's the first time I've gone in to see one, and that's the last time.' Joe didn't say anything."

Joseph remained aloof when the Ludlam clan met with the company at a small, catered get-together in the lobby after the Sunday matinee. Nor would he ever share any impressions of the play or of his son's highly praised performance with Marjorie. He had disapproved of Charles his whole life, and nothing would alter his attitude.

Ludlam was, however, even more excited about his father seeing the theater itself than about his attending the production. He was proud of having attained a piece of property he could call his own, and thought that this — at least — would impress his father. But it didn't.

Nor did Ludlam receive much solace from his relationship with Quinton during this period. The casual reference to Bellevue in the breakfast scene of *Reverse Psychology* was almost a precursor to the events that followed. It was shortly before the play's long-extended run that Quinton had himself checked in to that very facility. Though he had designed the costumes and supervised the sound for *Reverse Psychology*, it was noticeable to everyone that Quinton resented not being onstage. Peter Golub recalled, "He was very down on the other people" and "Charlotte's performance especially drove him crazy." He even once threatened that he would "not turn the sound on," according to Susan.

Though Ludlam and Quinton had taken to going off on their own during the old regime, new people called for new circumstances. It became more or less habitual for the two of them to join Susan, Forbes, and Golub for dinner following performances of *Reverse Psychology*, frequently at the Rosebay Cafe above the theater at One Sheridan Square. (While Forbes's husband-to-be, Phil Catoggio, usually joined them, Vehr never did. In addition to Vehr's private nature, as Susan observed, he increasingly withdrew after the departure of Pashalinski and Brockmeyer.)

According to Forbes,

> Even though the play was long and physically exhausting, it was also exhilarating. We would go into the Rosebay and carry on like crazy people afterwards. We all got really plastered some nights, but Everett was truly the wild man. He was drinking very heavily. Charles could drink or not drink — he could have one drink and that would be fine. He could have two drinks and that would be fine. But if Everett had one drink, he'd have to have a hundred drinks: He would drink until he dropped. And Everett was a nasty, Irish kind of drunk.

Golub noticed a pattern emerging regarding Quinton's drinking habits. Whether it was at a restaurant or a bar, everyone seemed to be having a grand time together when

Quinton suddenly turned hostile. "He would often throw his glass and go storming out of the place."

Quinton's drinking had gotten so out of hand that even he began to realize he had a problem: In the midst of a heat wave, while out drinking with a friend, he suddenly took himself to Bellevue. "I had heard about detox, but when I realized that they were going to put me in the hospital, I freaked out and they had to restrain me to keep me there for seventy-two hours," recalled Quinton.

Golub accompanied Ludlam on a visit to the hospital the next morning. "It was quite horrific," said Golub. "Charles was somehow goading Everett on, until Everett finally said, 'Charles, did you come here to visit or to drive me crazy?' Charles responded, 'Both.'"

Though Quinton resumed drinking after his release — and continued to "hit the bottle" until the subsequent March — he marks his episode in Bellevue as the turning point in his alcoholism. That first morning when he awoke to find himself in the hospital, "I was sick with embarrassment, and also from what they shot me up with," said Quinton. "When I realized they were going to keep me for a few days to evaluate me, I thought to myself, 'Oh, Jesus!' I made my bed as well as I could, and when the nurse came in, I said, 'See how well I made my bed?' In this heavy Jamaican accent, she said, 'Honey, you're not confused. You just drink too much.' And that's when I realized that everything wrong with my life was due to booze. After that moment, none of the drinking worked anymore."

Quinton eventually came to appreciate that his drinking was both a cause and a symptom of his unhealthy relationship with Ludlam. "It was fear that was keeping us together then. There was love there; but once you open up the bottle, anything can happen."

Despite any appearances to the contrary, Forbes sensed that "Everett was really my champion who wanted me to be in all the plays after *Reverse Psychology*. He was very disappointed that I didn't come back and do a play right away. But it just wasn't possible. I was now working with my new company." Susan felt that Ludlam kept trying to woo Forbes to be in future plays as Pashalinski's replacement. "They had a great sense of humor in common."

The first play that Forbes turned down was Ludlam's next, *Love's Tangled Web*. He had plenty of time to work on the script during the extended run of *Reverse Psychology* in the spring of 1981. He had developed by then what many would consider a highly peculiar writing method. While checking his clothes in a locker, Ludlam took index cards and a pen into a cubicle at gay bathhouses and worked out bits of dialogue with the door ajar, waiting for attractive tricks to pass by.

While he was shooting *Impostors* the year before, he told the film's director, Mark Rappaport, "how much he loved going to the baths, because he'd get a cubicle and sit there and write without wasting any time until 'Mr. Right' came along." It was an especially efficient routine since Quinton apparently had the impression that Ludlam was at the tiny office at One Sheridan Square, working away on the script.

Steven Samuels recalled that a great deal of *Love's Tangled Web* was written in this fashion. "There were times when he felt like the baths were the only place he could go and concentrate," said Samuels. "He very rarely worked at the office — that was not a particularly congenial environment. There were only a number of occasions when he would be dictating a play under a great deal of pressure and we would work together at the office. Home had all kinds of problems associated with it, primarily because it was small. And Everett liked to listen to opera, which drove Charles more or less up the wall. Music per se was not a major part of his life, and he used to complain a great deal about Everett's obsession with opera" — or his watching soap operas, for that matter.

With some regularity during this period, Ludlam arrived at the office directly from the baths and handed Samuels a fresh batch of dialogue on pink note cards for him to type into the script. Ludlam boasted to Samuels that he could have sex whenever he wanted, and never had to masturbate. "He felt that it was much better to be gay: You don't have to deal with pregnancy, or being rejected by women, because everyone in the gay world was inclined to have sex with anyone without rejection."

By the time Ludlam had started working on *Love's Tangled Web*, there had already been rumors about a new "gay cancer" or "gay plague." In less than a year it would be known as GRID, which stood for Gay-Related Immune Deficiency. Within just over a year, or by July 1982, this disease, now called AIDS, would become only too well known. Since the baths were deemed a rampant breeding ground for the virus, efforts were mobilized to close them in the coming years, and the gay community was rather divided on the attendant issues.

Ludlam himself evidently became ambivalent in his attitude towards the baths. Like many other gay men of his generation, he was not prone to exercising any caution or restraint when it came to fulfilling his voracious sexual appetite. But while Christopher Scott, Leandro Katz, Bobjack Callejo, and William Kohler would all testify to encountering Ludlam at the baths or backrooms of gay bookstores and bars during the early eighties, both Steven Samuels and Black-Eyed Susan had a different impression. Ludlam was very firm in telling Susan that he stopped going to the baths because of AIDS. And according to Quinton, both he and Ludlam stopped being promiscuous when he stopped drinking for good in March of 1982.

By working on some of the middle-period plays at the baths, however, Ludlam was potentially sacrificing his art to his libido. While both plays were written with sporadic bathhouse visits, *Love's Tangled Web* would prove to be as much of a flop as *Utopia, Incorporated*. Both its humor and its convoluted story line feel strained. Like *Reverse Psychology*, it is also a farce about heterosexuals; but it doesn't have the solid premise of its predecessor around which to build — or contain — the farcical developments.

Love's Tangled Web was also written and produced under a great deal of pressure. After the success of *Reverse Psychology*, Ludlam was fearful of the critics dismissing anything he might produce next: This, at any rate, was a widely perceived pattern. And with Christopher Scott supervising what was a new, more streamlined operation, there were additional responsibilities and increased financial obligations.

Steven Samuels believed that a good deal of the ambition to take over the theater component of Lincoln Center originated with Scott, as opposed to Ludlam. "Charles adopted it, but it came from Chris," said Samuels.

> Charles was very susceptible to influence, and he was most influenced by the people who surrounded and loved him. But I thought there was a tremendous discrepancy between their visions. Chris would never be happy unless he was working for a company that was as exalted in the eyes of society as his world with Henry Geldzahler was. But that was a very different world than Charles was functioning in at the time. And it was a very seductive vision for Charles. And I think he responded very clearly to the ambitions that Chris had for him. But that's where the problem between them ultimately resided.

Ludlam's original title for *Love's Tangled Web* was *Sylvia, or the White Zombie*. But Scott balked at this. In his eagerness for the Ridiculous to be taken more seriously, Scott wanted to disassociate the new company from the old, and he particularly wanted to avoid the campy connotations of "White Zombie." But given Ludlam's tendency to dig in his heels whenever he was criticized, this isn't what Scott told him. He instead suggested that the name "Sylvia" might alienate the Jewish segment of his audience. Though Ludlam liked his original title and didn't understand the objection, he relented when Scott dragged out their old friend, the *I Ching*, on which they had been relying for advice since they were young. It only confirmed Scott's apprehensions regarding the name; but it was to meet a deadline for an ad for the play — and at the spur of the marketing moment — that Ludlam came up with *Love's Tangled Web*.

Though a scene directly referred to *Hedda Gabler*, and Ludlam also mentioned Elia Kazan's 1949 film *Pinky* as a source, *Love's Tangled Web* was basically an original story. Beginning with *Reverse Psychology* and culminating with *Secret Lives of the Sexists*, it proved to be the second of a trilogy of contemporary sex farces. All three of these plays were marked by Ludlam's feeling less dependent on quoting others, and finally more confident in his own voice. As he told Samuels, there was a moment when he "suddenly realized that inventing your own dialogue is so much easier than finding all this stuff to quote."

There are hints of autobiography strewn throughout *Love's Tangled Web*. It's set on "Long Island's fashionable North Shore," where Ludlam grew up, and the wealthy household it focuses on specifically reflects Scott and his upper-middle-class WASP upbringing. As designed by Ludlam, the set featured furniture from the fifties, some of which was borrowed from Scott's personal collection. Ludlam may also have had his maternal grandfather in mind when he wrote the part of a lower-class Long Island gardener for himself.

The plot concerns Sylvia Woodville, a villainous heiress who pretends to be crippled in order to be the benefactor of her father's will. Having inherited the estate, she agrees to let her mother Eve and her brother Bertie stay on as her maid and butler. Bram, the gardener, had a fling with Sylvia in the past and he is still madly in love with her. (When Sylvia tells Bram that he sired her child, he replies, "Are you sure you were the mother?") But now, ten years later, he's pursued by Raeanne, a "paranormal," who devises a farcical masquerade to get him in the end.

A scene between Bram and Raeanne at the Woodville estate suggests that Ludlam was very conscious of his working-class background while he was writing *Love's Tangled Web*, and especially mindful of his good fortune in meeting Christopher Scott in high school:

RAEANNE: Why do we have to stay here? Why can't you just take me home?

BRAM: Raeanne, this is my first chance to get in with really high-class people and you want to go and ruin it.

RAEANNE: Then why don't you stay here and I'll walk home.

BRAM: How would that make me look if I stayed here and let you walk home?

RAEANNE: Why do you care so much about what these people think?

BRAM: These people are somebodies. Do you want to run around with a bunch of nobodies for the rest of your life?

RAEANNE: I like nobodies. I'm a nobody. You're a nobody. What's wrong with being a nobody?

BRAM: Because practically everybody is a nobody and almost nobody is a somebody.

RAEANNE: Maybe there's a good reason why almost nobody is a somebody. Maybe nobody wants to be a somebody. Maybe being a somebody isn't all it's cracked up to be.

BRAM: Do you want to be a clam digger's daughter all your life?

RAEANNE: That's one thing I'm sure of. I'll always be a clam digger's daughter. And proud of it.

Ludlam set out in *Love's Tangled Web* to write a parody about the wealthy suburban life he experienced in his youth; but he only knew about such a life indirectly, from his exposure to the Scott clan. This might explain why the play keeps slipping away from him, in a sense, with dangling plot lines, mistaken identities, and a gorilla popping into the scenario. Ludlam had a rationale, however, for the crazy-quilt effect the play had on its audience.

After distinguishing himself from the contemporary avant-garde, Ludlam claimed,

> I've tried to use plot in a twentieth-century way, just as some painters learned to use paints and canvas in twentieth-century ways. The plots of my farces are avant-garde in that they are abstract and expressionistic. All those zany, improbable events in these comedies shouldn't be taken literally; they're simply too ridiculous. . . . In the new play, *Love's Tangled Web*, the audience will not be able to recount the plot. It's like Feydeau — it's very, very complicated.

The play was episodic and it very deliberately parodied soap-opera structures. The recently released John Waters film, *Polyester*, was also a send-up of fifties suburbia, and Ludlam originally cast two actresses who were well known for their work with the camp filmmaker: Mink Stole (as Eve) and Cookie Mueller (as Raeanne). Though Mink Stole remained with *Love's Tangled Web* to the end, Ludlam replaced Mueller early in rehearsals. According to Susan, "Charles felt that Cookie wasn't as experienced as the rest of us, and that she simply wasn't used to stage acting."

At first, Ludlam invited Kate Manheim, Richard Foreman's wife and frequent star, to take over the part, but she bowed out during rehearsals. "Kate left because Richard was in France with a new production and she wanted to be there for the opening," recalled Susan. But Susan also remembered Ludlam saying that "Kate wanted him to give her more detailed directions than he was prepared to." The role of Raeanne ultimately went to Christine Deveau, a prized student actor from Carnegie-Mellon whom Ludlam had first directed in *The Country Wife* the previous fall.

In addition to Mink Stole and Christine Deveau, the rest of the six-member cast consisted of the surviving core group: Ludlam as Bram, Susan as the evil Sylvia, Quinton as her swishy brother Bertie, and Bill Vehr as Reverend Bates — a greasy-palmed minister whose allegiance is to the person with the most money to donate. Though the character of Bertie started out with very few lines, the role was expanded late in rehearsals, perhaps a maneuver to appease Quinton's hostility over not having appeared in the last play.

When the play opened on June 7, 1981, Frank Rich was more or less speaking for all the reviewers by writing,

> Not one of these actors . . . comes close to beating Mr. Ludlam at his own daffy game. . . . At all times, you never know when Mr. Ludlam will suddenly drop his pose of the moment, whatever it may be, to revert to the eye-rolling inanity of a misbehaving six-year-old. But even then, at its absolute silliest, his performance is shrewdly conceived and timed. If Charles Ludlam, the playwright, would only bring to this production the same discipline as Charles Ludlam, the actor, the disordered strands of *Love's Tangled Web* could yet be woven into a tight-knit farce.

Though Ludlam received rave notices for his own performance, the reviews for *Love's Tangled Web* ranged from tepid to scornful. (In *Newsday*, Long Island's own newspaper, Allan Wallach wrote that the play "is as slow as a ride on the Long Island Railroad on a day when a train has been derailed outside Penn Station.") They were disappointing enough for even Ludlam to realize it would be futile to keep the show running — it closed within three weeks.

The failure was particularly demoralizing for Christopher Scott, who left the company for good with the premature demise of *Love's Tangled Web*. This was partly because Scott was spreading himself too thin. During the year he had taken over exclusive responsibility for the business as Executive Director of the Ridiculous, he was simultaneously helping Geldzahler "rebuild" the New York Department of Cultural Affairs. And in the midst of all this, Geldzahler was breaking up with Scott and wanted him to move out. "After fifteen years together," claimed Scott, "I refused to leave the apartment until I received a community property settlement from Henry."

Scott's growing breach with Ludlam stemmed from a stormy relationship they developed in their final days of working together. According to Samuels,

> Once there was no Henry [Geldzahler], who was Chris Scott? This was a major problem for Chris. He needed to be perceived in the world as Charles's equal, his partner. It got to the rather ludicrous point where they were sitting in the theater having a knock-down-drag-out fight about whose name appeared how often in the program [for *Love's Tangled Web*], with Chris insisting that his name had to appear as frequently as Charles's did.

"Charles was no fun to work for," said Scott. "I realized that the only way to continue to have a relationship with him was to become a more serious member of the audience [by attending numerous performances of future productions]. That way, I got the best of it without the worst. And Charles eventually transformed himself from being this angry, psychopathic person into being a loving and gentle one."

In the meantime, Scott felt guilty about leaving Ludlam in the lurch. He had noticed how bright and efficient Steven Samuels had been in his many duties at the office, and he prepared him to become his successor. "I gave Steve the executive directorship, because I just couldn't do it anymore," said Scott. "At first, Charles was a little skeptical, because he thought Steve was too ambitious. But it was clear that he was very good, and Charles gradually came to trust him."

During *Reverse Psychology*, Samuels had been promoted from House Manager to General Manager. "I moved very quickly from cleaning the toilets to cleaning the books," quipped Samuels with his customary wit. But suddenly Scott asked him to assume even more responsibilities. The meeting between the two of them took place in the theater office, while Ludlam was upstairs at the Rosebay Cafe. Samuels recalled Scott running back and forth between them during the negotiations. When Scott finally returned from upstairs and said it was "a done deal," Samuels went up to talk to Ludlam.

Ludlam began by saying, "So, you're going to be the bookkeeper. And you're a professional, of course." Samuels replied, "No, Charles. And I need you to understand this: I know something about bookkeeping. But I'm not a professional." In a coy manner, Ludlam crossed his legs, put his hands across his knees, and said, "Well, you are now."

Samuels recalled the morning that a panicked Ludlam phoned him at 7 AM to ask if they had to close *Love's Tangled Web*. As far as Samuels was concerned, being asked to make such an important decision was when he knew he had become the business manager. Ludlam would later claim, "*Love's Tangled Web* was written, produced and directed in six weeks, and I really loved it. I wish it could have run longer, but it just wasn't making enough money to keep the theatre open. I suppose you could call it a critical failure. In other words, the critics failed it."

Samuels also felt that "*Love's Tangled Web* opened to the critics before it was really ready for them. By the time it closed, three weeks later, it was pretty exciting. Had it been in the shape it was when it closed, the reviews would have been significantly better."

Eventually, Ludlam would come to pin much of the blame for the failure of *Love's Tangled Web* not on the critics or on the timing of its opening, but on Black-Eyed Susan. According to Samuels, "Susan had disappointed Charles tremendously in *Love's Tangled Web*. He built the show around her in many ways and wanted it to be her showcase. If you simply count the lines in the play, you discover that the role of Sylvia is the real lead. Charles was playing what was essentially a bit part. Yet, of course, he stole the show."

While acknowledging that Ludlam would have been upset if he failed to steal *any* show, Samuels detected the development of an embittered attitude towards Susan following *Love's Tangled Web*. "Charles didn't feel that Susan was willing to take the kind of responsibility you have to take to be a star and carry a play," said Samuels. "And he felt she didn't take advantage of the opportunity." This, at any rate, would become Ludlam's justification for giving Susan smaller roles and Quinton larger ones in the coming years.

Looking back on *Love's Tangled Web*, Quinton claimed that "Susan was brilliant in that role. Charles and Susan just needed a break from each other. If she could have stood on her head and spit wooden nickels, he would have wanted quarters."

Dismissing the poor reaction to the play itself was a different, if familiar story. As

Quinton summarized it, "Everything is not your masterpiece, I don't care what Charles thought. You could give him gold, and he'd want platinum. But the ones that didn't go over so well were like his children that needed all the more support and attention."

There were other factors, however, that Ludlam needed to consider. As he would receive more and more outside work through the mid-eighties, Ludlam recognized the need to become less indispensable to the Ridiculous, so that the company could function with or without his presence. He frequently expressed aggravation over having to create works for other people to carry, and he specifically identified Susan and Quinton as star material. Yet he consistently felt let down by them in this respect. However, his characteristic ambivalence was also a part of the equation: How could anyone other than himself truly be the star?

In consort with Samuels, Ludlam decided against ever again renting the theater to other performers after the abrupt closing of *Love's Tangled Web*. He felt it would compromise the identity of the Ridiculous if attention were being paid to anything else at One Sheridan Square. Better to be dark than to underscore the fact that the Ridiculous had nothing on.

But he also adhered to his recent decision to avoid any revivals by intending to put on his still unproduced *Isle of the Hermaphrodites*, which he was calling *Henry III and His Court*, after its original source. It was a finished script, after all. Auditions were held, and there were even signs outside the theater to announce its impending arrival. But following an early reading — with Samuels cast as the magician, Georg Osterman as the Queen, Susan as the Duchess of Guise, and Quinton as St. Muggeroon — Ludlam despaired of the play ever working. Samuels sensed that Ludlam was particularly disappointed with the way he himself read a scene with Osterman. Ludlam seemed to have a fixed idea in his head of what he wanted, and Samuels never understood why he "couldn't believe that something might evolve and grow" as the actors helped develop the play further. "He was just terribly frustrated and full of doubt about it."

Ludlam next brought in some pages of the *Kharagos* scenario he had performed in France and periodically used for his *commedia* classes. There was a reading with Shorty, Vehr's lover, cast as a cockroach. But plans for staging this frivolous piece were also quickly abandoned.

During such fallow periods, Ludlam would always resume work on *The Sorrows of Dolores*, his epic film-in-the-making. On August 28, 1981, he wrote a letter to onetime lover Robert Beers, who was then working in the film department of the Museum of Modern Art. "Dear Robert," it began:

> Thanks for your kind offer of screening *The Sorrows of Dolores* at the Museum of Modern Art, but wouldn't you prefer a private screening chez moi before sticking your neck out for an as yet untried cineaste (or are cineastes men who chase after little girls and photograph them making peepee)? I could arrange such an evening. Would this weekend be all right? My projector only takes a four hundred foot roll, which means a brief intermission every fifteen minutes, but since the film is based on silent serials, it doesn't mar it. Perhaps it even adds to the effect.
>
> I loved reading the play with you the other night. Would you seriously consider acting with us again? And if not on stage, what about on the silver screen?
>
> Telephone me the moment you receive this letter and we'll make a date. Yours in the art without a muse, cinema . . .

Ludlam had recently encountered Beers at a dinner party hosted by Robert Reddy. "Reading the play" referred to the group's rendering of some Shakespeare scenes following supper. But after such a long hiatus, Beers never pursued the invitation to act again with the company. Nor would he later, when Ludlam approached him to be in *Salammbô*. What's more remarkable about the letter to Beers is that Ludlam was evidently talking about *The Sorrows of Dolores* as if it were ready for a preliminary screening in 1981, when, in fact, he would still be working on the film at the time of his death six years later. But there would periodically be showings of this work-in-progress for intimate gatherings in the intervening years.

August 28 also marked the death of Ludlam's beloved Aunt May, who succumbed to an embolism. Up until the day before, May had been helping the Ludlams by coming over to look after Joe — who had recently had a stroke — while Marjorie walked to the store for groceries. Since Ludlam and Quinton were otherwise behaving like a married couple, it may seem odd that Ludlam attended his aunt's funeral alone. Though Marjorie doesn't recall ever telling him, perhaps Ludlam got wind of the fact that his father constantly complained to her: "Why does he always have to bring Everett with him when he comes to visit?" One way or the other, Marjorie did what she could to dissuade her son from including Quinton on some of his trips to Long Island.

જ

The uncommonly long rehearsal period for *Secret Lives of the Sexists*, Ludlam's twenty-first play, began in September of 1981, though it would not open until the following February. The rehearsals occurred in the midst of major renovations at One Sheridan Square. A fan of the company who was a manager of a Trans-Lux movie theater donated some old seats with one stipulation: They needed to be removed within a twenty-four-hour period. The real chore was breaking up the existing concrete pews and carting away the debris. It proved to be a massive undertaking, involving many volunteers.

Ludlam also spent time that fall shooting a silent movie at Coney Island, as part of a larger project. The ten-minute black-and-white film, called *Museum of Wax*, features Ludlam as an escaped convict who tries to elude the police by blending in with the various wax figures housed in the museum.

The movie was being made for a fund-raising event to be held on Halloween. As produced by Coney Island, U.S.A. and presented at the World in Wax Musée — the oldest wax museum in the country — "Tricks and Treats at the Wax Musée" would prove to be an eight-hour extravaganza that included twenty-four performance pieces and drew several hundred spectators. Offbeat performance artists such as Paul Zaloom, Sandra McKee, Vanalyne Green, and Dick Zigun, the producer of the event, were among the other participants.

"Tricks and Treats" was a custom-made event for Ludlam. It was designed to recreate an earlier form of popular entertainment known as the "dime museum." Usually presented on fairgrounds, dime museums intermingled wax figures and other oddities with magicians, carnival freaks, and monologuists performing on jerry-built platforms.

In addition to showing *Museum of Wax*, Ludlam and Quinton performed a piece entitled "Escape From a Regulation Straightjacket as Used on the Murderous Insane." As reported by John Frick and Stephen Johnson in *The Drama Review*, the piece began when Ludlam ("in street clothes") and Quinton (dressed as a nurse),

> took their places in a booth. Quinton told Ludlam, whom he addressed simply as Charles, that he had been "bad" and deserved to be punished. He gave Charles a choice of punishments: the snake pit or the straightjacket. Ludlam chose the straightjacket, retreated to a corner of the room and pouted. Assuming a Christ-like pose with arms outstretched and head lowered to his right shoulder, he accepted the straightjacket, whimpering occasionally. For the next five minutes as Quinton laced Ludlam into the jacket, he lectured Charles on his transgressions and the

necessity of punishment. During the final minute of the act, Ludlam writhed on the floor, stretched, and went through various contortions, ultimately escaping from the straightjacket.... (According to a program note, Ludlam had based this act on one created by Harry Houdini, who began his career in a dime museum.)

Since it was so crucial to his childhood development and so fundamental to his theater, the carnival-like atmosphere of "Tricks and Treats" naturally found its way into the script Ludlam was working on that fall, in an astonishing monologue he wrote for Black-Eyed Susan. But it's hardly central to the story. *Secret Lives of the Sexists*, Ludlam's third sex farce on "modern life," is basically a mockery of sexual categorizations and all they imply—from heterosexuality and homosexuality to any variation in between. Though Ludlam was obsessed with hypocrisy in general, he became particularly annoyed whenever he detected it in reference to gender divisions. As Samuels described Ludlam's ambitions with *Secret Lives*, "He was going to stick it to all the frauds in the society." Ludlam more specifically set out to upend the sillier aspects of feminism, which had permeated the mainstream culture.

Even if his intentions were formulated, however, Ludlam didn't have a very firm notion of where the play was going to go at first. He was unhappy with some early draft pages, and *Secret Lives* ultimately had an extended developmental period, becoming one of the many that was still being written while it was being mounted, and benefitting from the process.

In the play, Ludlam portrayed Phil Landers, a butch "physical culture" trainer and aerobics instructor. Landers is straight, but he pretends to be gay in order to be hired by Zena Grossfinger (Black-Eyed Susan) to teach aerobics at her beauty parlor. During their interview, Zena asks Phil if he's gay.

> PHIL: Usually—sometimes I get depressed just like anybody else.
> ZENA: I mean are you straight?
> PHIL: Straight? Am I straight? You mean you have to ask if I'm straight? You can't see with your own eyes?
> ZENA: That's what I was afraid of. I'm looking for a gay man for this job. You see all my customers are women. I think it would be very bad for business if one of the customers became involved with a male employee. I couldn't consider hiring you if you were straight.
> PHIL: (*His voice breaking into falsetto as he crosses his legs at the knee and throws a limp wrist*) Straight? Am I straight? (*Wetting his pinky at his lips and*

tracing his eyebrows with it) You mean you have to ask, you can't see
with your own eyes?

ZENA: I'm so relieved. I don't want any trouble with jealous husbands. But I can
see you're safe.

PHIL: As a eunuch in the harem of a sheikh.

Unbeknownst to her daughter Nadine (Mink Stole), Zena's new beauty parlor venture
is being financed by her son-in-law, Buddy Husband (Bill Vehr). It's all part of a plan to
make Zena, a nightclub stripper, more respectable before she's reunited with Nadine,
whom she gave away at birth. In the meantime, unaware that Zena is her mother,
Nadine mistakenly assumes that Buddy is having an affair with her. Nadine's suspicions
are fostered by her sister-in-law, Fanny (Georg Osterman, performing in drag again).

Fanny is married to Izzy Husband (Everett Quinton), and she stands to inherit $200,000
when she has her first child. But the joke built-in to Izzy's name ("Is he [a] husband?")
betrays his fear of having sex with his wife — or with any woman for that matter.

FANNY: Are men never satisfied? Are they all insatiable?

IZZY: Not me. I'm satiable. Aren't you glad you never have to worry about me
going out after funsy-wunsy?

FANNY: Please, Izzy, we are mature adults. We don't have to refer to it as funsy-
wunsy anymore. It's perfectly acceptable to call it whoopie.

IZZY: Aren't you glad you have a husband who's never even looked at a woman?

FANNY: Oh Izzy, I am. But we've been married almost a year now. Don't you
think it's time we saw each other with our clothes off?

IZZY: It's just that I'm a modest person. Anyway clothes leave more to the
imagination.

FANNY: But we're married. We don't have to have imagination anymore.

In order to secure Fanny's inheritance, Izzy persuades his brother Buddy to try and
impregnate her, offering to share half of the proceeds with him. In one of the more
hilarious scenes, Fanny encourages Buddy to be a "dummy Izzy" as she practices
seduction techniques from a sex manual, while Izzy — sequestered in a closet — is
goading Buddy on to cooperate.

An equally absurd moment arrives when Nadine stages a seduction of the ostensibly gay
Phil following an aerobics class. She seeks "revenge on my husband . . . [who] had the
nerve to say I was a 'safe wife' because I'm not the type men go for." Since Nadine has

timed the seduction perfectly, Buddy catches them in the act. Wielding a gun, he threatens to kill both of them before forcing Phil out onto the window ledge.

The play becomes particularly preposterous when the women attend a radical feminist rally in Act III, and the men crash the meeting in drag. The rally is being organized by "Women Against Stenography," a group considered even more extremist than "Women Against Photography," who maintain that "women have the right to do what they want with their bodies — as long as they don't photograph it." Nadine becomes a rabble-rouser calling for "an end of the two-sex system once and for all ... we'd simply give all women a promotion and make them legally men." Zena attends the meeting to defend herself against the feminist attacks her striptease act has provoked.

Within the context of so many sexual convolutions and contortions, even a preposterous line such as the following makes sense: "I let a lesbian trick me into making it with her by pretending she was a homosexual man in drag who needed to be cured." Ludlam had not confronted "gayness" so directly in a play since *Caprice*, and *Secret Lives* became Ludlam's final word on the absurdity of all gender labels and any cultural or social restrictions they entail.

Steven Samuels avers that he inadvertently assisted Ludlam in writing the play. Ludlam had developed what ultimately became the bulk of the first half without yet knowing where it was headed. Samuels, who was reading Aristophanes at the time, was "quite struck by how much it seemed to be the same play, the same subject," as *Thesmophoriazusae*. According to Samuels, "I had always thought of Charles as our very own Aristophanes. There hadn't been quite so Aristophanic a playwright in many and many a year. And I just assumed that Charles knew Aristophanes backwards and forwards."

When Samuels pointed out the similarities between *Secret Lives* and *Thesmophoriazusae*, he was surprised to discover that Ludlam was totally unfamiliar with the work, and in fact, only knew a couple of the Greek dramatist's plays. But after Samuels brought it to his attention, Ludlam read *Thesmophoriazusae*. "He built a great deal of the [third] act out of the Aristophanes — most of the arguments, the debates that occur in the play."

Though it also appears in the third act, Zena's lengthy self-defense was inspired not by Aristophanes, but by Susan, who had recently started auditioning for work with other companies. By making many sarcastic remarks about the "commercial theater," Ludlam indicated his displeasure with the situation. But he was also egomaniacal enough to ask her why she wasn't using material from any of his plays for her auditions. Susan said quite simply that there was no monologue long enough to be suitable. This prompted Ludlam to write the speech for Zena, which he added to the script just a few days before the previews commenced.

Zena's monologue is perhaps the single, most archetypal speech and self-contained story Ludlam ever wrote. As such, it deserves to be quoted in its entirety.

> ZENA: Ladies. (*Boos, jeers*) Ladies, please hear me! (*Boos, jeers*) I am not accustomed to public speaking. My own voice sounds very far away to me at this moment, and I can hardly hear it my heart is pounding so and I'm afraid you can hear my knees knocking all the way out there. You see, I am more accustomed to speaking to men than I am to women — having spent so much time in their company as I have. (*A single boo*) So I hope you will excuse me if I speak to you the way I speak to the men I've had the business of doing pleasure with. "Okay, sports! What's in it for me?" Those were the words I learned at my Mamma's knee. You see I was a lady of the evening like my Mamma and her Mamma before her. Three generations of women who made their way in the world providing horizontal entertainment for lonely men — and boys. We were carny folk in those days, livin' out of trailers, travelin' from town to town. My Mamma was an exhibit in the sideshow, "Eve as God Created Her," twenty-five cents a peek, an act my Gramma thought of 'cause Mamma couldn't strip. She was all thumbs and had two left feet — couldn't dance and always got her zippers stuck. Between shows Mamma used to invite certain gentlemen to her trailer for tea. I had to hide in my bunk till they were through. Those gentlemen used to get real affectionate toward Mamma and call her doll and honey and love and stuff — and that's when I'd always hear Mamma say, "Okay, sport! What's in it for me?" Now this carny used to travel with a freak show. Every carny used to have a few. And Mamma used to tell me, "Keep away from those freaks. I don't want those freaks messin' 'round with you." But there was this guy they called the Human Worm. Didn't have no arms or legs but he was every inch a man. He was always tryin' to love Mamma. But she just wouldn't let him touch her. Well, one day I was sent to bed without supper for scarin' off one of Mamma's tricks. And I decided to run away. I headed for the road. Then suddenly this traveling salesman tried to grab me. I was only six years old — but well-

developed for my age. He tried to kiss me on the mouth. I remember
how the stubble of his beard scratched my face and the smell of liquor
on his breath. Why, that man slapped his hand over my mouth before I
even had time to say, "Well, sport, what's in it for me?" Suddenly he
laid on top of me without even taking off his clothes. He just started
grunting and sweating right there in the rain — in the mud! Suddenly
he groaned a fierce groan and let out a hideous breath. His whole body
shuddered and he went limp. He was dead! The Human Worm had
stabbed him with a knife held in his teeth. He pushed the salesman off
me and we headed back to my trailer with him crawlin' at my side.
That night we moved on. But my hero the Human Worm was never
the same again. He was haunted by what had happened. He had a powerful guilt. One day he said to me, "Zena, I'm going to turn myself in. I
can't live with this on my conscience. I'll probably be away a long
time." I begged him not to do it. But he wouldn't listen to my pleas. He
wanted to tell the police where he was. But he asked me one last favor
before he turned himself in. He said he had never had a woman... and
now he probably never would. Would I let him, just once? How could I
refuse this sad, heroic man who was aching for a woman? I let him. It
was a beautiful experience. And I didn't even have to ask, "What's in it
for me?" Then he went and dialed the phone with his tongue. Later on
I realized that something was changing. My body was full of life. I had
a healthy baby and that's when I became Zena Moline, the world's
youngest mother. But after a while I realized that I was no good for that
child. I didn't want *her* to grow up saying, "Okay, sport! What's in it for
me?" So I gave her up to those who'd raise her decent. So she'd know a
better life than the one I'd known. And ever since that day I've dreamed
of meeting her someday and being with my baby once again.

This otherwise ridiculous tale perfectly epitomizes Ludlam's lifelong fascination with
"carny folk." As Ludlam's occasional long-distance dramaturge Leon Katz observed,
"Charles had a genuine affection" for the freaks of this world — not to be mistaken for a
more prurient or indecent interest in the bizarre — which to some unknowable degree
stemmed from his identifying with them. Ludlam's description of "the Human Worm"
conforms with an actual armless and legless creature who appeared in Tod Browning's
1932 cult film *Freaks* — wielding a knife in his mouth as he squirms across the screen in
the film's final segment. The allusion to "the world's youngest mother" refers to a South
American girl who had ostensibly given birth when she was only six years old, as Zena

claims to have been in her story. Ludlam was recently reminded of this oddity by seeing a wax rendering of her at the Coney Island wax museum during the fall, when he was working on the script of *Secret Lives*. His absolute love of the carny world becomes a promise fulfilled in the play's denouement, when Phil runs off with Zena to join a traveling circus.

The script is loaded with puns and topical jokes skewering everything from the *Village Voice* ("This world is rotten and corrupt! It's everything the *Village Voice* says it is!") to another Off-Broadway theater company:

> FANNY: It's just like those plays in the 1950s where the homosexual commits
> suicide at the end.
> BUDDY: I love those plays. Why don't they do them like that anymore?
> FANNY: They still do over at Circle Rep.

Yet another funny bit of dialogue had some less than humorous undertones that hit rather close to home, however:

> BUDDY: Would anyone care for a cocktail?
> ZENA: No thanks. I don't drink.
> FANNY: Oooh, alcoholic, huh?

The rehearsals for the play were protracted. From the outset, Ludlam asked everyone to envision their characters as cartoons. He saw the play tumbling forward in an animated fashion, almost like the Keystone Kops. After a few weeks of working on it this way, Ludlam told Susan that she was losing the cartoonish approach and making her character "too real." Susan replied that she wanted "to come alive, and there has to be more ambiguity than a cartoon character has." An argument ensued. Ludlam accused Susan of deliberately defying him. But she proved relentless, and he ultimately accepted her interpretation.

In addition to its longer rehearsal period, *Secret Lives* had a more extended preview showing before it opened to the critics. After fourteen years of a more haphazard approach — often fiddling with a script until opening night — Ludlam was prompted by Samuels to appreciate the necessity of fine-tuning a work, before letting in the reviewers. This became yet another factor separating the new company from the old.

As Christopher Scott perceived, "*Secret Lives* was technically perfect and the first one that really worked like clockwork every time." This doubtlessly contributed to its popular success. After opening on February 9, 1982, it ran for four months. But in spite of monitoring its development more carefully than with previous shows, and then opening the play to the press when the production was as good as it was going to get, the reviews for *Secret Lives* were predominantly mixed.

While encouraging his readers to attend *Secret Lives* and citing "some wicked, crazy laughs in this raunchy jape," Frank Rich responded that "the evening quite literally drags on" and felt that the play "is in need of ample editing, both in writing and performance." Don Nelsen more or less shared Rich's ambivalent reaction in his review for the *Daily News* ("The comic level is not as consistently provocative as some earlier Ludlam pieces. . . . But sit through it. The big laughs are worth it."), as did Clive Barnes in the *Post* ("Of course here, the style is the thing, and this time out the style may not be enough.") Even Mel Gussow had some reservations in his broadcast review on WQXR, referring to "slow stretches and self-indulgent jokes" as well as more "priceless" moments.

Along with the public, the less mainstream reviewers were far more enthusiastic. In his analytical review for the *Village Voice*, Michael Feingold claimed that "the effect is as wholesome as Molière" and that "good sense and sweet nature are the moving forces behind [Ludlam's] work these days." (The erudite Feingold was the only critic who noticed the connection with *Thesmophoriazusae*.) Terry Helbing, in his review for the *Native*, found *Secret Lives* "easily the best offering of the Ridiculous Theatrical Company in the last decade." And while proclaiming that "criticism is beside the point," Sylviane Gold's well-considered review for the *Soho Weekly News* declared that behind the "jesting is a seriousness of purpose that is perhaps unique in our current theater."

Both the critics and audience members alike had nothing but praise for two scenes in particular, entailing the bravura performance skills of Susan and Ludlam, respectively. Offered as a prologue to the play, Susan performs Zena's striptease with a puppet of a devil. While his head is perched loftily on her shoulder and a cape hides the apparatus, the devil's arm (actually Susan's) undoes Zena's brassiere. Ludlam's ingenious conception for this stage business was inspired by an antique photograph of a French stripper with a puppet affixed to her shoulder.

Ludlam's star turn entailed perhaps his greatest feat of slapstick acrobatics yet. After Buddy forces Phil out onto a ledge and closes the window, Ludlam proceeded to perform a pantomime worthy of the Silver Screen's great comic, Harold Lloyd. As

Buddy and Nadine carry on a boisterous argument in front of the window, Ludlam's muted gestures become increasingly frantic, until he falls off the ledge and scrambles back. Ludlam's wig is ultimately removed by a pigeon, exposing his bald pate.

The farcical aspects of *Secret Lives of the Sexists* may have been what made the play such a hit with the public, even as they may have been what prevented the mainstream critics from appreciating the work's more serious overtones, which the "Downtown" critics apprehended. Indeed, as Steven Samuels confirmed, "One of the reasons for the major critics' complaints was the fact that, in some ways, it was their lives that were being skewered." Despite what the record allows, *Secret Lives* remains one of Ludlam's stronger plays that deserved to be the hit that it was.

During the play's extensive run, backstage life had become more sober for the company, both literally and figuratively. On March 3, or a month after the show opened, Quinton sought outside help and finally gave up alcohol. This followed nearly a year of his more halfhearted attempts to quit drinking. Susan recalled times during this period when Quinton would take antabuse, and other times when he deliberately refrained — in effect, planning to go on a bender. When Quinton quit for good, Ludlam stopped drinking as well. And in a matter of months, Ludlam would also relinquish marijuana, which had always been his intoxicant of choice. Though alcohol had not been the problem for Ludlam it was for Quinton, he quit to support his lover on the road to recovery.

Ludlam did not have to turn to any outside network for support, however. He told Samuels that he had an "iron will," and this "demonstrated just how firm he could be in disciplining himself. He was awfully successful, but nothing really changed about him: He was every bit as paranoid as he had been before he stopped drinking and smoking." Whenever he left his apartment, for instance, Ludlam would return a number of times to confirm the door was locked, driving friends crazy as they waited for him by the elevator.

Though there were no other outward signs of change in Ludlam, he definitely became even more productive than he had been before. One could argue that the unprecedented success the Ridiculous would enjoy in the coming years was due in part to his newfound sobriety. It was also due to the improved relationship with Quinton that accompanied the sobriety, an improvement that was instantly apparent to everyone who knew them — first and foremost because they no longer fought with each other in public.

As Richard Hennessy observed:

> Once they sorted out their problems, it was really amazing. I mean, I've never
> seen two people have such a positive effect on each other. I think Everett
> ultimately gave Charles a great deal of strength, and the other way around:
> Their relationship gave Charles great independence. I think he had been very
> vulnerable before that. As I watched Everett develop into a wonderful actor
> over the years, right in front of my eyes, I also saw how this made Charles
> stronger. It was extraordinary. They helped each other because they cured each
> other of each other's bad habits.

But even after Quinton stopped drinking, there was one thing he would not give up —
his love of dancing at bars and discos into the early hours of the morning. Ludlam was
less enamored of this nocturnal activity. One night, he finally refused to accompany
Quinton, saying, "I only dance when I'm paid to." At first, it was difficult for Quinton
to go off on his own — the dependency was still that pronounced. In fact, Quinton's
insecurity prevailed for quite some time, until he eventually recognized that his bond
with Ludlam had truly become permanent.

Ludlam told him: "Everything is fine — just keep on doing what you're doing," reassuring Quinton that he would always be there for him. They had been through it all by
then, and had finally reached that plateau many couples strive for, but few achieve. As
Quinton described that magical moment for himself in their relationship, it was more a
matter of realizing that they had been there all along for each other, and of accepting
that they would continue on together, no matter what was to come.

RIDICULOUS DIVA

It's not a certain society that seems ridiculous to me, it's mankind.
— Eugène Ionesco

Great artists are acknowledged but never forgiven.
— Charles Ludlam, *Galas*

In his March 1982 "Artistic Statement," written for fund-raising purposes, Ludlam codified his approach to playwriting while making certain concessions to both "pluralism" and the "avant-garde," phrases that appealed at the time to the grant-bestowing organizations to which he was applying. After congratulating himself for playing "to an ever-broadening audience" in the four years since he had taken up residence at One Sheridan Square, he wrote:

> During our years of work as parodists, we found new expressive possibilities in theatrical conventions considered oppressive by others. Plots of multiple complexity have become our specialty. The abstract element in farce makes it the most modern dramatic medium. Its ability to reflect on the human condition is seemingly limitless. But farce requires specialists. Strong ensemble acting is the real secret to its success. In the Ridiculous Theatrical Company, a collision of acting styles is an energizing factor, implying by its very diversity an affirmation of the pluralistic society.
>
> The immediacy of comedy and its audience rapport has served as a touchstone for our wildest experiments. We plan for the future to produce a series of modernist farces which will prove to be both avant-garde and popular.

By referring to "a collision of acting styles" as "an energizing factor," Ludlam was shrewdly attempting to turn a common criticism of the company into an asset. While his own acting was consistently praised by critics, the other players tended to be dismissed — when they were not deplored. However, his emphasis in the proposal on "ensemble acting" better described where the company had been than where it was headed. The departures of both Lola Pashalinski and John Brockmeyer two years earlier signaled a basic change in the dynamic of the Ridiculous — as did the costarring role that Everett Quinton was assuming both in the company and in Ludlam's life. Once Quinton stopped drinking and their relationship began to stabilize, Ludlam — his Pygmalion — rewarded him by making him a star.

The decision to go "on the wagon" contributed even more to the dissolution of the familial feeling that had always woven and smoothed the fabric of the group. Once they stopped drinking, Ludlam and Quinton ceased socializing with the other cast members after each performance. By the time of *Secret Lives of the Sexists*, instead of rushing to remove their makeup and departing together as they had in the past, the actors now lingered backstage before going their separate ways.

The sense of being a family, which had held the company together through the adventurous and uncertain 1970s, would continue to erode. *Secret Lives* would be Georg Osterman's last play with Ludlam after a decade with the Ridiculous. By the time of *Reverse Psychology*, Bill Vehr, a cofounder of the company, had already become noticeably aloof; after *Secret Lives*, he too would not appear in Ludlam's next offering.

Everyone, including Ludlam, accepted the reason Vehr gave for his withdrawal: He was breaking up with his lover, and did not want Shorty to be able to track him down at the theater. Shorty's fierce heroin addiction had finally become too much even for the even-tempered Vehr, who was beginning to fear his life might be in jeopardy. When Vehr moved to Brooklyn, Shorty was told he had returned to Ohio to live with his parents. Shorty showed up at the theater a number of times anyway, hoping to find him there.

Even what remained of the core company — Ludlam, Quinton, and Black-Eyed Susan — was breaking down. In complaining to Steven Samuels about Susan's performance in *Love's Tangled Web*, Ludlam had tried to justify his giving her smaller parts in recent plays so that Everett might play larger ones. Arguably, Susan had been the second biggest star of the company, consistently receiving the best notices after Ludlam himself. But now her roles were increasingly diminishing — only to disappear by the time of *The Mystery of Irma Vep* in 1984, which Ludlam would write for himself and Quinton alone. (The only previous two-person show by Ludlam, *The Ventriloquist's Wife*, had been written for himself and Susan.) As Samuels noticed, a somewhat peculiar situation existed at the Ridiculous, since the men as much as the women were in competition for the "great female roles."

According to Samuels,

> It was around this time that Everett began to sense his own potential, his own
> power as an actor, and his fierce competitiveness with Charles began to emerge.
> And it's about this time that Charles begins to make Everett a star. That was

certainly his intention in creating Solange for Everett in *Exquisite Torture*, which becomes the next show on the agenda. Everett has a major role in drag, and Susan was relegated to a less substantial role.

Although everyone knew Ludlam was deeply in love with Quinton and recognized talents in him that were unapparent to others, the company was wary of Ludlam's attempts to turn him into a real actor. But Ludlam cultivated those talents with the kind of patience that only a lover could lavish.

Once Pashalinski and Brockmeyer were out of the picture, Quinton felt he had the space he needed in which to flourish. Also emerging were the newcomers to the company, such as Deborah Petti and Ed McGowan, who struck others as protégés of Quinton rather than of Ludlam. Quinton was also starting to grow in other respects — steeping himself in Trollope, for instance, and otherwise trying to improve himself intellectually. Within a couple of years, he would even attempt to write a play of his own.

Exquisite Torture, the would-be breakthrough vehicle for Quinton as a performer, underwent a drawn-out creative process. Ludlam based the play on Salvador Dalí's obscure, surrealistic novel *Hidden Faces* (1944); the 1932 Garbo vehicle, *As You Desire Me*; and to a lesser degree on *Nerone*, Boito's rarely performed opera about Nero. It was written under a great deal of pressure since once again the company was financially troubled, and Ludlam needed another commercial success.

Ludlam began working on the script while *Secret Lives of the Sexists* was still on the boards at Sheridan Square. The unusual terminology of the new play's subtitle, "A Romantic Ecstasy," indicates that he wanted to depart from the strictures of farce, and that he was groping for a new form. In a press release for the play, Ludlam would describe *Exquisite Torture* as his "first foray into 'post-structuralism,' a theater of pure emotion"; he would define "an ecstasy" as "a new genre, a vehicle for overly emotional acting."

According to Samuels, "Charles was still following hard upon the notion of creating an incomprehensible plot: something that seemed to make sense minute-to-minute, but ultimately just evaporated in your hands." It was part of his continuing experiment with theatrical form, his ambition to tap into the great dramatic tradition and yet create something totally original, an "evanescent narrative." His experimentation had really begun with his first few plays and his so-called "epic" works: *Big Hotel*, *Conquest of the Universe*, and *Grand Tarot*. By *Utopia, Incorporated*, he operated from the idea that there

were certain paradigmatic plots which were so well known that they could be fragmented and used to create a new, self-disintegrating dramatic form. As Ludlam would
further explain in a 1983 grant proposal, "In *Exquisite Torture*, we sought to show that,
contrary to common opinions in experimental theatrical circles, narrative is not the
unmodern thing about the drama; but rather, modern playwrights have failed to
modernize their plots, as 20th-century composers and painters have modernized the use
of their basic materials." As a result, the play reads — for better or for worse — as a
kind of Cubist exercise in narrative.

Had Ludlam failed to identify Dalí's *Hidden Faces* as his primary source, probably no
one would have made the connection. Beyond the central relationship of Dalí's Count
Grandsailles and Solange de Cleda, whose love for each other transcends time and
space, very little of *Hidden Faces* appears in *Exquisite Torture*, which does indeed evapo-
rate even as it unfolds. And apart from the name Neroni, there is even less of Boito's
opera in Ludlam's play.

As modified by Ludlam, Dalí's French nobleman becomes the Italian Count Neroni, "the
last of the Neros," who is in the throes of "a terrible cash flow crisis." Solange de Cleda
becomes Solange de Choisy, and Ludlam provides a twist to the plot straight out of
Anastasia. When the play opens, Solange is discovered by her brother Frank, having just
performed her nightclub act under the name Venus Veronica. She had disappeared seven
years before, which strikes even this Solange — if Solange she be — as peculiar. "This is
a strange coincidence," she says. "Seven years ago I became the victim of amnesia."

Frank finally persuades Solange to return to Count Neroni. Neroni's scheming "nanny,"
Toinette, tries to persuade him that this Solange is an impostor. But he claims to
love her whether she's the authentic Solange or not. His financial straits are such, however, that before he and Solange can be truly reunited, he must pursue his fortune in
Southern California. In the meantime, he has rented his Italian villa to Barbara Bendix,
a wealthy American, and Rhea, her lascivious daughter. Disguised as a man, Solange
will stay behind to look after things.

The wayward plot quickly veers in many directions, entailing dream sequences, surrealistic occurrences, and preposterous developments. A waiter appears at a restaurant with
a birdcage on his head, and Frank arrives at the villa with a leather s&m mask covering
his face. Though Frank has come to visit Neroni, he meets Barbara instead. She
explains she "just stepped out of the bath" and proceeds to open her robe, exposing her

naked body. When Frank says he's leaving after this, their first meeting — which consumed all of a minute — Barbara responds:

> **Barbara:** If you ever come back, I'll marry you.
> **Frank:** That's damned civil of you. But I couldn't let you. You've never seen my face.
> **Barbara:** I don't need to. I love you for your personality.
> **Frank:** Well, since you're being such a sport about it, I'll marry you too.

In a dream sequence, Neroni finds himself in the midst of a classic actor's nightmare. "I'm onstage but I'm in costume for the wrong play, and I don't know any of the lines," he says upon discovering himself in California in the second scene of Act II. Frank tells the flustered Neroni that he had been dreaming but now he is awake. "This is real life, where there's no script and we make it up as we go along," says Frank. "I have a horror of improvisation. I don't even like to be in the same room with one," replies Neroni.

Frank dies in this sequence, only to reappear visiting Solange in the hospital. After learning that Neroni — who was impersonating Frank — agreed to marry Barbara, Solange shoots herself. Blind and on her deathbed, she mistakes Frank for Neroni and promptly dies herself. But even more inexplicably, she miraculously delivers a final song ("An illusory thing is love...").

Exquisite Torture is, in other words, every bit as incomprehensible and "evanescent" as Ludlam set out for it to be. Though successful with its audience during a three-month preview period, the play was poorly received when it opened to the critics in mid-October. Whether Ludlam acknowledged it or not, his problems with *Exquisite Torture* continued the struggle he had with creating the play in the first place.

According to Samuels, "The evolution of Everett's performance as Solange was slow, and the rehearsals were not easy. But the rehearsals for that show were torture because the script was completely unwritten. I got most of my [bit] parts literally two days before it opened." *Exquisite Torture* was the first show Samuels was in, and he had a "full dose of the rehearsal process, which was primarily listening to Charles talk about his birds and his fish and his plants, and what he had for breakfast and what he had for lunch. That could occupy two hours every day, which was absolutely mind-numbing."

Ludlam worked painstakingly with Quinton, whose transformation from a secondary to a lead player became something of a trial for those on the sidelines: While the rest of the cast tried to fend off boredom, Ludlam rehearsed Quinton exhaustively.

No one really realized just how extensively Ludlam was also working alone with Quinton. Lola Pashalinski recalled running into them at a bagel shop near Sheridan Square, and they invited her back to the theater to perform a scene from *Exquisite Torture* for her. From time to time she laughed, but sensed that Quinton was taking offense at her response. He became so "self-conscious," according to Pashalinski, that he and Ludlam had to stop and start over. This time, Pashalinski remained stone-faced, though Ludlam was actively trying to elicit her laughter. She left in the midst of what struck her as a "personal fracas" between the two of them. When Pashalinski called Ludlam later that day, Quinton got on the phone to apologize for acting "so crazy."

Late in the rehearsal process, H.M. Koutoukas — who was playing the nanny Toinette — exploded in front of everyone. He pulled off Quinton's wig and shoved it in his face. Then he turned to Ludlam and said, "If you had cast for talent instead of love, you would have never cast Everett." Quinton shot back, "If Charles had cast for talent instead of pity, he would have never cast *you!*"

Quinton and Koutoukas had been fighting with a vengeance during this period. Quinton once informed him, "You can't act!" to which Koutoukas replied, "I am not an actor! I am a force of nature!" Koutoukas made Quinton furious by maintaining an air of calm superiority.

In telling Ludlam that he was sacrificing his art for his lover, Koutoukas was essentially resigning from the show. But there may have been more to his stormy departure than this account suggests. Koutoukas had long been notorious for his inability to learn lines. During the rehearsals for *Exquisite Torture*, an exasperated Ludlam would often take Koutoukas aside to try to help him. Koutoukas's explosion over Quinton might have been his way out of an increasingly untenable situation.

Regarding his confrontation with Koutoukas, Quinton later explained that he was anxious about playing Solange, his most important role so far. "We were just these two egos acting like assholes," said Quinton about his problems with Koutoukas. "But it was a fluke. Because during *Exquisite Torture* I had prided myself on being a 'good boy' who was working hard and who was not drinking."

Ludlam had to scramble to replace Koutoukas at the last minute. With less than a week to rehearse, Eureka agreed to take on the part. When she showed up at the theater, she recalled,

> Everett grabbed me and said, "Here's your costume." I had no idea what I was doing or playing, but Everett was very worried that I wouldn't fit into Harry's costume, which was this hideous, black schmata or smock. But fortunately, I did fit into it, and that was all Everett cared about.

> Then Charles thrust a script at me, and we walked through part of it. But Toinette is in lots of scenes, and I never got through the whole show with the cast that night. Charles just sent me on my merry way to learn the script.

When Eureka showed up to rehearse only three days before the first public performance, Ludlam told her he was adding a scene for the two of them. Offhandedly, he assured her it would not be any problem, since he had adapted a scene from Shakespeare's *Coriolanus* involving the title character and his mother, Volumina. Ludlam was transposing them into Nero and his mother Agrippina. As if it were an afterthought, he mentioned that they would perform the scene in pig Latin — "We'll just improvise it," he added. They continued to work on their fractured dialogue for the first few weeks of previews. "It was different every night," according to Eureka, "before it settled into something." One night, Ludlam inadvertently stepped on the end of a long scarf trailing behind Eureka and almost choked her as she was making her grand exit as Agrippina. The misstep went over so well that he decided to keep it. "It became this bit that got bigger and bigger and bigger," said Eureka. "It was like everything else: It happened accidentally and then we just kept on doing it."

The free-spirited assembly of *Exquisite Torture* was a throwback to the earliest productions of the Ridiculous. But no matter how "off-the-wall" the play struck the audience — particularly after the critics declared it incomprehensible — those involved with the production sensed that it primarily concerned Ludlam's feelings towards Quinton and marked a shift in their relationship.

In terms of pairing Ludlam with Quinton as stars and as lovers, *Exquisite Torture* became the prototype for *Irma Vep*. The major theme of love transcending time and space and loss is exactly the same in both works. Then, too, *Exquisite Torture* and *Irma Vep* were both in a sense devised to make Quinton a star.

Though she found the play impossible to understand, Eureka did perceive that

"*Exquisite Torture* was all about Charles's obsession with Everett, and their relationship." Samuels noticed that "Charles had written a self-effacing part for himself, as opposed to that for Everett. Neroni was very low-energy: a totally different mode for Charles." In his role as director, Ludlam urged his cast into "languid" and "mysterious" performances. But unfortunately, the languor swept across the footlights into the audience as well.

Since cash flow was as much a problem for Ludlam as for Count Neroni, there were only three performances of *Exquisite Torture* each week during previews: one on Fridays and two on Saturdays. This schedule was intended to maximize the audience and to minimize the workload for the actors, who were not being paid. Though *Reverse Psychology* and *Secret Lives of the Sexists* had both been hits, the company was still facing a longtime deficit. As if sensing that the press would make fewer concessions — or more demands — than loyal fans had during previews, Ludlam delayed the opening from August until the second week in October. Once the reviewers pronounced it an inferior Ludlam work (even Mel Gussow called it "a trifle" on WQXR Radio), the run petered out.

"I don't always have the same level of approval from the audience and the critics," Ludlam once claimed. "But for me it is always the same problem. . . . What I do is create what *I* want and then let them come and judge me. The play must be what *I* want it to be, because I can't figure out how to make it what they want."

It is significant that the company's following was by now sizable enough to keep *Exquisite Torture* running as long as it did, albeit with only three shows per week. Samuels had begun to tap the company's regular fans by putting together a list and mailing them announcements of new shows. But Ludlam dismissed the idea he once had of making the Ridiculous a subscription-based theater company. He could never accommodate the constraints a subscription company entailed: announcing seasons in advance, having to close a successful play in order to bring in the next one scheduled, schmoozing with fans to help build an endowment for the company. Ludlam always had an abundance of ideas, but he could never be committed to the sequence in which they might be realized. No matter how streamlined the operation might become, the Ludlam style of theater had to remain spontaneous: subject to artistic inspiration and responsive to the needs of the moment.

Though it is not likely to prove more successful with posterity than in Ludlam's lifetime, *Exquisite Torture* is historically important in at least two respects: first, as the forerunner of *The Mystery of Irma Vep*, one of Ludlam's inarguable masterpieces and far and away his greatest crowd-pleaser; second, as the first Ridiculous production to be videotaped, paving the way for each subsequent show to be recorded as well.

Samuels had long been after Ludlam to capture his productions on video. At first, Ludlam was adamantly opposed to the idea. He was beginning to view his plays as a "treasure trove" of royalties for retirement — an annuity that circulated tapes would undermine. He relented only after Samuels explained to him that he could take the tapes home and guard them against any pirating.

Ludlam would eventually adopt video as a tool in the creative process — viewing tapes made during previews and then reworking productions before they opened. He even considered using video as a device for performance tune-ups of the other actors, with permanent monitors installed so he could watch what was happening onstage while he was in his dressing room. But he remained terribly ambivalent about the videos that were made. Beginning with *Exquisite Torture*, the early ones were shot with equipment Samuels had purchased for videotaping his newborn son. They were extremely primitive affairs, usually recorded from the lighting booth by whoever was running the sound or lights.

In the coming years, the Library of the Performing Arts at Lincoln Center would tape *Galas* and *The Mystery of Irma Vep*, and the Ridiculous itself would hire a professional to tape Ludlam's last show, *The Artificial Jungle*. Ludlam was eventually grateful that the tapes existed. Yet they always failed to capture the intimacy and immediacy of live performance. Like film, video was simply antithetical to the ephemeral moment — the combination of body, breath, and spectacle that comprises theater in general and Ludlam's theater in particular.

പ

For more than a decade, Ludlam had identified himself with Molière, the seventeenth century genius of French comic drama who — like Ludlam — had performed in his own repertory company. Having always intended to write a play specifically based on Molière's work, Ludlam now found his perfect inspiration in *Le Bourgeois Gentilhomme*, Molière's classic satire about a bourgeois determined to make himself into a gentleman. In Ludlam's brilliant variation, *Le Bourgeois Avant-Garde*, the protagonist, Rufus Foufas, is obsessed not with becoming a gentleman but with becoming "avant-garde." Due perhaps to the intensity with which he felt a connection to his great satirical forebear,

Ludlam created a play that is in many respects the most consummate or archetypal in the Ridiculous canon. It was also the first of three plays that marked an unprecedented string of hits for the company.

Le Bourgeois Avant-Garde was Ludlam's zeitgeist response to the art boom that had transformed New York's former manufacturing district of Soho and had begun to sweep through the East Village — as well as to the Yuppie phenomenon that was fueling this inflationary development. Though the play is an assault on all the arts as well as the art "scene" in general, it is also a vendetta against the concommitant need for labels to explain art. Labels were reductive, Ludlam believed, confining the artistic exchange to the viewers' preconceptions.

On a more personal level, *Le Bourgeois* represents Ludlam's ultimate revenge against his early sponsor Henry Geldzahler as well as Andy Warhol. His target was also the more shallow aspects of the fashionable art world they catered to — a world to which some mistakenly assigned Ludlam. He was satirizing the elitism he participated in when he powwowed a decade before with Christopher Scott and Geldzahler. There is no mistaking the implied gist of the play: that Ludlam is a real artist, superior to all he is mocking.

Ludlam despised the so-called avant-garde so vehemently because he felt that most of those parading under its banner were frauds. At best, they were merely recapitulating experiments that had already been tried by others. Ludlam, of course, viewed himself as being *truly* avant-garde. According to Samuels, who was fast becoming a principal intellectual ally, Ludlam considered himself the most advanced artist of his time as well as "the last modernist." Though he owed a certain debt to the absurdists, Ludlam also saw how they had painted themselves into an absurdly barren corner. He mostly ranted and raved against Beckett. But in an unguarded moment, he told Samuels that he thought Beckett's work was "truly phenomenal." The trouble was Beckett left absolutely no room for development, so Ludlam had "to go screaming in another direction."

For their shared vision of an inverted world — as well as their mutual interest in abandoned vaudeville techniques for expressing it — Ludlam perhaps had more in common with Eugène Ionesco, father of the Theater of the Absurd. Like Ludlam, Ionesco was leery of labels: He preferred "derision" to "absurd" — which comes much closer to describing Ludlam's own theatrical ethos as well. Ionesco could have been speaking for Ludlam when he said, "It's not a certain society that seems *ridiculous* to me, it's mankind."

Unlike the majority of his contemporaries who stressed their own originality, Ludlam insisted that he was forging something new by working with what had come before him, and lending it his own special imprint. He was ferociously competitive and considered his only real peers to be long dead. He could be quite contemptuous of his contemporary colleagues, and quite outspoken when he discussed the work of Robert Wilson, Joe Chaikin, and a good deal of what Ellen Stewart presented. (According to Edgardo Franceschi, Wilson once came backstage after a show and said to Ludlam, "You're the best," to which Ludlam replied, "I know.") Though Ludlam was intrigued by the startling, in-your-face work of the Wooster Group — some of whose members were among his friends — there were other associates in the theatrical community for whose work he had little or no respect. He was close to Richard Foreman and admired his highly stylized and idiosyncratic pieces. But he also came to feel that Foreman employed the same bag of tricks for every production, evincing no growth or change. Ludlam firmly believed that everything *he* did was new and different from anything he had done before.

What most infuriated Ludlam, however, was being lumped together or even compared with any other theater practitioners, when he considered his own work to be unique. Indeed, Ludlam was far more *sui generis* than the mainstream allowed. In only a few years, he would see *Vampire Lesbians of Sodom*, an Off-Broadway drag show by Charles Busch, whom many would compare to Ludlam. Ludlam returned from the performance enraged, griping that superficial elements of his work had indeed been stolen, but without any of their substance. Work like Busch's — and the wide array of cabaret bad-boy drag that would come to characterize much of Downtown theater — possessed an easy camp and glitter that lacked the more serious intentions underlying those ingredients when employed by Ludlam.

In 1983, Ludlam set out to use *Le Bourgeois* as an attack on a style of theater that others compared with his, since he believed that such comparisons both degraded what he had to offer and usurped the position that was rightfully his. As he explained in a press release, he wanted the play "to describe what happens when the avant-garde becomes more conservative than its audience," and to criticize "the kind of work that masquerades as avant-garde but is, in reality, merely confusing." Ludlam firmly believed he was performing "a public service" with *Le Bourgeois*, and had no qualms about saying so. He was educating the public by "showing up the frauds for what they were." He was also venting his outrage at the corruption of his style by others and attempting to ensure that his works would be seen on an aesthetic level above the rest.

On the other hand, anyone seeing *Le Bourgeois* could simply delight in its extravagant satire and high humor, to the exclusion of Ludlam's more high-minded aims. As with all of Ludlam's work, this division of aesthetic goals embodies a conundrum: Serious intentions are leavened — if not disguised — by the overriding conceit of the Ridiculous, which begins with inversions, ends in paradox, and, in the process, mocks all that it surveys, including the Ridiculous itself. The battle Ludlam waged throughout his life to make serious what was ridiculous — and vice versa — continues after his death. And given the inherent contradictions, even when his work is admired, it is usually not for the right reasons.

ಏ

By the time Ludlam started working on *Le Bourgeois*, he was trying to streamline his life. Much of the play was dictated to Samuels during afternoon sessions at the Morton Street apartment. Ludlam had set aside his mornings to be undisturbed. He would begin his day with internal reveries and by taking ritualistic care of chores. He would water the plants, feed his considerable aviary, and change the water in the fish tanks, which entailed an elaborate process of natural aeration. Ludlam was trying to create new strains of tropical fish and kept extensive breeding records. He was obsessive about surrounding himself with life, and the tiny apartment was just bursting with signs of it. (Ludlam once said that if the space had been large enough, he would have raised horses on Morton Street.) Any visitor was instantly impressed and amazed by the exotic environment.

Directly after visiting Ludlam and Quinton on March 30, 1982 (less than a year before work began on *Le Bourgeois*), Ludlam's onetime lover Wally Gorell made a journal entry while waiting for a subway train to meet Christopher Scott uptown:

> Everett declined the pears I brought by saying he thought of pears as horse food. He brought out oranges and talked of the trend toward lots of fabric and away from jewels. He says he's going to wear a black lamé gown with hundreds of yards of material cinched under a cummerbund with tails. Charles is breeding *Beta splendens* [Siamese fighting fish] in dozens of tanks around the living room. A gardenia in bloom scents the air. Charles arrives home with purple film cans and then runs out to score [some marijuana] before he has to splice them all together onto a single reel for tonight's showing [of *The Sorrows of Dolores*] at Jacob Burchardt's.

Ludlam dictated much of *Le Bourgeois* in this environment, with Samuels at the typewriter. (They also worked in the low-ceilinged cubbyhole of an office in the rear of the basement theater.) Occasionally Ludlam would rant at Quinton when he insisted on watching his favorite soap or listening to an opera.

Samuels had come to appreciate that although Ludlam was avid for inspiration from the pantheon of world literature, contemporary influence terrified him. "It was critical that I develop no response to anything he said when he was dictating, unless it was to praise him," recalled Samuels. If he had a suggestion to make, Samuels had to find an indirect way of slipping it into conversation so that the change would become Ludlam's *own* idea.

By any account, Ludlam was accustomed to taking the work of others and reconfiguring it. The basic outline of *Le Bourgeois Avant-Garde* is appropriated wholesale from the Molière play. But as Ludlam focused on the vacuity of the contemporary art world, his own sensibility made Molière's play relevant more than three hundred years after it was written.

Portrayed by Ludlam, Rufus Foufas, owner of the "Friendly Foufas Food Stores," is a wealthy grocer and an art patron easily preyed upon by artists and sycophants. Among the "artists" eager for Foufas's support are a composer, a choreographer, and Percival Hack, "a major director of the avant-garde" stage. The opening scene establishes the play's satirical look at the contemporary art world and, particularly, its propensity for supplying labels in lieu of substance. In a mode of satiric verbal attack familiar from vaudeville routines, the Composer and the Choreographer hurl epithets at each other:

> CHOREOGRAPHER: Although I think that serial music is just a bit passé. I mean
> it's sort of stuck back there in the muck of Modernism. I consider
> myself to be much more advanced. I am a Postmodern.
>
> COMPOSER: You mean you are a Futurist?
>
> CHOREOGRAPHER: No, the future was over by the early thirties.
>
> COMPOSER: Well I am a *Post*postmodernist.
>
> CHOREOGRAPHER: And what may I ask is that?
>
> COMPOSER: A Neomodernist.
>
> CHOREOGRAPHER: (*Indignantly*) Hurmph!
>
> COMPOSER: When Postmodernism died, a Modernist revival ensued.
> (*Triumphantly*) And we're right back where we started!
>
> CHOREOGRAPHER: How pretentious! You've done nothing but revive Futurism.
>
> COMPOSER: You ass! The future cannot be revived until it has been lived, and
> when it has been lived it is no longer the future!

CHOREOGRAPHER: Do you know what I think? I think you're nothing but a
    lapsed Surrealist posing as a Postmodernist.

COMPOSER: And I think you're a Constructivist posing as an Expressionist.

CHOREOGRAPHER: Dadaist!

COMPOSER: Fauve!

CHOREOGRAPHER: Cubist!

COMPOSER: Surrealist!

CHOREOGRAPHER: Pop artist!

COMPOSER: Op artist!

CHOREOGRAPHER: Conceptualist!

COMPOSER: Realist!

CHOREOGRAPHER: (*Reeling as if from a blow*) Ouch! (*Then winding up and
    striking back*) Minimalist!

COMPOSER: (*Doubling over as if he had received a low blow*) Ooof! Wait a minute.
    I am not ashamed to admit that my work has a certain affinity to
    Minimalism.

CHOREOGRAPHER: Particularly that one great affinity. Your work is definitely
    (*Accentuating each syllable of the word*) Minimal.

While recognizing that their patron Mr. Foufas is a "man ravenous for art" and "starved for culture," the Composer and the Choreographer complain that he's also a cultural moron who doesn't understand their work. ("And even when he does like something it's always for the wrong reason," says the Composer, echoing exactly what Ludlam thought about his own critics.) But as Percival Hack responds, "Vulgar and ignorant though [Foufas] may be, his applause has cash value far greater than all the aesthetes with their refined compliments and subtle appreciation who are too damned cheap to put their money where their mouths are." And as the Choreographer acknowledges, "anything is better than teaching."

The pandering Hack introduces Foufas to both Maia Panzaroff (pronounced "My-a Pants-are-off"), the "great Polish avant-garde actress," and Moderna 83 (his up-to-the-minute name incorporates the year in which the play premiered). Moderna is "one of the best graffiti artists working today in the Independent line," Hack explains. (By 1983, graffiti artist Keith Haring was highly fashionable and spawned many imitators.) According to Hack, Moderna "has gone beyond art with his invention of Artex . . . a convenient art-substitute. It is art without the usual fuss and bother. Art without anguish."

Moderna's garbled language, called "Newspeak," is itself a form of verbal graffiti. As

Hack defines it, Newspeak "is composed entirely of monosyllables which, while having no lexical meaning, convey inner emotional states." In the hilarious scene when they first meet, Hack interprets Moderna's remarks for Foufas. A long series of "Doy doy doy doy doy doy doy doy doy doy doy doy. Doy doy doy doy doy . . . [etc.]" is translated to mean, "He likes your shoes." But later, when Moderna says more tersely, "Doy doy," Hack explains, "He says that he could tell the moment he met you that you were a man of rare intelligence and understanding. That you were not only a great patron, but one of those rare spirits who are utterly ahead of their time. A superb judge of creative work and a harbinger of a new age of cultural achievement!"

Foufas is far more excited about finally meeting Panzaroff, given her international "avant-garde" reputation. He's been wooing the Polish actress from afar, through Hack. She's going to attend a soiree that Foufas is holding that evening in her honor. In hopes of seducing Maia, he sends his wife off to dinner at Beefsteak Charlie's. But suspecting foul play, Mrs. Foufas has the maid, Violet, spy on her husband's shenanigans.

Foufas is unaware that a diamond ring he had bought for Panzaroff was presented to her by Hack, as if it were a token of his *own* esteem. Now that Foufas is finally going to meet her, the devious Hack warns him against mentioning the ring.

> HACK: Among the avant-garde any mention of money is considered commercial and — how shall I say — vulgar.
> MR. FOUFAS: Is that so?
> HACK: When you see her, the way to really impress her would be to pretend that you didn't give it to her.
> MR. FOUFAS: Is that how the avant-garde do it?
> HACK: Yes. Pretend you think it's nothing. You see, the avant-garde scorn money.
> MR. FOUFAS: If that's what the avant-garde do, I'll do it too!

In keeping with the original Molière, Mrs. Foufas sees through the sycophancy her husband has fostered, but she cannot overcome his gullibility. The plot comes to center on the destiny of their daughter Prue, who wants to marry Newton Entwhistle. "She loves him and he has a good steady job at the bank," says Mrs. Foufas, who is in favor of the marriage. But Foufas won't hear of it. "I don't want our daughter making the same mistake we made," he says. "She should practice free love, have children out of wedlock by any number of different men, preferably famous artists and, like Isadora Duncan, write her memoirs and die in a fatal automobile accident!" He wants her to marry Moderna 83 and "live a bohemian life."

Also, as in Molière, it's Violet, the maid, who conceives of a scheme for Newton
Entwhistle to trick Foufas, thereby securing his unwitting approval to marry Prue.

> VIOLET: Tell him you're avant-garde.
> NEWTON: Well I don't know what avant-garde is.
> VIOLET: From what I gather, neither does anyone else.
> NEWTON: How do I prove I'm it?
> VIOLET: As far as I can see, anything can be avant-garde as long as it doesn't
> make any sense and goes against the natural way of doing things.

Newton is transformed into "Nicky Newfangle," whom Hack proclaims "the founder
and leading theorist of the post-avant-garde...a kind of antimovement. He synthesized
subsurrealism and unsound structuralism and came out with repressed expression-
ism.... And what's more, he wants to confer upon you the honor of membership in
the avant-derrière movement! This is a society of vanguard artists. He wants to see
you at once and hold the investiture ceremony immediately." Similar to Moderna 83's
"Doy doys," Newfangle's speech is comprised of sound effects, which Violet interprets
for Foufas. ("Barks like a dog; makes sounds of footsteps in a corridor; creaking hinge;
closing door; a woman's scream," reads the first of Newfangle's "lines" in the script.
"Makes sound of: cough; fart; hiccup; belch; sigh," reads another.)

Ludlam reserved his most scathing satire for the induction ceremony of the "avant-
derrière" movement. Everyone is now wearing a "fake ass" attached to the front of his
or her pelvis, and Foufas is instructed to kiss all of these prosthetic buttocks. Next he
"must eat the words avant-garde," actually licorice letters flown in on a string. After
chewing for a long time, he claims, "It's a little hard to swallow." But in order to remain
a member in good standing of the movement, he's told he "must always eat in the avant-
derrière manner.... Members of the avant-derrière do not consume food through their
mouths like the ordinary bourgeois herd!" They eat by means of "nutrient enemas."

When Mrs. Foufas asks what avant-garde actually means, Panzaroff explains that it's
"French for bullshit." Then the play closes as it opened, with the Choreographer and the
Composer exchanging a list of new art genres or labels, most of which are illogical, self-
canceling puns. These include "unimpressionablism," "abstract rejectivism," "anarcho-
formalism," "postpremodernism," "prepostmodernism," "lethargism," and "inhibitionism."

Though played to elicit the abundant laughter it received, *Le Bourgeois Avant-Garde* is
one of Ludlam's most earnest and heartfelt works. The play shoulders past its humor to

become the playwright's devastating response to having suffered for years the public's misapprehension of his work. Ludlam understood that the only way to achieve mainstream success in a media-driven culture was by conforming to its need to classify and assimilate: He could do no more than gesture to his ambitions in a two-sentence description compatible with brief listings in weekly entertainment guides. This was yet another reason for resisting such success. But it didn't prevent him from resenting the situation and then biting back.

Le Bourgeois's instant success belied the difficulties Ludlam experienced in crafting it. Once he had assembled his cast and realized that nothing was going right, Ludlam took the rare step of canceling rehearsals for a few weeks to rewrite the play extensively without his cast's participation. When rehearsals resumed, he presented everyone with a completed script, which was also unusual for Ludlam, if not unprecedented. The first act had been virtually eliminated, and the characters significantly changed.

Having withstood as much humiliation as he could from his abrasive director, Steven Samuels — who felt he was playing the Composer more fervently than Ludlam wanted — quit the play during the hiatus. Still in hiding from Shorty, Bill Vehr now felt less threatened about being discovered, and agreed to take over Samuels's role.

Samuels found it even harder to tell Ludlam that there were a couple of other performers he considered handicaps to the production. Since Samuels believed Ludlam was oblivious to their inadequacies, he felt compelled to bring his concerns to Ludlam's attention. He was shocked to discover that Ludlam had already identified these problems. While conceding that the actors might harm the production, Ludlam explained that there was simply nothing he could do: He just "loved them" — as people if not as actors — and found it impossible to replace them. This eye-opening incident gave Samuels new insight into the way Ludlam operated. "Nothing escaped that man, but nothing," he would declare years later. Ludlam was motivated at least as much by his personal relationships as by aesthetic considerations. For Ludlam, his life and its friendships were inseparable from his art.

Though Susan was not among those Samuels cited as a liability, she sulked and complained a lot about her relatively small part as Maia Panzaroff. Ludlam, in turn, grumbled about her whining. He told Samuels that he didn't really understand why she was so upset, since "she had the classic second act star's entrance." The character's thickly exaggerated Polish accent and overly earnest airs were custom-made for Susan, and she would come to make the most of the role during the show's long run. Whether she knew it consciously or not, Susan was actually responding to the ongoing transference of power to Quinton. While Susan was playing Ludlam's mistress in the play, Quinton was undertaking the noticeably larger part of his wife. Indeed, Quinton received his best notices yet as Mrs. Foufas.

When it opened in mid-April, *Le Bourgeois Avant-Garde* was hailed as "Mr. Ludlam's brightest prank since he assaulted analysands in *Reverse Psychology* three seasons ago" (Frank Rich, the *Times*), "one of his most felicitous theatre 'pieces,'" (Mel Gussow, WQXR Radio), "his most solidly funny writing of the past several years" (Michael Feingold, the *Village Voice*), and "another satirical hit" (Marilyn Stasio, the *New York Post*). Even Don Nelsen (the *Daily News*), who felt that the humor fell off in the second act, acknowledged that the play "does not patronize its audience because it is intelligently conceived and goes after a phoniness that is quite fashionable in our society."

In his rave review, Feingold recognized that Ludlam was "biting every hand that has fed him . . . exactly what a comic artist should be doing." Feingold presciently observed that Ludlam would reach a wider audience with this play than he had in the past: "The big scenes . . . produce that loud, blocklike laughter that tells you an artist is cutting across lines of class and taste." Feingold's forecast would apply even more to the runs of Ludlam's next two plays, *Galas* and *The Mystery of Irma Vep*.

Late in the extensive run of *Le Bourgeois Avant-Garde*, when ticket sales started to sag, the box office received a boost from a feature story on Ludlam in the all-important Sunday "Arts & Leisure" section of *The New York Times*. At last, a bastion of the mainstream press was paying significant respect to the company's lengthy history. After declaring that Ludlam was probably the only person in the history of the American theater to have written, directed, and acted in his own plays with his own company for as long as fifteen years, Sam H. Shirakawa wrote that the company "is gaining both a wide following and critical recognition despite occasional sneers from purists used to the conventions and mannerisms of the commercial stage. While there may be some disagreement at times about the quality of his company's work, there is little argument about Mr. Ludlam's unusual position in the American theater." Adopting false modesty to make an immodest point, Ludlam told Shirakawa, "All I'm doing down here is working within a comic tradition using character types that have been around for centuries. I'm just trying to make them live again in a way that's funny and thought-provoking. If I'm able to do that successfully, then I'm not just somebody in the comic tradition, but somebody who's advancing it."

Though Joseph Ludlam was still alive when this feature appeared in the July 3 edition of the Sunday *Times*, he was in no position to finally take any pride in his son's considerable accomplishments. Having suffered a series of strokes during the last few years, he had become incontinent and incapable of speech. When he became too much for Marjorie to handle and she put him in the hospital, an irate Ludlam accused her of abandoning his father.

For most of Ludlam's life, there appeared to be no love lost between father and son. But as everyone close to Ludlam confirmed, he had learned to let go of long-held resentments and tried to reconcile with Joseph once he realized how ill he was. According to Marjorie, he wept for days when his father finally succumbed to a major embolism and died on December 18, 1983, five months after the article appeared in the *Times*.

Perhaps out of deference to his father, Ludlam attended the funeral without Quinton. Marjorie found it "creepy" when he insisted on spending the night in Joseph's mechanical, hospital bed. This was possibly his way of trying to get closer to his father in death than he ever had been in life. It was only after Joseph's demise that Ludlam began to imply he took after his father rather than his mother, proudly proclaiming that he had derived both his sense of humor and independence from him.

c∕ɔ

Given the long-term success of *Le Bourgeois Avant-Garde,* it is surprising that Ludlam did not try to produce a new script free of the pressure that would eventually be on him. But once again, he procrastinated. Despite his astonishing prolificacy, he seemed to suffer perpetual writer's block, surmounted only when his back was against the stage wall and the curtain about to rise.

More and more, Ludlam spent any free time at home creating his own art: lush pastels and oil paintings of male nudes, religious icons, flowers, and still lifes. More than just a pastime or diversion, painting had become for him a kind of therapy; a way of emptying his mind of current anxieties and pressures. And like both D.H. Lawrence and Winston Churchill before him, Ludlam proved to be a consummate artist in this secondary vocation.

Ticket sales for *Le Bourgeois* continued to be brisk on weekends, but they started to plummet on weeknights, and the play ran longer than the grosses warranted. Although Ludlam *was* becoming more shrewd about the business aspects of running a theater, he insisted that he was performing a "public service" with this play in particular, and needed to continue to convey its message to an ever-wider public. More to the point, he hadn't yet written its successor. But the play he came up with in a matter of weeks — *Galas* — was in many respects the apotheosis of his career; and it made even the success of *Le Bourgeois Avant-Garde* seem paltry in comparison.

The year before, in June of 1982, an Off-Broadway sensation called *Torch Song Trilogy* had transferred to the Great White Way, making its author and star, Harvey Fierstein, something of a household name. With his semi-autobiographical and highly sentimental tale about the trials of being a drag queen, Fierstein was embraced by the mainstream more enthusiastically than any drag performer in decades, and Ludlam naturally resented his rival's capture of the limelight. The success of *Torch Song* prompted Fierstein to collaborate with Jerry Herman on a brassy Broadway musical about drag queens, which was on the verge of opening in the summer of 1983 amid a huge amount of advance publicity. It was called *La Cage aux Folles*.

The glorification of drag queen Fierstein — as well as Ludlam's detestation of his celebrity — may well have played a part in prompting him to write *Galas*. Considering that he had not introduced a new female role for himself since *Camille* a decade before, the timing of *Galas*'s creation suggests that it was more than just coincidence. Though Ludlam is primarily remembered as a "drag" performer, the fact is that *Galas* was only his second major female role. He would play only one other with the Ridiculous, later on in *Salammbô*.

Looking back on the genesis of *Galas*, Ludlam would claim, "I knew I wanted to play a female role, in order to prove that female impersonation could be taken seriously | as art in Western theater." For him, Fierstein's work was neither art nor to be taken seriously; both *Torch Song Trilogy* and *La Cage aux Folles* were merely symptomatic of the emperor's-new-clothes phenomenon so rampant in the art world Ludlam was mocking in *Le Bourgeois Avant-Garde*. Even more germane for Ludlam, both of Fierstein's offerings were specifically about *drag* performers. In his *Galas*, as in his *Camille*, Ludlam's female impersonation was about something else, something that transcended gender-based definitions. But, for the most part, the media failed to appreciate the difference. As Ludlam explained, "Every major comedian in the country does drag. You have to do it. You're not a comedian if you don't. Johnny Carson does it. Abbott and Costello did it. But to play a *role*, comedic or serious, of the opposite sex, that's different. It's more *Oriental*, it's more in the tradition of the Kabuki or the Elizabethan theatre."

ABOVE: Ludlam arriving at the Village Gate for the 1973 Obie Awards. That handsome devil with the dangling cigarette — behind Ludlam — is Robert Beers. Ludlam won his third Obie award for his performance in *Camille*. Photograph © Richard Currie.

TOP LEFT: The program cover for *Stage Blood* featured the play's ensemble, consisting of the Ridiculous troupe's core members (l to r): Bill Vehr, Lola Pashalinski, John Brockmeyer, Jack Mallory, Charles Ludlam, and Black-Eyed Susan. Program courtesy Teriananda.

CENTER LEFT: Designed to accompany Calvin Tomkins' extensive Profile on Ludlam in *The New Yorker*, Edward Koren's caricature of Charles was based on his get-up as Hamlet in *Stage Blood*. Illustration © The New Yorker Collection, 1976, Edward Koren, from Cartoonbank. All rights reserved.

BOTTOM LEFT: This scene from *Stage Blood* — perhaps Ludlam's most underestimated play — features Charles as Carlton Stone Jr. (portraying Hamlet), advising Black-Eyed Susan as Elfie Fey (portraying Ophelia).

BOTTOM RIGHT: A very hirsute Ludlam as Buck Armstrong, in *Hot Ice* (1974). Charles set out to play the part as if he were Puerto Rican. Photograph © Tom Harding.

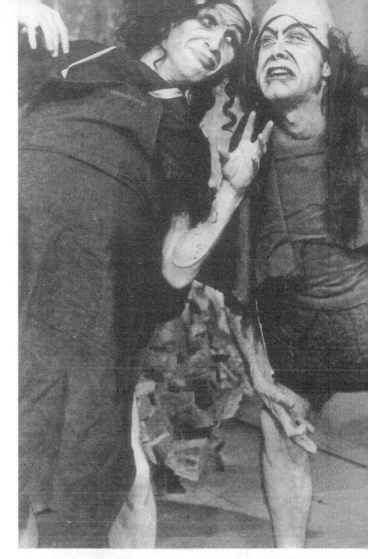

TOP RIGHT: Everett Quinton and Bill Vehr as Nihilumpen in *Der Ring Gott Farblonjet*, with costumes designed by Ludlam. Photograph © Martha Morgan.

BOTTOM LEFT: A backstage photo of Ludlam applying makeup to Robert Reddy, who portrayed another Nihilumpen in *Der Ring Gott Farblonjet* (1977). "It was during the run of *Corn* that Ludlam shrieked one night that he desperately needed some pipe cleaners before going on. 'When I came back with them, Charles said, "I'll put you in my next play for that,"' recalled Reddy. And he did." Photograph © Richard Currie.

BOTTOM RIGHT: A "faaaaaabulous" Stephen Holt, getting ready as a Valkyrie, before a performance of *Der Ring*. "Cathy Smith told me it was a big financial dip that caused the closing this week, but I think it was just because Charles was tired and bored with the whole thing. I don't know. Who can say? The *Ring* certainly had its run. . ." Photograph © Richard Currie.

Top: Photo-booth snapshots of Everett Quinton and Ludlam, taken at the beginning of their relationship. "Although everyone knew Ludlam was deeply in love with Quinton and recognized talents in him that were unapparent to others, the company was wary of Ludlam's attempts to turn him into a real actor." Photographs courtesy Everett Quinton.

Top right: Ludlam himself designed this flyer for his *Anti-Galaxie Nebulae* serial puppet show, performed for children of all ages.

Right: Eliot Hubbard's poster for *The Ventriloquist's Wife* features a demonic-looking Ludlam and his "Walter Ego" towering over the seriously endangered Black-Eyed Susan.

Top left: Georg Osterman (as Melanie) and Everett Quinton (as Moe) in the 1978 revival of *Corn*, which was performed in the company's new home at One Sheridan Square. Photograph © Les Carr.

Top: Ludlam's makeshift costumes for *Utopia, Incorporated* were, in many respects, more creative than the script: (l to r) Ludlam, Bill Vehr, Lola Pashalinski, Adam Kilgore, and Everett Quinton. Christopher Scott took this photo specifically to suggest vaudeville and the silent film era.

Middle left: Richard Currie caught Minette in a jaunty mood for this 1978 photo. "Though Ludlam would invite him to perform in many a Ridiculous production over the years, as Minette explained, 'I could make ten times as much money just staying home and providing some horizontal entertainment in bed. . . . This was just before Gay Liberation, which was when people found out they could get "it" for free.'" Photograph © Richard Currie.

Bottom left: While promoting his own version of *Medea*, this publicity photo of Ethyl Eichelberger shows the wildly coiffed performance artist with his obligatory accordian. Eichelberger once told Black-Eyed Susan that Ludlam was the only person he admired enough in the theater to work with — when he wasn't putting on his own plays. Photograph © Peter Hujar, courtesy Matthew Marks Gallery, New York.

RIGHT: A publicity still from Mark Rappaport's film, *Imposters*, with co-star Michael Burg giving Ludlam the hairy eyeball. "Mike was afraid that Charles was going to walk away with the movie, and he does." (Mark Rappaport.)

BOTTOM RIGHT: Ludlam as Scrooge and Everett Quinton as Marley's ghost in *A Christmas Carol*, Ludlam's most innocuous and straightforward adaptation, and the only play of his that his father saw. Photograph © Les Carr.

BOTTOM: An archetypal photo of Ludlam as a jester or vagabond, taken at the company's new home at One Sheridan Square, during a Halloween party in 1979. Ludlam was wearing a costume reminiscent of The Fool "card" he played in *The Grand Tarot*, featuring his signature red sneakers. Photograph © Richard Currie.

All photos on this page are by Patrick McMullan. Christopher Scott had hired McMullan to take what amounted to his first professional photo shoot for Reverse Psychology.

TOP LEFT: Charlotte Forbes and Ludlam in a scene from *Reverse Psychology*: "Every time we did the breakfast scene over the newspaper, it was a dare . . . who, who was going to get the biggest laughs?" (Charlotte Forbes.) Photograph © Patrick McMullan.

RIGHT: Head shots of the four stars of *Reverse Psychology*: Charlotte Forbes, Charles Ludlam, Bill Vehr, and Black-Eyed Susan. Photograph © Patrick McMullan.

BOTTOM: Christopher Scott with his gorgeous lover of the period, Scott Fritz. (Fritz stood on his toes to appear taller in the picture than he actually was.) Photograph © Patrick McMullan.

Top left: Christopher Scott designed this poster for *Love's Tangled Web* with a Fifties motif. Both in his appearance and his performance, Ludlam meant to evoke Cornel Wilde. The part of Raenne was given to Christine Deveau, the prized student actress that Ludlam had recently directed in *The Country Wife* at Carnegie Mellon.

Center left: The "eyes" have it: an astonished Zelda Patterson looks on as Ludlam inspects the mammary glands of Black-Eyed Susan in *Le Bourgeois Avant-Garde*, Ludlam's brilliant send-up of the contemporary art world. Susan recalled having to cross her eyes to prevent herself from laughing during this scene. Photograph © Anita & Steve Shevett.

Bottom far left: Ludlam, as Galas, on the phone: "I've been compromised and humiliated! I want an immediate and precise retraction. (*Pause*) Of course there's no truth in it! Every claim was a lie! I did not diet. Vermicelli was not my physician. *And I never eat macaroni!*" Photograph © Richard Currie.

Bottom left: A backstage photo of Everett Quinton in his striking fright wig as Bruna Lina Rasta, "a mad soprano, and Galas's maid," in *Galas* (1983). Quinton is holding up a photo of Ludlam as Galas, and that's Ludlam himself, over Quinton's right shoulder. Photograph © Richard Currie.

Top: Ludlam as Nicodemus Underwood (the one-legged butler who becomes a werewolf) and Everett Quinton as Jane Twisden (the fussy housekeep with a number of secrets) — two of their multiple roles in *The Mystery of Irma Vep*, which would prove to be Ludlam's greatest crowd-pleaser. Photograph © Anita & Steve Shevett.

Right: Ludlam may have used Everett Quinton as a model for his pastel drawing of a gypsy woman. "More and more, Ludlam spent any free time at home creating his own art: lush pastels and oil paintings of male nudes, religious icons, flowers and still lifes." Drawing courtesy Everett Quinton.

TOP RIGHT: A souvenir, backstage photo of Ludlam, the opera director — signed by Scott Reeve, one of the anthropomorphic players in the Santa Fe production of *The English Cat.* (1985.) Photograph courtesy Everett Quinton.

CENTER RIGHT: Katy Dierlam as Hanno, "a decadent Suffete who suffers from overweight and leprosy," in *Salammbô* (1985). "I'd get into my simple, brown, sack-cloth costume and then pass this five hundred pound naked lady applying body makeup to make herself look leprous. Your breath was taken away. But by the second or third day, it became perfectly normal — that was the scary part." (Steve Samuels.) Photograph © Richard Currie.

BELOW: That's Philip Campanaro as Matho, the Barbarian, trying to put the make on a hard-to-get Ludlam as Salammbô, the high priestess of the Moon, surrounded by her muscular entourage. "The bodybuilders shared the front dressing room. They all liked to grease themselves up before going out onstage: and prior to the posing scene that opened Act II, some of them were sure to pump up all of their muscles—including the one nestled in their loincloths." Photograph © Anita & Steve Shevett.

ABOVE: This quiet moment in a Ridiculous dressing room sharply contrasts with the more customary activity to be found there. Consider the chaotic, backstage environment of *Salammbô*: "In yet another dressing room, Ethyl Eichelberger tended to the wigs he managed, protecting them from the live doves that were employed in the play to augur the deflowering of Salammbô by Matho. The doves sometimes flew out of control both on- and offstage." Photograph © Peter Hujar, courtesy Matthew Marks Gallery, New York.

RIGHT: While this may look like a boardwalk cut-out of Robert Taylor in a DeMille epic for a tourist's head shot, it's actually Steven Samuels as Spendius, in *Salammbô*. Spendius's come-hither look was meant to indicate his lust for the barbarians. Photograph © Richard Currie.

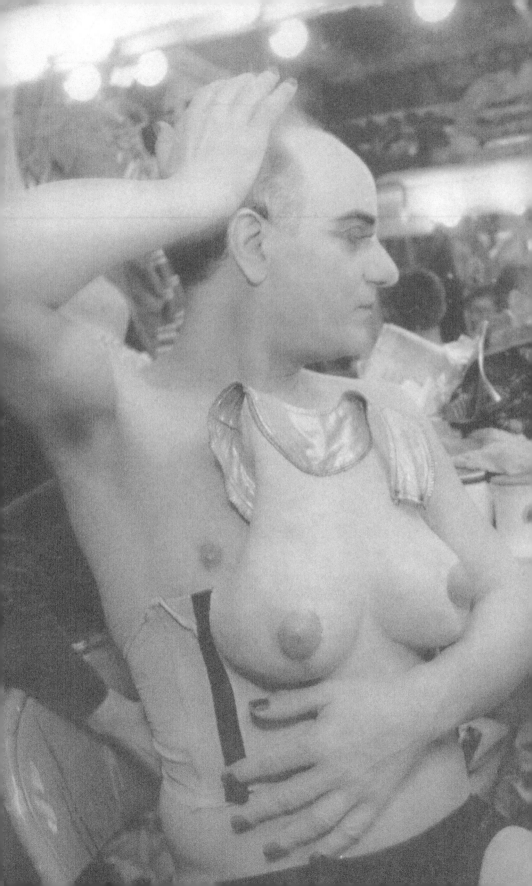

Top: The ensemble of *The Artificial Jungle* (1986), Ludlam's last play. All eyes are on hunky Philip Campanaro as Frankie Spinelli, the friendly neighborhood cop, who is apt to interfere with Roxanne's (Black-Eyed Susan) plan to murder her husband, Chester Nurdiger (Ludlam, playing "a lovable sap"), while her mother-in-law (Ethyl Eichelberger) looks on, aghast. Photograph © Anita & Steve Shevett.

Right: This production shot of Ludlam (with Ethyl Eichelberger) in *The Artificial Jungle* demonstrates just how rapidly AIDS was beginning to ravage him during the run of the play. Photograph © Richard Currie.

Opposite: Ludlam is trying on a breast-plate backstage and getting into character as the virgin priestess, Salammbô, in his extravagant play of the same name, for which he was pummeled by the critics. Photograph © Sylvia Plachy.

ABOVE: Charles with Ellen Barkin in the posthumously released film, *The Big Easy*. "As a gentleman lawyer of Old Dixie, he rolls his eyes and wraps the picture like a ribbon around his panama hat." (Pauline Kael.) (Ludlam told Black-Eyed Susan that he imitated Truman Capote's voice in the part.) Photograph from Photofest © Columbia Pictures.

RIGHT: The program cover for *The Artificial Jungle*, Ludlam's last play. "While it was borrowed from Camus, the final line of his final play can be interpreted as Ludlam's making peace with the universe. 'I'm dying,' says Slade, 'And I look up at the stars, the thousand unseeing eyes that look back on this speck of dust we call the world, and I ask — What was my crime compared to your indifference.'"

Top: As soon as Ludlam's death was announced, "a kind of shrine had spontaneously been created in front of the doors of the theater at One Sheridan Square. An adoring public had started bringing flowers, candles, cards, and letters expressing their undying appreciation and affection for Ludlam." Photograph © Richard Currie.

Right: The program for Ludlam's memorial service was designed by Robert Reddy. "Tonight we're going to celebrate the joyous work of Charles Ludlam."

The
Ridiculous Theatrical Company

Presents

TABU TABLEAUX

A Memorial for

CHARLES LUDLAM

ERIC BENTLEY ON THE THEATER OF CHARLES LUDLAM

TheaterWeek

April 23, 1990 $2.00/$3.00 Outside NYC

The Ladies in Question
Drag Crosses Over

ABOVE: Three years after Ludlam's death, *Theater Week* ran a cover story confirming that drag had crossed over into the mainstream. The five "Ladies in Question" on the cover were (clockwise from upper left): Lypsinka, Ludlam (in his *Galas* get-up), Everett Quinton, Ethyl Eichelberger, and Charles Busch.

Ludlam was also very much in touch with the female aspects of his own personality. "I think I'm an androgynous being to a certain extent," he claimed,

> And that the male characterizations are informed by a recognition — if not on the part of the character, on the part of the artist creating the character — of the feminine side of [one's] personality.

> Being male in real life, I play a variety of male roles. The female is this actress I find in myself who then in turn plays the role. It's not the actor playing a female role. It's the actor transforming [himself] into an actress and then playing a female role.

No matter how much Ludlam saw himself in Marguerite Gautier when he wrote and portrayed *Camille* in 1973, his identification with the great diva Maria Callas in *Galas* would prove even more natural for him — more genuine and more complete.

Speaking for many who idolized her, Leonard Bernstein once declared that Callas was "without any question, the greatest singer of our time." Callas was someone who transcended categories. Her range of roles was far greater than that of any other opera singer of her day. She was credited with reintroducing a style of singing (bel canto) that had not been heard in over a century, and with reviving a long-forgotten repertoire. Ludlam related not only to Callas's greatness as an artist, but also to the same forces which drove her.

He himself said,

> Like Maria Callas — I know I'm comparing myself to the great diva — sometimes things you do that seem terribly new and daring and revolutionary are really traditional things. You're restoring a tradition that's been lost, and they think you are doing something very radical because it's flying in the face of a current fashion that has no real roots in any kind of tradition.

Callas was most admired as a singer who achieved greatness despite her vocal flaws. Though she didn't have a consistently beautiful voice, even those who dwelled on her imperfections were impressed with the drama she brought to her characterizations. Her greatness lay in overcoming vocal weaknesses through the sheer intensity and dramatic thrust of her expression. ("Drama comes first," said Callas, "otherwise it's boring.")

Ludlam possessed his own version of Callas's characteristics. He had been told by his college professors that he would never be a star because he was odd and funny looking. And just as Callas had made a problematic voice seem beautiful, throughout his career Ludlam sought to reveal the innate beauty in whatever had been deemed unattractive by the culture or rejected by society.

More consciously, Ludlam identified with the public image of a Callas who was "a very controversial character, very fiery and opinionated." In the play, he specifically set out to defend her, to "show the human side, the behind-the-scenes reasons for her outrageous public behavior, and to indicate the extent to which she was really misunderstood." He was speaking for himself as well as Callas when he claimed,

> Part of the price of fame is that your image becomes simplified enough that a vast number of people can grasp it easily. You can never really be all of you. You could become a trademark, in a sense, or a quick idea that people think of—often one characteristic in a performer—that they light upon. I wanted to show the more complex background behind it, and why what people saw wasn't quite true, or how a foolish mistake or a slip of the tongue or a complex choice could be misconstrued.

Galas is, in other words, a quasi-autobiographical play. Ludlam saw Callas as he saw himself: the misunderstood artist, the archetypal diva who seems not only terribly demanding but capricious, high-handed, and temperamental. Ludlam very much related to Callas the perfectionist, who understood more about her talent than anyone around her. (She knew when her voice was going, for example; Ludlam sympathized with the motivations for her scandalous walkout in the middle of a performance.) Her desire to revive neglected, bel canto operas played very directly into Ludlam's own aesthetic of reviving theatrical traditions that had grown unfashionable. He further identified with aspects of Callas's private life, especially her struggle to maintain a romance while working in a physically demanding art form. And above all else, like Callas, Ludlam was convinced of his own greatness.

Explaining his reasons for creating *Galas*, Ludlam wrote,

> After *Le Bourgeois Avant-Garde*, I felt it was very important to strike another blow, to give the public an example of the alternative to the kind of theatre we critiqued in our modern Molière. So I decided in favor of a portrait of a modern woman in whose life I saw a narrative of universal relevance. *Galas* broadened the company's

range and proved that real feeling and even tragedy could be expressed in a comic theatre. Audiences easily accepted the narrative innovations.

Ludlam would later tell an interviewer that his primary inspiration for writing *Galas* was an "amazing gown" that Quinton had unearthed in a thrift shop. A press release for the play boasted that the script included "many anecdotes [about Callas] privately recounted to the playwright and never before made public." By all evidence, both of these contentions were pure publicity hokum. His real inspiration was *My Wife Maria Callas*, a memoir of Callas by G.B. Meneghini, her onetime manager and husband, which had just been published in 1982.

Though Ludlam had considered writing a play about Callas for years, as usual there were a number of other ideas he was contemplating when he finally decided on *Galas*. In a grant proposal prepared in December of 1982 for the upcoming season, Ludlam referred to plans for a different "biographical character study": *The Earrings of Lola Montez*. Of greater relevance were two one-act plays that Ludlam had conceived for Quinton and himself alone. The first, *Strongman Joe*, was rather like Fellini's *La Strada*, as it featured a carnival he-man bursting a chain by expanding his chest muscles. The second, *Bastard Amber*, was set in a dressing room and concerned an aging actress (Ludlam) and her maid (Quinton). Though neither of these plays was ever written, *Bastard Amber* became the basis of the relationship between the prima donna and her faithful maid, Bruna Lina Rasta, in *Galas*. And the notion of a two-person show for Ludlam and Quinton would evolve — after *Galas* — into the company's biggest hit, *The Mystery of Irma Vep*.

Because of the degree to which Ludlam empathized with Callas, it's hardly surprising that *Galas* emerges as his most serious play. He even subtitled it "A Modern Tragedy." The work's humor is subservient to the portrait of a great artist who was adored by her many fans, though misunderstood and pathetically abandoned at the end of her life. While deliberately evoking *Madame Butterfly* and *Tosca*, Galas's tragic suicide serves as a brilliant metaphor for how Callas dedicated her life to her art at the expense of personal happiness. "To live is to suffer, to endure pain," and "To have everything and lose it — now, that isn't funny," says Galas in the end. While the second line provoked sporadic laughter in the audience, it was meant rather to be taken seriously.

Though other liberties are necessarily taken to compress the life of Maria Callas into a two-act scenario, her suicide is the only real invention. The script is most remarkable for its ability to evoke so many of the high points in her life. It covers her first marriage to an Italian brick tycoon who became her manager; her rise to international stardom; the controversies surrounding various artistic and legal feuds with opera impresarios; her walkout in the middle of a performance of *Norma* at an opera gala opening in Rome; her dramatic weight loss; her leaving her husband for Greek shipping magnate Aristotle Onassis (and his in turn leaving Callas for Jacqueline Kennedy); and her death in 1977, in relative solitude and loneliness.

Though the jokes stand out in performance, they are far outweighed in the script by more earnest concerns. (Consider Galas's closing line before she stabs herself to death: "What do I do from morning to night if I don't have my career? I have no family, I have no husband, I have no babies, I have no lover, I have no dog, I have no voice, and there's nothing good on television tonight.") As in his epic Wagner parody, *Der Ring Gott Farblonjet*, Ludlam changed the characters' names to humorous effect, beginning with Galas itself. (In a program note, he wrote: "The characters in the play are real. Only their names have been changed to protect the playwright.") Her first husband, Meneghini, becomes Mercanteggini. Onassis becomes Aristotle Plato Socrates Odysseus, referred to as "Soc" for short. For the name of Galas's maid, Ludlam interpolated another figure from the opera world — a very obscure Italian soprano by the name of Lina Bruna Rasa, who spent much of her life in an asylum. Renamed Bruna Lina Rasta — and portrayed by Quinton with wildly frizzy hair and dark eye makeup — she proves to be an otherworldly and strangely prophetic creature. More than just a maid, she is also Galas's caretaker and advisor. In a purely comical moment, Galas asks, "How many Normas do I have?" and Bruna looks down her throat before replying, "eighty-six." (The joke also being a pun on the colloquial usage of "eighty-sixed," meaning ousted.)

The funniest scene entails an audience with Pope Pius XII, whom Ludlam has rechristened Pope Sixtus the Seventh. In addition to dismissing him as "just another bishop," Galas plays a game of one-upsmanship with the Pontiff as she is compelled to kiss his ring.

Though none in the audience could have known it, one of the relatively casual lines referred to a special moment in Ludlam's childhood. While applying eye shadow in front of a mirror, Galas announces that she's "gilding the lily!" As a child, Ludlam once wandered into his Aunt May's bedroom and asked what she was doing as he observed her painting her face. "I'm gilding the lily," she responded. Aunt May's otherwise inscrutable gesture made a permanent impression on the susceptible youngster: Indeed her remark remained with Ludlam the rest of his life, and the action it described helped define his sensibility and successes as an artist who gilded practically everything he touched with his own special alchemy.

Another significant instance of autobiographical identification occurs in the final scene, when Galas rants:

> The public, the public. When I sing well they applaud, and when I do not they boo and jeer. That's the public. Pah! You know, it's very strange, but there are certain nights when the public thinks that I am giving a great performance, but I do not feel that way at all. On such nights all compliments embarrass me. And yet there are certain other nights when I feel that the performance is going particularly well, and that I have attained a kind of perfection, but the public does not agree. This is what haunts me.

From his lonely childhood and frustrating associations with mentors, to his early successes and recent triumphs, Ludlam was desperately haunted his whole life by the feeling that he wasn't appreciated — or that when he was, it wasn't for the reasons he deserved to be. As Mercanteggini says in another line that Ludlam clearly applied to himself, "Great artists are acknowledged but never forgiven."

In a National Public Radio interview on October 13, Ludlam emphasized the ways he identified with Callas and with the ways she was misunderstood. "I'm also...willful," he told Tom Vitale, the host. "[Callas had] gotten a lot of bad publicity for doing things that the public...would interpret as being willful and arrogant and capricious. But, if you're a performer with high standards you saw that...in reality it was the pursuit of a certain kind of excellence."

As was also the case with *Camille*, no matter how much they laughed, many in the audience were deeply moved by the play's tragic ending. The magic of the effect depended entirely on the magic of Ludlam's performance — on the ineffable way he got to have his comedy and his tragedy too. Destined to run for eight months, *Galas* would garner more admiration for Ludlam as an artist than he had ever known before.

Galas was assembled remarkably quickly. Less than five weeks elapsed between the time Ludlam started work on the script and the first public presentation of the play. Larry Eichler, the company's production manager, became apoplectic when he learned of the many scenic effects Ludlam intended. To salvage the fading ticket sales for *Le Bourgeois* and quickly launch something new, Eichler thought they needed a "beer and potato chips" production — not the champagne Ludlam seemed to be pouring. Yet Ludlam didn't envision *Galas* as the grandiose opus it would become. He threw the work together almost as if it were merely another midnight frolic, just as *Elephant Woman* had been several years before.

The chaos of the first preview reflected the haste with which the play had been put together. Though it was based primarily on various interviews Callas had given over the years, Ludlam didn't come up with the play's ending until that afternoon, when he arrived at the theater to dictate the last scene to Samuels. Samuels retyped the messy pages and rushed them to a photocopy shop. Since neither Ludlam nor Quinton had any time to learn these new lines, Samuels had three oversized sets of the final three pages made: One set was taped to a wall in the wings, offstage right; another to the rear of a three-paneled dressing screen behind which Galas dies; the third to a marbleized countertop being used as a prop.

Though the rest of the performance ran smoothly enough during this first preview, the final scene between Galas and Bruna was a nightmare. Both Ludlam and Quinton randomly wandered around the set trying to find their places in the script. Occasionally Ludlam would go over to the countertop and lean on it, throwing lines back over his shoulder. In a frantic attempt to keep up, Quinton would retreat to the wings and study the pages tacked on the wall. The costume changes behind the screen — which would later be so fast that audiences would gasp with disbelief — took forever this first night, as Ludlam and Quinton lingered there to read their lines. The real problem was that when they were out onstage saying what they had just committed to memory, they were anticipating lines and jumping around in the script. They had a devilish time trying to get back on track. Samuels cringed in his seat as he watched, but, remarkably, the audience never seemed to realize anything unusual was taking place. Afterward, Ludlam told Samuels that they got through it all simply by going out onstage with "absolute conviction" in their roles and through sheer faith in their ability to somehow manage.

Confirming all this, Wally Gorell made the following journal entry after attending the first public performance of *Galas* on July 1, 1983: "Whenever one of them couldn't recall a line, s/he'd invent some reason to go behind the screen. Amazingly I had no idea [this was taking place]. Late in the scene the screen somehow got knocked over. Later when I inquired about the fluttering of pages when the screen fell down, I was told this story." In fact, photographer Peter Hujar was sitting in the front row, and when one of the pages had turned over during the mishap, he discreetly flipped it back.

Since *Le Bourgeois Avant-Garde* was still doing decent business on Fridays and Saturdays, it continued to play weekends throughout the balance of the summer. *Galas* went into previews to pick up the slack on Wednesdays, Thursdays, and Sundays. In the process, the Ridiculous came up with the notion of presenting a repertory of new plays. With the tandem runs of *Galas* and *Le Bourgeois* setting the precedent, they discovered that a new play created its own brand of excitement even in previews — especially with company loyalists who would see a work repeatedly and track its development. The house could practically be filled for the entire week, and at the same time Ludlam and his crew would have more time to work on new productions. This very effective strategy soon became house policy.

When *Galas* opened on September 15, 1983, it received universal kudos — except from John Simon, who deigned to attend a Ridiculous production for the first time in years, only to knock it in a single paragraph in *New York* magazine. But it wasn't the very favorable nature of the reviews that proved so exceptional; rather it was the sheer volume of coverage. Besides all New York and many regional papers and magazines, this Off-Broadway play received national and even international attention, as well as generating radio and television interviews with Ludlam.

A rave in *Time* magazine (dated October 31) was something of a fortuitous accident. T.E. Kalem, the magazine's regular theater critic, was absent; his replacement, Richard Corliss, was a Ridiculous fan who took it upon himself to cover the play. In his review, Corliss was more or less speaking for all the critics when he wrote:

> By the climax, Ludlam has moved from funny halfway to sublime. He does not
> keep the satirist's distance from Galas: He inhabits her, and turns ramshackle farce
> into full-throated melodrama. Leading a band of faithful players who dare only to
> flirt with competence, producing his extravaganzas on shoestring budgets, Ludlam
> is a star in the vanishing tradition of the actor-manager. The Ludlam line may go
> back even further, to the capering Pantaloons of Renaissance Italy. With reckless
> energy and a wickedly contemporary show-biz savvy, this clown prince is putting
> the art back in *commedia dell'arte*.

Ludlam received another stroke of good fortune merely because *Galas* opened in the midst of the centennial season of the Metropolitan Opera. Since the play was about one of the greatest figures of twentieth century opera, music lovers and critics in town for the celebration were naturally intrigued and drawn to it. Martin Bernheimer and

Donna Perlmutter, the respective music critics for the *Los Angeles Times* and the *Los Angeles Herald-Examiner*, gave their readers glowing reports of both Ludlam and his play early in November.

The phenomenal media response to *Galas* continued when Eleanor Blau featured it in her "Broadway" column for a Friday (or "Weekend") edition of *The New York Times* later in November, including a coveted Hirschfeld caricature (Ludlam's first and only) in full Galas regalia. As if to guarantee a much longer run, *Galas* was cited as one of the "Ten Best Plays of the Year" in both *Time* magazine and *The New York Times*. Chris Chase's early Cable News Network review was matched late in the play's run by Marcia Steiner's cable TV interview with Ludlam. There was even a full page devoted to Ludlam and his *Galas* in the February 1984 edition of *Torso* and a feature promoting the play in *Mandate*, both gay porno magazines. Ludlam also won a Drama Desk Special Award for Outstanding Achievement in the Theater, "in recognition of fifteen years of Ridiculous productions."

The play's long run, of course, led to problems maintaining its relatively large cast. Susan remained miserable about her minor role as the ex-mistress of Odysseus, and her gloom infected the whole company. Though Ludlam had to be aware of the embarrassing position he had put her in (even a number of the reviewers mentioned that Susan was being underutilized), he insisted that *she* was trying to humiliate him by being so ornery and difficult. Ludlam's onetime lover John Heys, who portrayed Odysseus, remembered:

> It was absolutely painful to see the way Charles treated Susan during *Galas*. She could do *nothing* right. She had only one scene with Charles. Every night, you'd watch her go out onstage, totally focused and dedicated. But then she'd come off with this stricken look on her face. It was like Charles had just attacked her during the scene. . . . But I felt like she took that abuse because she wanted to, she had inured herself to it.

From Susan's perspective, the situation confirmed that Ludlam was particularly insensitive and competitive with other women whenever he was in drag. According to Heys, "Charles truly *was* Maria Callas. Over the years, there were always complaints that whenever you're onstage with Charles, he's going to totally upstage you. Sometimes he'd be aware of it, but other times it might be unconscious."

Heys was especially excited by the many celebrities who came to see *Galas*. In what became a nightly ritual, he'd peek through the curtain before the show went on, and come backstage to report: "Paloma Picasso is in the first row. . . . Jill Clayburgh is here tonight with her husband David Rabe. . . . Michael York is in the audience. . . ." The longstanding Ridiculous cult reached a chic peak with this production.

In the middle of the run, Heys left the show to perform a solo piece in Germany. Though Heys gave a few weeks notice, it was clear that Ludlam resented it. "He was not very gracious about it," Heys claimed. "He adopted this 'How can you be leaving me?' attitude." Heys had initially told Ludlam that he was going on his annual pilgrimage to Morocco "to pick dates — both kinds," and not that he was going to perform in Germany. "Charles was terribly resentful of his lack of commitment, both professionally and personally," recalled Samuels. "He could never understand people not having the same commitment he did, or not giving up their lives for their art — or for that matter, for *his* art."

Heys was quickly and smoothly replaced by Ethyl Eichelberger, who was already involved with the production, handling its many wigs — as he had for *Exquisite Torture*. It proved more of a problem when Bill Vehr suddenly became very ill and had to be rushed to the hospital one night. Though he had been coughing for some weeks, Vehr wasn't one to complain, nor to take very good care of himself. He was diagnosed with tuberculosis, placed in a ward for a lengthy recuperation, and, having no health insurance, was forced to sell a beloved Ken Tisa print to help finance the stay. Vehr was replaced by Samuels and later by Adam Kilgore, until he was well enough to return to the production.

There was also a week in January when Susan came down with such a bad case of laryngitis that Penny Arcade had to fill in for her. With only a day to learn her lines, Arcade went to Morton Street to pick up a copy of the script. She recalled:

> Charles greeted me at the door, and then gave me a tour of his apartment. Strangely, he was completely focused on his tropical fish, instead of the script or the play. He was also focused on his anger at Susan. Charles had taken her laryngitis as a personal attack, a betrayal. He complained that he had written this part for her, a minor cameo, really, because Susan had begged him to be in the play.

They agreed to meet at the theater the next afternoon, presumably for Ludlam to provide Arcade with some direction in a part she had never even seen performed. But warning her not to upstage him — and her reassuring him that she wouldn't — seemed to be the extent of their "rehearsal." Arcade even had to specifically ask that Ludlam indicate her entrances and exits.

"That night, I returned for the performance," continued Arcade.

> I shared the dressing room with Emilio Cubeiro [who played Mercanteggini], and in a scene I had with him, the stage was set with a few chairs. At the end of the scene, as I was leaving the stage, Emilio hissed at me, "Penny! Where are you going? You have to move your chair." Well, the backstage space was notoriously dangerous, with wires like spaghetti, ready to trip you at every turn. Back in the dressing room I expressed my surprise that Charles hadn't told me about moving the chair in the dark, and hadn't walked me through it. While laughing sympathetically, Emilio said, "You know, Charles has a mean streak as wide as the Hudson River!"

Indeed, the rest of Arcade's memory of her involvement with *Galas* demonstrated just how cruel Ludlam could be. "I could tell that my performance went well, and my two scenes were really fun," said Arcade.

> Charles and Everett approached me after the show with a large bouquet of roses. Susan was with them, hanging back a little. As he presented me with the flowers, Charles proclaimed loudly, "You were magnificent!" Then he quickly glanced sideways at Susan, as if to be sure she was still there, before saying, "You completely brought the character to life. Finally, I could see the part played as I had written it, and meant for it to be played." I suddenly realized that I had an additional, unscripted role in their offstage fag/fag-hag melodrama.

Arcade's week in *Galas* marked the first time in sixteen years that Susan was able to see a Ridiculous performance from the audience perspective. Though she always knew that Ludlam was very careful in designing the arc of his own performance, only then did it become apparent to her that the others had modified their own to conform with his. Despite any ill will that prevailed between them at the time, Susan claimed, "I realized then that if I had never known Charles, I would have been a tremendous fan of his theater."

The great Brazilian soprano Bidú Sayão proved to be a very special enthusiast of *Galas*. When she went backstage following the performance, Ludlam bent down and kissed the hem of her white mink coat. The great diva asked Quinton if he would mind her giving him a bit of advice. In her thick, Portuguese accent, Sayão said, "I knew Lina Bruna Rasa quite well, and she had much bigger boobies." Several days later, Ludlam received a famous studio photo of Sayão in her *Traviata* costume: The picture was signed, "To Charles Ludlam. From one 'Camille' to another."

Perhaps the most amazing response from Ludlam's fans occurred on a particularly rainy evening late in the run. The Minetta Creek — a small Manhattan stream that had long been buried by urban development — flowed directly under the basement at One Sheridan Square. Whenever a torrential rain persisted, the subterranean creek would rise and the sewers overflow, causing the toilets in the restrooms to release gushes of water and all kinds of disgusting effluents. Early during one night's performance the sewage started to spill into the theater. At first, people in the first few rows moved to higher territory in the rear of the raked auditorium. The performance was halted and Ludlam announced that it would have to be canceled, ". . . unless you'd like us to do it Venetian style?" The audience cheered, encouraging him to continue. But soon the backstage toilets had started to overflow as well, flooding the raised stage and risking the destruction of thousands of dollars worth of costumes.

Galas brought Ludlam to a new level of accomplishment and recognition. He had risen above the venal and self-indulgent avant-garde with his sensibility and his spirit intact. But characteristically, he had reservations and resentments regarding his triumph. Though Ludlam reveled in *Galas* and in the adoration it brought him, he was also ambivalent about, once again, being perceived primarily as a drag performer. He especially resented the way in which the previous decade of his theater was being dismissed. It was as if he had achieved nothing between *Camille* and *Galas*, as if the most productive period of his life — containing his highly experimental and accomplished work — had been erased from the minds of both the crowds and the critics.

With the overlapping successes of *Le Bourgeois* and *Galas*, Ludlam barely had a moment's respite. There is a telling passage in *Galas* when the diva says she's breaking down and her husband recommends that she take a vacation. But after looking at her datebook, he discovers that she's booked solid for the next year. It was about to become the same for Ludlam. There was no time to do anything but work for the foreseeable future. For Ludlam, as for Galas, any difference between life and work had been erased, but unlike the tragic, neglected diva, Ludlam's reputation would continue to soar until the very end.

ONE FOR THE AGES

It is original, not in the paltry sense of being new, but in the deeper sense of being old; it is original in the sense that it deals with origins.
— G.K. Chesterton

Mothers are always the first to know, but the last to find out.
— Charles Ludlam, on being gay

The double-barreled sensation of *Le Bourgeois Avant-Garde* and — more emphatically — *Galas* led to more outside opportunities for Ludlam in the last three years of his life than he had known in the first forty. In addition to writing five more plays, four of which he produced, he would appear in two network TV shows and one syndicated series, direct two operas in Santa Fe, star in the title role of *Hedda Gabler* in a controversial production of the Ibsen classic in Pittsburgh, and have a featured part in a major Hollywood film.

Since Ludlam was always convinced of his own greatness, he took all of this galloping success in stride. Then too, since this level of celebrity came relatively late in his abbreviated life — after he had endured the indignity of having little more than local fame — it never really went to his head, as it might have had it had arrived twenty or even ten years earlier.

It's quite possible, however, that the first of these mainstream breakthroughs — marking the television debut of Charles Ludlam — might have come about even without the national spotlight that was suddenly thrown on him and his *Galas*. The moving force behind it was Hofstra colleague Madeline Kahn. Though she hadn't worked with Ludlam since college, when they both had played small roles in *The Tempest*, Kahn had attended Ridiculous productions over the years and "very much admired the risks Charles was taking." Occasionally they talked about doing something together, but nothing ever came of it until early in 1984.

At the time, Kahn had her own TV sitcom on ABC called "Oh, Madeline!" When she learned the series was going to be canceled, and had only a handful of episodes left, Kahn asked the producers if she could do something "unusual" with them. "I was experiencing the difficulties that came with trying to be innovative in the mainstream world with the kind of censorship that was going on," said Kahn. "And when I would see what Charles was doing in his theater, it would stand out even more clearly in my mind."

Kahn specifically told her producers that she wanted to shoot an episode with Ludlam guest-starring as a woman. With her persistence, they finally agreed. But ultimately, according to Kahn, "ABC couldn't see their way clear, so they had Charles play a man *disguised* as a woman. His wig was pulled off in the end so the public could rest assured he was really a man and we wouldn't have to worry [about any homophobic backlash or controversy]."

No matter how much Harvey Fierstein had recently done to boost drag performance into the mainstream, it was Dustin Hoffman's wildly successful *Tootsie*, released just a year before, which had given cross-dressing a respectability and popularity it had never known. By having Ludlam portray a man who dresses as a woman out of economic necessity, the episode of "Oh, Madeline!" was following the *Tootsie* formula exactly, and it's easy to surmise that it probably would not have happened if not for the Sidney Pollack film. (It is tempting to speculate that there might never have been a *Tootsie* — or even the runaway success of Harvey Fierstein for that matter — if not for Ludlam's *Camille* ten years earlier.) But apparently it was still a daring leap for network television, which then, as now, feels compelled to cater to its conservative and timid advertisers first.

The hilarious episode was designed to showcase Ludlam and his special talents, according to Kahn's wishes. It remains one of the best extant examples of Ludlam's estimable skills at portraying a woman.

Suspending performances of *Galas* for the first week in February 1984, Ludlam flew out to Los Angeles to shoot the "Oh, Madeline!" episode, which aired on ABC at the end of the month. Kahn's husband in the series (played by James Sloyan) is a popular romance novelist who writes under the female pseudonym of Crystal Love. In this particular episode, his publisher wants him to make what would amount to Crystal's first public appearance to promote her new book, especially because a highly visible newcomer by the name of Tiffany Knight has "taken over the romance market." An incredulous Kahn responds, "You mean that *ridiculous* woman with the feathers, the hair, the makeup? She looks like an explosion at the Rose Parade." Though the public thinks Tiffany is really a woman, she's portrayed, of course, by Ludlam. (While the role of Tiffany was designed as "a cross between Barbara Cartland and Joan Collins," Ludlam played the part with his Tallulah Bankhead voice.)

To save her husband's career as a romance novelist, Kahn consents to impersonate Crystal Love at a book signing, which is crashed by Tiffany. Thinking her own secret is also Crystal's, Tiffany intends to expose her as a man when they're both guests on a TV talk show. But the opposite occurs when Crystal inadvertently yanks off Tiffany's wig, revealing Ludlam's bald head.

While the scenario might sound lame, it's executed with a great deal of wit and aplomb, including some rather risqué *double entendres* and subtle puns that had to be stretching any codes of decency ABC was imposing on itself for the sake of its sponsors. ("Oh, Madeline!" probably failed as a series because it was a tad too highbrow for the average sitcom watcher.) But in retrospect, what's most fascinating is that the network hemmed and hawed over the matter of revealing Ludlam's gender up until the last minute. In his column for the *Daily News* on January 29, Harry Haun notified his readers that *Galas* would be dark for the week so that Charles Ludlam "can drag himself to Hollywood. . . . An old history classmate of his from Hofstra, Madeline Kahn, asked him to guest on her series, 'Oh, Madeline!' and he will — without compromising any standards: He'll play a woman novelist of the Barbara Cartland school of Romance." Haun ended his item with this juicy tidbit: "To date, the net hasn't decided whether to reveal his true gender."

Even harder to fathom is Richard Hack's "Stranger Than Fiction" item in the *Hollywood Reporter*, concerning a half-page ad ABC procured in *TV Guide* to promote the episode. "The ad shows a picture of series star Madeline Kahn holding a blonde wig and staring in disbelief at a man wearing a dress and large gypsy earrings," explained Hack a few days after the episode aired.

> The strange part is that the man isn't Ludlam, the dress isn't Tiffany's and the blond wig belongs to Madeline. . . . Instead of blowing the trumpet at the small-screen debut of a man whom *New York*[er] magazine devoted 28 pages to profile, ABC not only didn't mention his name in the ad, but illustrated the layout with the photo of a nameless other. If this is an example of network homophobia, someone should tell ABC that this is 1984. If it isn't, then ABC owes us all an explanation.

Regardless of how he felt about these silly, would-be controversies, Ludlam simply had a ball doing "Oh, Madeline!" According to Kahn, perhaps there was some "attitude" manifested by others involved with the show who failed to "understand or appreciate Charlie's particular gifts. But Charles wasn't offended by any of it. He had the most wonderful time and he was just a joy to work with, a very generous artist." As others recalled, he returned from Hollywood "thrilled" with the entire experience. He especially enjoyed working with the costumers and teaching *them* tricks of the trade, such as stuffing his bra with birdseed to better simulate realistic mammillary movement.

Ludlam was also quite pleased with how he came across on the show. His work in "Oh, Madeline!" led the following year to his cameo appearance — yet again, in drag — in the season premiere of "Miami Vice," one of the most popular television series at the time. Then in 1986 he would have the leading (and straight, if it could be called that) role in a southern gothic episode of "Tales From the Dark Side," a nationally syndicated horror series.

But no matter how much outside work started pouring in, Ludlam's first commitment remained with his own theater. His second was increasingly focused on Everett Quinton. He brought both of them together, as it were, by writing his next play exclusively for the two of them: *The Mystery of Irma Vep*. As Samuels said, it was designed "as much to advance their relationship as to advance Charles's artistry."

The only other two-character play Ludlam had ever written and produced was *The Ventriloquist's Wife*, with Black-Eyed Susan. She had to feel a sense of betrayal when she learned of *Irma Vep*, which would prove to be Quinton's ultimate triumph over her. Susan helped paint a tree on the set, but for the first time in nearly two decades, she was compelled to seek other acting work. She commenced a long association with John Jesurun, beginning with his performance piece, *Red House*. And Ethyl Eichelberger wrote *Hamlette* for Susan, with a special midnight showing scheduled specifically so Ludlam could attend. After watching her performance, Ludlam told Susan that he loved her in drag in the title role.

Though it was written for only two actors, *The Mystery of Irma Vep* is not exactly a two-character play. Giving new definition to the notion of the quick-change artist, it was designed for two actors to share seven different roles between them. It would become the biggest hit of Ludlam's career. And although everyone claimed it would never work without Ludlam and Quinton's *tour de force* performances, it has emerged as Ludlam's biggest hit following his demise, with any number of productions being staged regularly throughout the world.

Irma Vep, as it became known, was an anagram for "vampire." By labeling the play "A Penny Dreadful," Ludlam revealed at least part of his inspiration. Benét's *Reader's Encyclopedia* defines a "penny dreadful" as "Any cheaply printed paperbound book of adventure or mystery popular in England and America, particularly in the 19th century. As with the Dime Novel, penny dreadfuls were inexpensive and known more for the sensationalism of their stories than for any literary merit."

Ludlam further identified a host of sources as the basis for his convoluted story, including the popular films *Rebecca*, *Wuthering Heights*, *Gaslight*, and *Nosferatu* (the German version of *Dracula*), as well as *Romance of the Mummy*, a 19th-century French novel by Théophile Gautier, and *She Who Sleeps* by Sax Rohmer, author of the Fu Manchu series. Ludlam had always combined references from both low and high culture in his plays. But in this, his twenty-fifth, he accomplished the far more astonishing feat of contributing something of his own to high culture by focusing on the low.

Featuring a werewolf, a vampire, and an Egyptian mummy, the story concerns Lady Enid Hillcrest (Ludlam), the new bride of Lord Edgar Hillcrest (Quinton), who is still in love with his deceased first wife, the eponymous Irma Vep. The two other principal characters are Nicodemus Underwood (Ludlam), the one-legged butler who is transformed into a werewolf depending on the phases of the moon, and Jane Twisden (Quinton), the fussy housekeeper who is hiding a number of secrets.

Though the emphasis is clearly on gothic tales and horror stories, Ludlam also incorporated elements from higher up the cultural ladder. The script is laden with Ibsen references on practically every page: While working on the play, Ludlam also steeped himself in the works of the great Norwegian dramatist, in preparation for his playing the title role in *Hedda Gabler* that summer in Pittsburgh.

But *Irma Vep* was primarily based on the theatrical convention of the quick change. When he was still working on the script, Ludlam told Joseph Hurley for the June issue of *New York Theater Voice* (a short-lived theatrical monthly),

> This time I started with the device and worked back to the play. Usually, I start with a sketch or at least an outline, but this time it was just the idea that two people are doing all the parts, and they have to do quick changes, and I'm not always entirely sure that the plot makes any sense. . . . I may in fact open with a plot that doesn't entirely work, a plot I haven't totally solved.

Ludlam had the idea for *Irma Vep* a good while before he started writing it. But once he sat down to work on it, it came tumbling out of his overactive mind. It evolved in bits and pieces, with scenes very much out of the sequence in which they would finally appear. In a rare development, Ludlam began by typing the script himself, at home. But if Ludlam was a lousy speller, he was an even worse typist.

Samuels was by now doing more and more of the company's business on a computer, and Ludlam was impressed by how much it improved the office organization. But from the very beginning, Ludlam resisted the computer revolution: He said that personally he would rather "go back to the quill pen." To emphasize his point, he proclaimed himself one of the Luddites, a group of English rebels who opposed the rise of technology during the Industrial Revolution. On the most basic level, Ludlam was simply not mechanically inclined. Though he eventually purchased a telephone answering machine, he was so intimidated by the gizmo that he delayed hooking it up for months.

The real challenge to writing *Irma Vep* had little to do with writing implements, however. Since there are so many characters and situations but only two actors, it was structurally complex in ways that could only be worked out with mathematical precision. It is unquestionably the trickiest of all of Ludlam's plays to perform.

In one of the key scenes, Ludlam knew that he wanted to appear onstage as his two major characters—Lady Enid and Nicodemus—simultaneously. But he couldn't figure out how to do it. He awoke in a panic in the middle of the night and phoned Leon Katz, who immediately had the solution: wear a two-sided costume and perform the scene in a doorway.

Some years earlier, Ludlam's dentist happened to mention that he could create "a monster's denture" for him should it ever prove useful. As Ludlam told Hurley,

> When I realized the trouble I was facing with Enid and Nicodemus, I phoned him and said "Doctor Cone, this is the moment!" and I took him all the pictures I could find of Fredric March in *Dr. Jekyll and Mr. Hyde* because I always loved the way those teeth were... and he made it for me in the lab. It fits perfectly and it looks absolutely real. I pop the teeth in, and they distort the mouth without destroying Lady Enid's makeup, but the whole thing is so complicated and the changes are so fast that I'm sure sooner or later I'll wear them on as Enid.

The six weeks of rehearsals for *Irma Vep* were practically as madcap as the play itself. Since Ludlam lacked an ending for the play a couple weeks before previews were scheduled to begin, and because a lot of rehearsal time was required to work out the furiously fast costume changes, Samuels tried to persuade him to postpone the first public performance by at least a week. But Ludlam wouldn't hear of it—not at first, anyway.

However, there *still* was no ending a few days before the first preview was scheduled.

Ludlam arrived in the office one morning, intending to dictate the final pages to Samuels, but he was stymied. Samuels accompanied him to lunch to hash over the problem. Ludlam just couldn't figure out which of the characters should be responsible for the death of "little" Victor, an offstage figure whose demise is a driving force in the story's subplot. They spent much of the day walking around the Village and going from coffee shop to cafe as they tried out "every possible" angle to arrive at a plausible explanation for this plot development.

Finally over dinner, Ludlam revealed the inevitable and only solution: Jane the housekeeper kills "little" Victor. When Samuels realized that Ludlam had really known this all along, he wanted to know why "we had been beating our brains out all that time." As Ludlam divulged, the problem was more moral than structural: He simply could not face the concept of someone having killed the child, so he was desperate to find an alternative. But there wasn't any.

At last, only two days before previews were to begin, the entire play could be rehearsed. But with some costume changes occurring in five or ten second intervals, it proved impossible to work out all the stage business in such a short time. They fumbled with the staging until 3 AM that night. When Quinton discovered himself locked in the mummy case, one of the more prominent props in the play, Ludlam finally relented and agreed to put off the previews. Once the decision to postpone was made, Ludlam went to the other extreme and acted as if they could extend the rehearsal period indefinitely. But the operating expenses were accumulating, and Samuels insisted they start playing to audiences the following week.

Having realized how effective it was to have extensive previews of *Galas* before opening to the press, this now became a calculated maneuver to maximize a play's run and improve it in the process. Thus a pattern emerged to creating the company's most successful works: initiation of previews in the spring; a summer hiatus; a remounting of the show for the critics in the fall; and then on to a regular run. The summer breaks would prove necessary, anyway, to accommodate the outside projects that suddenly presented themselves to Ludlam in the wake of his celebrated *Galas*. In the case of *Irma Vep*, Ludlam was already slated to perform *Hedda Gabler*.

In the meantime, two problems emerged during the month of spring previews. Though audiences adored *Irma Vep* right from the start and this seemed to militate against making any changes in the script, many people had questions about various developments in the plot. (The most prevalent one was: How or why did the characters suddenly show up in Egypt?) Though Ludlam was annoyed with such reactions, he had a second and far more pressing concern. Since he had promised "two new productions" during the year in his grant agreement with the New York State Council on the Arts, he felt obligated to insert another play into the schedule by the close of their season, which began in July and ended the following June. (*Galas* had begun its previews the previous spring and technically belonged to the earlier season, so only *Irma Vep* qualified as a new play for the year.) As Ludlam told Marcia Steiner on her local TV show during this period, "The way I do plays is I announce the opening, and then I write the play. So it's like a duel: You're a coward if you don't show up."

In a mad scramble to produce something by June 30, Ludlam wrote his version of *Medea* in two days, during the first week of May. "Recited" may be a more appropriate term for describing how he went about writing it. Ludlam knew the play inside out. He was particularly familiar with Judith Anderson's portrayal in the Robinson Jeffers translation, as he had listened to the recording time and again over the years. While Samuels frantically typed it into the computer, Ludlam dictated the entire play to him, sometimes working directly from a copy of Jefferson's text. Basically, Ludlam was performing the piece as Samuels got it down. But this would prove to be the only performance of the Greek tragic figure Ludlam would ever give.

As soon as he had finished his rather straightforward *Medea*, Ludlam decided that he would never be able to stage it. If it had been difficult for him to follow through with the murder of Victor in *Irma Vep*, how could he ever bring himself to portray a woman who murders her *own* children? Though his rapidly composed adaptation of *Medea* had seemed like an efficient solution to his NYSCA obligation, once he envisioned acting the role night after night, he just couldn't face it. And in a journal he would keep during the first few days of working on *Hedda Gabler*, Ludlam made a connection between "the murder of her unborn child and [Hedda's] suicide."

Ludlam gave no explanations for his obsession with this subject and the irrational behavior it sometimes engendered. But perhaps his overreaction to fictional child murderers had to do with the question of whether or not he had fathered the baby Deborah Rosen might have aborted more than two decades earlier. Samuels recalled that whenever he talked about his own son, Adrian, Ludlam would become uncomfortable. "He would start babbling about his fish and his birds," said Samuels. "It was very reflexive. There was a sense in which he needed to compete with me as a procreator."

But once he decided not to stage *Medea*, Ludlam had little more than a month left to produce another play. Briefly, he resurrected the idea of doing something with Oscar Wilde's *Salomé*. Ludlam earlier accounted for this play's hold on him: "Against a background of satiric religious discussion," he wrote,

> Wilde set the tragedy of woman's sexuality, which in this aspect is synonymous with homosexuality: Both risk the possibility of rejection by the male. . . . Just as the male or female cells carry within them the sexually determining factors, so too the individuals, regardless of sex, carry within them both sets of sexual characteristics, to pass on to their progeny or for their own use in self-realization. The ability to recognize opposites in ourselves is the basis of art, definitely of drama. It is part of imagining and imitating. Few people dare to enact their fantasies in art; fewer dare to realize them in the flesh.

Notwithstanding his unusual insights into *Salomé*, Ludlam ultimately felt the play could not be staged. On the premise that Wilde himself had been inspired by Gustave Flaubert's *Salammbô*, Ludlam turned to this 1862 historical novel concerning a virgin priestess in ancient Carthage. Though he initially worked directly with Wilde's text of *Salomé*, Ludlam's notebooks incorporated more and more of the Flaubert. This became a way of remaining true to what had originally drawn him to the Wilde years before, while freeing Ludlam from any slavish imitation of the script. It also permitted him to generate some fresh ideas of his own. But no matter how Ludlam approached *Salammbô*, it proved too much of an extravaganza to be assembled fast enough, and so it was postponed for a year.

Having exhausted these other possibilities, Ludlam finally satisfied what he perceived as his NYSCA obligation by writing a play about a playwright — named Charles Ludlam, no less — who is under enormous pressure to write a play. *How to Write a Play*, his twenty-seventh opus, is a coyly autobiographical enterprise, based on the urgent circumstances in which he suddenly found himself. Not surprisingly, he transformed his own situation into a classic "Kaufman and Hart" farce.

Set in the playwright's apartment, which he shares with Everett Quinton, "his roommate and man Friday," the play begins in the morning, with Charles feeding his fish and birds, and watering the plants. He explains that he has only three weeks to write a play to fulfill a grant commitment: "or else we have to give the forty thousand dollars back." He tells Everett that they're not doing *Salammbô* next: "I just didn't feel that three weeks was enough [to convey] the splendor of the ancient world. The battle scenes. For that, we need at least four weeks."

Though Charles endeavors to glue himself to his desk center stage and write a play, he must endure one hilarious interruption after the other. First there's Everett, with his morning banter. Next, Natalie the maid arrives to clean the apartment. The UPS man makes a couple of deliveries. Madame Wong, a macrobiotic cook, enters to begin preparing meals for Charles during his intensive writing period. A composer by the name of Ima Poussy elbows his way into the apartment, trying to persuade Charles to use him as a musical collaborator. A neighbor, Mrs. Hornblatt, makes an appearance to ask Charles to feature her patently untalented daughter Rosalie in one of his plays. By the afternoon, or the end of Act I, a group of Gay Seniors shows up — as does the fire department, to put out a blaze in the adjacent apartment.

The shenanigans continue in the second act. A South American general, who was involved in a coup in Uruguay and has "absconded with half the national treasury" — and who is an enormous fan of Charles and wants to endow his theater — arrives. The catch is that he saw Charles as Galas and thinks he's really a woman; so Charles must now assume drag while serving dinner. It all builds in pure farcical fashion: Charles divulges his real gender, which the general claims to have known all along (akin to the ending of *Some Like It Hot*); and Madame Wong reveals that she's actually in cahoots with the government and plans to arrest the general.

After the others have left Charles and Everett alone, the play's denouement says it all:

> **CHARLES:** Madame Wong working for the C.I.A.? I had no idea.
>
> **EVERETT:** You heard what she said about her connections. Madame Wong has the biggest Tong in China.
>
> **CHARLES:** Oh my God! I've got to write this play! I can't do it! The deadline is up, and I'm completely dry. I'm burned out.... It's writer's block. I haven't got an idea in my head! There've just been too many distractions! (*He collapses in despair*)
>
> **EVERETT:** Why don't you just write about all the distractions and interruptions that happen to you when you're trying to write a play?
>
> **CHARLES:** (*Brightening*) That's a brilliant idea! I'll do it!

Ludlam wrote *How to Write a Play* in less than a week, and the focused intensity helped produce one of his more solid and delightful farces. Though most of it sprang whole cloth from Ludlam's imagination, the subplot regarding the South American dictator was taken directly from Feydeau's *Un Fil à la Patte*. Some passages were even lifted word-for-word. Once again dictating the play to Samuels, Ludlam placed a volume of Feydeau in front of him and, pointing with his finger, said, "Start typing here."

While *How to Write a Play* exaggerated the lunacy of Ludlam's daily existence, there was another development during the course of launching it that was practically as crazy as anything that occurs in the play. Just before the rehearsals were scheduled to begin, Ludlam had his annual June meeting with NYSCA, with Samuels in tow. When Ludlam told Gigi Bolt — the NYSCA representative who would later become head of the theater program at the NEA — that he was frantically putting together a new play to fulfill the previous year's agreement, she was concerned and dismayed. She told him that NYSCA was there to provide relief, not pressure. She made it clear that Ludlam should have come to them earlier, explained the extenuating circumstances (the unexpectedly long run of *Galas*), and simply requested an amendment to the grant agreement.

As they left the meeting, a somewhat dazed Ludlam suggested to Samuels that perhaps they should abandon *How to Write a Play*. But as they were already so far along, Samuels convinced him to go through with it, in the event that they encountered a similar predicament the following season. Given the time constraints, rehearsals were confined to less than two weeks. Ultimately, there would only be two performances — plus a well-attended dress rehearsal — the last weekend in June, before Ludlam took off for Pittsburgh.

Considering how compressed the schedule was, it's remarkable that Ludlam wrote a play with sixteen characters, and even more amazing that he managed to assemble such a large cast so quickly. Accentuating the ways in which the play was autobiographical, he cast it with people from every period in the company's history, making it a kind of homecoming.

Charlotte Forbes, who hadn't performed with the Ridiculous since *Reverse Psychology*, was Claudia, the company manager who introduces the character of Charles to the South American general. "Charles had to *beg* me to do it," said Forbes. "He just wooed me to death." She was finally enticed by the "promise of only three performances," and the lack of any longer commitment to the project. For Forbes, as for others, it was more of a "hoot" — a way to have fun with Ludlam and the gang, as opposed to anything more rigorous.

Not having worked with the company since his dismissal during rehearsals for

Caprice nearly a decade before, Jack Mallory returned for *How to Write a Play*. Ludlam built the dynamic of his abusive relationship with Mallory into the character of Ima Poussy. Even though he only gave three performances, Mallory considered it his "best role" with the Ridiculous.

In addition to featuring other company regulars such as Black-Eyed Susan, Bill Vehr, Ed McGowan, and Deborah Petti, the cast of *How to Write a Play* introduced a new-comer by the name of Katy Dierlam. An acquaintance of Samuels from Bennington, Dierlam had become his administrative assistant at the Ridiculous a few months earlier. Since she weighed five hundred pounds, "The minute Charles laid eyes on her, he dreamed of ways to put her in a play," said Samuels. Dierlam was cast as Natalie, "a cleaning woman of heroic proportions" (reads a stage direction) who does a G-string striptease in the midst of the mayhem.

How to Write a Play never opened for review. Its three historical performances were attended predominantly by the company's most die-hard fans — Minette, for one, saw it twice. Though there was talk of a subsequent production, presumably after *Irma Vep* opened to the press in the fall and enjoyed a successful run, it never came to pass.

In the meantime, with Leon Katz behind the wheel, Ludlam rode out to Pittsburgh on July 1 to begin three weeks of intensive rehearsals for *Hedda Gabler*. Chatham College was presenting the play as part of the second season of the American Ibsen Theatre (aka, the National Ibsen Symposium), which had been cofounded by Michael Zelenak and Rick Davis. The team had met with Katz in New Haven during the winter to discuss their plans for the 1984 summer season. With *Hedda* as the drawing card, it would also include repertory productions of Ibsen's *Little Eyolf* and Schiller's *The Robbers*.

Zelenak and Davis wanted to emphasize the comic elements they felt were lurking in *Hedda*. And with Katz prodding them, they also came to see the demands of the role in terms of a kind of nineteenth century acting style: working from the outside-in, as opposed to the psychologically-based Method acting that has predominated since. After being stumped and unable to come up with the name of a single suitable actress, it was Katz who suddenly blurted out, "Well, what about Charles Ludlam?" They leaped at the suggestion. Davis had already played host to Ludlam in Appleton, Wisconsin five years earlier, when *The Ventriloquist's Wife* was performed at Lawrence University.

As recorded in his "Hedda Journal" — a handful of brief notebook entries he made during the first week of rehearsals — Ludlam reported:

> Leon [Katz] tells me that anything one says about Hedda is true and that the opposite is also true. He recommended me for the role because he felt that I was the only actor who could play the contradictions in turns, thereby imply a human being/motive somewhere behind them. That I would accentuate the contradictions rather than flattening them out — Attempts at a consistent characterization lose Hedda.

Ludlam had always admired Ibsen and been particularly taken with the complex character of Hedda Gabler, who, despite her feminine qualities, had the drive and ambitions of a man. When he was offered the part, his instant response was, "Ah, my role!" A feature in the *Pittsburgh Post-Gazette* would later report that he was "agog with excitement" about doing it. In defense of the drag dimension, he said, "It saves us from literalism, which is the great enemy of art." Earlier he had told the *Village Voice* for a notice on the upcoming event: "Hedda's a man trapped in a woman's body, a woman with a man's mind. It's perfect to do in drag. And it needs a virtuoso performer."

Later that spring, Mel Shapiro was approached to direct the production of *Hedda*. Shapiro was familiar with Ludlam's work, and delighted when they told him who the start would be. Remarkable though it seems, this was the first (and last) time Ludlam was directed by anyone else on the stage since his split with John Vaccaro back in 1967. Though he was coming fresh from *Galas* and many expected him to behave like the diva he had been portraying, Ludlam proved extremely cooperative with Shapiro and the rest of the cast. According to Davis, who served as dramaturge on the production, Ludlam was even deferential: "He seemed to work very consciously at removing his other hats and becoming a collaborator." But then, Shapiro directed Ludlam with "a very light touch."

There was nothing special about the salary Ludlam received to suggest he was the star. But with Quinton along, he was put up in an old apartment building called Webster Hall, while the rest of the cast stayed in campus dormitories. Rehearsals were held five hours a day, six days a week; but Ludlam was having chronic stomach problems that summer and a number of the sessions ended early.

Though Ludlam ultimately gave a very precise and unvaried performance, there was a funny incident during the first preview when he confused several scenes in his mind, and started dressing for the wrong one. By the time he realized his error and began changing back into his correct costume, he was late making his entrance. He came rushing on-stage only partially dressed, saying in character, "Thea, would you zip me up, please?"

Ludlam made quite a splash as Hedda, playing the part in a grand and physically aggressive manner. When a stage direction called for Hedda to open the drapes, Ludlam didn't simply open them, he *threw* them back. He did not sit down on the chaise longue, he *collapsed* onto it. Rather than just grabbing Thea's hair, he *lunged* at it. Through his interpretation, it became a very self-consciously theatrical role.

But as more than one reviewer noted, the edge Ludlam gave to his performance separated it from the rest of the cast and hence the overall production was lacking a coherent style. "At the time, Charles and Mel were not really aware of that [discrepancy in the performance], and were surprised to hear that reaction," recalled Eric Bentley, who was a participant in the Ibsen Festival and had caught Ludlam's performance. "The other actors played *Hedda* absolutely straight. Charles was such an ironic personality, you never knew how literally to take what he said; but he seemed to think he fit in with that. He thought he was not a drag queen, but a female impersonator who could actu-ally be mistaken for a woman."

While one review was quite positive and another an outright pan, both hinged entirely on reactions to Ludlam. On the other hand, a number of advance feature stories in the local papers were geared to stir up controversy: The critics' invitation promised a "daring, risky new interpretation of the ever-popular Ibsen classic *Hedda Gabler* [that] will make theatrical history."

The controversy continued at a much-heated symposium on Saturday morning, August 11, where Bentley gave the keynote address. In addition to Bentley and Katz, several heavy-hitters of theatrical scholarship were on hand to discuss the great Norwegian playwright, including Richard Gilman and Martin Esslin. Ludlam was present to answer any questions that were posed. According to Bentley, the event was dominated by "an egotistical feminist" who was outraged that Hedda had been played by a man. While a number of those present "wondered how the other characters could possibly ignore this Hedda's strange posturing," Leon Katz defended the radical casting choice by pointing out that "Hedda Gabler is neither a man nor a woman, [but] a *character*." When a male member of the audience said that he had always expected "Hedda Gabler to be more beautiful," a noticeably crestfallen Ludlam tried to disguise his humiliation, retorting, "Well, I do my best."

Despite considerable criticism, Ludlam remained proud of his performance, and his Hedda became legendary. He so coveted a pair of shoes he had worn in the production that he eventually acquired them from the Ibsen Festival as a memento.

಄

After the final performance of *Hedda Gabler* on August 19, Ludlam returned to New York to remount *The Mystery of Irma Vep*. It opened to the press six weeks later. In response to feedback from its preliminary run in the spring, he kept working on the script until the weekend before critics began to attend. In the process, he made what had already been a crowd-pleaser during previews into a masterpiece for the ages.

To some extent, the secret of the production's ingeniousness relied on both classic magicians' tricks for distracting the audience, and on puppeteers' techniques for throwing the voice. Ventriloquism was frequently utilized to make a character's voice appear to be trailing off on one side of the stage, while the actor was actually changing costume behind the scenery and about to reemerge as a different character on the other.

Needless to say, the entire effect depended on the timing. When the first outside production of the play surfaced (in Toronto in 1985), the actors reported how proud they were to have their costume changes down to twenty seconds. For Ludlam and Quinton, who accomplished their changes in just five to ten seconds, this would have seemed like an eternity. To make it all possible, there were three dressers strategically positioned backstage. (Ludlam always said that *Irma Vep* had been "choreographed like Kabuki.")

After the show became one of the hottest tickets in New York and settled in for a long run, certain people were granted permission to watch it from backstage. They included the sculptor Nancy Graves, a generous financial contributor to the company, as well as Curt Sanburn, a reporter from *Life* magazine who was planning a "spread" on Ludlam and the Ridiculous in conjunction with the next show. From the backstage perspective, *Irma Vep* resembled a boxing match as much as a play: With rolls of paper towels cluttering the wings, the dressers would blot the sweat from the actors while helping them in and out of their tear-away costumes (Velcro was one of the secrets), and then hurling them back into the ring. The show was so physically exhausting that Samuels persuaded Ludlam to offer only one performance on Saturdays, instead of the two they had been giving during the spring preview period.

While the reviews for *Galas* had surpassed in volume anything the Ridiculous had known before, the same could now be said about the response to *Irma Vep*. The critics were obviously intoxicated and quite eager to spread their euphoria.

"Don't bother to read this," declared Clive Barnes in the opening sentence of his review for the *Post*. "Just make plans to go to One Sheridan Square and arrange tickets. . . . You quite conceivably will have seen nothing like it before." Frank Rich took a similar, hard-sell approach in his review for WQXR Radio: "If you've never been down to the Company's tiny theater at Sheridan Square, this is definitely the time to go," he broadcast. "In every way, *The Mystery of Irma Vep* is the strongest possible reminder of why the Ridiculous Theatrical Company is one of the most lovable institutions in the New York theater."

The New York Times review was written by Mel Gussow, as opposed to Frank Rich, and although it too was a rave, there was some concern about a limit to its impact because Gussow wasn't the chief critic. But Rich's radio review four days later simply doubled the exposure.

The rave reaction ranged over the entire spectrum of critics and publications, from Michael Feingold in the *Village Voice* ("One of the best times I've had in the theater in quite a long stretch") to Richard Corliss in *Time* magazine ("Deft as a textbook travesty, delightful enough to take your mom (or your mummy) to, *Irma Vep* serves as a spiked tonic to the young theater season. It's penny wonderful"). Even beyond the Los Angeles coverage of *Galas*, Dallas and Denver were now taking notice, along with the *Nation*, *Vogue*, and a seemingly endless variety of national and regional publications. In the months ahead, reviews of this Off-Broadway production would appear in countless local papers — from Atlanta, Georgia, to Bloomington, Indiana — to say nothing of the numerous foreign language reviews abroad. More than one London paper enthusiastically reported that negotiations were under way to import the show there. And as with *Galas* before it, *Irma Vep* would inevitably appear on both *The New York Times* and *Time* magazine's "Best of the Year" lists.

There was much well earned praise for the cozy, booby-trapped set designed by Ludlam, and for the equally ingenious costumes designed by Quinton. But since the major thrust of the show concerned its quick-change artistry and because it was so brilliantly executed, the performances of both Ludlam and Quinton were particularly emphasized by the reviewers who almost consistently employed the words "*bravura*" and "*tour de force*" to describe each of them. As if to convey just how magically Ludlam and Quinton peopled the stage with multiple characters, some reviewers reported that they portrayed six, seven, or even more figures between them. To cover all the bases, Mel Gussow wisely provided a range in his review: "What makes it singular is that every one of the myriad characters — men and women, more than 6, less than 12 — is played by Mr. Ludlam and Everett Quinton."

Shortly after *Irma* opened, Ludlam ran into Martin Gottfried who told him, "Now you've done it, Charles! You'll never top this!" With typical hubris, Ludlam replied, "It may be true, but at least I have the satisfaction of knowing no one else ever will either."

Though Quinton had begun to receive major recognition in *Galas*, now he was suddenly being perceived as a star in his own right. Just as Ludlam had received a Hirschfeld caricature the previous year as *Galas*, Quinton now received his as Lord Edgar in *Irma Vep*.

"I realized how much I didn't know and I was shocked at how much I had to learn," a beaming Quinton told Enid Nemy for her theater column in the weekend section of Friday's *New York Times*. "I've just recently learned to hold the stage.... I've just recently learned to deal with characterization on a broader level, and I'm still learning how to handle my voice."

Though he had no theatrical training prior to meeting Ludlam and joining the Ridiculous eight years before, the thirty-two-year-old Quinton was now a force on the New York stage to be reckoned with in his own right. According to Samuels, "Part of what drove *Irma Vep* was that Charles had someone in his face every night who was struggling to steal the scenes from him, and Everett sometimes succeeded." But rather than feeling threatened by the situation, Ludlam reveled in it. After all was said and done, he had engineered it in the first place: Quinton's success reflected not only the depth of Ludlam's love for him, but also a newfound security in Ludlam himself and a willingness to share the limelight.

There was another way Quinton was trying to grow however, which, Samuels claimed, provoked some testiness in Ludlam. During the period of *Galas*, Quinton began working on a play of his own. It was based on someone once having told him that Pinocchio was homosexual. In Quinton's elaboration on the idea, a Catholic schoolgirl befriends the gay Pinocchio. When a distressed nun finds out about their association, she sets out to murder the little wooden boy and procures a flamethrower for the purpose.

According to Samuels, Ludlam was "at various times incensed" after he learned about the play, which Quinton was calling *Feed Them to the Christians*. "He might laugh about it," said Samuels. "He might say, 'I thought *I* was the playwright here!' But there was a double-edge to the jokes he made and you could tell he really meant it. Charles did not want his authority challenged that overtly."

Though Quinton did not recall any friction over his attempts to write a play, he apparently sensed it might pose a threat to Ludlam. As Samuels recalled, he had kept his play "a secret" from everyone — including his lover — for quite some time.

Samuels also had playwriting aspirations, but he temporarily abandoned them by the time of *Galas*, "primarily because Charles was very paranoid and I was much too involved with our working relationship to want to make him feel that I was competing with him as a playwright." It's telling that Samuels and Peter Golub were working on a large musical project together, but doing so surreptitiously. "There was no question that Charles would have felt threatened," said Samuels.

A few years earlier, Samuels had written a play and wanted to apply for a grant. The NEA requirements stipulated that any play submitted had to have a reading by a professional theater company. Samuels, somewhat intimidated by the prospect, asked Ludlam if he could just *say* he had had a reading at the Ridiculous. But Ludlam had insisted upon actually going ahead with it. To fill out a cast of ten, a number of people were involved, including Ludlam himself, Quinton, and Black-Eyed Susan.

"It was fairly clear Charles didn't think there was much going on in it," said Samuels. "But he said, 'I could do something with this. On the other hand, I could do something with anything.'" Samuels chose a path of less resistance by turning to fiction instead. This would in no way jeopardize his relationship with Ludlam, who had never considered writing a novel.

Curiously, there was a time when Ludlam warned Samuels that any association with the Ridiculous might work against him, that people "might look askance" at him based on his connection with the company. This was when the Ridiculous was in something of a slump, before the sustained success they were now enjoying. Ludlam may have been thinking about the dismissive way his fellow actors were treated by the reviewers. He was also possibly thinking of Pashalinski, who was having difficulty establishing herself as an actress in anything beyond the Ridiculous genre because of her long-term association with the company. Ludlam's aesthetic was so misunderstood that it could be perceived as a hindrance.

Ludlam once asked Samuels, "If you make any money as a writer, would you put it into the Ridiculous?" Samuels told him he would probably support his own work first. "Charles did not take that well," remembered Samuels. "He was shocked that I might actually have something else to do with my money besides give it to him."

Not that Ludlam needed any money at the time. With the heady and glowing success of *Irma*, the whole world seemed to be opening up to him. Suddenly, it wasn't so much a matter of whom Ludlam knew, as it was a matter of who wanted to know him. The phone at the Morton Street apartment started to ring constantly. In the futile attempt to try and maintain some morning solitude for his personal routines, Ludlam established a designated hour for receiving phone calls, between 11 AM and noon. But it became increasingly difficult to reach him since the phone was constantly busy. There were endless requests for interviews, many of which were granted, including permission for *Life* magazine to track Ludlam's habits for a future article. And this was when Joseph Papp began courting Ludlam, eventually asking him to direct *Titus Andronicus* for the New York Shakespeare Festival. This was also when Ludlam was invited to direct *Die Fledermaus* at the Santa Fe Opera in the summer of 1986, and to craft his own libretto for the production.

While *Irma Vep* was playing to packed audiences at One Sheridan Square, there was talk about moving it to Broadway. Ludlam was approached by a producer who took him to lunch. But as with *Corn* more than a dozen years before, Ludlam proved resistant to the move. Ever since his early experiences with John Vaccaro, Ellen Stewart, and Adela Holzer, he had a pathological fear and distrust of both contracts and producers. In the case of a transfer to Broadway, where more and more multiple producers were becoming necessary to finance any given project, it would mean losing even more control. It would also require company members to join Actors' Equity, which could jeopardize future operations. There was also the intimate nature of the show to be considered in relation to the size of the theater. Why move *Irma Vep* when it clearly could have a long life with significant financial rewards in his own venue, under his own control? As Samuels summarized it, "There was no ambivalence in Charles's desire for success. It was rather over what he might have to give up in order to have it." If a key value for Ludlam remained a matter of succeeding on his own terms, his resistance to a Broadway transfer of *Irma Vep* was an indication of just how savvy he still was.

He received yet another invitation to move *Irma Vep*. As the recently appointed head of the nascent American National Theater, Peter Sellars invited Ludlam to Washington, D.C. to discuss bringing *Irma Vep* there as soon as possible. Adding that "This will be yours," he also showed Ludlam a smaller space at the Kennedy Center where the Ridiculous might introduce new works in the future. Having once joined Ludlam and Sellars for breakfast in New York, William Kohler claimed that "Charles was afraid he'd end up with the short end of the stick." Thus nothing ever came of Ludlam's pending affiliation with the American National Theater, nor of Sellars' additional plan to costar him and Carol Channing in a production of Congreve's *The Way of the World*. Ludlam failed to see any advantage in having a second home in Washington anyway; and according to Samuels, he never took any of his talks with Sellars very seriously.

While Ludlam proved stubborn about not moving *Irma Vep*, he was also resistant, at first, when regional companies began asking if they could mount their own productions of the show. If it was hard enough to consider relinquishing control in the course of working with other producers, the thought of others performing the work on their own seemed out of the question. Walter Gidaly, Ludlam's longtime lawyer, recalled having any number of lengthy discussions with Ludlam before finally convincing him to grant David Daniels, a producer, the right to present the play in Toronto at the Adelaide Court Theater during the summer of 1985. Productions followed at the Capital Rep in Albany, the Pegasus Theater in Dallas, the Remains Theater in Chicago, and many other cities during the mid-eighties. Eventually *Irma Vep* would become the longest-running play in the history of Brazil, playing continuously there for eight years. (In the special licensing agreement Gidaly drew up for *Irma Vep*, he included a clause that may very well be unique in the history of theatrical contracts: It guaranteed that the play would entail cross-dressing, by stipulating that both actors had to be of the same gender.)

Not all of the early attention prompted by *Irma Vep* proved welcome, however. Marjorie Ludlam became livid when a friend at a senior citizens meeting handed her a feature story about the play that referred to Quinton as her son's lover. "So I called Charles," said Marjorie nearly a decade later. "I was mad. I said, 'Why did you have to put it in the paper?' And then Everett got mad at me, and I don't think he's ever really been friendly with me since."

Marjorie was so riled, in fact, that she didn't properly convey the source of her anger. While both Ludlam and Quinton were under the impression that Marjorie had just learned they were lovers from the article, she was rather upset over their willingness to discuss their relationship with the press. Given Quinton's many visits to Greenlawn with Ludlam, when filmmaker Mark Rappaport heard about this phone call, he said, "Who did she think Everett was? Your favorite actor?" And even though it was based on his misunderstanding the nature of Marjorie's anger, Ludlam could have been speaking for an entire generation of gay sons in the post-Stonewall era when he bitterly concluded, "Mothers are always the first to know, but the last to find out."

かな

Ludlam realized he had a gold mine with *Irma Vep* from the beginning, but he started making plans in the fall for his next play to be introduced in rep during the spring. The question was: What would he put on? It was only natural for Samuels to argue in favor of *How to Write a Play*, since it would have been its virtual premiere. But Ludlam viewed *How to Write a Play* as an "evergreen" that could be easily inserted into any future schedule. He felt far more drawn to *Salammbô*, which he was already beginning to envision — and promote — as his "Cecil B. DeMille" production.

At least part of the motive behind the timing of *Salammbô* could be found in Ludlam's rebellious nature, as demonstrated repeatedly by his interactions with teachers and other authority figures throughout his life. After proving that he could be a mainstream success on such an enormous scale with *Irma Vep*, Ludlam now needed to remind the press, the public — and maybe even himself — of what the Ridiculous was *really* about. He was very deliberately throwing it in their faces by going back to his beloved epic structure, knowing full well that it was a risky and unpopular form — or would be prior to *Angels in America* (whose author Tony Kushner has acknowledged his debt to Charles Ludlam). Ludlam's previous epic outing, *Exquisite Torture*, had been an exquisite failure. Ludlam loved *Irma Vep*, but as far as he was concerned, it was strictly entertaining. *Salammbô*, on the other hand, would be more representative of his art. No matter how much he was being recognized for his genius, Ludlam knew the situation would turn around and bite him sooner or later. He'd get the first bite with *Salammbô*.

One can almost hear Ludlam himself talking in a letter that Gustave Flaubert wrote, anticipating a harsh reaction to his novel: "*Salammbô* will 1) irritate the bourgeois — which is to say, everybody; 2) upset the nerves and hearts of sensitive readers; 3) anger the archaeologists; 4) seem unintelligible to ladies; 5) give me the reputation of being a pederast and a cannibal. Let's hope so!"

Though Ludlam had happened upon *Salammbô* somewhat inadvertently via Oscar Wilde, it was custom-made for his Ridiculous "epic" imprint. "I think I use the word *purple* or *diamond* in every sentence of my book," Flaubert wrote in another letter while working on *Salammbô*, which he described as "historical hashish." Because there was more legend than fact surrounding the pre-Christian city and civilization of Carthage, the author had embarked on an enormous research project and become a leading expert on the subject before starting his novel, which took five years to write. While many of the characters were based on real-life figures, such as Carthage's general Hamilcar, his daughter Salammbô was entirely Flaubert's invention. Matho, the barbarian military captain who falls in love with her, had also been a real historical figure.

Flaubert knew to expect a violent reaction to his novel because he had included the most gruesome details in his recreation of barbarian customs and warfare. His description of the leprosy-ridden Hanno, Hamilcar's rival for power in Carthage, makes for one of the most repulsive figures in literature. But Flaubert did not anticipate that the book would be poorly received by the critics for being top-heavy with confusing battle scenes, or that he personally would be compared to the Marquis de Sade. Nor did he know that *Salammbô* would at the same time become a *cause célèbre* and even have an identifiable influence on Parisian fashions. Shortly after it was published, the Empress Eugenie was among the first to consult with Flaubert about having a dress made in the style of his controversial heroine.

Though Ludlam also set out to stir up controversy with his staging of *Salammbô*, he had not expected to be pummeled by the critics and rejected by the public to the degree that he would be. While clearly provocative, the production also represented his faith in the educative value of the theater, and his belief that, after nearly two decades, he had developed an audience capable of seeing his work in terms of the innovations he had intended. As with some of his first few plays (*Big Hotel, Conquest of the Universe, The Grand Tarot, Eunuchs of the Forbidden City*) as well as a couple from the middle period (*Der Ring Gott Farblonjet* and *Exquisite Torture*), *Salammbô* would be an epic. But it would also be his most extravagant and beautiful epic. Ludlam luxuriated in his conception of ancient Carthage, and despite the disappointing way in which the play was ultimately received, many near to him were under the impression that *Salammbô* remained his favorite of all the plays.

To better accommodate his grandiose designs, it was the first time Ludlam employed an assistant director. (Phillip Warner — the brother of Peter Golub's girlfriend, Cristina — was recruited for the job.) A large part of the conceit was to try to create a thoroughly lavish atmosphere. With the box office boom from *Galas* and *Irma Vep*, Ludlam could afford to invest as much as $80,000, making *Salammbô* far and away his most expensive production. (*Irma Vep*, by comparison, had cost roughly a quarter of that, and during the eighties, most other productions would range from $20,000–$35,000.) Due to the company's non-Equity status and the generosity Ludlam inspired in others, the $80,000 went much further for staging effects than it would have with another company. Edgardo Franceschi's set designs utilized a lot of *trompe l'oeil* and faux marble. Quinton's costumes were more ravishing and spectacular than any he had designed before. The production would be excessive in the same over-the-top way that Fellini's *Satyricon* had been.

Since both plays would run in rep at first, the need to store the sets for *Irma Vep* in the already cramped wing space at One Sheridan Square placed significant limitations on what Franceschi could design for *Salammbô*. But in accordance with Ludlam's wishes and despite the spatial restrictions, his sets for this production proved to be the most extravagant the Ridiculous had ever known.

The single most striking feature of *Salammbô*, however, was that Ludlam filled out the large cast with bodybuilders rather than actors. From the very beginning, he had pictured the barbarian hordes in terms of rippling torsos and bulging muscles, clad only in skimpy loincloths. While he saw the play as his "gift to the world celebrating my reading of all of Flaubert," and while he set out, like Flaubert, "to accomplish in art what is unattainable in life," his use of bodybuilders was partially in response to the AIDS epidemic. "*Salammbô* is one for the boys, believe me!" he declared in an interview for a gay publication. "We decided that we gays have been through enough in the last couple of years. We are going to give them a little something."

As alarming as AIDS was, by 1985 the right-wing response and political backlash were in some respects even more dismaying. Society's increasing acceptance of homosexuality — which had been earned through long, hard battles over the previous two decades — was suddenly being undone. With its drag and bodybuilder components, *Salammbô* was also Ludlam's in-your-face response to this calamity; his highly exaggerated expression of what was being lost. Ludlam would tell a baffled Wally Gorell that *Salammbô* is "my AIDS play, which says everything I want to say on the subject."

When he was interviewed by Alan R. Yoffee for an article in *Au Courant* magazine, to be published in conjunction with the play's press opening in November, Ludlam launched into his perennial argument about how the Ridiculous was not gay theater, per se.

> I think the distinction between gay theater and what I do, which some people call "queer theater," is that gay theater is really a political movement to show that gay people can be admirable, responsible members of the community. It shows their problems. I don't do that. I've written plays that have had gay characters: *Caprice* was about a gay fashion designer. My theater does use certain elements of this deviant, deserted point of view to interpret to the world, but it's not gay writing about [being] gay.

> Because I am homosexual, it becomes significant to homosexuals on that level, I suppose. But I don't think it's me trying to prove that gay people are these remarkable members of society who are going to be bourgeois, because I don't think that's necessarily right. If they want to, fine. I don't doubt that they can be teachers and office workers who are reliable, but maybe depicting them as dangerous characters would be more interesting. Maybe we're not as housebroken as those plays want to make it seem.

With *Salammbô*, Ludlam was going to put the "sex" back into homosexuality. And this was precisely at a time when there was an enormous amount of pressure — even within the gay community — to appear "safe" and assimilationist. *Salammbô* began its previews a few weeks after the Off-Broadway opening of William M. Hoffman's *As Is* and a few weeks before Larry Kramer's *The Normal Heart*, the first two significant AIDS plays, which together served as a clarion call to the world about the epidemic. (Given Ludlam's own imminent death from AIDS, it's particularly poignant to note that Hoffman paid homage to him in *As Is*: A stranger in a bar tries to pick up the play's protagonist by saying, "Do you like movies? There's an Alfred Hitchcock festival at the Regency. Or maybe we could see the new Charles Ludlam. . . .")

Ludlam would later claim,

> I certainly couldn't have called [*Salammbô*] an AIDS play; it had nothing to do with that. But it was about *the official religion*, which was a state religion, a fascist state that stated, "All who touch the veil must die!" Then you had to die to prove that they were right — in the play — that society always has to be right, even if they're dead wrong in actuality.

Just when the gay world suddenly had compelling reasons to become more monogamous or even celibate, Ludlam was going to celebrate the lascivious promiscuity it had
reveled in before — primarily by putting a lot of raw muscle onstage. Finding the
champion athletes was another matter, however. Initially, Ludlam advertised in various
publications for "muscular" actors. But those who responded were hopelessly scrawny
in comparison to what he had in mind. Matthew Epstein, a friend and an agent at
Columbia Management, came to the rescue. He referred a couple of bodybuilders who
had been spear-carriers in various operas. They in turn brought some pumping buddies
along to auditions at the Ridiculous. Ludlam was so enthralled and tongue-tied by the
erotic fantasies they sparked that he couldn't bring himself to ask them to remove their
shirts and display their physiques. It was left to Larry Eichler, the production's stage
manager, to make the request.

No one ever knew how many of the bodybuilders were going to show up for a particular
performance of *Salammbô*, and a small army of them passed through the theater during
the course of the run. Though there were usually eight, there could be as few as five or
as many as nine onstage on any given night. Sometimes someone would arrive and
announce, "Oh, so-and-so isn't going to come anymore, so I brought so-and-so along,"
and newcomers would just slip into the production in this arbitrary fashion. Ludlam
pretended to be shocked by such amateurish behavior, but he was secretly titillated:
excited by the prospect of becoming visually acquainted with yet another well-oiled body.

Needless to say, some of the men were pretty unusual characters. One of the short-lived
ones, named Roger, had been a porn star who also appeared in *Village Voice* ads for
gyms and various erotic products. Roger was somewhat unpredictable and could be
dangerously out of control. At one performance, he claimed that two members of the
audience were lesbians who were heckling him, so he interrupted the scene to "moon"
them. There was the French Canadian, Pierre Asselin, who choreographed the bodybuilders' poses, but his accent was so impenetrable that he always provoked laughter
when he spoke onstage. There was also another who spoke only Spanish, but fortunately, Phillip Warner knew the language and could convey Ludlam's directions to him.

While one of the bodybuilders was an accomplished ragtime pianist and rather cultured,
most of them were not particularly educated. Another named Jerry didn't have an
especially large body, but Ludlam hired him because he thought he could act. According
to Samuels, "It was the ones who had a spectacularly naive quality that appealed to
Charles the most. The less experience they had, the more charming they proved to be.
Rehearsals might have been prolonged just for the pleasure of their company."

Rehearsals for *Salammbô* began in the winter while *Irma Vep* was at the height of its run. They continued for almost four months, usually three-hour sessions, a few afternoons a week at One Sheridan Square. This atypically long time frame was not only due to the scope of the show, but also to the difficulties Ludlam was having with the script — not to mention the ongoing physical demands of continuing to perform in *Irma Vep*. He was writing and rewriting, delivering the scenes in dribs and drabs. All of the actors had problems with the play, both during rehearsals as well as the run, and Ludlam kept trying to address them. Though he still derived more pleasure from strutting around the stage and being adored as an actor, Ludlam long before had realized his writing would survive him: He had learned to take it more seriously than he had in the beginning.

While contending with the many complaints that surfaced as *Salammbô* was being created, Ludlam acknowledged that epics were harder than more tightly constructed plays both to put on and to sustain. He understood that you had to keep on introducing fresh business to prevent the performers and the play from becoming stale. But he never anticipated the many cast changes he would have to endure between the play's preview period in the spring and its reopening in the fall.

To all evidence, *Salammbô* had the most chaotic backstage environment of any Ridiculous production. Given the cramped quarters at One Sheridan Square, as well as the size and diversity of the cast, it was even more of a circus-like atmosphere than *Der Ring Gott Farblonjet* had been a decade earlier. Not only were there eighteen cast members, but several of them were twice the size of regular players.

The bodybuilders shared the front dressing room. They all liked to grease themselves up before going out onstage; and prior to the posing scene that opened Act II, some of them were sure to pump up all of their muscles — including the one nestled in their loin-cloths. One time, a couple of them disappeared into the bathroom just before curtain time, and the heavy breathing that ensued let everyone know they required some privacy. Given their special diets, the bodybuilders also tended to release an inordinate amount of flatulence. Not only was incense burned during the performance to try to disguise the odor, but the doors were always opened at intermission as well to help ventilate the air.

As if to complement the bodybuilders, there were also the drag performers. Ludlam, as Salammbô, and Quinton, as her handmaiden Taanach, shared the second main dressing room with Samuels and John Heys. Heys also was in high drag as Schahabarim, "an old eunuch priest," and Samuels portrayed Spendius, a Greek slave who conspires with the barbarians to bring down Carthage. In yet another dressing room, Ethyl Eichelberger (who was playing Hamilcar) tended to the company's wigs, protecting them from the live doves that were employed in the play to augur the deflowering of Salammbô by Matho. The doves sometimes flew out of control both on- and offstage.

But the most improbable sight of all to conjure is that of the obese Katy Dierlam, alone in the petite dressing room that normally served as Black-Eyed Susan's. Dierlam, the only authentic female in the cast, was portraying the grotesque Hanno, "a decadent Suffete who suffers from overweight and leprosy."

"It was unimaginable backstage," said Samuels. "I'd get into my simple, brown, sackcloth costume and then pass this five hundred pound naked lady applying body makeup to make herself look leprous. Your breath was taken away. But by the second or third day, it became perfectly normal — that was the scary part." It was the use of Dierlam, wearing only a loincloth onstage, that prompted some scathing commentary and a heated exchange of letters in the *Village Voice*.

But problems surfaced with *Salammbô* long before the press was invited in the fall. Though there had been a longer than usual rehearsal period, Ludlam knew the play still wasn't working when previews started in April. In the midst of performances, he would run off for a costume change and scrawl messages on his mirror with lipstick — as was his custom — so he could remember specific acting notes to give people later. He had particular difficulties with Emilio Cubeiro, who had played Mercanteggini in *Galas* and was now portraying Matho, the lead barbarian who consummates his passion for Salammbô. Cubeiro drove Ludlam crazy, repeatedly asking picayune questions regarding the psychological motives of his character, which seemed entirely superfluous given the epic nature of the play. And although, as Ludlam had commanded, Cubeiro had grown a beard for his role in the spring, he had the audacity to shave it off during the summer hiatus. Ludlam so resented this that he replaced him in the fall.

There had already been a number of cast changes during the preview period. Michael Belanger, who had played the Choreographer in *Le Bourgeois Avant-Garde*, was originally cast as Spendius. But he injured himself when he stumbled into a pothole while jogging, and couldn't walk, let alone perform. With a day to learn the part, Samuels replaced him early in the previews. He recalled that Phillip Warner was rehearsing him in the late afternoon, a few hours before curtain, when Ludlam came into the theater and sat in the back. "He made me so nervous," said Samuels, "I suddenly couldn't remember any of my lines." Ludlam in turn panicked, saying that they would have to get somebody else right away. But Warner intervened, saying, "I'm handling this,

Charles. He'll get it, but you're driving him crazy. Just go away." And he did. Samuels performed the role during previews and opened with it in the fall.

But apparently just about everyone was having a rough time with *Salammbô* from the beginning. Adam Kilgore, who had returned to the Ridiculous for the first time in years, was only around for the previews. "I just hated my role," recalled Kilgore. "I had this long scene where I was ranting and raving in chains. It was very difficult and it was even painful. Friends who came to see me said they couldn't understand how I figured in the plot or who my character was supposed to be. I went to Charles and said maybe he should redistribute some of the lines. By the time it opened, I wasn't in it."

John Heys also had difficulty apprehending his role of Schahabarim. "I read the Flaubert before we started rehearsing and I didn't understand it or see what Charles saw in it," admitted Heys.

> But I always took Charles's direction with the utmost gravity and tried to follow what he was saying. Still, whatever I did in *Salammbô*, it just wouldn't work for him. There were nights when I knew I played the scene to the maximum of my capabilities, and I thought that we were really cooking, we were communicating, and giving-and-taking on these lines. But it was never good enough for Charles. There was never a night when I felt like I did anything right.

Everyone noticed that Heys indeed had problems with *Salammbô*: Sometimes he'd just go dead onstage. But instead of finessing the situation, Ludlam became more impatient with him. As others observed, he was "basically torturing John backstage" and "always on his case": giving him the same notes over and over again, constantly whining at him, calling him "Hazel," even though Heys made it clear he despised that fey nickname. Whereas Susan had customarily been the punching bag for Ludlam in previous productions, Heys was now serving that function in her absence.

For solace, Heys even turned to Susan and Vehr who tried to be supportive, "because they had been through it all before with Charles," said Heys. But since they weren't in the play themselves, they could only do so much. With hindsight, Heys acknowledged, "I was a large part of the problem because I felt so lost in that play, mostly because people I had worked with before, such as Bill and Susan, were not in the cast. I was looking for someone and there were always just these enormous bodies everywhere, constantly admiring themselves in the mirror. It was crazy. It was just too much."

Heys had dinner frequently with Ludlam and Quinton during *Salammbô*. Ludlam would talk about his ideas for future plays and about *The Sorrows of Dolores*, the film-in-progress he was perpetually editing. Ludlam was also pursuing Heys's concept for a one-man show based on Diana Vreeland, which Ludlam agreed to direct.

"There were also a lot of fights between Everett and Charles backstage," recalled Heys, "whenever Everett felt that a scene didn't work to his advantage or that Charles wasn't being generous onstage." Quinton was obviously miserable in *Salammbô*. No doubt it had something to do with the fact that he had a relatively small part as the heroine's maid, in contrast with his starring multiple roles in *Irma Vep*. While Ludlam performed onstage, Quinton acted out his own mini-dramas and angry fits in their dressing room. While muttering under his breath, he would throw things in his makeup case or toss his jewelry on the table and constantly threaten to quit, reminding everyone of what it had been like back when he was drinking.

For Ludlam, the chief frustration was his inability to get the production to come together in the way he envisioned. And with so much ill will backstage, everyone seemed to be sabotaging the finished product. *Salammbô* also failed to gel because of its abbreviated performance schedule. Since *Irma Vep* was still a sellout on its regular Wednesday through Sunday schedule, *Salammbô* was introduced in April on Tuesday nights only, without the opportunity to try changes out the next day. This prevented the fine-tuning the play required during the spring preview period.

Hoping that *Salammbô*, his magnum opus, would somehow take the shape he wanted before opening to the press in the fall, Ludlam took off for Santa Fe in the summer of 1985 to direct his first opera, Hans Werner Henze's *The English Cat*. At last, he was being accorded the national attention and respect he deserved for his wide-ranging, out-sized theatrical talents. It's impossible to imagine how much more he might have achieved, if only AIDS had not already begun to alter the life that Ludlam and everyone else — had known.

EVERY DAY A LITTLE DEATH

It is not our folly which makes me laugh: It is our wisdom.
— Montaigne

The invention and wit are nonstop
— John Rockwell

Despite the travails he was experiencing with the creation of *Salammbô*, Ludlam could console himself with the ongoing phenomenon that was *Irma Vep*. Its level of success had been gratifying from the outset. But as the months went by and it continued to play to packed houses, it provided Ludlam with a kind of reassurance he had never had in the past, assuaging some of the anxiety that always lurked behind any success he had known before.

Prior to *Reverse Psychology* in 1980, Ludlam hadn't received any royalties for his plays, although the company did pay his rent. (Unbeknownst to everyone else, there were a few times when Black-Eyed Susan was unemployed and the company paid her rent as well. When she offered to pay it back, Ludlam told her they would "take it out in secretarial fees.") By now, however, everything had become more standardized. Ludlam was earning 5 percent of the gross in royalties; plus he and Quinton were each taking home $500 a week as actors; and all the other actors were receiving a minimum of $125 a week.

With money accumulating in the bank for the first time in his life, Ludlam could suddenly entertain dreams of moving into a larger apartment while maintaining a separate studio for work. With more substantial living quarters, he imagined establishing a salon for friends and intimates on Mondays, or the "dark" nights at the theater. To maximize the company's income, Ludlam talked about taking over the Rosebay Cafe above the theater and opening his own restaurant there. He also considered turning the theater into a quasi Ripley's Believe-It-Or-Not museum or daytime attraction spot, as well as turning the company's storage studio on West 10th Street into a shop selling old costumes — or better yet, just renting them out for Halloween. Another potential project, which he mentioned every now and again, was the notion of reviving old vaudeville diversions, or "Greenwich Village Follies," and creating what he expected would become the supreme New York drag show. With his best marketing prowess, he even conceived that the name for this show would simply be the box office telephone number — 691-2271.

Though it's tempting to imagine how some of these plans might have panned out,

Ludlam was far too busy to ever realize any of them in the two hectic years of life remaining to him. Perhaps one of the greatest tributes to his genius was how quickly certain influential members of the music world recognized his talents and embraced him as a colleague.

While practically everyone else had a different impression, Steven Samuels claimed that Ludlam actually had strong misgivings about the use of music in the theater taking any sort of precedence over dialogue. "He was a very firm, vocal advocate of words on the stage, and he came to speak with great derision of opera," said Samuels. "He was only involved with opera at the end of his life in terms of wanting to renovate it and make it into a more interesting theatrical experience than he thought it was. While Quinton was far more obsessive about operas, Ludlam complained a lot about being bored with them."

Nevertheless, even before the prestigious Santa Fe Opera invited Ludlam to direct a work, Matthew Epstein had conceived of a production of Offenbach's *The Grand Duchess of Gerolstein* for the Long Beach Opera, with Ludlam directing Madeline Kahn in the title role. Though both Ludlam and Kahn were initially interested, they ultimately proved reluctant. The project evolved far enough for Michael Feingold to work on a new translation of the libretto, and to audition three of the numbers for Kahn, who came to feel the role was not right for her. But as Feingold also inferred, the decisive factor was that "Charles didn't want to do it."

The Santa Fe connection came about somewhat circuitously through Earl Wild, the virtuosic pianist. Along with Michael Rolland Davis, his companion and recording producer, Wild first saw Ludlam in *Galas*, which was the case for a great many people in the music world. They were so bowled over by the show that they went backstage after the performance and invited Ludlam and Quinton for dinner at their place a couple of weeks later. It was the first of several get-togethers at their apartment at West 55th Street and Sixth Avenue. Ludlam was sure to bring a different exotic flower as a gift each time. As they became better acquainted, Wild was struck by how much "Charles was, underneath, quite serious about many things, though you never would have perceived it if you hadn't known him."

Wild and Davis proceeded to see every Ridiculous show at least twice — except for *Salammbô*, which they saw once and considered "a disaster." Of greater significance, Wild "insisted" that John Crosby, a longtime friend, accompany them to *Irma Vep* when they went to see it again. According to Wild, Crosby was instantly impressed and asked if they thought Ludlam would be interested in directing the upcoming *Die*

Fledermaus for his Santa Fe Opera Company. "We of course pushed it like crazy," said Wild. "We said it would give the opera a shot in the arm."

Crosby, who founded the Santa Fe Opera in 1957, remembered the circumstances somewhat differently. "Earl had raised the question with me of Charles directing an opera prior to my seeing *Irma Vep*. He felt Charles was extremely gifted and someone whose work I ought to know." As soon as he saw *Irma Vep*, Crosby agreed. Though he went backstage and met Ludlam that night, Crosby deferred approaching him with the idea of directing *Fledermaus*. He had Wild "float the idea" by Ludlam first, so he could decline gracefully if he wished to. But Ludlam leaped at the invitation.

Crosby recognized that Ludlam "had a great sense of high comedy, but always with exquisite taste, and with a very marvelous sense of timing." Crosby's novel approach to *Fledermaus* was to go back to its original source as a French farce, which had been made into both an English play by W.S. Gilbert (as in Gilbert & Sullivan), and a comic operetta by Johann Strauss. Crosby appreciated Ludlam's interest in theatrical history, and he wanted him not only to direct *Fledermaus*, but also to readapt the libretto for the opera on the basis of Gilbert's play.

Though *Fledermaus* was slated for Santa Fe's 1986 summer season, Crosby offered Ludlam the assignment a good year and a half in advance. In the meantime, he lost the director who was scheduled to stage the American premiere of Henze's *The English Cat* at Santa Fe in 1985, and he instantly thought of Ludlam as a last-minute replacement.

"I remember thinking *The English Cat* would be something Charles would enjoy doing and something he would realize wonderfully," said Crosby. He thought Ludlam would be particularly good for "the magic and the inventiveness of it." Crosby also felt that Ludlam and Henze would mesh well. "Henze had a tremendous acquaintance with the theater and with works of art," he said. "He was probably one of the few contemporary composers who would have a deep appreciation for Charles's exceptional talents. So there was every reason to believe they would get along fine, and indeed they did."

Ludlam did not get along so well with the fifteen singers in the cast, however. He was accustomed to directing actors who would introduce business of their own for him to respond to, in a more improvisational manner. Opera singers, on the other hand, are used to being given explicit instructions by their directors, who act like traffic cops as much as anything else, telling them when to move and where to go. The cast of *The English Cat* simply didn't know how to deal with Ludlam, who struck them as aloof. But the worst of it was, the singers kept their complaints to themselves. Although there were clearly "disappointed expectations" on both sides, Ludlam never really realized what was wrong. Each side was expecting the other to contribute more, but in different ways.

Ludlam and Quinton flew to Santa Fe for four weeks of rehearsals, beginning on June 17. The hospitable opera company was providing them with a house and a car, but Ludlam had never learned how to drive and Quinton's license had expired. With little else to do and simply to avoid feeling lonely, Quinton attended most of the rehearsals. But after his ongoing kudos in *Irma Vep*, it was hard on Quinton's self-esteem to be idle while everyone else was working. Though he and Ludlam didn't socialize with any of the singers, Earl Wild was in Santa Fe during the rehearsal period, and Ludlam also quickly befriended Henze, the composer.

Ludlam did get along quite well with at least one of the singers, however, by the name of Peter Kazaras. A tenor who had three different roles in the opera as a sheep, a dog, and a fox, Kazaras recalled,

> Charles and I had a great time together. Even in the first run-through, I would come up with things of my own. And as soon as he saw it, he would immediately pick up on it and start giving me stuff. "That's good," he would say, "but if you exaggerate this, and take away a little bit more there, then you'll be able to really make it build to here."

> But basically, the others just sat around and watched Charles. Everyone was saying, "This guy doesn't know what he's doing and he's not telling us what we can do." Frankly, after a while, a lot of people in the cast were angry with Charles. He was deferential to a point that was counterproductive. He was so in awe of what he was doing that he was reluctant to go at it hammer and tongs. Everyone started keeping more to themselves, and there was this slow, growing pond of resentment.

Though the atmosphere during the rehearsals for *The English Cat* remained cordial on the surface, there was an icy undertone that emerged between Ludlam and his cast. The friction had started early in the process and Ludlam was quite relieved when the composer finally arrived. He felt like he had a compatriot, a coconspirator in Henze, who was obviously delighted with Ludlam's *commedia* concept for staging the opera. Ludlam also marveled at what appeared to be Henze's infinite capacity for marijuana consumption. According to Ludlam, Henze was perpetually high: For the first time, he had actually met someone who might be able to smoke him under the table, so to speak, if only he were still indulging himself.

Beneath it all, Kazaras had the distinct impression that Ludlam was intimidated by the prospect of directing this, his first opera. Ludlam never verbalized such fears with anyone, but he did talk about feeling uncomfortable and more restrained whenever he was working with new people who were veritable strangers. He also complained about the "union situation." This was the first time he had ever directed a piece in accordance with union regulations, and he found it a trying experience. There were times when he thought they were just getting somewhere, but they would have to stop for allocated breaks or the end of scheduled rehearsals. He mentioned instances when even the singers expressed a desire to continue, but the union representative would put his foot down. He also complained about the time lost when musical needs took precedence over acting considerations during the rehearsals.

Since the set design featured a lot of oversized furniture — to "shrink" the cast members onstage and give them the illusion of more cat-like dimensions — some of the staging decisions were ultimately made simply by the arrival of the scenery. According to Kazaras, "We realized by the time we opened that we had a show there. But the general feeling was, 'Well, how did it happen?'"

The range of reactions from the critics was schizophrenic. In *The New York Times*, John Rockwell referred to "Charles Ludlam's absolutely delightful staging" before declaring it "a triumph" and explaining: "The invention and wit are nonstop, yet Mr. Ludlam never tilts over into campy excess.... This is a vision of animals as people that couldn't be more winning." Michael Walsh in *Time* magazine also had high praise for "The delightful storybook production by Charles Ludlam... turns the opera into a tragi-comedy in the vein of a 19th century melodrama, but one with a pointed moral." And in the *Daily News*, Bill Zakariasen proclaimed Crosby's choice of Ludlam "an inspired stroke.... Most remarkable is [Ludlam's] comprehension of singers' personalities and how to move them for optimum effect."

On the other hand, Martin Bernheimer of the *Los Angeles Times* found Ludlam's direction "ponderous" and "curiously subdued." And Andrew Porter was even more damaging in the *New Yorker*: "It may be that in a production more astutely focused than the very mild one Charles Ludlam presented in Santa Fe, *The English Cat* will seem less feeble from a dramatic point of view."

Since the Santa Fe production marked the American premiere of an important new opera (it was first performed in Henze's native Germany in 1983), there was a seemingly endless barrage of reviews. When Ludlam received an enormous package of the clips back in New York, he was struck by the diametrically opposed responses: They demonstrated perfectly his long-held conviction that whether they were praising you or damning you, critics simply were not to be trusted.

Even more remarkable than the contradictory reactions to Ludlam's staging of *The English Cat* was a follow-up "Critic's Notebook" piece by John Rockwell that appeared in *The New York Times* on August 29 — or four weeks after his rave review — concerning the friction that had surfaced during the rehearsals. After reiterating that the production "was wonderfully fresh, sweet and sensitive — a 'thinking man's' *Cats*, as I called it in my review," Rockwell reported,

> Imagine my surprise, then, when I [subsequently] heard from sources within the company that there had been constant tension between the singers and their director. Mr. Ludlam had never directed an opera before, and apparently prefers the practice — common in the theater but uncommon in American opera — of improvising with the performers, thinking up the production as he goes along. . . .
>
> The rehearsals were stormy, but that's common enough. The theater is full of tales of crises before the first night in which everyone reconciles in the glow of a triumph. But even after the production had been proclaimed a success, the cast reportedly cold-shouldered Mr. Ludlam when he came backstage to offer congratulations.

While defending Ludlam as well as his own initial response to the production, Rockwell went on to indict the singers. "It's hard to escape the conclusion that the Ludlam incident suggests something stale about the operatic art," he wrote.

> If American opera singers (and symphony players) are so stuck in conventional ways of doing things that they can't distinguish real innovation from mechanistic efficiency even when they are part of it, it's just as bad as if they are practicing an art so abstruse that the public can't hope to appreciate its inner beauties. In either case, the performing artists themselves are so cut off from true theatrical excitement that opera as theater . . . is more moribund than we feared.

Perhaps the most salient point to be gleaned from the reviews for *The English Cat* is that a number of prominent music critics who were unfamiliar with Ludlam's work gave him glowing notices — as well as the benefit of any doubt. It emerges as powerful testimony to how far Charles Ludlam — and his reputation — had come.

✑

Towards the end of the rehearsal period for *The English Cat*, after the "techs" had commenced, both Ludlam and Quinton were flown down to Miami, literally for twenty-four hours, before flying back to Santa Fe. Each received $1,500 plus travel expenses for cameo appearances in an episode of the popular TV series, "Miami Vice." It was a special, two-hour season opener, featuring a number of New York theater personalities, including Julian Beck, Peter Allen, and Penn Jillette, of Penn & Teller fame. Ludlam had only a handful of lines as a hard-boiled female nightclub owner-cum-drug dealer; Quinton was his/her sidekick.

Originally, their scene was supposed to be shot in New York earlier in the summer, before they were to leave for Santa Fe and *The English Cat*. Since so much time had elapsed, Ludlam just assumed that they had simply been cut from the show, when it was rather a matter of the production being terribly behind schedule.

As Ludlam later reported the frantic circumstances:

> I was up all night with this opera tech, which was over at 2:30 AM, and I had been up very early that morning. Then we had to be driven to Albuquerque — an hour and a half away — for a 5:30 flight into Miami through Dallas, which got us into Miami at 12:30 PM.

> By the time we did this *Miami Vice* thing, Everett and I had been up almost forty-eight hours. Then they didn't have our costumes ready, so we had to go out with the designer and shop and find appropriate outfits. Suddenly the Teamsters went on strike and this location they wanted for the nightclub scene couldn't be used, so they had to build a complete set from scratch. We didn't really start shooting until about 7:30 at night.

> When we got on the set, they said, "Let's rehearse." I said, "Rehearse what?" They shouted, "You mean no one gave you a script?" I said, "No!"

> They're on a very high-pressure kind of schedule, with a lot of people all hyped up into hysterics.

Ludlam was suddenly on a kind of a merry-go-round himself, leaving behind his most precious *Salammbô* in order to direct *The English Cat* for a month and then fitting in this single day's work on "Miami Vice." If his talents were being somewhat wasted on both projects, he would still show the world what he was capable of with his version of the forgotten Flaubert classic. But unfortunately, very few would come to appreciate what Ludlam thought was there.

Though *Irma Vep* had resumed performances on August 2, 1985, or shortly after Ludlam and Quinton returned from Santa Fe, principle energies were devoted to reworking *Salammbô*. The major change in remounting the production for its fall opening concerned the replacement of Emilio Cubeiro, who had played Matho, the male lead. As Ludlam told Samuels, he required "a special kind of leading man to make me feel like a woman" when he was in drag. And although the macho Cubeiro seemed to fit the bill in *Galas*, Ludlam found him "stiff" and "tiresome" in *Salammbô*. To be his successor, Ludlam recruited Philip Campanaro, who had played one of the bit bodybuilder roles during the spring previews.

A plumber and sometime stripper from a working-class background in Yonkers, Campanaro had a girlfriend when he came to the Ridiculous and he appeared to be straight—despite rumors of his swinging both ways during the course of the run. With his swarthy, beefy, Italian good looks and his natural way of saying "dese," "dem," and "dose" (for "these," "them," and "those"), Campanaro was, in short, a big, lovable lummox. And Ludlam was, in short, infatuated with him. It was Campanaro's thick New York accent that brought down the house every night, especially in the spring when, as the barbarian Iddibal, he would earnestly but ludicrously deliver a long-winded message, at the end of which he would say, "I have tol' dit." Though his heavy accent as Matho would be mentioned in practically every review, it was only sometimes with endearment, more often with scorn.

While the need to replace Cubeiro seemed to precede the desire to promote Campanaro, it was equally clear that Ludlam was enamored of Campanaro. In some respects, he represented Ludlam's ideal performer—someone with no training, whose untutored responses were sincere and malleable. Ludlam felt he could make something of Campanaro, and he did.

With the sudden need to find a replacement for Iddibal, the lowly barbarian Campanaro had played in the spring, Ludlam had a brainstorm and brought Arthur Kraft back to the Ridiculous. Though "Crazy" Arthur hadn't performed with the company since he had participated in the *Tabu Tableaux* benefit a decade earlier, he had remained almost as much of a fixture at the theater as Minette over the years, and Ludlam had always retained a soft spot for him. Ludlam had also used Kraft as one of the featured players in *The Sorrows of Dolores*.

In *Salammbô*, Kraft would get laughs just by showing up. His enfeebled, elderly condition was in sharp contrast with the bodybuilders who surrounded him in his single scene. Kraft was also quite blind without his glasses, and his bottle-thick spectacles were absurdly anachronistic with ancient Carthage. Though he only had a few lines, they were sizable enough for Kraft's notorious problems with memorization to present an obstacle. But since, as Iddibal, he was essentially delivering a proclamation, Ludlam had another inspiration: Kraft could read his lines from a scroll. Not that this really helped matters. Kraft's eyesight was so poor, and he was so nervous onstage, that he had as much difficulty reading his lines as he did trying to memorize them. He would often get lost and resort to improvising, as he constantly did for his far more substantial role in his first Ridiculous production, *Turds in Hell*, almost twenty years earlier.

And, as in *Turds*, Kraft's behavior onstage was absolutely unpredictable. The other actors were in constant terror, wondering what might come out of his mouth and how they would have to respond. (According to fellow performer John Heys, "If you gave Arthur an inch onstage, he'd take six feet.") Ludlam on the other hand found it exciting, because it was true to the moment, and, ergo, *real* theater. Though he wasn't in the scene himself, Ludlam had to rush to the wings every night to see what crazy business Crazy Arthur might be perpetrating.

While Ludlam made some cast changes in hopes of improving the production, there were others over which he had no control. Right after the awful reviews appeared, there was an upheaval when John Heys abruptly left the play. He phoned Ludlam from Massachusetts — where he claimed he had just gotten a "decorating job" — to announce that he was quitting. Ludlam was livid. "I wrote this role for you and now you're doing this to me!" he screamed over the phone. "You're not an actor! You don't care about your acting or your craft!" he added before hanging up on Heys.

Though he exploded on the phone, Ludlam was actually more ambivalent about Heys's departure than he admitted — perhaps even to himself. The anger he displayed was disguising the sense of relief he also felt. From the beginning of *Salammbô*, Heys was having a hellish time in the play and his sour mood had infected everyone, including Ludlam. But it's typical that Heys left instead of being dismissed. Ludlam often said,

"People leave before I can fire them." With the recent ousting of Cubeiro as the exception to the rule, it was rare for Ludlam to ever dismiss someone from a production. He was not, however, above being ornery with someone if he was unhappy with their work, thereby provoking them to quit.

Nor was Ludlam above dissembling to serve his own purposes. Though he evidently told Heys that he had written the role of Schahabarim with him in mind, initially he had offered the part to Ethyl Eichelberger, who would also handle the wigs for the show. Since Eichelberger was doing more of his own work at the time, he declined the invitation, only to accept — in the interim — the smaller role of Hamilcar. But now Eichelberger replaced Heys in the role that was written for him in the first place.

Though he apparently had mixed feelings about Heys leaving the play, Ludlam had every reason to be particularly annoyed by the timing of his departure. He felt that Heys had remained with the production just long enough to be included in the reviews. But as usual, only Ludlam seemed to exist for the critics; and along with just about everyone else, Heys was rarely mentioned. Nevertheless, the response of the critics was enough to make anyone involved with the production seek solace in Massachusetts. Though *Salammbô* seemed to go over quite well with the company's devoted fans during the lengthy preview period, it received the most devastating reviews Ludlam had seen in years — if not in his career — when it finally opened to the press the second week in November. What he considered to be his best and most important play was virtually being denounced as his worst.

Ludlam's longtime champion Mel Gussow all but declared it such in his discussion for the Sunday "Arts & Leisure" section of *The New York Times*, where he observed that *Salammbô* "falls below *Eunuchs of the Forbidden City* and other lesser Ludlams." Gussow also berated Ludlam for "sidelining many of his funniest Ridiculous colleagues," and specifically for excluding Black-Eyed Susan from the production while employing a lot of amateurish bodybuilders instead.

In his review for the *Times*, Frank Rich focused his objections on a lack of balance between the more earnest representation of Flaubert and the campy interpretation it was given, "with the consequence that the two halves of its creator's artistic personality end up sabotaging each other." While the chief criticism amounted to a sense of outrage over the production's vulgarity and excess in general ("self-indulgent" appeared in more than one review), many reviewers cited the grotesqueness of the nude, scabrous, five-hundred-pound Katy Dierlam in particular. There was also an almost consistent complaint about how the elevated purple prose — as rendered from Flaubert — was being butchered by the bodybuilders who obviously had no acting experience, even though this had been one of Ludlam's humorous conceits. Almost unanimously, the critics used their coverage of *Salammbô* primarily as an excuse to resend their readers to *Irma Vep* — which was playing on other nights — instead.

Ludlam was especially upset by what he perceived as Frank Rich's "coding" in both his print and WQXR Radio reviews, where he claimed the show was for the most "hard-core" Ridiculous fans only. As far as Ludlam was concerned, it was the same as saying, "Don't go unless you're gay."

After several years of accelerating success, the critical failure of *Salammbô* also had its "up" side: It reestablished the sense in which the Ridiculous was not just this lovable, lunatic, Downtown company, but a provocative and dangerous one as well. As Ludlam told Eichelberger one night in the wings before going on stage in *Salammbô*, "You know, in the early days the foundations would never give me any money because they would have been afraid I would do this. And now that they've given me the money I've gone ahead and done it."

Ludlam even received a savage attack in the most unlikely of places: the *Village Voice*. Under the headline "The Reaganization of the Ridiculous," it appeared in Erika Munk's weekly column, "Cross Left," which focused on the political aspects of her chosen topics. While dwelling on her disgust with the image of Katy Dierlam, Munk labeled Ludlam a "misogynist" and lambasted him for his "peculiar homage [to Flaubert], turning an already peculiar sensibility inside out by concentrating its revulsion on women." Munk closed her discussion with the bizarre accusation that Ludlam had become right wing. "What strikes me," she wrote, "is that the mean-spirited edges he's showing are precisely those which American society now encourages. The right might call *Salammbô* pornography. Surely they wouldn't recognize its callousness as a reflection of their own, directed toward the same victims."

Munk's onslaught was part ludicrous, part baffling, and mostly infuriating. It was Dierlam herself who rushed to defend Ludlam in a letter that appeared in a subsequent issue of the *Voice*. "There is no one to blame but myself," she wrote. "I asked to play this role. Charles Ludlam is no more a misogynist than any other man, and as a director he has the courage to push beyond the conventional boundaries of role and gender.

"Fat is not so horrible as Erika Munk thinks it is," Dierlam continued. "To me, nothing so truly reeks of Reaganism as the reversion to conventional ideas of what's acceptable in a woman's appearance and what is not. Are we all to be condemned to the dreary confines of current political imagery?"

As if doing penance for both the shabby treatment they gave Ludlam and the controversy they stirred up when *Salammbô* opened in November, the *Voice* ran a "Centerfold" feature on the play three months later. It was written by Guy Trebay, who, in great detail, described his experience attending the sixty-ninth performance of *Salammbô* from a backstage perspective.

It may seem incredible that the play had such a long run, considering it was panned practically across the board. But the fact is, if *Salammbô* often sold out during its previews in the spring, it continued to do a brisk business for a number of weeks after the negative reviews appeared. This was due, in part, to its limited schedule. *Salammbô* never played a full week, adhering to a schedule of performances on Tuesdays through Thursdays while *Irma Vep* continued on the weekends and, well into its second year, surpassed the close of *Salammbô* in the spring of 1986. But it was also the case that Ludlam had enough followers by now who would want to see a Ridiculous failure as much as they wanted to see a Ridiculous success. As Michael Feingold ended his brief notice on *Salammbô*: "Very simply, so much goes on in the piece, of so many clashing tonalities and such widely varied resonances, that my advice would be to distrust any critic's view of it, even mine, and see it for yourself. Goodness knows you aren't likely to see anything like it ever again."

Ludlam told Edgardo Franceschi, "The critics don't get it, but this is my 'Don Giovanni.'" And as confirmed by the more positive reviews that appeared in January and February in out-of-the-way newspapers and gay magazines, *Salammbô* also improved the longer it ran, and as the many cast changes sorted themselves out. Once they knew it was going to close, everyone invested more of their energies to finally achieve the play Ludlam kept on saying it could be. Many involved with the production, including Ludlam himself, felt that the closing performance was the best.

Indeed, *Salammbô* is another instance where the play reads much better than it came across onstage. Though it is written in the same style, it is not as unruly or defiantly incoherent as some of Ludlam's earlier epics. The density of the writing, though appropriate to Flaubert, was simply at cross-purposes with the bodybuilders' diction and lack of delivery skills. Much of the script was lost in the presentation and, inevitably, the story eluded the audience. With Campanaro's thick, "dese"–"dem"–and–"dose" accent in mind, consider Matho's description of Salammbô:

> She is unlike any other daughter of man. Her eyes under her great curved eyebrows are like suns beneath triumphal arches. Remember when she appeared how all the lamps paled? And between the diamonds of her collar glimpses of her nipples shone resplendently. And how the odor of perfumes floated behind her as from a temple. She was more fragrant than wine, more terrible than death.

As ticket sales for *Salammbô* fell off precipitously in January and February, its weekly loss had been underwritten by the profits from *Irma Vep*. But with eighteen cast members each receiving at least $125 a week, there was no choice but to finally close it in March, after the eightieth performance. Though Ludlam put up no resistance, he was terribly despondent about its having been such a failure. After the closing performance, the company watched the video that had been taped that night, and viewing it seemed to make him even sadder. He knew he would have to write in a more popular vein to have the kind of success he was still having with *Irma Vep*. But he retained his conviction that an appreciation of his more difficult works — of his real art — would continue to grow as well.

℃

Ludlam's breakthrough into network television with "Oh, Madeline!" initiated what suddenly began to look like an alternate career as a Hollywood actor. To merely summarize the sequence of other projects with which Ludlam had become involved during this period is to convey just how congested his life had become. In October 1985, or a month before *Salammbô* opened, he had been approached to star in an HBO special that was being packaged by Michael Loman, a writer and producer. Though plans for this project ultimately petered out, Ludlam received some preliminary fees when he signed an agreement on October 18, as negotiated by Paul Martino, an agent at ICM.

On November 30, Ludlam was flown down to New Orleans to meet with the creators of an upcoming feature film starring Dennis Quaid and Ellen Barkin. As directed by Jim McBride and written by Dan Petrie, Jr., the film's working title was *Nothing But the Truth*. In the film, Quaid played a New Orleans homicide detective compelled by Barkin, an investigator with the D.A.'s office, to track down corruption in the police department. Ludlam was cast in a featured role that Paul Bartel had also been considered for:

Lamar Pamentel, an unscrupulous Southern lawyer with gentlemanly airs who represents "sleazebags."

As handled once again by Martino, the contract with Ludlam was signed on December 12, 1985, and gave him $3,750 a week. Though there was a four-week guarantee, Ludlam completed his work in less than a month — having flown back to New Orleans on December 14 for on-location shooting. Quinton flew down four days later, on his birthday, to join him. As Quinton recalled, Quaid first greeted Ludlam on the set with "Hello scumbag," and Ludlam was understandably offended. But after Quaid took it upon himself to apologize for the remark, they got along fine.

Quaid of course had no way of knowing that Ludlam, in a character part, would fare much better with most reviewers than he himself would as the lead. When the film was finally released as *The Big Easy* in August of 1987 — three months after Ludlam's death — Pauline Kael registered some contempt for the film and all of the players except two: "John Goodman, who generally remains in the background of the shots, and the great Charles Ludlam, who thrives on broadness. As a gentleman lawyer of Old Dixie, he rolls his eyes and wraps the picture like a ribbon around his panama hat."

(Ludlam also made a cameo appearance as a disgruntled, beret-clad director of porn movies in *Forever, Lulu*, a quirky and pretentious Tri-star picture that, in retrospect, is most noteworthy for featuring Hanna Schygulla, Deborah Harry, and Dr. Ruth Westheimer, as well as for presenting Alec Baldwin in his film debut. *Forever, Lulu* would be released in April 1987, the month before Ludlam's death.)

After Ludlam's final day of shooting *The Big Easy* on December 27, he returned to New York with Quinton in time for New Year's Eve. Following the holidays, they resumed their back-to-back runs of *Irma Vep* and *Salammbô*. In the meantime, John Crosby of the Santa Fe Opera was repeatedly asking Ludlam to complete his new version of *Die Fledermaus*. Though it wouldn't be performed until the summer, Crosby required a long lead time to send the script to the cast who were dispersed at opera houses throughout the world. He was finding Ludlam no less delinquent and every bit as hard to pin down as Paul Taylor had in 1977. Crosby was also struck by the extent to which Ludlam confined their communications to the telephone, as opposed to any written correspondence.

Adding yet more work and pressure to his already busy schedule, Ludlam starred in an episode of "Tales From the Dark Side." This nationally syndicated television show was shot during the spring in New York, while Ludlam was in the midst of rehearsals for *The Artificial Jungle*, his twenty-ninth and final play.

Before conceiving of *The Artificial Jungle*, Ludlam had other ideas for the company's next presentation. When *Salammbô* had opened to such sour notices in November, he had been talking about remounting *How to Write a Play* and simultaneously introducing previews of *Houdini* in the spring. He never dreamed that *Irma Vep* would continue to draw audiences until April, preempting these plans. (By the time it closed, *Irma Vep* had given a grand total of 331 performances.)

By playing the legendary magician, Ludlam expected to prove that he could become every bit as celebrated portraying a real man as he had a real woman in *Galas*. While exploiting his lifelong love of magic and stage illusions, he imagined that his *Houdini* would surpass even *Irma Vep* in popularity and critical praise. In preparation for what he saw as his greatest role yet, he started practicing new tricks. He had already conquered Houdini's renowned escape from a straightjacket — only Ludlam had the help of Velcro.

Ludlam also had plans to shoot a documentary about creating the play. He envisioned "The Making of *Houdini*" as being aired on PBS. He concocted elaborate plans for producing it, beginning with a visit to Houdini's hometown. He wanted to avoid the process of random shooting followed by heavy editing — which is the way most documentaries are assembled. Instead, Ludlam was going to work out a complete script in advance, focusing on his study of magic tricks. One gag he came up with entailed his breaking free from handcuffs only to emerge from the theater and discover he had locked his keys in his car.

But seeing as Ludlam's designs for both the play and the documentary were so grandiose, Quinton persuaded him to do something less imposing right after *Salammbô*, and *Houdini* was shelved for later on. Inspiration for *The Artificial Jungle* came from at least two sources.

Black-Eyed Susan recalled that Ludlam invited her to lunch during *Salammbô*'s run. He told her that he wanted her in his next show, and asked what she would like to play. She mentioned Joan of Arc, but Ludlam failed to share her interest in the subject. His eyes lit up, however, when Susan mentioned that she had always wanted to play Lady Macbeth.

The plot to *The Artificial Jungle* concerns a husband who is murdered by his wife and her paramour. This is the same basic premise not only of Émile Zola's *Thérèse Raquin*, which Ludlam acknowledged as his source, but also to the "Tales From the Dark Side" episode he had already agreed to make. (Originally based on a true story that consumed all levels of Parisian society in the 19th century, Zola's scandalous 1867 novel inspired any number of books, dramas, and movies, including James M. Cain's extremely popular novels *The Postman Always Rings Twice* and *Double Indemnity*.)

As written by Dick Benner, the "Tales From the Dark Side" episode, called "The Swap," presented a grisly twist on Zola's theme. Ludlam would once again be playing a Southern figure, this time a grotesque millionaire named Bubba, whose "mama was the greatest conjuror woman Louisiana ever saw." Though his hunchbacked body is horribly deformed and covered with hideous warts, Bubba has a pretty young wife named Anna Belle (Maria Manuche). Along with Claude (Jim Wlcek), the "white-trash farm boy" and hired hand, Anna Belle executes her scheme to murder Bubba and inherit his estate. They have no idea that Bubba has been working on his mother's "recipe for making one spirit trade bodies with another," and that, in effect, he becomes Claude during the course of the murder.

As Quinton recalled, Ludlam enjoyed working on "The Swap" and was pleased with the way it came out. On the assumption that the camera tends to exaggerate any choices one makes as an actor, he deliberately underplayed the character. Because Bubba is such a bizarre creature to begin with, Ludlam's toning down his performance proved to be the right decision. It remains one of his better characterizations available to posterity.

Whether prompted by his involvement with "Tales From the Dark Side" or by Susan's having told him that she wanted to play a murderer, Ludlam quickly turned to the Zola novel as the next source to plunder for his company. Though it's telling that most of the critics would refer to *The Postman Always Rings Twice* and *Double Indemnity* in their reviews, *The Artificial Jungle* adheres far more closely to the original Zola novel. On the other hand, Ludlam himself would describe the play as a "pastiche of the *film noir*" genre.

Though Ludlam's primary goal with *The Artificial Jungle* was to produce a crowd-pleaser and earn back some of *Salammbô*'s losses, another important ambition was to establish a new core company. It had been seven years since Pashalinski and Brockmeyer had left the Ridiculous, and given the perpetual casting nightmares he had just endured with *Salammbô*, Ludlam was beginning to miss the stability a core group afforded him.

An even more important motive for assembling a new troupe of regular players was that Ludlam's career outside the theater had blossomed, and he was eager to pursue it. This meant there would have to be other Ridiculous stars who could sustain productions with or without his presence at One Sheridan Square. Ludlam saw Susan, Quinton, and Eichelberger as having potential drawing power, and the stunning notices they would each receive when *The Artificial Jungle* opened in September would strongly reaffirm such hopes. He also wanted Philip Campanaro and Katy Dierlam to become members of the new core.

But Ludlam was not going to repeat mistakes of the past, and his concept for a new nucleus of players entailed more freedom on both sides of the equation. For his own part, Ludlam would never allow himself to feel obligated to write roles for specific people, as he had during the first half of the company's history. The others would also have more liberty to come and go as they pleased. Susan was already doing more outside work — not only with John Jesurun, but also with Ethyl Eichelberger. Indeed, Eichelberger would eventually write the *Saint Joan* for Susan that Ludlam had denied her. Moreover, Eichelberger enjoyed increasing success as an actor in his own plays.

In keeping with the notion of a more relaxed core troupe, there was no role for Dierlam in *The Artificial Jungle*. Campanaro, however, was cast as Frankie Spinelli, a neighborhood policeman and good friend of the character Ludlam played. In spite of his crush on Campanaro — or maybe because of it — Ludlam told Susan that it was dangerous to "project one's fantasies onto someone else." Referring to Campanaro, he said it wasn't fair to treat a person as an object of desire, because it demeaned who they really were and prevented them from ever becoming real to you. He added that he had specifically made this mistake in the past with Randy Hunt, the young freeloader who played musical beds with seemingly half the company years before. The wisdom behind such insights reflected just how much Ludlam had matured through his stabilizing relationship with Quinton. It didn't prevent him, however, from at least trying to improve Campanaro's mind. As if to compensate for the copy of L. Ron Hubbard's *Dianetics* that Campanaro kept on his dressing table during the run of *Jungle*, Ludlam gave him Thomas Mann's *Magic Mountain* to read.

If it seemed like Susan was being phased out of the company in recent years, *Jungle* proved an ingenious vehicle for bringing her back. She was cast as a wife who conspires with her new lover (Quinton) to kill her husband (Ludlam). Such a dynamic was tailor-made to mitigate the friction that had built up among the three of them offstage. In the play, it was now Susan and Quinton in cahoots against Ludlam, instead of him and Quinton conspiring against her. And as many of the reviewers would note, Ludlam's own role in *Jungle* seemed subservient to theirs. This was part of his larger scheme to make them stars in their own right who could carry the Ridiculous in his absence.

ロ

Ludlam rapidly wrote *Jungle* without availing himself of Samuels as a typist. As with *Corn* and a handful of other plays, its compressed composition was a boon to the finished product, making for one of his most tightly woven scripts. A pet shop setting was Ludlam's variation on Zola. His vision of the store was based on a real shop he frequented on Rivington Street, but Ludlam also may have had his own apartment in mind. With the birds, the fish, and the plants, it presented an intense profusion of life everywhere; and, as designed by Ludlam's old friend Jack Kelly, the wonderfully playful set incorporated elements of the Morton Street address. With colorful piranhas in a fish tank to facilitate the plot's pivotal murder, comparisons with *Little Shop of Horrors*, the long-running Off-Broadway musical, would prove inevitable.

In the play, Chester Nurdiger (Ludlam) runs a pet shop on the Lower East Side with his wife Roxanne (Susan) and his overprotective mother (Eichelberger, in drag). As his surname implies, Chester is a prototypical "nerd," and Roxanne is going out of her mind with boredom. To relieve Roxanne of the more "disgusting" aspects of her pet shop duties ("handling tubifex worms," "cleaning the rat cages," etc.), Chester agrees to hire some help. Enter Zachary Slade (Quinton), a mysterious drifter who is instantly smitten with Roxanne.

After she takes out a life insurance policy on her husband, Roxanne exploits Slade's passion by compelling him to assist her in murdering Chester, whom they ultimately feed to the piranhas in the fish tank, center stage. As in Zola, when Mother Nurdiger overhears Roxanne and Slade talk about having murdered Chester, she has a massive stroke, leaving her paralyzed and unable to communicate. Also in keeping with Zola — as well as *Macbeth* — Slade and Roxanne are finally undone by their own guilt.

As he consumes poison in the last scene, Slade's closing line is borrowed directly from Camus' *The Stranger*. Most of the more memorable lines, however, are intentionally reminiscent of hard-boiled fiction and particularly James M. Cain. Consider Roxanne's "Love is a disease, and you gave it to me," or, "I didn't get these lips from sucking door-knobs." She instructs Slade to "Kiss me until I bleed," and in terms of their murderous plans, advises, "We're on this train together... right to the last stop." And although Chester is perceived as an insipid milksop who "wouldn't hurt a fly," Roxanne sarcastically adds, "Not unless he happened to bore it to death." (As Frank Rich would observe in his review for the *Times*, "If James M. Cain didn't actually write all of Miss Susan's blow-torch zingers... somewhere he is wishing he had.")

In addition to all the funny repartee, much of the humor was to be found in the staging. The piranhas were actually stick puppets that would bounce around in their aquarium as if in response to the characters' dialogue, providing a repeatedly hilarious sight gag. In a humorous subplot, Chester used ventriloquism to sell mute parrots as talking birds to his unsuspecting customers. And when Mother Nurdiger had her stroke, the tall and lanky Eichelberger did a gravity-defying back flip that consistently brought down the house.

Eichelberger's acrobatics were his own invention. He was the one performer whom Ludlam trusted implicitly and always relied on to come up with his own business. He hardly directed him at all. Eichelberger, in turn, told Susan that Ludlam was the only person he admired enough in the theater to work with — when he wasn't putting on his own plays.

In the play's final scene, the otherwise paralyzed Mother Nurdiger scrawls letters on a tabletop to try and expose her son's murderers to Frankie, the visiting cop. During the previews, Campanaro kept telling Eichelberger to restrain his performance, maintaining that the scene really belonged to him. Though Eichelberger was too "ladylike" to argue the point, he finally exploded one night in the dressing room when Campanaro again raised the topic. The conflict ultimately prompted Ludlam to intervene and confirm that Eichelberger should carry the scene, as he did primarily with his eyes.

This was an exceptional incident, however. Along with the rest of the cast, Ludlam rather enjoyed the backstage atmosphere during *The Artificial Jungle*. It felt like the company was a real family again for the first time in years, and they could revel in the good will that seemed to predominate — at first, anyway. No one, including Ludlam, realized that he was already infected with the HIV virus, and that his condition would rapidly deteriorate over the course of the winter and the run of the play.

℘

Following a brief but intensive rehearsal period, *The Artificial Jungle* previewed for only a few weeks beginning in late April. The last week in May, Ludlam was in a Hollywood studio "looping" some of his lines (that is, rerecording his voice on the soundtrack) for the final print of *The Big Easy*. On May 27, he flew directly from Los Angeles to Albuquerque to work on *Die Fledermaus* in Santa Fe. Once again, Quinton accompanied him. But since he had renewed his driver's license in the intervening year, this time Quinton could drop Ludlam off at rehearsals and tootle around Santa Fe on his own.

Though both Ludlam and John Crosby tried to put a positive spin on the situation, there were some underlying tensions by the time Ludlam arrived in Santa Fe. While Crosby had wanted Ludlam's new adaptation of the opera by the fall of 1985, he only received the first draft sometime in the winter. But there were major problems with the script Ludlam delivered, and it still required a lot of work.

Crosby thought he had made it clear that much of the spoken dialogue in Gilbert's play had found its way into the sung numbers of the original Strauss operetta, and that Ludlam would have to be sure and make allowances for this when he readapted the libretto. But to all evidence, Ludlam never bothered cross-referencing his script for *Fledermaus* with the lyrics for the operetta, and Crosby had to prod him to rework his adaptation during the spring.

When Ludlam and Crosby finally got together in Santa Fe the last few days in May, they worked at cutting the redundancies in the lyrics and the libretto. Sometimes Ludlam would simply tell Crosby, "Look, you know this work a lot better than I do, so whatever you think is right, just go ahead and do it." Act III in particular required a lot of work. According to Crosby, "The third act of any operetta always needs to be reenergized for some reason." In the case of *Fledermaus*, it was a matter of the endless ways one could approach the comic situations, and Crosby told Ludlam, "You're the master of that, so take it and run with it."

Since this was a new production of *Fledermaus*, there continued to be tinkering during the first two weeks of rehearsals in June. After his experience with *The English Cat* the previous season, Ludlam was sure to provide more direction this time around. And as the conductor of *Fledermaus*, Crosby was even more involved than he had been with *The English Cat*, and he observed Ludlam more closely. He felt that Ludlam was especially good at detecting the cast members' innate talents and eliciting them through experimentation.

Joyce Castle, a mezzo-soprano who played the trouser role of Prince Orlovsky, recalled that "Charles dealt with each of us as we were. He wanted us to go with our own personalities, and he didn't want puppets. In a strange way though, I thought he was shy." Castle found Ludlam particularly timid in relation to what she had been expecting. More than a year before, right after Crosby hired her for *Fledermaus* and told her Ludlam would be directing, she went to see *Irma Vep*. "Good lord!" exclaimed Castle, recalling the experience.

> I just sat there, and this *thing* started happening onstage. I had never seen any-thing like it in my life, and I had been in the business a *long* time. It was a major thrill for me that I would be working with that guy up there who was doing all that madness. But I was also scared, because he was so awesome. I knew I was in the presence of a genius and I figured my work was cut out for me.

At Crosby's prompting, there was no end to the funny business that Ludlam invented for Act III, which was where he really left his imprint, and which made his *Fledermaus* an instant hit with operagoers. In the scene when Frosch, the drunken jailer, poured himself some tea, he seemed to believe an offstage tenor's voice was coming from the teapot: When he returned the lid to the pot, the voice stopped, and whenever he again removed it, the singing resumed. In an even more hilarious bit of staging, Ludlam had Eisenstein make his entrance with Frosch hiding underneath his costume. When Eisenstein raised a hand, another one came up from the cape to pull it back. Ludlam also conceived of an imaginary hole in the stage that everyone would stumble over throughout the third act.

Ludlam and Castle developed an especially congenial rapport. When he first observed her in her full drag regalia — consisting of a white uniform, monocle, mustache, and riding crop — he stopped short in his tracks, surveyed her appearance, and then said in a seductive tone, "*Now* you look good to me, Joyce!"

Though Ludlam got along fine with the entire cast this time, it was far from smooth sailing with John Crosby. They had what are euphemistically referred to as "artistic differences" — in this case stemming from the coming together of two very strong per-sonalities who inevitably clashed. It culminated in a rift over questions of authority, which had been a problem for Ludlam all his life. After Ludlam requisitioned an addi-tional costume for Rosalinda in Act III, Crosby reminded him that he was only the director of the opera, and not the head of the company. Following a particularly thorny confrontation midway through the rehearsal process, Crosby refused to communicate directly with Ludlam any further. And on opening night, Ludlam felt totally rebuffed when he went to shake Crosby's hand and the gesture was not reciprocated.

Peter Golub arrived in Santa Fe just in time for the opening of *Fledermaus* in early July. He stayed with Ludlam and Quinton in the house that had been provided for them, and he was struck by how quiet and moody Ludlam seemed. According to Quinton, Ludlam had been returning from rehearsals totally exhausted and rolling his eyes in disbelief. But despite all these reported difficulties, the *Fledermaus* Ludlam assembled was an enormous hit with critics and audiences alike. (Bill Zakariasen in the *Daily News* claimed, "The glorious bag-of-tricks direction by Charles Ludlam ... is thus far the best I've yet seen given this operetta masterpiece.") "Even though it was a major success," claimed Golub, "Crosby never said a word to Charles after the opening, and he was just crushed." Ludlam returned to New York two days later, vowing he would never work at Santa Fe again.

Both Quinton and Samuels confirmed that Ludlam felt horribly mistreated and neglected by Crosby. But Crosby was apparently oblivious to the extent of the problems between them, and had no recollection of any feud. From his perspective, they had "a mutually respectful working relationship." If anything, he was pleased by how well *Die Fledermaus* was received, and even proud of how Ludlam's comic ingenuity made the usually lethal third act so vital and alive.

No matter how upset Ludlam continued to feel about Crosby after he returned to New York, there was hardly any time for brooding. *The Artificial Jungle* resumed previews in August of 1986, prior to opening to the press in September. In the meantime, there was a far more distressing development when Ludlam had a routine checkup with his dentist, who discovered that he was riddled with thrush. Ludlam knew this to be a common precursor to full-blown AIDS, but he simply refused to believe the evidence — even after a doctor confirmed that he did indeed have an opportunistic infection. It had, after all, been some years since he had had any compromising sex with anyone other than Quinton, who was also monogamous during this period. Ludlam told Samuels that he wasn't even having much sex with Quinton during the last couple of years. "They became like an old married couple," said Samuels, "having sex only occasionally."

Hoping against hope, Ludlam put off having an HIV test for a couple of months. It wasn't confirmed that he was positive until November, when he found out that not only did he have AIDS, but that he also had practically no T cells left. By then, *The Artificial Jungle* had settled into what appeared would be a long run, following the loving and respectful reviews it received when it opened on September 21. They were predominantly raves, recognizing the play for the sturdy piece of theater it was.

"The ingeniously complicated plot leads to a series of wonderful surprises, nuggets of stage magic that stun the audience and leave them howling," wrote Howard Kissel in the *Daily News*. In the *Post*, Marilyn Stasio claimed, "Ludlam leaves no details unattended in this brilliantly packaged parody of the suspense melodrama." Allan Wallach in *Newsday* found it "surely one of the funniest comedies Ludlam and his Ridiculous Theatrical Company have done in their 20 years."

In the *Times*, Frank Rich declared, "Both as writer and director, Mr. Ludlam remains our master of the ridiculous," adding that "Unlike David Mamet, who missed the joke by highlighting ponderous psychosexual implications in his screenplay for the remake of *The Postman Always Rings Twice*, Mr. Ludlam seeks to remind us that a good chiller may be simply that and no more." Rich did have some reservations about the play's length, and claimed it "isn't always top-rung Ridiculous, but, with this troupe, second-rung is more than funny enough." Though one might conclude from such remarks that he had a mixed reaction to the play, four months later (on January 16, 1987), Rich would make a point of promoting it in a Friday *Times* feature entitled "Critics' Choices for a Wintry Weekend," in which he declared the play "a typical tour of its creator's sensibility, which embraces parody, camp and, most of all, a serious commitment to the durable traditions of the theater."

Ludlam seized a feature story about *The Artificial Jungle* (in the September 22 issue of *Women's Wear Daily*) as an opportunity to pontificate on the common dismissal of his work as being "camp." "Anything with such a bad reputation as 'camp' has to have a power and be important," he told the writer Rob Baker. "But 'camp' is really a sexist term used against homosexual artists to imply their work is not good because it's Gay. If heterosexuals do the same thing, it's biting social satire. But if homosexuals do it, it's dismissed as 'camp.'"

Following the attention bestowed on *Galas* and *Irma Vep*, it is clear from the coverage of *The Artificial Jungle* all across the country that the Ridiculous Theatrical Company was firmly established in the national landscape. In his review for the *Associated Press*, Michael Kuchwara pronounced it "an off-Broadway treasure." Robert W. Butler wrote in the *Kansas City Star*, "Visitors to the Big Apple who want to experience something truly weird without endangering themselves might check out what the Ridiculous crew is up to." And in the *Denver Post*, Alan Stern debunked the notion that the Ridiculous

was merely a cult phenomenon by declaring in his opening sentence, "What a cult —
Ludlam's biggest fan is *The New York Times*."

In retrospect, the reviews of *The Artificial Jungle* acquire a special poignancy, as many of
them refer to the company's near twenty-year history and read like the eulogies they
effectively became. Consider how Mel Gussow ended his "Stage View" discussion of the
play for the "Arts & Leisure" section of the *Times*:

> Mr. Ludlam and company are often larger — and funnier — than life. As
> entertainers, they have brightened more evenings with their jocularity and their
> iconoclasm than any other theatrical troupe of their longevity. Though Mr.
> Ludlam has acted in a few movies, his plays have not been filmed. They — and
> he — exist live on stage. In that sense, he could be considered the Alfred Lunt
> of the Ridiculous theater.
>
> From *Bluebeard* to *The Artificial Jungle* has been a delirious passage. The wit
> was always there, but over the years, Mr. Ludlam has become more polished as a
> playwright and director (from the beginning, he was a droll comic actor, and
> others have adopted his style). Though he can be a titanic Fool, he knows exactly
> what he is doing, and to whom he is doing it. The work begins as parody, but at
> its best it becomes its own entity. Just as *Irma Vep* transcended Daphne du
> Maurier, *The Artificial Jungle* turns *Double Indemnity* into a revenge comedy of
> high risibility and "reckless immediacy."

Even though *The Artificial Jungle* was written and produced before Ludlam was diagnosed with AIDS, irony topples over irony when one recognizes just how much his last
play appeared to be addressing the status of his own health. As Chester Nurdiger,
Ludlam dies in the play, only to come to haunt the other characters in the last act.
While it was borrowed from Camus, the final line of his final play — in essence, the
final line of his extensive oeuvre — can be interpreted as Ludlam's making peace with
the universe. "I'm dying," says Slade,

> And I look up at the stars, the thousand unseeing eyes that look back on this little
> speck of dust we call the world, and I ask — What was my crime compared to
> your indifference. I committed a senseless murder. But in its very senselessness it
> is in harmony with the universe, which is itself senseless and ultimately stupid.
> In an aeon or two, who will be left to accuse me?

Even Ludlam's devotion to Houdini during the last two years of his life acquires extra symbolic weight in terms of his unexpected AIDS diagnosis. Houdini had a strong belief in the afterlife, and he was famous for performing death-defying acts. In a similar spirit, Ludlam really believed that he was going to defy AIDS and survive by carefully monitoring his diet and adhering once again to a strict macrobiotic regimen.

Though there were already early experiments with AZT and other drugs by the time he was diagnosed on November 21, 1986, it's hardly surprising that Ludlam chose not to pursue any medical assistance. To match his lifelong, obsessive fear of death, he had no faith in doctors and a pathological fear of hospitals. What is astonishing is that once he learned he had AIDS, Ludlam did absolutely nothing to alter the incredible pace his working life had recently assumed. It's as if the only way he could continue at all was by pretending he had as much time left as he had always had. It's even more remarkable that he continued to refuse to see a doctor even as his condition rapidly worsened later in the winter.

Terrified it would harm their mutual and respective careers, Ludlam and Quinton decided not to tell a soul that Ludlam had AIDS. Prior to his entering the hospital in April 1987, the only other people who knew were Ethyl Eichelberger and Quinton's therapist. Thus ensued five months of keeping the rather dreadful secret to themselves, even while Ludlam was still performing in *The Artificial Jungle* and remained very much in the public eye during the first three of those months. Only in retrospect did the many colleagues and friends who continued to see him on a daily basis realize how blind they had been to his deteriorating condition. It was simply unfathomable to them that Charles Ludlam, at the height of his remarkable career and only forty-three years old, had AIDS, which was an even swifter death sentence at the time than it would become over the next few years. As prompted by Ludlam himself, they were all involved in a kind of communal denial of enormous proportions.

Though Ludlam was losing weight very rapidly and noticeably over the winter, he had become fanatical about his macrobiotic diet and everyone accepted this as the reason. Sometimes when he was confronted on the matter, he would even indicate that he was thrilled to be shedding so many pounds and feeling healthier thanks to the diet. But when it came to having a meal with Ludlam during this period, other things he said seemed to indicate something else — once again, only in retrospect.

Peter Golub recalled having Ludlam and Quinton over for dinner one night. He had prepared a roast and, at first, Ludlam took a bite of the meat. But as if catching himself, he said, "That's a high-risk piece," as he quickly returned the morsel to his plate.

Lola Pashalinski remembered being concerned and asking Ludlam about his health during a phone conversation. After explaining that he was allowing himself only a teaspoon of oil a week, Ludlam launched into a zealous sermon, proselytizing on the virtues of macrobiotics. When the hefty Pashalinski replied that the diet had never worked for her, Ludlam responded, "Miracles happen every day." Given the solemn tone of his voice, the remark took on a special resonance for Pashalinski. As a follow-up to the conversation, he sent her some macrobiotic literature.

Ludlam and Quinton spent both Thanksgiving and Christmas with the Ludlam clan in Greenlawn, as they did faithfully every year unless they were working outside New York. This particular Christmas dinner was given at his brother Donald's house, a few blocks from Ludlam's childhood home. As Quinton recalled, Marjorie was quite distressed that they brought their own macrobiotic food and refused to partake of any of the feast that Laura, Ludlam's sister-in-law, had prepared.

But in addition to the macrobiotic defense, everyone close to Ludlam was aware of how much he was doing, which in and of itself was enough to dispel any conjecture that he might have AIDS. Given how overextended Ludlam suddenly seemed, Samuels remembered feeling "frightened for Charles at the time," without even knowing he was ill. While *The Artificial Jungle* was up and running (entailing two performances on Saturday nights, as usual), Ludlam was working on *Houdini*, pursuing his plans with the New York Shakespeare Festival for the production of *Titus Andronicus* he was slated to direct in the summer, and also collaborating with Donald Thompson. A wealthy, would-be producer, Thompson had approached Ludlam the year before to rework *Der Ring Gott Farblonjet* for an entirely different production on Broadway. In addition to all of this, Ludlam had made a commitment to screen *The Sorrows of Dolores* at the Collective for Living Cinema on April 30. Though he had been working on the film for nearly a decade, it still wasn't finished.

Preparations for the pending new production of *Der Ring Gott Farblonjet* actually began before Thompson even knew about Ludlam's 1977 adaptation of the opera cycle. Thompson had long been a fan of Wagner's *Ring* and independently conceived of a condensed version with new music that might become a perpetual, Off-Broadway attraction along the lines of *The Fantasticks* (in which, incidentally, Thompson would invest later). Thompson had approached Peter ("P.D.Q. Bach") Schickele with the idea, and he, in turn, referred him to Ludlam.

Thompson contacted Ludlam with the notion of his readapting the opera cycle in a more straightforward manner, and he readily agreed. He was fronted $10,000, and planned to deliver the manuscript in the spring. But as Quinton recalled, Ludlam quickly tired of the assignment once he realized — following some luncheon sessions with Thompson — how much he would have to "clean up" his original adaptation. And then when plans for *Titus Andronicus* suddenly materialized, Ludlam asked Thompson if he could postpone the Wagner project till the fall of 1987. While neither of them realized what little time he had left, Thompson told him to take all the time he needed.

Titus Andronicus got far enough along in the development process for Ludlam to attend meetings with various designers and casting people at the Public Theater. He talked about having Vincent Price in the title role, as well as casting his wife Coral Browne. Price was reportedly flattered when he heard about the offer, but ailing and confined to a wheelchair, he was incapable of performing on a stage. (When Ludlam had his mind set on something, little could deter him: He evidently considered having Price play the part *in* a wheelchair.)

When he attended a meeting with Jerry Marshall, a fill-in props master at the Public Theater, Ludlam brought with him some very firm ideas of how he wanted the production to look. He had conceived of a two-tiered colonnade creating a rear wall, with large, classical Roman statuary above the arches. As he sketched out his ideas on a piece of paper to demonstrate what he had in mind, Ludlam further specified that he wanted the statues to lose various appendages — with attendant blood stains — as the play progressed, in keeping with the Grand Guignol aspects of the drama.

"I was impressed by how clear he was about what he was seeing on the stage," said Marshall, who was particularly excited about the project since the precision of Ludlam's vision would inevitably make the designers' work that much easier. Marshall was also struck by how solicitous Quinton was of Ludlam during the meeting. Quinton — who had recently won an award for his costumes for *Salammbô* — was onboard as the costumer for *Titus*, and he deferred to Ludlam on any and all questions the other designers put to him.

On March 31, 1987, Don Nelsen ran a feature in the *Daily News* regarding Ludlam's plans for *Titus*. "Laurence Olivier? Bah. Gielgud, Scofield, Brando and the rest of the so-called elite bag? Twaddle. The most versatile actor in the Western world is a man named Charles Ludlam," began Nelsen's puff piece. As quoted by Nelsen, Ludlam described his approach to the play:

> I'm going to try to emphasize the surrealist elements because a lot of the excessive blood and gore in it isn't really possible. . . . The actions have a more symbolic quality, though they can be made to seem very graphic and frightening. A lot of these things have subliminal meaning. For instance, all the dismemberments are really about the state coming apart. If I can bring up those values, I think it can make a lot of sense.

There was another story on Ludlam and the play a month later in the "Broadway" gossip column of the Friday *New York Times*. Beyond identifying *Titus* as Ludlam's "favorite Shakespearean play," Nan Robertson interviewed Joseph Papp, who told her, "If you want someone to deal with extremes of human behavior, you go to Charles Ludlam [who's] also extremely erudite and knowledgeable." While revealing that he had considered having Ludlam play Tamora, the Gothic queen in the play, Papp added, "directing this Shakespeare will probably make enough demands on [him]."

And demands there were. It's difficult to believe that Robertson's column would appear in the *Times* on Friday, May 1, 1987, or the day *after* Ludlam finally entered the hospital. There would be a brief notice in the "Broadway" column exactly two weeks later to announce that the "eagerly awaited" production of *Titus* had been postponed until the following season.

The events leading up to his admission into the hospital would ultimately prove nothing less than harrowing. The fact is, Ludlam had begun to exhibit signs of serious illness back in January. His performance as Chester Nurdiger had become increasingly strained and lifeless, and he simply didn't have the energy required to maintain the role anymore. *The Artificial Jungle* was more or less forced to close early in February.

A couple of weeks before it closed, Ludlam had appeared on First City, a local access cable show, giving what would prove to be his last television interview. It was a fifteen-minute segment, encompassing two discrete video clips of *The Artificial Jungle*, which it was promoting. Though Ludlam seemed chipper and engaging, his responses were somewhat slower and more low-key than in earlier television interviews. He looked like a man in his sixties as opposed to his early forties. His face was noticeably shrunken and sallow, which only accentuated the intensity of his penetrating eyes.

In spite of his condition, and even though there were only the rudimentary beginnings of a script, rehearsals for *Houdini* commenced shortly after *The Artificial Jungle* closed. But Ludlam was so ill during the first week of rehearsals that practically nothing could be accomplished. He would hold the rehearsals whenever he felt well enough to show up. But inevitably he reached a point where he was too exhausted to even rise from his seat in the auditorium and work onstage.

Here was a man who had always railed against anyone in the theater who failed to work when they had a cold. He himself had been like a bull who went on no matter how he was feeling. Only in retrospect did it seem suspicious that *Irma Vep* had to close down for a week when he had a severe case of the flu and failed to rebound as quickly as usual. That episode, a year and a half earlier (and some months after his stomach problems during the rehearsals of *Hedda Gabler*), might very well have been the juncture at which his HIV-positive status converted into full-blown AIDS.

Though he had every confidence his health would improve and the play would eventually be realized, the rehearsals for *Houdini* were abruptly abandoned with little to show for them. It just became obvious there wouldn't be another production until Ludlam recovered from his "cold." For the first time in years, the theater was dark and without the prospect of presenting anything in the foreseeable future. Fortunately, *The Artificial Jungle* had earned enough money to sustain the business operations for the time being. But as Steven Samuels succinctly summarized the situation: "Nothing made any sense at that point." As the weeks dragged on, it gradually became apparent that there wasn't any forward motion on any of the many projects that Ludlam had been juggling for the past two months.

Ludlam did, however, keep after Walter Gidaly, his lawyer, to schedule a meeting with the owners of the theater at One Sheridan Square and renew the company's lease. Though the optional extension on the original lease was in effect until February 28, 1988, Ludlam felt compelled to ensure the company's distant future a year ahead of time. While suppressing his private worries that he might expire before the existing lease did, it was probably this fear of encroaching death that compelled him to act on it so swiftly.

Accompanied by Gidaly and Samuels, Ludlam went to the meeting late in February. He was thinner than ever and coughing most of the time. When the theater owners proposed a five-year renewal, Ludlam came back with a request for a twenty-year lease. This was practically unheard of under any circumstances, but at the height of what had been a prolonged real estate boom in New York, it was more than just audacious — it was outrageous. What Ludlam was really petitioning for was the company's future as well as his personal legacy, his immortality. What he settled for was a ten-year lease, which would go into effect on March 1, 1988.

Also in February, as Pashalinski recalled, Ludlam came to see her perform in *Cleveland and Halfway Back* at the Ensemble Studio Theater. Though he greeted her backstage afterwards, it was the first time Ludlam avoided any mouth contact when embracing her. She found this strange, of course, and only made sense of it a couple of months later, when she learned he was in the hospital with AIDS.

On February 22, Ludlam went to the Collective for Living Cinema to see a reel of short films Leandro Katz had taken of *The Grand Tarot* when it was performed in 1970. As compiled by Katz for this screening, the seven-and-a-half minutes of silent footage were a beautiful yet poignant reminder of the earliest period of the Ridiculous. After the screening, Ludlam had dinner with Quinton, Pashalinski, and Pashalinski's lover Linda Chapman at Souen, a vegetarian restaurant he had frequented for years. He could hardly eat a thing. He reserved what little energy he had for sermonizing on a macro-biotic lifestyle — still — and pointedly referring to its transcendental properties.

By March, Ludlam had become increasingly hermetic and unreachable, even by phone. He would often be too tired to take calls, and he became less and less responsible about returning them. When someone did manage to connect, Ludlam would be gasping for breath in his pathetic struggle to communicate. Samuels remembered asking him more than once if he had been to a doctor, saying it wasn't just a flu anymore and it sounded like it could be pneumonia. But Ludlam insisted it was just the flu.

Deep down, Ludlam certainly understood that it was more serious. The closest he came to seeing a doctor was when he visited his macrobiotics guru, an Oriental woman in lower Manhattan, who prescribed a holistic treatment for pneumonia. It consisted of acquiring a live carp, removing certain entrails and placing them on his chest, to absorb their nutrients as they dehydrated. As instructed, Quinton managed to locate a live carp at the Essex Street market and, as far-fetched as it sounds, they actually applied this cockamamie, voodoo-like remedy.

As he became increasingly unavailable during March and April, word spread that Ludlam was busy finishing *The Sorrows of Dolores* for its April 30 showing. Though the shooting of the film had essentially been completed by 1982, there had always been talk of additional sequences, which he never got around to filming. The existing footage still needed to be edited, however. He also wanted to complete *Museum of Wax*, another silent film that had already been shown in Coney Island but required titles and credits as well as some additional editing. Working by hand and with minimal equipment, he was trying to achieve all this by himself in his apartment. But once he realized how futile it was, he had Daphne Groos, the Ridiculous props mistress, come to the apartment and help.

Since Peter Golub was composing the score for *The Sorrows of Dolores* and needed to have his work completed in time for the screening, he kept pestering Ludlam about their getting together so he could coordinate his music with the film. But whenever Golub phoned to say he wanted to come by, Ludlam told him that he was too tired. "It was very frustrating for me," said Golub, "because I wasn't able to get precise timings on things.

"Every time I spoke to Charles, I was pressuring him to see a doctor," he continued. "Earlier he would argue that the macrobiotics would work for him and he'd get better. But eventually he would agree and say maybe he should see a doctor."

On April 30, or the day of the scheduled premiere of *The Sorrows of Dolores*, Quinton phoned Samuels to say Ludlam was much worse and he feared that they would have to put him in the hospital. Not having seen Ludlam since their lease-renewal meeting two months before, and having spoken with him only rarely in the interim, Samuels rushed over to help Quinton deal with the situation. Not knowing what to expect, he stopped by the office to grab a fistful of money from the petty cash fund. Though Ludlam had some medical insurance through the Screen Actors Guild, Samuels wanted to be prepared.

But nothing could have prepared Samuels for what he discovered when he arrived at Morton Street around noon. "It was truly appalling," recalled Samuels. "It was all much worse than I could have possibly imagined. He was truly skeletal, like an Auschwitz victim, and he couldn't get out of bed."

While lying on a futon on the floor, Ludlam was producing labored rasps. He could hardly breathe. Samuels remained behind with Ludlam as Quinton went with Daphne Groos to get her car and begin preparations for taking him to the hospital. "I cannot tell you how horrible it was to watch Charles try to move from the bed to a chair," continued Samuels.

> It must have taken him fifteen minutes. Every time he moved a muscle or shifted position, he had to stop to desperately try and catch his breath. Merely putting on his shoes became a Herculean effort. I began to get quite crazed. Everett had come back by now, and I said to them, "This makes absolutely no sense. He's not even going to make it down the hallway, let alone into the elevator and out into the street. There's just no reason to put him through this. Call for an ambulance. Get people to come and put him on a stretcher so he doesn't have to go through this."

> The really scary thing was that I couldn't understand what kind of cocoon-like world they had entered and were now living in. But it was very far removed from the rational, day-to-day activities of ordinary mortals.

Despite Ludlam's obviously deplorable condition, Samuels had to badger them into agreeing to call for an ambulance. He came to realize that they were still denying how severe things had become and trying to keep his illness a secret. Since Ludlam did not even have a doctor who was aligned with a particular hospital, Quinton dialed 911.

When the paramedics arrived, they took one look at Ludlam and one of them said, "ARC or AIDS?" Barely able to speak but mindful that Samuels was present, Ludlam replied, "Can we discuss this privately?" At that point, Samuels claimed that his brain just disconnected and he "entered the Twilight Zone or something," since he still failed to comprehend that Ludlam had AIDS. But looking back at that fatal moment, he recalled the expression of terror on Ludlam's face. "I think he knew he would never be back home again," said Samuels.

In the middle of the afternoon on April 30, a gray and overcast Thursday, Charles Ludlam was admitted to St. Vincent's Hospital, located only eight short blocks north of his apartment on Morton Street, and only a few blocks north of his theater at Sheridan Square. He would die there exactly four weeks later.

TOODLE-OO, MARGUERITE!

In eternity there is no distinction of tenses.
— Sir Thomas Browne

There is no ignominy in death. There is complete ignominy in an unreplenished, mechanized life.
— D.H. Lawrence

When British screenwriter Dennis Potter was interviewed on the BBC in April 1994, he knew that he was dying of pancreatic cancer and had — at most — two months to live. "We tend to forget that life can only be defined in the present tense. It *is*, and it is *now* only," he told interviewer Melvyn Bragg. "Things are both more trivial than they ever were and more important than they ever were — and the difference between the two doesn't matter," Potter claimed, as he was suddenly confronting his own death. "But the *nowness* of everything is absolutely wondrous." Potter went on to explain how his death sentence was liberating in at least one respect: "The fact is that if you can see the present tense, boy, do you see it! And boy, can you celebrate it!"

As his lifelong devotion to the theater and to the spontaneous moment emphasizes, Ludlam was more consistently in touch with "the present tense" than most mortals are, or, perhaps, can afford to be. And he literally spent his life celebrating it. Such celebration had no room for doctors or hospitals or death warrants. Ludlam was simply not going to let go of life willingly: His career and achievements testified to how much he loved it, first and last.

It seems likely that if Ludlam had sought some sort of medical attention sooner, his life would have been prolonged — though it's harder to say for how long, or what the quality of his additional days might have been like. It is certainly the case that Ludlam only submitted himself to a hospital when he no longer had any choice in the matter, as Steven Samuels's harrowing description of the morning of April 30 confirmed.

When he performed in his own version of *A Christmas Carol* in 1979, Ludlam told Black-Eyed Susan that playing Scrooge, who was confronting his own death, had frightened him at first. But he added that it ultimately made him realize you only have one life to live, and you had better make the most of it

While surveying all of his plays, it's germane to note that Ludlam dealt with the notion of an afterlife in at least three of them. In the prologue to *Caprice* (1976), he conceived of a "Wayfarer" who is actually a Bodhisattva, a Buddhist who has passed through several reincarnations and is ready for nirvana but chooses to remain on earth instead, to help others diminish human suffering. In *The Mystery of Irma Vep* (1984), he was concerned with a love that transcends time and space—in a sort of Nietzschean sense of the "eternal return." In something akin to a Catholic "miracle," the deceased title character communicates with the world of the living through a portrait of herself that bleeds. And in Ludlam's last play, *The Artificial Jungle* (1986), he himself plays a murder victim who repeatedly returns to haunt his murderers.

As formulated by Nietzsche, the notion that Christianity teaches people how to die rather than how to live is also quite relevant to Ludlam, who had long admired the German philosopher's writings. Though Catholicism was a major aspect of his youth and a subtextual influence on much of what he wrote, Ludlam quickly came to see the hypocrisy between its tenets and many of its practices. He left the fold as a young adult, never to return. Even though he understood that the ornamentation and trappings were a way of controlling the flock, Ludlam did retain a lifelong fascination with the theatricality of Catholicism, as well as with its iconography (tacky, plaster saints were a staple of his interior decorating). He also sustained an abiding interest in religion in general. But given his persistent, sacrilegious attitude and ridicule of Catholicism in his work, his decision to have a Catholic funeral (he planned it from his hospital bed) was arguably his most *ridiculous* act of all. On the other hand, anything less than the solemn grandeur of a Catholic farewell would have been lacking and inappropriate.

⁊

While Quinton rode with Ludlam in the ambulance at 1 PM on April 30, Samuels walked to St. Vincent's Hospital. As soon as Ludlam was ensconced in a room, Samuels rushed down to the theater to collect the guest list for the screening of *The Sorrows of Dolores* that night. He then met with Daphne Groos, Ed McGowan, and Peter Golub as they were scrambling to ready the film for its presentation. But they were all in a state of shock, and the few hours they had to assemble the premiere passed in a blur.

The 8:00 PM showing was a joint benefit for both the Ridiculous and the Collective for Living Cinema, where the screening was held. As an advance flyer described the film:

"Shadowgraph Photoplays" presents Charles Ludlam's haunting motion picture
THE SORROWS OF DOLORES (1987), starring Everett Quinton. Nine years in the

making! A cast of thousands! The entire production personally directed and
photographed by Mr. Ludlam, with graphics and animations by Arthur Brady.
Featuring Minette, Arthur Kraft, Lola Pashalinski, John D. Brockmeyer, [and]
Black-Eyed Susan.... 16 mm, b/w, silent. Musical score and sound effects by Peter
Golub. A Ridiculous Theatrical Company production.

Though Ludlam had managed to cut some of his precious footage in the last few weeks,
he never really finished editing *The Sorrows of Dolores* as he might have, and the audience had difficulty following the film. In its unfinished state, it proved to be a lethargic
movie with overlong sequences and a murky story line. Ludlam wasn't in the picture,
per se. But everyone could recognize him in a brief appearance he made à la Hitchcock.
It's little more than a flash on the screen, when he appears nude in a mirror during an
hallucination Dolores (Quinton) has in a train car.

Since he had already had some months to adjust to Ludlam's deteriorating condition,
Quinton was relatively composed at the screening. Samuels, however, was still reeling
from the news of the day. While acknowledging that Ludlam was ill and unable to
attend, he also tried to suppress the gravity of the situation in hopes of keeping all eyes
focused on the film. Then, just before the showing, the Collective's programmer Robin
Dickie announced to a nearly full house that Ludlam was indeed in the hospital. This
was when, where, and how Christopher Scott — and practically everyone else of the
inner circle — learned that Ludlam was sick.

As word spread that Ludlam was in the hospital, there was no end to the parade of visitors. Those closest to him made many visits over the course of the next month. At first,
John Brockmeyer didn't want to intrude. He waited until Everett conveyed that Ludlam
had asked about him. While Samuels was there every afternoon, Quinton sat vigil like a
sentinel, manning the evening shift. The two of them served as hosts as much as anything else. Ludlam was in a large, private room, and there were times when it was so
crowded with guests that it felt like a party was being thrown.

Ludlam was well treated by the hospital staff — more for his angelic spirit than for his
being a celebrity. Though he had been a thoroughly demanding friend and colleague in
life, he proved to be an undemanding patient. This was due, in large part, to his embarrassment over being ill and his feeling like a burden. In his final weeks, Ludlam made
peace with everyone and exuded a bottomless love and compassion. But beneath the
surface he was in a perpetual state of turmoil, and he never really came to accept the
circumstances of his impending death.

Nor was he the only one still engaged in denial. Despite the precautionary warning signs posted on the door to his room, for several days there were those who refused to believe that Ludlam had AIDS. When Samuels raised the topic with Black-Eyed Susan, he recalled, "She went absolutely ballistic and insisted that wasn't the problem." Coupled with his own hope, her doubt was compelling enough for Samuels to latch on to — until he put the question to Walter Gidaly, Ludlam's lawyer, who confirmed that it was definitely AIDS.

On the other hand, it was painfully obvious to any visitor that Ludlam had pneumonia — more specifically, Pneumocystis carinii, which was a frequent cause of death for people with AIDS during the first decade of the epidemic. He was hooked up to a respirator as soon as he was admitted into the hospital, and he remained on one until the end. As the days turned into weeks, he developed a scar on the bridge of his nose from the oxygen mask he was forced to wear.

While seemingly everyone who ever knew or worked with Ludlam visited him in the hospital, there were at least two notable exceptions. Ethyl Eichelberger couldn't bring himself to face Ludlam in his failing state and never came by. Even more startling, Marjorie never made the trip from Long Island to see her son at St. Vincent's.

Reluctant to deliver the news himself, Ludlam had Quinton call his mother to tell her that he had AIDS. The usually feisty Marjorie was dumbfounded by the news. Quinton felt that, in fact, she was angry, but couldn't allow herself to show it.

Samuels happened to answer the phone when Marjorie called Ludlam for what proved to be their last conversation, a few days before he died. Even though Samuels held the phone for him, Ludlam had all he could do to keep whispering, "I love you too, Mamma, I love you too."

Since it was difficult for Ludlam to talk, he had a pen and pad on his bed table and often communicated via notes. When he had only one or two guests, which was usually the case, they passed most of the time by reading aloud to him. It's a tender sort of irony to realize that he spent the last month of his life very much like his earliest years, when his mother read to him every day.

Initially, visitors would take turns reading *Around the World With Auntie Mame*, Patrick Dennis's sequel to his phenomenally successful book about another larger-than-life figure who, like Ludlam, believed that life should be celebrated at every turn. The variety of subsequent books serves as a potent reminder of the wide-ranging tastes that shaped Ludlam's life and work. Samuels read Zola's *The Masterpiece*, which concerned the author's friendship with Cézanne. Christopher Scott read some Balzac tales and recalled skipping over a long passage about venereal disease, since it was hitting too close to the hospital bed. Lola Pashalinski remembered telling Ludlam that she had just been cast in a production of Ezra Pound's version of *Elektra* at the Classic Stage Company, and he said he would love to see the script. Along with Quinton and Black-Eyed Susan, she read a good deal of the play during her next visit, until Ludlam fell asleep.

Quinton read a biography of Gypsy Rose Lee written by her son, Erik Lee Preminger. He recalled that when he reached the last chapter, concerning her death, Ludlam looked over his shoulder and shook his head, indicating he didn't want to hear it.

In addition to the readings, flowers were another motif in Ludlam's hospital room. Susan brought some rhododendrons from John Brockmeyer's garden in Staten Island, and Ludlam held them to his chest for quite a while, staring at them with great intensity. Brockmeyer himself picked some dandelions from the garden and placed them in a vase on the windowsill. When he said they would last for a couple of days, Ludlam made a gesture with his eyes, as if to say that he wasn't sure he would.

Even though he was uncomfortable and sometimes in a great deal of pain — for which he took morphine — Ludlam never reached a point where he would have preferred to die. He nevertheless dealt directly with certain practical matters associated with his passing. He had Walter Gidaly come to the hospital and draw up his will. "However sick he was in body, his mind was still functioning a hundred percent," said Gidaly. "He was very much Charles Ludlam. He always delegated. He always knew what he wanted and he was very specific about it."

Ludlam divided his estate into three parts, shared equally among his lover Everett, his mother Marjorie, and his brother Donald. Looking to the future, he specified that his mother and brother's shares should be passed on to Donald's daughters, Roslyn and Cara. Samuels recalled that Ludlam had also wanted to leave a single dollar to his estranged half brother, to prevent him from contesting the will. But even while he had no memory of this bequest, Gidaly claimed it would have been a superfluous maneuver.

Ludlam was equally meticulous and detailed about planning his own funeral, which essentially became the last show he ever directed. Quinton, himself a lapsed Catholic, was surprised when Ludlam told him he wanted a Catholic service. He remembered asking him if he was serious. Ludlam dictated everything, from which prayers were to be read and what music he wanted played, to who should speak.

There was, however, an even weightier matter, which Ludlam appeared to be over-looking: naming his successor as head of the company. But as Samuels discovered a good year later while editing his papers, Ludlam *did* write something that would make his wishes known. The single-page document was based on a conversation that actually transpired between Quinton and himself. Ludlam probably wrote it sometime in March, at a moment when he was feeling ill and realized his days might be numbered. Samuels found the page buried in the unfinished script for *Houdini*, which Ludlam had stopped working on at the time:

> CHARLES: You must continue the theatre.
>
> EVERETT: But I can't write. I don't know how.
>
> CHARLES: Steal lines. Orchestrate platitudes. Hang them on some plot you found somewhere else.
>
> EVERETT: But I don't know how to make it funny.
>
> CHARLES: You don't have to worry about that. Funny is in the eye of the beholder. You know yourself from doing the same play every night. Some audiences are solemn and others laugh. Let the audience be the judge of what is funny.
> The art of playwriting can be passed on from father to son. Stefan Brecht should have continued in his father's footsteps. Remember Dumas *père et fils*.
>
> EVERETT: But I'm not related. I don't come from the same gene pool as you.
>
> CHARLES: It's not genetic. It's technology. And you don't have to do everything yourself. Delegate responsibility. There are plenty of talented people around.
>
> EVERETT: But they won't do what I tell them.
>
> CHARLES: They will if you pay them.
>
> EVERETT: But the audiences want *you*.
>
> CHARLES: They'll like some plays and they won't like others. It was ever so.

Some months earlier, in conjunction with the run of *The Artificial Jungle*, the cast members had joined Ludlam for a group interview on National Public Radio. In response to being asked if the Ridiculous could continue without Ludlam, everyone emphatically said "No." Later, when they got home, Ludlam let Quinton know how furious he was with their response.

To offset the dismal concerns of preparing for his demise, Ludlam and Quinton kept looking at newspaper ads for a country house they talked about acquiring after his release. They planned to get away from the pressures of the city and further recuperate in the country. Everyone, including Ludlam, seemed to believe he would recover from his bout of pneumonia and achieve still more in his already accomplished life. He told Christopher Scott that he had carefully observed hospital protocol, and that there was hilarious material for a play there, which he was working out in his head.

Late in his term at St. Vincent's, there was a brief interlude when it appeared as if Ludlam actually was getting better. Regular visitors observed that his coloring had improved, and that he had been placed on a smaller respirator. When his housekeeper came to visit and burst into tears, Ludlam reassured her that he was on the mend. No one seemed to realize that many AIDS patients appear to rally shortly before the end.

It was during this period that Jeremy Gerard, a theater reporter for *The New York Times*, phoned Ludlam to discuss his last-minute withdrawal from the production of *Titus Andronicus* in Central Park. Though he had great difficulty talking, Ludlam put a positive spin on the situation. He said he was already feeling better and that he would be back at work soon. AIDS was never mentioned, of course. But like many who had contact with Ludlam in his final weeks, there was no mistaking the evidence; and Gerard claimed that he knew Ludlam had AIDS. He also recalled crying as he put the receiver down. Gerard would begin the research for his front-page obituary of Ludlam in the next few days.

Two weeks before his death, the *Village Voice* kept calling Samuels to say that Ludlam had to attend the Obie Awards ceremony, on May 18. If the truth be told, Ludlam had grown weary of attending the Obies every year and paying homage to other people whose work he did not respect. Even though the specific winners traditionally remained confidential until the presentation, the *Voice* eventually sent word that Ludlam was receiving a lifetime achievement award, and no excuse would be acceptable for his failure to show up.

Ross Wetzsteon, an editor at the *Voice* and chairman of the Obie Awards committee, finally understood that Ludlam was hospitalized and unable to attend. He proceeded to ask if they could arrange a special telephone hookup, so that Ludlam might accept his award from his room. Though everything was being done to suppress the urgency of Ludlam's condition and to disguise the fact that he had AIDS, Samuels finally had to explain that he had pneumonia and simply couldn't speak. This was more than Ludlam and his associates wanted to reveal for public consumption. But Wetzsteon's persistence had left them no choice.

The heart of the Obie citation read,

> We're often told that America has no classical theater, but for 20 years New York has had the honor of possessing a theater that's classical in form, witty in substance, and innovative in content; a theater that keeps the old plays and the old traditions of dramatic structure alive by rethinking and reinventing them until they come out brand-new; a theater that is at once a popular entertainment and an intellectual delight.... For 20 years of joy and excitement, for daring limits, overstepping boundaries, arousing controversy, and provoking delight, this year's Obie for sustained achievement in the Off-Broadway theater is awarded to Charles Ludlam.

With Samuels, Black-Eyed Susan, Peter Golub, and Ed McGowan bolstering him, Quinton accepted Ludlam's "Sustained Achievement" award — his sixth and final Obie. Though a stunned Susan won her own award for "Sustained Excellence of Performance," the Obies ceremony was understandably a melancholy occasion for everyone close to Ludlam.

The week after the awards, on Wednesday, May 27, Quinton called Paul Martino, the ICM agent who had handled Ludlam's Hollywood contracts, and said, "If you're going to come, it had better be today." Martino arrived in the evening and recalled that Susan was massaging Ludlam's feet. A good many visitors had been to see him earlier in the day. Samuels interrupted his reading to Ludlam as three friends arrived independently of one another. Ludlam momentarily perked up when Stuart Sherman mentioned that he had recently discovered a recording of works by Nietzsche, and that he would tape it before his next visit. A theatrical publicist with a jovial spirit, George Ashley's presence helped lighten the otherwise somber mood. A Hare Krishna and dear old friend named Govinda brought a chain of braided roses, from which Ludlam seemed to derive much pleasure.

In time, Quinton would refer to that evening as "closing night." It was fortuitous that Susan, Pashalinski and Brockmeyer — three cofounders of the Ridiculous — had each been to visit on this, Ludlam's final day. Theater director Larry Kornfeld and his wife Margaret were the last to leave prior to Everett, later that night. Though he had plans to see a movie with his friend Bob Pollack, and he also wanted to prepare for a TV commercial audition scheduled for the next morning, Quinton had an odd feeling and asked Ludlam if he should stay later than usual. Ludlam said no. But he in turn made an unusual request. For the first time during his month in the hospital, Ludlam asked Everett to turn off the lights before leaving. It was a theatrical gesture, as if he knew he were going to die later that night, and wanted the stage to fade to black.

The nurse who was on duty phoned Quinton shortly after 1 AM to report that Ludlam had just expired. She explained that he was holding her hand at the time, and had what appeared to be a peaceful passing. Quinton called Samuels and Phillip Warner. According to Samuels, Quinton was remarkably calm: "It was as if he was dead himself, an empty shell going about his necessary business."

Marjorie and Donald Ludlam entrusted Quinton with the funeral arrangements. After accompanying him to the funeral home to select the casket and schedule the wake, and then going to the hospital to collect Ludlam's belongings, Samuels spent the bulk of Thursday at the theater on the phone, notifying members of the company and the press of Ludlam's death. Though Jeremy Gerard was told — like everyone else — that Ludlam had died of pneumonia, he called back at least twice to ask if the cause had been AIDS. Given Gerard's persistence, Samuels ultimately referred him to Walter Gidaly.

While acknowledging that Ludlam had AIDS, Gidaly said the family was opposed to his mentioning it in the obituary. There was also the justifiable concern for how such news might affect Quinton's ongoing career. But Gerard now kept after Gidaly, phoning him back once or twice until he agreed to speak with Marjorie and Donald, who instantly gave their approval.

Looking back at that pivotal moment, Gerard explained, "We [journalists] were at a crossroads in terms of reporting on AIDS. It was crucial, especially with people of stature, that we take the stigma away from it." Indeed, Ludlam died a year and a half after Rock Hudson, whose death marked a turning point in AIDS awareness and in the still young history of the epidemic. Only five weeks after Ludlam's obituary appeared on the front page of *The New York Times*, Michael Bennett would receive the same privileged treatment when he too died of AIDS.

But Gerard insisted that the notice of Ludlam's death would have appeared on the front page of the paper with or without any reference to AIDS. The culture staff at the *Times* had simply been one of his greatest champions from the beginning of his career; and with this single, parting gesture they were doing what they could to perpetuate his legacy.

In spite of the paper's continued admiration for Ludlam's achievements, the opening of his lengthy obituary seemed to emphasize the AIDS connection. The first and second of twenty-four paragraphs read:

> Charles Ludlam, one of the most innovative and prolific artists in the theater avant-garde, who seemed to be on the verge of breaking into the mainstream of American culture, died of pneumonia early yesterday. He was 44 years old and had been suffering from AIDS.
>
> Mr. Ludlam's death stunned a theater community that is struggling daily — mostly, until now, in private, personal ways — with the devastation of AIDS. The announcement of his death and the causes was made by his lawyer, Walter Gidaly.

In spite of its obvious warmth towards Ludlam, the *Times* encomium offended many by stating that Ludlam only "seemed to be on the verge of breaking into the mainstream of American culture." (A quoted contribution from Joseph Papp reinforced the idea: "We lost an extraordinary artist who was just on his way to a tremendous breakthrough in theater and opera.") However, the mere placement of the obituary on the front page of the *Times* — a rare honor usually reserved for figures whose reputations transcend national, let alone local boundaries — refuted such a notion and more than suggested that Ludlam had indeed entered the mainstream. On the other hand, perhaps it was apt for any concept of the "mainstream" to elude Ludlam at the time of his death, considering how much he had flirted with it, and at the same time resisted it, thoughout his life.

In the *New York Post*, Clive Barnes wrote that Ludlam was "a mixture of mayor and guru.... He had a talent to amaze.... He had a masterly sense of the ridiculous and genius sense of theater ... his whole theater style, became first a cult, and then something closer to a movement ... his entire theatrical being promoted a specific style of theater that was as much a way of looking at art as it was a way of looking at life...." Barnes ended by saying, simply, "The man is unrepeatable."

Mel Gussow paid tribute the following week in the "Arts & Leisure" section of *The New York Times*. He referred to Ludlam as

> a brilliant, one-man way of theater.... Inventing himself and his troupe, he created a performance genre.... [His] recklessness led some people to misinterpret his work as anarchic. It was spontaneous, but it was also highly structured — and

always to specific comic effect. Though Mr. Ludlam was a titanic Fool, he was not foolish. He knew exactly what he was doing. . . . Mr. Ludlam was an original theater artist, and, as such, his art will survive — in his plays, in our memories of performances and also in the actors whom he trained and who became his comic co-stars. . . .

The *Village Voice* devoted more than an entire page to commemorating Ludlam. Michael Feingold was quick to take his uptown colleagues to task for misperceiving Ludlam in a variety of ways.

> He was not, as has wrongly been assumed by the daily press, an avant-garde artist in the least; he was the reviver and purifier of a thousand traditions that had fallen into corruption, banality, and disrepute. He reinvented the burlesque tradition, the vaudeville and silent-film tradition of physical comedy, the tradition of playwriting as an ongoing conversation with a faithful audience, the tradition of repertory acting. . . . The papers described him as having been on the verge of entering the mainstream, but Charles's theater *was* the mainstream; it's the rest of our institutions that lallygag on the verge, giving us patchy, one-sided versions of this or that aspect of the theater, while Charles Ludlam gave us the whole experience.

Demonstrating a brand of hubris that only Ludlam himself might have surpassed, Feingold added, "In person, I have to confess, he always scared me a little; he was the only American theater artist whom I have ever really thought of as my intellectual superior."

Though Feingold's was the most personalized, like all the other death notices and tributes (including ones on ABC TV and NPR), it seemed geared to ensure that Ludlam's work and aesthetic — his legacy — would carry on into the future. On the other hand, Steven Samuels was one of many who imagined that, even though the plays would flourish, the company would simply have to fold. He was instantly disabused of this notion on Friday, the day after Ludlam died.

The dramatic moment occurred at the wake, which was held at the Perazzo Funeral Home, on Bleecker Street, just east of Sixth Avenue. Samuels met the iron-willed Marjorie for the first time, in front of the open coffin. As soon as they were introduced, Marjorie said, "You *will* keep the company going, won't you?" She filled in the ensuing pause by turning to the coffin and gesturing to her son's body, as she added, "He would have wanted you to!"

"When he died, my feeling had been that I would have a few months to straighten things up and close things down," said Samuels. "I had been one of those people who thought the company couldn't continue without Charles. But as soon as she said that to me, I said, 'Of course we will, Mrs. Ludlam. We'll do everything we can.'"

The coffin was set at an angle in a fairly large chapel in the rear of the funeral parlor. Quinton had laid Ludlam out in a natural-colored linen suit, with a pastel shirt, and a boldly colored, striped tie that Susan had given him a month before for his last birthday. There was a rosary in his hands, which were placed across his chest.

Like Marjorie, Quinton didn't cry at the viewing. While he embraced and comforted a sobbing Samuels, he said, "I can't cry anymore. There just aren't any tears left." It was Susan who struck many as Ludlam's widow. "She was in the most elaborate mourning clothes," recalled Samuels. "We stayed until we were told to leave, and we were each given one last opportunity to say goodbye, as it were. I remember going up and wanting to touch Charles, but not being able to. I reached out, but all I could do was touch his sleeve. Susan was the last. She spread out her dress and knelt before him."

After leaving the wake, a number of people happened to walk by the theater at One Sheridan Square and discovered that a kind of shrine had spontaneously been created in front of its doors. An adoring public had started bringing flowers, candles, cards, and letters expressing their undying appreciation and affection for Ludlam. Countless contributions continued to appear over the next week.

This unexpected display of public grief was perhaps the most palpable manifestation of just how beloved Ludlam had become in the community. It elicited a special story by Jeremy Gerard in *The New York Times* two weeks later, in which it was revealed that the company had "about 300 patrons who contribute money regularly." Such figures provided further testimony to the substantial devotion that Ludlam had prompted from his most generous fans.

A painter of the photo-realism school, David Fisch would permanently capture the shrine in front of the theater a year later, in an oil painting he dedicated to Ludlam called "Merlin's Laugh." (Fisch himself would die of AIDS in 1994.) Two years after Ludlam's passing, the city would dedicate the tiny little strip of road in front of the theater to him, in a public ceremony and installation of a new street sign that read "Charles Ludlam Lane."

లు

Ludlam's funeral was held on Saturday morning at St. Joseph's Church on Sixth Avenue and Washington Street, a short block away from the theater. It was presided over by James Gardiner, a young priest whom Ludlam had selected, having been impressed after attending other funerals Gardiner had officiated at.

In a letter to David Hockney detailing the funeral, Christopher Scott reported, "Before the mass . . . Thomas Lanigan Schmidt went back to the chancery and ordered the priests to put on their most elaborate vestments and use tons of incense. He also told them the congregation would not tolerate a mechanical reading of the liturgy and that they should be mindful to speak with absolute sincerity, which they did."

While addressing the standing-room-only crowd, Gardiner introduced a bit of levity at the beginning of his service. "Charles is ready for heaven," he said, "but is heaven ready for Charles?" Various friends and relatives read passages from the bible, and Susan spoke passionately of her relationship with Ludlam. But it was Leon Katz, the last to speak, who brought the house down as he closed his eloquent eulogy with the final line from *Camille*: "Much will be forgiven you, for you loved much. Toodle-oo, Marguerite."

At that moment, it was as if a switch had been thrown and the congregation was instantly electrified, leaping to their feet as one and rocking the church with a spontaneous, deafening applause. It was the last standing ovation for Ludlam.

The applause continued as fans of the company lined the sidewalks for several blocks along Sixth Avenue, spurring on the funeral cortege as it began its two-hour journey to St. Patrick's Cemetery on Lloyd's Neck in Huntington, Long Island, where Ludlam was to be buried beside his father, grandparents, and beloved aunts. It was a sunny, prematurely hot and sultry day. One of the limousines broke down on the freeway, disrupting the caravan and forcing its passengers to double up in other vehicles. While Marjorie rode with Donald and his family, Quinton was in another limo with his sister Mary Ann and Steven Samuels. Lola Pashalinski, Bill Vehr and John Brockmeyer rode together, and Christopher Scott, Black-Eyed Susan, Thomas Lanigan Schmidt and the Kornfelds were in another limo.

Set in a lovely, hillside cemetery with enormous trees, the graveside ceremony was brief. On the premise that it was more final and cathartic to observe the grave being covered,

Thomas Lanigan Schmidt persuaded Christopher Scott to stay on when the others departed. Noticing how hunky the gravediggers were in their tight tee-shirts, Scott told Schmidt that Ludlam would have appreciated this final touch. Scott smoked a joint while the two of them lingered on in the cemetery before walking to the train station in Huntington. Though it felt to Schmidt "like it was a thousand miles away, and like it was a thousand degrees outside," the walk to Huntington was additionally poignant for Scott since he and Ludlam had spent formative years of their youth with Jan Reynolds at that very station.

Those who returned to the city convened at the Rosebay Cafe above the theater. Since the oval-shaped theater sign over the doors tended to yellow with exposure to the elements, there was always a fresh one on reserve. It was Ed McGowan who suggested they put the new one up immediately, as if to reassure themselves that the company would indeed continue. Bill Vehr told Samuels he would like to direct plays, and the two of them talked about how ironic it was that the proceeds from the works, which Ludlam had imagined he would retire on, would now prove a source of income for them, in the form of ongoing work under the Ridiculous banner.

Scott arrived at the Rosebay just as the group had begun to disband. He accompanied a subdued Quinton to fetch provisions at the Integral Yoga health food store on West 13th Street, across from the Gay Community Center. He marveled at how they were stopped on every block along the way by virtual strangers who offered their condolences to Quinton.

$$\mathit{e}\mathit{\backsim}$$

Under the familiar name *Tabu Tableaux*, there was a memorial for Ludlam on July 13, held at the onetime Entermedia Theater, which had recently been refurbished and reopened as the Second Avenue Theater. As planned by Quinton, Black-Eyed Susan, and Bill Vehr, scenes were performed from seven of Ludlam's plays, along with alternating tributes by various members of the theatrical community. Lola Pashalinski was the emcee, introducing the scenes as well as the speakers with her own commentary.

"Welcome to *Tabu Tableaux*," she began, after a group of Ludlam-esque "Rheinmaidens" opened the program.

> Tonight we're going to celebrate the joyous work of Charles Ludlam. That was the first scene from *Der Ring Gott Farblonjet*. . . . The scenes we're performing tonight

represent just fragments of Charles's immense creativity, and there are friends and colleagues here who, I think you'll agree, indicate the diverse appeal of Charles's work. Our first guest is one of the great actor-directors in film and theater: I'm proud to introduce Geraldine Fitzgerald.

The other speakers included Eric Bentley, Madeline Kahn, Judith Malina, Joseph Papp, and Richard Hennessy, who delivered a poem he had written for Ludlam. In addition to *Der Ring Gott Farblonjet*, the other scenes were taken from *Conquest of the Universe*, *Eunuchs of the Forbidden City*, *Bluebeard*, *Secret Lives of the Sexists*, *Salammbô* (the controversial, "Hanno at the Baths" scene), and Ludlam's unfinished script for *Houdini*. In this last, which closed the program, Quinton played Dr. Saint, a medium who attempts to contact Houdini for his widow, portrayed by Black-Eyed Susan. It ended with an enormous projection of Ludlam in chains, trying to break through from the netherworld.

The three-hour event was interspersed with additional offerings. Quinton hosted a slide-show representing the company's twenty-year history. Leandro Katz showed his silent film clips from the 1970 production of *The Grand Tarot*, while Satie piano compositions played in the background. Vicki Raab opened the second half of the evening with her rendition of the title song from *Reverse Psychology*, accompanied by Peter Golub on a grand piano. Golub also wrote a *Requiem* for the event, which was sung by Joyce Castle. The piece was written to a lengthy passage from *Turds in Hell*, which was printed in the program designed by Robert Reddy. Though the words were credited to Ludlam and Bill Vehr, Leon Katz pointed out that they were actually taken from Joyce's *Ulysses*. How wonderfully apropos this final misattribution was, considering that Ludlam had borrowed from any and all sources in his plays.

There were 1,100 people at the memorial and still others who wanted to attend but could not be accommodated. The free tickets had been distributed by the Ridiculous box office, and they were gone within a matter of days. Samuels reserved a number for family members and certain VIPs, including critics such as Frank Rich.

As soon as the memorial was over, Leon Katz was approached by a reporter who inquired, "There are so many people here and yet it seems like they're all relatives and close friends who loved Charles. How is that possible?" It was a moving and stirring observation, one that perfectly summarized Ludlam's impact on his public at large.

The only sour note at the otherwise loving tribute occurred when a projected image of Ludlam as Camille prompted some derisive and awkward laughter from several people who clearly failed to appreciate either the humanity or the humor behind Ludlam's impersonation. While Ludlam had to combat misapprehensions regarding his use of drag during his lifetime, the misconceptions would only escalate after his death. In the media's rush to give Ludlam his posthumous due, too much emphasis has been placed on the drag component of his art, and too many strictly vacuous drag performers have been perceived as his disciples. No matter what they may have done to extend the legend of Charles Ludlam, such comparisons tend to diminish the far greater complexity behind both his theories and his work, and to undermine his devotion to comedy as a cleansing agent and a tool for demystification.

Ludlam identified with Camille on any number of levels during each of the more than five hundred times he portrayed her. What no one including Ludlam could have foreseen was the extent to which his own life would come to resemble hers in the end. Just as Camille dies prematurely of consumption, Ludlam would die before his time of AIDS, shortly after his forty-fourth birthday. In view of this, one of Ludlam's lines for Camille acquired a special relevance fourteen years after it was written: "I shall not live as long as others so I have promised myself to live more quickly." Posterity can only be grateful that Ludlam kept the same promise, and managed to accomplish so very much in his abbreviated time on the stage of life.

NOTES

Unless otherwise stated, excerpts from all plays (with the exceptions of *Whores of Babylon* by Bill Vehr, as well as *Bluebeard, Camille, Galas, The Mystery of Irma Vep,* and *Stage Blood*) are reprinted from *The Complete Plays of Charles Ludlam.* (New York: Harper & Row, 1989).

Excerpts from *Bluebeard, Camille, Galas, The Mystery of Irma Vep,* and *Stage Blood* are reprinted with permission from *The Mystery of Irma Vep and Other Plays.* (New York: Theatre Communications Group, 2001).

Unless otherwise indicated in the text or in this Notes section, all quoted statements in the book are based on the author's personal interviews with the subjects cited.

Apart from several letters and journal entries generously provided to the author by Christopher Scott, Lola Pashalinski, Richard Currie, Stephen Holt, and Teriananda, all personal correspondences reprinted herein are the property of the Charles Ludlam Estate, and are reproduced here with the kind permission of Walter Gidaly, Esq.

INTRODUCTION: *A Lifetime to Explain*
XII "God, if I hadn't discovered theater early on." Calvin Tomkins, "Profiles," *The New Yorker* (November 15, 1976): 55–6+

XII "The problem isn't that I've influenced them." After returning from an interview during which he was asked about his influence on others, Ludlam shared this thought with his company's business manager, Steven Samuels.

XIV "One of the problems with accepting a tag like avant-garde." Sam H. Shirakawa, "The Eccentric World of Charles Ludlam," *The New York Times* (July 3, 1983): "Arts & Leisure," 3+.

CHAPTER 3: *Flaming Creatures*
49 "I have this feeling he'd be good, too." Though the words are ascribed to Jerry Benjamin, they were recollected by Ronald Tavel.

55 "Most of the audience, who had never before." Fred W. McDarrah, "American Flag Burned in Theatre Spectacle," *Village Voice* (April 14, 1966): 7.

Chapter 4: *Glitter and be Gay*

63 "heavily made-up performers." Stuart W. Little, *Off-Broadway: The Prophetic Theater.* (New York: Coward, McCann & Geoghegan, Inc., 1972), 192.

63 "The present underground theater." John Gruen, *The New Bohemia.* (New York: Shorecrest, Inc., 1966), 88.

64 "To view the theater of the Ridiculous." Stefan Brecht, *Queer Theatre.* (New York: Methuen, New York & London Ltd., 1986), 53.

65 "We adopted a position of deliberate unfashionableness." Charles Ludlam, *Ridiculous Theatre: Scourge of Human Folly: The Essays and Opinions of Charles Ludlam,* ed. Steven Samuels. (New York: Theatre Communications Group, 1992), 114–115.

66 "It only costs me $50.00 a year for costumes." Frank Keating, *Queen's Quarterly: The Magazine For Gay Guys Who Have No Hangups.* (New York: Queen's Quarterly Publishing Co., Inc., Summer 1969), Volume 1, Number 3, 44.

71 "Of course, I play Marilyn." John Gruen, *Close-Up.* (New York: Viking, 1968), 30.

74 "an explosion of talent that leaves." Michael Smith, *Village Voice* (November 1967).

75 "a travesty of science-fiction cheapie movie spectaculars." Martin Gottfried, "Public Privacy," *Women's Wear Daily* (December 8, 1967).

75 "The curtain does not go up until Ondine." Ultra Violet, *Famous for 15 Minutes: My Years With Andy Warhol.* (New York: Harcourt Brace Jovanovich, 1988), 124–125.

80 "transvestite frolic, horrible fun." Brecht, *Queer Theatre,* 78.

81 "In his current two intermissionless plays there are enduring." Allan Edmands, "Dramatorgy," *East Village Other* (January 5, 1968): 13–14+.

86 "The author heaps ingredients onto the stage." A.D. Coleman, "Theatre: Big Hotel" *Village Voice* (January 18, 1968).

86 "A triumph of the theater of the ridiculous." Dan Isaac, *Show Business* (December 30, 1967): 15.

Chapter 5: *With the Force from My Emerald Eye*

93 "The Emerald Empress is discovered reclining." Bill Vehr, *Whores of Babylon.* (From an unpublished photocopy of the script), 7.

94 "It is a woman who is speaking to you." Ibid, 16.

94 "Some dreams are too intense." Ibid, 17.

99 "personally found it approached a kind of ideal." Martin Washburn, "Theatre: Turds In Hell," *Village Voice* (December 5, 1968): 47.

100 "They were half an hour late for the midnight performance." Frederick Ted Castle, *Gilbert Green: The Real Right Way to Dress for Spring.* (New Paltz, NY: McPherson & Company, 1986), 123.

104 "The main thing about Candy and Jackie Curtis." Ludlam, *Scourge,* 21–22.

106 "someone else's dream that, imagine!" Brecht, *Queer Theatre*, 80.

111 "I began to feel I was pouring everything into an abyss." Ludlam, *Scourge*, 22–23.

CHAPTER 6: *A Well-Made Play*

115 "Took a winter off [to write] a play." Ludlam, *Scourge*, 24.

116 "Bluebeard is an intellectual." Ibid, 24.

122 "Ludlam's consistently amusing linguistic conceits." Mel Gussow, "Laughs Pepper Ghoulish 'Bluebeard,'" *The New York Times* (May 5, 1970): 58.

123 "the details of the story, which are absurd nonsense." Martin Washburn, "Theatre: Bluebeard," *Village Voice* (April 16, 1970): 44+.

123 "They do not mark out new ground." Richard Schechner, "Two Exemplary Productions," *Village Voice* (April 23, 1970): 44+.

129 "It is fixed biologically or bio*ill*ogically at birth." Ludlam, *Scourge*, 151–152.

129 "The play is a gothic thriller featuring the slick art-nouveau acting." Althea Gordon (alias for Charles Ludlam), "The Play that Answers the Question, 'Is a Third Sex Possible?,'" *Gay Power*: 9+.

132 "If you spot any kids wearing sneakers." Ludlam's remark was recalled — and doubtlessly paraphrased — by Christopher Scott.

138 "Mr. Ludlam is an exploded pack of Tarot cards, a one-man harlequinade." Mel Gussow, "Stage: 'The Grand Tarot,'" *The New York Times* (March 4, 1971): 28.

140 "No one ever forgets their first meeting with Charles." Ronn Smith, "Ethyl Eichelberger," *Theatre Crafts* magazine. January 1989 issue, 28–33; 51–52.

145 "When the company got to London." Ludlam, *Scourge*, 26–27.

145 "Everything [else] at the festival was Grotowski-oriented." Ibid, 27.

146 "They put us in a PTA meeting hall." Ibid, 27.

149 "the only avant-garde theatre in Berlin." Ibid, 28.

149 "The German press received [*Eunuchs*] with gratitude." Ibid, 28.

151 "The critics in London seemed annoyed with me." Ibid, 29.

CHAPTER 7: *In The Forbidden City*

160 "Money is endangering the Ridiculous Theatrical Company." Martin Gottfried, *Women's Wear Daily* (April 10, 1972): 16.

160 "an exuberant and robust work, one of Ludlam's most polished." Mel Gussow, "Ludlam's 'Eunuchs' Arrives," *The New York Times* (April 7, 1972).

161 "I'm at a loss how to convey the idiosyncrasy, charm, and distinction." Michael Smith, "Theatre Journal," *Village Voice* (April 13, 1972): 61.

161 "I feel that I'll define what ridiculous is as a genre." Michael Smith, "Theatre Journal," *Village Voice* (March 30, 1972).

161 "The sex scenes are too broadly played." Fran Lebowitz, "All That Glitters Is Not Gold, Honey," *Changes* (June 1972): 28.

171 "across and under and back-and-forth." The convoluted description of the space at Sammy's Bowery Follies was Black-Eyed Susan's recollection.

174 "Yuck! The stuff they teach you in drama school nowadays." Ludlam's remarks here were reconstructed two decades later by Wally Gorell, to whom they were made.

180 "The fun is not primarily in the script." Mel Gussow, "Stage: The Ridiculous Company's Musical 'Corn,'" *The New York Times* (November 24, 1972).

181 "Ludlam has constructed the play with even more than." Michael Smith, "Theatre Journal," *Village Voice* (November 30, 1972).

CHAPTER 8: *The Ultimate Masochism*

185 "I developed such an identity with the role." Tomkins, "Profiles," *The New Yorker* (November 15, 1976): 55–6+.

185 "had a lot to do with my feelings about love." Ludlam, *Scourge*, 36.

187 "I wanted the audience to keep in mind." Ibid, 41.

187 "I pioneered the idea that female impersonation." Ibid, 40.

188 "Drama at its greatest is paradox." Ibid, 46.

192 "I had to convince myself that I was beautiful." Ibid, 41.

193 "When the audience laughed at my pain." Ibid, 41.

193 "This is no facile female impersonation." Mel Gussow, "Ludlam Star of 'Camille' In Title Role," *The New York Times* (May 4, 1973).

194 "I have seen many stage Camilles. Susan Strasberg." Emory Lewis, "'Camille' Parody a Daring Tour de Force," *Bergen County Record* (May 3, 1973).

194 "the company is perfectly in key with Ludlam's own performance." Michael Feingold, "Half (Cough Cough) in Jest," *Village Voice* (May 10, 1973).

194 "Charles isn't playing an old drag queen." Michael Smith, *Village Voice* (May 17, 1973).

194 "When the dying Camille shivers in the third act." Ernest Leogrande, "Night Owl Reporter," *New York Daily News* (June 12, 1973).

196 "few [of the participants] ranged as far as Ludlam's." Michael Iachetta, "An Off-Broadway Camille in Drag," *New York Daily News* (July 17, 1974).

204 "This is not one of Mr. Ludlam's tightest scripts." Mel Gussow, "The Theater: Hilarious 'Hot Ice,'" *The New York Times* (February 11, 1974): 48.

204 "brilliant, hillarious, outrageous new play." Michael Smith, "Theatre Journal," *Village Voice* (February 14, 1974): 57.

205 "That fine hairline between comedy and tragedy." Clive Barnes, "Stage: An Oddly Touching 'Camille,'" *The New York Times* (May 14, 1974).

207 "a master of theatrical parody [who] has the ability to breathe new life." Elenore Lester, "The Holy Foolery of Charles Ludlam," *The New York Times* (July 14, 1974): "Arts & Leisure," 1+.

207 "Tradition isn't a stale thing that holds you back." Tom Topor, "Theater Pitching Tent on Old Camp Grounds," *New York Post* (July 6, 1974): Entertainment Page Two.

207 "to lampoon life, to fracture the square." John Stern, "People Are Talking About...," *Vogue* (August, 1974).

207 "an artist in a field of paper daisies." William A. Raidy, "Ludlam's 'Camille' Funny Outrage," *Long Island Press* (May 14, 1974).

207 "Tallulah Bankhead, Lillian Gish, Bette Davis, Maria Callas." David Richards, "The Sublime May Be Passe, But Should It Be Ridiculous?," *Washington Star-News* (August 9, 1974): D-4.

208 "the very essence of a drag show; the difference." John Simon, "Campille," *New York*: 74.

208 "If this is 'camp,' you are welcome to it." Richard Watts, "The Ridiculous 'Camille,'" *New York Post* (May 14, 1974): 21.

208 "Ludlam's artistic career seemed to have ended." Brecht, *Queer Theatre*, 93.

208 "Ludlam's descent into professionalism." Ibid, 86.

216 "an example of the literary side of the Ridiculous." *Theatre of the Ridiculous*, ed. Bonnie Marranca and Gautam Dasgupta. (New York: Performing Arts Journal Publications, 1979), 8.

217 "Such amazing things happened when I was writing." Tomkins, "Profiles," *The New Yorker* (November 15, 1976): 55–6+.

218 "Laughs are freefalling, but the play is less wild." Mel Gussow, "Ludlam's 'Stage Blood,' 'Hamlet' With Happy Ending," *The New York Times* (December 9, 1974).

218 "If our commercial theatre lifted its embargo." Dick Brukenfeld, "'Hamlet' as We Like It," *Village Voice* (December 16, 1974).

218 "Having hit upon an idea that captures the very essence." Martin Gottfried, "Clowning 'Stage Blood' With the Ridiculous," *New York Post* (December 9, 1974): 21.

218 "it's undermined by the performing of the Ridiculous." Allan Wallach, "Too Ridiculous," *Newsday* (December 9, 1974).

218 "is one of the funniest men in the New York." Emory Lewis, "Stage: Amusing Whodunit," *Bergen County Record* (December 9, 1974).

219 "appears to have become more disciplined, more fastidious." Julius Novick, "'Stage Blood' Is Anemic Parody," *The New York Times* (January 12, 1975).

220 "I wanted to write a ghost story." Ludlam, *Scourge*, 50.

220 "With hand puppets, it's your hand that's acting." Ibid, 58.

CHAPTER 9: *Caprice Itself*

231 "Twyfford was more of an s&m type." Ludlam, *Scourge*, 59.

237 "lesser Ludlam . . . far below the author's *Bluebeard*." Mel Gussow, "Stage: 'Caprice' by Charles Ludlam," *The New York Times* (April 16, 1976).

237 "measure up . . . is because the play does not afford Ludlam the comic actor." Gerald Rabkin, "Chez Charles," *Soho Weekly News* (April 22, 1976).

237 "People have preconceptions about what you should be doing." Ludlam, *Scourge*, 59.

239 "was an ill-fated production." Ibid, 58.

240 "does things with his shoulders and his hands." Hal Crowther, "Ludlam's 'Camille' Is Bewitching Burlesque," *Buffalo Evening News* (April, 1976).

246 "a small, wiry, nervously energetic man." Tomkins, "Profiles," *The New Yorker* (November 15, 1976): 55–6+.

250 "It was influenced by Joyce." Ludlam, *Scourge*, 63–64.

255 "I hold these conversations with myself." Ibid, 67.

256 "Ludlam the playwright-director-designer has denied." Gerald Rabkin, "Ho-Jo-To-Ho, Already!," *Soho Weekly News* (May 5, 1977): 29.

256 "certain individual scenes drag on too long." Michael Feingold, "Let Ludlam Ring!," *Village Voice* (May 9, 1977): 83.

257 "Having successfully avoided the Ridiculous." Douglas Watt, "Wagner's 'Ring' Is Lost Along the Way," *New York Daily News* (April 19, 1977).

257 "I was warned when I took this job that, sooner." John Simon, *New York* (May 16, 1977).

257 "Give Mr. Ludlam points not only for nerve, but for." Mel Gussow, "Stage: A Ridiculous Thing Happened to 'Der Ring,'" *The New York Times* (April 19, 1977).

259 "I watched it forty times and I couldn't even think of an improvement." Ludlam, *Scourge*, 65–66.

260 "was like climbing Everest. It was a turning." Glenn Loney, "Theater of the Ridiculous Wings West," *Los Angeles Times* (April 9, 1978): Calendar, 68.

260 "Despite 10 years of almost continuous performance." Mel Gussow, "Ludlam's a Success In a Ridiculous Way," *The New York Times* (July 22, 1977).

CHAPTER 10: *A Talent Like This*

268 "Where he goes, Walter is a traffic stopper." Mel Gussow, "Ludlam, No Dummy, Takes a Partner," *The New York Times* (November 18, 1977).

270 "settled in for a very welcome week-long run." Anna Kisselgoff, "Dance: 'Aphrodisiamania' Is Decadent Delight," *The New York Times* (November 30, 1977).

275 "a diabolically comic *coup de theatre*," Mel Gussow, "Stage: 'Ventriloquist's Wife' Is Presented," *The New York Times* (December 28, 1977).

275 "a superb ventriloquist — recalling in some of." Clive Barnes, "Ludlam's New Show Is Magical," *New York Post* (January 5, 1978).

275 "All feats of skill I don't understand or can't." Erika Munk, "No Dummy," *Village Voice* (January 9, 1978).

289 "an evening of lackadaisical Ludlam." Mel Gussow, "Theater: 'Utopia, Inc.' From Charles Ludlam," *The New York Times* (December 5, 1978).

289 "a confused plot, laborious action, and a lot." Michael Feingold, "Utopia Limited," *Village Voice* (December 11, 1978).

289 "an anemic letdown from past triumphs." Marilyn Stasio, "'Utopia, Inc.' Isn't Even Ridiculous," *New York Post* (December 2, 1978).

289 "The puns come so thick and fast that one's reactive groaning becomes rhythmic." Gerald Rabkin, "Not On Farce Value," *Soho Weekly News* (December 7, 1978): 90.

290 "A sense of parody and a sense of fun are everywhere." John Russell, "Art People," *The New York Times* (December 29, 1978).

297 "in a class with such vintage Ludlam extravaganzas." Mel Gussow, "Stage: Black-Eyed Susan Wed to 'Enchanted Pig,'" *The New York Times* (April 24, 1979): 10.

297 "Ludlam here has all the makings of a success." Don Nelsen, "Fun With a Pig Tale," *New York Daily News* (June 5, 1979).

297 "a masterpiece of childish nonsense." William A. Raidy, *Newark Star Ledger* (July 26, 1979).

297 "will cure the most ennui-struck sophisticate." James Leverett, "Fable and Fact," *Soho Weekly News* (May 3, 1979).

297 "perhaps Ludlam's most compact, elegant production." Jan Hoffman, "The Uses of Disenchantment," *Village Voice* (April 30, 1979): 89.

297 "it ranks as one of the best plays in the RTC." Terry Helbing, *The Advocate* (September 6, 1979).

302 "saw something about my acting, was sensitive to an aspect of it." Ludlam, *Scourge*, 210.

304 "I don't think you're getting it....I had no idea." Ludlam's words, here, were recreated by Black-Eyed Susan in the course of recalling this anecdote about his direction of Vicki Rabb.

311 "If you say you're not a gay theatre they say." Steve Warren, "Creator of the Ridiculous: Interview with Charles Ludlam," *The Sentinel* (February 8, 1980).

314 "I'm not out to write the Great American Play." Ludlam, *Scourge*, 107.

CHAPTER 11: *Secret Lives*

317 "The supreme theatre is intuitive." Ludlam, *Scourge*, 156.

326 "If you ask me, it may be time for Charles." Frank Rich, "Stage: Ludlam's 'Reverse Psychology,'" *The New York Times* (September 16, 1980).

327 "It's all about sex, love and possessiveness." Donald Miller, "Director brings unusual brand of theater to CMU," *Pittsburgh Post-Gazette* (November 18, 1980): 25.

334 "I've tried to use plot in a twentieth-century way." Ludlam, *Scourge*, 105.

335 "Not one of these actors … comes close to beating." Frank Rich, "Stage: Ludlam's Latest, 'Love's Tangled Web,'" *The New York Times* (June 8, 1981).

337 "*Love's Tangled Web* was written, produced and directed in six weeks." Ludlam, *Scourge*, 112–113.

341 "took their places in a booth. Quinton told." John Frick and Stephen Johnson. "'Tricks and Treats' on Coney Island," *The Drama Review* (Spring 1982): 26, No. 1, 132–36.

347 "some wicked, crazy laughs in this raunchy jape." Frank Rich, "Theater: 'Secret Lives of the Sexists,'" *The New York Times* (February 13, 1982).

347 "The comic level is not as consistently provocative." Don Nelsen, "Secret Lives of the Sexists," *New York Daily News* (February 23, 1982).

347 "Of course here, the style is the thing, and." Clive Barnes, "'Secret Lives' Delight in Ridiculous," *New York Post* (February 13, 1982).

347 "slow stretches and self-indulgent jokes." Mel Gussow, wqxr Radio (February 11, 1982).

347 "the effect is as wholesome as Moliere." Michael Feingold, "Dire Straights," *Village Voice* (February 23, 1982): 85.

347 "jesting is a seriousness of purpose that is perhaps unique." Sylviane Gold, "Cult-sure," *Soho Weekly News* (February 23, 1982): 61.

CHAPTER 12: *Ridiculous Diva*

358 "I don't always have the same level of approval." Ludlam, *Scourge*, 183.

361 "to describe what happens when the avant-garde." Ibid, 116.

368 "Mr. Ludlam's brightest prank since he assaulted." Frank Rich, "Stage: 'Le Bourgeois,' Comedy After Moliere," *The New York Times* (April 15, 1983).

368 "one of his most felicitous theatre 'pieces.'" Mel Gussow, wqxr Radio (April 15, 1983).

368 "his most solidly funny writing of the past several." Michael Feingold, "The Triumph of Anarcho-Formalism," *Village Voice* (April 26, 1983).

368 "another satirical hit." Marilyn Stasio, "Ludlam Hilarious as an Ass of the Arts," *New York Post* (April 25, 1983).

368 "does not patronize its audience because it is intelligently." Don Nelsen, "'Bourgeois': Act I Has All the Laughs," *New York Daily News* (April 19, 1983).

368 "is gaining both a wide following and critical recognition." Sam H. Shirakawa, "The Eccentric World of Charles Ludlam," *The New York Times* (July 3, 1983): "Arts & Leisure," 3+.

370 "Every major comedian in the country does drag." Ludlam, *Scourge*, 137.

371 "I think I'm an androgynous being to a certain extent." Ibid, 137–138.

371 "Like Maria Callas — I know I'm comparing myself to the great diva." Ibid, 119.

372 "a very controversial character." Ibid, 117.

372 "Part of the price of fame is that your image becomes simpified." Ibid, 118.

373 "After *Le Bourgeouis Avant-Garde*." Ibid, 117.

375 "[Callas had] gotten a lot of bad publicity for doing." "Galas" feature on National Public Radio Morning Edition, with Tom Vitale (October 13, 1983).

377 "By the climax, Ludlam has moved from funny halfway to sublime." Richard Corliss, "Off-Off-Broadway's Daffy Diva," *Time* (October 31, 1983).

CHAPTER 13: *One for the Ages*

385 "can drag himself to Hollywood. . . . An old history classmate." Harry Haun, *New York Daily News* (January 29, 1984).

385 "The ad shows a picture of series star Madeline Kahn." Richard Hack, "TeleVisions," *Hollywood Reporter* (March 2, 1984).

386 "Any cheaply printed paperbound book of adventure." William Rose Benet, *Benet's Reader's Encyclopedia*, Third Edition. (New York: Harper & Row, 1987), 749.

387 "This time I started with the device and worked back to the play." Joseph Hurley, *New York Theater Voice* (June 1984).

388 "When I realized the trouble I was facing with Enid." Ibid.

391 "Against a background of satiric religious discussion." Ludlam, *Scourge*, 164.

395 "Leon [Katz] tells me that anything one says about Hedda is true." Ibid, 171.

395 "Ah, my role!" Jim Davidson, "Hedda Gabler Another of Actor's 'Flamboyant Female' Roles," *The Pittsburgh Press* (July 19, 1984): C-1.

395 "It saves us from literalism, which is the great enemy of art." Frederick Price, "Actor Says Offbeat Role Enhances Ibsen Play," *Pittsburgh Post-Gazette* (July 1984).

395 "Hedda's a man trapped in a woman's body." As quoted in an unsigned item ("Ludlum [sic] to Star in Ibsen Production") in *The Pittsburgh Press* (May 17, 1984): B-9.

398 "Don't bother to read this." Clive Barnes, "Calling All Vampires to Sheridan Sq.," *New York Post* (October 8, 1984).

398 "If you've never been down to the Company's tiny theater." Frank Rich, WQXR Radio (October 9, 1984).

398 "One of the best times I've had in the theater." Michael Feingold, "When We Undead Awaken," *Village Voice* (October 16, 1984): 113+.

398 "Deft as a textbook travesty, delightful enough to take." Richard Corliss, "Tour de Farce," *Time* (October 15, 1984).

399 "What makes it singular is that everyone of the myriad characters." Mel Gussow, "Stage: 'The Mystery of Irma Vep,'" *The New York Times* (October 4, 1984).

399 "I realized how much I didn't know." Enid Nemy, "Broadway," *The New York Times* (October 12, 1984).

404 "*Salammbô* will 1) irritate the bourgeois." Herbert Lottman, *Flaubert: A Biography*. (Boston: Little, Brown & Company, 1989), 163.

404 "I think I use the word *purple* or *diamond* in every sentence of my book." Ibid, 149.

404 "historical hashish." Ibid, 158.

405 "gift to the world celebrating my reading of all of Flaubert." Ludlam, *Scourge*, 190.

405 "to accomplish in art what is unattainable in life." Ibid, 134.

405 "*Salammbô* is one for the boys, believe me!" Ibid, 133.

406 "I think the distinction between gay theater and what I do." Alan R., Yoffee, "The 'Ridiculous' World of Put-On Artist Charles Ludlam," *Au Courant* (November 4, 1985).

406 "Do you like movies?" William M. Hoffman, *As Is: A Play*. (New York: Random House, 1985), 17.

406 "I certainly couldn't have called [*Salammbô*] an AIDS play." Ludlam, *Scourge*, 247.

CHAPTER 14: *Every Day a Little Death*

417 "Charles Ludlam's absolutely delightful staging." John Rockwell, "Opera: In Santa Fe, Henze's 'English Cat,'" *The New York Times* (July 29, 1985).

417 "The delightful storybook production by Charles Ludlam." Michael Walsh, "When the Style Is No Style," *Time* (August 19, 1985): 61.

417 "an inspired stroke.... Most remarkable is." Bill Zakariasen, "High Notes in High Places, *New York Daily News* (August 14, 1985).

417 "It may be that in a production more astutely focused." Andrew Porter, "Musical Events: Melodious Cats," *The New Yorker* (September 2, 1985): 58+.

418 "was wonderfully fresh, sweet and sensitive — a 'thinking man's'." John Rockwell, "Critic's Notebook: Is the Music Customer Always Right?" *The New York Times* (August 29, 1985).

419 "I was up all night with this opera tech."Ludlam, *Scourge*, 219–220.

422 "falls below 'Eunuchs of the Forbidden City' and other lesser Ludlams." Mel Gussow, "Watching Ludlam Stumble and Osborn Fall Flat," *The New York Times* (November 17, 1985): "Arts & Leisure."

422 "with the consequence that the two halves of its creator's." Frank Rich, "Theater: Ridiculous's 'Salammbô,'" *The New York Times* (November 12, 1985).

423 "peculiar homage [to Flaubert], turning an already peculiar sensibility." Erika Munk, "Cross Left: The Reaganization of the Ridiculous," *Village Voice* (November 19, 1985).

424 "There is no one to blame but myself." Katy Dierlam, "Letters: Fat Chance," *Village Voice* (November 26, 1985): 6.

424 "Very simply, so much goes on in the piece." Michael Feingold, "Theater," *Village Voice* (November 19, 1985).

434 "The glorious bag-of-tricks direction by Charles Ludlam." Bill Zakariasen, "If This Is His Worst, We Can't Wait to See His Best," *New York Daily News* (August 5, 1986).

435 "The ingeniously complicated plot leads to." Howard Kissel, "Dial 'L' for Laughter," *New York Daily News* (September 22, 1986): "New York Live."

435 "Ludlam leaves no details unattended in this brilliantly." Marilyn Stasio, "Wildly Hilarious 'Jungle' Farce," *New York Post* (September 23, 1986).

435 "surely one of the funniest comedies Ludlam." Allan Wallach, "Ludlam's Merry Look at Murder," *Newsday* (September 22, 1986).

435 "Unlike David Mamet, who missed the joke by highlighting." Frank Rich, "Theater: Ludlam's 'Artificial Jungle,'" *The New York Times* (September 23, 1986).

435 "a typical tour of its creator's sensibility." Frank Rich, "Critics' Choices for a Wintry Weekend," *The New York Times* (January 16, 1987): "Weekend."

435 "Anything with such a bad reputation as 'camp' has to." Rob Baker. "Benigni and Ludlam: Classy Clowns," *Women's Wear Daily* (September 22, 1986).

435 "an Off-Broadway treasure." Michael Kuchwara, *Associated Press* (September 25, 1986).

435 "Visitors to the Big Apple who want to experience." Robert W. Butler, "What's Going on Off Broadway?," *Kansas City Star* (October 19, 1986).

436 "What a cult — Ludlam's biggest fan is *The New York Times*." Alan Stern, "Check These Off-Broadway Shows," *Denver Post* (November 30, 1986).

436 "Mr. Ludlam and company are often larger — and funnier." Mel Gussow, "Stage View: Charles Ludlam And the Importance of Being Ridiculous," *The New York Times* (September 28, 1986): "Arts & Leisure," 4.

440 "Laurence Olivier? Bah. Gielgud, Scofield, Brando and the rest." Don Nelsen, "The Bard As Never Before," *New York Daily News* (March 31, 1987).

440 "If you want someone to deal with extremes of human behavior." Nan Robertson, "Broadway," *The New York Times* (May 1, 1987): "Weekend."

CHAPTER 15: *Toodle-oo, Marguerite*

454 "Charles Ludlam, one of the most innovative and prolific artists." Jeremy Gerard, "Charles Ludlam, 44, Avant-Garde Artist of Theater, Is Dead," *The New York Times* (May 29, 1987): 1.

454 "a mixture of mayor and guru. . . . He had a talent to amaze." Clive Barnes, "Unrepeatable Man," *New York Post* (May 29, 1987): 34.

455 "a brilliant, one-man way of theater. . . . Inventing." Mel Gussow, "Stage View: The Man Who Made Theater Ridiculous," *The New York Times* (June 7, 1987): "Arts & Leisure," 5.

455 "He was not, as has wrongly been assumed by the daily press." Michael Feingold, "The Great Continuum," *Village Voice* (June 9, 1987): 88.

455 "You *will* keep the company going, won't you?" Ludlam, *Scourge*, 263.

456 "about 300 patrons who contribute money regularly." Jeremy Gerard, "The Ridiculous Theater, After Ludlam," *The New York Times* (June 13, 1987): 9.

INDEX

NOTE: RTC refers to Ridiculous Theatrical Company

476

483

492

495

94268055R00303

Made in the USA
Middletown, DE
18 October 2018